# FAMILY AND JUSTICE IN THE ARCHIVES

# Family and Justice in the Archives

## HISTORICAL PERSPECTIVES ON INTIMACY AND THE LAW

EDITED BY
*Peter Gossage & Lisa Moore*

Concordia University Press
Montreal

Cover design: Sébastien Aubin, OTAMI-
Design: Garet Markvoort
Copy editing: Saelan Twerdy
Index: Natalie Greenberg
Proofreading: Saelan Twerdy
Cover illustration: Jean-Louis Forain, *Court Room Scene*, date unknown. Pen and black ink with brown wash on cream laid paper, 39.1 × 29.3 cm. Gift of Christopher and Georgina Mills, Ottawa, 1996, in memory of Andrew Phillip Cowan Mills. National Gallery of Canada, Ottawa. Photo: NGC.

*Family and Justice in the Archives* is set in New Caledonia, David Berlow's 1988 digital version of W.A. Dwiggins's classic Caledonia typeface, originally designed for the Mergenthaler Linotype Company in 1938. Dwiggins chose the name Caledonia, the Roman name for Scotland, to express the face's basis in nineteenth-century Scotch Roman typefaces.

Printed and bound in Canada by Imprimerie Gauvin, Gatineau, Quebec

This book is printed on Forest Stewardship Council certified paper and meets the permanence of paper requirements of ANSI/NISO Z39.48-1992.

Concordia University Press's books are available for free on several platforms. Visit www.concordia.ca/press

First English edition published in 2024
10 9 8 7 6 5 4 3 2 1

978-1-988111-43-8 | Paper
978-1-988111-44-5 | E-book

*Library and Archives Canada Cataloguing in Publication*

Title: Family and justice in the archives : historical perspectives on intimacy and the law / edited by Peter Gossage & Lisa Moore.
Names: Gossage, Peter, 1956- editor. | Moore, Lisa (Editor), editor.
Description: First English edition. | Includes bibliographical references and index.
Identifiers: Canadiana (print) 20230540651 | Canadiana (ebook) 20240370708 | ISBN 9781988111438 (softcover) | ISBN 9781988111445 (ebook)
Subjects: LCSH: Domestic relations—History.
Classification: LCC K670 .F36 2024 | DDC 346.01/5—dc23

Concordia University Press
1455 de Maisonneuve Blvd. W.
Montreal, Quebec H3G 1M8
CANADA

*Concordia University Press gratefully acknowledges the generous support of the Birks Family Foundation, the Estate of Linda Kay, and the Estate of Tanneke De Zwart.*

*This book has been published with the help of a grant from the Federation of the Humanities and Social Sciences through the Awards to Scholarly Publications Program (ASPP), using funds provided by the Social Sciences and Humanities Research Council of Canada. Funding has also been gratefully received from Concordia University's Aid to Research-Related Events, Exhibition, Publication, and Dissemination Activities (ARRE) Program.*

*For our families*

# TABLE OF CONTENTS

# FIGURES AND TABLES

# CONTRIBUTORS

JUANDREA BATES is a historian whose scholarship explores the development of family policy and citizenship rights in Latin America. Her research ranges from issues surrounding immigration policy to juvenile justice, domestic violence, and child protection in the past and present. She holds a PhD in History from the University of Texas and is now an Associate Professor in the Department of History and Legal Studies at Winona State University. She is currently working on a book manuscript entitled *Raising Argentina: Family Policy, Inequality and Justice in Buenos Aires 1871–1930*.

ISABELLE BOUCHARD is a professor of history in the Département des sciences humaines at the Université du Québec à Trois-Rivières (UQTR). Her research focuses on the political, economic, and legal history of Indigenous communities in the Saint Lawrence Valley during the nineteenth century. Her dissertation (Université du Québec à Montréal, 2017) was awarded the Fondation Jean-Charles Bonenfant Prize as well as the Canadian Historical Association's John Bullen Prize.

EMMA CHILTON is a recent graduate from the Bachelor of Arts and Science Program at McMaster University. Emma has worked on several legal scholarship projects and is a proponent of public legal education. She is particularly interested in the intersections of personal relationships and legal structures.

GINGER FROST is University Research Professor of History at Samford University. She is the author of six books, including *Living in Sin: Cohabiting as Husband and Wife in Nineteenth-Century England* (2008) and *Illegitimacy in English Law and Society, 1860–1930* (2016), both from Manchester University Press. A former fellow of the National Humanities Center (2002–2003) and member of the Institute of Advanced

Study (2009–2010), her most recent book is *Mixed Marriage: Class, Religion, Race, and Nation in England, 1837–1939* (2024).

JEAN-PHILIPPE GARNEAU is a professor of Canadian history at the Université du Québec à Montréal (UQÀM). His research focuses on the history of law and justice within the context of colonial Quebec. Favouring social and political approaches to studying legal institutions, his most recent publications have examined lawyers and families in Lower-Canadian society.

SHELLEY A.M. GAVIGAN is Professor Emerita and Senior Scholar at Osgoode Hall Law School, York University, Toronto. With graduate degrees in Law and in Criminology, her scholarship is significantly interdisciplinary, located primarily in legal history, socio-legal studies, feminist legal studies, and social justice. A lawyer by training, she began her legal career in community legal clinics in Saskatchewan and her ongoing research continues to address law and justice in the history of that region.

FABIENNE GIULIANI is an associate researcher at the Centre d'histoire du XIX^e siècle at the Université Paris 1 Panthéon-Sorbonne in France. Drawing from the expertise she gained from her doctoral research on incest during the nineteenth century, she worked at the Agence Nationale de la Recherche on the DERVI initiative (*Dire, Entendre, Restituer les Violences Incestueuses*, or Telling, Hearing and Reporting Incestuous Violence), in collaboration with other historians and anthropologists (2019–2022). Her research looks specifically at how the notion of norms intersects with the histories of law, justice, sexuality, the family, and medicine.

PETER GOSSAGE is a professor in the Department of History at Concordia University and a scholar of family and gender in Quebec. He is co-author, with J.I. Little, of *An Illustrated History of Quebec: Tradition and Modernity* (Oxford University Press, 2012) and co-editor, with Robert Rutherdale, of *Making Men, Making History: Canadian Masculinities across Time and Place* (UBC Press, 2018). In his research, he frequently draws on court records, jurisprudence, notarial deeds, and other legal sources for insights into the intimate worlds of Quebec families, primarily in the period from 1840 to 1960.

RIYAD SADIQ KOYA is completing a doctoral dissertation entitled "Indian Indentured Labor, Imperial Citizenship, and the Geography of Legal Pluralism, 1834–1955," at the University of California, Berkeley. His previously published works include "The Campaign for Islamic Law in Fiji: Comparison, Codification, Application," *Law and History Review*, 32, no. 4 (2014): 853–881; and "Slavery, Abolitionism, Indentured Labour: The Problem of Exit and the Border between Land and Sea in Colonial India," in *South Asian Migrations in Global History: Labor, Law and Wayward Lives*, ed. Neilesh Bose (London and New York: Bloomsbury Academic, 2021), 113–38.

EMILEE LORD works to improve policy and social systems with history, data, and technology. Previously, she completed a Fulbright Fellowship in Medellín, Colombia, and a Press Fellowship in the United States House of Representatives. She graduated in May 2019 from Davidson College in North Carolina with a double major in History and Hispanic Studies.

NAAMA MAOR is a legal and social historian of the United States whose research weaves together a study of intimate life and legal regimes. An Assistant Professor in the Department of History at Tel Aviv University, Maor explores the intertwined development of the welfare state and the carceral state by tracing the history of juvenile justice institutions. Before receiving a PhD from the University of Chicago, Maor was a broadcast journalist and spent a year working at a reformatory for boys.

MÉLANIE MÉTHOT is a professor at the University of Alberta, Augustana Campus and the recipient of a SSHRC Grant for her research on bigamy in Canada, as well as another more recent one for her project dealing with bigamy in Australia. Méthot is the founder of the Augustana Conference on Undergraduate Research and Innovative Teaching.

LISA MOORE is a PhD Candidate in the Department of History at Concordia University. Her dissertation explores gender and juvenile justice in postwar Quebec through an examination of the regulation of girls brought before the Social Welfare Court of Montreal. She has professional experience in the history and heritage sector, including as a Concordia-based editorial assistant, as a research assistant for the SSHRC-funded project *Familles, droit et justice au Québec, 1840–1920*, and as a researcher for the Montreal Museum of Fine Arts.

JAMES MORAN is Chair and Professor in the Department of History at the University of Prince Edward Island. He researches and writes about the history of disease, medicine, and mental health. Recent publications include *Madness on Trial: A Translatlantic History of English Civil Law and Lunacy* (Manchester University Press, 2019), and "A Tale of Two Bureaucracies: Asylum and Lunacy Law Paperwork," *Rethinking History* 22, no. 3 (2018).

CHANDRA MURDOCH is an SSHRC postdoctoral fellow at Osgoode Hall Law school and holds a PhD from the Department of History at the University of Toronto. Her research examines the development of the Indian Act in nineteenth-century Ontario through Indigenous political responses to the law. She received the R. Roy McMurtry Fellowship in Canadian Legal History for 2018–19 and was a Junior Fellow at the Centre for Criminology and Sociolegal Studies at the University of Toronto from 2018–2020.

JANE NICHOLAS is a professor of history at St. Jerome's University in the University of Waterloo. She is the author of *Canadian Carnival Freaks and the Extraordinary Body* (University of Toronto Press, 2018) and *The Modern Girl: Feminine Modernities, the Body, and Commodities in the 1920s* (University of Toronto Press, 2015). Her chapter in this collection is part of a new SSHRC-funded project on child death and grief in Ontario.

MARY ANNE POUTANEN teaches history at Concordia University and interdisciplinary studies at McGill University. She is a member of the Montreal History Group and of the Centre for Interdisciplinary Research on Montreal at McGill. Her research focuses on licit and illicit subsistence strategies that popular-class women instituted in nineteenth-century Montreal. Her monograph *Beyond Brutal Passions: Prostitution in Early Nineteenth-Century Montreal* (McGill-Queen's University Press, 2015) was awarded the Prix Lionel-Groulx by the Institut d'histoire de l'Amérique française in 2016.

LORENA RIZZO is a historian of Southern Africa (Namibia and South Africa) with special interests in gender history, history and theory, and visual history. Among her publications are *Gender and Colonialism: A History of Kaoko in North-western Namibia, 1870s–1950* (Basel: Basler Afrika Bibliographien, 2012); *Photography and History in Colonial Southern Africa: Shades of Empire* (London and Johannesburg: Routledge/WITS University Press, 2019); and *Women and Photography in Africa: Creative Practices and Feminist Challenges*, co-edited with Darren Newbury and Kylie Thomas (London: Routledge, 2020).

GAIL SAVAGE is a professor emeritus of history at St. Mary's College of Maryland. She is the author of *The Social Construction of Expertise: The English Civil Service and its Influence, 1919–39* (University of Pittsburgh Press, 1996) and essays on the history of divorce in England. She is completing a manuscript, *Breaking Up is Hard to Do: Divorce and Divorce Law Reform in England, 1828–1937*, and is in the beginning stages of research for a new project on transnational marriage during and in the aftermath of the Second World War.

JOHN WERTHEIMER is the William R. Kenan, Jr. Professor of History at Davidson College in North Carolina. He has a BA in History from Oberlin College in Ohio, as well as an MA and PhD in History from Princeton University in New Jersey. He specializes in the legal histories of the United States and Latin America. His publications include *Race and the Law in South Carolina: From Slavery to Jim Crow* (Amherst, MA: Amherst College Press, 2023) and *Law and Society in the South: A History of North Carolina Court Cases* (Lexington: University Press of Kentucky, 2009).

# FOREWORD

In May of 2019—before anyone had ever heard of COVID-19—we invited a lively, eclectic, international group of historians, legal scholars, and others to Montreal for a three-day symposium entitled *Family and Justice in the Archives: Histories of Intimacy in Transnational Perspective—Famille et justice dans les archives: Perspectives transnationales sur les histoires de l'intimité* (https://familyandjustice.cieq.ca/). People travelled from Australia, Argentina, Alberta, and many other places, near and far, convening on and around Concordia University's downtown campus on those warm spring days. Together, we listened to and discussed over fifty papers, in French and English, on topics ranging from family honour in nineteenth-century Venice to debt and insolvency among Western Canadian farm families in the 1930s, to battered women syndrome in contemporary India, and including a spellbinding keynote lecture by Constance Backhouse entitled "Intimacy and the Law: The Promise of Archival Records." We enjoyed each other's company in the way academics with shared interests and a longer or shorter acquaintance like to do: over morning coffee or a buffet lunch at the conference centre, over beer or wine at one of the local pubs—the outdoor *terrasse* at Brutopia on Crescent Street comes to mind, but there were many others—and at a festive Monday evening banquet on an elegant mezzanine at the Montreal Museum of Fine Arts.

The big idea for that richly rewarding symposium—and now for this book—took shape in the context of a team research project, funded (like our 2019 event) by the Social Sciences and Humanities Research Council of Canada. The project was called *Familles, droit et justice au Québec, 1840–1920* (Families, Law, and Justice in Quebec, 1840–1920) and the team of investigators consisted of Donald Fyson (Université Laval), Thierry Nootens (Université du Québec à Trois-Rivières), Eric Reiter, and Peter Gossage (both of Concordia University). The idea was that our framing of legal archives as a privileged window onto the intimate lives of Quebec families in the nineteenth and early twentieth centuries might usefully be placed into conversation with scholars and projects using similar sources—that is to say, court records and related documents generated by the legal apparatus of the state—to explore similar questions for other times and places.

As it turns out, the idea of encouraging an international dialogue in the space defined by the three conceptual pillars of our project—family, justice, and archives—resonated with a lot of people, some of whom we had known for years, while others crossed our paths for the first time in 2019. We drew, in particular, on the generous contributions of colleagues in the Department of History at Concordia University, including Rachel Berger, Sarah Ghabrial, Wilson Chacko Jacob, Nora Jaffary, Barbara Lorenzkowski, Mary Anne Poutanen, and Shannon McSheffrey. We benefited enormously from the support, collegiality, and insights of many members of the research networks to which we belong, especially the Centre interuniversitaire d'études québécoises (CIÉQ) and the Centre d'histoire des régulations sociales (CHRS) whose overlapping membership includes Louise Bienvenue, Isabelle Bouchard, Noémie Charest-Bourdon, François Fenchel, Jean-Philippe Garneau, Ollivier Hubert, Sherry Olson, Martin Petitclerc, Jean Trépanier, and Brian Young, who offered a marvelous impromptu toast at the banquet. We were able to count on a terrific program committee that included Michelle McKinley, David Niget, and Sylvie Perrier, in addition to others already named. And we were strongly supported by a dynamic group of graduate students and post-docs at Concordia, especially Paul D'Amboise, Sophie Doucet, and Leslie Szabo, as well as by Alycia Manning and Donna Whittaker in the History Department office, without whom it's fair to say nothing much would ever get done.

As a volume of essays, *Family and Justice in the Archives: Historical Perspectives on Intimacy and the Law* seeks to build on the transnational discussion begun in Montreal five years ago. This is not so much a set of proceedings, then, as a careful selection of the most innovative and provocative papers prepared for the symposium, revised several times and in some cases considerably expanded for publication, and grouped into a series of thematic sections in such a way as to encourage comparisons and highlight connections across time and space. We are thrilled by the prospect of its publication with Concordia University Press and confident this book will stand on its own as a fresh contribution to legal history, to family history, and to law and society studies long after those inspiring days in 2019 fade into distant, pre-pandemic memory.

As co-editors, we have been working together for some time now and wish to acknowledge some of the many debts acquired along the way. First and foremost, we have had amazing cooperation from our eighteen contributing authors, some of whom experienced the pandemic in very direct and personal ways. We thank them all sincerely for sharing their insights, of course, but also for the patience and generosity they have displayed throughout this adventure. Special thanks are due to Ginger Frost, who took time to review our initial proposal and to provide some key suggestions about its ultimate framing, focus, and structure. Having co-chaired the symposium that inspired this collection, Eric Reiter remained involved and accessible throughout the ensuing process, providing timely advice and support at virtually every stage, including critical readings of at least two iterations of our introductory essay. He has our most sincere thanks. This, moreover, is a book about intimacies encountered *in the archives*, so we would be remiss if we failed to thank the many archivists and librarians who have provided vital assistance to our contributors and facilitated their countless discoveries at repositories on several continents, including here at home the Bibliothèque et archives nationales du Québec and at Library and Archives Canada.

We are also grateful for the encouragement and guidance we have received from the team at Concordia University Press, beginning with director Geoffrey Little, who attended our symposium and whose encouraging response to our proposal secured our allegiance to this newest member of the Canadian scholarly publishing community. We owe a very special thanks to acquisitions editor Ryan Van Huijstee, who went above and beyond to ensure a smooth and productive peer-review process and whose clarity, insight, and enthusiasm have been invaluable to us as co-editors. Saelan Twerdy did double duty as copy editor and editorial coordinator in the production phase of this project, which benefited enormously from his skill, patience, and attention to detail. We are grateful to the three external readers for the time and care they invested in their assessments, for their generous and unambiguous support for the project, and especially for challenging us to dig a little deeper in order to make this the best book it could possibly be. Steven Watt translated three chapters from the original French with his characteristic skill, precision, and efficiency; he has our thanks as well.

We will close with some more personal acknowledgements, firstly from Lisa Moore: I owe an enormous debt of gratitude to my friends and family for their constant guidance and support. I thank my grandmothers for first igniting my interest in history and my parents for encouraging me with love and enthusiasm through all my academic endeavours. I am most grateful to Corey and little Owen for their trust and understanding, and for the strength, joy, and laughter they never fail to provide. Finally, I thank my co-editor, Peter, for over a decade of truly invaluable mentorship. It has been a real pleasure working together on this collaborative project, and I have benefited immensely from his insight and expertise. And from Peter Gossage: I am proud to be Lisa's co-editor and sincerely grateful for her careful, intelligent, and generous collaboration, upon which I have relied since day one of this project. I thank my friends, colleagues, and students in the Department of History at Concordia University for their many and various encouragements and for fostering such a stimulating and progressive intellectual environment. Family has always been a major focus in my scholarship and I thank every member of the extended Adams-Gossage family for their unfailing support and for the profound sense of belonging they provide. And as ever, my deepest and most intimate debts are to Annmarie, Charlie, and Katie, who fill my life with love, joy, and meaning every single day.

PG and LM, Montreal and Calgary, April 2024

# FAMILY AND JUSTICE IN THE ARCHIVES

INTRODUCTION

# Family and Justice in the Archives

## *Historical Perspectives on Intimacy and the Law*

*Peter Gossage and Lisa Moore*

"There's no place for the state in the bedrooms of the nation," quipped the Canadian Minister of Justice, Pierre Elliott Trudeau, in 1967 as he introduced sweeping changes to the Canadian Criminal Code in areas such as homosexuality and abortion.[1] Soon to emerge as one of the most influential leaders of his generation, Trudeau was staking out a political position and calling for a new, more progressive framework for the legal regulation of sexual relations and reproductive choices. His aspirational slogan is contradicted, however, by two centuries of history that demonstrate the profound and pervasive role of the state in regulating sexual, affective, and domestic intimacies across the world. Indeed, the state has occupied a significant place in the bedrooms of virtually every nation, establishing and enforcing the legal parameters for marriage, parent-child relations, inheritance, sexual morality, domestic violence, and reproductive rights, among many related matters. Individual citizens frequently turn to the state, its laws, and its judicial apparatus as the ultimate arbiters of conflicts arising in intimate settings, including shocking cases of seduction, rape, incest, and bigamy and long-simmering struggles over family honour, parental authority, and inheritance. The complex and varied legal systems that regulate what goes on in "the bedrooms of the nation" and in other intimate spaces, moreover, have been studied at length by jurists and others specializing in family law.[2]

Women and men throughout history, meanwhile, have defined their intimate worlds on their own terms, often resisting and challenging official rules, definitions, and prescriptions. Stable domestic partnerships, for instance, might or might not be afforded the recognition and privileges associated with formal, state-sanctioned marriage, depending on a range of factors, including race, nationality, and sexual orientation, that have varied dramatically over time and from one jurisdiction to another. This, indeed, is the context in which the struggle for recognition of LGBTQ+ marriage rights was waged and won in the generation following Trudeau's bold declaration and the decriminalization of queer sexualities to which it was tied.[3] Half a century earlier, young Russian women who had married foreign soldiers and journalists stationed in wartime Moscow, as shown in this volume, were not recognized as legally married by the Soviet state, which refused to let them emigrate to join their husbands.[4] Earlier still, the Australian bigamists we will meet in another chapter had chosen to live outside the moral and legal boundaries established by British and colonial law and enforced by Australian courts.[5] But the personal intimacies in which they believed and for which they struggled were no less real and profound for all that.

*Family and Justice in the Archives* brings together sixteen essays that explore the legal regulation of intimacy in the nineteenth and twentieth centuries. Our aim is to focus attention on legal archives as a privileged window onto domestic, sexual, and affective intimacies across time and space. We seek, furthermore, to stretch the boundaries of that discussion beyond a single national context, presenting work that spans five continents and highlighting certain universal themes that draw these studies together, rather than the cultural, geographic, and jurisdictional differences that separate them.[6] While the scholarship in this area is vast and touches every period of human history, we have chosen to tighten the focus by limiting the temporal range for this book to the nineteenth and twentieth centuries. This is the era for which we, as historians and editors, can claim some specialized knowledge.[7] More importantly, it is the period that saw the rise of industrial modernity and democratic liberalism, of colonial and nation-building projects on a global scale, and of those judicial and regulatory institutions that so fundamentally characterize the contemporary nation-state. Indeed, the relationship between nation-building and the regulation of intimacy is a recurring theme throughout this volume and something which has been demonstrated especially well in Canadian settings by scholars like Adele Perry, Sarah Carter, Carolyn Strange, and Tina Loo.[8]

In preparing this book, our objective has been to assemble studies with common themes and concerns but located in different spaces, jurisdictions, and time periods. The geographic range of these essays is therefore intentionally broad, juxtaposing a number of Canadian contributions with others focused on Argentina, Australia, England, France, Guatemala, Mauritius, Russia, South Africa, and the United States. The diversity of settings reflects the approach we took in organizing an international symposium on the legal regulation of intimacy at Concordia University in 2019.[9] That event engaged scholars from various disciplines and all career stages, including every contributor to this collection, in a series of transnational conversations about the challenges and opportunities offered by the use of legal records to explore family life. Building on that central premise, this volume represents a coming-together in a Canadian setting of an international group of like-minded scholars, ready to share their insights and findings across the boundaries of time and space.[10]

Spanning five continents and two centuries, the essays collected here share a fascination with judicial sources: "*ces archives indiscrètes*"[11] that allow us to explore domestic intimacy in its material, bodily, emotional, sexual, and other dimensions. In this sense, our contributors are all engaged in a research praxis inspired by a number of pioneering scholars who have shown the value of legal sources for the study of society, culture, and family. Cultural historians of early-modern France, such as Arlette Farge, Natalie Zemon Davis, and Robert Darnton have been especially influential in showing how legal records both reveal and hide everyday intimacies.[12] The focus of these scholars on narrativity within archival sources, daily life and privacy, and micro-historical approaches to the past are important models for the work featured in this volume. North American legal historians were also quite early to recognize the powerful lens offered by the law—and especially by the archival traces left by nineteenth-century court cases—to anyone seeking a better understanding of family, gender, and sexuality in former times. Michael Grossberg and Constance Backhouse were among the first to use this approach with legal records relating to marital property, sexual violence, seduction and paternity, contraception and abortion, the status of "illegitimate" children, infanticide, and a host of related topics, in their important books on family, gender, and the law in the United States and Canada.[13] Likewise, scholars in archival theory, particularly but not exclusively within post-colonial studies, including Farge, Carolyn Steedman, and Ann Laura Stoler, provide important conceptual frameworks within which to pursue the questions our contributors ask.[14]

In tracking the international scholarship that has emerged at the intersection of law, history, and intimacy since the 1980s, we are struck by the range, volume, and diversity of the work. Specific topics related to our central theme have been explored in many important studies within various national contexts. Marriage choice and parental opposition to children's nuptial decisions, for example, have been examined by Patricia Seed in the context of colonial Mexico as well as by Shannon McSheffrey for medieval London using the records of ecclesiastical court systems.[15] The legal regulation of women's sexuality has also been the focus of many studies, including those of Joan Sangster, Mary Anne Poutanen, and Nora Jaffary, who rely on judicial case files to investigate the regulation of female sexuality in twentieth-century Ontario, sex work in nineteenth-century Montreal, and pregnancy prevention and abortion in colonial Mexico.[16] The specific role that families played in the process of regulating "deviant" behaviour more broadly is the subject of Thierry Nootens' 2007 monograph, which explores how families in nineteenth-century Montreal sought recourse from the justice system to manage troublesome relatives, often suffering from addiction or mental illness, and to mitigate the financial risk they posed.[17] In that same vein, many historians have considered the law's involvement in governing the economic affairs of families through investigations of inheritance, the guardianship and care of children, as well as conflicts surrounding spousal support and family allowances.[18]

Historically, families have sometimes been framed nostalgically as safe, supportive havens from the dangers and demands of an increasingly hostile and risky outside world.[19] But the cross-cultural prevalence of domestic violence casts serious doubt on any such naïve reading of family life in the past. There is an especially rich literature that observes this troubling topic from a legal perspective. One of the most important examples is Backhouse's comprehensive study of over one thousand sexual assault cases heard before Canadian criminal courts between 1900 and 1975.[20] Violence against children, especially as inflicted by mothers and fathers, has also been examined in earnest by Marie-Aimée Cliche for the context of Quebec, Fabienne Giuliani and Anne-Emmanuelle Demartini for France, and Elaine Farrell and Cliona Rattigan for Ireland.[21]

Such studies, obviously, are damaging to any nostalgic view of domestic life in the past, as are the many excellent historical explorations of marital breakdown and divorce. These include Roderick Phillips' extensive examination of the evolution of divorce laws in the West from the Middle Ages to the twentieth century as well as James G. Snell's investigation of the ways women navigated the Canadian legal system to secure divorces in the early 1900s.[22] The relationship between fractious families and the nascent juvenile justice system is another topic that has generated interest from scholars around the globe, but especially those working in North America, France, and Belgium. Studies in this area analyze the evolution of laws relating to youth protection and delinquency as well as the domestic, socioeconomic, and gendered aspects associated with the legal regulation of children and adolescents.[23]

The affective dimension of family relationships is yet another area that historians have begun to observe through the prism of the law. The significance of emotion in legal settings has been revealed using case records related to adultery and injury as well as death and mourning by scholars like Laura Hanft Korobkin, William Reddy, Eric Reiter, and Julie-Marie Strange.[24] Along these same lines, the question of family honour and status has historically been addressed in judicial settings, as demonstrated by Kathryn Sloan in her study of seduction cases involving minors in postcolonial Mexico and Eric Reiter in his work on moral injury disputes in the British colony of Lower Canada.[25] Family identity, moreover, whether collective or individual, has garnered attention from historians such as Jane E. Mangan and Jessica M. Marglin, who have both explored the ways in which families used aspects of the law to adapt and survive within societies transformed by colonialism.[26]

## *Perspectives on Intimacy*

As all of these examples reveal, scholars across the globe have for some time now been unpacking the stories of intimacy revealed in processes of legal regulation to develop rich new insights about family, gender, sex, power, culture, identity, and daily life. Located initially in the private spaces of lineage, estate, family, household, and bedchamber, those intimacies were both dramatic and quotidian, material and emotional, and invariably tied up in gendered and generational hierarchies of power and privilege. That being said, there is a need to more fully articulate our conception of "intimacy" as a central, unifying concept for the present volume. We offer here a diverse collection of essays, all of which focus on the archival traces left by various legal processes in a range of different countries since 1800. But why "intimacy" rather than some other formulation, such as "private life" or "the domestic sphere"—both expressions that are widely used in this literature?

At one level, our contributors are united by their interest in matters occurring in the "private" realms of love, sex, marriage, and the family, which then cross a certain threshold into the "public" sphere of social and legal regulation. It is our explicit intention, however, to avoid the reductionist public/private dichotomy, the limitations of which have now been established by a generation of feminist scholars.[27] Literary scholar Lauren Berlant captured a similar intention when they argued, in 1998, for a renewed and reimagined approach to intimacies of every kind. "A related aim of this reframing of intimacy," they wrote, "is thus to engage and disable a prevalent US discourse on the proper relation between public and private, spaces traditionally associated with the gendered division of labor. These categories are considered by many scholars to be archaic formations, legacies of a Victorian fantasy that the world can be divided into a controllable space (the private-affective) and an uncontrollable one (the public-instrumental)."[28] Framing this book around sexual, affective, and domestic *intimacies* as they intersected with legal and judicial institutions and processes, then, is an effective way of articulating the constant interaction of the private and the public, the personal and the political, without falling into a "separate-spheres" trap. Indeed, this effort to transcend those weary dichotomies might be carried even further with reference to a paradoxical concept such as "intimate publics": an idea widely associated with Berlant, but which was also used by feminist legal scholar Robyn Wiegman for her 2002 study of child-custody litigation arising from new reproductive technologies in the United States.[29]

The influential American economist Viviana Zelizer has used similar language to challenge prevailing notions about the incompatibility between personal, private, and affective relationships on the one hand and the role of money, the market, and economic rationality on the other.[30] The antithetical opposition widely assumed between love and money, family and the market, private and public "spheres" is simply wrong, in her view, since "in everyday life, people constantly mingle intimacy and all sorts of economic activity—production, consumption, distribution, and transfers of assets. Intimate relations between spouses, between lovers, between parents and children, and even between doctors and patients depend on joint economic activity. No loving household would last long without regular inputs of economic effort."[31] Just as importantly for our purposes, it regularly falls to public authorities, especially the civil courts, to assign monetary value to emotional attachments, as for instance in the case of legal settlements for wrongful death. Framing these and similar settings as areas of intimacy in which economic logics play a fundamental but neglected role is a significant contribution, made forcefully in Zelizer's provocatively titled 2006 monograph *The Purchase of Intimacy*.

The study of intimacy, then, unites researchers across a range of disciplines and has gained currency since the turn of the millennium as a framework in which to situate explorations of sex, love, marriage, and domestic life. Feminist and poststructuralist historians of empire in particular, as legal scholar Michelle McKinley observed in 2014, "have perceptively shown that regulating sexuality and intimate life was one of the central technologies of imperial rule."[32] Over the past two decades, the regulation of intimacy as a technology of imperial governance has emerged as a lively and important thread within post-colonial studies. One of the leading scholars in this field, the anthropologist and historian Ann Laura Stoler, published an important article in 2001, situating her own work (primarily on the Dutch East Indies) with respect to a body of literature that shows "how intimate domains—sex, sentiment, domestic arrangement, and child rearing—figure in the making of racial categories and in the management of imperial rule."[33] That insightful essay led to the 2002 monograph *Carnal Knowledge and Imperial Power: Race and the Intimate in Colonial Rule*, a landmark study that moved sexual and domestic intimacies away from the periphery and into the very centre of imperial projects of rule. Stoler offered in that book a definition of "the intimate" that begins with *The American Heritage Dictionary* ("1. Marked by close acquaintance, association, or familiarity...") and continues as follows: "[The] notion of the 'intimate' is a descriptive marker of the familiar and the essential *and* of relations grounded in sex. Its Latin etymology ('innermost'), which it shares with its homograph 'to intimate,' is more telling still. It is 'sexual relations' and 'familiarity' taken as an 'indirect sign' of what is racially 'innermost' that locates intimacy so strategically in imperial politics and why colonial administrators worried over its consequence and course."[34]

Several of the contributors to this volume, including Riyad Koya and Lorena Rizzo, engage with matters of race and imperial politics, which are key components of Stoler's definition but not our main concern for the moment. We must attend, rather, to the *multivalence* of intimacy as a concept and specifically to its dual meanings as "a descriptive marker of the familiar and the essential *and* of relations grounded in sex." Stoler's main title (*Carnal Knowledge and Imperial Power*) might suggest that she and other post-colonial scholars are preoccupied mainly with this second valence and especially with the regulation of sexual desire, specifically between European men and Indigenous, racialized women.[35] Sexual intimacy, certainly, is a recurring theme in that body of work and, indeed, in the present volume, seen for instance through the growing moral panic over incest in nineteenth-century France or the attention paid by colonial courts to the adulterous or bigamous relations of young married women in northwestern Canada and southeastern Australia.[36] But intimacies in this view are also grounded in the *familiar*, which shares its Latin root with *family* and which allows for a broader conceptualization of "the intimate." This, in the end, is the meaning to which we subscribe, one that embraces not only sexual relationships but also those based on affect (as with one's most intimate friends), on spatial proximity (as with housemates or neighbours), and certainly on kinship or family, as with the many parents, grandparents, children, siblings, aunts, uncles, and cousins we will encounter in the pages of this book. Thus, studies focusing on the transmission of property and status from one generation to the next, on guardianship arrangements for minor children who have lost their mother or father, and on litigation pitting adolescents in search of greater autonomy against their parents have their place here as well.[37]

Intimate settings—sexual, domestic, and affective—are generally a locus for strong emotions, both positive and negative. The "Perspectives on Intimacy" in our title, we hope, will suggest some of the emotional content of the relationships examined in this volume. Legal archives are usually (as with court records) grounded in conflict, or sometimes (as with wills and pre-nuptial contracts) in efforts to prevent conflict. They can be relatively silent on the positive emotions associated with intimacy, such as love, loyalty, pride, and solidarity. But we will also get hints of these more tender feelings in the pages that follow, and sometimes in surprising places: in the intimate lives of Montreal sex workers, for instance, whose networks of love, friendship, and mutual support are Mary Anne Poutanen's primary focus (Chapter 8). The courts are better known for regulating conflicts arising from negative emotions such as anger, jealousy, lust, shame, humiliation, and even grief, as in the case of the wrongful death suits studied by Zelizer. We can understand more about the emotional landscapes of earlier times by studying challenges to parental authority in Argentina (Bates, Chapter 6), the judicial regulation of masculinity in the Anglo-American world (Chilton and Moran, Chapter 10), or everyday violence towards girls and women as revealed by infanticide cases in Ontario (Nicholas, Chapter 14). We are inspired, then, by the possibility of placing this volume into conversation with recent work in the legal history of emotions, an exciting new field of scholarship to which our colleague Eric Reiter has made important contributions, most notably his 2019 monograph *Wounded Feelings*.[38]

## *Family and Justice*

Our main title, *Family and Justice in the Archives*, sets into place the three thematic pillars that support and define this volume. We have just devoted several pages to the rich historiography surrounding legal regulation of family life, with particular attention to the concept of intimacy as it has been deployed in this area. Next, we will articulate how the theme of "justice" is mobilized in these sixteen essays. As it happens, the metaphor of pillars is especially apt here, given the predominance of neo-classical designs, with their imposing columns, in the architecture of so many nineteenth and twentieth-century courthouses: those *palais de justice* (palaces of justice, in the evocative French phrase) that were the setting for many of the stories to be told in the chapters below. For lest there be any misunderstanding, it is to *legal* constructions of justice, rather than to broader moral, ethical, or philosophical ones, that we refer in our title, and to which we have invited the contributors to attend.[39]

This, of course, is the sense in which every Western democracy has a Ministry of Justice responsible for its courts, prisons, police service, and so on. Legal historian Douglas Hay, writing about England in the journal *Crime and Justice* some four decades ago, situates the emergence of those institutions—the modern state apparatus for the administration of justice—in the eighteenth and nineteenth centuries.[40] And it is the sense in which Donald Fyson, applying a similar lens to a British colonial possession in the same period, uses the phrase "everyday criminal justice": meaning both "the structure and operation of the lower-level civil and criminal courts, and … the experiences of people who came before the justice system."[41]

The "justice" in our title, then, encapsulates our focus on the administration of justice as a function of the emerging liberal state; on the ways in which the various institutions and officers of justice, including courts, prisons, police forces, lawyers, judges, and notaries, have participated in processes of social, legal, and moral regulation[42]; and especially—and this echoes Fyson's idea of "everyday" justice quite closely—on "the experiences of people who came before the justice system." Justice, after all, as Eric Reiter has reminded us, "can be what the state metes out; but it can also be crafting informal rules and norms that fit with individual views on the way things should be."[43] From that perspective, we are especially interested in the ways so-called "ordinary" people used the justice system to further their own goals and interests, as with Montreal sex workers examined by Poutanen, or pushed back against the normative, state-sanctioned understandings of propriety and respectability embedded in marriage laws, as with the Australian bigamists studied by Méthot. The regulation of intimacy by state authorities, in other words, was never a one-way street. And the state's frequent incursions into "the bedrooms of the nation," as we shall see, were met with indifference, defiance, and sometimes outrage as often as with compliance and resignation.

Hay and Fyson are among the many historians who have focused on criminal justice in their efforts "to situate historical crime in an intelligible context of class relations, collective mentalities, and economic structure," as Hay phrased it in 1980.[44] In legal circles, criminal justice has traditionally been treated as an important branch of *public law*, meaning the set of rules that govern relationships between individuals and society, between citizens and the state.[45] From this perspective, systems of criminal justice establish the boundary between acceptable behaviours and those which, by their transgressive or reprehensible nature (as defined by legislators) merit prosecution and punishment by the police, the courts, and the prison system. Crucially for present purposes, crime and criminal proceedings intersect with "the intimate" in ways that have piqued the interest of historians for some time now. The list of specific criminal offences occurring, by definition, within the intimate worlds of sex, marriage, and family varies from one jurisdiction to another, of course, but is invariably long and would in most countries include bigamy, incest, infanticide, seduction, prostitution, and rape.[46] To this list, sadly, must be added crimes rooted in gendered, domestic, and intimate-partner violence. These are shocking offences which, whether or not they were covered by specific provisions of the criminal law (such as Guatemala's 2008 "Law Against Femicide and Other Forms of Violence Against Women," discussed in Chapter 16 by Emilee Lord and John Wertheimer), have been studied to great effect, especially for what such cases can reveal about patriarchy and its inherent, sometimes tragic inequalities of power, opportunity, and personal security.[47]

In defining the "vertical" relationships between individuals and the state, the realm of public law also extends to legal regimes governing citizenship and legal capacity. Scholars of colonialism have explored the extent to which settler states used their legislative and administrative power to impose restrictive and exclusionary notions of citizenship, in studies that often push the boundaries of "family and justice" by highlighting the sorts of intimate and domestic relations that were specifically excluded by racist colonial regimes.[48] Our contributor Lorena Rizzo, for example, uses the South African state's recourse to photography as a lens through which to explore "a plethora of laws that curtailed the political and residential rights of all those classified as non-white" in the years immediately following unification in 1910. In the process, as she observes, "the legal and moral boundaries of the nation were drawn in order to define who belongs and who does not."[49] Similarly, the legal question of who does or does not belong arose once again during the world wars of the twentieth century, most immediately in the international debates over the citizenship status and mobility rights of women married to citizens of hostile nations. During the First World War, for instance, women born in England who had taken a German or Austrian husband lost their status as British subjects and were classified as enemy aliens, with enormous consequences for their social status and material well-being, as Ginger Frost shows in Chapter 12. "Family and justice," in the end, could just as easily mean "family and injustice" for individuals forced into legal limbo by the international conflicts of the twentieth century, as Gail Savage also shows in Chapter 13, this time for Soviet women who married British men during the Second World War.

Historians of sexual and domestic intimacy have also, and not surprisingly, been drawn to the realm of *private law*, which traditionally refers to the set of rules governing relationships between and among individuals.[50] Most obviously, private law includes family law and therefore the vast spectrum of legislation and jurisprudence concerning marriage, divorce, parental obligations, adoption, child custody, inheritance, and a host of other topics. Indeed, as Michael Grossberg writes in the opening lines of *Governing the Hearth* with reference to the United States, "[a] specialized law of the family was one of the most significant products of the nineteenth-century legal order."[51] A full treatment of this topic, that is to say, of the emergence of the specific area of law that Grossberg calls "domestic relations," for the many countries discussed by our contributors, is beyond the scope of this volume. But we certainly catch glimpses in many of the essays collected below. A good example is the contribution by Jean-Philippe Garneau (Chapter 5) in which he examines the legal instrument of *la tutelle*—a form of guardianship for the minor children of deceased parents, based on French civil law but applied in the British colony of Lower Canada—and its use by families of different origins and configurations in the 1820s and 1830s. Also set in Lower Canada, Isabelle Bouchard's essay (Chapter 1) places the emphasis on the transmission of wealth, status, and opportunity—in a word, inheritance—as it was mobilized across three generations of a single Indigenous family governed by the same regime of private law as their French-Canadian neighbours.

Bouchard's chapter also helps us make another, less obvious point, which is that private law covers a much broader terrain than what Grossberg calls domestic relations, embracing the bodies of law that govern contracts, property, and torts as well. As we shall see, Bouchard's chapter draws heavily on a collection of notarized contracts, many of them involving real estate transactions, and on her knowledge of the laws governing real and moveable property in a British province with French legal traditions, including the seigneurial system of land tenure. Under the heading "torts," private law also provides the framework within which citizens might institute civil proceedings against each other for various sorts of wrongs. Historians are now learning that civil litigation on a range of private matters can produce judicial paper trails that are every bit as rich in intimate detail and narrative potential as the most sensational criminal case. These include grievances rooted in slights to sexual propriety or family honour; protracted disputes between relatives over rights to inherited property; and litigation launched by heartbroken parents for civil damages over the wrongful death or injury of a cherished child.[52] The contribution by James Moran and Emma Chilton to this volume (Chapter 10) is an excellent example of this approach, drawing as it does on civil litigation in two different common-law jurisdictions as a window onto nineteenth-century conceptions of masculinity, paternal authority, and mental capacity in the Anglo-American world.

The distinction between opposing realms of "public" and "private" law has been a useful reference point for this discussion. But in legal studies, as in family and gender history, the traditional public-private binary is not without its limitations and, indeed, its critics.[53] The basic division it proposes—"vertical" relationships between individuals and the state (public) as opposed to "horizontal" relationships among individuals (private)—is clear and convenient, but in practice the boundary is anything but hermetic and there are many issues that cross over. This is especially true in the area with which this book is involved: the regulation of intensely *private* activities by resolutely *public* institutions. We are reminded in this connection of a 1950s civil case in which the key issue was a father's responsibility for his teenaged son's failure to act responsibly as a driver. The outcome was a hit-and-run accident that left a young girl permanently disabled, resulting both in the suit for compensatory damages (which was eventually upheld by the Supreme Court of Canada) and criminal charges against the joy-riding youth. The horizontal ties among individuals are important here and include the intimate father-son relationship on which the civil case turned, but also the conflictual ones linking the culpable driver with his innocent victim and the two fathers to each other, as plaintiff and defendant in this civil case. But this was also a highway accident that raised issues of safe driving and public safety and led to the teenager's arrest on charges of negligence, drunk driving, and fleeing the scene of an accident, so the vertical relationship between citizens and the state was also very much in play.[54]

If there is a generalization to be drawn from this brief reconnaissance at the crossroads of intimacy and the law—the place where our titular themes of "family" and "justice" overlap—it has perhaps already been articulated by one of our contributors. As Garneau puts it, "families' engagement with the law contributed to the ongoing symbolic and material construction of power within and surrounding the domestic unit."[55] Legal regimes and traditions, in other words, have played a fundamental role in allocating rights and responsibilities within domestic, residential, and kin groups, just as they have in setting the rules by which families and their members were governed by the state and its various institutions and agencies. But individual women and men might also challenge and resist the legal frameworks and restrictions imposed by state actors, as with the transnational marriages studied by Savage, who rightly emphasizes "the creativity of individuals who sought to shape their own lives," even "in the midst of global war."[56] Our authors share these convictions about the complex and dynamic relationship between family and justice across time and space. And their contributions here serve to push these ongoing conversations in exciting new directions.

### *In the Archives*

The intimacies explored by our contributors are made accessible through the written traces left by public proceedings that occurred in legally sanctioned spaces of social regulation, from notaries' offices to criminal or civil courtrooms to legislatures. The emphasis throughout this book on family, justice, and *the archives* suggests a final point that needs making, as we prepare to step aside and let these authors speak for themselves. "It was social and cultural historians," Alecia Simmonds reminds us,

> who, from the 1970s onward, turned to legal archives to uncover the voices of the disenfranchised. Following them, it was post-structuralist historians, in the 1980s and 1990s, who dispelled the fantasy that legal sources were authentic whisperings across the centuries from the lips of the lower orders. As Natalie Zemon Davis famously argued, the testimony in legal records is a collaborative, somewhat fictive venture, scripted by lawyers, litigants and scribes according to notarial formulae and with an eye to legal success. Legal records must be treated with caution.[57]

We share completely in this plea for caution, with its emphasis on the risks and pitfalls of legal records as source material for historians, whether social, cultural, poststructuralist, or otherwise. We also applaud scholars like Athena Athanasiou who have pushed the "archival turn" in exciting new directions, building initially on the epistemological challenge launched by Jacques Derrida in the 1990s and then on the powerful and persuasive contributions to archival theory made by Carolyn Steedman and Ann Laura Stoler.[58]

All of the contributors to this volume, we submit, would acknowledge the constructed nature of archives (and/or *the archive*). They have also embraced the particular challenge of decrypting the documents left behind by the workings of the legal and judicial apparatus, where so much of the content can be formulaic and transactional. Some, like Lorena Rizzo, are particularly explicit about the archival theory that informs their work. Rizzo calls for "an approach that understands intimacy not only as a matter of social relations, predominantly located in the domain of the private and the domestic, but as something that is *embedded in the archive itself*."[59] In a somewhat different register, Shelley Gavigan is no less reflective in considering the nature of the archival materials that form the basis of her study. For her, the main challenge is "how to interpret the words of vulnerable people, often women and children, who were required to describe their intimate experiences in inhospitable public contexts, to men they did not know and who did not share their life experiences and struggles."[60] Gavigan is among the many contributors to this collection who are skilled at "reading against the grain" with empathy and imagination in order to discover things about the past—and especially about intimacy and patriarchy in the past—that are interesting, useful, important, often forgotten, and just as often unexpected.

In the end, "legal archives" turns out to mean different things to different people, as is reflected in the range and variety of source material consulted by the scholars who answered our call and whose work is assembled here. There is a solid core of studies based on court records, whether originating in civil litigation (Chilton/Moran), youth court proceedings (Maor), or in criminal trials (Poutanen, Gavigan), including the records of capital murder cases that might lead to executions (Nicholas, Koya). There are several chapters that combine court records with newspaper coverage of "intimate" crimes that fascinated the reading public, such as those for incest (Giuliani) in France and for bigamy (Méthot) in Australia. Legal records of a more administrative nature are also in the mix, such as petitions by youths to minor officials in Argentina (Bates) and a selection from the vast trove of notarized deeds (Bouchard, Garneau) that has informed and enriched Quebec social and legal history for at least half a century.[61] We also encounter government files held by Canada's Department of Indian Affairs (Murdoch); both the British Home Office (Frost) and its Foreign Office (Savage); a set of photographs collected by South African immigration officials for identification purposes (Rizzo); and a series of on-the-street interviews conducted in urban Guatemala about recent changes to domestic-violence legislation (Lord/Wertheimer). This is a considerable and heterogeneous array of archives, united by its dual focus on the "legal" and the "intimate" but divided by geography, jurisdiction, and in so many other ways. Taken as a whole, it is itself an archive that presents many challenges but also some rather amazing possibilities, as our contributors—all careful, responsible scholars—demonstrate in the essays collected here.

A related feature of this volume is the extent to which our contributors have drawn on transcriptions of oral testimony: first-hand narratives collected in various legal settings and written down mainly by court stenographers and clerks, but also by presiding judges in their notes and by crime reporters in their published articles. At least half of the authors make use of depositions or other transcriptions of testimony presented by plaintiffs, defendants, and witnesses in criminal, civil, and administrative proceedings. These were most often the stories of "ordinary" people caught up in some branch of the justice system and about whom other written records would in most cases simply not exist. As Steedman reminds us, such accounts most often contain a sort of "formulaic self-narrative" extracted by a trained interlocutor seeking answers to legally informed questions which, as often as not, are omitted from the transcription.[62] Accused of murdering his lover over her infidelity and an unpaid debt, for instance, a defendant in 1840s Mauritius provided the following brief account of himself: "I am Beecon, sometimes called Beekam, I do not know my age, I am a labourer in the service of Mr. Cordonau of Plaines Wilhems. I am a native of Calcutta."[63] Steedman's observation that one "can certainly hear the legally required questions that structure these autobiographies" rings very true in this instance.[64]

Elsewhere in this volume are many more first-person narratives culled from legal archives and dealing with various kinds of intimate experiences. These range widely, from the exasperated mother Anna Shultz (a pseudonym) of Denver explaining her reasons for turning her teen-aged son Otto over to the juvenile justice system (Maor), to the aggrieved son Richard Watson of Ontario who challenged the mental capacity of the father who had disinherited him in favour of his brother William (Chilton/Moran), to Catalina Solis of Buenos Aires, a fifteen-year-old dress-shop worker who sought legal relief from the arbitrary authority of her overbearing and sometimes violent father (Bates). In presenting these materials as historical evidence, our contributors demonstrate their persistent interest in listening to the "voices of the disenfranchised" (to return to Simmonds' framing) while remaining fully attentive to the lessons of the archival turn and especially (borrowing from Gavigan once again) to the inherent difficulty of interpreting the words of "vulnerable people" forced into the "inhospitable public context" of a courtroom confrontation, deeply imbued with legal routines and formulae and with rules of evidence and procedure.[65]

In many cases, moreover, the stories we encounter in legal archives—especially but not only in criminal court records—are difficult and disturbing ones, frequently involving violence, dispossession, deception, and abuse. This raises important ethical concerns for the scholars who undertake the research and who have shared their work in this volume. Jane Nicholas is the author who has articulated these issues most clearly for our readers in her discussion (Chapter 14) of Ontario women accused of infanticide. In addition to considering the practice of naming subjects, Nicholas reflects upon the importance of addressing with sensitivity the physical and emotional impacts of violence on the women she studies, referencing Louise A. Jackson's assertion that historians "have a duty to [their] subjects to 'use them as a source' in a responsible way" and "to acknowledge the interconnectedness of body, pain, experience, voice."[66] Each of our contributors shares this sense of responsibility and is acutely aware of the ethical implications of employing archival sources to probe the intimate lives of their subjects. Riyad Koya, for example, acknowledges the graphic nature of the testimonies given in the femicide trials he analyzes and proceeds with caution in relaying those accounts in his chapter. Similarly, Mélanie Méthot is attentive to the tendentious press coverage received by women accused of bigamy and warns her readers of the falsehoods often constructed by court reporters to describe these women. Insofar as our contributors are willing to reveal the most private details of their subjects' personal and domestic lives, they are also conscious of the boundary between historical significance and exploitation and approach their research with circumspection.

◆◆◆

*Family and Justice in the Archives* is organized into five sections, each with its own brief introduction. Rather than grouping the essays by shared geography or time period, we have adopted a thematic structure designed to encourage reflection and discussion of common themes and issues across boundaries of time, space, and legal tradition. The four chapters in Part 1, entitled *Colonial Encounters*, explore the regulation of domestic and sexual intimacies in two very different regions of the British Empire in a period extending from the late eighteenth century to the early twentieth. The circumscribed and contested rights and identities of Indigenous people, such as the Abenaki of Lower Canada, and other racialized groups, such as Indian and Chinese migrants to southern Africa, are front-and-centre in these studies of race, gender, and intimacy in colonial contact zones.

The regulation of relationships between parents and their children is the common thread uniting the three chapters in Part 2, entitled *Intergenerational Justice*. The emergence of child-protection laws and institutions, including guardianship arrangements and youth courts, and their deployment in urban settings from Montreal to Buenos Aires (by way of Chicago, Denver, and Memphis) are the focal points here, as is a growing sense of intergenerational tension pitting sometimes arbitrary forms of parental authority against youthful claims on agency and autonomy.

In Part 3, *Intimacies in the Courtroom*, readers will experience something of the drama of the nineteenth-century courtroom: that theatre of justice in which vulnerable women and men could be forced by lawyers and judges to recount their most intimate personal experiences. Two of these chapters focus on criminal proceedings—there are cases of seduction, prostitution, and a wide range of other offences in which intimate relations played an unexpected role—while the third draws on a set of civil suits that challenged a man's mental capacity and thus invoked Victorian standards of masculinity, grounded in "manly" virtues such as reason and self-control.

From one legal institution, the courtroom, we turn in Part 4 to quite a different one, matrimony, with three chapters grouped under the heading *Marriage Regulation*. Much more than a vow of love and commitment between two private individuals (or more, in societies and legal traditions that allow polygamy), legal matrimony creates a web of relationships involving kin, community, and most significantly here, the state, which might intervene to sanction bigamous unions or to strip fundamental citizenship and mobility rights from those, especially women, who chose foreign partners in war-torn Europe during the twentieth century.

In the final section of the book, entitled *Everyday Violence*, our contributors examine the legal regulation of intimate, sexual, and domestic violence in three different settings: nineteenth-century France, Ontario at the turn of the twentieth century, and Guatemala in the very recent past. The topics (incest, infanticide, and intimate-partner violence) and approaches are different, but the chapters collected here all share a preoccupation with the asymmetrical power dynamics that fostered violence and abuse in certain families, and with legal cultures grounded in patriarchy and inflected with the sort of *machismo* that accepted a certain level of violence as "ordinary" and that have been notoriously slow to change.

*Family and Justice in the Archives*, then, invites readers to participate in an international conversation about the legal regulation of domestic and sexual intimacies, as seen through the archival traces left behind by a wide range of state agencies in Canada, Britain, France, Argentina, South Africa, the United States, and a number of other countries. As broad and inclusive as this volume may be, finally, it is reasonable to anticipate that some readers will be disappointed by its silences and omissions. We gestured toward queer intimacies earlier in this introduction, a topic which has drawn many excellent scholars towards legal sources and especially into the archives of the criminal courts, where ample evidence has been found to document the state's repression of same-sex desire transnationally and throughout the period covered by this book.[67] But there is, alas, no chapter on the LGBTQ+ experience at the intersection of intimacy and the law: a topic which deserves a book—indeed, many books—of its own. Nor do our contributors address aging and elder care, another important area in which the state has played an increasing and often problematic role in the period covered by this book. Old-age pensions and related social-security legislation emerged in Western liberal democracies in the postwar years and publicly regulated long-term-care facilities took over from families as the setting—for better *and* for worse, as the COVID-19 pandemic has shown so dramatically—for the intimate lives of so many senior citizens.[68]

Some readers will be disappointed at these lacunae and at others they may identify for themselves. Certainly, there is much more work still to be done. For our part, we are pleased to celebrate the insights offered by our contributors, to highlight the depth and breadth of the essays they have prepared, to modestly suggest the overall thematic coherence of the present volume, and to encourage others to pursue further projects and publications that will broaden the international conversation around histories of intimacy and the law still further.

# PART 1

## *Colonial Encounters*

*The four chapters in this opening section examine how colonial subjects on two different continents navigated complex and sometimes overlapping structures of law which sought to narrowly circumscribe their legal rights and identities. Each contributor engages with the clash of legal systems and understandings of marriage, family, and kinship within the British Empire, especially as between settler regimes—sometimes complicated by several layers of European colonialism—and the beliefs, customs, and practices of Indigenous and other racialized peoples. There are profound and inter-related dissonances that emerge from the contact zone between Indigenous and settler understandings of family property in Canada, for instance, and from troubling stories of Indian indentured labourers embroiled in legal proceedings over sexual violence in colonial East Africa.*[1]

*Chapter 1, by Isabelle Bouchard, explores two generations of the Gill family's experience as prominent members of an Indigenous (Abenaki) family on the Odanak reserve in Lower Canada. This was British colonial territory in the nineteenth century, but also a place where French seigneurial laws of land tenure remained in force until 1854, with profound implications for access to property and social status. In a similar register, the impacts of Canada's notorious Indian Act (1876) on property and inheritance rights for Indigenous people, and especially Indigenous women, are examined by Chandra Murdoch in Chapter 2, where the context is Ontario in the final decades of the nineteenth century. Limitations were placed on Indigenous individuals' legal capacity to transmit property, but Murdoch's investigation reveals that community members, including women and political leaders, nevertheless sought and sometimes secured alternatives to the discriminatory inheritance laws set out by the Indian Act.*

*From northern North America, the discussion moves to more southerly parts of the British Empire, stopping first on the small East African island of Mauritius. As different and distant as one can imagine in most respects, Mauritius shares with Canada its successive histories of French and British imperialism and the related forms of legal pluralism. And both places experienced, as Riyad Koya shows in Chapter 3, the profound impact on intimate lives of racist and segregationist colonial laws. Koya asks what law ought to govern the family life of Indian migrants, particularly indentured labourers accused of murdering women who may or may not have been their legal "wives" under British law. Turning then, in Chapter 4, to twentieth-century South Africa, Lorena Rizzo investigates a range of administrative archives that used the medium of photography to classify individuals by their racial origins "in a context marked by racial segregation, internal colonization and the rise of ethnic nationalism."*[2]

*Indeed, the fundamental question of who gets to be a legal* person *in colonial and post-colonial settings runs through the chapters in this first section, with inequalities based on race and gender highlighted by all four authors, and with profound repercussions for marriage, inheritance, and other dimensions of family life.*

## CHAPTER 1

# Land Ownership and Inheritance among the Abenaki of Odanak

## *The Process of Family Reproduction in the Gill Household*[1]

*Isabelle Bouchard*

In the first half of the nineteenth century, the Abenaki of Odanak, an Indigenous community located south of the St. Lawrence River near Trois-Rivières, managed the lands granted to them under the French regime as a veritable seigneurial estate.[2] On behalf of their community, the Abenaki chiefs acted as the owners of the so-called *seigneurie de la mission*, which included sections of the seigneuries of Saint-François and Pierreville. The grants of 1700 and 1701 did not explicitly give them the authority to distribute land *en censive*. But on their own initiative, starting in 1800, the Abenaki of Odanak adopted the "fief and seigneurie" model as the basis for granting lands to *Canadien* (French-Canadian) farmers.

Since managing a seigneurie required "daily and constant attention,"[3] the chiefs hired a legal representative to oversee the administration of their estate. This middleman was given authority to grant *censives* and collect seigneurial dues from *censitaires* on behalf of the Abenaki. Members of the Gill family played this role from 1811 to 1855, exercising considerable influence over how lands held by the Abenaki of Odanak were managed. Augustin Gill served as the legal representative of the Abenaki in the 1810s and 1820s; his son, Louis, took over in July 1832 and continued in the role until 1855.[4]

Augustin's paternal grandparents, Samuel Gill and his wife Rosalie, were individuals of English origin adopted by the Abenaki Nation in the late seventeenth century. They were among the captives taken during raids carried out in New England between 1690 and 1760, some of whom were permanently integrated into the communities of the St. Lawrence

Valley.[5] Like his father, Joseph-Louis (1719–1798), before him,[6] Augustin Gill was appointed a chief of the Nation. And upon his death in August 1851, at the age of 80, Augustin was "buried in the church of the Abenaki."[7] However, unlike his grandfather and father, Louis Gill would not become a chief. In the early nineteenth century, the Gill family's membership in the community increasingly came into question because of their lifestyle (farmers living outside the village) and their marriages with French-Canadian women. In the late 1830s, Indian Affairs permanently removed Augustin and his sons from the list of annual presents, which served to identify community members entitled to receive presents from the Crown prior to the mid-nineteenth century.[8] Nevertheless, several members of the Gill family would continue to maintain close ties with the Abenaki of Odanak.

This chapter addresses the process of family reproduction in the household of Augustin Gill and Marie Félicité Plamondon during the first half of the nineteenth century. The process reveals much about the social status that Augustin was seeking to achieve and pass down to the next generation, especially the factors and strategies promoting the family's continued hold on the position of "seigneurial agent." The tactics employed by Augustin reveal his understanding of the role played by the colonial state, through the administration of civil law, in securing property rights rooted in the seigneurial regime. They also reflect the importance of kinship relations for the customs governing access to Abenaki territory.[9] The circumstances surrounding the intergenerational transfer of family assets in the Gill-Plamondon household therefore highlight the coexistence of different land tenure regimes in Lower Canada up to the mid-nineteenth century, as well as the role played by the corresponding legal traditions in the organization of family life.[10] This diversity of land tenure regimes was rooted in legal pluralism, "which, in a colonial context, presupposes an inevitable degree of penetration of the legal orders."[11]

Although much has been written about inheritance practices in rural Quebec,[12] such work consistently overlooks the situation among First Nations. Nevertheless, some Indigenous communities in the St. Lawrence Valley developed a land tenure regime that combined collective and individual (or family) ownership.[13] The intergenerational transfer of family assets is a complex process that can span "several decades corresponding to different phases of the family life cycle."[14] Accounting for all of the actions taken by the Gill-Plamondon household requires a meticulous reconstruction of its economic development, including the lands it acquired, the nature of the properties it accumulated, and the favoured means of passing them down. Alongside patterns of land inheritance, I look at other means of establishing the next generation, including apprenticeships and education. The study of matrimonial alliances and kinship networks also sheds light on family reproduction, and especially efforts to ensure that the Abenaki consistently chose a member of the Gill-Plamondon family to serve as their legal representative.[15]

In Lower Canada, notaries played a central role in the application of French civil law and helped ensure its preservation following the British conquest of New France. A great deal of their work was related to the transfer of family assets, a process governed by the Custom of Paris. Notarial deeds, produced by the most visible legal practitioners in the Lower Canadian countryside, therefore constitute a key source for studying family life in Quebec.[16] In the first half of the nineteenth century, like their French-Canadian neighbours, members of the Abenaki community of Odanak used the services of notaries. The deeds produced for the Abenaki showcase the means of inheritance planning used to transfer individual land holdings within the "dish" or "common pot," that is to say the "seigneurial" lands that the community reserved for the use of its members.[17] Notarial records therefore provide an important window on the material dimension of the intimate sphere, including the acquisition and transfer of land.

Compared to other members of the Odanak community, the Gill family began using the services of these legal practitioners to register their marriage contracts and land transfers much earlier, starting in the 1760s. My analysis of the Gill-Plamondon household is based on a collection of just under sixty notarial deeds in which Augustin Gill acted in a personal capacity, sometimes alongside his wife.[18] I also gathered genealogical data from the parish register for the church of Saint-François-du-Lac.[19] The Gill family's early use of notaries was most likely a result of the kinship networks they developed with French-Canadian families beginning in the mid-eighteenth century.

## *Marriage Alliances and Kinship Networks*

Through his own marriage and the marriage alliances secured by his family, Augustin Gill was closely related to the two *Canadiens* responsible for administering Abenaki lands in the first decade of the nineteenth century. In January 1800, Joseph Gamelin dit Chateauvieux, a merchant from Saint-François-du-Lac, was named "seigneurial" prosecutor and continued to hold this position until he resigned voluntarily in early 1810.[20] During the same period, Jean Plamondon was hired to survey several pieces of land granted to *censitaires* in the so-called *seigneurie de la mission.*[21] Thanks to his kinship ties to the Plamondon and Gamelin families, Augustin Gill was able to secure the position of legal representative responsible for managing the "seigneurial" lands of the Abenaki in October 1811.

On 1 May 1797, Augustin Gill married his second wife, Marie Plamondon, in the parish of Saint-François-du-Lac. Roughly twenty-six years old, the groom was identified as a carpenter and joiner.[22] On other occasions, he was described as a master blacksmith and master craftsman.[23] However, farming would prove to be his primary occupation.[24] He would also acquire various titles of distinction—"gentleman" (*notable*) or "esquire" (*écuyer*)—in addition to his diverse occupational identities.[25]

Augustin's bride was the daughter of Jean Plamondon, a surveyor from Ancienne-Lorette, and Félicité Girard dit Breton.[26] Following the death of his wife, Jean's work brought him to the Lake Saint-Pierre region. In the summer of 1783, he surveyed the boundary between the seigneuries of Saint-François and La Lussaudière, as well as a piece of land owned by Joseph Gill, Augustin's maternal uncle, in the fief of La Lussaudière.[27] This meeting led to the surveyor taking Catherine Gill, Augustin's sister, as his second wife on 17 November 1783.[28] However, the minor children from his first marriage, Marie and Jean, did not immediately follow their father to Saint-François. Rather, they remained in the care of their maternal uncle in Charlesbourg.[29] In January 1791, Jean Plamondon reconvened the assembly of relatives and friends to consider a request "to collect them and raise them in his home and under his care."[30]

The April 1797 marriage between Augustin Gill and Marie Plamondon, who was about eighteen years old at the time, further strengthened the alliance between these two families. Catherine Gill attended the signing of the marriage contract in her capacity as Marie's stepmother.[31] This union also meant that Augustin's brother-in-law, Jean Plamondon, became his father-in-law as well. When Jean and Catherine died suddenly in 1810, Augustin was appointed tutor to their minor children—testifying to the level of solidarity associated with such marriage alliances.[32] The

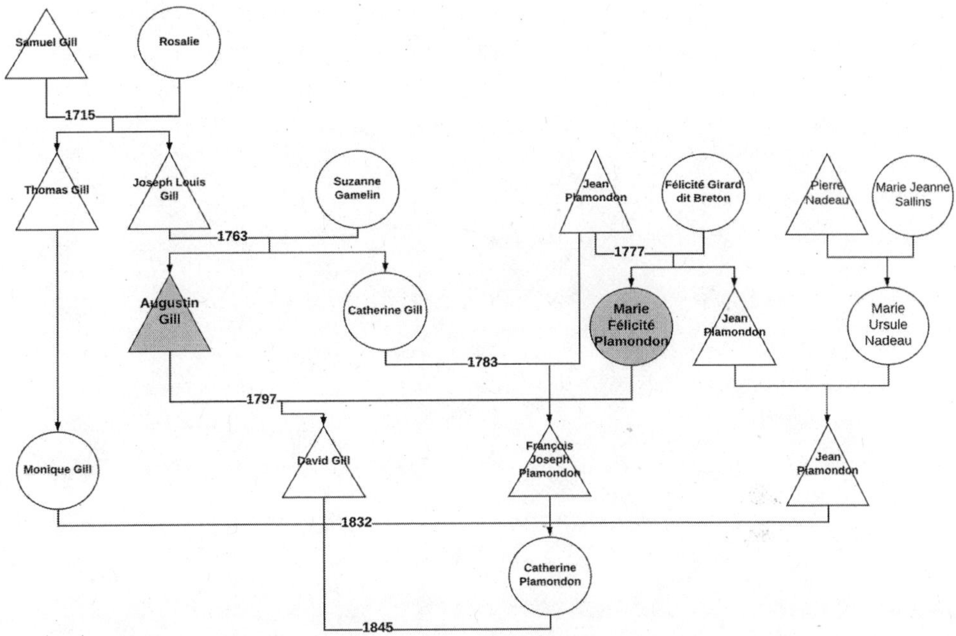


Figure 1.1 Gill-Plamondon kinship network. Source: Genealogical chart prepared by the author using Lucidchart.

next generation would see further marriages involving members of these two families.[33]

Unlike Jean Plamondon, a surveyor who arrived in the region shortly before the turn of the nineteenth century, the Gamelin dit Chateauvieux family had been established in the seigneurie of Saint-François since the early eighteenth century. Joseph's grandfather, Pierre Gamelin, was the nephew of the seigneur of Saint-François and served as the area's first militia captain.[34] In 1700, his dwelling was located across the Saint-François River (the Alsig8ntekw) from the Abenaki village.[35]

The Gamelins had shared a social network and been forging alliances with the Gills since the mid-eighteenth century. In November 1763, Augustin's father, Joseph-Louis Gill, had taken Suzanne Gamelin as his second wife.[36] Suzanne's brother (Joseph) had married Catherine Annance in February 1768.[37] The latter was the granddaughter of Samuel Gill and therefore also a cousin of Augustin Gill.[38] Two of Augustin's other first cousins (François Louis and Antoine) would also marry nieces

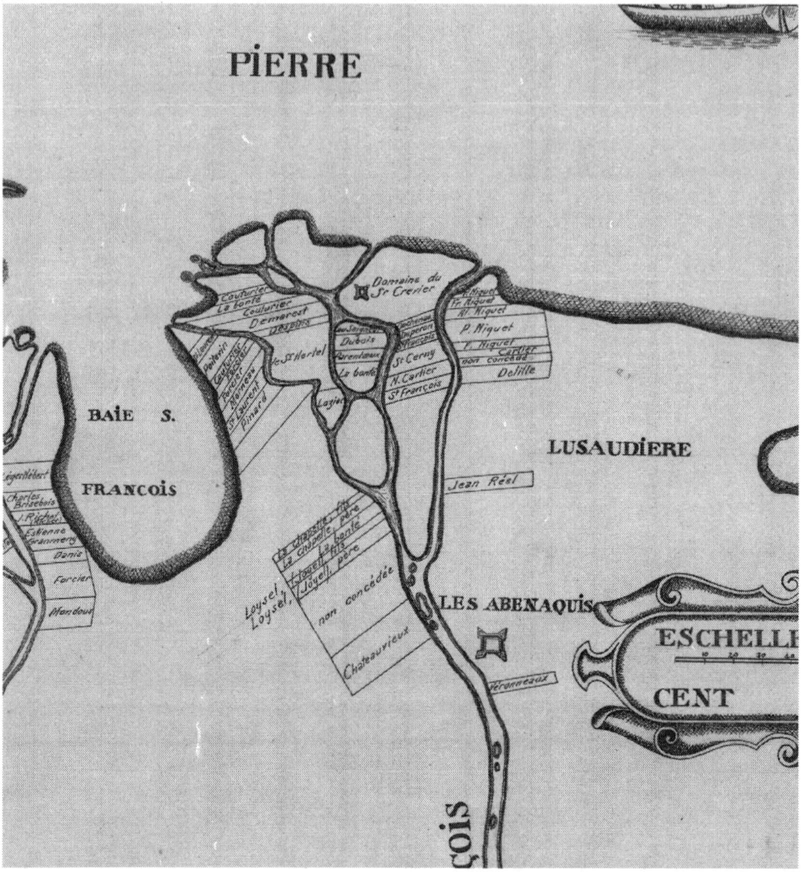


Figure 1.2 Map detail from *Suite du Gouvernement des Trois Rivières*, Gédéon de Catalogne, 1709. Source: Bibliothèque et Archives nationales du Québec – Quebec City, Gédéon de Catalogne, *Suite du Gouvernement des Trois Rivières qui comprent en dessendant le fleuve St Laurent depuis les isles de Richelieu jusqu'à la sortie du Lac St-Pierre levée en 1709 par les ordres du Roy ministre et secrétaire destat par le Sr Catalogne Lieutenant des troupes et dressée par Jean Baptiste Decouagne*, 1709. BAnQ-QC Reference: D197, SS2, S4, P600.

of Joseph Gamelin.[39] These complex linkages meant that the two families were tightly connected by the early nineteenth century.

Augustin Gill was therefore closely related to both Joseph Gamelin (his maternal uncle) and Jean Plamondon (simultaneously his brother-in-law and father-in-law). Through the kinship networks that connected him to two key actors in the introduction of the "fief and seigneurie" model to

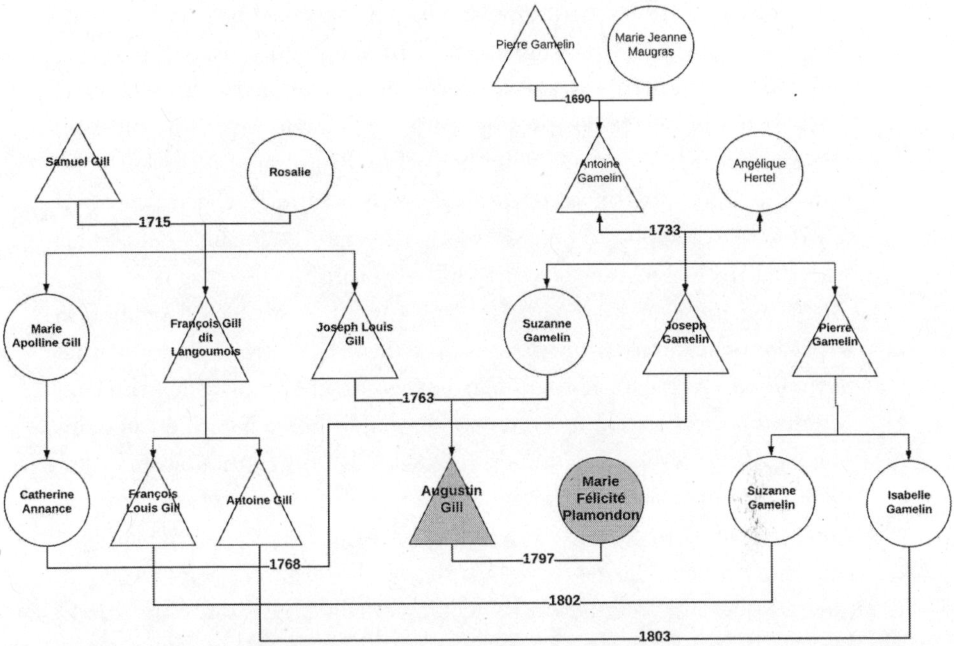


Figure 1.3 Gill-Gamelin kinship network. Source: Genealogical chart prepared by the author using Lucidchart.

Abenaki lands, Augustin Gill had access to valuable expertise on seigneurial management and territorial organization. This knowledge would allow him to serve as "seigneurial agent" for eighteen years and to pass the position on to one of his sons.

## *Land Acquisition and the Intergenerational Transfer of Property*

Understanding the Gill-Plamondon household's inheritance strategies requires close attention not only to the nature of the property acquired and transferred, but also to the rights attached to it. Like other inhabitants of the St. Lawrence Valley, Augustin Gill could acquire land *en censive* in one of two ways: a direct grant from a seigneur or the negotiated transfer of already granted lands. Meanwhile, his ties to the Abenaki community allowed him to acquire property within the domain (previously ungranted lands) of the so-called *seigneurie de la mission*. Such lands were not subject to seigneurial dues (*cens et rentes*) but were—at least in theory—reserved for members of the Odanak community.

The couple's efforts to acquire land began a few days before their wedding. On 19 April 1797, Augustin Gill purchased a *censive* measuring one-and-a-half arpents in area (twenty-six feet of frontage by twenty-five arpents in depth) in the seigneurie of Saint-François for the sum of 1,600 *livres*.[40] Joseph Gamelin helped Augustin pay for the land[41] by providing a loan of 1,300 *livres*, to be repaid through the rights owed to his wife in relation to her late mother's estate. Augustin's debt to his maternal uncle was transferred to his father-in-law and ultimately paid off by the surveyor in 1804.[42] His wife's family's financial contribution toward procuring this property appears to have been arranged at the time of their wedding. The couple's marriage contract specified that the land acquired by Augustin a few days earlier would be included in the community of property.[43] In addition to knowledge on seigneurial management and territorial organization, kinship networks therefore provided Augustin Gill with access to the capital necessary for acquiring land outside the Abenaki village, as well as the credit required to make such a purchase before his father-in-law could actually access the sums due to his wife.[44]

In addition to this land obtained from the Crevier family in the fief of Saint-François, Augustin Gill also acquired lands held *en censive* in that portion of the fief belonging to the Abenaki. In 1810, the legal representative of the Abenaki granted three small properties of various sizes.[45] These lands were adjacent to ones acquired by other members of Augustin's family, including his brothers.[46] Furthermore, in January 1829, he acquired a fourth such tract, consisting of half the *censive* measuring three arpents by thirty arpents that had been granted to César Annance dit Cathness, one of the Nation's chiefs, in 1810.[47]

Between 1816 and 1820, Augustin Gill also acquired eight properties from within the previously ungranted lands belonging to the Abenaki and reserved for members of the community. They were mainly located on islands in the Saint-François River: Au Pin, Pierrotte, and Sébastien (the latter island was also known as Sasabaskin). Records of these privately executed transactions have been preserved because they were registered with notary Joseph Badeaux on 16 November 1824. The corresponding deed also records the undated acquisition of a property measuring ninety square arpents, which was apparently ceded to Augustin by the chiefs in appreciation of his efforts in managing the Nation's affairs and which he was free to dispose of as he saw fit.[48]

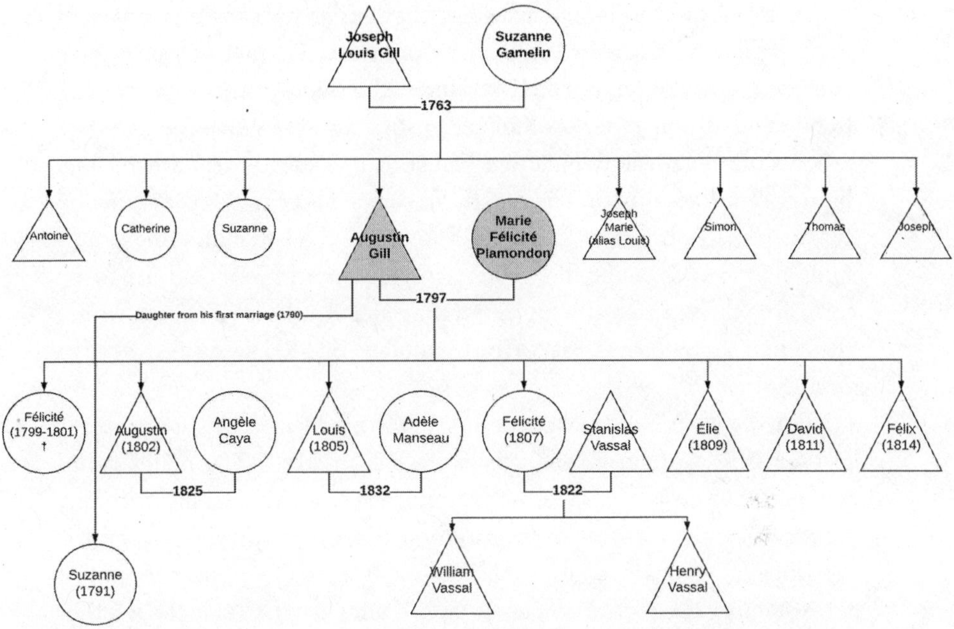


Figure 1.4 Children of Augustin Gill and Marie Félicité Plamondon. Source: Genealogical chart prepared by the author using Lucidchart.

Augustin Gill and Marie Plamondon had seven children—five boys and two girls—between 1799 and 1814, although one of their two daughters died in infancy.[49] The intergenerational transfer of the couple's lands began on the eve of the eldest son's wedding.[50] The couple used a deed of gift (*donation entre vifs*), the principal mode of inheritance in Lower Canada since the mid-eighteenth century. The nature of the different properties would, however, determine which heirs received them.

On 1 April 1825, Augustin Gill and his wife transferred two properties to their two oldest sons, Augustin and Louis. The latter were to equitably divide the land between them and farm it together.[51] Although the properties were transferred free of charge, the beneficiaries were prohibited from selling, exchanging, or transferring the land without the written consent of both parents, who guaranteed by these conditions their parental control.[52]

Located in the seigneurie of Saint-François, the first property (measuring four by twenty-five arpents) included the land first acquired by the couple, along with two additional tracts purchased the previous month.[53]

As the result of various land transfers, the property was by then adjacent to those owned by two of Augustin's brothers. The act of conveyance specified how the land; which bordered the Saint-François River, was to be divided. The elder brother (Augustin) was to receive the half (two arpents frontage) where buildings had already been erected. Meanwhile, he was required to have a house, barn, stable, and cowshed constructed for his younger brother (Louis), and to house the latter until these new buildings were completed.[54] The second property (four and a half by forty arpents)—which also bordered the Saint-François River, but within the Abenaki domain—was to be equitably divided between the two brothers.[55]

Four years later, in May 1829, the couple made a gift of land in favour of their three youngest sons, who were still minors.[56] The beneficiaries were to receive all movable and immovable property, along with any rights, cash, or claims belonging to their parents at the time of the latter's death. In this way, Élie, David, and Félix Gill were set to inherit the estate of their great-uncle, Joseph Gamelin, of whom their father had been made universal legatee in 1824.[57] In particular, this inheritance included lands located in the fief of Saint-François.[58] Like their older brothers, they were required to assist each other with the construction of homes and buildings on the property, while sharing common expenses.

As was often the case with such contracts, this deed of gift carried with it an obligation on the part of Élie, David, and Félix to provide for their parents' needs. Until the latter's death, the three beneficiaries were required to supply them with lodging, heat, food, attention, and care.[59] The parents were free to stay with any of their three sons and "to move from one to another whenever they see fit."[60] Caring for their ageing mother and father would have represented a significant burden for the beneficiaries, especially since the size of the associated lifetime annuity reflected an expectation of maintaining a high standard of living. The sons were required to support a varied diet that included grains and legumes (flour, corn, peas), meat (bacon, hocks, fattened beef, mutton), spices (pepper and salt), tea, coffee, and alcohol (wine and rum). They also had to provide their parents with a servant girl and a dairy cow, and to keep a "fully harnessed summer and winter carriage on hand for their use."[61] Furthermore, the beneficiaries were required to bury their parents in the cemetery of the parish where they died and to have two church services celebrated for each of them.

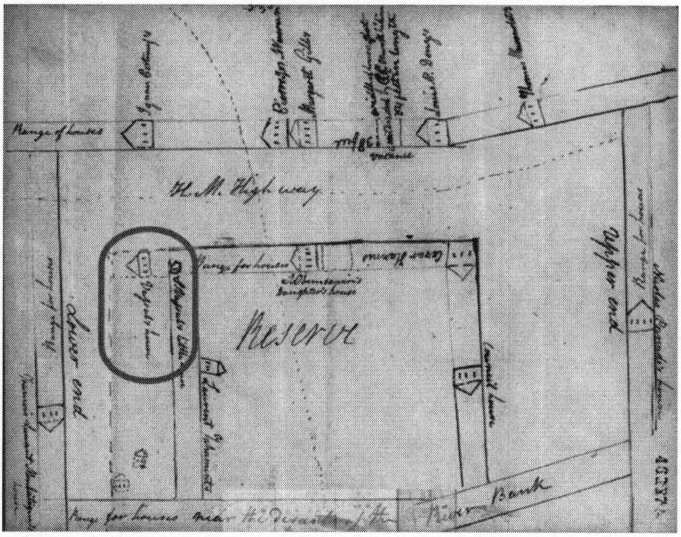


Figure 1.5
Map of the village of Odanak, 1842. Source: Library and Archives Canada, "Regulation relative to the village lots or emplacements in the village of St. François, with an explanatory sketch, as agreed to by the Abenaquois Chiefs & Warriors on the 27th July 1842," RG10, vol. 597, reel C-13379, pp. 46353–46357.

Contrary to what many historians have observed in rural Quebec, property was also transferred to the couple's only daughter.[62] In April 1825, Félicité inherited the home in which she was already living.[63] In this case, the nature of the property explains the choice of heir. Located in the Abenaki village, the house was on the ninety arpents of land granted by the chiefs. Since land and resource rights on the domain were tied to membership in the community, the couple chose to transfer this property to the only one of their children who was still considered a community member.[64]

Félicité Gill secured membership in the community through her husband. In August 1822, she had married Stanislas Vassal,[65] who was employed by Indian Affairs[66] and also worked in the fur trade.[67] The grandson of a French soldier,[68] Vassal had an Abenaki mother and was considered a member of the community, having been raised among the Abenaki since birth and having adopted their ways, habits, and language. Although his status was also based on adoption, it was his lifestyle that set him apart from his father-in-law and brothers-in-law.[69]

Beyond seeing to his daughter's needs, Augustin Gill also helped finance his son-in-law's business activities. Describing himself as a merchant (*marchand*) or trader (*commerçant*), Stanislas personally (i.e., not on behalf of a company) employed two non-Indigenous workers in the late 1820s.[70] In July 1829, Augustin Gill gave him a loan of fifty *livres* at the prevailing rate for "various advances of money and supplies."[71] If Augustin were to die before the loan was repaid, it was to be transferred to his grandson, William (also known as Guillaume).[72]

Félicité was the only daughter of Augustin Gill and Marie Plamondon to reach adulthood. However, Augustin had another daughter, Suzanne, from his earlier marriage to an Abenaki woman.[73] Suzanne was described as infirm, which likely explains why she does not appear to have ever married. In addition to providing for the twilight years of their father and mother, the three youngest sons were also required to take turns housing, feeding, and "humanely" caring for their half-sister.[74] However, no property was transferred to this daughter, who had no descendants.[75]

Ultimately, the couple's direct heirs were not the only ones to benefit from the properties acquired by the household. On 15 July 1811, Augustin Gill ceded, to Jacques Joseph Gill, one of the *censives* in the so-called *seigneurie de la mission* that he had acquired the previous year.[76] This gift was made just prior to Jacques Joseph's marriage to Marie Gill, the daughter of one of Augustin's first cousins.[77] At the time, Augustin was identified as Jacques Joseph's friend. Augustin and his wife would also be named godparents of the first child born to the younger couple.[78] Although I have been unable to establish any kinship ties between Jacques Joseph and Augustin,[79] their relationship was close enough for Augustin to provide for the needs of his "friend" by giving the latter a property (measuring three arpents, with six rods of frontage) for him to farm.[80] Moreover, the property was adjacent to those ceded to Jacques Joseph's brothers (Joseph Marie, also known as Louis, and Antoine Gill) in 1803.[81] However, this gift was made in exchange for an annual lifetime annuity of six bushels of wheat.[82]

## *Other Means of Establishing the Next Generation*

Augustin Gill and Marie Plamondon completed the intergenerational transfer of their family assets in 1832, when Louis Gill married Adèle Manseau and took over from his father as the legal representative responsible for managing the "seigneurial" lands of the Abenaki. In order to keep this position in the family, Augustin Gill relied on forms of family reproduction other than inheritance, including education and the transfer of know-how.

Since the mid-eighteenth century, the Gill family had shown appreciation for the benefits of literacy and schooling. Joseph-Louis Gill could read and write in French, and he ensured that his children received an education.[83] In 1774, he enrolled four of his sons in Moor's Indian Charity School, located in New Hampshire.[84] Joseph-Louis Gill also passed on his knowledge of the Abenaki language to his children.[85]

Instances where the Gill-Plamondon children were parties to notarial deeds—in particular, their marriage contracts—attest to their ability to sign their names, regardless of gender.[86] They may have attended the school run by François Annance, nephew of Joseph-Louis Gill, in the Abenaki village between 1803 and 1826.[87] Literacy and numeracy were essential skills when it came to managing a seigneurial estate. Augustin likely began sharing his knowledge with his son around December 1824, when the latter was appointed treasurer.[88] Like his father, Louis Gill had sufficient education to keep the books for the *seigneurie de la mission* and engage in correspondence with Indian Affairs.[89]

Apprenticeship represents another form of intergenerational transfer not involving inheritance. For instance, there was a forge located on the property in the fief of Saint-François that was transferred in 1825. Augustin Sr. reserved it, along with "all other carpentry shops," for his own use.[90] Meanwhile, a contract signed in January 1828 between Louis Gill and his brother-in-law, Stanislas Vassal, describes the former as both a clerk and a trained blacksmith.[91] His father therefore seems very likely to have passed down his know-how.[92] The presence of the forge may also explain why, in the early 1840s, Louis decided to reconsolidate the farm that had been split between him and his older brother.[93] Thus, in addition to receiving a farm, being trained as a blacksmith ensured he could support himself. Furthermore, during Augustin's time as "seigneurial agent," the work was unpaid. By contrast, Louis Gill was able to secure financial compensation in the form of a ten-percent commission on the sums he collected.[94]

## *Conclusion*

Although his second wife was French Canadian, Joseph-Louis Gill lived in the Abenaki village his entire life. But his sons settled outside the village. As they developed kinship networks with French-Canadian families, they acquired lands that were subject to seigneurial dues. And as

Figure 1.5 Map of the village of Odanak, 1842. Source: Library and Archives Canada, "Regulation relative to the village lots or emplacements in the village of St. François, with an explanatory sketch, as agreed to by the Abenaquois Chiefs & Warriors on the 27th July 1842," RG 10, vol. 597, reel C-13379, pp. 46353–46357.

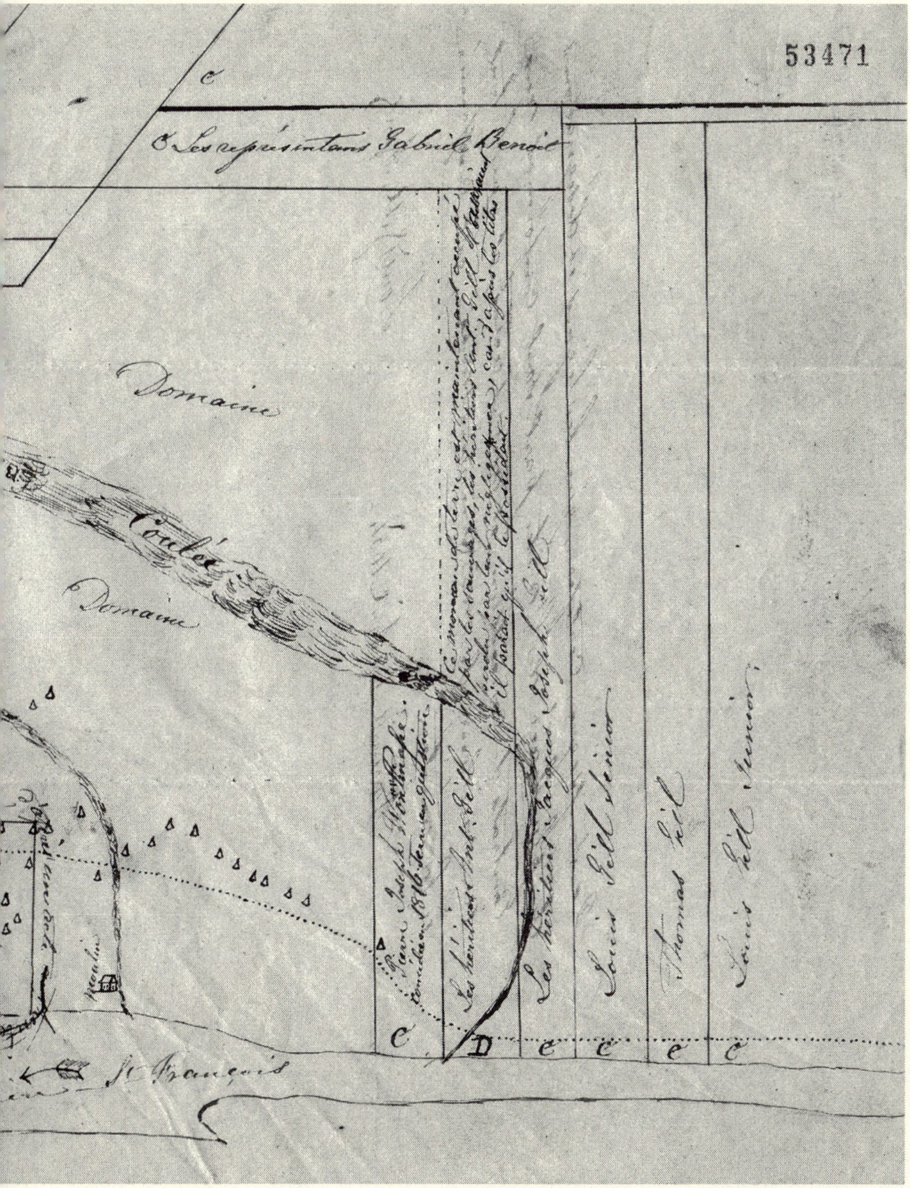
53471
Les représentans Gabriel Benoit
Domaine
Coulée
Domaine
St François
Louis Gill Senior
Thomas Gill
Louis Gill Senior

they adopted French-Canadian modes of property ownership and corresponding ways of working the land and using its resources, they began to identify themselves in notarial records as farmers of the parish of Saint-François, rather than as "Abenaki Indians."[95]

Notarial deeds provide a window on the private life of the Gill-Plamondon household and on how the parents sought to pass on the social status acquired by Augustin to the next generation. These judicial sources reveal how strategies for transferring family land were based on both the nature of the asset and the gender of the heir. Agricultural land held *en censive*, on which a livelihood could be earned, were mainly (but not exclusively) passed down to sons. Such land and the way of life associated with it also assigned a settler identity.[96] As a result, both the Abenaki community and the inhabitants of Saint-François-du-Lac perceived Augustin Gill, his brothers, and his sons as belonging to "White society." Louis Gill was therefore able to earn various titles of distinction and to rent a pew in the parish church.[97]

The *censives* acquired by Augustin Gill and his brothers were, for the most part, adjacent to one another. This allowed them to establish "Gill Village"—an area along the Saint-François River close to the centre of Saint-François-du-Lac that was home to multiple members of the family.[98] Eager for the next generation to continue pursuing inheritance strategies that extended beyond the nuclear family, Augustin required his male heirs to cooperate with each other and secured the right to oversee any land transactions they might make.

To their only daughter, Augustin Gill and his wife left the house and land he owned in the Abenaki village. Through their daughter's marriage to an individual regarded as a member of the Indigenous community, the couple ensured that this property would remain in the hands of one of their direct heirs. Following the death of her first husband and before her second marriage to a French Canadian, Félicité Gill transferred the land to her youngest son, Henry Vassal.[99] After growing up in the village and attending the Nicolet Seminary, he was appointed the Abenaki community's agent in 1873, thereby continuing the family tradition of accepting positions of power in Odanak.[100]

The adoption of the "White" mode of property ownership and the development of kinship relations with French-Canadian families did not mean that Augustin Gill had fully severed his ties to the Abenaki community. Since access to property and resources was at stake, Augustin contested his family's exclusion from the official list of those entitled to presents as members of the community, citing both his grandparents' adoption and the various positions held by his relatives in Odanak.[101] Remaining a chief until his death, Augustin Gill continued to play an active role in the political life of the community and in the management of the land its members collectively controlled. In addition to a share of his land holdings, he passed down to his second son the skills and knowledge required to take over the management of the *seigneurie de la mission.* Louis would continue serving as agent until the abolition of the seigneurial regime in 1854.

The inheritance strategies pursued by Augustin Gill and Marie Plamondon over the course of their married lives serve to showcase the personal, family, and community dynamics at work in the definition of membership in the Abenaki community of Odanak. This chapter has shown how the couple took advantage of the porous nature of identity boundaries in the period before the 1850s, when legislation formally defining who qualified as an "Indian" was first adopted.[102] In this respect, the Gill-Plamondon household's family reproduction strategies were most likely different from the inheritance practices of other members of the Abenaki community. Ensuring that male heirs could pursue farming was probably not the aim of most Abenaki families, given how notarial records identify hunting as the primary occupation of a great many men from the community. Moreover, Augustin Gill sought to maintain a position of power in the community, especially by taking over a key role in the management of Abenaki lands. Further research is needed to understand what specific strategies and aims were adopted by Abenaki individuals and families with respect to the intergenerational transfer of property, as well as how these strategies and aims relate to efforts for maintaining the land held in common by the community.[103]

CHAPTER 2

# Inheritance and the Indian Act

## *Political Action and Women's Property on Southern Ontario Indian Reserves, 1857–1900*[1]

*Chandra Murdoch*

What can be passed on to loved ones after death, and who controls these decisions, engage some of the most heated and personal aspects of family law in the archives. On Ontario Indian reserves in the late nineteenth century, these questions were a matter of both individual struggle and political engagement. Women and political leaders, on reserve land that represented a fraction of their traditional territories,[2] worked through and against the colonial system of inheritance laws imposed on them and their communities by the Indian Act.[3] Wills and estate law provide an avenue for understanding how the Department of Indian Affairs (DIA), through the Indian Act, sought to regulate an emotionally intimate and economically important aspect of family life—how individuals could pass on real and personal property to their families and other people they cared for. They show how the government imposed, through the law, a racist and gendered structure of paternalistic decision-making around inheritance for those deemed status Indians. Examining wills and estates also shows how alternatives to the law were fought for by Indigenous people in Ontario. They sought to ensure family security under a different set of colonial laws than those rooted in the French civil law and seigneurial land tenure examined by Isabelle Bouchard in the previous chapter.[4]

Between 1857 and 1894, the Canadian government altered and amended inheritance laws affecting Indigenous people several times. Through these amendments, inheritance provisions in the law were expanded, while control over them was given to the Superintendent General of Indian Affairs. As decision making on wills and estates became consolidated in the hands of the Superintendent General (a power most often delegated, in practice, to the Deputy Superintendent General), Indian Agents were tasked with increased surveillance of family life on reserves on their behalf.[5] The effects of this law have been longstanding as, to this day, the federal Minister of Indigenous Services is required to approve the wills of status Indians living in Canada.[6]

To outline the impacts of these changes to inheritance law, I examine the actions taken by three groups of Indigenous people in nineteenth-century Ontario: the Grand General Indian Council of Ontario,[7] band councils and reserve leadership, and women on reserves who advocated for the interests of themselves and their families. To do so, I draw on files in the Headquarters Records of the DIA that deal with inheritance, wills, and estates on reserves in Ontario from 1880 to 1900, as well as the meeting minutes of the Grand General Council. I argue that, while these files confirm the expansion of the DIA's control over inheritance, they also demonstrate how individuals, band councils, and one intra-reserve political group imagined and argued for alternatives to the limited options presented through the developing legal and regulatory systems of the Indian Act.

Women's property holds a distinctive place within these records. For this chapter, I examined all the files I could locate and access in the Headquarters Records that dealt with estates or wills from 1870 to 1909. This included 274 files from across Canada, and I focus on the 212 files from Ontario. Women are strongly represented within these files as both testators and devisees through their relationships as daughters, siblings, and widows. Of the 212 files I examined, 141 involve women directly. The files also contain a notably higher volume of direct correspondence by women to the DIA than I have found in other areas of my research into the nineteenth-century Indian Act. Within an archive that emerged with the intention of state regulation of Indigenous land on reserves, these women's letters demonstrate their own perceptions of property rights. In this chapter, I focus on cases that deal with women's property in order to highlight the gendered context in which the endeavour to secure control over Indigenous inheritance decisions unfolded. As struggles over control of inheritance took place between the DIA and Indigenous leaders, women's property was a concern for all levels of settler and Indigenous governance involved.

Family law within the Indian Act has been most robustly understood through the impacts of the exclusion of women from Indian status, and thus reserves, through discriminatory marriage clauses, as well as the devastating impacts of child removal through mandatory schooling clauses.[8] This is understandable, as both have had longstanding and violently injurious effects on Indigenous women and communities.[9] Wills and estate administration are, however, an understudied aspect of the Indian Act that affected the possibilities for families living under it, intersecting with the above issues through the establishment of increased surveillance of family, parental, and marriage relationships by Indian Agents.[10]

The transmission of property on reserves was already greatly constrained by law through the type of land title the government imposed there. As the government removed Indigenous communities from their traditional territories and onto small pieces of land over the nineteenth century, reserve lands were vested in the Crown. Individual properties could be obtained through a system of "location tickets," granted by the Superintendent General, which established a life interest only. The DIA, at least initially, only permitted this property to be willed if individuals enfranchised (gave up their Indian status), and then only to children or lineal descendants (who would obtain a fee simple title).[11] These provisions contrast dramatically with the situation of men and unmarried women under the common law and Ontario legislation, who enjoyed broad testamentary freedom. Other than the obligation of those holding land in fee simple to provide dower for their widows, there were few restrictions on what men could bequeath in their wills; and even then, legislation passed during this period simplified barring dower when land was sold.[12] This testamentary freedom was considered one of the fundamental rights of free-born (propertied) men in Ontario and the other common-law provinces of Canada.[13] The difference in how Indigenous property was treated and Indigenous communities' inheritance decisions were overseen by Indian Agents highlights the paternalistic control imposed through Indian status.

However, within these constraints, family farms were established, deep connections to land and place were lived through generations, and investments were made in housing and farm buildings that would have had both economic and emotional importance to those wanting to pass them on to their loved ones. Indigenous people fought to maintain control over who could inherit these properties through multiple political avenues. The Grand General Indian Council of Ontario strategized to have wills and property rights included in the limited rights accorded by the state to status Indians through the Indian Act.[14] While they achieved some notable successes on this front, the legislation consolidated and increased control over inheritance in the hands of Indian Agents and the Superintendent General. Band councils on individual reserves operated within these new laws, often affirming wills and inheritance decisions outside of norms imposed by the DIA. Finally, women advocated for their rights by writing wills, hiring legal representatives, and advocating their cases to the DIA and band councils. Their cases demonstrate the gendered context of the jurisdictional struggle over inheritance decisions on reserves.

## *The Indian Act, Wills, and the Grand General Council*

The Grand General Indian Council of Ontario was a political organization that operated in Southern Ontario from 1870 into the early twentieth century.[15] Initially called by the Haudenosaunee at Six Nations, the council met almost every two years across the region on different reserves to review legislation on Indigenous people put forward by the government and to provide feedback to them about the laws.[16] Their meeting minutes show a direct engagement with the law as it developed, dealing with both the legislative precursors to the Indian Act as well as its many amendments. As Chiefs and band councillors themselves, Grand General Council delegates put forward their priorities for how band governance should operate. It should be noted that after 1882 Haudenosaunee participation at the Grand General Council ended. Thus, the council's feedback on the law is clearly not representative of all Indigenous communities in Ontario, particularly as the council mainly represented reserves from the South of the province (see Figure 2.1).[17] Even between the primarily Anishinaabeg leaders participating after 1882,[18] council minutes show multiple viewpoints on how the relationship between the state and reserve leaders should operate. The meeting minutes do, however, offer an example of inter-reserve organizing and negotiation around the onslaught of legislation geared towards Indigenous people in the late nineteenth century and offer important insights into how settler laws on inheritance were debated.

Wills and inheritance were a consistent area of focus in the Grand General Council's requests to change the law. By tracing nineteenth-century legislation on inheritance that became incorporated into the Indian Act, and the subsequent amendments to this legislation, we can observe how the Grand General Council engaged with the law as the government shifted and expanded it to benefit the DIA at the expense of reserve governance. Colonial legislators first assumed the right to recognize wills made by Indigenous persons in *The Gradual Civilization Act* of 1857.[19] They stipulated that limited wills would become part of the package of rights legally accorded to those who enfranchised. Inheritance was further elaborated on in the 1869 *Gradual Enfranchisement Act*—the law that the Grand General Council first met to oppose at their inaugural 1870 meeting at Six Nations.[20] Property on reserves was held by individuals through a "location ticket" which granted a life interest in the property. Those undergoing enfranchisement processes were allowed to will this property to their children only; and, if no will was made, the property would descend according to provincial laws.[21] The beneficiary would obtain a fee simple title to the property, although widows in these cases would also only obtain a life interest in the property.[22] For those not enfranchising (the vast majority), the property would devolve to the children, with the requirement that they care for their mother. If there were no children, the property would revert to the Crown after undefined "support" for the widow was granted.[23] At Six Nations, the Grand General Council resoundingly rejected the law, with this latter clause rejected through a motion by Chief Simcoe Kerr of Six Nations, on the grounds that it "deprives the widow of her husband's property and takes land without reason, and deprives the Indian of the right to transfer or lease his land."[24]

Figure 2.1 (*overleaf*) Map of participating communities at the Grand General Indian Council of Ontario, 1880–1900. Historic names used in council minutes are in brackets (not shown are unspecified communities from "Manitoulin Island," "Lake Superior," and "Lake Huron" First Nations, as well as "Delawares of Grand River," "Pottawatomies of Muncey," "Nahnahbedabing," "Non-treaty Indians of Saugeen," "Pottawatomies of Walpole Island" and "Wahnahtabung"). Map created by author and Jesse Purcell, adapted from Google Maps.

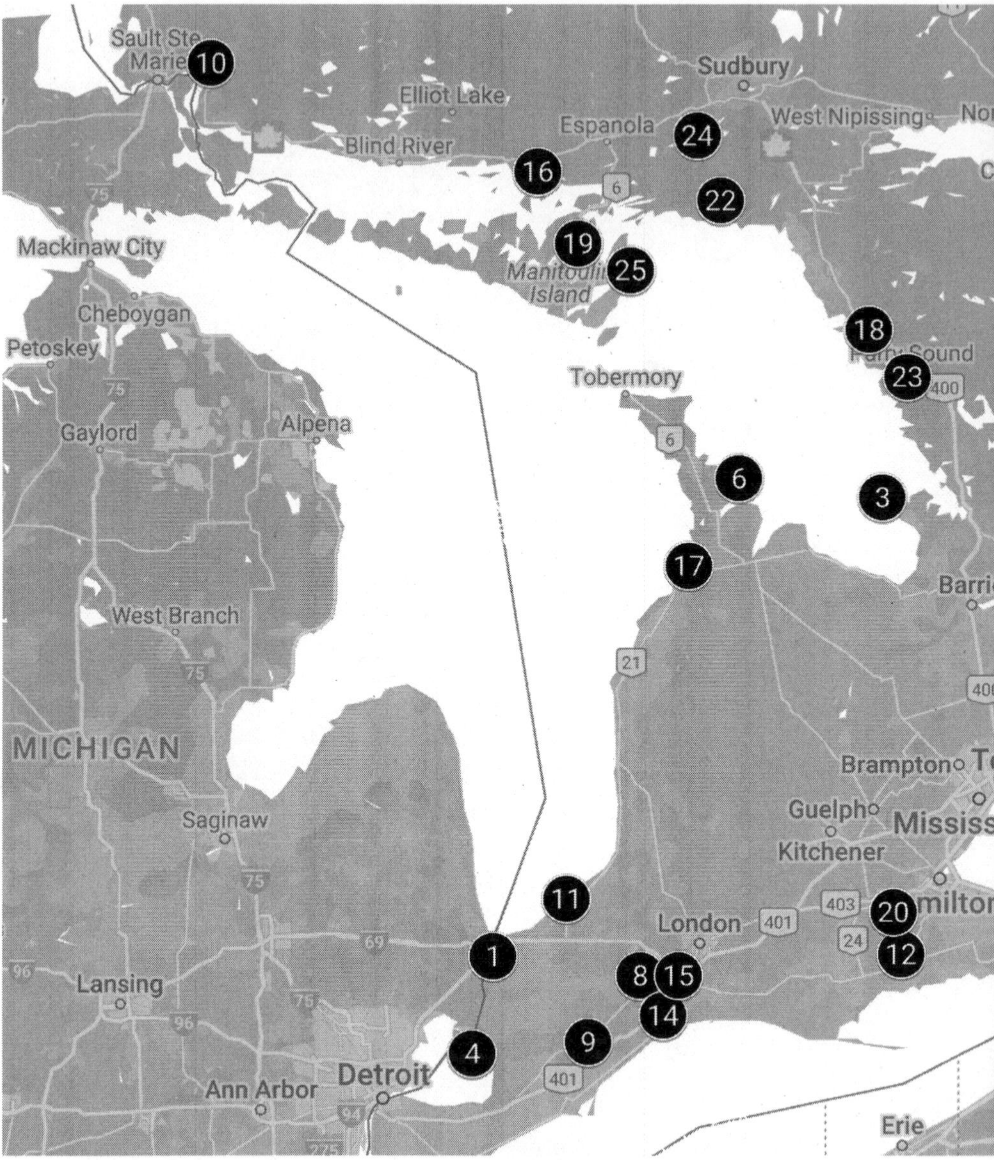


MAP LEGEND:

1. Aamjiwnaang First Nation (Chippewas of Sarnia)
2. Alderville First Nation (Alnwick)
3. Beausoleil First Nation (Christian Island)
4. Bkejwanong (Walpole Island)
5. Chippewas of Georgina Island First Nation (Snake Island)
6. Chippewas of Nawash Unceded First Nation (Cape Croker)
7. Chippewas of Rama First Nation
8. Chippewa of The Thames First Nation (Caradoc)
9. Delaware Nation at Moraviantown (Moravians of the Thames)
10. Ketegaunseebee (Garden River First Nation)
11. Kettle and Stony Point First Nation
12. Mississaugas of the Credit First Nation (New Credit)

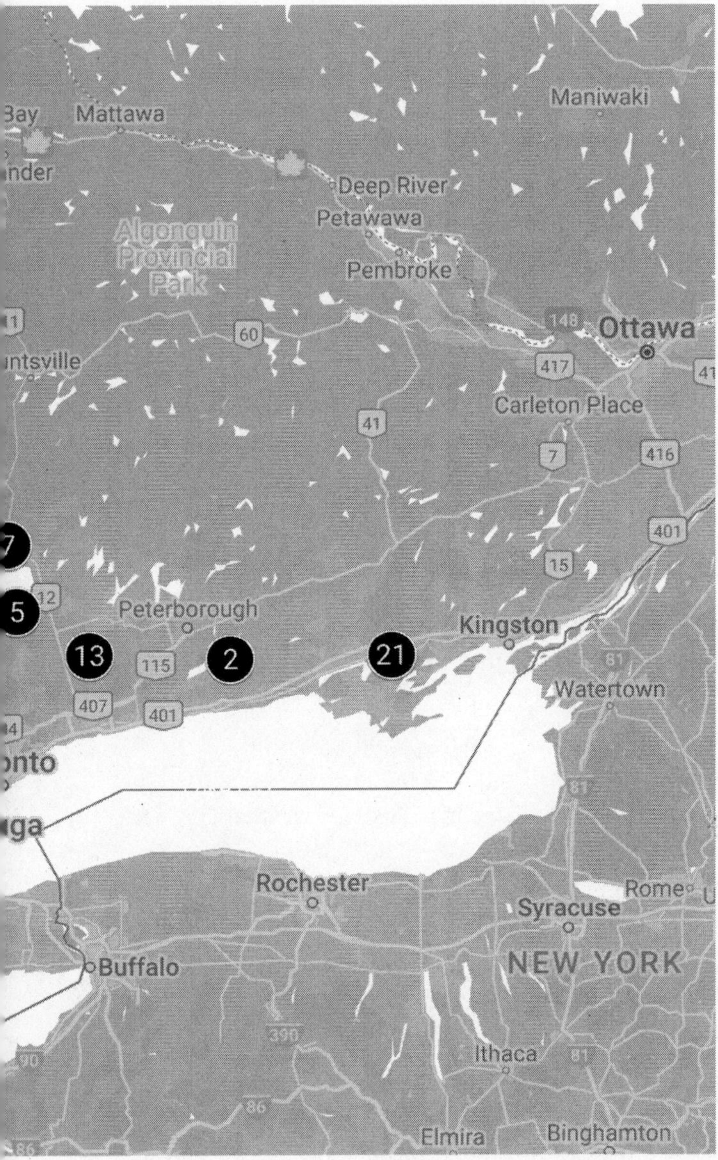


13. Mississaugas of Scugog Island First Nation (Scugog)
14. Munsee-Delaware First Nation (Muncey of the Thames)
15. Oneida Nation of the Thames
16. Sagamok Anishnawbek First Nation (Saganook)
17. Saugeen First Nation (Chippewas of Saugeen/Sauble)
18. Shawanaga First Nation
19. Sheguiandah First Nation (Shegoyenday)
20. Six Nations of the Grand River
21. Tyendinaga Mohawk Territory (Mohawks of the Bay of Quinte)
22. Point Grondine (Grondine)
23. Wasauksing First Nation (Parry Island)
24. Atikameksheng Anishinawbek First Nation (Whitefish Lake)
25. Wiikwemkoong Unceded Territory (Wikwemikong)

The 1876 Indian Act allowed for located land to be transferred more broadly—to a member of the same band.[25] It also provided greater protection for widows than earlier legislation by standardizing the process through which women could inherit their husband's property, thus removing the discretionary aspect of DIA involvement.[26] Here one-third of all property (including locations, goods, and chattels) would descend to the widow and two-thirds to any children.[27] In cases of death without issue, the entire estate would descend to the widow for her lifetime, and if there were no children or widow, the property would descend up to a first cousin. At the 1882 Grand Council held at New Credit, delegates argued that this prescriptive inheritance clause did not go far enough. According to Council minutes, "a long discussion took place, most of the Delegates arguing that it was very necessary that a provision should be made that a civilized and educated Indian" be allowed to will property to any family or band member.[28] The reasoning in the council minutes was that the "uncertain and arbitrary provision" over the transmission of property "had a tendency to discourage an Indian in accumulating property, as by it he is not permitted to distinguish between members of the family or relatives who have been friendly and of assistance to him and those who have been the reverse."[29] The Council passed a motion that "Indians be allowed to make a legal will."[30] A motion was also carried that a second cousin may be allowed to share in a deceased relative's property if this person was the closest living relative.[31] The minutes of the council meetings, as usual, were sent to the DIA by the Secretary of the Grand General Council.

Both of these suggestions were incorporated into the 1884 Indian Act. The government overhauled inheritance clauses in this version of the law and allowed for wills to be written by status Indians (for both locations and personal effects) to any member of the owner's family as long as they were able to reside on reserve and were no further removed than a second cousin. If no will was written, the formula from previous legislation would take effect, meaning one-third to the widow and two-thirds to the children.[32] Importantly, as we will see below, these wills were subject to approval by the band, followed by approval from the Superintendent General. These changes, which largely followed the proposal on wills from their previous meeting, were approved of by the Grand General Council in their 1884 council at Cape Croker.[33]

We can continue to see the Council's influence in terms of the evolution of the law in the 1890s. The Council's minutes for 1891 are missing, but their recommendations are outlined in a letter sent from the Deputy Superintendent General of Indian Affairs, Lawrence Vankoughnet, to the Deputy Minister of Justice suggesting amendments be made to the law.[34] Vankoughnet noted that the Grand General Council proposed to the government that the Indian Act be amended so that children outside of the reserve be allowed to inherit moveable property. His opinion was that "The law as it at present stands appears to be rather hard on such parties especially in the case of daughters who marry members of other bands or white men" and that there "appears to be no sufficient reason why they should not be allowed to share in the personal property," though he disagreed that they should share in real estate on reserves.[35] The council also wanted restrictions removed regarding who could inherit land. They advocated removing sections of the law that barred inheritance any further than a second cousin.[36] These suggestions largely became incorporated into the 1894 Indian Act, which provided that "Indians may devise or bequeath property of any kind in the same manner as other persons" as long as the devisee of any property was allowed to reside on reserve.[37]

These significant changes to inheritance clauses in the late nineteenth century—greater protection of widow's property, the ability to write wills, and, finally, the removal of some restrictions on the persons to whom property could be willed—were all amendments to the law advocated through the Grand Council. They are remarkable in that they are some of the few areas where the Council was able to have the government align the law according to their demands.

However, the changes to inheritance laws in the Indian Act also became more restrictive through these same amendments. The first way this happened is that, as legal protections for widows grew, so did their surveillance. In 1884, a widow's ability to inherit a life interest in property became contingent on her "good moral character," as well as living with her husband at the time of his death.[38] Her right to keep land as a guardian for her children's inheritance was also dependent on these provisions.[39] This became more strongly worded in the 1894 amendments, where the Superintendent General was deemed to be the "sole and final judge" of her character,[40] a judgment that would in practice be decided with input from the local Indian Agent. In order to obtain this knowledge, Indian Agents, often at the request of their superiors, became more vested in the surveillance of families, women's "morality," and questions around the "legitimacy" of children. Secondly, the 1894 amendments also removed the necessity for band consent to be acquired before wills could be approved, consolidating this power exclusively in the hands of the Superintendent General, who became, once again, the "sole and final judge" of any transmission of property questions. [41] In the pages below, I will consider how these changes impacted the surveillance of families and women's property, and the changing role for band councils in administering wills.

The 1894 Grand General Council held at the Moraviantown reserve voted to "take a careful look" into how the inheritance provisions had been recently amended.[42] A motion put forward to retain the amendments was lost, and President Albert Tobias of Moraviantown "said that he disapproved of the Superintendent General assuming all and every responsibility and entirely ignoring Indian Councils."[43] A second motion was carried, put forward by John Chechock of New Credit and Scobie Logan of the Munceys of the Thames, that the law be amended so that "the property of deceased Indians descend to the nearest of kin, if none, then to revert to the band."[44] Other council members voiced opinions that the Superintendent General's powers should be struck from the law and that the band in council should instead be the "final judge" on decisions conferring property on reserve.[45] These views echo the Council's work in many other instances to maintain band control at the local level when dealing with the legislation put forward by the government. In terms of inheritance, their moves over this period to protect widows' interests, to have individuals' wills respected, and to enshrine in law a measure of flexibility in terms of who could receive property were echoed in many ways by local band councils, of which Grand Council delegates were members.

## *Inheritance, Indian Agents, and Band Councils*

Band council decisions had an impact on how wills and other property transmission cases unfolded, despite the law on inheritance that increased the power of the DIA in the late nineteenth century. The Department had to contend with how band councils, which operated according to their own values and were often at odds with the limitations of the Indian Act, decided on wills and allocated property. This process was overseen by Indian Agents, who were responsible for both approving band council decisions as well as implementing decisions on inheritance that came from their superiors. At times the DIA conceded to band wishes, while at others it actively went against them. This negotiation of power can help us understand how the control of inheritance decisions operated, outlined in the law but brought to life in the interactions between Indian Agents and band councils.

In the period between 1884 and 1894, prior to the change in law that removed band council consent, the negotiation between the DIA and band councils is quite visible in the records, as the requirement for them to approve wills opened up points of contention the Department had to address. However, band involvement in inheritance cases did not end abruptly after 1894. Following the change in law, band councils participated in these issues in several important ways. One example was in their dealing with cases of intestacy, where property was supposed to be divided according to the Indian Act but would sometimes come before the band council.[46] In some communities, band governments retained jurisdiction over inheritances, as Indian Act provisions had not yet been applied. For instance, Susan M. Hill describes how, at Six Nations, the Confederacy Council operated through their own decision-making processes to deal with wills until 1912, when the DIA imposed control over these.[47] Band councils also had a say in where on-reserve location tickets were granted and this also influenced the outcome of some inheritance cases.[48] Finally, if a case came before the council dealing with a death that had occurred before the change in law, their approval was still required. All of these involvements in inheritance cases demonstrate how band councils were negotiating property transmission, against efforts by the federal government to assert sole jurisdiction after 1894.

We can see in band council decisions concerning which wills to approve (and how to deal with property in cases where no will was written) a willingness to take into account family structures and relationships that would not have been validated by the DIA and did not align with Indian Act limitations. Alternative family structures and relations of care outside of the immediate family were sometimes recognized by band councils in decisions about the transmission of property through wills or otherwise. For instance, in an 1883 case from Alnwick a woman willed her property to a young boy, through his father, who agreed to care for her as long as she lived.[49] They were not relatives by blood. The band approved of this arrangement and approved of her will.[50] In another example, from Walpole Island in 1888, the band made arrangements for an elderly widow from a previous marriage to live with the descendants of a second marriage and be provided for during her lifetime.[51]

At times, band council decisions were also able to have inheritance concerns brought forward that would have otherwise been overlooked at the level of the Department. For example, in an 1884 case from Six Nations, a woman had died intestate shortly after having ousted a first partner from her home and married another man.[52] She had built and furnished the house on a forty acre property she had purchased in the Tuscarora Concession.[53] Her sisters, after her death, brought the case to the Indian Agent, J.T. Gilkinson, because they worried that her two sons from the first marriage were not going to receive the property and that the new husband was not leaving the property or caring for them adequately.[54] When Gilkinson brought the case to the Superintendent General, he was asked to further investigate the family. He found that the sons were "illegitimate," and that the second husband was the father of an infant daughter who would be the legal heir.[55] The case became further complicated when he found out that this daughter had not survived her infancy.[56] The Superintendent General advised Gilkinson to defer the case to the Six Nations Confederacy Council.[57] In late April, the Confederacy Council decided that after the second husband was compensated for any improvements, the two boys should inherit the property. When the husband successfully challenged the decision through the Department, a recommendation was made that the boys' interests be accounted for.[58] The records I was able to find do not show what the end result of the case was, but through it we see both the Council's willingness to grant the property to the boys regardless of their status of legitimacy according to the state, and how their actions influenced the recommendation from the Department of Justice to account for the interests of the boys. It is also an example of how Indian Agents were employed to investigate family relationships for their department superiors.

The discretionary power of the Superintendents General meant that band decisions were at times deferred to. Of course, this was always very constrained by how and when the paternalistic system of DIA approval of inheritance decisions would be implemented, but we continue to see through the three examples below how alternative arrangements to the Indian Act were upheld and approved by councils when they were granted authority. These cases show how at times a degree of flexibility within the law was available when band councils had a role in decision-making around inheritance.

In March of 1882, the Chiefs in council of the Oneida of the Thames reserve upheld the decision of a woman to grant land to her niece and two nephews, as her husband "was never kind to her in health or sickness."[59] She had inherited the house and thirteen acres of property nine years earlier from her father, and three weeks before her death had made a verbal statement that the property should go to her young relatives. Tensions over her husband's refusal to leave the property brought the case, through the Indian Agent, to the attention of his superiors. The case ended up being referred by them to the Department of Justice (a common procedure when points of law were not clear). Upon reviewing the case, the Deputy Minister of Justice decided that because female property ownership, and thus widowers' rights, were not explicitly dealt with in the Indian Act, the husband had no claim,[60] and recommended that the Superintendent General exercise the discretionary powers given to him in the law. Through this "discretionary power," the Superintendent General ended up deferring back to the council to reach a decision. This settled the case in favour of the niece and nephews after a suitable guardian was selected.

In an 1899 case from the Rice Lake band close to Peterborough, a man willed his property to his grandmother.[61] The Law Clerk at the Department of Justice advised the DIA that the will was not valid because he had no relative closer than a brother or sister, and that the property should revert to the band, but that they might allow her to stay.[62] The band council allowed the woman to stay on the property.[63] Similarly, in a case from Six Nations in 1898, the Confederacy Council decided that a widow's will granting half a property to her granddaughter be upheld.[64] The Department did not approve of the will as under the Indian Act the widow would only have been able to inherit one-third of the property, but ultimately confirmed the granddaughter's right to stay there, effectively deferring to the will of the council.[65]

Although the "legitimacy" of marriages and children were not always taken into account by council decisions, these were often the DIA's first point of inquiry in their examination of wills. Surveillance into family relationships existed prior to the 1894 change in law but intensified after the necessity for band consent was removed. Even in straightforward cases, the Department would verify family relationships through the Indian Agent.[66] The cases above demonstrate the frontline position of Indian Agents in bringing cases of concern to the DIA's attention, while the examples that follow show their direct influence in the outcomes of certain cases. We also continue to see, through these cases, the desire of some bands to uphold ideas of the family that were different from that of the Department.

A straightforward example of how Indian Agents were granted decision-making power can be seen in a case from Rama on Lake Couchiching in 1897. Here, the Indian Agent brought a will to the attention of the DIA in which a woman had divided her twenty-eight-acre property between her son and her daughter's son.[67] The Indian Agent, D.J. McPhee, disputed the will as the grandson was "illegitimate" and not a member of the band, and asked how to proceed with the property division. Hayter Reed, the Deputy Superintendent General, responded by saying that if her death was after 1894 it was not necessary to consult the band and asked that McPhee himself resolve the case.[68] The grandson's inheritance was invalidated on McPhee's recommendation.

The moral views of Indian Agents also had an impact on the outcome of cases. In an 1898 case from Six Nations investigated by Indian Agent E.D. Cameron, the illegitimacy of the inheritors was a driving factor for his pushing the Department to overturn the Chiefs' decision.[69] The Chiefs had approved a will, but as the mother and father were not married when their children were born, Cameron insisted that they were "not entitled to the property as decided."[70] The Department was not initially willing to intervene in the case. This greatly frustrated Cameron and he continued to press the case, sending five letters reiterating the illegitimacy of the inheritors to his superiors.[71] The inheritance was eventually overturned in 1908.[72] Cameron investigated another case from Six Nations in 1898 where the issue of whether "pagan" marriages could be considered legal affected the inheritance.[73] Here he also had the Department overturn the decision of the Chiefs after conducting an inquiry.[74]

The cases above show how the involvement of Indian Agents was a significant component of how control over inheritance practices on reserves operated as the DIA sought to assert jurisdiction over decisions about the transmission of property after death. They also reveal how band councils worked to support alternatives that individuals were putting forward through their wills, in some cases successfully. Councils confirmed the legitimacy of partnerships and children born outside of legally recognized marriages or, put another way, moved to ensure that Anishinaabe and Haudenosaunee principles of family law continued to operate.[75]

## *Women and Inheritance*

Indigenous women throughout the 1880s and 1890s advocated for their inheritance rights and those of their families. Their advocacy took many forms: writing wills to ensure that their property devolved to their loved ones, writing letters to the DIA to make claims for property or against decisions they found unjust, and hiring barristers to advocate for their rights. The records of their actions provide examples of how they managed family relationships within and against the deeply unequal layers of gendered and racialized property laws vested in the Indian Act. These documents also testify to the political disenfranchisement of Indigenous women through the band council and Indian Agent systems.

Women were particularly discriminated against in the Indian Act through marriage provisions that unequally expelled them from status, but also as they were not able to vote for or serve as political representatives on band councils. An 1895 letter from a Tyendinaga woman against a band decision on inheritance states clearly "my matter is overlooked because I have no vote."[76] Women historically held important decision-making roles within Indigenous communities and continued to have important influence over politics on reserves.[77] Their actions were integrated into webs of care and family responsibilities that were specific to their nations and communities.[78] Their ability to secure their own inheritance rights and the rights of their families were navigated through these layers of responsibility and restriction.

Wills were written frequently by women. Some were written before they were sanctioned by the Department; the earliest that I found was from Walpole Island in 1868.[79] These wills often articulated their testators' desire to disregard the Indian Act's limitations and instead claim full testamentary freedom, examples of which we have already seen in the cases dealt with by band councils. Women were also very active in presenting their inheritance rights and those of their families to the DIA. They wrote to make claims against unjust decisions by Indian Agents and band councils by sending letters (a telegram in one case), as well as contacting band councils directly.[80]

Some women presented claims to the Department to protest the discriminatory inheritance clauses in the Indian Act. For instance, a woman from Caradoc in 1882 submitted a claim through the Indian Agent that she should be allowed to inherit a part of the hundred acres her late uncle left on the New Credit reserve after having lived there to care for him during his illness.[81] Her claim was, unsurprisingly, dismissed by the Department because she was not a reserve resident. In 1895, another woman from the same reserve took a slightly different approach. She wrote directly to the band council to fight her loss of inheritance due to her marriage status.[82] "I lived with and cared for my mother till she died last fall on the Reserve and worked hard" she wrote, noting "I have lived continuously on the Reserve since my childhood excepting about two years."[83] She also wrote to her member of parliament who contacted the DIA on her behalf.[84] Again the Department dismissed her claims along Indian Act lines, but these cases nonetheless show that women's ideas of inheritance were not limited by Indian Act stipulations and that they advocated for themselves against these laws.

Women also wrote to the DIA to have their rights under the Indian Act affirmed, using the law as an avenue to advocate for maintaining property rights. This was the case for a woman from Tyendinaga in 1888 who wrote directly to Lawrence Vankoughnet, the Deputy Superintendent General, about her deceased father's property, stating "The Chiefs informed me that in accordance with the Indian Act...I was entitled to two thirds [of the property], which I expect to get."[85] In a case from Sarnia in 1899, two sisters brought a claim to the DIA to share in the property that had been granted to their brother alone, implicitly aligning their claim with the Indian Act against the decision of the band.[86]

Some women hired legal professionals to advocate for their rights during this period. There are at least eleven examples of barristers and solicitors involved in the inheritance case files I examined, with ten being hired by women.[87] This was for multiple purposes. A Tyendinaga woman did so to obtain rents she believed were due to her from her brother's estate in 1899. In an 1898 case from St. Regis, a woman and her husband sent their will through a barrister to the DIA, hoping for an extra layer of assurance that their wishes might be granted. In the 1897 case of a woman from Six Nations, she hired a barrister to advocate for her young nephew who had inherited a property. At Six Nations in the 1890s, Indian Agent E.D. Cameron held extensive investigations into inheritance cases in Brantford, and women and families would sometimes be represented by barristers there.[88] These files do not demonstrate conclusively whether legal professionals helped women achieve their goals, as many final decisions are missing. Generally, they were based in towns close to the reserves, but little information is available as to the process by which they were hired or what payment was involved.[89] Although it is beyond the scope of this chapter, the involvement of legal professionals in Indian Act cases deserves further study as it points to strategies families adopted outside of band council and DIA authority.

Wills written by women and their ability to devise property were scrutinized by DIA officials, and their relationships were policed. When Indian Agent John Scoffield of Saugeen recommended a will be approved in 1897, the Superintendent General Hayter Reed replied asking for clarification regarding the relationship between the two women involved. Was the first married? If not, had she left any children? "It would be well," Reed chided Scoffield, "in any future case of submitting a will to give full information regarding the parties interested, so as to avoid unnecessary correspondence."[90] This type of routine bureaucratic scrutiny into intimate family relationships runs through these files. The surveillance of family relationships by Indian Agents also disproportionately affected women through the requirement that their "moral character" be investigated. If Indian Agents did not mention the "moral character" of widows in inheritance cases directly, the Deputy Superintendent General was quick to demand this information.[91] At times, even claims brought by women themselves ended up drawing increased investigation into family relationships.[92]

Aspects of Indigenous women's property transmission that would not have been questioned for non-Indigenous individuals also came before the Department. In one case, a woman's ability to dispose of property in her lifetime was investigated. When a Six Nations woman in 1883 gave away her personal property to the white man living with her, and her farm to "a young Indian," this was investigated through the Department of Justice.[93] The Department of Justice found that "there is nothing in the Indian Acts to prevent a woman or man (Indian) from disposing of their personal property as they think proper during their lives."[94] Nevertheless, the fact that both the Indian Agent and his superiors thought it necessary to have this clarified in law reveals how narrowly Indigenous women's rights to property were interpreted. The ability of a woman of the Sarnia Reserve to will her off-reserve property to her niece in 1895 was also investigated through the Department of Justice. It was found that the will was subject to the 1894 Indian Act and thus to the approval of the Superintendent General.[95]

The cases examined here demonstrate a diversity of legal and political action by women. Whether they advocated through Indian Agents, band councils, MPs, or barristers for their rights, or through the wills they wrote themselves, their actions contradict the narrow conception of property imposed on them by the DIA and the Indian Act. Navigating an "architecture of paternalism" through which they were forced to negotiate the futures of their families, women advocated for their rights and those of their families forcefully and consistently.[96]

## *Conclusion*

The political actions of three groups of Indigenous people—the Grand General Council, band councils, and individual women—help to outline the shape and operation of paternalistic decision-making power over inheritance on Ontario reserves in the nineteenth century. At the level of the law as it was written (contested and altered to some degree by the Grand General Council), the Department of Indian Affairs ultimately legislated control away from band councils over wills on reserves. While, at least on paper, this consolidated power in the hands of the Superintendent General, in practice the power to make decisions on estates was delegated to Indian Agents who were tasked, sometimes at the request of the Department and sometimes through their own volition, with increased surveillance into family relationships. Band councils nonetheless continued to act according to their own values around estate law in ways that did not align with Indian Act limitations. Women were disproportionately affected by the law, by the unjust and invasive surveillance it brought forth, and by legal restrictions on their ability to vote or officially participate in reserve politics. They nevertheless advocated for fairness and for their rights to be recognized through multiple platforms. These cases show that despite the developing legislative and regulatory system, alternatives to the restrictive clauses around the devolution of property in the Indian Act were put forward by women and those in leadership positions on Southern Ontario reserves. In a context where settler society benefitted from the "incredible, almost incalculable wealth" generated by their territories,[97] these alternatives posited several important things: that within the (deeply restricted) legal spaces of reserves, bands should retain control of decision making on wills; that the legitimacy of marriages and children should not be prioritized over relationships of care; and that both women and men should be able to live undisturbed with their families, decide on how to allocate their properties, and that their children should, at bare minimum, be allowed to do the same.

CHAPTER 3

# Strangers before the Law

## *The Intimate Lives of Indian Indentured Labourers in Colonial Mauritius*[1]

*Riyad Sadiq Koya*

In April 1847, an Indian labourer, Virapatrim, was brought before the Court of Assize at Port Louis, Mauritius. Virapatrim was accused of murdering another Indian immigrant, Taylamen, with whom he had previously had intimate relations. Carpaye, Taylamen's mother, was summoned to the court as a witness to the murder. Citing the 1831 *Code d'Instruction Criminelle* (Code of Criminal Procedure), Virapatrim's counsel objected that Carpaye's testimony was precluded by her status as Virapatrim's mother-in-law. However, the court held that Taylamen must be proven the "lawful wife of the prisoner" for Carpaye's testimony to be excluded. Accordingly, the judges asked Carpaye to describe the marriage of Virapatrim and Taylamen. Their marriage, she offered, had taken place in Mauritius. "There was a meeting of friends—a banquet," in which Virapatrim had presented a *collier* (necklace) to Taylamen. "This is the manner," Carpaye stated, "in which we marry in India." The Chief Judge, James Wilson, asked, "Can a marriage, that is, what ceremony constitutes the legal tie of marriage, be proved in this manner?" A second judge asked, "Could a marriage celebrated in this form, be held to be a good marriage?" The third judge concluded: "No evidence of a legal marriage." A decision was reached: "Repel objection to the witness' admissibility." Carpaye was then permitted to testify to the murder of her daughter.[2]

Virapatrim, Carpaye, and Taylamen were part of a larger wave of Indian immigrants arriving in Mauritius after the abolition of slavery in the British Empire in 1834. Drawing on earlier patterns of labour recruitment, Mauritian planters initiated a new stream of indentured migration, later formalized as a publicly regulated system in 1842. The large numbers of Indian indentured labourers arriving in the colony rendered them, I argue, "strangers" in Mauritius. The estrangement of Indian indentured labourers was multifarious. Indentured migration was initially conceived as a form of seasonal migration, whereby Indian labourers were regarded as "sojourners," rather than settlers or citizens.[3] Indian labourers also developed a reputation for desertion, absenteeism, and vagrancy, and were frequently accused of "wandering." The criminalization of their "vagrancy" confirmed their estrangement from Mauritian society.

As the transcript of Virapatrim's trial suggests, the intimate practices of Indian indentured labourers were also estranged from the laws of Mauritius. Although invested with rights of mobility as British subjects, Indian indentured labourers entering the colony were brought under the jurisdiction of Mauritian courts administering legal codes derived from French law. A series of capital cases in the late 1840s involving the murder of Indian women by Indian men brings into focus the ambivalent legal status of marital ties between Indian immigrants, based on unfamiliar law and practice in British India. Indian labourers relied on interpreters and judicial officers to render their testimony legible. Indian indentured labourers lacked fluency in the language and procedure of Mauritian courts and were reliant on interpreters and judicial officers to render their testimony legible. They were "strangers before the law," whose presence posed novel questions to the mixed legal system of Mauritius.

## *Strangers in Mauritius*

Georg Simmel described the stranger as "... the man who comes today and stays tomorrow—the potential wanderer, so to speak, who, although he has gone no further, has not quite got over the freedom of coming and going." Simmel imagined the stranger as a trader—which might appear to preclude consideration of the Indian indentured labourer as a "stranger."[4] Yet dress, language, custom, and religion distinguished the Indian indentured labourer from Mauritian society. Such differences were magnified by mass immigration into the colony after the abolition of slavery in 1834. The arrival of large numbers of Indian indentured labourers raised questions of policing acts of desertion, absenteeism, and vagrancy. Marina Carter and Khal Torabully posit Indian "vagabondage," or "vagrancy," as "the most common form of revolt by Indian labourers."[5]

Although multiple streams of migrants had left India for Mauritius prior to the nineteenth century, the advent of British rule after 1810 expanded labour recruitment from the subcontinent. The first British governor, Robert Farquhar (1810–1822), inaugurated the transportation of Indian convict labour to Mauritius. Clare Anderson estimates that 1,500 convicts, including only six women, were transported between 1814 and 1837 and engaged primarily in public works.[6] "They looked different," Anderson writes, "they wore different clothes, they spoke different languages."[7] The equalization of sugar duties in 1825 prompted Mauritian planters to expand the recruitment of labour for the sugar industry.[8] Satyendra Peerthum has documented the recruitment of Indian labourers on individual and group contracts from 1826.[9] The 1875 Royal Commissioners would later comment upon this durable history of contract and convict labour by noting that "the [indentured] immigrant from India … when he came to Mauritius, was not the entire stranger he was in the West Indies and Demerara …."[10]

The abolition of slavery accelerated Indian immigration into Mauritius. A private system of recruitment operated between 1834 and 1839, during which some 25,403 Indian labourers arrived in the colony, including 961 women.[11] At this early stage, colonial planters were optimistic about the "virtues" of Indian labourers. As Carter and Torabully point out, Mauritian planters found that the new system was "mutually advantageous to the employer, the labourer and the sending and receiving countries alike."[12] "However," they argue, "as the numbers of arriving Indians increased, the concern of employers shifted from a desire to increase immigration to the perceived need to enforce 'discipline.'" Consequently, "the rhetoric and stereotype of the Indian also changed."[13] Allen confirms this shift over the longer term, noting that earlier generations of Indian slaves and *gens de couleur* "… had generally been praised for their industry, sobriety, intelligence, grace, and docility … Such positive, albeit paternalistic views of Indian character did not long survive the advent of Indian immigration."[14]

The large numbers arriving in Mauritius prompted widespread debate on vagrancy. In 1836, Governor William Nicolay forwarded to the Colonial Office for approval two ordinances passed by the Mauritius assembly to expand policing powers over newly emancipated apprentices and immigrant labourers.[15] Hollier Griffiths, a Mauritian planter and merchant, identified a key rationale for the ordinances, arguing "that the immigration of a considerable number of strangers would render more difficult the maintenance of public tranquility."[16] Griffiths objected, however, that the restrictions upon entry of Indian labourers proposed by the ordinances infringed on their rights as British subjects.[17] In reply, the Procureur Général, P. D'Epinay, argued the necessity of internal police powers to preserve "public tranquility." He wrote: "This is, above all, applicable to the lower class of Indian labourers, who, by their manners, their usages, their customs, and their religion, are perfect strangers in every other country but their own."[18]

The emergence of a publicly regulated system after 1842 did little to assuage planter concerns about Indian vagrancy. Some 93,690 Indians were transported to Mauritius between 1840 and 1850; 13,827 of that total were Indian women. The 1846 and 1851 censuses demonstrate a population surge from 56,245 to 77,996 "Indians."[19] This rapid influx contributed to their estrangement. In an 1845 despatch to the Colonial Office, Governor William Gomm referred to Indian labourers as a "densely-crowded population of strangers."[20] The "love of wandering" attributed to this "crowd" led to increased demands to impose stricter vagrancy laws.[21] In 1845, Mauritius appointed a Committee of Labour to investigate desertion and absenteeism, attributed to a "love of change" and a disinclination to work.[22] In 1847, Ordinance 22 introduced a new tax and a ticket system for "old immigrants" who had completed their contracts.[23] Ordinance 7 of 1849 further provided for the arrest of "deserters" without warrant. Organized "vagrant hunts," Allen observes, often failed to distinguish the deserter from the vagrant. Allen further notes that Ordinance 4 of 1864 treated desertion itself as an act of vagrancy, making the breach of contract an "offense against society."[24]

Beyond vagrancy, other factors estranged Indian indentured labourers from Mauritian society. The first was the provision of a return passage. A guarantee against the permanent "exile" of strangers in a new land, the return passage facilitated the maintenance of rural ties to the Indian homeland.[25] Rural ties were further reinforced by the employment of returnee labourers, particularly *sirdars*, as recruiters from their home villages. The *sirdars* played an enhanced role as "labour intermediaries," recruiting bands of labourers for specific plantations and then supervising their employment on the estate.[26] These factors reinforced perceptions that indentured migration was "seasonal." In Arjan de Haan's terms, the maintenance of "rural connections"—here across the border between land and sea—made Indian labourers "unsettled settlers" in Mauritius.[27] In large numbers, as both "unsettled settler" and "vagrant," the Indian labourer was a stranger to Mauritian society.

## *Stranger Intimacy*

The intimate practices of Indian indentured labourers were similarly estranged from Mauritian society. This estrangement was often framed, as by d'Epinay above, as a difference of manner, custom, usage, and religion. The perception of indentured labour as "seasonal" tempered the expectations that labourers might settle, marry, and establish families in Mauritius. However, the low proportion of women recruited to Mauritius provoked concerns about "stranger intimacy" within the world of the plantation barracks, which appeared to resemble the homosocial worlds or "bachelor societies" of other frontier locations.[28] Writing about transient immigrant male labourers along the Pacific coast of North America, Nayan Shah has demonstrated that "stranger intimacy" was apprehended, variously, through the perceived moral threat of male strangers, the anonymity and transience of their encounters, and their attempts to form enduring bonds.[29] Similar bonds, both transient and enduring, were formed in the plantation barracks on colonial Mauritius.

As mentioned earlier, very few women were conveyed by the private system of recruitment in the 1830s. Marina Carter estimates that women represented only one or two percent of the immigrants to Mauritius in this period. This statistic indicates, again, the seasonal character of early migration, with women remaining in the home villages while men, as proverbial sojourners, earned income abroad. The Government of Bengal official J.P. Woodcock, who traveled with recruits to Mauritius, commented that of the "few" Indian women proceeding to Mauritius, many were "not generally the legitimate wives of the labourers, but persons with whom an illicit intercourse had arisen in Calcutta and who had been induced by money, or some powerful influence, to attach themselves to the fortunes of their protectors."[30] Woodcock's distinction between "legitimate wives" and women "induced" to migrate reinforced perceptions that Indian women would not willfully cross the border between land and sea to labour on overseas plantations.

Thomy Hugon, who would later become the Protector of Immigrants in Mauritius, favoured a policy of family migration to redress the population imbalance. He commented in 1839 that a fixed proportion of women "… could only lead to shocking abuses in India and Bengal, especially where it would be so easy to carry off women from the banks of rivers."[31] Family migration, he argued, would be enhanced by legislative action to recognize the legality of Indian marriages: "The real obstacle there (and a very serious one it is) to many natives emigrating to Mauritius with their families, is the want of any law to secure to the husband the possession of the wife; the latter amongst most eastern nations is more the property than the companion of the former."[32] As the Protector, Hugon later influenced Mauritian legislation by promoting the conjugal rights of Indian husbands.[33] Article 9 of Ordinance 3 of 1856 included a provision to forestall the inducement of Indian wives to leave their husbands, imposing a fine or imprisonment with hard labour upon any person convicted "of having enticed away the wife of any Indian immigrant."[34]

After the suspension of migration in 1839, planters and their lobbyists promoted family migration.[35] Initial efforts to recruit women after the resumption of emigration in 1842, however, were underwhelming. To stabilize family life on the plantations, Mauritian planters encouraged returnee recruitment, including the employment of female recruiters.[36] Carter argues that returnees created "an independent dynamic of family immigration and of circular migration."[37] However, the returnee dynamic would be supplemented by the award after 1852 of a £1 bonus to immigrants who returned with their wives or the wife of another labourer already in the colony.[38] The bounty was discontinued by 1866, in part due to concerns that recruiters were arriving in Mauritius with multiple wives.[39]

For Mauritian planters, the presence of Indian women "stabilized" the largely male workforce. In contrast to other indenture colonies, most Indian women who migrated to Mauritius largely were not engaged on indenture contracts. Instead, "they joined those estates to which bands of men were assigned with whom they might choose or be told to attach themselves."[40] While Indian women were largely "free" of labour obligations, they were consequently dependent economically upon Indian men.[41] Often, that man was a *sirdar*.[42] Dependence contributed to women forming transient, short-term relations based on the stability of financial support. Women sometimes cooked for multiple men within their living quarters. Such arrangements might also include sexual services. As Carter notes, these "alternative domestic arrangements" led contemporary observers to depict Indian women "as promiscuous and fickle, occasioning 'great disorder upon some of the estates,' by leaving 'the men with whom they cohabit, to immediately take up with others for the sake of the money or the jewels they thus obtain.'"[43] Such arrangements were often perceived as "adultery" or "polyandry," and appeared to explain the increasing prevalence of "wife murder."[44]

Indian women arrived in Mauritius both singly and in the company of husbands and relatives. Upon their arrival, they were assigned to plantation estates by the Protector of Immigrants. The Protector was mandated to allot families to the same estate. The fate of single women was more ambiguous. Scarcity meant that Indian men often petitioned the Protector for the assignment of a spouse. The Protector played a key role allocating sexual partners, imbuing the intimate relations of Indian labourers with a strong transactional dimension.[45] Marriages arranged by Indian migrants in the colony similarly appeared to resemble the "forced sale" of women.[46] For colonial officials, the sale of wives, including children, indicated a widespread immorality within the indentured population. This focus on immorality often misrepresented the novel domestic and household relationships pursued by Indian labourers under the demanding conditions of indenture. The intimacy of strangers was more often recognized as "cohabitation" rather than marriage.

Through the *Anti-Slavery Reporter* and several published pamphlets, abolitionists played a key role in framing the "stranger intimacy" of indentured labourers. John Scoble, who had exposed abuses towards Indian labourers in British Guiana, wrote in 1840 of the "frightful disparity of the sexes" in Mauritius. Scoble argued that this disparity resulted in "the most horrible and revolting depravity and demoralization."[47] He also raised concerns that the conveyance of Indian men to Mauritius induced family separation.[48] As Carter notes, the "continuing sexual imbalance" after the resumption of emigration in 1842 "led Anti-slavery Society members to renew their efforts against indenture, and cast a further slur upon the character of female recruits."[49] Writing to the Colonial Office in 1845, Scoble alleged that Indian labourers in the plantations barracks were guilty of "horrible practices"—a euphemism, Anil Persaud suggests, for same-sex relations.[50] In a subsequent letter, Scoble claimed that "by far the larger proportion introduced into Mauritius from 1843 to 1844 … were prostitutes, picked up on the streets of Calcutta and Bombay." Furthermore, he suggested, married and unmarried women were "herded together with the men in large buildings or barracks, and that the usual results were the consequence—promiscuous intercourse and debauchery."[51] At the direction of the Colonial Secretary, the stipendiary magistrates visited each individual estate to report on housing conditions, the provision of separate accommodations for married couples, and the existence of "revolting offences" among the labourers.[52] Scoble's allegations, however, were largely unproven.

## *Capital Cases and the Legal Archive*

Capital cases involving Indian immigrants in Mauritius and other British colonies are not easily discoverable through legal digests or law reports. They were often not reported; if they were, the cases were largely summarized. However, the disclosure of capital cases to imperial authorities appears to have been mandated for colonial governors.[53] The "report" of a capital case arrived in the form of a despatch from the colonial governor to the Colonial Office. A governor's despatch often reported only minimal details, simply declaring the execution of the capital sentence. The transcript thickened in cases where the capital sentence was appealed, as the colonial governor might document his decision regarding commutation. Documentation might include a trial transcript, the record of an appeal, the judge's notes, copies or excerpts of relevant ordinances, recorded statements and "confessions," or a petition for clemency.[54] By the 1840s, incoming correspondence was bound in large volumes, indexed in the order of the despatch number assigned by the government of Mauritius. Despatches were also assigned a file number by the Colonial Office. The volumes themselves, however, were unpaginated. From 1838, the bound volumes were maintained at the Public Records Office in London—the "most likely site," notes Carolyn Steedman, for the contraction of "archive fever."[55] Since 2003, the volumes have been held at The National Archives at Kew.

In terms suggested by Arlette Farge's investigation of archival practice, I have used these records to assemble a series of cases: cases which had previously been placed in a series by colonial officials.[56] These series resemble, but are not identical with, the series known as "wife murders" with which Indian indentured labourers became widely identified over the course of the nineteenth century.[57] Here, the series might be termed "the growing crime of murder" or "murders of Indian women by Indian men." Colonial officials identified these series as they debated the deterrent effect of capital punishment, in a context where the incidence of violent crime was understood to be rising.

Indeed, a flurry of capital cases had arrived before the Court of Assize in 1847 and 1848, duly reported by the governor, Sir William Governor Gomm, to the Colonial Office. Commenting on Virapatrim's sentence, Gomm took note of chief judge James Wilson's concern at the "growing prevalence of this crime [murder] among the Indian population of this colony."[58] Wilson observed a series of five murder cases at the "short assize" in which Virapatrim had been tried. In one case, a mother was acquitted of the murder of her infant child on grounds of insanity. Another case of murder was dismissed for a procedural defect. Within this series of five cases were three cases involving the murder of Indian women. In each, Wilson noted, the women had lived with the "Prisoners" as "wife or mistress." One case had resulted in a conviction for manslaughter with ten years' imprisonment. A second case lacked sufficient evidence to convict. Virapatrim's case was the third in the series; his sentence would also be commuted.[59]

Like Wilson, Gomm constructed a series from the reported cases. In his despatch of 30 December 1848, Gomm connected two recent murders committed by the sugar estate labourers Gojunday Valoo and Beecon. Their capital cases, discussed below, reveal that in both cases, "the victim of the crime proved again an Indian female"; both had resulted in an execution. Notably, Gomm's series was not formed exclusively of "wife murders." In Valoo's case, the victim, Chelayee, was determined to be Valoo's cousin. The governor associated the two cases with "several others" previously reported to the Secretary of State, many of which had been appealed successfully. Gomm hoped that the executions of Valoo and Beecon, "the retribution exacted by the law," would have an "enduring effect" on the Indian population. For Gomm, the murders demanded the firm hand of British justice. He noted the "comparative impunity…secured to classes of offenses not visited as capital in regions of India unapproached by British Legislation." [60] This impunity would be remedied by consistent application of capital sentencing. A transition appears within Gomm's series, from commutation to execution, with Indian immigrants subjected to the force of the law.[61]

Gomm's remarks on British legislation invite attention to the jurisdictional questions posed by the capital cases. In crossing the sea, Indian indentured labourers entered a new colonial jurisdiction. Although they remained within the British Empire, the legal system of Mauritius, a former French colony, was mixed. The dispute over Carpaye's testimony suggests the peculiarity of the legal situation in Mauritius. Her testimony was nearly excluded by the *Code d'Instruction Criminelle*. Rather than an artifact of the previous French administration, this code had been enacted by the British administration in 1831 based on the principles of French criminal law. The *Code d'Instruction Criminelle* was not revised until the passage of Ordinance 10 of 1850, which introduced the jury trial to Mauritius. It was finally repealed by Ordinance 29 of 1853.[62] The judicial system itself was reorganized by an Order in Council of 23 October 1853.[63]

The Penal Code applied in Mauritius played a key role in the capital cases. It was in part based on the French Penal Code, which was adopted in 1791 and subsequently modified by Ordinance 6 of 1838, again under British administration.[64] A key feature of the 1838 code was the distinction between manslaughter and murder. The charge of murder, which carried the weight of a capital sentence, rested on a finding of "determined intention" or, as emphasized in the trial transcripts, "malice aforethought." This concept, with a long history in both French and English law, guided the legal process from initial investigation and confession to trial and sentencing, and figured prominently in the governor's deliberations over the commutation of a capital sentence.[65]

The continuation of French law in Mauritius had been stipulated by the 1810 Articles of Capitulation. The eighth article of this international agreement "expressly preserved to the inhabitants their religion, laws, and customs."[66] Subsequent proclamations that same year confirmed that French law would remain local law. Such allowances followed upon similar dispensations for French Catholics in Grenada and Quebec in the aftermath of the Seven Years' War. Hannah Weiss Miller has argued that concessions to French law and the Catholicism of "new subjects" are suggestive of an emergent legal pluralism in the late eighteenth century.

This pluralism, she argues, was similarly applied with respect to Hindu and Muslim subjects in British India. "Passage of the Quebec Act" in 1774, she argues, "thus marked a moment when a truly imperial subjecthood was imagined and realized—a subjecthood that could accommodate the various peoples of the British Empire and that countenanced flexible rights."[67]

Soon after adopting the assumption of the diwani system of revenue administration in the Mughal province of Bengal, the East India Company made concessions to the religious usages of its newly subject population. The judicial plan forwarded by Warren Hastings in 1772 had specified that "in all suits regarding inheritance, marriage, and caste, and other religious institutions the laws of the Koran with respect to the Mahomedans, and those of the Shaster with respect to Gentoos, shall be invariably adhered to."[68] In administering "Gentoo" and "Mahomedan" laws, British judges consulted translations of key texts from the Hindu and Islamic traditions. They also conferred with native jurisconsults to aid in the interpretation of these works.[69] Over time, published case reports, digests, treatises, and handbooks contributed to the textualization of religious personal laws.[70] In the late 1840s, little of this apparatus was in evidence at the Mauritius Court of Assize.

Although British subjects, Indian indentured labourers in Mauritius became entangled in procedures and practices derived from French law. A key figure was the *Juge d'Instruction*. An archetypical figure of the inquisitorial method of French criminal procedure, the *Juge d'Instruction* played a pivotal role in securing confessions from prisoners.[71] In the confession, the accused and other parties to the crime were named—often inaccurately—before the law.[72] These confessions were cited as proof of premeditation or the intent—"malice aforethought"—of the accused. Immigrants and their advocates sometimes contested the validity of their confessions, claiming their estrangement from the vagaries of French criminal procedure. Additionally, with the legality of Indian marriages in the colony having yet to be clarified, the intimate relations of Indian labourers were identified as "cohabitation." To confirm bonds of intimacy, witnesses were questioned on length of co-residence, evidence of a ceremony, reputation for fidelity, and previously existing marriages. This evidence, however oblique, offers a bleak portrait of the intimate lives of Indian immigrants under indenture.

## *The Trial of "Andy Apin," alias Virapatrim*

Virapatrim had been employed as a *sirdar* on the Queen Victoria estate in the Flacq district. After his term expired, he would return to the estate, where Taylamen, his erstwhile spouse, continued to live. Taylamen resided with Moutou Carpin, who had succeeded Virapatrim as *sirdar* upon the estate. Witnesses described a previous visit when Virapatrim was confined at the estate hospital. Several months later, Carpin reported Virapatrim's return to the estate to Gustave Giquel, a Creole *sucrier*. Virapatrim, it was feared, was planning to lure a band of labourers to another estate, a phenomenon described as "*embauchant*." Under orders of the estate manager, Giquel arrested Virapatrim and again confined him at the estate hospital. Virapatrim escaped and rushed to Carpin's hut to confront Taylamen. On her refusal to leave Carpin, he killed her. Leaving the hut, he assaulted Taylamen's mother, Carpaye. He was then accosted and subdued by another labourer on the estate, Marimoutou.[73]

Virapatrim was swiftly brought to trial in April of 1847.[74] Appearing before the Court of Assize in Port Louis, Virapatrim was asked to identify himself. The defendant—identified as the "Prisoner" in the trial transcripts—was to be recognized by his "Christian name." Consequently, court proceedings identify the "Prisoner" as "Andy Apin," with an "alias"—"Virapatrim." At the outset of the proceedings, "Apin" stated "I am also called Virapatrim."[75] A witness insisted: "the prisoner was called Andy Apin."[76]

Witnesses testified to the intimacy between Virapatrim and Taylamen. Upon the admission of her testimony, Carpaye, Taylamen's mother, confirmed that they were married. She described their wedding banquet; she pronounced this banquet and the presentation of a necklace as constitutive of marriage. At the time of his trial, however, she did not consider Virapatrim to be her son-in-law. That status was reserved for Moutou Carpin, who had provided "assistance" for Carpaye.[77] Other witnesses vaguely perceived the marriage of Virapatrim and Taylamen. Giquel, who had witnessed Virapatrim's attack on Carpaye, stated, "I knew that the prisoner had relations (intimacy as with a husband) with the woman Taylamen and that these relations had finished."[78] Frederick Gustave Gimel, the estate accountant, encountered Virapatrim immediately after the assault. He testified:

> He then told me, that he had bought the woman for some hundred rupees, part of which he had borrowed to make up the sum. That having been confined in our hospital, while there, he felt "*son coeur viré*" (his heart turn) and he formed the project of assassinating his wife (i.e. the woman Taylamen) and with that design he had removed a plank, and got out—that he was nearly naked—but he took some linen which he found there and went to the hut of his wife. Being there he asked her to go with him to the "Camp de Masque," where he staid [sic]. She refused.[79]

When further questioned by an assessor, Gimel claimed not to know the marital status of Virapatrim and Taylamen.

Virapatrim was not called as a witness; his perceptions of Taylamen are not directly known. Witnesses did remark, however, on his mental state after the assault. Gimel testified that Virapatrim denied any feelings of regret. Virapatrim further confessed to Gimel his desire to kill his rival, Moutou Carpin. Gimel continued: "The Prisoner said to me that his right over his wife was so great, that even if he were dead she had no right to give herself to another…I think the words he use [sic], were in Creole '*moi pour tuer ma femme*.'"[80] Similarly, Giquel observed: "I saw him beside the body of the deceased. He was quite—*très posé*. He avowed that 'he had killed the woman that he had bought her and that as she had left him, he found it quite natural that he should kill her.'"[81]

Witnesses, charged with confirming Virapatrim's intention to murder Taylamen, reported little of the affect of their "marriage." In testimony before the Court of Assize, their marriage appears to resemble either a gift or a sale. The marriage is made "good" either by the gift of the necklace or, alternatively, the payment of a hundred rupees. Giquel offered a more rudimentary assessment: sexual intimacy confirmed Virapatrim's status as a husband. Virapatrim's conception of the marriage also appears transactional, with little duty of care or expression of intimacy for either Taylamen or Carpaye. Having departed the estate, he failed to provide maintenance. While this provoked a shift of allegiance for Carpaye, Taylamen's views are unknown.

Taylamen's status upon the estate is also curious. Having traveled with her mother, she seemingly was among those Indian women who arrived in Mauritius without a contract of indenture. Giquel offered that he had not seen Taylamen's name on an engagement. Taylamen's shift in affections between Virapatrim and Carpin, two *sirdars* upon a single estate, raises questions about her allotment. Were her affections bargained by the estate? Had she been trafficked? Or was her choice of partners merely a personal one, contingent upon a gift received?

The key issue in Virapatrim's case was whether he had committed murder or manslaughter. Virapatrim's counsel sought to disprove his intent to murder. The transcript summarizes the argument:

> Mr. Anselme for Prisoner, dwelt on the peculiar position of the prisoner, the ideas he, as an Indian, entertained as to the power of the husband over the wife. The illegality of the confinement in which he was placed. The exasperation thereby created. The consequence, loss of mental self control, and that there was no proof of premeditation which reduced the crime from murder to manslaughter.[82]

The judges at the Court of Assize similarly were disturbed by Virapatrim's confinement. Had Virapatrim arrived at the estate with the intention to murder Taylamen? At the conclusion of the trial, the chief judge, James Wilson, indicated his "regret" at the circumstances of Virapatrim's case. "Particularly that of the charge against the Prisoner of designing to *embaucher* (inveigling away) the Indians having been made by his successor in the profession of the affections of, and actually living with Taylamen, his former wife or associate."[83] The judges recommended the commutation of the capital sentence and the sentencing of Virapatrim to twenty years' imprisonment with hard labour. Despite his belief in the deterrent effect of capital punishment, Gomm endorsed the commutation.

## *The Trial of Beecon*

A woman named Puddoo had resided with the labourer Beecon at the Stanley estate in the district of Plaines Wilhems. Puddoo subsequently left Beecon for the hut of Gones Gontaye, a labourer at a neighbouring estate. Beecon asked permission of the manager, Cordonau, to retrieve Puddoo. Having obtained a pass, Beecon proceeded to the neighbouring estate and arrived at Gontaye's hut. He promptly seized Puddoo, battering her as they returned to the Stanley estate. They spent the night together in Beecon's hut. In the morning, Beecon confronted Puddoo and asked if she would remain with him; she declined. Beecon then asked if she would return 400 rupees to him. When Puddoo refused this second demand, he took her life.[84]

At the outset of the December 1848 trial before the Court of Assize, Beecon was asked through a "Hindostanee" interpreter to identify himself.[85] He stated: "I am Beecon, sometimes called Beekam, I do not know my age, I am a labourer in the service of Mr. Cordonau of Plaines Wilhems. I am a native of Calcutta."[86] Unlike Virapatrim, Beecon was not identified by a Christian name. Four witnesses were called at the trial. Gones Gontaye testified candidly to the relationship between Beecon and Puddoo, claiming that Puddoo had sought "refuge" from Beecon. When Beecon arrived to retrieve Puddoo, "He took her by force. He struck her and took her away in the direction of his hut." "I never saw her alive afterwards," Gontaye confirmed. Gontaye also recalled that he "had received orders from my master, to let the woman go."[87] He did not disclose to Cordonau that Beecon had beaten "the woman."

Cordonau also testified at the Court of Assize. Cordonau claimed not to know how long Beecon and Puddoo had "cohabitated" or whether they had arrived from India together. Cordonau had granted the pass for Beecon to retrieve Puddoo. Two days prior to the "murder," Beecon had informed Cordonau "that his wife (or woman) had left him and taken 400 Rupees away with her, of his; and 140 Rupees belonging to a man named Ballock."[88] Cordonau directed Beecon to inform a police officer. The next day, Beecon requested the pass "to go and fetch his wife" at the neighbouring estate. After Beecon's assault upon Puddoo, Cordonau went directly to Beecon's hut, where he found the labourer seated while eating. He believed Beecon to be of "mild and tranquil disposition," and did not think him capable of the murder. After examining the scene of the crime, Cordonau returned to Beecon, who remained outside his hut. Upon reproach, Beecon claimed "that was the way in India."[89]

The third witness, Henry Brumeau, proved crucial to Beecon's conviction. Brumeau, *Juge d'Instruction* for Plaines Wilhems, had not observed the events; Brumeau had taken Beecon's "confession." As Brumeau was introduced, two confessions were read before the court, one taken at Plaines Wilhems, the other at Port Louis. In the first, Brumeau reports that Beecon claimed to be a native of Calcutta. Beecon identified the body as an "Indian woman," Podo [sic] "with whom he had been cohabitating for upwards of two years."[90] He confessed to having "murdered" "Podo" and offered the motive that she had "run away," taking with her 400 hundred rupees that had been buried in a hole in his hut. Beecon confessed that he had traveled to the neighbouring estate to locate Puddoo and then returned to Beecon's hut where they "passed the night together." The next morning Beecon asked Puddoo what her intentions were, "that if she Podo [sic] did not wish to continue with him she might go where she liked." However, Beecon offered a condition: "she must return the money which she had stolen from him."[91] "Exasperated" at her refusal to continue to live with him or return the money, Beecon then "killed" "Podo." He further stated that "he does not regret what he has done but on the contrary would be ready to do the same over again."[92] These details were restated in the second confession.

The Court of Assize returned a verdict: Beecon was guilty of murder and sentenced to death. The verdict, however, was not unanimous. One "voice"—an assessor, another vestige of the French legal system—found Beecon guilty instead of manslaughter. Consequently, Beecon's counsel, Clement Ulcoq, composed a memorial to Gomm appealing for commutation. Noting that the conviction had not been unanimous, Ulcoq argued that Beecon's confession suggested an absence of "premeditation or malice prépensé." He further pointed to Beecon's "excellent character" as established by the deposition of Cordonau, for whom Beecon had been employed for five years.[93] After consulting Judge Surtees, who confirmed that two of the three assessors had concurred on the question of premeditation, Gomm denied Ulcoq's petition.

Throughout, there is little discussion of the "marriage" of Beecon and Puddoo. The focus of the proceedings was to render judgment on Beecon's intention to murder Puddoo. Beecon's final assault upon Puddoo is revealed to have been preceded by a longer pattern of domestic violence. Beecon claimed his actions hinged on the question of property: he had offered her freedom on the condition that the 400 rupees were returned. Or perhaps, in Beecon's view, Puddoo was herself property, with a value of those same 400 rupees. Ulcoq emphasized that Beecon had been seized by a "sudden paroxysm of passion" when informed that the rupees would not be returned. Cordonau's testimony undermined this argument: "this was the way in India." Beecon's declaration of custom, however, would not serve as an adequate defense to the charge of murder before the Court of Assize at Mauritius.

## *The Trial of Gojunday Valoo*

Gojunday Valoo, a labourer on the Mapou estate, had seen Chelayee with "many Malabars."[94] He warned her on several occasions not to have sexual intercourse with other men. He again saw her with a "Malabar" named Pagarin. He then resolved to kill Chelayee. Late in the evening, he sharpened his weapon. The next morning, he went to her hut, bringing with him an offering of rice. Finding Chelayee inside the hut with her daughter, Mardhaye, Valoo did not hesitate. He struck Chelayee with his weapon, and she fell to the ground. Mardhaye ran from the hut, screaming. Her mother was dead.[95]

Before the Court of Assize in December 1848, Valoo's identification was facilitated by a Tamil interpreter, George Hambert. He identified himself as a field labourer, employed on the Mapou estate owned by Mr. Aubin. He did not know his age but stated that he was born in India.[96] A range of witnesses were called to testify to the crime. The first witness called by the Crown was Mardhaye. Having known Valoo prior to the crime, Mardhaye clarified his relationship to her mother. This was not a case of "wife murder": Valoo and Chelayee were cousins. Two other witnesses, Sazure and Amavasi, testified directly to the assault. They did not, however, comment on Valoo and Chelayee's relationship.

Aristide Aubin, a "planter" at Bois Rouge, testified. Valoo had been brought before Aubin after the assault. Aubin asked if Valoo had killed Chelayee; Valoo answered that "it was true." Aubin related that Valoo was convinced that Chelayee had "behaved improperly." Valoo "had seen her with many Malabars, and he had resolved to kill her." On cross-examination, he confirmed that he had employed Valoo for about forty days, that there were no complaints against him, and that he did not appear to have a "violent disposition." Aubin attested that Valoo had stated that he had seen Chelayee "with a Malabar named Pagarin, and that at that moment he had resolved to kill her." Aubin offered a caveat, however: he could not "swear" that this was what Valoo had said, as Valoo's sentiments had been translated by another "Malabar."[97]

As in Beecon's case, key testimony with respect to intent was provided by Henry Brumeau. Valoo's "statement" to Brumeau was introduced as evidence.[98] Brumeau had interviewed Valoo with the assistance of two interpreters, one of whom, Edward Kumpholtz, translated from Tamil. Valoo had identified himself as "a native of Trichinapoly in India." Though Valoo did not know his age, Brumeau surmised that he "appears to be about thirty five years." Valoo claimed he was Chelayee's cousin. He lived in a separate hut from her; however, he would "take his meals" with Chelayee and Ramin, an "Indian" with whom she "cohabitated." He confirmed that he had departed for Chelayee's hut with the intention of "murdering" her. He entered the hut to find her with Mardhaye, whereupon he assaulted Chelayee. The previous evening, he sharpened his weapon for that "purpose."

Having confirmed Valoo's intent to murder Chelayee, Brumeau's statement also clarified Valoo's motive. He had discovered Chelayee "in the act of cohabitation" with another Indian labourer, Pagarin. Brumeau recorded that Valoo had warned Chelayee "on three different occasions" and that despite these warnings, Chelayee "continued to have sexual intercourse with several Indians" on the estate. Chelayee had further declared to Valoo "that she was her own guide and could do what she pleased with herself."[99] Valoo made a second statement to Brumeau two days after the assault. On this occasion, Valoo was identified by his emigration pass number—no. 23607. Valoo clarified that he had no defense; Brumeau therefore appointed the advocate Evenor Dupont as Valoo's counsel.

The Court of Assize convicted Valoo of murder. Included with the transcripts was an excerpt of Ordinance no. 6 of 1838, the Penal Code of Mauritius. In transmitting this "extract" to the Colonial Office, Gomm confirmed the distinctiveness of local law. Article 216 read: "Manslaughter committed with premeditation or by lying in wait is Murder," with premeditation defined as "determined intention."[100] Valoo had murdered Chelayee with a sharp object. He had sharpened that object prior to his confrontation with Chelayee, confirming his intention.

Valoo appealed his capital sentence to Governor Gomm, offering two key claims. Valoo's counsel argued that the sole evidence of his intent was his confession before the *Juge d'Instruction*. No other witnesses had confirmed premeditation. The petition also introduced a novel explanation for the violence, arguing in part that Valoo was "actuated…by a mistaken feeling of propriety and honor, on account of the promiscuous intercourse of the unfortunate deceased with several men; which conduct your Petitioner, according to the usages of his native country, erroneously supposed that he had a right to resent and to punish, as chief of the family; but he is now better informed." Valoo's acknowledgement of his "mistake" gestured to a change of jurisdiction; in Mauritius, Valoo's "feeling of propriety and honor" lacked the sanction of either custom or law. Valoo was a stranger before the law.[101]

Valoo's change of status was confirmed by the court's decision upon his petition. The court noted that:

> Supposing the fact to be as alleged by the prisoner, that the usages of his native country had induced him to conceive that he had a right, as chief of the family, to act as he had done for the purpose of punishing the misconduct of the deceased: that is no excuse in the eye of the law–a stranger coming, a free agent into another country, enters by that compact into an implied compact to abide by its laws.[102]

Valoo was not only a stranger, his arrival was voluntary, and not coerced, the assumption being that indentured labour was "free" labour. As a free migrant, he was thus obliged to abide by the laws of his new country.[103]

A coda of sorts is appended to Valoo's file. Gomm rejected the appeals of both Valoo and Beecon; their capital sentences were confirmed. As they awaited their execution, Gomm corresponded with the Bishop W.B. Allen Collier. The capital sentences had weighed upon Gomm, but he found "inappreciable consolation" in the news that the Abbé Laval, who had counseled the two prisoners, had succeeded in "awakening a donning [sic] of religious and even Christian feeling of contrition and hope in the breasts of the benighted criminals."[104] Thereafter, having become familiar by means of their conversion to a "Christian feeling of contrition," Valoo and Beecon were put to death.

## *Conclusion*

This series of capital cases within the legal archive highlights key dynamics in the intimate lives of Indian labourers in Mauritius, including rivalries between *sirdars*, the economic dependency of women, and the exchange of sexual partners. Multiple views on marriage also emerge. Marriages might be formed by gift or by sale, as a kind of debt, as a form of care, as a means for security, and as an (uneven) exchange of sexual and household labour. The emotions or feelings between partners are sparsely described. Where affect is broached within the transcripts, it is mixed with violence, as evidence of intent or "malice aforethought." Witnesses are asked to testify to the blunt impact of a weapon, rather than the trauma they experienced as spectators to sexual violence. Perhaps the paucity of affect speaks to the strain of life under indenture. It may also indicate the disinterest of the law in the affective bonds between "co-habitating" subjects.

The titular phrase "before the law" invokes the short story by Franz Kafka, and meditations on that story by Jacques Derrida. In that story, a "man from the country" (a stranger?) waits at a portal for entry to the law. The door is patrolled by a guardian, who does not permit access. In Derrida's reading, "before" has multiple meanings: "topographic" (in front of the door), a sense of prejudging or prejudice, an interrogation of judgment itself, what precedes judgment, and how judgment may render justice. I would like to focus here on the guardian. Derrida suggests initially that the guardian is analogous to the judge, with the doorway resembling a trial: "To appear before the law, in the French, German, or English languages means to come or to be brought before the judges, the representatives or the guardians of the law, in a trial, and there to act as a witness or to be judged."[105] Elsewhere, Derrida suggests the possibility of multiple guardians: "Behind the first guardian there are others, an unspecified number of others; perhaps there are more than can be counted, each more powerful than the last...."[106]

The experience of a labourer such as Beecon is suggestive of the multiplicity of guardians, and of law. Beecon appears before the estate manager to request a pass, "confesses" to the *Juge d'Instruction*, appears at trial before the judges of both the Court of Assize and the Court of Appeal, petitions the governor of Mauritius for clemency, and, finally, offers another kind of "confession," a confession of the soul, to the Abbé Laval. Strikingly, Thomy Hugon, who had been appointed Protector of Immigrants in 1847, makes no appearance in any of the cases discussed here.[107] However, each of the guardians offers judgment of the stranger. The judgment is not singular. Rather, judgment is based on, variously, implied physical force, paternalistic authority, the terms of the labour contract, the status and role of the labour intermediary, prescriptions for the issuance of a pass, the codified rules of criminal procedure, a "French" penal code, British subjecthood, and, finally, pastoral guidance.

For Indian women, however, appearances before the law were abbreviated. Oral contracts were difficult to prove or enforce in a court of law. Dependent economically on men, their claims to maintenance were impaired by the invalidity of their marriages. Consequently, Indian women were often secluded from the judgment of the Mauritian legal system.[108] Carpaye, however, offered a poignant reminder of the economic dependence of women and the choices they exercised to achieve precarious security. She also testified to the physical violence suffered by her daughter and to the final assault which took her daughter's life. Her testimony had been permitted by the court's invalidation of Taylamen's marriage, yet her claim for a customary celebration of marriage resonated for decades, as Mauritius and the British Empire laboured to afford hospitality to strangers and their intimate practices.[109]

CHAPTER 4

# The Materiality and Visuality of Intimacy in a South African Colonial Archive

*Lorena Rizzo*

In the early twentieth century, the South African segregationist state began to pursue population policies that drew distinctions between rights-bearing citizens and disenfranchised subjects. The main preoccupation was to classify men and women along the lines of race, gender, and nationality and thereby impose a hierarchy of political, social, and economic privilege.[1] These political and legal concerns are reflected in an extensive archive comprised of textual and photographic records documenting the bureaucratic registration and identification of Africans, Indians, Chinese, and Europeans, who moved in and beyond the reach of South Africa's expanding political and economic dominion. I have thought and written about these archival documents on several occasions, but return to them here in order to trace some of the historical specificities of *intimacy* in a context marked by racial segregation, internal colonization, and the rise of ethnic nationalism.[2] However, before exploring the problem of intimacy—that is, the multiple meanings or "multivalence of intimacy"[3] as they emerge from an archive of mobility and containment in South Africa in the early decades of the twentieth century—I would like to introduce the material at hand by way of briefly discussing two particular archival files. My entry point to the case studies documented in these files is each time a photographic image.

The first one (Figure 4.1) is a photograph submitted by a woman called Marie Schiffer Lafite, who in 1914 applied for an identity certificate that would enable her to travel from South Africa to Mauritius in order to visit her relatives.[4] The photograph and application were part of a file compiled by the immigration officer in Cape Town, and it includes an assemblage of written and visual information. It tells us that Schiffer Lafite was, at the time, a shop assistant by profession, originally from Mauritius,

Figure 4.1
Marie Schiffer Lafite.
Source: Western Cape Archives and Record Service (KAB), PIO 1 – 147 E, File on Marie Schiffer Lafite.

first a resident of Cape Town and then Port Elizabeth, in what is today the Eastern Cape. She had moved to the Cape Colony in 1902, and after her first husband left her, remarried a French hairdresser called Lafite. Given that her intended journey required official approval, Marie Schiffer Lafite was submitted to an idiosyncratic process of certifying her identity and sanctioning her mobility. According to the information compiled in a standardized application form, she was declared to be a British subject by birth; thirty-two years old, female, married; fluent in English and French; "creole/coloured"; and—given her provenance from Mauritius—alien. Alongside the photograph and the form, the file likewise includes affidavits submitted by Schiffer Lafite herself and authored by two of her acquaintances in Port Elizabeth, who attested to her impeccable social reputation, pleasant personality, and exemplary manners.

Proceeding from the information thus assembled over a period of several days, the immigration officer eventually issued a certificate to Schiffer Lafite that approved of her journey and granted the right to return to the Cape Province after an estimated absence of one year.

The next pair of images (Figures 4.2 and 4.3) is, again, part of a file produced by the department of immigration in Cape Town, this time in 1922. The photograph and the graphic composition pertain to the documents submitted by Eva Wing, who applied for an identity certificate for herself and her children in order to accompany her husband, Lai Wing, on an extended journey to China, and return to the Cape after three years.[5] As was the case for Schiffer Lafite, the portrait photograph submitted by Eva Wing was taken in a professional photo studio and all photographic subjects, including the infants, appear in impeccable attire, lined up in a careful group composition and distinguished from a low-keyed studio backdrop. Alongside this image and a series of individual portraits, the file also includes a graphic composition of affixed cutouts from the children's photographs, and recorded dates, names, and fingerprints. Standardized questionnaires and forms provide itemized information about the Wing family. Lai Wing, the husband, was forty-four years old at the time and was said to be a trader of Chinese descent. He was married to thirty-two-year-old Eva, a "coloured" woman, born in Cape Town as a British subject (up until her marriage to a Chinese man), mother and homemaker, who spoke English. In 1922, when Mrs. Wing applied for the certificate, the family resided in Port Elizabeth.

What do these two case studies tell us about histories of intimacy, and how is the intimate constituted in this particular archive? The two files just discussed are, perhaps obviously, suggestive for an analysis that conceives of intimacy as something that pertains to the domain of the social, and is located in the private, domestic, affective space of the family—in which questions of romance, emotions, sex, and the body surface in more or less explicit ways.[6] While we do indeed catch a few glimpses at the personal, familial, and broader social worlds inhabited by Marie Schiffer Lafite and Eva Wing—and I will come back to these later on—our desire to retrieve subjugated intimacies and make these women's lives and embodied experiences legible in an act of biographical reconstruction will rapidly lead us astray.[7]

This is why I propose instead to pursue a historical inquiry that attends to the conditions under which the South African state recorded,

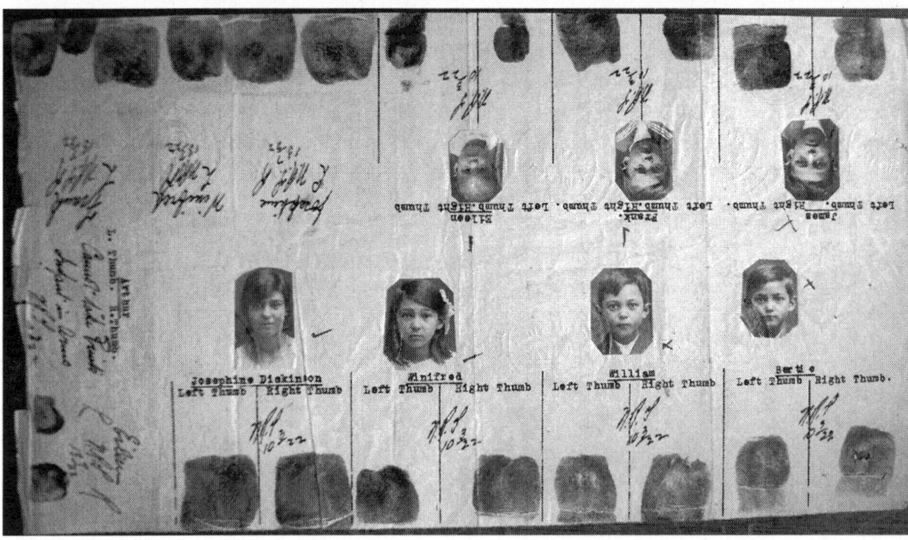


Figure 4.2: Wing family portrait. Source: KAB IRC 1/2/4 73 C, Eva & Lai Wing.

Figure 4.3: Wing genealogical graph. Source: KAB IRC 1/2/4 73 C, Eva & Lai Wing.

refracted, authorized, and dismissed bodies and social selves, and how the intimate corporeality thus produced and circulated helped constitute a particular South African notion of the body politic.[8] Such an approach is sensible, given that the files considered here and today stored at the Western Cape Archives and Records Service in Cape Town, form part of a public archive that records and authenticates a particular kind of history, whose subject is first the South African state and its related acts of sovereignty.[9] What we encounter here, in other words, is a particular constellation of textual and visual remains—the material fabric of what Athena Athanasiou calls "sedimented intimacies"—that sustain the temporalities and historical ontology of an emerging South African nation.[10] Attending to the nation's intimate archive will, by implication, shift attention towards the pulse of the archive's materiality—to the cadence and tone of archival tangibility by which a sense of intimacy in our encounter with the material and visual traces from the past is enforced, shaped, and mediated.[11] Archival research and historical methodology are grounded in our embodied engagement with texts, images, and objects that help us immerse ourselves in the worlds and lives of historical subjects. We draw nearer and, provided our response is empathic, strive to understand a particular past—at this point the lived experience of mid-twentieth century South Africans and their response to and contestation of their being drawn into the realm of state administration and surveillance.[12]

However, the particular archive I will discuss constitutes a problematic site for historical hermeneutics, precisely because our desire to become an intimate of this past is strongly mediated through the material and visual practices of the segregationist state. This ought not to deter us on principle but shall simply serve as a reminder that in this particular South African archive, intimacy sits uncomfortably at the interstices of state bureaucracy and regulation, history and memory, archival assimilation, counter-narrative, public authentication, and voyeuristic intrusion.[13]

## *The Boundaries of Intimate Belonging*

Marie Schiffer Lafite and Eva Wing were two women whose idiosyncratic encounter with the South African bureaucracy in the 1910s and 1920s, respectively, mainly circled around three issues—social status, race, and mobility. This was no coincidence, given that South Africa was only just entering a process of political formation. The unification of the former

British colonies and the two Boer republics had just been enforced in 1910, and the central state began to consolidate a confusing assemblage of different legal regimes and administrative policies and procedures inherited from its political predecessors within a single body of rules. This consolidation was geared explicitly toward defining the emerging South African nation and its racial fabric.[14] The programmatic credo of a "white man's land" became the guiding political imaginary that would henceforth frame the preoccupation with registering and classifying subject populations, determining individual identity, and controlling people's disposition and mobility.[15] Consequently, the first two decades after Union saw the imposition of a plethora of laws that curtailed the political and residential rights of all those classified as non-white. Chinese exclusion, the multiple forms of discrimination against Indians, and the political disenfranchisement of so-called "natives," that is, Africans, had mushroomed since the mid-nineteenth century, but they were carried over and exacerbated in national legislation passed during the 1910s and 1920s.[16] However, while the ideological constitution of the South African segregationist state was, from its very beginning, a project that made the question of inclusion and exclusion essentially a matter of nationality and race, it remained conditioned by imperial parameters and the political economy of transnational migration.[17] The entanglement of empire and nation, race and nationality, resulted in the emergence of uneven legal norms, an idiosyncratic legal culture and, more importantly, a complex administrative and bureaucratic practice that engendered the definition and regulation of racial and national identities, citizenship, and belonging.[18]

South African Union had inaugurated a process of political and legal standardization, but throughout the inter-war period things remained fluid and there continued to be great regional and institutional variation. Administrative procedures and the application of laws were decentralized and matters concerning an individual's classification were decided more at the local than the national level.[19] Within a regulatory system that remained ill-defined, the question of a person's political, legal and cultural status—the meaning of citizenship in the broadest terms—was therefore characteristically resolved in complex struggles over residence and mobility. As a dominion within the British Empire, South Africa was liable to imperial legislation that granted some political rights by birth or naturalization, although still contingent on gender and age. Moreover, since there was reluctance to offend metropolitan sensibilities openly, yet nevertheless a strong urge to pursue the national project of racial differentiation and hierarchization, the question of race and citizenship was made precisely conditional of mobility and migration, both within and beyond the South African territory.[20]

The files compiled on Schiffer Lafite and the Wing family provide rich evidence for how laws on race, nationality, citizenship, and migration were applied and actualized in the context of South African administrative practice in the 1910s and 1920s. However, the main interest here is to explore if and how we can understand these processes in terms of a sedimentation of intimacy, while acknowledging the concept's ambiguity in terms of meaning and its multiple constitutions at the level of the material, visual, and discursive. A focus on intimacy promises to nuance our understanding of South African nation building, and to do so in a way that attends to both the political and the affective.[21] These were not separate, but mutually dependent domains in which the legal and moral boundaries of the nation were drawn in order to define who belonged and who did not. As we shall see, the main idiom through which these intimate boundaries were articulated was the language of race, gender, and the body.[22] Intimacy, in other words, sensitizes us toward a series of official concerns with the most private spheres of life, and helps to highlight the extent to which the arrangement of these intimacies was bound up with the differential logic of a racialized nation.[23] My main concern in what follows is to substantiate the intimate entanglement of the gendered, racialized body and the body-archive of an incipient South African nation by way of foregrounding the material and visual practices on which it was based.[24]

## *Epistemologies of Belonging in the Cape Colony*

At the time when they applied for official documents, Marie Schiffer Lafite and Eva Wing were both residing in the Cape Province, more specifically in Cape Town and Port Elizabeth. The files compiled about these women, their families, and broader social environments were the product of a political and administrative regime engendered by both the process of national consolidation and its resonance at the regional and local level. South African Union in 1910 had brought change to the Cape, although characteristic features of Cape colonial society endured. Cape

Town in particular had gone through significant economic and social transformation since the 1870s. Up to the late nineteenth century, the British colony was characterized by a predominantly rural population mostly employed in farming, either pastoral or agriculture. According to census figures, approximately 720,000 people lived here in 1875, divided into 236,000 "whites" and 484,000 "coloureds," meaning Khoikhoi, people of Asian or mixed descent, and former slaves.[25] Cape Town itself, while the largest city in Southern Africa, was relatively small and counted 45,000 inhabitants.[26] The economy was dominated by merchant capital, retail business, and farming, and the export of agricultural commodities such as wool, wine, and brandy. Industrial activity in towns and cities was concentrated on the production of food, clothing, and shelter, and required little machinery and labour. Seasonal work was characteristic, limited to agriculture, commerce, and fisheries across the province, while self-employed artisans, small retailers, washerwomen, domestic workers, drivers, and carriers diversified the urban labour force.[27] The social structure and racial divides in Cape colonial society were based essentially on white bourgeois dominance and Black subordination that had their roots in slavery and colonial conquest.[28] In Cape Town, a small number of merchant families controlled property, commerce, capital investment, and credit, and members of the white bourgeois elite held key positions in government and the judiciary; while at the lower ranks of society people of African, Asian, and Afrikaner (Boer) descent remained locked in structural poverty. However, while social stratification was rigid, racial divides were particularly strict in the countryside, but less so in urban contexts.

The Cape was known for its colour-blind franchise since the mid-nineteenth century and the technical equality of all before the law since the abolition of slavery in 1838. Inter-racial mixing, especially among the middle and lower classes, was common, and racial and ethnic categories remained fluid. While there was de facto segregation across government and many social institutions, and a close correlation between colour and social standing, British administrators, missionaries, and vast sections of the urban public held the liberal belief in the civilizing mission and the potential equality of Blacks, once the latter embraced the values of Victorian bourgeois society.[29] This relative fluidity, however, was coming under threat and the situation had changed for the worse by the 1890s. The "mineral revolution," triggered by the discoveries of diamonds and gold in the Cape in the 1870s but especially on the Rand around

Johannesburg in the 1880s, was the main force behind the economic and demographic changes in the Cape and beyond.[30] Cape Town experienced a period of renewed prosperity among the merchant elite; infrastructure was expanded and building activity flourished, and the local economy diversified, especially in the industrial sector. Yet along with the economic upswing came growing migration to the towns and cities and rapid urbanization, which shifted the fragile demographic balance of Cape colonial society and exacerbated the problem of poverty. Against the backdrop of structural social transformation, the discourse and practice of segregation expanded, even if it came into effect de facto rather than de jure.[31] The separation of Black and white was applied more consistently across government and social institutions, and the debate on poverty was increasingly racialized. While Black urban residents were perceived as the bearers of disease, filth, and crime, the white urban proletariat was concurrently moved to the centre of political attention and social welfare. Growing socio-political tension was beginning to produce a climate of partisan ethnic mobilization, among British, Afrikaner, and coloured.[32] Although Cape Town had become one of the most cosmopolitan cities in Southern Africa, by the early twentieth century the contours of racial segregation were being outlined more explicitly.[33] In 1902 parliament passed the Cape's Immigration Act that reflected the gradual rise of anti-immigrant sentiment.[34] African migration from rural hinterlands or Mozambique was curtailed, and limiting the presence of "unwanted" Africans or "natives" in cities and towns across the Cape, among them Cape Town, Port Elizabeth, and East London, was seen as key to the preservation of white economic and social hegemony. Racial segregation was institutionalized and increasingly enforced by law in schools, hospitals, and prisons, while African urban residents were confined to "native" locations.[35]

By 1910, while a truncated non-racial franchise persisted and working-class interracial socialization remained common, the similarities between the Cape and the rest of South Africa, including the former Boer republics, outweighed the differences.[36] After the First World War, which had dominated white and, to a certain extent, Black life, Cape Town entered a phase of modernization and renewed economic growth, which transformed it from a small commercial port to a modern industrial city. Compared to the Rand, though, the Cape was not wealthy and the economy remained modest in scale. The search for cheap labour and seasonal work continued, and migrants driven by poverty flocked to towns and cities, among them many Africans and Afrikaners.[37] While the construction of a unified political entity was underway, histories of regional divisions, racism, political and social conflict, and the emergence of ethnic particularisms endured, especially among British and Boer constituencies.[38] Nevertheless, throughout the 1910s and 1920s, a sense of South African identity began to emerge, especially among whites, and—as mentioned before—the state actively promoted a "white man's land" ideology. Immigration became critical within the politics of whiteness, though the Cape had aspired to attract high numbers of European and British immigrants since the early 1900s.[39] In view of growing anxieties about the relative size of the Black and white population, the focus shifted toward pre-emptive measures, and the Immigration Regulation Act passed in 1913 codified an essentially restrictive legislation that would henceforth hinder African and non-white immigration to South Africa. While the act was geared toward aligning regional legislation, it accommodated provincial autonomy, preserved legislation that enabled temporary labour migration (a critical factor to mining and industrial capital), and maintained racialized access to land ownership, trade, and interregional mobility.

## *Intimacies of the Body, Intimacies of the Nation*

The profound economic and demographic changes, enduring high mobility (both national and transnational), and the tightening politics of segregation of the emerging nation-state required the Cape authorities to actually implement a programmatic agenda and provide an institutional apparatus that would produce and maintain an archive of ethnicized and racialized belonging. While the political imaginary of a "white man's land" might have seemed straightforward to those who embraced it, its translation into applicable policy and administrative procedure that would help to delineate the contours of distinctive groups and individuals remained less obvious in the Cape. Marie Schiffer Lafite's and Eva Wing's documentation, two examples among hundreds of comparable cases processed by the immigration department, and often supplemented by the police and magistrate courts, illustrate the idiosyncrasy of political and social membership requirements, and the changeable criteria by which racial and gendered inferiority or superiority, privilege, and power were defined during the interwar period.[40] In other words, the taxonomies of rule and epistemologies of inclusion and exclusion were literally and metaphorically in the making—haunted from within and without by the nation's "undesirables."

Let me return to the archival files and begin with situating the documents that relate to Marie Schiffer Lafite within South African discourses of race, gender, and nationality, and explore in more detail how notions of intimacy emerged in this particular case. Schiffer Lafite approached the immigration office in Cape Town in 1914 because of her planned journey to Mauritius, where she had been born in 1882. As described earlier on, applying for a document of passage that sanctioned an individual's transnational mobility resulted in the administrative segmentation of the body and its reconstitution as a particular kind of person within the framework and idiom of the racialized nation-state. Remember Lafite was hence classified as female, married, "creole/coloured," fluent in English and French, and alien. A closer look at the archival reference—the file's location within the larger archive of migration—reveals, crucially, her administrative positioning under the category "E," European. In other words, what seemed at first sight a rather straightforward process of classification based on a prescribed taxonomy proved ambiguous. Contrary to expectations, the fragments of information on Schiffer Lafite ran counter to the logics of bureaucratic systematization, and they indeed provide hints to the complexity of the emerging nation's archival intimacies. Her marriage to a Frenchman determined her derivative legal and gendered status, but also her potential proximity to Europeanness/"whiteness."[41] Her appearance—"colour" in contemporary parlance—and provenance, on the other hand, were more problematic and constituted the potential grounds on which the state could fix her condition of un-belonging, alienation, and extraterritoriality.[42] The combination of categories applied are, in fact, suggestive of the implicit socio-political matrix and ideological concern that shaped the immigration officer's perception and placement of Schiffer Lafite, and was linked to one of the main concerns of immigration policy in the early years of Union: Indian Ocean mobility and migration.[43]

Marie Schiffer Lafite inhabited the world of a diverse diaspora from South Asia and the islands off the southeast African coast. These movements of people, which began in the mid-nineteenth century and were marked for decades by the political economy of indentured labour, but likewise rested on voluntary migration, as discussed by Riyad Koya in

Chapter 3, involved significant mobility of men and women, many of whom were attracted to the sugar plantation economy of South Africa's Natal province.[44] Notwithstanding Koya's important contribution, the history of Mauritian participation in these cultures of mobility remains uncertain, and the immigration officer's ambiguous classification of Schiffer Lafite in terms of race and ethnicity is telling.[45] On the one hand, the term "creole" explicitly references a space of hybrid colonial cultures and registers of (racial) identification associated with the southeast African archipelagos but, on the other hand, "coloured" remained a term, especially in the Cape, that allowed him to translate the ambiguity and fluidity of race into local registers.[46] Yet administrative flexibility and candour did not go further, and ultimately gravitated toward homogenization and the state's concern to limit Indian and "other Asiatic" immigration and presence in the country—including from Mauritius. British subject status protected Schiffer Lafite against racial discrimination, and her proven language proficiency prevented the authorities from sanctioning her subject status to an education clause included in the 1913 Immigration Act.[47] But the newly established national framework introduced additional criteria for the exclusion of unwanted immigrants and residents—i.e., the category of alien—and made Schiffer Lafite's request for the right to travel and, more importantly, to return to the Cape more doubtful than it appeared at first sight.[48]

I will explain at a later stage what may have tipped the balance in favour of Schiffer Lafite's application and show that her success was precisely the result of her ability to map a terrain of counter-intimacy while she diligently navigated the domain of state bureaucracy and the pitfalls of gendered and racial classification. For now, I wish to add more texture to the nation's intimate archive by attending to the second case study discussed here—the application of Eva Wing. This material takes us into another facet of South African history of documentation, in which those classified as "Chinese" occupied a pivotal place.[49] Chinese immigration to the South African colonies and republics goes back to government-driven labour schemes initiated in an attempt to solve labour shortage problems on the mines after the South African War (1899–1902).[50] Compared to the Transvaal and the Witwatersrand mining complex, which attracted most indentured workers, Chinese who migrated to the Cape Colony during the late nineteenth and early twentieth century had predominantly done so as "freemen." In a climate of growing anti-immigrant and anti-Asian sentiment, and although numbers were very small, Chinese presence at the Cape was as politicized as it was in other parts of South Africa. Chinese immigration was seen as both an economic problem—given that they were seen as rivals of the "white" labour force—and as a moral threat to the nation.[51] In 1904, the colony passed one of its most restrictive pieces of legislation, the Chinese Exclusion Act, which introduced the first individual race-based process of registration.[52] The act made immigration to and residence in the Cape illegal for all "classes" of Chinese, indentured or free, except for those who were granted exemption permits. As a result, and because the permit system targeted almost every aspect of people's lives, Cape authorities began to produce a cumbersome archive of control, surveillance, and identification. The Wing family's file inserted itself smoothly into a paper regime, which by the 1920s had become meticulous and extensive.[53] The documents assembled listed names, place of residence, birth and migration history, profession, gender, and race, and they included recommendations by neighbours, business partners, and acquaintances, most of whom were "white" and acceptable enough to certify the family's respectability.[54] Based on the information thus recorded, the Wing family could be placed within the small milieu of Chinese traders, businessmen, clerks, and artisans, who predominantly lived in the Cape's coastal towns, especially in Port Elizabeth and Cape Town.[55] As a "mixed" couple, however, they seem to have been exceptional and might therefore have attracted the immigration officer's special attention.[56] Eva Wing's application, which was meant to enable herself and her children to join her husband on an extended trip to China and return to the Cape after several years, was fraught with risk. She had lost her status as British subject when she married Lai Wing, and her husband's recognition as a registered Chinese immigrant provided some protection of his professional activity, but gave little guarantee for the right of residence and mobility of a family, which was disenfranchised in any case.

I have reconsidered the Wing family's file here for how it sheds light on the constitution of another kind of intimacy within this archive—one that rested on men paying special attention to women's bodies. The photograph of the collage, which included the children's portraits, their names, birthdays, and fingerprints, resonates with anxieties over the balance between "white" and "non-white" in South Africa at the time—in other words, policies that were increasingly articulated in numerical terms and within the logics of demography.[57] Children from mixed marriages complicated the simplicity of racial categories, especially if they involved individuals who transcended the tripartite system of white, Black, and coloured.[58] Furthermore, those born into Chinese families were often stigmatized and subjected to racist assumptions about promiscuity and boundless reproduction—beliefs that seemed to legitimize massive bureaucratic intrusion into the most intimate domains of people's sexual and emotional lives.[59] However, while these violations must have been unacceptable to Eva Wing and her children, breaking boundaries on one level helped establish them elsewhere, in as much as they defined the moral boundaries of the body politic. Women's bodies and their reproductive function were critical here, precisely because they became the markers of social, racial, and national boundaries.[60] The file on the Wing family exemplifies, perhaps in an exceptionally graphic way, the material and visual practices through which the bureaucratic apparatus translated a crude epistemology of the nation based on race and miscegenation, demography, and female reproduction into specific forms and formats of documentation that made racialized and gendered bodies legible for the segregationist project. What is made visible here is not simply a process of rationalization and bureaucratization, i.e., the genesis of registration systems aligned with the constitution of modern states; nor is it simply a question of the nation-state establishing sovereignty in the domain of international migration.[61] Rather, the file on Eva Wing and her family was the result of an administration which in its everyday gendered practice and intimate encounter with those marginalized and disenfranchised under the banner of South African nationality became increasingly rude, judgmental, and cruel.[62]

What has just been said does not, however, prevent us from shifting attention toward those being administered within the South African nation's intimate archive and asking if there are counter-intimacies we might be able to retrieve. I believe there are, and I suggest that these counter-intimacies circulate on the performative plane and are lodged in the photographs included in each file.[63]

## *Photographic Counter-Intimacies*

I opened this chapter by introducing Marie Schiffer Lafite's and Eva Wing's files with photographs included in them. The use of photography as a means of identification and surveillance has been widely covered in the history and theory of photography.[64] In the colonial context more specifically, the medium has been identified as a tool of empire that was often complicit with colonial epistemic violence, especially in the domains of policing and control.[65] While the "repressive" use of photography in archives of mobility and surveillance in twentieth century South Africa was common, it was not coherent, and contingent on both institutional circumstances and the shifting social status, gender identity, and racial classification of those placed under regulatory regimes. Photographs of migrants and mobile sections of the population were part of the state's broader archive of visual registration supplied by immigration, native administration, police, and the penal system.[66] Chinese exclusion and anti-Indian immigration laws had produced paper regimes that included photography early on, while the bureaucratic sanctioning of African and "native" mobility remained, by and large, non-photographic up to the mid-twentieth century.[67] In other words, visibility and invisibility were distributed unevenly, while photography's relationship to power—with its intricacies of visual representation and legibility—remained complicated.

The photographs included in Marie Schiffer Lafite's and Eva Wing's files were submitted by the women themselves, an instance that indicates the persistent acceptability of original photographic images within the bureaucratic domain in the inter-war period.[68] The transition of private photographs into the public domain—in fact, the strategic use of these images by those who applied for travel permits and identity certificates—was critical, since the medium thus remained beyond the representational control of the state and could still serve as a form of individual self-expression. Schiffer Lafite's and Wing's photographs resembled each other. They were in line with Victorian pictorial conventions and registers of bourgeois respectability that had been embraced by wide sections of Cape colonial society: the professional studio space, formal dress, elaborate backdrops, and selected accoutrements were part of this particular aesthetic disposition.[69] However, once these images entered the administrative domain, their material and visual effects shifted, whereby the function of the portraits in the women's embodiment and performance of sociality and belonging countered the logic and script of administrative categorization.[70] This is particularly the case in the Wing family photograph, in which the careful staging referenced nuanced hierarchies and relations within the family and constituted the familial as the domain of social security, emotional bonding and intimacy, respectability, and well-being. Beautiful and sophisticated portraiture, in short, enabled both women to interrupt the teleological narration and categorical abstraction of the racialized nation and to set the particular against the generic, the specific against the essential, and the situational against the normative. These photographs played a role in Marie Schiffer Lafite's and Eva Wing's intervention in the negotiation of gendered and social categories and the constitution of their personas in this archive. While the immigration officers were confined to the domain of the archive, the portraits submitted by the women transcended the narrow imaginary of the nation and its institutional scaffold. They constituted counter-intimacies, mediated through particular modes of subjectivity that pertained to spaces of aesthetic, social, and cultural practice, which continued to elude the state apparatus. In terms of the politics of racial segregation, gender marginalization, and nationalist alienation, Marie Schiffer Lafite and Eva Wing could hardly claim recognition as citizens and strive for inclusion into a South African nation in the making. Instead, they had to resort to aesthetic and affective strategies, using their embodied presence in the photographs as a means of performing an alternative, intimate form of citizenship and belonging.[71]

## *Conclusion: The Materiality and Visuality of (Un)Belonging*

This chapter has inquired into the material and visual practices in a South African archive of mobility and containment with a view towards understanding the ways in which notions of intimacy emerged in the context of South African nation building in the early twentieth century. Proposing an approach that understands intimacy not only as a matter of social relations, predominantly located in the domain of the private and the domestic, but as something that is embedded in the archive itself, has shed light on a particular South African iteration of national intimacy—that is, a nation's intrinsic need to define who belongs and who does not. Furthermore, the chapter has argued that within South Africa's intimate project of national constitution, the state bureaucracy literally and metaphorically turned its gaze towards the body, and thereby exposed its dependency on deeply racialized and gendered intimacies—such as the figure of the coloured alien in Schiffer Lafite's case, or the children of "miscegenation" in the Wing family's case.[72] Defining the national intimates via the bodies of those submitted to the state's identification and surveillance regimes helped establish an organic notion of the body politic that would repudiate its internal and external others as contaminating threats to be held off—among them "natives," coloureds, Indian, and Chinese. However, during the interwar period, South Africa's project of a "white man's land" remained conditioned by British imperial legislation and a theoretical equality of all in front of the law, and there were hence important limits on implementing total disenfranchisement based on race. Immigration thus emerged as a critical domain in which to enforce the boundaries of citizenship and belonging and, throughout the twentieth century, the South African state would continuously expand the scope of outward seclusion and internal alienation.[73]

There are, however, further questions raised by our interest in intimacy that concern the intrinsic politics of the archive and the ethical implications we face when engaging colonial archival collections today. The history of racial segregation, the focus on bodies subjected to repressive paper and image regimes, and the hyper-intimacy it thereby engendered can produce deep discomfort and fear of historical voyeurism once we encounter the fragments of people's lives in archives. Explaining the (discursive) dismembering of bodies—the domiciliation of itemized individuals in single files—and the reassembling of the nation—the seriality of thousands of immigration files—in terms of rationalization and the emergence of modern state bureaucracies only partly and temporarily diverts attention from what haunts these archives from within. This sense of discomfort ultimately emerges, I believe, from a problematic conjunction of nation and history that precisely rests on the archive's logic of dissection and re-assemblage, of dismembering bodies and pasts, and reconstituting a present inevitably oriented toward the traumatic memory of a history of colonialism, race, and racism, and the precarity of (un)belonging.[74] The immigration files considered here, their inclination to merely reproduce the state's claim to control mobile bodies and draw the boundaries of the nation, is indeed a reminder of the archive's constitutive relationship with sovereignty, rendered in the state's preferred idiom—the law.[75] It is against this backdrop that the chapter considered the possibility to retrieve counter-intimacies, even if they remain constrained within the archive. Paying close attention to the photographs enclosed in the immigration files and considering them as snapshots of intimate citizenship constituted in the context of diasporic socialization, emotional attachment beyond the colour line, and aesthetic expressions of respectability and belonging helped underscore both the limits of a unifying domain of archivability and the incommensurability of intimacies beyond the nation-state.[76]

# PART 2

# *Intergenerational Justice*

*To what extent and for what reasons have the state and its judicial apparatus intervened in parent-child relations? What can the archival records generated by civil courts and the juvenile justice system teach us about the intergenerational dynamics of earlier times? Such are the questions that animate the three chapters in this section, which focus attention on intergenerational justice as seen in the "tutorship" arrangements that protected vulnerable minors in Lower Canada, in court challenges to parental authority launched by adolescents in industrializing Buenos Aires, and in stories of "unfit and unworthy" parents so identified by the nascent youth-court system in large American cities.*

*In Chapter 5, Jean-Philippe Garneau approaches this discussion from the standpoint of* la tutelle parisienne*: the Parisian form of tutorship applied in what is today Quebec, with its heritage of French civil law. This was a type of legal guardianship used in very different ways—depending especially on gender, social class, and ethnicity—by recently widowed mothers and fathers in Lower Canada in the 1820s and 1830s. As in two contributions to Part 1 of this book (Chapter 1, by Isabelle Bouchard, and Chapter 3, by Riyad Koya), we find ourselves here at the intersection of French and British legal traditions, this time with the resulting hybridity playing out in the intimate world of parental rights and obligations with regard to minor children. Striking differences between the ways French-Canadian and Anglo-Celtic families applied these provisions of the law are at the heart of Garneau's analysis, as are culturally specific understandings of masculinity and paternal authority.*[1]

*From Lower Canada, we move south to the United States and Argentina, with two chapters that explore the state's emerging role in the regulation of conflict between parents and their children. Juandrea Bates situates her discussion (Chapter 6) in Buenos Aires at the turn of the twentieth century. The Argentine capital was growing quickly at this time (there were already 1.6 million people living there in 1914) as its labour market was transformed by industrial capitalism. In this setting, hundreds of young people—many of them employed as waged labourers—used civil suits to challenge the unconstrained authority of their parents. Some sought relief from violent and abusive situations, while others simply wanted more autonomy to spend their own wages or choose their own romantic partner.*

*In Chapter 7, Naama Maor examines intergenerational justice through the lens of the specialized youth courts that were established in every major city in the United States—and many others worldwide—during the Progressive Era. Using judicial archives from Chicago, Denver, and Memphis, Maor shifts attention away from "wayward" youth themselves and towards their parents, whose failings were increasingly framed by legislators and the courts as contributing to their children's delinquency. By focusing on the state's preoccupation with "unfit and unworthy" parents, on the ways in which these parents understood their parental responsibility, and on cases where they either welcomed or resisted state intrusion into their intimate family affairs, she makes an important new contribution to the growing literature on the juvenile justice system in Europe and North America.*[2]

## CHAPTER 5

# Administering Minor Children's Inheritance

## *Domestic Authority and Masculinities in Lower Canada, 1825–1835*[1]

*Jean-Philippe Garneau*

Family historians are well aware of the law's role in shaping the lives and destinies of nineteenth-century households. Both older and newer rules governing marriage, inheritance, and wills continued to express a certain (highly gendered) vision of the nuclear and extended family. Granted, as notions of private life and a private sphere gained ground, family strategies did increasingly diverge from the letter of the law, to the point that the (male) head of household likely enjoyed unprecedented latitude. However, families' engagement with the law contributed to the ongoing symbolic and material construction of power within and surrounding the domestic unit. Without a doubt, legal practitioners contributed to this construction. Their arrival on the scene often coincided with the brokering or expression of decisions that confirmed or reshaped the roles and prospects of family members and other interested parties. This study explores the involvement of legal professionals by focusing on a specific type of legal proceeding: the tutorship of minor children, an aspect of French law that drew on ancient civil law traditions. This normally consensual recourse to the courts sought to protect minor heirs by appointing a legal representative empowered to act on their behalf. The following analysis emphasizes how this encounter with legal practitioners provides examples of domestic authority in action, at a time of family instability caused by the death of one of the parents, especially the male head of household. Ultimately, I highlight their role in shaping representations of masculinity in early nineteenth-century Lower Canada.[2]

A predominantly French and Catholic province within British North America, Lower Canada nonetheless shared in a transatlantic colonial experience with neighbouring colonies, especially its patchwork of social and legal cultures.[3] Lower Canada therefore provides a particularly interesting—though by no means unique—context of study.[4] Somewhat exceptionally, family law rooted in France theoretically applied to all settlers in this former French colony. But, especially after 1815, at-times massive immigration from the British Isles and the emergence of Anglo-Celtic communities[5] profoundly transformed the social and cultural composition of the colony's main towns and cities, as well as that of certain rural areas. Dating from the nineteenth century, the first censuses of the city of Montreal clearly show that this growing diversity was not limited to individuals of English or Scottish origin.[6] Nevertheless, the latter acquired significant economic and political influence. In addition, British identity likely served as a unifying force, especially in the lead-up to the Rebellions of 1837–1838.[7] To my mind, the diversity of concepts and customs governing both legal and family matters in Lower Canada cannot be overemphasized. And yet, the intercultural dynamics implied by this diversity have received little attention, especially in relation to the history of the family in Quebec.[8]

However, as I discuss below, paternal authority was constructed very differently depending on the origins and gender of the heads of household who initiated tutorship proceedings in the district of Montreal during the first third of the nineteenth century. My analysis leads to a twofold conclusion. On the one hand, the courts largely treated women the same, although there could certainly be variations on a theme. On the other hand, fathers who initiated tutorship proceedings were almost exclusively French Canadian. The liberal model of masculinity, based on the autonomous will of fathers, clearly stood apart from the more communitarian and traditional model favoured by *Canadien* families, which is to say Lower Canadians of French origin. But before going into more detail, I should review the principles underlying both the Parisian model of tutorship and legal practice in the district of Montreal.

## *Domestic Authority and the Parisian Model of Tutorship*

Like most aspects of Old Regime French law, the tutorship of minor children had been introduced during the earliest days of New France. In 1763, the advent of a new regime cast doubt on the basis of private law in a British colony with an overwhelmingly French-speaking and

Catholic population. The British Parliament sought to clarify the situation in 1774: French property and family law would prevail, subject to certain significant compromises I will address a bit further on. Contrary to the situation following the English conquest of New Netherland,[9] French law therefore theoretically applied to all subjects in the colony, regardless of origin.[10] In particular, tutorship would persist, unaffected by any major legislative changes until the adoption of the Civil Code of Lower Canada in 1866.[11]

Despite their Roman origins, the rules governing tutorship in Lower Canada can only be properly understood in light of the principles underlying the Custom of Paris. Upon the death of either parent, Parisian law provided for the appointment of a legal representative for any minor children who qualified as heirs. Under the Custom of Paris, equality of inheritance meant that each child could actually claim a share of the parental estate. Since the same legal tradition dictated marriage in community of property, the death of either spouse gave rise to the inheritance of a portion of the family's assets. The mother's or father's inheritance normally represented half of their common property, along with any separate property (*biens propres*) belonging to the deceased spouse (for instance, inherited land). Given that parents still often died prematurely in the nineteenth century, tutorship remained an important component of the inheritance practices of young families. This type of legal proceeding, which provided for the management of minor children's inheritance, normally began with an inventory of the property of the deceased and ended with a passing of accounts when the children reached the age of majority or were otherwise emancipated. Legal scholars from the period explain how, following natural law, the surviving spouse would be appointed tutor on the advice of an assembly of seven relatives and friends convened by a judge.[12] Most of the time, the latter was content to ratify the assembly's "unanimous" decision. The presiding magistrate would only intervene in cases of conflict or irregularity, or when the chosen tutor declined the appointment. Finally, the Custom of Paris also provided for the appointment of a so-called subrogate tutor. Usually chosen from among the relatives of the deceased, this *légitime contradicteur* was specifically tasked with supervising the postmortem inventory and valuation of property.

The legal process set in motion by the appointment of a tutor therefore provides historians with valuable information on family assets.[13] But the study of tutorship itself also sheds light on the reconfiguration of domestic authority, on the behaviour of family members (especially that of the surviving spouse), and on those individuals (uncles, brothers-in-law, or even close acquaintances) who were closest to the minor children. The Custom of Paris mainly treats tutorship as a means of settling the matrimonial regime upon the death of a spouse. Indeed, this legal proceeding was one of the requirements for dissolving the community of property. However, it is important to note that tutorship was not exclusively reserved for this type of regime. Analogous to guardianship in English law, it was required whenever minor children received an inheritance.[14] Naturally, the death of both parents also gave rise to tutorship proceedings and other efforts to preserve the "property and person" of orphaned children. In such cases, there was a clearer need to appoint an individual to exercise parental authority, alongside material considerations.

The Anglo-Celtic elites established in Lower Canada saw French customary law as a major irritant, especially as it related to marital property and the rights of widows and orphans. For several decades, the Custom of Paris lay at the heart of a conflict—the course and flashpoints of which have been detailed by Evelyn Kolish—that divided the population along national lines.[15] British colonists could take some limited comfort in the fact that English rules for validating wills had been introduced in 1774. This legislative change opened the door to a kind of customization of the colony's legal framework, a situation facilitated by the fact that most common-law judges and many lawyers were of British or American origin. Contrary to judicial practice under the previous French regime, no *procureur du roi* ensured that the legal protection of all minor children was duly administered.[16] In the early nineteenth century, French Canadians were prone to accusing "English" legal practitioners of undermining Lower Canada's French legal heritage, especially where wills were concerned.[17] However, little is known about the actual situation behind the public discourse, since few studies have looked at the day-to-day activities of civil courts or even of public notaries.[18] One notable exception to this rule is Bettina Bradbury's work, which reveals the almost visceral desire among British elites to be exempt from the legal provisions of the Custom of Paris.[19] They therefore tended to focus their attacks on the perceived adverse effects of French law on issues surrounding marriage settlements and wills. Essentially, they sought to liberate male property from the restrictions imposed by the customary rights of widows and orphans. Nevertheless, certain key dimensions of the issue remain poorly understood, including those related to inheritance practices and to how the courts dealt with matters of family property.[20] Tutorship proceedings constitute one of these missing pieces.

## *Legal Practice and Practitioners in the District of Montreal*

Along with other non-contentious proceedings, including those involving the curatorship of incapacitated persons, the tutorship of minors was placed under the jurisdiction of the Court of King's Bench. In 1794, such courts were established in each of the colony's three main urban centres. My research focused exclusively on cases in the district of Montreal,[21] which extended far beyond the city itself to encompass a vast rural area.[22] Between 1815 and 1840, the court handled roughly 600 to 800 cases of all types per year—except for 1832–1834, when its workload doubled amid successive waves of cholera.[23]

Before going any further, I wish to address a few issues I encountered with these judicial documents, especially since the identifying information recorded by legal practitioners is crucial to the analysis that follows. Generally speaking, the Lower Canadian judicial archives rarely mention an individual's "national" origin. The court showed little interest in the ethnocultural identity of parties to its proceedings, whether out of a concern for ensuring equality before the law or because local knowledge did not meet the threshold for legal regulation. Although information available on genealogical websites allowed me to clarify a certain number of cases, I was unable to systematically determine national origin or religious affiliation with certainty for all individuals.[24] Nor is finding the mother's name an easy task. One cannot rely on the nominative index prepared by the clerks, a shortcoming that speaks volumes about the court's patriarchal understanding of domestic authority. Indeed, most of the time, these indexes provide the name of the widower or deceased father, and sometimes those of the minor children. Only exceptionally do they include a woman's name, such as when a minor daughter sought emancipation by marriage. It therefore becomes essential to proceed from the index to the judicial case file itself in order to ascertain the mother's identity, provided the practitioner bothered to note it; many did not, even though this information was crucial for the proper administration of the Custom of Paris.

Applications and minutes related to assemblies involving relatives and friends usually provide the following information: the identity of the applicant; the names of the father and mother, their place of residence and sometimes their occupation; the first name and age of the minor children (not always); the names of those attending the assembly and, in some cases, their relationship to the minor children. The ambiguity surrounding the social circle of the minor children also extends to adult children and those from previous marriages, whose names are not always provided.

The legal practitioners who laid out the picture of the family revealed by the case files were all men. However, they came from different ethnocultural backgrounds.[25] Families were less likely to use the services of lawyers or clerks, although those who were hired tended to be English speaking. By contrast, applications and minutes were frequently prepared by notaries, who were predominantly French Canadian. Meanwhile, certain work habits—such as sometimes neglecting to record the name of the deceased mother, or the relationship between the minor children and either the applicant or the participants in the assembly—were more characteristic of Anglo-Celtic legal practitioners. The sources give the distinct impression that practitioners writing in English were more focused on information regarding the husbands and sons, compared to other members of the nuclear or extended family.

The case involving the minor children of Alexander McDonald and Mary McDougal provides a good illustration. Both parents died intestate while living in Soulanges, a rural parish not far from Montreal that was home to several Anglo-Celtic families. In July 1825, their eldest son visited the city to retain the services of Irish Catholic notary Richard O'Keefe, with the aim of selling part of the estate. Since a portion of the inheritance belonged to siblings who had yet to reach the age of majority, the notary was required to oversee the appointment of a tutor. The application, which fails to mention the mother's name, was written in English and authorized by Judge Louis Charles Foucher. However, because the family lived more than "five leagues" from Montreal, the minutes of the assembly of family and friends had to be prepared by a Soulanges-based notary named Joseph B. Mailloux. The oldest brother was appointed tutor and a cousin on the father's side was named subrogate tutor. In addition to recording the mother's name, the French-Canadian notary used the term "half-brother" (*frère consanguin*), indicating the involvement of children from two different marriages.[26] Enough similar cases exist[27] to suggest that this example reflects the divergent representations of the family and gender that prevailed not only among legal professionals, but throughout society.

## *Analyzing Proceedings Through the Lens of Ethnocultural and Gender Identity*

My analysis of proceedings initiated by families is based on a comprehensive review of tutorship case files from the district of Montreal for the years 1825 and 1835. The diversity of proceedings included in these archives reflects the range of scenarios and events a Lower Canadian family could experience in any given year. I cannot hope to do justice to all this complexity in one short chapter. Having consulted some 1,700 files from the two years on which the sample is based, I identified 1,111 cases involving a widower or widow, including 736 involving the appointment of a tutor and 375 subsequent proceedings in which the tutor most often played some role. By comparison, only 238 cases involved the death of both parents, including 111 where a tutor was appointed for the orphaned children.[28] The following discussion looks at the appointment of tutors, first from a general perspective and then with a specific focus on cases where only one spouse had died.

### THE APPOINTMENT OF TUTORS IN DIFFERENT LANGUAGE COMMUNITIES

Given that French Canadians made up the vast majority of the population in the district of Montreal, it is not surprising that the tutorship of minors overwhelmingly involved French-speaking families. An analysis of cases where a tutor was appointed, whether following the death of one or both parents (847 cases), reveals that 84.7 percent of French-speaking families sought the advice of relatives and friends. This proportion is even slightly higher than that of the French-Canadian population in Lower Canada.[29] Such proceedings were especially popular among rural families in the district of Montreal, even if the countryside was slightly underrepresented in cases that came before the court.[30] Of course, French-speaking households predominated in rural areas (accounting for slightly more than nine out of ten families). Most often with the guidance of the local notary, tutorship proceedings clearly reflected

Table 5.1: Distribution of tutorship appointments according to the father's socioprofessional status: Montreal (city and suburbs), 1825, 1831–1832, 1835

| *Couples* | *English-speaking* | | *French-speaking* | | *Bilingual* | *Other* | *Total* | |
|---|---|---|---|---|---|---|---|---|
| Public figures and other elites | 16 | 12.2% | 10 | 7.5% | 5 | 1 | 32 | 10.3% |
| Professionals | 5 | 3.8% | 6 | 4.5% | 3 | 0 | 14 | 4.5% |
| Merchants | 31 | 23.7% | 9 | 6.7% | 9 | 2 | 51 | 16.4% |
| Tradesmen and service providers | 50 | 38.2% | 79 | 59.0% | 19 | 1 | 149 | 47.9% |
| Farmers and yeomen | 3 | 2.3% | 2 | 1.5% | 0 | 0 | 5 | 1.6% |
| Workers and day labourers | 7 | 5.3% | 18 | 13.4% | 3 | 1 | 29 | 9.3% |
| Undetermined | 19 | 14.5% | 10 | 7.5% | 2 | 0 | 31 | 10.0% |
| *Total* | 131 | 100.0% | 134 | 100.0% | 41 | 5 | 311 | 100.0% |

Sources: Tutorships and Curatorships Fonds, CC601, S1, BAnQ-VM; Généalogie Québec, Civil Status Registers (https://www.genealogiequebec.com).

the continuity of traditional practices.[31] Furthermore, the majority of these rural French-Canadian households were engaged in agriculture (at least two-thirds, and up to eighty percent after the proportional distribution of unknown cases).

In the city and suburbs of Montreal, the distribution largely reflected the relative demographic weight of the local French Canadian and Anglo-Celtic populations. To expand the urban sample, I added cases from 1831 and 1832 to those from 1825 and 1835.[32] Across all four years, just over forty percent of families applying to have a tutor appointed were English-speaking. Adding in mixed couples and those of other origins (Italian and German), which represented upwards of fifteen percent of the total, a little more than half of cases in Montreal involved a spouse who was not French Canadian. Socio-professional diversity was also greater and more balanced among families in the city (Table 5.1). Many urban families undoubtedly came from modest backgrounds, alongside some that were a little better off and others that belonged to the upper echelons of society. However, the latter group was over-represented, with a particularly strong presence of those English-speaking families who dominated the commercial sector, as well as public figures and other members of the elite.[33] With few exceptions, unskilled workers from the British Isles showed little interest in a type of legal proceeding with which many of them would have been completely unfamiliar. By contrast, the vast majority of French-speaking families were either middle-class or, to a lesser extent, from the popular classes.[34]

There were other key differences between the two main groups. To begin with, non-French-speaking families were somewhat more likely to appoint a tutor to children who had lost both parents. Furthermore, such orphans were often boys interested in learning a trade, or else young women preparing to get married. Sometimes, the deceased parents had never set foot in Lower Canada and their identity was not always disclosed. Such cases often involved distinct life trajectories. For instance, the secretary of the London Children's Friend Society for Canada was appointed tutor to some thirty boys between the ages of ten and seventeen who arrived from England in the fall of 1835. This individual was no doubt tasked with finding a trade for the boys with the help of the city's charitable organizations.[35] In this way, tutorship became wrapped up in the social regulation of so-called "vagabonds" in Britain and Ireland, giving an imperial dimension to the local administration of a judicial proceeding based in French law. By contrast, the appointment of tutors for French-Canadian orphans in no way resembled a transnational adaptation of a scene from *Oliver Twist*. Rather, such children and their siblings tended to be too young to provide for their own future and the corresponding tutorship proceedings were more likely to involve older relatives and friends.

## TUTORSHIP PROCEEDINGS INVOLVING WIDOWS AND WIDOWERS

Clearly, tutorship could have very different meanings for families in the district of Montreal, depending on their ethnocultural background. Yet the vast majority of tutorship proceedings involved the mother or father of minor heirs, following the death of the other spouse. Considering whether the process was initiated by a widow or a widower not only adds a gendered perspective to the analysis, but also provides a clearer overall picture.

Most often, these cases involved the initial appointment of a tutor. As explained above, such an appointment provided the surviving spouse with the legal authority to act on behalf of minor children. Although the appointment itself was never in doubt, the case files from 1825 and 1835 nevertheless describe practices that could vary considerably depending on the gender of the surviving spouse and the family's ethnocultural background. Whereas, among French Canadians, fathers were more likely than mothers to pursue a court-approved appointment, Anglo-Celtic fathers almost never initiated such proceedings following the death of a wife (see Table 5.2). The few English-speaking widowers who went before the court appear to have been advised to do so by a French-Canadian legal practitioner—especially notary Nicolas-Benjamin Doucet, who was well known for having published a civil law commentary for the province's English-speaking population.[36] It is also possible that French Canadians who were close to the family sometimes influenced an Anglo-Celtic widower. This appears to have been the case with Stanley Bagg, a Montreal merchant and defeated candidate in the bloody 1832 by-election in the riding of Montreal West.[37] In February 1835, shortly after the death of his wife, Ann Clarke, he was appointed tutor to their fourteen-year-old son. One of the teenager's uncles by marriage, a French Canadian, was named subrogate tutor. However, an inventory of the late mother's property does not appear to have been prepared, nor were any other legal applications made in the context of this tutorship. In any case, I should note that although they were of English origin, both the father and his late wife had been born in Montreal.[38] Although exceptional, this example demonstrates how individuals sometimes strayed from group norms. That being said, the almost total absence of Anglo-Celtic fathers in the case files related to tutorship proceedings (including but not limited to appointments) seems to be explained by the rarity—if not the nonexistence—of maternal succession. Perhaps some wives' wills exempted the widower from initiating such proceedings, by naming the husband universal legatee.[39] Overall, the situation would seem to reflect a conception of the family in which the husband was the uncontested head of household, regardless of class. By entering into a marriage contract, many English-speaking Protestant couples were able to opt out of the matrimonial regime of the Custom of Paris and keep family assets in the hands of the husband. But such couples represented only a small fraction of all Anglo-Celtic households, most of which would not have had a written marriage contract. And few married women in Lower Canada wrote a will or had their last wishes drawn up by a notary.[40] In short, the well-known legal practices of some Anglo-Celtic households cannot fully explain the widespread absence of English-speaking fathers in the case files.

Table 5.2: Appointment of tutors following the death of the first spouse, district of Montreal, 1825 and 1835

| *Couples* | *English-speaking* | | *Bilingual and Other* | | *French-speaking* | | *Total* | |
|---|---|---|---|---|---|---|---|---|
| Widowers | 7 | 9.3% | 14 | 56.0% | 358 | 56.3% | 379 | 51.5% |
| Widows | 68 | 90.7% | 11 | 44.0% | 278 | 43.7% | 357 | 48.5% |
| *Total* | 75 | 100.0% | 25 | 100.0% | 636 | 100.0% | 736 | 100.0% |

Sources: Tutorships and Curatorships Fonds, CC601, S1, BAnQ-VM; Généalogie Québec, Civil Status Registers (https://www.genealogiequebec.com).

The situation was markedly different for English-speaking mothers. Proportional to the English-speaking population of the district of Montreal, Anglo-Celtic widows appeared before the court just as frequently as their French-Canadian counterparts. Their presence was even more conspicuous in the city, where they accounted for over half of appointments involving a mother (88 out of 169). Once again, these numbers are not particularly surprising. They merely reflect the flip side of paternal dominance within Anglo-Celtic households. The death of the father was the real event—the one that could create headaches for associates and business partners, the one that precipitated the involvement of the friendly society, the one that led to the family being harassed by creditors alerted to the death of the head of household. Indeed, the financial reckoning that accompanied the death of a husband led many a widow to appear before a judge seeking the tutorship of her minor children. In most cases, she herself was appointed, although this was less often the case than for widowers. In most of these cases, the deceased had not made a will. But sometimes, when he had indeed committed his last wishes to paper and named his wife as testamentary executor, he may also have taken pains to recommend she be appointed tutor to the couple's minor children. For example, Nathaniel Smith was among the handful of husbands whose wills specified that their widow "should be appointed Tutrix."[41] Granted, testamentary tutorship was not recognized in Lower Canada and—in theory at least—the surviving spouse's appointment had to be confirmed by the court.[42] And it is possible that a study focused on wills rather than tutorship files would uncover cases where one or more trustees were given responsibility for administering the late father's estate.[43] This would have served to put the transmission of the family inheritance on hold, along with the need to go before the court regarding the tutorship of any minor children.

In any case, the way in which mothers were treated does not appear to have varied substantially from one group to the other. For some widows, being appointed tutor would have had clear advantages, theoretically allowing them to oversee the administration of a portion of often significant family assets. However, hard evidence that mothers were actually able to play this role is currently lacking. Meanwhile, tutorship proceedings clearly showcased the high level of supervision imposed on women when they ventured into the public sphere of legal practitioners. In a legal aberration, those pregnant with a posthumous child were assigned not only a subrogate tutor but also a "curator in ventro," thereby reinforcing the level of male supervision over female tutors and the property of their minor children.[44] Seventeen years after her appointment as tutor to her children, Josephte Fonteneau had to be appointed once again—this time for her youngest child, with whom she had been pregnant at the time of her husband's death. A few days later, she was involved in proceedings to retroactively approve a sale of land that could otherwise have been declared invalid because no tutor had previously been appointed to this child.[45] Of course, such cases tended to consist of legal formalities and mainly served to line the pockets of notaries and to fund the court's operations. But this careful oversight, apparently at the insistence of a legal practitioner, also reflected very real power relationships that extended to the level of close associates. The fact that the assembly of relatives and friends was almost always exclusively composed of adult men[46] could only serve to reinforce male dominance in the context of already unequal gender relations.

In the same vein, subrogate tutors appear to have played a more active role in cases where mothers were appointed tutor. Indeed, in cases where the widow did not remarry, a subrogate tutor was more likely to be appointed and to play a significant role. French-Canadian women regularly had to accept the involvement of one of their late husband's relatives, often a grandfather or a paternal uncle of the minor children, whose presence implied claims on the family land. By contrast, Anglo-Celtic women appear to have been more likely to have to work with one of their husband's associates or confidants. From this perspective, the case of Pélagie Larochelle is interesting because it involved an ethnically mixed family. The wife of a Montreal merchant of English origin, Pélagie was appointed tutor to her four minor children just days after her husband's death (the speed with which the tutorship was established further emphasizes the stricter legal framework imposed on many widows). One of the merchant's brothers, the children's paternal uncle, was appointed subrogate tutor. A few days later, Pélagie granted a general power of attorney to the brother. In all likelihood, the latter took over the family business.[47] Meanwhile, in the 1830s at the latest, a new distinction was made between the familial and fiscal aspects of tutorship. This principle, which was just emerging in Lower Canada but well-established in France,[48] guided a division of responsibility whereby the mother attended to the children's personal needs (*tuteur à la personne*), whereas a male tutor was given power over their property (*tuteur aux biens*).[49] In practice, such arrangements had likely long existed. However, the ideology of separate spheres served to emphasize the underlying distinction, which began to be explicitly acknowledged in court proceedings.

It is therefore not surprising that the exercise of male authority was more conspicuous in cases where widows remarried. Unlike widowers who found a new spouse, these women were automatically stripped of their status as tutor. And although such mothers were most often reappointed, they had to serve jointly with their new husband, the minor children's stepfather. In some cases, remarriage led to conflict. After being appointed tutor to her eight minor children, Thérèse Victoire Simard, the widow of a farmer from L'Assomption, married a local carpenter and settled in the village. A few short weeks later, the paternal uncle who had been appointed subrogate tutor insisted on holding a new assembly, to which the mother was not invited. Had it not been for a judge from the city who insisted that Thérèse be notified, she would most likely have been stripped of her public duties as tutor. As with many other mothers who remarried, the minor children's stepfather was appointed joint tutor based on his status as husband.[50] In the case of Jane Allan, marital authority appears to have been applied even more rigorously. A Scottish immigrant who arrived in the colony as a widow, she went on to marry a fellow Scot living in the seigneurie of Beauharnois. The newlyweds were most likely in the process of seeking out an apprenticeship for Jane's fourteen-year-old son, "to whom no tutor *or guardian* ha[d] ever been named or appointed." Advised on French-Canadian customs by a legal professional who was careful to draw analogies to more familiar legal concepts (references to guardianship also come up in other proceedings), the new husband sought to be appointed tutor to his wife's child. However, unlike in the case of Thérèse Victoire, the stepfather became the sole tutor, and no subrogate tutor was appointed.[51] That being said, both arrangements likely played out in similar ways. In practice, joint tutorship granted the stepfather the power to act alone on behalf of the minor children.

Other situations demonstrate how the court helped oversee the weakening of mothers' authority in the public sphere. Take the case of seventeen-year-old Fleure Deniger, whose widowed mother quickly ceded authority over her daughter's affairs after taking a day labourer from Montreal as her second husband. In December 1825, the latter requested that a "tutor ad hoc" be appointed for Fleure who, being a minor, was preparing to marry John Trim, a Montreal widower of African descent and a former slave.[52] The stepfather's application was unusual because Fleure's mother could have easily consented to the marriage without the need to appoint a tutor.[53] But there was another dimension to this story that tutorship was likely meant to address: Fleure had just given birth to a daughter from a premarital affair with John, who would have been about seventy years old at the time. Whatever her views on the matter, Fleure's mother was not given an opportunity to address the court. Rather, John's entourage—he clearly had strong ties to the local Anglican community—dominated the proceedings. Only English-speaking men appeared in court. The assembly of relatives and friends appointed Joseph Shuter, a Montreal merchant named as godfather to the "natural" child, as Fleure's tutor ad hoc. The unlikely couple ultimately got married in Montreal's Christ Church Anglican Cathedral. A few years later, when her youngest child was baptized as a Catholic, Fleure was using her husband's name. Before his death, John willed all his assets to the couple's children (in usufruct, reserving ownership for the following generation).[54]

## *Conclusion*

The Deniger-Trim case was highly unusual. Nevertheless, it demonstrates how men and women could sometimes cross the never entirely watertight barrier separating ethnocultural communities or racial identities in Lower Canada, as Isabelle Bouchard's contribution to this collection (Chapter 1) shows as well. Such cases of intermarriage also suggest that French-Canadian women willingly accepted the English ways of their husbands—even when the latter were of African origin. That being said, barely five percent of cases involving the appointment of a tutor featured a mixed couple. For every Stanley Bagg or Pélagie Larochelle, hundreds of fathers and mothers stayed true to the customs associated with their ethnocultural identity, customs that the court system either upheld or reshaped in its own ways.

Not surprisingly, the case files also serve to underscore the supremacy of male and paternal authority. Clearly, the day-to-day practice of tutorship bolstered male dominance in the public sphere inhabited by legal practitioners. However, this dominance was legally expressed in different ways. Even if the barrier between ethnocultural groups was not watertight, the national origin and cultural heritage of the men involved in tutorship cases still played a decisive role.[55] Among Anglo-Celtic fathers, regardless of class, there was an almost universal rejection of tutorship. The heads of certain wealthy English-speaking Protestant households may have relied on marriage contracts and wills, among other legal tools, to eschew the Custom of Paris and uphold male domestic authority. But most Anglo-Celtic households in Lower Canada would have rarely, if ever, called on the services of legal professions to help implement family financial strategies. As a result, these households were subject to French matrimonial and inheritance laws, including those related to tutorship proceedings. And yet, court records show that hardly any Anglo-Celtic widowers were subject to such proceedings.

By avoiding the proceedings provided for in French law, they were also spared the hassles associated with the assembly of relatives and friends, which their French-Canadian counterparts nevertheless willingly embraced. Granted, the latter group of men also had the means to impose their will, no doubt just as emphatically. But for French Canadians, the death of a wife initiated negotiations that regularly involved the family of the deceased. Tutorship proceedings required the head of household to engage with the complexities of Parisian matrimonial and inheritance law, not to mention the claims of various family members. Most French-Canadian fathers managed to remain in control of a process that favoured their interests, provided they exercised a degree of shrewdness or drew on sage advice. But they still needed to secure the support of close relatives. As was also somewhat the case for women, the authority of French-Canadian men who were appointed tutors rested on a ritual that engaged broader kinship and community networks. In addition to initial discussions with the family of the deceased, the associated legal proceedings opened the head of household's domestic affairs to public scrutiny. Although they did not experience the same treatment as widows involved in tutorship proceedings, these men nevertheless found themselves in the role of "supplicant," to use the language found in legal sources. Other types of tutorship proceedings, not covered by this study, show that even after being appointed as a tutor, French-Canadian fathers—just like widows—still had to seek permission from the court to manage the assets inherited by minor children. By contrast, no Anglo-Celtic fathers appear to have been required to undertake such proceedings.[56]

While some have emphasized the patriarchal outlook shared by men of various origins, it is just as important to highlight the distinct constructions of domestic authority and masculinity that clearly differentiated French-speaking and English-speaking Lower Canadians. Unlike personal diaries or elite correspondence, the records of legal proceedings reveal little about the thoughts and attitudes of individuals. The rather dry style normally used in legal documents stands in stark contrast to the stirring prose of a politician like Louis-Joseph Papineau, a renowned orator and leading figure of the Lower Canadian Patriot movement.[57] Nevertheless, tutorship case files do bring to light distinct forms of masculine behaviour in relation to domestic authority and family property, approaches that were at least partially based on ethnocultural identity. Given that institutions can be understood as a crucible for the ongoing construction of masculinities,[58] tutorship proceedings can provide precious insight into the gendered expression of domestic authority. In fact, the colonial justice system appears to have helped shape—or at the very least reinforce—two models of domestic masculinity that coexisted during the period of study. One of these models, which was no doubt present throughout the British Empire, clearly emphasized the father's individual autonomy. From this standpoint, it is easy to recognize this refusal of French tutorship practices as an expression of rational self-control and of the exclusive domestic authority exercised by male household heads over the management of family capital, despite the community of property prescribed by the Custom of Paris. This Victorian model of masculinity, more broadly depicted by John Tosh,[59] is strikingly in tune with the lunacy investigation legal proceedings Emma Chilton and James Moran examine in Chapter 10 of this collection. Resorting to the *juge des tutelles* would simply amount to adopting irrational behaviour and abdicating one's masculine authority.

The other model, which held sway among the colony's small property owners, appears to have been more dependent on kinship and better aligned with the legal paternalism characteristic of French law. This binary construction of domestic masculinity is reminiscent of the distinction that Mary Beth Norton draws between monarchical and republican patriarchal models in the context of the American Revolution.[60] More recently, Elizabeth Mancke and Colin Grittner have contrasted two forms of masculinity in early nineteenth-century Nova Scotia, describing how a conception rooted in morality and community slowly gave way to a capitalist ideal of male independence.[61] In light of the legal proceedings involving families from the district of Montreal, I would argue that traditional community-based masculinity continued to hold its own alongside the more resolutely liberal model. Granted, by carrying on their legal traditions, French Canadians reaffirmed their national identity, whether consciously or not. But by appearing before the *juge des tutelles*, as Anglo-Celtic women often did, French-Canadian fathers found themselves in a subordinate position on the British gender spectrum, which associated masculinity with the exercise of full autonomy by both the head of household and the political subject. I also believe that this duality was fostered by legal practitioners who were sensitive to the ethnocultural differences present in Lower Canada. Supported by the same court system, the two models coexisted in a colonial society disrupted by mass immigration, as well as by political disputes that would soon come to a head in this corner of the British Empire.[62]

CHAPTER 6

# Wayward Daughters and Unnatural Fathers

## *Generational Conflict, Youth Culture, and Parental Authority in Buenos Aires, 1890–1930*

*Juandrea Bates*

Nineteen-year-old Maria Elena Galluzzi and sixteen-year-old Ana Maria described their father, Ernesto, as a cruel and abusive man who cared little for his family. When Maria Elena was four and her sister just an infant, Ernesto had abandoned them and their paralyzed mother. The girls detailed growing up in abject poverty, "living on bread for weeks at a time." Ten years later, Ernesto returned, but time had done little to alter his callous ways. He moved his mistress into the one-room apartment the family shared and refused to work. According to his daughters, his only contributions to the household were the "slaps, hits, and fits of abuse" he aimed at their mother, who died six months into this ordeal. In a petition lodged in Buenos Aires' Civil Tribunal, Maria Elena vividly recounted the pain and shame it caused her dying mother to share a table with her husband and his concubine.[1]

Although Maria Elena and Ana Maria condemned the suffering their father had caused the family, it was not his cruelty that prompted them to appear in court on 21 December 1918, intent on stripping him of his parental rights. Instead, the sisters insisted that financial issues catalyzed their suit. After their mother's death, the sisters had found work in a glass factory, and Ernesto had begun confiscating their wages to support himself and his new lover. This was the final straw that brought Maria Elena to the court. "The wages I make are my own," she declared. "It is not possible for us to live in a house and support our father and this woman. We would prefer to spend the time in prison."[2]

His daughters' suit might have surprised Ernesto. In the decades between Argentina's independence in 1816 and the period of national consolidation that followed 1860, the country had no national legal codes. In preparing their rulings, judges drew inspiration from a complex and often contradictory combination of community norms, Spanish imperial laws, and legal treaties published in France and Italy. Argentina's 1869 Civil Code provided the nation with its first coherent set of laws regarding family, and it gave men unfettered authority over their wives and minor children.[3] This gendered and generational hierarchy, referred to as *patria potestad*, meant that a married woman could not acquire property, administer businesses, contract employment, or select a domicile without her husband's consent. Minor children, those under the age of twenty-two, faced even more constraints. In exchange for financial support, fathers controlled youths' upbringing, finances, property, labour, education, and domicile. Both legal theorists and judges reasoned that men's authority over their kin was a natural right by which men's financial support and protection of their dependents entitled them to control and submission. The Defender of the Minor, a city official responsible for overseeing all legal proceedings involving those under twenty-two, proved particularly hesitant to intervene in the familial conflicts of the urban poor, defining the domestic sphere as a realm in which civil authority ought not to interfere. The law sanctioned corporal punishment, and courts even allowed fathers to intern their sons and daughters in penal institutions for misbehaviour or insubordination. By nature of their minority, Maria Elena and Ana Maria were not even supposed to appear in court alone, much less file petitions.

If his daughters' suit alarmed Ernesto, the support they received probably shocked him more. Maria Elena's supervisor from the glass factory and two neighbours testified to the girls' good conduct and morality. Likewise, the Defender of the Minor decried their father's depravity, suggesting, "A guardian must be appointed to protect these girls' moral and physical safety."[4] When Ernesto's attempts to fight the suit resulted in growing legal costs, a donation from the Sisters of the Society of Saint Vincente allowed the Galluzzi sisters to continue. Moreover, the girls' focus on their wages struck a chord with court officials. While the law restricted civil judges' authority in the private realm of family, the girls' focus on wages made their father's failings legible to the state. They presented their father's misuse of their wages as a breach of the natural contract between parents and offspring. Court officials adhered to this logic. The *fiscal*, a public prosecutor charged with presenting arguments and jurisprudence to the judge, contended that since Ernesto had not supported his daughters since infancy, he had inverted the natural order of families. This reasoning framed his official recommendation. "*Patria potestad* must be removed," he argued, "as it is not being practiced as the law indicates…and with the wages these girls earn, they can provide for themselves."[5] The judge agreed and awarded temporary tutorship to a maternal aunt, thereby freeing the girls from their father's control.[6]

The Galluzzi sisters were not the only young *porteños* (residents of Buenos Aires) who came before civil judges with complaints about their parents at the turn of the twentieth century. Rather, a quantitative analysis of the records produced by Buenos Aires' Civil Tribunals reveals a dramatic rise in the amount of litigation related to parental rights after 1890. An in-depth examination of fifty such disputes from each decade between 1870 and 1930 (300 in total) indicates that minors played key roles in this growing litigation. Before 1890, young people rarely filed suits against parents or guardians. In the decades following 1890, however, hundreds of adolescents filed and, as time went on, a growing number of them found favour with judges.[7]

Maria Elena and Ana Maria's legal petition, and others like it, reveal intimate aspects of family life cast against the backdrop of a city beset by rapid change. In the last decades of the nineteenth century, Argentina's immersion into Atlantic markets as an exporter of wheat, wool, and beef ushered in an expansion of domestic production and the advent of industrial manufacturing in Buenos Aires.[8] Over a forty-year period, more than six million European immigrants entered the country. As the nation's primary port and with a burgeoning industrial sector, Buenos Aires grew from 177,787 people in 1869 to more than 1.5 million in 1914. By the outbreak of the First World War, Argentina's GNP rivaled that of Spain and Switzerland.[9]

At the dawn of the twentieth century, Argentine elites boasted of their accomplishments but found themselves beset by a new host of problems. The city's growing population strained housing and infrastructure. Concerns about sanitation, crime, and public order mounted. Dependence on agricultural exports, foreign capital, and overseas markets created seasonal unemployment, exacerbated by abrupt economic downturns. Low wages and the swelling cost of living drove women and children into the industrial labour force and prompted unionization and politicization among working-class men. Socialist and anarchist unions boasted more than 500,000 members nationally by 1904. Protests and general strikes revealed the power of these unions and resulted in violent conflicts with the police. In 1919, one such demonstration triggered seven days of conflict. This *Semana Trágica* resulted in more than 120 dead and more than 400 wounded.[10] Rather than recognize the problems inherent in the country's economic structure, elites fixated on what they called "the social question"—how to incorporate the rapidly growing, largely immigrant population into existing social and economic structures without ceding their own power. Efforts to uplift and pacify the poor took varying forms, from the draconian expansion of the police and penitentiary systems to increased education spending and the expansion of welfare agencies aimed at stabilizing family life among the poor.[11]

In recent years, historians have demonstrated that young people featured prominently in the urban landscape as well as the anxieties wrought by development. An 1895 census counted 1,586,933 youths under fourteen in the country.[12] Concerns over working-class youth galvanized a generation of legislators and reformers. In 1884, Law 1420 mandated public schooling for youths under twelve, while the nation's first labour legislation in 1907 limited the hours those under sixteen could work in factories. New juvenile detention centers aimed to reform orphaned or abandoned youth alongside those convicted of crime.[13]

Young people rarely leave behind extensive documentation on how they navigated a shifting terrain of urbanization, industrialization, and the development of increasingly intrusive state bureaucracies. But, read carefully, petitions like the one filed by the Galluzzi sisters offer insight into just such things. On one level, their suit provides a window into the work experience, leisure pursuits, and social networks of youth during this transformative period in Argentine history—as well as how macro-historical shifts in demography and the economy affected family dynamics. Read from another angle, their petition, with its casual references to a childhood filled with hunger, fear, and abuse, provides a record of the "everyday violence" Jane Nicolas so brilliantly brings to the forefront in her investigation of infanticide in Ontario elsewhere in this volume (Chapter 14). Like most legal records, my sample of civil disputes overrepresents moments of conflict. Yet, at the same time, these case files provide evidence of the positive emotions fostered by domestic intimacy, including the tenderness shared between the Galluzzi girls and their mother in the final years of the matriarch's life, along with the solidarity and determination displayed by the sisters in the wake of their mother's death. Finally, the case provides a glimpse into the girls' understandings of the law, legal culture, and the boundaries between state and private power. These insights can only come from an approach that recognizes that young people like the Galluzzi sisters came before the court in a position of profound vulnerability. The success or failure of their petitions often hinged on whether they could craft a narrative that would make their lives as poor young women intelligible to elite adult men. The cases then provide a window into the narratives and logic young people and their allies believed would find favour with judges.

This chapter uses these family disputes to explore how the changes brought by modernization shaped youth's experiences, their relationship to their kin, and the way they thought about power relationships in the household. Together these cases reveal that demographic and economic shifts opened a host of new opportunities for youth to exercise autonomy and freedom. At the same time, a shift from contract to wage labour allowed young people to challenge the logic underpinning legal notions of parental authority, and new social welfare agencies provided allies that allowed young people to take their complaints from the living room to the courtroom. Together these shifts transformed civil courts from a space that reinforced the absolute authority of patriarchs to one that offered young people like the Galluzzi sisters a space to protest their father's treatment and advocate for a better future.

## *Kin, Community, and Youth in Buenos Aires*

In 1869, when Argentina's first civil code awarded fathers total authority over their offspring, the nation had just emerged from more than fifty years of civil war. The territory that would become the federalized district of Buenos Aires more closely resembled a collection of small towns than a booming metropolis.[14] City residents, rich and poor, were spread between roughly two dozen *barrios*, or neighbourhoods, many of which had been sovereign towns before the city federalized in 1888. Each had its own population nucleus that included a plaza, churches, markets, a police station, justice of the peace, and workshops.[15] Most residents spent their days secluded in these local communities, with little reason to travel to the rest of the city.

In these barrios, long-standing kin and community networks helped to reinforce traditional family structures. Young people lived and laboured under the close eye of kin and community.[16] Fathers' control of family finances bolstered their authority. The formal economy provided few opportunities for a woman to find work without her husband's permission.[17] Likewise, poor children often found themselves contracted out as domestic servants and apprentices. These labour agreements, forged between parent and employer, left youth without formal means to protest such arrangements. In exchange for their efforts, they received little more than food and clothing. Any wages they did earn were paid to their parents.[18]

In the final decades of the nineteenth century, demographic forces, disease, and urban planning reshaped the city. The population jumped from 177,000 in 1869 to 649,000 in 1895. A series of epidemics swept the south and west of the city in the 1870s and 1890s. Many elites fled congested neighbourhoods for less crowded estates along the city's northern edges.[19] Tanneries and meat processing plants filled their absence in the south. These disruptions were exacerbated by urban planning projects that ripped working-class housing out of the city centre, pushing arriving immigrants into increasingly crowded neighbourhoods in the south or west.[20] As the capital's population soared to 1.5 million by 1914 and 2.5 million by 1930, pastureland became crowded *conventillos* (or tenement buildings) and dirt paths were paved into city streets.[21] A growing system of streetcars and trams connected formerly insulated barrios. The city boasted more than four hundred miles of streetcars by 1910, carrying more than 300 million passengers annually.[22] By 1913, the city's first subway line opened, carrying 170,000 passengers on its first day of operation.[23]

As the population boomed, so did opportunities for youthful adventure. The country's first amusement park, *Parque Japonés*, opened in 1911, providing daytime entertainment alongside the city zoo, botanical gardens, and parks.[24] *Porteños* could admire the latest European fashions displayed in shop windows in upscale shopping districts on Avenida

Florida and Santa Fe.[25] A theater district emerged, delighting patrons with nightly dramas, short comedies, and vaudeville acts. Cafés, restaurants, and bars sprang up to fill patrons' bellies and their cups after an evening of entertainment. Billiards and music halls offered after-dinner entertainment, while *milongas* and other dance halls offered young Argentines the prospect of close dancing in dark saloons.[26] In this way, the spatial transformation of the city brought young people away from the insular neighbourhoods of their parent's youth and into a large metropolis where they could escape the watchful eye of relatives.

Civil cases give brief glimpses into the excitement the growing city created for young people, along with the trepidation it caused their parents. Eighteen-year-old Carlos Faustima explained that on his days off, he often wandered the city, taking a trolly to join friends at a park, billiards hall, or dance hall. Such freedoms, however, caused conflict with his father, Ruiz, who characterized the money Carlos spent on trolleys and shows as waste. The patriarch argued that Carlos' refusal to stay close to home was proof that he was becoming "antisocial" and "prone to idleness and vice," traits he argued Carlos had picked up from spending time with friends from outside the neighbourhood, or as he called them the "worst sorts of people."[27] Sixteen-year-old Hector Mendez was also excited to explore the city. His mother explained that he was in the house for only a moment each evening before disappearing with people whom she had never met. Worse, once he was gone, she complained, he stayed out until all hours of the night. Hector tried to assure his mother and later a judge that he was doing nothing wrong and had been going to dinner and passing time with friends.[28]

Youth mobility caused even greater tension between parents and daughters. Sixteen-year-old Lorena Constanza Satari and her mother, Constancia, regularly disagreed about whether it was acceptable for girls her age to leave home unaccompanied by a relative. Lorena reported that she enjoyed taking the tramway from her parents' home in Flores to walk in the fresh air of Palermo Park and look in the windows of the shops downtown. At her mother's insistence, she came home before dinner and never even entered a theatre or café without her older cousin present. Nonetheless, her mother loathed the idea of her daughter taking a tramway to another part of the city, insisting it would be more proper for the teen to spend her time at the plazas in their neighbourhood under the watchful eye of her mother and aunts. Constancia explained that "It is well known that those areas can entrap a girl her age in a world of disgrace."[29]

The anxiety felt by long-time city residents was often worse for immigrant parents. Immigrants comprised two-thirds of Buenos Aires' working class by 1914,[30] and they regularly used courts to settle family disputes, filing forty-two percent of the petitions in my sample. Many new arrivals hailed from patriarchal societies and found themselves frustrated by the way migration undermined their authority over their children. They worried that their new city with its saloons, tango clubs, crowded apartment buildings, and public plazas would corrupt their sons and daughters.[31] Seventeen-year-old Luz de Carmen Novo explained when she told a judge, "My mother is not from here and she does not understand the way of life in the city. She went on to explain that her "[father] is a very traditional man," who "believes that he can do as he pleases with all of his children.... Here young people have more choices and freedoms."[32] To pursue such freedoms she came before the civil court to request the judge allow her to leave her parents' house and live with a female friend and her mother.

The tensions between immigrant parents and their offspring seemed particularly acute when youths arrived in Buenos Aires before their parents. Many young people made the trip across the Atlantic with relatives, family friends, or alone. They found jobs and set up households in Buenos Aires, perhaps even sending money back home to help their parents make the voyage. This was the case for Giovanni Martel. Fourteen-year-old Giovanni crossed the Atlantic accompanied by his maternal uncle Angelo Ricci, a man only four years his senior. His parents remained in Italy for three years, during which time Giovanni and Angelo lived together, "in a state of complete content," and sent part of their wages back home. In 1904, however, the serenity of the household came to an end when Giovanni's parents and siblings arrived in Buenos Aires. During his three years of independence, Giovanni had become active in local unions and accustomed to meeting with friends after work. This did not sit well with his father, Lorenzo, who expected the teen home immediately following work and forbade him from consorting with peers his family had not met. One night, Giovanni returned home to find his door locked from the inside. He was enraged and shouted "for all to hear" that he had paid for the apartment, and that his father who had not yet found steady work, had no rights to it. Unable to overlook the embarrassment in front of their neighbour, Lorenzo tried to re-establish his authority with his fists. The police officer who broke up the fight informed Lorenzo that under the 1869 Civil Code, parents could apply to the Ministry of Minors to sequester insubordinate children in juvenile detention centres for a period of thirty days. Lorenzo followed his advice and filed a complaint. However, he dropped it before there was a ruling. It is unclear if he had a change of heart, worked out the tensions with his son, or realized that his son was the only member of the family earning a steady paycheck.[33]

## *Work, Wages, and Generational Conflict*

Disagreements over work often exacerbated struggles over youth's autonomy in turn-of-the-century Buenos Aires. Family pressure to find employment was strong, particularly for boys. For example, in 1917, José Gentile appeared before the Defender of the Minor, asking the official to lock up his nineteen-year-old son, Salvador, because he would not keep a job. He hoped this punishment would make him into a man "dedicated to industrial pursuits."[34] In my sample, sixty-eight parents approached the court because their sons refused to work, making this their most common complaint.

Although parents did ask judicial officials to deposit their daughters in correctional facilities, they never listed a lack of employment as the cause. Instead, they typically said that young women ran away from the house, took up with lovers, or were insubordinate. This gendered difference in the complaints parents made about their daughters suggests one limitation of these judicial sources, as parents, along with their children surely crafted their statements to appeal to the gendered expectations of elite judges. Working-class families relied on the labour of girls as well as boys, and many girls worked outside the household. Many girls reported that their parents pressured them to find employment. Rosa Helena Núñez, for example, complained that her mother pressured her and her sisters to find work. When the sixteen-year-old fainted during her twelve-hour shift in a textile mill, her boss sent her home. Despite still being sick the next day, she reported to work, explaining that her parents threatened to beat her if she missed her shift. A year later, when Rosa lost her job, her parents locked her out for two days. Her father denied locking her out and insisted that conflict in the home centred around his daughter's “willfulness, rebelliousness,” and the potential that she would corrupt her young sisters. Nevertheless, he mentioned the termination of Angelina’s employment twice in his response, suggesting that girls’ work could cause intergenerational conflict, even if parents did not report it as such.[35]

Shifts in labour practices among *porteño* youth at the turn of the twentieth century exacerbated tensions over work. After 1890, Argentina’s growing manufacturing sector provided new employment opportunities to over 410,000 men, women, and minors in Buenos Aires and the surrounding towns.[36] Alongside women, young people often found employment in large, modern factories. Many working-class families were eager for children to earn wages in factories. Cities like Buenos Aires faced a rising cost of living and seasonal unemployment cut into working men’s real wages.[37] While domestic service and apprenticeships saved parents the cost of raising children, they rarely contributed to the family’s cash income. Parents recognized that factory work allowed minors to contribute to family finances immediately and might allow them to make more money in the long term. As a result, the turn of the century witnessed a shift in youthful employment away from contract labour towards employment in skilled crafts and factories. My sample of 300 cases between 1870 and 1930, which included many sibling groups, contains employment information for 242 youths. A sample of 200 marriage petitions lodged between 1870 and 1930 provides the occupations for another 292 young people.[38] Together, these sources indicate that from 1870 to 1890, working-class youths most often listed domestic servant, apprentice, or day labourer as their occupation. This was particularly true for those under eighteen. This began to change after 1890, and by 1900, the overwhelming majority of youth who appeared before the court mentioned employment in factories, shops, or mills. Textile factories, seamstresses, and unnamed factories became the top employers for young women. Adolescent men most frequently became mechanics, dockworkers, and machine operators.

For youth in Buenos Aires, labouring outside the household was not new, but wage labour represented a fundamental shift in the experiences of labour for young people. Through the eighteenth and nineteenth centuries, poor families often used the Defender of the Minor’s office to contract out their children’s labour as apprentices or domestic servants.[39] Most servants lived with their employers, as did apprentices. Keeping young employees within the domestic realm reinforced generational hierarchies and isolated them from their peers. Once parents signed these agreements with employers, minors had little choice but to oblige. Employers could use corporal punishment in the face of insubordination and could solicit the help of the police in tracking down servants or apprentices who ran away. In these arrangements, wealthy families often took minors' labour in exchange for training or sustenance. When the positions did pay wages, they were small and delivered directly to parents or, in the case of orphans, to the Defender of the Minor himself. Either way, these labour arrangements left children voiceless with little control over their earnings.

Manufacturing offered a new atmosphere. The concentration of large factories on the city's southern edge meant that many young people took advantage of the city's cheap transit to work far from home. Since manufacturing tasks were often separated by gender and experience, youths often worked alongside their peers. Although hours could be long and tedious, many recalled their time in factories as one of homosocial camaraderie. For example, when pushed to leave her job, Patricia Rossi indicated that she enjoyed the solidarity and friendships she found at work. Her coworkers joined her on her across-town commute each afternoon and went window-shopping on their days off.[40]

In some families, new opportunities in industry created tensions over where young people worked. Many youths appeared eager to rid themselves of the intense oversight and limited freedom of domestic service and apprenticeship contracts. For example, one young woman, Alessiani Rosa de Cuero, approached the Defender of the Minor and later civil judges asking that they release her from the control of her father so that she might terminate the labour contract he had signed with a family in the wealthy barrio of Recoleta. She reported that her employers "worked her as a slave until my hands bleed." Promising to remain diligent and industrious, she suggested that she might obtain employment in a cigarette factory where her older cousin worked. Another young domestic, Dolores, approached court officials with a similar request testifying, "I have been living like a slave. I cannot work there any longer. I would rather be in jail."[41]

Dolores' reference to prison was not hyperbolic. Hector Mendez de Rosa had sent his daughter Maria Carmen Rosa to work as a domestic servant for a wealthy family in their neighbourhood in 1892 when the girl was just ten. At twelve, she fled the position, turning up at her father's apartment one afternoon when he returned from work. Begging her father to terminate the contract with her employer, she offered to find work in a factory with her older brother. Her father insisted that factory work would "leave her exposed" and "submit her to poor influences."[42] He preferred to find her work with another family in the area, a decision Maria Carmen resisted. Over the next four years, she continued to flee any position in which her father contracted her to work. Two other employers dismissed her for insubordination. In 1907, the Defender of the Minor warned that she would be sent to a correctional facility if she absconded again. A month later, the police found her living in an alley, and the Defender of the Minor made good on his threat. With her father's consent, he sent her to live in a women's prison, where she stayed for the next six years.[43]

While some youth struggled to enter the industrial labour force, others pushed to stay in domestic service. For example, in 1907, fourteen-year-old Manuela Fernandez began working as a domestic servant for a family that was "kind and fair," allowing her to "receive such an education that she could now read and write." In 1908, however, her father wrote to her and demanded that she leave that position and join her cousin in a factory to help support their family. The girl ignored his letters. She could not feign obliviousness, however, when he showed up at her employers' home, "causing a disturbance and a great deal of embarrassment."[44] In response, Manuela approached the court and begged the Defender of the Minor to let her remain as a domestic servant instead of sending her to live at home. Other youths made similar claims. Fifteen-year-old Flora Gonzalez explained that, although her employer only paid her eight pesos per month, she would rather stay there as he also provided room and board. She saw this as a welcome alternative to living with her uncles, who had confiscated her salary and left her with nothing to eat.[45]

According to the 1869 Civil Code, civil authorities should have decided in favour of allowing Alessiani, Dolores, Maria Carmen, Manuela, and Flora Gonzalez's fathers to determine their daughters' employment. Interestingly, however, this was not the case. Manuela and Flora, the girls who asked to remain in their positions as domestic servants, found favour with the court. Alessiani, Dolores, and Manuela, the girls who sought industrial work, did not. Such rulings were part of a larger trend. Judges generally favoured minors' continued work in domestic service.

They looked at parents who allowed or advocated for minors' employment in industries with more suspicion.

The difference in judicial reactions provides insight into how industrialization and wage labour shifted larger understandings of parental authority. Argentine jurists had long framed *patria potestad* as an exchange of rights and responsibilities. Men held authority over their dependent wife and children because they supplied protection and financial support. Domestic service and apprenticeships did not contradict this logic. According to nineteenth-century judges, these contracts assured minors' continued support and protection as it placed them under the authority of an alternative patriarch. These substitute father figures took on the responsibility of a child's support, education, and moral upbringing.[46] As such, civil judges, reform agencies, and particularly the Defender of the Minor, advocated for labour contracts obligating youth, particularly girls, to serve as domestics in elite homes. As late as 1919, the Defender of the Minor argued, "I know of no better place to raise and educate a child than with a family whose honour has been accredited. I cannot write of the morality of a factory owner."[47]

Factory wage labour did not fit so neatly into this paradigm of parental support and minor obedience. Youths obtained positions in wage labour through their own agreements with employers. Employers wanted the freedom to lay off workers during recessions and had no interest in signing contracts or engaging youths in lengthy apprenticeships. They paid workers, including minors, on a daily or weekly basis.[48] Without signing contracts, young people were free to select employers at will, and parents could not easily get help from the police to force their children to return to work. Moreover, earning wages encouraged minors to believe they could be self-sufficient or make valuable financial contributions to another household. They then approached civil courts arguing that this financial solvency should allow them to cast off the authority of parents.

The case of Maria Elena and Ana Galluzzi mentioned at the outset, makes this clear. In explaining why her mother was hesitant to leave her father, even after he took a mistress, Maria Elena emphasized that her mom was "debilitated, and this prevented her from doing all but the smallest amount of work."[49] The teen went on to say that before she took a job, they could not protest Ernesto's mistress because they feared losing any money he might give them. Ana Maria and Maria Elena's employment enabled them to challenge their father. The two young women insisted they could support themselves and argued that their earnings would prevent them from becoming a financial strain to their aunt. Another minor, fifteen-year-old Flora Moreno, argued similarly, "My father does not conduct himself as a father should." She went on to explain, "For three years, I have fed myself and provided my own care and sustenance." She concluded, "With my earnings, there is no reason to live under the control of a man who does not labour for himself."[50]

Working in factories also gave minors a chance to make allies outside their family, kinship group, or ethnic community. For example, Maria Elena's employer hid her wages and offered her and her sister, Ana Maria, a place to stay. When their father complained that Maria Elena "had begun corrupting her younger sister, keeping her out all night," her boss testified "she is a good, hard-working poor thing, terrorized by the tyranny of her father."[51] Likewise, when Guzman Realés requested that the court remove his mother's *patria potestad* over his younger brother, his supervisor testified to the young man's industriousness, the length of his employment, as well as his morals.[52] The courts took employers' references and testimony seriously. In Guzman's case, the judge referenced his employer's testimony twice in his decision to strip Guzman's mother of her parental rights. Considering that the majority of these cases were based on witness testimony from family members and neighbours, people who might have been hesitant to intervene in domestic disputes and whose loyalty would more likely lay with parents, having a respectable witness to testify on their behalf could be an indispensable asset to minors' cases.[53]

As was the case in other large industrializing societies, factory work encouraged many young people to challenge their parents' authority and push for more autonomy.[54] Disputes over how adolescents spent their wages surfaced in seventy-three of the ninety-two cases lodged by minors in my sample. For example, in 1915, fifteen-year-old Catalina Solis claimed that her father's attempts to seize her earnings brought her before the court. Working in a dress shop, Catalina made sixty pesos per week, the entirety of which her father confiscated as soon as she returned home. Insisting "My money is my own," she argued that she should be able to use it on herself and her sister. Catalina's refusal to turn over her wages resulted in physical confrontations with her father. When he threatened to beat Catalina's sister unless she gave up her earnings, the young woman initiated a petition to strip him of his parental rights.[55]

These conflicts also occurred between young men and their families, although not at the same rates. While training as a mechanic, eighteen-year-old Juan Mendez earned ninety pesos a week, a large portion of which he gave to his mother. However, when she encouraged Juan's younger brother to leave school to work, he protested that she was spending too much of his money on herself and initiated a suit to become tutor of his siblings.[56]

Most youths agreed to turn over a part of their wages to their parents but leveraged these contributions to increase their influence among kin. Young people seemed particularly concerned about their siblings. Historically, Argentine jurists have looked at relationships between siblings with suspicion. Legally, brothers and sisters were joined by their competing interests as inheritors of parental estates. The 1869 Civil Code created several barriers to prevent older siblings from gaining custody or legal guardianship over younger brothers and sisters.[57] However, youth's testimony in court petitions shows a good deal of tenderness between brothers and sisters. Young people often cited concern over their siblings as the explanation for why they fled domestic servant positions. For example, Juan Guiloff repeatedly ran away from his apprenticeship. Each time, officials found him living with his two younger brothers, who had also run away. When caught by the police, Juan explained, "I need to ensure that my brothers and sisters have been cared for."[58] Likewise, when Teresa Paulina and her brother Andrés escaped from their positions as domestic servants, the Defender of the Minor found them together, at first with an aunt and, later, living in the street.[59]

Young people often tried to use their wages to shape parents' treatment of their siblings or raise them independently. Jose Luis Lozano, for example, ran away from home at age fifteen and found work as a mechanic in a textile shop. Two years later, he returned home and demanded that his father surrender custody of his younger brother. Likewise, seventeen-year-old Joaquin Patricio informed the court, "My earnings do not make me wealthy, but they will be enough to support my brother and I outside the tyranny of my father."[60]

Other young people withheld wages to try to shape their parents' romantic and sexual behaviour. For instance, Catalina willingly gave some of her money to her father, but she refused to pay for his drinking and "immoral use of women."[61] In a similar case, sixteen-year-old Maria Blanco had been giving her pay to her mother for years but refused to support her stepfather. Maria Elena and Ana Maria Galluzzi, Maria Blanco, Catalina Solis, and Juan Mendez all protested supporting their parents' lovers. Questioning the sexual morality of women in custody suits had been a common strategy since the 1870s.[62] Holding men to a similar standard, however, was rare. In the past, most attempts to strip fathers of parental rights had been based on abandonment. Employed minors after 1900, however, frequently argued that they had the right to withhold wages from fathers who demonstrated sexual immorality. For example, Catalina alleged that in expecting her to support his frequent drinking binges and his mistress, her dad was exposing her to laziness and vice.[63] Likewise, Maria Elena justified hiding her wages by pointing out that her father had brought his mistress to live with them while their disabled mother was still alive.[64]

Furthermore, when the court sided with Catalina and Maria, it sent a powerful message. In the past, judges rarely considered men's moral failings as a factor in determining whether they should exercise parental rights. As long as men provided financial support for their offspring, the law promised them authority over dependents. However, the rise of wage labour among youth undermined the financial justification of men's authority. This economic shift paired with growing anxiety among elites about the potential of working-class men corrupting future citizens shifted how judges viewed parental rights in working-class homes. In judges' eyes, men's immoral behaviour did disqualify them from controlling their daughters' wages.

## *Youth Initiatives in the Competitive Charity Market*

Just as industrialization shifted labour relations among the young, the rise of new state agencies and philanthropic groups helped bring household tensions out into the open, providing young people with the ideological justification and material support to challenge parental authority in court. Before the turn of the century, social welfare programs in Argentina's capital were largely restricted to a single organization, the *Sociedad de Beneficencia,* a philanthropic organization financed through a combination of private donations and government subsidies. This would change quickly after a two-year economic crisis from 1890–1892 put thousands out of work and armed uprising called into question the legitimacy of the ruling oligarchy.[65] To bolster legitimacy, national officials poured money into welfare institutions, both public and private. By 1918, there were more than one hundred different institutions in the city of Buenos Aires alone. Relief efforts focused particularly on youth, creating reformatories, orphanages, daycares, schools, milk banks, and clinics.[66]

In her analysis of archival records from juvenile courts, Naama Maor (Chapter 7) skillfully highlights the strategic decisions parents made to balance conflicting family interests when confronted with the juvenile justice system in the United States. Civil court records in Buenos Aires reveal young people making similar calculations about the benefits of involving state and philanthropic agencies in disputes among kin. Far from passive recipients of reformers' programs, youth often initiated contact with emerging social welfare agencies. For adolescents struggling with their parents, the Defender of the Minor was typically a first choice. Maria Blanco's appeal is a perfect example. When the sixteen-year-old and her mother went to the court to protest her stepfather's abuse in 1914, their request for an alternative guardian was denied. Instead, Maria was placed as a domestic servant in a wealthy family's household. However, two years later, eighteen-year-old Maria made her way back to the Defender of the Minor's office alone. The family where she had been working left her in Buenos Aires while they vacationed in the country. Maria claimed, "Considering my age, I should always be under protection and guardianship as I am a poor little thing (*criatura*) and at my tender age I know of dangers that face me."[67] She requested that she be able to live in the custody of her mother's friend, Francisco Gomez. Gomez made a similar argument, saying that without proper supervision Maria would not be, "protected from the dangers that can befall her as a young girl (*niña*)."[68] Considering that Maria was eighteen years old, six years older than the required age for marriage, Maria's use of the word *criatura* and Gomez's use of *niña* are particularly striking. Emphasizing Maria's need for proper education and protection won her the support of the Defender of the Minor as well as the judge, who released her into Gomez's custody.

Minors also found assistance among expanding state and private reform agencies, especially the city's *Patronato de Infancia*, a municipal agency providing food, education, and medical care to children. In 1915, Jesus Rodolfo appeared before the Defender of the Minor in collaboration with Francisco Guzmaras, an officer of the *Patronato de Infancia.* Jesus claimed that his mother used his wages to support her improper, immoral lifestyle. He feared that without intervention, his mother might lead his sister, Ana, into a life of prostitution and loose morals. Jesus was probably a little hesitant to approach the court. Two years earlier, his mother, assisted by the police and the Defender of the Minor, interned Jesus in a correctional facility. But Francisco appeared equipped with a series of medical testimonies regarding the importance of proper care for children at Jesus and Ana's age. He had also collected testimonies from witnesses about the mother's behaviour. As a result, Jesus' request was granted.[69]

## *Conclusion*

In recent years, historians have become increasingly interested in exploring the ways that Latin American children have "lived, learned, and loved as they grew into adults."[70] Civil cases provide a provocative window onto these histories as they detailed changing work experiences, relationships with employers, how minors used their income, conflicts with parents, the creation of alternative households as teens sought refuge with employers or relatives, and minors' frequent moves to protect and care for their siblings. Beyond simply detailing these experiences, these cases reveal that minors played a vital role in shaping their own lives, family dynamics, and urban development. In deciding what wages they would share with their parents, minors challenged familial power dynamics and enforced morality in working-class homes. Moreover, in appearing before state bureaucracies and private reform organizations and manipulating ideas of youth and the need for protection, minors influenced how growing bureaucracies, charitable organizations, and legal systems functioned.

CHAPTER 7

# Unfit and Unworthy

## *Parental Delinquency in Progressive-Era Juvenile Justice*

*Naama Maor*

Speaking at the annual meeting of the National Education Association held in Des Moines, Iowa in 1921, Judge Ben B. Lindsey of the Denver Juvenile Court outlined a far-reaching doctrine: the "Parenthood of the State." Its principles had implications not only for the relations between the state and children, but also between the state and parents. Having spent two decades on the bench championing the nation's newly established juvenile courts, Lindsey framed the idea of state governance of juvenile life as a humanitarian necessity and civic imperative that no parent could rightfully oppose. Addressing parents directly, he declared: "We, the people, or in our aggregate capacity—the state—permit you, the parent, to retain the custody of and the responsibility for your child." But the state affirmed parental custody not because it recognized the child belonged with "you" as a parent, or because it would "satisfy the love or cravings of your parental heart." Rather, mothers and fathers were allowed to keep their child because it would most effectively "safeguard the rights and best interests of the child itself."[1] Parents' own interests were beside the point.

Their legal responsibilities, however, were very much the point. When Judge Lindsey pronounced the state a "super-parent" to all its children, he did not mean to relieve legal guardians of their duties. Because society had a vested interest in the well-being of its youngest members, the state had an obligation to keep parents in line to assure "the home performs its functions where it is careless and that it is helped where it is helpless."[2] State regulation was therefore needed to carry out this vision not only through humanitarian, welfare-oriented measures, but also through a coercive, even punitive, state apparatus.

Lindsey's comments reflected the social thought and legal frameworks undergirding a wave of government policies concerning the welfare of children enacted in the late nineteenth and early twentieth century in North America and Western Europe.[3] Included in these reforms was the creation of specialized juvenile courts that removed children from criminal proceedings and separated them from adults. As recent scholars who examine these socio-legal developments through a comparative or transnational lens suggest, juvenile courts and the institutions designed to treat delinquent youth reflected turn-of-the-century attempts to centralize and systematize solutions to social problems and crises through government action.[4] The judge's statements revealed that these reforms and policies did more than reimagine relations between state and child. They also reformulated relations between state and parent—and, inevitably, parent and child.

This chapter explores how the new American juvenile justice regime shaped the relationship between the state and the family in the early twentieth century. Rather than focusing on state-child relations—which have been at the center of most histories of juvenile justice—this study shifts the focus to state-parent relations.[5] It argues that juvenile court proponents formulated, codified—and, in some cases, criminalized—cultural narratives about parental delinquency and dysfunction. The founding principles of this nascent legal regime were the evaluation and treatment of delinquent, dependent, and neglected children and their families on a case-by-case, putatively scientific basis. Inspired by the era's developing notions of childhood and adolescence, and changing ideas about the causes of criminal behaviour, juvenile justice proponents studied environmental conditions to understand the cause of child delinquency. Primary among them were the children's parents.

Changes in attitude towards children—that they were deserving of protection and education, rather than punishment—and towards criminality—that it was primarily the product of nurture, rather than nature—prompted the state to reconceptualize parental roles and the responsibility it could place on parents when their offspring misbehaved. As juvenile courts sought to identify categories of delinquent parental behaviour as part of their preventive or punitive measures they, in effect, created expansive legal archives rife with definitions of improper and, consequently, proper parenting.

To trace the production of these concepts, I analyze the archival records of three trailblazing juvenile courts in the United States. The first two, Chicago's (1899) and Denver's (1903), shaped the laws and practices that quickly spread across the nation and beyond. The third, located in Memphis (1910), was among the first established in the segregated American South, shaping the meaning of juvenile justice under Jim Crow.[6] Each of these courts produced legal archives that are varied in their reach and scope of documentation. Chicago's records, for instance, consist primarily of legal filings and probation reports produced by court personnel. Denver's and Memphis' cases, on the other hand, contain a rich tapestry of materials that only sparingly appear in Chicago—epistolary evidence produced by the subjects of these courts—most importantly, letters written by parents and children to court officials or to each other. Exploring these diverse case files reveals how, in the process of inspecting children's homes, court officials rendered some parents "unfit" or "unworthy," and designed a mechanism for penalizing supposedly dysfunctional caretakers. In so doing, reformers, legal experts, social scientists, and bureaucrats turned these minors' mothers and fathers into objects of study, reform, and policing, all in the name of child protection.

Although these unprecedented interactions with state agents meant that some parents could, for the first time, rely on some form of government assistance, many others were forced to cede parental authority to the "professionalized" parent, a representative of the state. To illustrate the tension between promise and loss under such a system, I will conclude by tracing the criminalization of parents deemed responsible for their children's alleged criminality and immorality. Subject to a new category of offenses—contributing to the delinquency or the dependency of a minor—parents faced increased responsibility for their children's waywardness.

## *"Not an Isolated Child"*

When the Chicago Juvenile Court—the first of its kind in the United States—opened its doors in 1899, the court was celebrated as a monumental step towards distancing children from the criminal justice system.

Judge Julian Mack, who would act as the court's second presiding judge, claimed that the institution revolutionized "the attitude of the state toward its offending children."[7] Mack echoed his predecessor, Judge Richard Tuthill, who hoped that "the boy who has known nothing but the club of the policeman and the cell of the police station and jail" would realize that the state had his best interest at heart.[8] The court's goal was to *protect* children from the criminal system, or in Macks's words, "to shut the prison door before the child shall enter, and to lift up the child so that he may never be in danger of entering it."[9] Its guiding principle was that children differed from adults both in their culpability and in their capacity for reform. They were malleable persons, who, with proper care, would grow up to be productive members of society. Within a quarter of a century, these views informed the creation of juvenile courts worldwide. In the United States, every city of more than 100,000 inhabitants established a specialized court by 1925.[10]

Juvenile courts largely grew out of the conditions of urban life. Progressive-Era reformers assumed that cities, particularly rapidly expanding industrial centers, fostered the waywardness of children. They offered a world of temptation and danger.[11] At the same time, reformers claimed that the urban environment could also house potential solutions to the problem of childhood delinquency. As they studied the city and its effects on children, Progressives turned urban centers into laboratories of social justice.[12] County courts appointed judges to deal with cases involving children and adolescents. They hired probation officers and trained social workers to study families of delinquents and supervise their reform process. This change in approach toward delinquent, dependent, and neglected children formed one part of a wave of child-centred reforms. Others included compulsory education, restrictions on child labour, and the implementation of new health standards for the care of infants and children.[13] As state after state enacted laws designed to protect children from injury, exploitation, neglect, or abuse on city streets, in the workplace, and at home, a new regime for regulating the lives of children coalesced.

Central to this broader regulatory regime was the concept of the "best interests of the child," said to guide the efforts of juvenile justice actors.[14] Yet, without a clear definition of the child's best interest, officers of the court had substantial leeway when exercising their power over young offenders.[15] Agents of this new legal system—judges, probation officers, and social workers—possessed extensive authority to determine what constituted the best interest of a child, and affected not only the minors who were brought into the court but entire families, subjecting adults to new forms of governance.[16] Although some of these actors were public officials with professional credentials in law or social work, others performed these roles as volunteers whose claim to expertise was founded on their experience with social reform and private charity work. These juvenile court representatives, many of whom were middle- and upper-class women, promoted a class- and gender-based ideal of both motherhood and fatherhood.[17]

In addition to claiming they acted in the child's best interest, reformers and policymakers justified the expansion of state authority by stressing the need to protect society from current and future criminals and to raise moral and industrious American citizens. According to historian Michael Grossberg, such arguments reflected a tension between a "fear for children" and a "fear of children."[18] Other studies examining the juvenile court movement—the ideologies, motivations, and practices of its major proponents—assert that Progressives sought to control the working-class and racialized minorities in an attempt to protect themselves from the social disorder brought by rapid urbanization, industrialization, and immigration in the late nineteenth century.[19] Self-proclaimed "child savers," these revisionist accounts suggest, were not benevolent and humanitarian reformers, but creators of a system that labeled children as "troublesome" and subjected them to arbitrary punishments.[20] Juvenile courts, according to this interpretation, constructed the very category of juvenile delinquency that it claimed to prevent and treat.

As they aimed to eradicate the problems of children who were deemed delinquent, the architects of American juvenile justice systems—social scientists, lawmakers, reformers, and public officials—sought to first identify and conceptualize the causes of youth waywardness. Moving away from their predecessors' assumptions that criminality reflected the inherent failings of "degenerate classes," Progressive-Era reformers focused instead on studying and treating the environmental factors that they viewed as the root of juvenile delinquency.[21]

Foremost among these contributing factors was the child's family. Reformers, social scientists, and court officials claimed that unfit homes and unworthy parents bred criminality in still-impressionable children. Through the process of examining the homes of their young wards, probation officers, social workers, and the social scientists who influenced their approach to juvenile delinquency classified parents as negligent, ignorant, or mischievous due to their children's misbehaviour. As Julia Lathrop, the nationally renowned social reformer and the first Director of the United States Children's Bureau opined, "[t]he new method [of treating delinquent children] should take into account not an isolated child." It should think of a "child in a certain family and amid certain neighborhood surroundings, and a judge should base his action upon the value or the danger to the child of his surroundings."[22]

The state officials with whom parents most commonly interacted were probation officers. Tasked with inspecting the homes of wards of the court to "consider the habits, conduct and morals" of their families, probation officers provided "full consideration to every detail."[23] Their reports helped the judge determine the future of the child in question—primarily, whether they could be returned to their homes or should be committed to state institutions. Probation officers assessed parents' ability to "control" their child and scrutinized every environmental factor that may have led to the child's delinquency. A full "history of the case" included the parents' race, nationality, religion, occupation, and estimated income.[24] During their home visits, officers also recorded impressions of the family's residence as well as other observations that did not fit neatly into the official forms. As the bureaucratic nature of the juvenile justice system continually evolved, the collected data included citizenship status, migration history, language skills, and the habits of family members, such as drinking, gambling, or using "vile" language.[25]

During those meetings, parents would have to demonstrate that they were sufficiently attuned to American law and culture and versed in middle-class social values and practices.[26] A mother who was identified as a German immigrant living in Chicago, "could speak no English," according to the probation officer and was "unable to see why the boy should go to school every day." Parents' indifference towards court officials or their child's acts was often described in terms of failure to understand the law of the land and local customs. One case summary clarified that "[w]hen the mother understood that in America it was wrong to let the boy pick coal from the tracks, she kept him away" from the tracks.[27] A record of a different Chicago family noted the parents never learned English and that the mother "has always continued to wear the old peasant costume, and the home, a very poor two-room apartment, looks very foreign."[28] In passing this judgment, probation officers flagged the family's inability to assimilate as a main cause of concern.

The living conditions that parents provided for their children were closely inspected. Probation officers surveyed the physical features of the child's home, writing observations on the neighbourhood, the number of rooms in the house, home ownership, and "the standard of cleanliness, industry and living."[29] The home of one Lithuanian family in Chicago was described as "a poor, dirty home in a very poor neighborhood,"[30] while another family had "a wretched home, a five-room cottage, damp and dirty, in a very poor neighborhood near the city limits, surrounded by swamps and standing water."[31] Such observations were meant to help the court determine a family's problems and provide guidance to the mother and father. In demanding to know the cause of the dependency or the delinquency of a child, Judge Tuthill asserted, the probation officer "becomes practically a member of the family and teaches them lessons of cleanliness and decency, of truth and integrity."[32] Indeed, when officials such as Chicago's Chief Probation Officer T.D. Hurley boasted the idea of a "return to paternalism," they were describing the treatment children received from the state, which also extended to their family.[33]

Influencing parents to make adjustments to their lives was thus central to the court's child-saving mission. In a 1909 report, one judge instructed probation officers to persuade parents "that the purpose of the officers of the law is to assist them in bettering their own condition and the condition of their children." Then parents would be "apt to accept the advice and suggestions tactfully offered."[34] In the words of a Chicago probation officer, a "great good would be accomplished if some way could be devised by which the surroundings of the child could be corrected and by which, if possible, the parents could be educated to be more serious and to be cleaner both physically and mentally."[35] The goal of the court, then, was to influence children by re-socializing them as well as dictating the terms of their home life, in effect policing and surveilling parents through a classist ideology of hygiene and moral discipline. With the founding of new juvenile courts, a complex web of influence was formed, with judges trying to impart a worldview on probation officers, who in turn sought to impart a worldview on both children and parents, who in turn would be expected to influence each other. It was believed that by relying on this form of transitive property, a vision of juvenile justice could be achieved.

Chicago's innovative court served as a model for other institutions across the country and worldwide as well as a site of study and experimentation of the conditions in which children's mischief thrived. With over a decade of experience of working with delinquent, dependent, and neglected children and their families, the Cook County Juvenile Court produced an unprecedented source-base to be used by researchers who were interested in uncovering the causes of delinquency in minors. Between 1899 and 1909, the court handled 14,183 delinquency cases—11,413 involving boys and 2,770 involving girls. Drawing on these records, particularly the family histories that probation officers included in the files, researchers and social reformers Sophonisba Breckinridge and Edith Abbott of the Chicago School of Civics and Philanthropy published in 1912 a canonical study that helped construct categories of delinquent parents' characteristics.[36]

Breckinridge and Abbott's *The Delinquent Child and the Home* outlined the most common profiles of children deemed "delinquent," classifying them into several groups and focusing on the environment in which they grew up: the child of the immigrant; the poor child; the orphan or homeless child; the child from the degraded home; the child from the crowded home; the ignorant child; the child without play; or the child from the comfortable home. These categories indicated what kind of homes were viewed as potentially breeding immorality and criminality. Although Breckinridge and Abbott found that delinquent children grew up in households of various economic conditions, the majority of the children that they discussed came from families who struggled with great financial instability and who lived in neighbourhoods that supposedly housed the city's criminal and immoral classes and its corrupting forms of amusement.[37]

In addition to classifying children and their parents under these categories when evaluating the conditions that led to delinquency, Breckenridge and Abbott also divided parents into several groups according to their reaction to the court. The first class was parents who initiated the process or seemed happy to cooperate with the state because they realized the advantages of doing so. The second class consisted of those who wanted to cooperate but whose unfavourable living conditions made it impossible. In the third class, Breckenridge identified parents whose central problem was an inability to understand why court intervention was required or willfully neglected the child's needs. The fourth class consisted of parents who had means to provide for their children but chose not to. Finally, the last class was comprised of families in a state of "drunkenness, immorality, crime, filthy, and degraded homes" in spite of their economic stability.[38]

Drawing on this study and others of its kind as well as on their own experience handling cases of wayward children, judges and probation officers endeavoured to evaluate the "worthiness" of the parents who came before them. The problem that these state officials faced, Breckinridge explained, was "discovering how far it may be safe to leave the children brought before [the court] under supervision in their old surroundings, or how far the conditions from which they have come as delinquent boys and girls are irremediable and necessitate their removal to new conditions."[39] In some cases, however, parents played an active role in negotiating the terms of the intervention.

Take, for instance, Anna Schultz, who filed a complaint against her fifteen-year-old son Otto at the Denver Juvenile Court on 21 June 1916. Anna alleged that Otto caused her trouble and refused to go to school or work. According to Anna, her teenage son spent most evenings out with friends instead of being home. "I cannot depend on Otto for anything," she disclosed to the court, admitting that her son's behaviour had "gone from bad to worse." Nearing the end of her rope, the mother asked Judge Lindsey to commit her son to a state institution for wayward boys. "We do not wish to send Otto there as a punishment," she explained. Rather, she and the family thought it would be "the only way to make a good boy out of him." Involving the legal system in her family affairs was not a decision Anna took lightly. Nor was she eager to see her son go off to a state institution.[40] Anna's pleas found a sympathetic audience at the Denver court. A probation officer assigned to the Schultz's case described Anna, a widowed German immigrant, as a hard-working woman who, after raising five children alone, had been humiliated by her son's misconduct. The probation officer praised Anna's morality and was convinced that she was a woman worthy of the court's assistance after reading a reference letter written on her behalf.

Many parents, however, did not enjoy the benefit of the doubt from court officials, or meet their standards for good parenting. Unlike Anna, who was regarded as a well-intentioned mother struggling to find her way out of a difficult situation, Margaret Snow was labeled as "hostile," uncooperative, and potentially immoral. Her son, fourteen-year-old Clifford, first appeared in the Denver Juvenile Court to answer to a truancy charge in 1913. According to a probation report, when Clifford's mother learned of his first infraction and was asked to cooperate with the court, she informed the probation officer that she would "pay no attention" to the court's orders. Although Margaret cooperated with the officer in the years that followed, it was not enough to change the court's impression of her or her family. An investigation into the Snow household led the officer to conclude that the conditions there were dire. Both parents worked for meagre wages and habitually took Clifford out of school "on the least excuse." The officer did refer to the parents as hard-working but concluded that they could not keep track of their son. In fact, his account suggested that it was because both had to work that they failed to monitor Clifford and prevent his downfall. Finally, the officer chose to disclose in his report to the court that several of the family's children were born out of wedlock—a detail that had no bearing on Clifford's behaviour but implied that the family was of questionable moral standing and therefore could not provide the proper care and guidance that Clifford needed to rehabilitate.[41]

The cases of Anna Schultz and Margaret Snow exemplify two very different parental experiences with the Progressive-Era juvenile justice system. Both mothers struggled to discipline their sons and compel them to go to school. Both clearly had some hesitation in their interactions with juvenile court officials. However, only one was scrutinized for her parenting skills and moral judgment. Whereas Anna's appeal to the court for assistance signaled good mothering, Margaret's reflected poorly on her abilities as a mother. That her children were conceived outside of marriage served as sufficient proof of her failure as a mother, but the court also condemned Margaret for working outside the home to provide for her family instead of tending to her children and household.

Margaret's case illustrates the material and emotional dilemmas parents faced when confronted with the new juvenile justice regime. Should they seek court intervention to aid in the discipline of an unruly child? If they cooperated with state agents, would it help them regain control over their children? Would it undermine or reinforce their authority? How would letting court officials into their homes and relating stories of their parental challenges to government representatives influence the treatment that their children would receive? Would they, the parents, be held criminally or morally responsible for the children's misbehaviour or misfortune and what price would they have to pay for it? Would their homes be deemed unfit and they themselves deemed unworthy of the care of their children?

First-hand narratives of mothers and fathers whose lives were inspected and upended by the juvenile justice system are uncommon in court records. Much of the epistolary evidence that did survive speaks to the transient nature of many of the subjects of juvenile courts, as they were usually letters from parents whose children got into trouble in a remote city or parents who could not accompany their children to court. Their defensive narratives reflect a realization that they were at a disadvantage not only because they could not advocate for their children in a legal proceeding but because they would be judged for their inability to be there. However, the few surviving narratives reveal the internal turmoil of parents who were trying to balance the interests of their troubled children with the interests of the rest of the family. They provide a window into parents' relationships with their children, not only in opposition to an interventionist state that labelled them "unfit," "unworthy," or "delinquent" but also within their kin and community networks.[42] They often provide an admission that they were struggling to maintain their authority.

Parents who confessed their powerlessness hung their offspring's misconduct on external forces that derailed their efforts. When Keith and Curtis Carlson ran away from their home in Water Valley, Mississippi to Memphis, Tennessee, their mother Ruth assumed her boys had been "led off by older boys" who were "of a comon [sic] class of people."[43] Rachel Parsons from Cleveland, Tennessee tried to convince the Memphis court that her son Harold was corrupted by "the old moving-picture shows." In a twelve-page letter detailing every method of discipline deployed to disabuse him of this addiction, she blamed this "abomination" for his disobedience.[44]

A significant portion of the correspondence contained within the case files include letters from parents who tried to justify their inability to attend a court hearing. They seemed to have realized that their absence would reflect poorly on them and jeopardize their ability to keep their children at home. Mothers detailed their role caring for others—infants, elderly, or infirm family members—or described working outside of the home. Fathers invoked work responsibility even more frequently, insisting they could lose their job for missing even a few hours of work, or stated they were away from their family chasing new employment opportunities. An Italian immigrant whose eleven-year-old son was brought to the Denver court repeatedly noted he could no longer miss work to deal with the boy's misbehaviour. With a wife and six children, rent to pay, and only half a day off work each week, he could not "waste [his] time" attending to this matter. He suggested his son be committed to a reform school, hoping that it would "punish him and he will do better."[45] A different father explained he sent his two sons, aged ten and thirteen, on their own to their court hearing because he did "not like to loose [sic] the time [at work] unless it is absolutely necessary as it takes all I can… to make a living."[46]

As they grappled with their children's behaviour, parents recognized the potential consequences of the court's involvement in their lives, ranging from surveillance to separation and even to criminalization. They were also aware their entanglement with law enforcement could stain their reputation both within their own communities and in the eyes of state officials. As parents tried to make sense of their children's conduct and consider their most favourable course of action, they articulated two sets of concerns. First, they worried about the nature of the children's behaviour. Second, they shared concerns about how their children's behaviour reflected on the parents themselves. Much like reformers and state officials, parents feared their sons and daughters would grow up to be idle, uneducated, and immoral. Their narratives reflect a concern that without proper education and moral guidance, without learning a trade or understanding the value of hard work, their children would not be able to stand on their own two feet. But working-class parents were worried about more than their children's future. From a more immediate vantage point, they feared disobedient children would be a burden on the family instead of productive household members, whether they lived in the city or rural outskirts.

Whereas some parents were willing to admit to court officials they were unable to control their children, they also expressed concern that their offspring's legal entanglement would negatively impact their own standing within their communities. As Anna Schultz of Denver explained in a letter to the court, she "always held back in taking" the step of committing her son to an institution "on account of the disgrace" she thought it would bring to the family.[47] Others had little choice in the matter. Eugene Kaczynski's fifteen-year-old son Bernard ran away from St. Louis along with a group of outlaws and was arrested in Memphis. Eugene, a Polish immigrant, admonished young Bernard in a note sent to his son after he was captured and placed in a detention home. Bernard's escapades had made "the whole family ashamed" of him, Eugene wrote. He expressed hurt that Bernard "took [his] lunch and said [he] was going to work" but instead ran away, leaving his family wondering where he was until the Memphis police informed them of his arrest. As the father feared, word of Bernard's predicament had already spread.[48]

To avoid such shameful scenarios, parents pleaded with court officials to refrain from publicizing their cases. It is difficult to ascertain whether they were trying to protect their own reputation, that of their children, or both. When Eddie Dunbar's mother wrote to her son, who had been committed to an industrial school in Colorado for committing a robbery, she refrained from sending letters directly to the institution. She did not want the postman to know where Earl was and therefore asked her son if she could send the letters to the school superintendent instead. Tell him "that the rural carrier is our neighbor," the mother from Illinois requested.[49] The record provides no indication as to how Eva accounted for Eddie's whereabouts to her family and friends.

But even if parents felt shame over their inability to discipline their own children, especially as it reflected on them in their communities, their statements rarely disclosed a sense of guilt over their children's behaviour. They insisted they had done all they could to care for their children and should not be accountable for any youthful indiscretion. A mother and father from rural Colorado whose son ran away and was arrested in Denver admitted they could not get him to pull his weight around the house. They tried securing a summer job for him, but "he was always lazy." Instead of working, he ran away. "We brought him up from an infant and did everything we could for him to try and make a good boy of him," the parents emphasized, but they no longer felt they could help their son on their own. "We have tried our best and cannot do any more for him," they explained. "We think it best that he be not returned…to get in with his evil companion." They suggested that he stay in Denver under the care of a state institution, learn a trade, and work.[50]

At stake in these cases was how to best approach the correction of a child who had misbehaved. In debating these options, some parents played a more active role than others, refusing to serve as objects of study and reform by juvenile court officials. If deemed unfit, parents could lose authority over their offspring, who could be committed to a state institution. However, with the invention of a new category of laws that targeted adults as the objects of policing through the juvenile court, the stakes for parents had significantly changed.

## *Policing Parents through Juvenile Courts*

In addition to their efforts to reform parents and homes that were deemed "unfit," Progressive-Era reformers, lawmakers, and state agents developed a host of disciplinary measures to police parents. The invention of a new category of criminal offenses that held adults responsible for contributing to children's delinquency or dependency—commonly known as "contributory laws"—provided the most direct and punitive instruments by which state officials constructed categories of delinquent parents and penalized them for allegedly failing to perform their duties.[51] First enacted in Colorado in 1903 and 1905 and quickly replicated across the country and outside of the United States, these new laws provided the legal vehicle through which prosecutors and judges could seek justice against individuals whose willful neglect or misconduct created the breeding ground for children's illegal behaviour or impropriety.[52]

Contributory laws corresponded with the two central classifications of minors brought to early-twentieth-century juvenile courts: delinquent and dependent children. In Colorado, the original language of the 1903 "Act to Provide for the Punishment of Persons Responsible or Contributing to the Delinquency of Children" charged any parent, legal guardian, person who had custody over a child, "or any other person" who was responsible for, encouraged, or caused the delinquency of a minor with a misdemeanor.[53] Vaguely and succinctly defined, this category of offenses relied heavily on the legal definition of juvenile delinquency outlined by Colorado state law the same year. According to the Act, a "delinquent child" was a minor sixteen years old or younger who was "incorrigible"; who visited a "house of ill-repute," gambling place, saloon, liquor store, or pool room; who wandered in railroad yards or the streets at night; who hitched rides on trains; who used vulgar language or performed "immoral conduct" in public; or who simply violated "any city or village ordinance."[54] If the district attorney could make the case that an adult encouraged a child to commit any of these acts, the case could be brought to the juvenile court. This sweeping category of child delinquency allowed juvenile judges to cast a wide net over adult defendants. The punishment for contributing to the delinquency of a minor was a fine of up to one thousand dollars, imprisonment in a county jail for a period not exceeding one year, or both.

Two years after the enactment of the first contributory law, Colorado passed another contributory law, this time charging adults who were deemed responsible for a child's dependency or neglect. The purpose of this law was to target fathers and mothers who failed to properly care for their children, depriving them of basic physical needs such as food, clothing, or shelter, leaving them unattended, or placing them in any form of danger. Unlike the commonly known "non-support" laws that were enacted at the same time criminalizing male breadwinners' failure to support their wives and children, contributing to dependency was a more capacious and less severe category of offenses. It was utilized as a warning to "dysfunctional" parents and other adults who came into contact with the children and risked their well-being.[55] In Colorado, these cases were punishable by a fine of up to one hundred dollars and a jail sentence of up to ninety days, whereas the punishment for a non-support conviction was up to one year in a penitentiary.[56]

Contributory laws were designed first and foremost to discipline parents or any adult who acted as a child's guardian or custodian. Since social scientists, judges, and probation officers criticized parents who failed to support their children and argued that careless or vicious parents were largely responsible for child delinquency, they found it fitting to punish mothers and fathers for depriving their children of proper education, guidance, and care. With the threat of a fine or imprisonment, it was argued, the state could "compel parents to perform their duty."[57]

By formulating a category of offenses that could be broadly construed, contributory law advocates introduced a mechanism of punitive prevention to exist alongside direct punishment in cases involving parents. Juvenile courts interpreted parents' "contribution" to delinquency to include not only encouraging children to commit illegal acts—such as stealing or scavenging for coal at the railroad yard—but also creating morally-corrupt conditions that could foster children's delinquency.

Parental delinquency consisted of a range of acts committed in the presence of children, including having "immoral relations," "using vile, profane and obscene language," or consuming intoxicating drinks.[58] In effect, the court was under no obligation to establish that a child had committed a crime or an act that was deemed immoral in order to charge the parent; all the court had to establish was that the parent created conditions that *could* foster criminal acts. When children did, in fact, commit a crime, the parent could be charged without any prior knowledge or involvement; a boy who stole coal without active inducement from his parents, for example, was nonetheless a boy who stole coal because of his parents.

Taken at face value, contributory offenses did not appear to be morals policing measures, but they served as such. It was in this offense that prosecutors and judges found a new route to bring to justice adults suspected of crimes against children, especially sexual offenses. Within the family, however, contributory laws were routinely deployed to police and punish cases of fornication or adultery. Not only parents but their partners too were subject to these laws, suggesting that sexual impropriety between two adults led to the neglect or corruption of impressionable children. Most often it was a mother and her male partner who drew the law's attention and discipline. In one such Denver example from 1922, a woman and the man with whom she had been in a relationship were charged with contributing to her daughters' dependency by providing a "bad environment" for the girls. Yet another mother from Colorado was charged in 1921 with contributing to the dependency of her child, alongside the man she had been seeing, their offense being "living in adultery" and creating an "immoral environment" at home.[59]

Expanding the scope of parental liability for children's crimes or indiscretions, these new laws left no infraction without a responsible party. It is unsurprising, then, that they appealed to lawmakers across the United States. By 1919, the legislatures of thirty-two states enacted similar laws, and several other countries showed interest in these acts, including Canada, England, Japan, Germany, Bulgaria, Sweden, and Austria.[60] Sanford Bates, Commissioner of Corrections for the State of Massachusetts, asserted that contributory laws were a natural outgrowth of the juvenile justice movement. In a criminology journal, Bates asked his readers, if one of the goals of creating children's courts was that "the responsibility of the child is reduced," would it not be fitting that "the responsibility of some other person of agency is increased?" In other words, if the juvenile court relieved the child from responsibility due to his age and inadequate upbringing, "must we not transfer the responsibility to those persons who are in turn responsible for the state of facts which predisposed him to delinquency?"[61] With new legislation that shifted this responsibility, the courts could shield children from criminal charges, and instead pursue cases against their parents. By constructing contributory offenses, in other words, juvenile justice proponents created a mechanism by which the responsibility for a crime was not eliminated but rather redistributed.

## *Conclusion*

When Judge Lindsey of the Denver Juvenile Court articulated his commitment to the principle of the "Parenthood of the State," he lamented the "indifference, ignorance, and…criminality" that allowed American youth to succumb to corrupting influences and lead a life of lawlessness. He was pointing his finger not at the parents of these children but at a society that had become alienated from its young population. "We justly punish many a parent for the crime of contributing to the dependency or delinquency of a child," Lindsey noted, "But the criminality of the state…is far greater than that of the parent."[62] The juvenile court movement that Lindsey was a central part of was supposed to be a corrective to this negligence. It reflected a belief in the legal authority and the moral obligation of the state to intervene on children's behalf. In the shadow of this important transformation in the relations between the state and the child, stood parents who were trying to understand what role they would play in this novel regime. Their initial experience of this new system was that they were now being conceptualized as the cause of their children's delinquency.

Once parents were pulled into the orbit of the juvenile justice system, they left their marks on the records of this novel apparatus. They appear in the family histories composed by probation officers, where they were evaluated for their ability to provide what state officials considered a proper home and the level of care their offspring deserved and needed; they emerge in court officials' narratives as stumbling blocks in the path of their children's reformation or rehabilitation.[63] At times, more compassionate depictions of these parents contextualize their struggles, rendering them the victims of the socio-economic conditions in which they operated. While most of these documents fail to capture the unmitigated voices of the subjects of court proceedings, as we examine the labels imposed on parents and children, we can uncover their form of resistance to the classification as dysfunctional or delinquent and to the interventionist policies affecting them.[64] First-hand accounts, however, do exist in these legal archives and though the context of their production is important, they also provide an invaluable glimpse into the struggles of work and life of individuals who came into contact with court officials. They also help reveal the circumstances that brought parents to solicit the assistance of state authorities.

Undeniably, some parents knowingly and willingly relied on the juvenile court to help them maintain or reclaim their parental power or attend to the needs of their offspring. But their decision came at a price. External intervention meant not only undermining parents' ability to assert authority or their labeling as "unfit" or "unworthy." In some cases, it could lead to their prosecution. As shown by the creation of the category of contributory offenses designed to place the responsibility for a child's misconduct on an adult, parents stood to carry this responsibility.

# PART 3

# *Intimacies in the Courtroom*

*In this third section, our contributors focus on the public theatre of the courtroom, especially in cases where sexual intimacies—revealed, for example, in prosecutions for seduction or prostitution—were on trial, bringing patriarchy, social class, and other hierarchies of power into stark relief. There is a difficult irony in our title, "Intimacies in the Courtroom," since, in general, courtrooms are anything but intimate. They are austere, imposing spaces in which the (properly) awesome power of the state is on full display. And yet they are also places in which vulnerable private citizens can be compelled by court officials to reveal, under oath, the most intimate details of their personal and domestic lives, especially when the "improper intimacies" of Shelley Gavigan's title (Chapter 9) are in play.*

*Mary Anne Poutanen's study of prostitution in early nineteenth-century Montreal (Chapter 8) follows up on her award-winning monograph on that theme.*[1] *Her focus here, however, is much more squarely on the court proceedings through which sex work was criminalized and on the judicial case files generated by criminal trials targeting brothel-keepers, prostitutes, and their families in this colonial town. Poutanen skillfully combines these judicial records with genealogical and other sources to reconstruct the close kinship ties that often existed among sex workers and to shed light on their familial relationships and private lives. She also engages with Lorena Rizzo's concept of "counter-intimacies" (see Chapter 4) to emphasize the agency, creativity, and solidarity of the women she traces in this rich set of documents, using this legal archive to explore "the performance of subjectivities in the everyday beyond the control of state authorities but which involved personal forms of citizenship and belonging."*[2]

*In Chapter 9, Gavigan uses a similar method, examining case files drawn from the archives of nineteenth-century criminal courts in Canada's North-West Territories. Much like Poutanen, her focus is on women in the courtroom and how they occupied this space in a range of capacities as victims, defendants, and witnesses. Her investigation illuminates both the fraught relationship between family and justice and "the animating presence of patriarchy," in cases involving broken promises, spousal violence, and other conflicts arising in familial and domestic settings on what she has called elsewhere the "Aboriginal Plains" of Western Canada.*[3] *Indeed, given the colonial setting, the constant interaction between settler and Indigenous cultures, and the role of the nascent Canadian state in regulating the "improper intimacies" that Gavigan has located in a surprisingly wide range of cases, a strong resonance with the essays presented in Part 1 of this volume, under the heading "Colonial Encounters," seems worthy of emphasis here.*

*Courtroom dramas of a different kind are played out in Chapter 10, by Emma Chilton and James Moran. Their concern is with conceptions of manhood and masculinity as revealed through civil cases in which the mental capacity of individual men (and, by extension, their rational masculinity) was directly challenged in court. The patriarchal perspective reinforcing this understanding of masculinity and mental competence was deeply entrenched within British imperial law during this period, and as the chapters by Poutanen and Gavigan reveal, shaped women's experiences in the courtrooms of Montreal and the North-West Territories as well. Chilton and Moran's chapter is also noteworthy for the explicitly transnational approach they employ, as they draw their examples from two different jurisdictions within the Anglo-American world. Indeed, they demonstrate how the transfer of British lunacy law to both New Jersey and Ontario reinforced "rational self-conduct and the responsible management of personal capital" as the primary benchmarks for determining a man's mental competence.*[4]

## CHAPTER 8

# Intimacies in the Neighbourhood

## *Revisiting Sex Commerce, Families, and Criminal Court Records in Early Nineteenth-Century Montreal*

*Mary Anne Poutanen*

Rosalie Paquet and Éloi Benêche *dit* Lavictoire had a long-lasting but complicated history together, both having been charged in 1831 and 1837 for keeping a house of prostitution on St-Constant Street in Montreal. Police arrested Rosalie at least three more times for the same charge and at the same address. Éloi made another appearance at court in 1841 for an assault on Adélaide Cinqmars, who accused him of forcing his way into Rosalie's brothel, where she worked, wounding her in the face, and evicting her from the house.[1] Court documents offer no indication as to what Rosalie thought about this attack or her role in it. Éloi may have set out, at Rosalie's request, to discipline Adélaide for some transgression, to assert his male authority over the women who worked in the brothel, or to make an example of Adélaide. It is also possible that Rosalie's relationship with Éloi had soured and he was acting out his rage and/or jealousy. It is clear, however, that the sex trade had been at the heart of their relationship for a long time.[2]

Rosalie lived on St-Constant Street for more than a decade, advertising her establishment in Lovell's Directory as a boarding house[3] and reporting to the census-taker in 1842 that five unmarried women between the ages of fourteen and forty-five lived there.[4] The following year, Rosalie and Éloi married at Notre-Dame Church. Although a mason by trade, Éloi was selling groceries on Visitation Street by 1843. In 1845 he took up residence in a single-story wood house on Lagauchetière Street, a move that brought him geographically and perhaps emotionally closer to Rosalie.[5] In declining health a year later, Éloi dictated his last will and testament to notary Jean-Daniel Vallée, who attended him at his bedside in their home, likely Rosalie's brothel. He died six days later on 14 February 1846 at the age of thirty-eight, leaving his property and funeral arrangements to thirty-six-year-old Rosalie.[6] They had no children. Rosalie lived another thirty-two years, never having remarried, before dying at the age of sixty-eight, likely from tertiary syphilis, at Longue-Pointe in the St-Jean-de-Dieu Lunatic Asylum where she had been residing for three years.[7]

This account of Rosalie and Éloi's life together is based on a diversity of historical sources that originated with criminal justice documents—in particular, police registers, prison lists, court records, and grand jury presentments—and then followed by parish records, city directories, census returns, and notarial documents. All these sources contribute in different but important ways to some understanding of their relationship. Court records, I argue, provide a window onto the key liaisons that women who marketed sex forged with loved ones, fellow sex workers, clients, neighbours, elites, and various members of the criminal justice system, albeit from the perspective of what were viewed as illicit acts. Women are highly visible in lower court documents, turning to the criminal justice system to meet some of their needs: to discipline wayward neighbours; to charge others who had committed criminal acts against them; and to seek incarceration as a strategy to not only ensure food and shelter but also medical and palliative care. Many of the same women and men also appear in court proceedings as plaintiffs, defendants, witnesses, and bondsmen in cases involving assault and battery, uttering threats, larceny, rioting, slander, and sexual assault. Consequently, I have a much more comprehensive portrayal of how they negotiated the criminal justice system and used it for their own purposes. Other sources offer information that situates them in their families. Genealogy resources, for example, show how sex work fitted into individual and family life cycles and therefore why women turned to prostitution to earn a living. These personal histories ultimately draw attention to another reality, reminding us that the women who marketed sex were also wives, lovers, mothers, daughters, sisters, kin, friends, and neighbours. Moreover, they led complicated lives, like any other residents of Montreal. Notarial documents—such as leases, marriage contracts, inventories, sales, and promissory notes—offer glimpses into the business arrangements and relationships that some of these women forged. When Rosalie Paquet purchased a cariole and cowhide from Francis Donaldson, notary Charles Desève recorded the transaction. She agreed to pay £10 for the items in weekly instalments of twenty-four shillings.[8] With this acquisition, Rosalie performed her imagined material success in the public by touring about the city in her newly acquired cariole; Éloi, in turn, began to self-identify as a bourgeois.

Using data from research I conducted for my 2015 monograph, *Beyond Brutal Passions: Prostitution in Early Nineteenth-Century Montreal*, I re-examine in this chapter the utility of court documents in reconstituting the lives of women such as Rosalie Paquet and the intimacies they fashioned. I also re-consider some of the challenges such historical records pose in depicting a complex portrait of the women in their multiple roles, in addition to how the employment of a range of historical sources brings us closer to elucidating and complementing their relationships as seen in judicial documents. Women's history has already demonstrated the importance of using an integrated approach to study sex work that not only combines data from a broad variety of historical records but also cautions us against placing too much weight upon elite discourses without considering everyday experiences and practices, as well as resistance to new definitions and enforcement of respectable sexual behaviour. Central to these intimacies is the knowledge that women had about criminal justice and how they navigated this system. Such an approach highlights the intersections of sex work, class, ethnicity, race, gender, and sexuality in the context of transnational history, empire, and migration and reinforces the relationship of court records to patriarchy and women's agency. Drawing on Lorena Rizzo's exciting research, which resonates with much of my own work, I am borrowing her concept of counter-intimacies: that is to say, the performance of subjectivities in the everyday beyond the control of state authorities but involving personal forms of citizenship and belonging.[9] Equally important are the studies by Shelley Gavigan (Chapter 9) and by Riyad Koya (Chapter 3) in this collection, exploring other forms of everyday intimacies that reinforced patriarchy in British colonial settings.

I begin with a brief discussion of prostitution in early nineteenth-century Montreal. Next, using examples of sex workers and their families taken from the judicial archives, I consider the strengths and weaknesses of court documents and the importance of linking them to a range of other historical records that highlight aspects of their daily lives with respect to work and intimacy. Finally, I suggest other potential avenues of exploration in determining a more comprehensive picture of the women who marketed sex.

## *Sex Work in Montreal*

Lower court documents demonstrate that prostitution was more than an exchange of money for sex. It constituted an assortment of encounters, interactions, and relationships between the women and their husbands and lovers, parents, children, relatives, neighbours, other sex workers, clients, police constables, night watchmen, magistrates, and even gaolers. Women who marketed sex were kin to local labouring and artisanal families and embedded in all of the city's neighbourhoods. They had a notable presence in public space where they rubbed shoulders with men, women, and children of all social classes and all ethnic and racialized groups while they went about their activities of daily living. They navigated the streets and green spaces—sometimes "living rough"—often in pairs or in groups, shared church pews, frequented urban amusements, shopped in the same stores and marketplaces, acted as ambassadresses to male newcomers unfamiliar with the town, and sought drink, food, and shelter in local taverns where they also negotiated the price of sex. Prostitution not only provided an essential source of income for many women, but it also contributed to the urban economy by encouraging men to spend money on hospitality services such as meals, beverages, and lodging.

Sex work was ubiquitous in the urban landscape although not uniform. Red-light activities were more entrenched in those parts of Montreal with greatest demand. The town centre, for instance, was home to the Quebec Gate Barracks which housed as many as 1,500 soldiers at any one time, two public markets, a small commons, wharves where sailors, who manned the hundred or so British ships, disembarked every shipping season, and a legion of taverns and inns. These businesses provided havens for neighbours and others seeking a welcoming place with their fire and featherbeds, pots of soup and glasses of warmth, as well as soldiers, sailors, artisans, and labourers in search of women marketing sex. The town was also home to numerous brothels and sites of solicitation.

Given that the average age of marriage for men in Lower Canada was 25.5 at mid-century, such a late age of marriage, according to Leah Leneman and Rosalind Mitchison, signalled a sizable cohort of men who were sexually mature but unable to marry.[10] Many of them embraced a sociability predicated on pleasure, alcohol consumption, public entertainment, visits to neighbourhood brothels, or rambles through public spaces in search of streetwalkers. This bachelor subculture, a consequence of migration and subsequent loosening of family ties, was normalized in fraternal work relations by a shared sense of masculinity, camaraderie, and familiar cultural practices. Middle-class single men also embraced a similar masculinity, although one enhanced by privilege, which challenged the limits of respectable bourgeois behaviour. Alcohol consumption was part and parcel of their exercise of manhood. Military officers, for example, arrived on horseback or in carriages at the front doors of brothels at all hours of the night without regard for the disturbances they created. Others paid extra fees for sex commerce in private or with several women at the same time. As US historian Timothy Gilfoyle has argued, such a "sporting male culture," was "organized around various forms of gaming—horse racing, gambling, cockfighting, pugilism, and other 'blood' sports—defended and promoted male sexual aggressiveness and promiscuity."[11]

Streetwalkers solicited along Montreal's thoroughfares, in squares and green spaces such as the Champs-de-Mars, at local markets, the military barracks, in taverns, stables, various outbuildings, the main streets of the *faubourgs* or suburbs, and in the fields and farms that surrounded the city. They navigated these spaces in pairs or in groups made up of kin, friends, and casual acquaintances (sometimes including men), looked after each other by sharing resources, and sometimes fought with or stole from those outside these intimate circles. To persevere in a hostile environment, they established bonds of mutual dependence, often in moments of need. The women sought to procure the daily requirements of shelter, food, warmth, emotional support, and comfort in a world characterized by danger, poverty, homelessness, hunger, cold, and social ostracism. Such ties were linked to a wide range of behaviours that suggested intimacy, warmth, and love, on the one hand, and tension, anger, and mere tolerance on the other. Homeless women turned to the local prison to meet some of their subsistence needs. Although prison conditions were terrible, they were not necessarily worse than those that women who lived "rough" encountered.

Brothels were differentiated by location, structure, size, patronage, and services. Court depositions show that Montreal women operated houses of prostitution in buildings made of stone or of wood, in the cellars of the Sainte-Anne's Market, rooms in taverns, abandoned buildings, as well as in apartments, single rooms, and even attics in multi-family dwellings. While brothel-keepers usually established their businesses in partnerships with other women, a significant number did so with men, usually spouses or lovers with whom they cohabited, as we saw with Rosalie Paquet and Éloi Benêche *dit* Lavictoire. A few operated them with family members. Henri Breton and Marie-des-Anges Duclos, who had married in Laprairie in 1801, for instance, kept a city brothel together with their son Henri and two daughters Emélie and Amable. In 1822, they were charged with keeping a disorderly house although Amable was dropped from the indictment before the petit jury rendered a guilty verdict; the parents were sentenced to prison and the pillory and Henri and Emélie to incarceration only.[12] Their brief flirtation with brothel-keeping seemingly ended, for most of them. A year later, Henri married Françoise Paris; Emélie wedded carter Antoine Charron in 1830. Unlike her siblings, Amable, who was named for her maternal grandmother, marketed sex for the next twenty years, both on city streets and in houses of prostitution.

Complainants' descriptions of the interiors of brothels show that most were small, crowded spaces which accommodated an assortment of people involved in complicated and ambiguous relationships. Overcrowding added to unpredictability and risk. Those kept in spacious stone buildings with servants, cooks, security men, and sex workers to service an elite clientele were much less common. The respective inmates, from the women and men who kept the bawdy houses, spouses and lovers, sex workers, clients, servants, and security personnel to children and relatives wielded varying levels of power which were rooted in gender relations. Court records reveal that women negotiated these relationships in an environment marked by conjugal violence, drunkenness, clients' threats and assaults, parental coercion of daughters, as well as brothel-keepers' intimidation of sex workers. Although more difficult to detect explicitly given the nature of court documents with their focus on illicit acts, brothels were also characterized by loving relations between husbands and wives, lovers, parents and their children, and brothel prostitutes.

## *Historical Sources of Intimacy*

Seeking evidence of the private lives of sex workers in historical sources is challenging and requires a great deal of resolve, as my pursuit of traces of Rosalie and Éloi's intimate relationship indicates. Fortunately, Montreal is exceptional among North American cities in the high quality, conservation, and access to nominal and genealogical sources, which has allowed me to identify individuals, reconstitute aspects of their lives, and distinguish some of their kinship ties. Rosalie and Éloi were together for at least twelve years before marrying in 1843 and another three years before Rosalie was widowed. She was thirty-four years old at the time of the nuptials in Notre-Dame Church; Éloi was thirty-six. Rosalie's father had died in 1837 and her mother not until 1847 but it appears that she did not attend their wedding, nor did any of her siblings. Éloi's parents were both deceased before his marriage. A relative on his mother's side, Jacques Perrier, witnessed the ceremony but no other family members did. The groom signed the parish record, but the bride did not. Therefore, judicial records with the addition of other historical documents make it possible to paint a portrait of the couple and their extended families. It is much easier to locate key material for individuals like Rosalie and Éloi because Catholic parish records contain more information than those for Protestants. Moreover, Protestants with common English family names are much harder to differentiate and were more mobile; many remained in Montreal for a short time before resettling in Upper Canada or in the United States. Nonetheless, early nineteenth-century court records include the legal names of women sex workers in addition to the names of husbands for those married or widowed, making it easier to track individuals.

Parish records reveal that Rosalie was born in St-Vincent-de-Paul, Île-Jésus in 1809, a middle child of labourer Ignace Paquet and Marie Saumur *dite* Mars who bore seventeen children, of which nine survived infancy. Her parents had wed in 1800 in St-Martin, Île-Jésus. Éloi was born in 1807 in nearby Ste-Geneviève to carpenter Jean-Baptiste

Benêche *dit* Lavictoire and Josephte Perrier who had married in 1788. He was the second youngest in a family of three girls and six boys. By 1825, the Benêche *dit* Lavictoire family had moved to Montreal.[13]

Court documents disclose that Éloi's sister Marguerite had operated a brothel in Montreal around the same time as Rosalie and Éloi. She married carpenter François Proulx in 1814, a month after they had visited notary Thomas Barron's office with their parents, siblings, and friends to draw up a marriage contract. After fifteen years of marriage, Marguerite and François separated. In November 1829, Proulx placed an advertisement in *La Minerve* announcing that because Marguerite had deserted him, he would no longer be responsible for her debts.[14] By the time that forty-one-year-old François died in May 1832, they had been living apart for three years. In 1836, Marguerite married plasterer Charles Bonnier. She never had children. Three months following her marriage to Bonnier, Marguerite was accused of keeping a brothel on St-Dominique Street.[15] Marguerite's career in sex work may have already started around the time of her separation from François Proulx. Referred to as "Madame Lavictoire" by city constables, she incurred few charges for keeping a disorderly house but was, according to police records, a well-known brothel-keeper in Montreal.[16] The eldest sister and first-born, Marie-Louise Benêche *dite* Lavictoire also earned a living by establishing a house of prostitution. While it is unclear when she opened her brothel, in 1829 Marie-Louise signed a three-year lease for a one-story wood house and stable on St-Constant Street for which she paid £18 per annum. Various items of furniture such as tables and chairs, two cupboards, five washstands, and three beds, in addition to bedding, kitchenware, and decorative objects were included in the agreement. The gold-framed mirror, six gilt frames and prints, carpet, and a sofa with a chintz cover would have made her business more attractive to a particular clientele.[17] It was not until 1832 that Marie-Louise was first accused of keeping a disorderly house with brothers Éloi and Barnabé on St-Constant Street where she was still living.[18] Marie-Louise, her brother Eustache, and their father Jean-Baptiste died in June and July that year, likely from the global epidemic of cholera, which had been raging over the summer in Lower Canada. A younger sister, Scholastique, made a brief appearance in the judicial documents, accused in 1837 of the same offence, having been apprehended in a building on St-Dominique Street, possibly her older sister Marguerite's brothel.[19] Four months later, thirty-six-year-old Scholastique was dead. It would appear that at least five members of the Benêche *dit* Lavictoire family turned to sex work as a means to earn a living—some were firmly embedded in the trade and others only briefly—perhaps at the insistence of male family members who would have provided security in their establishments.

Some of the Benêche *dit* Lavictoire siblings do not appear to have been involved in the sex trade. Brother Étienne, who self-identified as an innkeeper and a boarding-house keeper, was married to Marie-Angélique Beauchamps and had five young children at home. Their youngest son was named after Éloi; when he died in 1832, the next son was also baptized Éloi, suggesting that Étienne's relationship with his brother had been close. In 1830, for example, the Hudson's Bay Company hired both Éloi and Étienne as voyageurs to winter at the Portneuf trading post together.[20] The oldest brother Eustache had married Marie-Louise Beauchamps in 1817, a sister of Marie-Angélique who would wed Étienne in 1821. To add another element to this already complicated family history, Étienne Benêche *dit* Lavictoire was one of several plaintiffs who in 1831, at the same time that many of his siblings were operating their own houses of prostitution, objected to the presence of five brothels on Vitré Street.[21] This family reconstitution raises a number of key questions. Given that the various Benêche *dit* Lavictoire disorderly houses on St-Constant and St-Dominique streets were only steps away from the five he identified as brothels on Vitré Street, was Étienne acting for them by trying to limit competition with his accusation? As in the case of Rosalie Paquet, was his boarding house a cover for a house of prostitution and the complaint designed to ensure his own business interests? Or was he warning his brothers and sisters that if they did not end their involvement in the sex trade, he would make similar legal denunciations against them?

Judicial sources are especially valuable because they demonstrate how popular-class[22] women and men understood the law, engaged with the criminal justice system, and navigated the different spaces that made up their lives: from workplaces on the streets, in brothels, and in taverns and inns, the private and intimate spaces that accommodated relations with kin, lovers, friends, and neighbours, to the prison and courts that constituted the criminal justice system, an underworld made up of pawn shops, lodging houses, brothels, and taverns, and the liminal places where danger lurked. They employed diverse subsistence strategies that crossed licit and illicit boundaries and resorted to an armamentarium of approaches to discipline neighbours. By focusing on women's everyday experiences, in what Donald Fyson describes as "the banal, the routine, the ordinary, the everyday,"[23] we have a much better sense of the world the women inhabited, the subsistence tactics they employed, and the myriad ways in which they engaged with family members, neighbours, elites, and state authorities. Court documents allowed me, for example, to discover Margaret Delany, a long-established sex worker, who in April 1841 sought shelter at the police station for herself and her five children. As a single parent, she tried to keep them with her despite the family's utter destitution.

For women like Margaret, the task of seeking out the necessities of life brought many of them together in a common purpose. Court records give impressions of the complex and ambiguous relationships of kinship, friendship, and solidarity that they established with the women and men who shared their world and their neighbourhoods. These bonds involved mothers, daughters, sons, sisters, and cousins, husbands and wives, and women and men such as soldiers, vagrants, police constables, and night watchmen in relationships that ranged from the casual to the intimate, transcending the client/prostitute paradigm. Some men provided sex workers with protection, shared money, alcohol, and food, scavenged for food and searched for shelter with them. Their shared poverty straddled the fine line between criminal activity and self-help. Moreover, these men likely profited from their remuneration in sex commerce. Nevertheless, they would have provided sexual and emotional solace to each other in ways not unlike that furnished in families, especially if they were estranged from their own kin. Take, for example, the poignant story of Mary Kelly, separated from her husband because he had been incarcerated in the city jail, and who found herself in dire straits. A vagrant man offered Mary lodging in his hut on the beach "so imperfectly constructed as to be pervious to wind and rain and hardly to deserve the name of a shelter." She died there from hypothermia and malnutrition; her companion—profoundly distraught by her loss—had been reduced to tears.[24] There are several examples in judicial documents demonstrating that street-walking allowed families to stay together. The Love family—Andrew, Francis, Matthew, and Maria—survived "living rough" precisely because they looked out for one another, each contributing to the family's subsistence, including Maria's solicitation, and when necessary even served jail time together after their father Andrew Love, a labourer, had died in 1840.[25]

Judicial documents highlight some of the subsistence strategies that sex workers employed to get them through arduous periods. These involved sex, which was more than likely coerced or endured in exchange for a meal, a drink, or security. These paradoxical liaisons were fraught with danger and would have required extraordinary judiciousness on the part of the women if they were to remain safe. Thus, streetwalkers interacted with men as clients, spouses (legally married or cohabiting), or protectors in relationships that could be exploitative, combative, congenial, or mutually beneficial.[26] Court records not only identify married couples but also the circumstances of their lives at particular moments. Take, for example, Catharine Hicks and Michael Riley or Louis Bonin and Henriette Mercier, who were homeless, arrested, and jailed for vagrancy.[27] Family members and neighbours sometimes sought to discipline those cohabitating together. William Lemon, Henri Latreille, and Marie Anne Labonne wanted one Charbonneau and his lover, the well-known sex worker Véronique Fleury, arrested for vagrancy because "in keeping Véronique Fleury at home with him, Charbonneau would cause a huge scandal."[28] Similarly, labourer Charles Leclerc asked that police apprehend his daughter and her lover following an argument he had with Alexis Dumont over her well-being. They were, he argued, homeless and "roamed the streets like vagrants."[29]

Court records also provide an important window onto women who shared a female subculture and travelled through public space in groups, forging a "community" of outcast women[30] similar to the "radical community of women" that historian Maria Luddy argues existed amongst the "wrens of the Curragh."[31] Her study of these women, who lived as camp-followers on the margins of society near the Curragh army camp in the county Kildare in Ireland—sex workers, vagrants, ex-convicts, and alcoholics—formed a radical community. Their lives, she contends, were organized around women and children to the exclusion of men. In Montreal, some groups of women shared the same ethnicity and others were mixed, each fashioning complex bonds. As Marilyn Wood Hill has suggested, the relationships between New York City sex workers were likely characterized by competition, jealousy, and antagonism on the one hand, and by female solidarity on the other. They "assumed an emotional centrality in each others' lives, which often led to deep, mutual friendships characterized by strong female bonding and a special sense of solidarity."[32]

Some sex workers established long-term and intimate bonds with soldiers. Historian Judith Fingard identified similar relationships between soldiers and streetwalkers and between soldiers and abandoned wives in Halifax, Nova Scotia.[33] A number of soldiers' wives who were economically dependent upon their husbands became unofficial wives of replacement soldiers when regiments departed, leaving spouses behind.[34] Others turned to prostitution when husbands left the city for military postings elsewhere. Take, for example, Montreal resident Catharine Daly. She was married to a British soldier of the 37th Regiment when he deserted her after being garrisoned at Kingston in Upper Canada. Catharine was arrested for sex work sometime later.[35]

The sex trade also provided opportunities for women to leave unhappy marriages, particularly when husbands were addicted to alcohol or had a penchant for violent behaviour, to deal with a spouse's desertion, and to institute informal divorce whilst earning a living. Isabella Tomlinson is a case in point. Husband Thomas Rousby accused her of having left him and their children to establish a brothel. When he went to the house to demand she return home, Isabella refused and allegedly assaulted him.[36] Although it is impossible to determine why she had abandoned their marital bed, Isabella's departure surely represented a separation or self-divorce. Sex work on the streets served the same purpose for some women. In 1831, for instance, Julie-Archange Daigneau left her four daughters Marie-Elmire, Archange, Marie-Henriette, and Caroline with her husband Jean Dérouin and moved out of the family home. Julie-Archange had been pregnant and a minor when she married Jean Dérouin ten years earlier in June 1821. Their four daughters were born within the first seven years of marriage. It is unclear why Julie-Archange left. Jean claimed that she had simply abandoned him and her children for a life on the streets.[37] A year following her departure, Jean died, presumably in the cholera epidemic, yet Julie-Archange did not return home. What happened to her four daughters, the youngest being only four years old at her father's death, is unknown. In the case of desertion, Mary Martin, whose shoemaker spouse George Powell lived in Halifax and had been absent from Lower Canada for twelve years, turned to sex work to support herself and children.[38] It is ironic that prostitution, embedded in significant risk owing to the prevalence of excessive alcohol use and misogyny, provided a means for women to escape spousal abuse. There was, however, no guarantee that a woman who chose to leave an abusive husband would be free of his brutality. After Thomas Day forced his brothel-keeping wife Mary Ann Turner out of the family home, thus reinforcing his supremacy in the household, he continued to mistreat her: "she succeeded in escaping from him but he was determined to catch her and blacken her eyes. That he has frequently come to her house with a view to annoy and injure her and hath on some occasions struck her and on others torn some of her clothes as he could lay his hands upon."[39] Day entered into a six-month recognizance in the amount of £40 to keep the peace.[40] That said, some of the married women who kept houses of prostitution with spouses also encountered drunkenness and violence from them at home.

Brothel-keeper Louise Corbeille's long history of emotional and physical abuse at the hands of husband Antoine Delaunay is but one example of many. Not only had he threatened to kill her but had on several occasions thrown knives at her head.[41] When Louise Corbeille's interventions failed to stop the violence, she sought legal remedy to deal with his mistreatment. While the act of laying a complaint before a justice of the peace served to limit publicly the right of a husband to discipline his wife, it was likely a strategy of last resort. Women may not have wanted the court to treat their husbands severely given that incarceration would have resulted in their inability to earn a wage, which would have been devastating to the household economy or could have provoked further violence from a vengeful husband. Why take these risks? Gregory Smith has argued that their objectives were straightforward: "aside from seeking to halt the abuse itself, these women were seeking some recognized, authoritative power (in this case that of the state) to add weight to their own personal opposition to harsh physical treatment."[42] Court records tell us little about the expectations women had with respect to their husbands' behaviour when making a complaint.

Since women's work in the home also included, as Bettina Bradbury has argued, tension management associated with difficult life situations, how might we understand Éloi Benêche *dit* Lavictoire's single episode of aggression against a sex worker that I noted at the beginning of the chapter? Had Rosalie become more effective at containing Éloi's wrath?[43] Was it Éloi's strategy to warn Rosalie and therefore to silence her? Kathryn Harvey's examination of wife battering in Montreal after the mid-nineteenth century offers additional insights into spousal abuse, showing that conflict around "drink, struggles over money, jealousy, and authority over children" precipitated assaults.[44] The brothel was no different and men who were husbands or lovers committed acts of violence. Such aggression was surely a consequence of their legal and social right to physically admonish their wives in an atmosphere of tensions and strains associated not only with daily living in the brothel but also with alcohol abuse, perhaps intimidation of wives who may have been uncomfortable about operating a brothel especially if it involved children, and jealousies associated with sex commerce.

Criminal justice records make it possible to tease out the complex, sometimes ambiguous, coercive, and at times intense relationships that sex workers established with others. I draw on Jane Nicholas' detailed telling of Annie Robinson's trial in her essay "Suffering for Compassion: Everyday Violence and Infanticide in Ontario, 1820–1920s" (Chapter 14) to try to make sense of Adélaide's intimate and emotionally charged narrative. These mediated historical sources focus on those moments when sex workers broke the law, were perceived as doing so, or were maliciously prosecuted, making interpretation sometimes difficult. How do we understand silences? For example, if we return again to Éloi Benêche *dit* Lavictoire's violent attack on Adélaide Cinqmars, what does it suggest about the role Éloi played in the brothel? Was this an act of intimidation at the behest of Rosalie to keep sex workers in line? What factors may have resulted in Adélaide's resistance? What did she hope to achieve by laying a complaint before the magistrate against Éloi? How do we comprehend her encounter with Éloi in the everyday? Was she speaking for herself or was she voicing the unease of fellow sex workers in Rosalie's brothel? How do we even locate their "voices" in mediated sources?

While I recognize that depositions were constructed to maximize the goals of the plaintiffs and to follow certain well-established narratives, a careful reading of these sources reveals that many featured detailed accounts of the events, sometimes in very colourful and distinctive language and in the plaintiff's or the accused's own words. Influenced again by the methodologies developed by historians of women, I approach criminal justice documents by reading against the grain to locate women's voices and experiences in order to piece together individual accounts. This technique, as cultural historian Stephen Robertson has elucidated, "focuses on moments of misunderstanding and conflict—ruptures in the legal process, departures from legal forms, formulas, and language, and information that has not been shaped to fit the terms of the law. In those moments, in those places in texts, can be found the voices of ordinary people." Hence, my study engages with the records in order to understand who turned to the law for justice, how it was understood, the ways in which it was practised, negotiated, and subverted, and what it can tell us about intimacy in brothels, in families, on city streets and green spaces, and in neighbourhoods. As Robertson contends, "It is not the way law works as a means of social control but the gap between laws and their enforcement that has framed the way that historians have thought about the law." [45]

Rosalie would have had to pay close attention to her relationships with neighbours as well. Sex workers were integral to city neighbourhoods where they shared housing, purchased goods at nearby markets and stores, frequented local taverns, attended church services, and worked on city streets, in green spaces, and in houses of prostitution. Rosalie operated her brothel at the same address in the 1830s and 1840s. To do so required that she and the inmates not only establish affable and responsive contacts with neighbours but also follow a code of behaviour of the neighbourhoods where they lived and laboured. There are some examples of women who, like Rosalie, kept disorderly houses for long periods without attracting either the attention or wrath of the community. To do so meant that brothel-keepers and the women who provided sexual services had to negotiate with neighbours to stay in business. Neighbours relied on a variety of responses to discipline those whose comportment did not tally with their expectations: they spoke to brothel inmates and streetwalkers, assaulted them, gossiped, rioted in the offending establishments, and laid complaints before a justice of the peace. As studies have shown, most plaintiffs were not interested in pursuing cases at court to a verdict—they usually abandoned the process by failing to appear in court to privately prosecute the defendants—choosing instead to use depositions and contact with the criminal justice authorities to pressure women who transgressed local norms to conform or leave.

Catherine Crumbie had maintained her brothel in the same neighbourhood until an altercation between neighbour George Mackin and one of her inmates forced her to move her business elsewhere. Mackin described his version of the confrontation in a deposition, claiming to have struck the "notorious harlot" across the cheek after being "rudely insulted" when she used "language the most abominable" in reference to his wife. The next evening, the "notorious harlot" apparently went to his home where she threw stones at the building and uttered the following insult: "Come out here you Dublin Jackson (Jackeen),[46] I have a knife here for you and I'll run it through yours guts."[47] When George Mackin made an official complaint to the authorities, he effectively banished Catherine Crumbie, Maria Jordan, Catherine Brutton, and Mary Macdonald from their residence on Salaberry Street. Having lost their neighbours' endorsement, they were arrested, imprisoned, and charged with keeping a disorderly house.

The proximity of sex workers' lives also meant that they derived support and protection through the relationships they established with each other. A "subculture of solidarity" and intimacy existed amongst sex workers, cultivated by the risks they shared: participating in an illicit marketplace, unwanted pregnancies, venereal disease, arrest and imprisonment, a non-respectable status, and of course potential and real violence.[48] Camaraderie is inferred when sex workers were protective of or loyal to one another or when they left one brothel to move together to another. Take for example, siblings Félicité and Marguerite Bleau who both worked at Angélique Paré's bawdyhouse or on city streets until Marguerite died of tuberculosis in the city gaol. Following her sister's demise, Félicité sought out another group of women for companionship and safety. Consider also the homeless sex workers who formed communities of outcast women in city streets and green spaces. Women also transgressed these relationships of friendship. They appeared in court documents as plaintiffs, defendants, and witnesses in cases involving assault and battery, uttering threats, larceny, rioting, slander, and sexual assault. Consequently, we have a much more comprehensive picture of how they negotiated the criminal justice system, used it for their own purposes, and ultimately expressed their friendships with others. The marketplace of sex in Montreal, as elsewhere, was competitive and rivalries and disputes between sex workers sometimes resulted in theft, violence, and defamation. Insults and gossip served to regulate women's behaviour, including for those who marketed sex.

Judicial records cannot provide a complete picture of sex work. Women who were able to evade formal judicial scrutiny—perhaps a consequence of police corruption or of informal settlements with neighbours—are obviously not represented in these documents. Were those arrested less able, as historian Clare Lyons ponders, "at manoeuvring through a system of informal rules, corruption, and bribes?"[49] Given the reality of unreported crime, it is difficult to determine how representative court records are, since not all of the documents have survived and clandestine, casual, and high-status sex workers are likely under-enumerated. There are also key epistemological limitations to these documents. For instance, I know little about sexual practices or indeed the fees that sex workers charged for the services they provided. Nor could I always ascertain with any certainty which complaints were the consequence of malicious prosecution. It was sometimes difficult to determine if the women who were accused of keeping a disorderly house or being a disorderly person actually worked in sex commerce. We know from historical studies that unmarried women's involvement in intimate, non-commercial heterosexual relations was sometimes recast as prostitution. It was also challenging to differentiate between women who engaged in sex for pleasure or who were coerced. Moreover, sex workers would have engaged in intimate sexual relations with men for whom they had affection at different points in their lives, indeed even at the same time that they were working.

It is worth remembering, finally, that women who marketed sex were engaged in the business of hospitality, albeit an illicit one. Did some women operating brothels catering to elites depend upon credit to purchase goods for their establishments? How many leased buildings that involved the formal services of a notary? If not, how did they rent their establishments and from whom? Were sex workers renting the same buildings and from the same individuals? Was the cost of renting higher or was it offset by the offer of sexual services that they may have been negotiated with the lessor? In other words, what sorts of relationships did women establish with those from whom they rented or purchased goods? Some women in the sex trade achieved notoriety, but few attained a high standard of living, and all aimed at a low profile to ensure tolerance of their neighbours. They were concentrated in popular-class neighbourhoods with access to military barracks and the riverfront. The well-known city constable Louis Malo advertised a "pleasure garden" and bowling alleys in the 1850s, and an exceptionally handsome array of furniture, financed by the dealer that was transferred every few months within a network of women working in the sex trade. It was bourgeois furniture in a popular-class location, and the transfers were engineered when one or another went to jail.[50] This may have been the case for Éloi's sister Marie-Louise, who rented a house on St-Constant Street from the gentleman William Scott along with an array of furniture, kitchenware, bedding, and decorative objects.

Historians of prostitution have argued that brothel-keepers participated in a network of sex commerce which extended beyond the confines of their households and comprised landlords, merchants, and tradesmen. Joel Best has shown for St. Paul, Minnesota how brothel-keepers had to maintain these ties or risk denunciation by dissatisfied businessmen and women who normally profiteered from the sex trade.[51] Such links remain uncharted in Montreal. Depositions reveal that keepers of disorderly houses leased space in buildings owned by prominent city families. While it is unclear if these notables knew to whom their properties were rented, some plaintiffs claimed that they did, although none were prosecuted for doing so. Grand jurors of the January 1840 Quarter Sessions of the Peace expressed their criticism of elites' willingness to lease their buildings for illicit purposes: buildings which "[t]hey regret to remark are the property of persons of family and respectable standing, who cannot but be aware of the character of the individuals to whom their dwellings are leased or of the traffic carried on by them."[52] Neighbours, who complained to authorities about local houses of prostitution, incriminated landlords by deliberately citing their names in depositions. Take the example of surveyor William Hall and High Constable Adelphe Delisle who accused Monique Panneton and Sophie Morrison of establishing a brothel in a house belonging to either the prominent notary public Joseph Labadie or his wife, Marie-Louise Grénier.[53] By identifying property owners, complainants raised a possible link between them and sex commerce, which likely served to pressure proprietors to act against brothel-keepers and their inmates.

The city's population was small enough, prostitution tended to be a public activity, and proprietors likely would have been cognizant of rumours or complaints issuing from neighbours and lessees. Some landowners would not have been directly involved in renting their properties since houses were customarily let out to individuals who, in turn, sublet parts of the buildings including rooms or apartments. Nonetheless, certain proprietors leased property routinely to brothel-keepers. Over a fifteen-year period, merchant George Wurtele rented houses to at least five known keepers of disorderly houses. Such proprietors likely stood to gain financially because they could hypothetically charge madams higher rents for their property. Another example is Jacob Marsten, who had a reputation for leasing property to sex workers. As Montreal's high constable, it would have been extremely difficult to claim at court that he was unaware to whom he let out the apartments. His penchant for renting to sex workers came to light after Marsten accused Jean Lebeau of assaulting him while on police business to quell a riot. Two witnesses, Antoine Delaunay and François-Xavier Poitras, suggested that Marsten had simply acted to put an end to the drunken revelry taking place in his own house that he had let to sex workers Fanny and Elizabeth Proulx. Delaunay and Poitras also accused him of leasing another of his houses to a woman by the name of "Renois" who was reputed to keep a brothel.[54] Likewise, Montreal's sheriff Frederick William Ermatinger rented one of his houses, located in the centre of St-Charles-Borromée Street, to the local hangman Benjamin Field, a man of African descent born in the United States. Field had only recently been discharged from prison after Thomas McCord had sentenced him in 1820—already his second offence—to an astonishing four years of incarceration for keeping a disorderly house.[55] No other person had been imprisoned for more than six months for brothel keeping. Field reopened a brothel in Ermatinger's house with the assistance of Richard and William McGinnis, Mary Field (a daughter who was married to Anthony Billow), Jane Graham (wife of Henry Garret), and Ellen Purcell.[56] As the city's sheriff, Ermatinger would have known about Field's earlier foray into sex commerce. For re-offending, Benjamin Field returned to prison for another two years.[57] Surely, Field's occupation and his racialized identity played key roles in both of these unusual and protracted prison terms for a victimless crime. Frederick Ermatinger, on the other hand, remained the city's sheriff. Pointe-à-Callière proprietor Pierre Morreau clearly knew exactly what his tenant Élisabeth Duffault was doing with his property and condoned it. He served as a bondsman for her when police arrested her for keeping a disorderly house. Duffaut took out a surety to keep the peace for six months; Morreau put up £10 and Élisabeth's husband Louis Cabarra provided the other £10.[58]

## *Conclusion*

Judicial documents have allowed me to piece together a surprising wealth of data and to ask questions about women's personal relationships and daily experiences. Nonetheless, there are silences and obvious limitations in these records as Éloi Benêche *dit* Lavictoire's brutal attack on Adélaide Cinqmars demonstrates. Judicial records, however, provide a window onto intimate relationships, friendships, acts of kindness and solidarity, moments of sadness, joy, fear, and rage, and episodes of intimidation and violence. They remind us that sex workers were also wives, lovers, mothers, sisters, daughters, kin, friends, and neighbours who led complex lives, similar to all Montrealers. If we look closely, they allow us to see sex workers in their full humanity. Judicial documents can also highlight aspects of popular-class private life such as family and marital relations, informal divorce, and relationships between neighbours as well as representatives of the criminal justice system. Other sources, such as parish records, city directories, census returns, and notarial records are complementary; they situate individuals in families and in business relations to reveal why women turned to sex work. Finally, research has shown me the importance of approaching my subjects with sensitivity—not sentimentality.

CHAPTER 9

# Improper Intimacies, Impossible Promises, and the Prerogatives of Patriarchy

## *Family and Justice in Nineteenth-Century Criminal Courts in Canada's North-West Territories*[1]

*Shelley A.M. Gavigan*

On the evening of 12 April 1882, Jack Cameron returned to his home at "The Forks" near the Prince Albert settlement in the District of Saskatchewan in the North-West Territories (NWT) from an overnight trip to find his house in ruins, and not by natural causes. He had no personal knowledge of how it had happened. The District of Saskatchewan, where Cameron lived, was home to First Nations and Métis communities and a small population of white settlers.[2] The Métis were not listed in the 1881–82 Census of Canada;[3] however, the 1884–85 Census of the NWT revealed that almost three quarters of the 5,373 people (72.6 percent) who lived in the census sub-district of Prince Albert were Indigenous.[4] This region was home to the largest number of Métis communities in the NWT, many of whom had arrived from Manitoba in the 1870s.[5] Despite their central role in founding the Prince Albert settlement, as Paget Code has noted, the Métis did not hold the reins of political or economic power in the community.[6]

Jack Cameron was a homesteader, possibly newly arrived.[7] The ownership of the lot on which his house stood was disputed (and claimed by another man). Was his house pulled down because of this land-based dispute, a form of self-help not unknown in the NWT?[8] Cameron said he thought that this was what had happened. Two and a half months later, he learned that the land dispute was not the reason his house had been pulled down, but rather a more personal and intimate grievance, driven by a husband's anger over Cameron's "improper intimacies" with his wife.[9]

On June 28, four local farmers—George Finlay, William Craigie, Thomas Righton, and Malcolm McLeod—were brought before Justice of the Peace James Campbell in Prince Albert to face the charge that they did "on or about the night of the 11th day of April last past unlawfully & maliciously pull down the dwelling house of John M. Cameron situated on lot 22 Township 47 his homestead at the 'Forks.'"[10] Cameron told the Court that he had been unable to find out "who did this thing" until two days earlier; until then, "I did not suspect these men at all."[11] The people who had pointed him to Mr. Finlay were Finlay's wife, Charlotte, and her parents, Joseph and Mathilda Pocha.[12] They had come to him on June 26, shortly after Mr. Finlay had "dismissed his wife from his house."[13] The theory of the defence seems to have been that the case was motivated by a grudge held by Cameron and his witnesses against Finlay. Cameron acknowledged in cross-examination, "I had some trouble with Finlay on account of his wife some time ago. Finlay accused me of improper intimacy with his wife. Previous to that I had not made any statements to my knowledge about her character."[14] Defence counsel W.R. Gunn confronted Cameron with a document, apparently a written apology to Finlay that he had signed. What was that about, Mr. Cameron?

> I signed that to save my own character. I did not wish it to go to court. I said if Finlay pardoned me, I would never bother his house again. I did not go on my knees to ask pardon. I have not exactly had a grudge against Finlay ever since. I thought he was rather hard but misled. I did not to my knowledge make any statements to John Smith about Finlay's wife, such as that I had seen her on the floor naked & could make her prostitute herself at any time. To the best of my knowledge, I did not say so. I am positive that I did not.[15]

Joseph Pocha testified that his son-in-law, Finlay, had asked him if he could keep a secret: "we went and pulled down Cameron's house last night," to which Pocha had responded, "...you have done very wrong. It's just as good to kill a man when you have done that to his house."[16] Pocha also testified that Finlay said he wanted to drive Cameron out of the country and had threatened to tar and feather and set Cameron on fire.

Mr. Pocha also said that Finlay told him that his wife, Pocha's daughter, had slept with Jack Cameron and another man.

Twenty-seven-year-old Charlotte Finlay had been born in Manitoba and would have come with her parents to the Territories. The Pochas were a prominent Métis family of the Prince Albert district, said to have been good hunters "noted for their courage and resource."[17] Joseph and Mathilda Pocha stood by their daughter against the husband who had thrown her out of her home, even when her husband told her father that she had slept with other men—whether they believed him or not. It was clear from Joseph's evidence, and that of his wife Mathilda, that Finlay's in-laws were angry at his treatment of Charlotte. Mathilda recounted that she had been with her daughter in the Finlay home when George "was clapping and making a laugh" and said, "I wonder what Jack will say when he comes to his house and finds it down...there were four of us that went and pulled it down."[18] In response to a question by Mr. Finlay's counsel, Mathilda was unequivocal: "My reason for telling is on account of Finlay's treatment of my daughter. I feel angry with Finlay. He, Finlay, told me with his own mouth."[19]

There was enough evidence for the Justice of the Peace to commit Finlay and his co-accused to stand trial. On 17 July 1882, Finlay was released on a Recognizance with a surety to appear at the next sittings of the Court in Prince Albert. He and the other men were tried by Stipendiary Magistrate Hugh Richardson with a jury on 25 October.[20] The transcript of the trial does not form part of the archival record. The *Prince Albert Times* reported that "three witnesses testified to a confession on the part of one of the accused, and threats beforehand" and "the judge charged strongly against one of the accused, Finlay, but the jury acquitted him."[21] The Pochas had sought justice for the man whose home had been demolished with apparent impunity by their daughter's husband. Stipendiary Magistrate Richardson clearly believed them and would have convicted him. The jury voted to acquit. Their names do not appear in the court file and it is not known whether any of them was Métis.

Jack Cameron lost his house and his case against the aggrieved husband and abettors. Charlotte Finlay lost her home. It is possible that Charlotte was pregnant when her husband "dismissed her" from their home in late June 1882. While there is no record of Charlotte Finlay (Findlay) in later censuses, Joseph Pocha's household in 1891 included "Ellen Finley," "GC" [grandchild], aged nine, whose mother was born in

Manitoba.[22] Charlotte's parents must have taken her in, and the baby girl born not long after.

## *Law, Patriarchy, and Ideology in Court Records: Questions of Context, Method, and Analysis*

What would lead a researcher to think that a privately prosecuted criminal charge by Jack Cameron against George Finlay for malicious damage to property would really be a case about a wife's alleged improper intimacy? On its face, this "damage to property" case in the court records offers no hint of patriarchal, familial, or intimate relations, or indeed intimate violence, unlike offences of abortion, carnal knowledge, incest, rape, or domestic assault, to cite but a few. In this chapter, I pursue the question of how historians can avoid making the kind of mistake Jack Cameron made when he surveyed the detritus that had been his home. He thought the dispute about title to land lay behind the destruction.

A close reading of court records reveals that sites of intimacy are to be found in unexpected places. So where do we find them? How do we identify sites of conflict born of intimacy in these inhospitable contexts? Or, as Felice Batlan incisively puts it, how do we gender "the seemingly ungendered"?[23] My approach has been to widen my lens and study a broader range of records beyond the ones that expressly "shout" gender relations or violence—to look into cases of theft, fraud, break and enter, perjury, extortion, mischief and damage to property, wounding animals, etc. Some, such as George Finlay's case, involve a husband's response to alleged infidelity,[24] while other alleged intimate violence or wrongs underpin charges of theft,[25] assault on another man,[26] and extortion.[27] A Regina man, Michael Krauss, expressed his sense of grievance that Fanny Haman had named him as the father of her deceased newborn by laying an Information accusing her of perjury.[28]

In addition to questions of method, issues of theory and framework are engaged when one is challenged to identify and analyze what these archival records reveal of society's wider assumptions about familial and gender relations. This chapter reflects my attempt to take up this challenge and to think through the meaning of "intimacy" in the context of patriarchal social and familial relations as revealed by the criminal court records of the North-West Territories.

The administration of justice in the NWT largely rested initially with the North-West Mounted Police (NWMP) whose senior officers were justices of the peace *ex officio*.[29] Before the construction of courthouses, court hearings were held in NWMP posts, and terms of imprisonment were served in NWMP cells. The principal "statisticians" of the NWT criminal courts were the NWMP who recorded and reported the numbers for the NWMP Commissioner's annual reports. Lay justices of the peace supplemented the NWMP JPs and, until 1886, three legally trained Stipendiary Magistrates traversed the vast expanse of the Territories to try criminal and civil complaints. The court documents upon which I largely rely are those of Hugh Richardson, Stipendiary Magistrate and, after 1886, Justice of the newly created Supreme Court of the North-West Territories.[30]

In these records, the perils of life and harsh climate on the Plains emerge in stark relief: of vulnerability exacerbated by isolation, far from neighbours, towns, and medical aid. These perils were further exacerbated by the law, as one finds few convictions of men accused of forms of sexual assault and sexual interference with children. If a wife or mother took ill or died in childbirth, and the father's land or livestock were at a distance, motherless children could and did find themselves alone and fending for themselves for long stretches of time. One encounters husbands, fathers, and employers (masters) being prosecuted and, on occasion, convicted for dereliction of their patriarchal obligations in relation to their wives, children, and wards, and other "wronged" husbands on the wrong side of a prosecution in the aftermath of a failed prosecution against other men.

However, just as the Montreal sex workers in Mary Ann Poutanen's contribution to this volume (Chapter 8) engaged and used the law, women in the Territories also turned to law for redress of injury and violence, aided in some cases by a male relative who commenced the criminal process against another man, often the woman's husband. Some women, including a few Indigenous women, went to law on their own, as Informants in their own right, to complain about a man's violence or ill treatment. Still other women were taken to law, not as accused persons, but as witnesses for or against their aggrieved or abusive men, to testify against the men whom they may once have loved or thought they did.

The stories of intimacy found in court records[31] are stories that have been told publicly—to police, to justices of the peace, magistrates, judges, and to juries—inevitably involuntarily, subject to scrutiny and judgment, then as now. This is seldom fair or neutral terrain. But, even in the context of nineteenth-century Western Canada, it appears that the sites of and relationships between law and patriarchy were more complex, uneven and contradictory than one might expect if one sees law as only a unidirectional, unidimensional expression and enforcer of patriarchy.

Legal historians face moral and ethical issues about whether to name,[32] and how to interpret the words of vulnerable people, often women and children, who were required to describe their intimate experiences in inhospitable public contexts, to men they did not know and who did not share their life experiences and struggles. Women in the NWT court records, a trio of whose cases and names I use and whose stories (as found in these documents) I tell, had diverse experiences of forms of intimacy. In each, one can identify the animating presence of patriarchy—not necessarily expressed evenly, effectively, or without contradiction or resistance, but still informing, shaping, and present. In this chapter, I attempt to highlight women's voices, experiences and expressions of agency and to focus on their relationships, to keep the intimate stories publicly told in focus, whilst also attempting to imagine how it must have *felt* for a young wife required to describe in court in the presence of her husband how she had been unfaithful to him, and why. And then to return home with him, as was Florence Wilson's experience—to which I now turn.

## *Florence Wilson and the Impossible Promise of Happiness*

On 20 June 1894, W.K. (William) Wilson and Florence Wharton were married in a small ceremony at his mother's home in Qu'Appelle Station, NWT, at which the presiding minister is reported to have made a "short but pointed address."[33] Florence, daughter of a widowed laundress, was fifteen. The groom, a successful local carpenter and contractor, at twenty-six, was ten years her senior. Florence turned sixteen one month later. By her seventeenth birthday in the following July, Florence would be the mother of three-month-old William, born 18 April 1895.

On 8 January 1897, less than three years after their wedding, William turned quickly to law to retrieve Florence, who had left the family home on the evening of 7 January. He was able to convince four men—his brother, a justice of the peace, and two members of the North-West Mounted Police—to begin a criminal process in which George Shaw, a blacksmith and boarder in the Wilson home at Qu'Appelle Station, was accused of an offence contrary to section 185 of Canada's recently introduced *Criminal Code*, known informally as "defiling a woman."[34] The Justice of the Peace issued a warrant for his arrest, which was executed that same evening by NWMP Constable M.J. Della Torre in the town of Wolseley.

At a hearing on 9 January before J.P. Gisborne, Constable Della Torre deposed that he had received a wire from Staff Sergeant Fyffe, advising that a warrant had been issued for George Shaw of Qu'Appelle Station and instructing him "to arrest Shaw and hold Mrs. Wilson who was supposed to be in his company."[35] Della Torre deposed that he found Mr. Shaw and Mrs. Wilson in the sitting room of Hall's Hotel in Wolseley. He arrested Mr. Shaw, brought him to Qu'Appelle and "handed Mrs. Wilson over to Mr. Robinson." The legality of her detention was surely questionable. (Mr. Robinson is not identified elsewhere in the court record; it is possible that he was J.B. Robinson, a fellow local contractor and colleague of W.K. Wilson.)[36]

The Information alleged that Shaw "did entice Mrs. Florence Wilson, wife of William Wilson of Qu'Appelle Station, away from Qu'Appelle Station for the purpose of unlawful carnal connection."[37] It would be a stretch to think that William Wilson found his own way to section 185, one of the new provisions introduced as part of a "litany of procuring offences, designed to protect girls and young women from the wiles of procurers, brothel keepers and other sexual exploiters, including parents and guardians."[38] Wilson's problem was that adultery and alienation of affection were not criminal offences.[39] The criminal process was more inviting for the result he sought.

In his deposition, Wilson identified himself as the husband of Florence Wilson, who he said was not yet twenty years of age and to whom he had been married "two years ago last June." He testified that nine months earlier George Shaw had come to his house to board, that it had been Shaw's idea to do so, and that they had had amicable relations until Shaw left earlier in the week. Wilson maintained that all had been well at home: he had "never noticed any undue familiarity with my wife…" and added that "[m]y wife and myself were friendly could not be more so. Never had any trouble with my wife."[40]

Florence Wilson may well have had her own views on the state of their marital friendliness, but she did depose that they were amicable.

She made a long deposition in which she took full responsibility for the relationship with Shaw and of the arrangements she and he had made together:

> I allowed him to take personal liberties with me. ...In the first instance I made advances to George Shaw, I spoke to George Shaw in an improper manner using terms of affection that I ought not to have applied to anybody but my husband. ... Up to the time George Shaw left there had been nothing wrong or immoral between us. I expected to live with George Shaw the same way I would live with a husband. This was agreed between us. Several times we talked on this subject, he told me all the happiness that would happen from our living together, he did not cease talking about the enjoyment and happiness that would result from my going with him. If it had not been for his talking and shewing the happiness it would be living with him I would not have gone with him. Up the time I went away with Shaw I was absolutely a moral woman as far as he was concerned.[41]

Florence said that after Shaw left, she also left to meet him at the town of Wolseley. Her train ticket was likely not for Toronto, but for Wolseley, which might have been how her husband was able to track her down.

> Shaw met me at the train. He told me to get off the train as he had not sold the team. I then went to Hall's hotel with Shaw. We first went to the sitting room and the proprietor show [sic] me our bedroom. George Shaw went first into the bedroom and I followed him and stayed with him all night. I naturely [sic] that we should sleep in separate bedrooms. I asked Shaw which was my bedroom and he said this was it. I told him I would rather to go to a room by myself he asked me to stay where I was. This was the first occasion I was unfaithful to my marriage vows and I was unfaithful.[42]

When asked by the Justice of the Peace if he wanted to say anything, George Shaw declined. Mr. Shaw did not wax eloquent in his defence. His is a silence difficult to interpret. Did he love Florence? Had he intended to go to Toronto with her to make a new life together? Did he fight for her? Did he give up? Had he meant any of his promises to her?

Leaving aside the dubious merit to the criminal charge under section 185, Florence's forthright evidence before the Justice of the Peace left him with little choice but to dismiss the charge, which he did. One hopes she did not have to pay too dearly for her expression of agency and assertion of responsibility. One cannot but admire the courage it would have taken to speak those words in a room full of men, one of whom she had left and one of whom she was leaving.

George Shaw may have walked away from court on 9 January a free man, but word of the case and its disposition seems to have made quick news in the community. In a coy item that leaves little doubt that the justice's dismissal of the charge was not determinative, the *Qu'Appelle Progress* reported in its "Local and General" column the following week,

> On Saturday night [the 9$^{th}$], there was quite a run on the egg and whip market, a number of citizens having decided to pay their respects in a marked manner to a young man who was supposed to leave on the evening train. Hearing of the intended "send-off," with the aid of some acquaintance, a team was procured and he was quietly driven out of town, which is not likely he will visit again for many months, much to the disgust of those assembled at the depot to bid him a fond adieu.[43]

Having successfully dodged the horse whipping planned for him by the unnamed citizens of Qu'Appelle Station, it is possible nonetheless that George Shaw remained in the Assiniboia East District, if he is the same George Shaw found in the 1901 Census record for the sub-district of Winlaw.[44] There he is listed as a twenty-five-year-old single farmer, living with his brother's family. If he was Florence Wilson's George Shaw, he would have been twenty-two at the time he talked his eighteen-year-old landlady into believing that she could find happiness and a good home with him in Toronto.

From the 1901 Canada Census record of the Wilson household, one can infer that Florence had returned home to her husband and their twenty-month-old son. And she stayed. In December 1900, she had had another baby, James.[45] By 1906 Florence, now twenty-eight, had had a

Figure 9.1: W.K. Wilson (undated, likely in the 1930s). Source: Photograph courtesy of Bruce Farrer, Secretary, Qu'Appelle Masonic Lodge no. 6 AF & AM.

Figure 9.2: Hugh John Wilson as a young man (undated). In 1929, W. Bro. (Worthy Brother) H.J. Wilson served as Worshipful Master of the Masonic Lodge. Source: Photograph courtesy of Bruce Farrer, Secretary, Qu'Appelle Masonic Lodge no. 6 AF & AM.

third son, Harvey, but little James must have died, as he is not listed in the census record.[46] For his part, William Wilson remained a successful contractor who built several homes, churches, and schools in Qu'Appelle and neighbouring communities.[47] He was a prominent member of the Qu'Appelle Masonic Lodge no. 6 AF & AM from 1905 when he joined until his death in 1936, having twice served as Worshipful Master (President).[48] His younger brother, Hugh John Wilson, the Informant in the criminal charge against Shaw, would also become a prominent member of the Qu'Appelle Lodge, also serving as Worshipful Master in 1929 and holding other high offices, as well as an appointment as editor of the *Qu'Appelle Progress*.[49]

Figure 9.3: Qu'Appelle Chapter no. 88 Order of the Eastern Star, 1938. Florence Wilson (Mrs. W.K. Wilson) is in the second row, second from the right. Source: Photograph courtesy of Bruce Farrer, Secretary, Qu'Appelle Lodge no. 6 AF & AM.

The affair with George Shaw appears not to have tarnished Florence's stature in Qu'Appelle, at least in the long run, perhaps fading in the collective memory. Years later, she was noted for her community work in support of the war effort in the First World War, and still later as one of the founding members of the Qu'Appelle Chapter no. 88 of the Order of the Eastern Star (OES). She is a radiant presence in a photo of the group taken in 1938, two years after her husband's death. In the1940s, she served twice as Worthy Matron (President),. the highest office in an OES Chapter—evidence of not only her capability but of the high regard in which she was held by the women who were her peers.[50]

## *Mrs. Crispen, Mrs. Glenn, and the Prerogatives of Patriarchy, Class, and Power*

The patriarchal family enjoyed pride of place in the legal instruments of the Territories, ranging from the organization of title to settler homesteads to the definition of Indian in the *Indian Act*.[51] As Chandra

Murdoch's research so clearly illuminates in Chapter 2 of this collection, women from the South Ontario Indian reserves actively challenged and engaged with the "deeply unequal layers of gendered and racialized" Indian legislation and, often supported by those in leadership positions in their communities, fought hard for their property rights and to define for themselves their rightful heirs—with some measure of success.[52]

The ascribed roles for settler women in the Territories were forms of domestic servitude and dependence before and after marriage. The head of the household was the husband, and the farm was his farm, as Sarah Carter has demonstrated so vividly:

> It is readily apparent from gazing at any township map how land law and policies were used to shape a society of male heads of households and dependent females, how the land was not neutral, how ideas about proper gender roles were embedded in the landscape. For most women the only way to get land was to get a man, or have a husband die....[53]

And even then, not without a fight. Well into the twentieth century, the use of the word "ours" was said by a Saskatchewan judge to be simply a husband's "diplomatic and ambiguous" euphemism for the "forthright and challenging 'mine.'"[54]

As pivotal as "the family" would be to the settlement of the Territories, the court records suggest that it is important to situate the family within the broader notion of households, given that it was common for wives, mothers, and their children to share their homes with boarders, lodgers, domestic help, hired men, and immigrant child labourers—all living under the patriarchal authority of the head of the household, the husband, father, and employer.[55] George Shaw had been one such boarder. Annie Crispen was one such domestic servant.

It is not clear how Annie Crispen[56] and her husband Richard found their way to Joseph Glenn's home in Indian Head in 1898. Glenn, a thirty-seven-year-old husband and father[57] and apparently prosperous farmer and businessman, later testified that Richard Crispen had approached him for work. Glenn hired the couple for a year, and they commenced their employment on 28 February 1898. Richard worked at Glenn's farm as a labourer; Annie lived and worked as a servant in the Glenn family home in town and slept in the basement. The Crispens were a young couple (Annie, 19; Richard, 26) having been married for about one year when they began to work for Joseph Glenn at the end of May.

However, by the end of summer, Glenn had terminated their employment. Shortly thereafter he was in court charged with indecent assault of Annie, and later he in turn charged Richard with two counts of extortion. The unravelling of their employment relationship derived in part from Annie's allegations and in part from Richard's response.

On 17 March 1898, Annie wrote to "my darling husband" that on the night before, Mr. Glenn had down come to the basement and asked her "if [she] was getting lonesome" and then "hauled" her over to her bed and asked her to give him "some play" for which he said he would give her a silk dress. She told her husband she had pushed Mr. Glenn off, given him a piece of her mind about her sense of self-respect and asked whether he had any respect for his own wife.[58] She ended the letter by asking her husband to "make some arrangement for us quitting here as I cannot stand anything like that but [added] I suppose we will have to do for the best."[59]

In his reply to "my darling wife" in a letter dated 27 March, Richard counselled Annie in terms that reflected his own subordinate position and indebtedness to Glenn:

> …[N]ow you can depend that if ever such a thing occurs with Glenn while we are under his employ just as soon as we get in position I will prosecute him as far as I can under all circumstances from this on if he ever attempts to try such a low degrading thing like that as he has tried this time[.] [I]f I had not owed Glenn $125.00 and he agreed to take it out in work I would not stay one day longer but I want to pay him that before I leave him as I have agreed to. Glenn may not try such a thing again with you.… .[60]

But in April she said it had happened again, recording the incident in a small notebook: "He said he had not had any for some time and that I might take pity on him and give him some play as he called it."[61]

On 15 November 1898, Richard Crispen laid an Information and Complaint against Joseph Glenn for two counts of indecent assault on Mrs. Annie Crispen. The hearing into Crispen's Information took place on 25 November before two local justices of the peace, George Thompson and Thomas E. Donnelly. The story of what transpired between June and November and the explanation for why it took so long for Mr. Crispen to lay the charge does not appear in this court file. A fuller, if undoubtedly partial, account of the June to November period would have to wait until a later hearing involving a different criminal prosecution against Crispen himself.

At Glenn's hearing Annie recounted under oath the two incidents. She also said she had spoken of the assault with NWMP Sergeant Fyffe. When asked in cross-examination whether she had cried out on either occasion, she answered no. When asked if she had said anything of the assaults to Mrs. Glenn, she also answered that she had not done so, as "Mrs. Glenn was always cranky."[62] She admitted that if she had cried out, it would have been possible for others upstairs in the house to hear. She also admitted that she had heard something about a deal between Glenn and her husband for a team [of horses]. Richard testified at the same hearing that he "too had spoken to Sgt. Fyffe about 'the affair.'"[63] Despite the two references to Fyffe, there is no indication that the NWMP sergeant did anything in response to a complaint against Mr. Glenn.

Glenn categorically denied Mrs. Crispen's allegations of indecent assault. He might have thought that, having denied under oath the accusations made by Annie and Richard Crispen, he would not be committed to stand trial—that his word would carry more weight than that of his former servants, the farm labourer and the domestic. Perhaps he thought he could count on his relationship with George Thompson, who was one of the justices of the peace presiding at the hearing. Nevertheless, at the end of the hearing, he was committed for trial and released on his recognizance of $100.00 together with a surety in the same amount.

For his part, Richard had testified that the reason he "did not take proceeding when my wife first told me was because we were hard up... ."[64] It is possible that Richard had been cowed at the prospect of confronting the older man, their employer. His early response and actions suggest as much. However, a second hearing, this time seeing Richard Crispen accused of extorting Glenn, advanced a different story.

The next day, 26 November, Glenn laid an Information and Complaint against Richard Crispen for two counts of extortion.[65] The "Glenn vs Crispin" hearing, also before Justices of the Peace Thompson and Donnelly, took place on 28 November. For this hearing, Glenn had marshalled several former employees as witnesses, some of whom testified that they had either heard Crispen refer to a settlement he had made with Glenn or of the words he said in their presence.

The extortion prosecution of Crispen was based on a letter and a conversation that followed. In a letter marked "Exhibit A" in the Joseph Glenn file (not the Richard Crispen file), Crispen wrote to Glenn, "Kindly call at my place by the $15^{th}$ of Sept or I will shove you as far as the law will put you if you do not come and have a settlement with me. You thought you were making a great fool of me by making the statements you made to me [–] if we do not have a settlement by that time you may stand the consequences."[66]

The second count relied on a conversation between the two men that took place in the presence of others on 17 September, in front of a livery stable in Indian Head. Glenn said that he had ended the Crispens' employment at the end of August, paid him for services rendered, and that Crispen had taken "stuff" from the farm for which he owed Glenn. Richard's response to this asserted indebtedness ($67.90) gave rise to the second count of extortion. Crispen is said to have replied, "I'll tell you what I'm going to do as you have indecently assaulted my wife[:] unless you give me a clear receipt for what you have me charged with I'll push you as far as the law will allow."[67] Glenn's reply: "I told him he was a low lifed brute and if he was worth it I would smash him right now" and walked away.

Under cross-examination by Mr. Hamilton (presumably Crispen's counsel), John Shannon, Glenn's former employee, elaborated on how the exchange ended:

> Glenn replied to him [,] ["] you miserable brute if you were worth touching I would tramp you in the street. ["] I can't say whether the words Glenn says he used were used or not, I have not talked to Mr. Glenn about the evidence to be given. I can swear positively that Crispen said to Glenn unless he gave him a receipt for what he owed him he would push him as far as the law would go.[68]

During his deposition at the extortion hearing, Glenn also advanced his theory (and defence) of the indecent assault charges for which he had been committed to stand trial. Once again before Justices of the Peace Thompson and Donnelly, Glenn made a lengthy deposition. He swore under oath that he and Crispen spoke on 23 June "about the matter of the indecent assault."[69] Glenn suggested that he took the lead in the encounter, confronting Crispen: he asked Richard "if he had circulated the report" that he, Glenn, had indecently assaulted Mrs. Crispen. Glenn testified that Richard admitted doing this because his wife had told him it had happened. However, when Glenn proposed that they go together to speak with Mrs. Crispen, Richard apparently told Glenn "it was unnecessary" as he said that his wife had denied the assault, that she had made it up in an attempt to get her husband to bring her out to the farm. Glenn said he pressed Richard further, accused him of spreading the story that Glenn had given him a team of horses "to settle the matter." Again, Glenn said that Richard admitted it but said it was a lie. Glenn said that he offered to have a settlement and "let him go" but that Richard "pleaded to remain the balance of the year," that he would tell the others what he had just admitted and said that Glenn "would have no more trouble." Glenn added that a couple of days after this conversation, Crispen approached him at the farm and told him, "he had had a [racket?] with his wife, saying he would teach her to tell him a lie, he said she said it was for the purpose of getting moved out from town to the farm and that he had given her a G -D licking for it."[70] At the end of the hearing, Crispen was committed to stand trial on the two extortion charges.

On 10 December 1898, Crown Prosecutor T.C. Johnstone indicted Joseph Glenn on two counts of indecent assault upon Annie Crispen. At his trial only two days later, Glenn, unsurprisingly, was acquitted. The court record is silent as to the evidence led at trial. On that same day, 12 December, Johnstone indicted Richard Crispen on two counts of extortion. Again, the evidence at trial is not in the court record. Crispen was convicted, his sentence deferred by Judge Hugh Richardson, and he was released on a recognizance of $200.00, with his older brother William acting as surety in the same amount. Despite the serious nature of the offence of extortion, it may be that Richardson expressed his own thoughts about the weightiness of Crispen's crime through the light sentence he imposed. For its part the local newspaper, *The Regina Leader*, opined that Glenn had faced a "foul charge" that was "scandalously untrue, and Crispin [sic] narrowly escaped severe penalty for attempted blackmail; he was let go on a suspended sentence."[71]

In 1912, Joseph Glenn, still a prosperous farmer and businessman, was elected as a Conservative member of the Saskatchewan Legislative

Assembly. He served as a Member of the Legislative Assembly for nine years. Richard Crispen was then serving in a different public institution, having been convicted in another matter of perjury and fabrication of evidence and sentenced to twelve years. The *Regina Leader* chortled its delight and recalled the earlier "foul charge" against Glenn whilst incorrectly reporting that Crispen had been "given a heavy sentence" for that offence.[72]

## *Conclusion*

The cases in the Territorial court records challenge me to revisit my own approach to conducting research on gender relations, patriarchal relations, familial relations in law—or, at least, remind me to set aside any assumption that gender and patriarchy are anywhere but everywhere.

The court records I study offer evidence of the complex nature of patriarchy and its constant if somewhat uneven relationship to law. The cases in this chapter reveal different patriarchal familial relations. Not every patriarch or patriarchal right prevailed. In this chapter, the parental loyalty of the Pocha parents' words was rebuffed by a jury determined to acquit their son-in-law notwithstanding the judge's charge for a conviction. Wilson and Crispen, the two husbands who criminally prosecuted other men, failed in court. Finlay, the aggrieved husband who took matters into his own hands, was acquitted by a jury. Only Richard Crispen was convicted of extortion for his bombast toward his employer, the man he accused of indecently assaulting his wife.

And, as for the women—Mrs. Finlay, Mrs. Wilson, Mrs. Crispen, and even the invisible Mrs. Glenn—the results were mixed at best. For these women, the public accounts of their intimate and familial lives must have been a dreadful experience. Florence Wilson offered a brave account of her relationship with husband and lover and, in the end, the criminal charge against her lover was dismissed. However, even as she stood up to law, Florence Wilson was in the hands of more powerful institutions: marriage and motherhood. One hopes that she was able to cherish the memory of the courage of her words.

Perhaps no case more than Annie Crispen's illustrates the concern and argument of this chapter about the importance of patriarchal relations—as power and ideology—in these legal cases of "improper intimacies." Annie turned to her husband with a complaint that their employer had abused her. His response was to say nothing, do nothing, because of their (or his) indebtedness to the man who had given them work (and paid them as a couple). Despite Crispen's bravado, that he would push Glenn as far as the law would allow, Glenn ended the employment relationship, likely evicted them from the house on the farm, and cleared part but not all of Richard Crispen's indebtedness to him. Richard, with a pregnant wife, started a new job still in debt to the man whom his wife said had sexually interfered with her twice.

Richard had gone to law, armed with his wife's words, as well as his own. Glenn's power (and resources) were surely determinative of the path to court and the conclusion. When Richard appeared to have secured an interim victory, Glenn also went to law. He did not pursue a claim for defamation, libel, or slander, but rather a tit-for-tat criminal prosecution for extortion. He pulled out all the stops and "smashed" Crispen, not in the street but in court. The asymmetrical nature of their respective patriarchal power, in which class power clearly trumped familial for a working-class patriarch and his wife, could not have been clearer.

Equally, the importance of "unexpected" legal places where gender-related and patriarchal relations can be found is further demonstrated by Joseph Glenn's prosecution of Richard Crispen and by Jack Cameron's prosecution of George Finlay. The deeper story of "improper intimacies" emerges from the cases of extortion and malicious damage to property. Had I not looked more broadly and more closely in the court records, I would have missed them, and others.

CHAPTER 10

# Civil Law, Mental Capacity, and Masculinity in Transnational Context

*Emma Chilton and James Moran*

In an early nineteenth-century New Jersey trial, Dr. James Kennedy was asked to testify to the mental state of his patient, Philip Lerch. Was Lerch "of sound and disposing mind and memory"?[1] Dr. Kennedy responded, "I can't answer that question. I am not sufficiently acquainted with his money matters to answer it."[2] On the face of it, it is striking to see a medical professional downplaying his medical expertise in his assessment, especially since Dr. Kennedy had been Lerch's attending physician during his "lunacy." Why did this doctor think that finances were the area in which a man demonstrated mental capacity? Can this emphasis on business capacity be surprising when we remember the extent to which a man's status has been historically tied to economic power?

The intersections of civil law and mental capacity as played out in court settings in Ontario and New Jersey offer an exceptional vantage from which to evaluate family, justice, intimacy, and masculinity in transnational perspective. In his influential book *Manliness and Masculinities in Nineteenth-Century Britain*, John Tosh argues that certain "enduring masculinities" can be identified in nineteenth-century England, such as male household authority and "the sexual rite of passage of young men on the threshold of authority."[3] Tosh argues that, as forms of enduring or "resilient masculinity," these two aspects of male behaviour "persisted through substantial changes in class formation between 1750 and 1850."[4] The structure of lunacy investigation law that developed in England over several centuries and that was imported successfully into colonial settings like Upper Canada/Ontario and New Jersey likewise reinforced forms of resilient masculinity of the sort described by Tosh—namely, rational self-conduct and the responsible management of personal capital.[5] However, somewhat paradoxically, lunacy investigation law supported these forms of enduring masculinity by applying legal power to scrutinize and discipline male authority.

The legal archive upon which this chapter is based is assembled from a series of mid-to-late nineteenth-century civil suits heard in New Jersey (US) and Ontario (Canada).[6] For both jurisdictions, the legal cases centre on the relationship between property ownership and mental capacity. In Ontario, the court considered whether individuals had the mental competence or testamentary capacity to make legal documents. Most of the Ontario cases examined here concerned documents made at the end of life (i.e., wills). In New Jersey, the court cases (civil trials in lunacy) considered the mental competence of individuals to govern themselves and their property—to decide whether or not they were *non-compos mentis*.[7] In both places, tests of mental capacity were based on procedures, legal paperwork, case law, and statutes informed by an English legal tradition that stretched back to the fourteenth century.

The English law of lunacy investigation, originating as part of the King's rights over the property of the mentally alienated, developed through the Court of Wards and subsequently the Chancery Court into a sophisticated legal mechanism which, by the eighteenth century, greatly influenced the way that madness was understood and responded to in England.[8] As part of the English colonial inheritance, this body of law was transplanted successfully throughout the English Empire, taking root in colonies such as New Jersey and Upper Canada (Ontario).[9] The trials of *testamentary capacity* and of *non-compos mentis* that emerged and developed in English colonies and post-colony jurisdictions thus formed part of "law's empire,"[10] that massive body of law that consolidated and reinforced European rule in colonial and post-colonial contexts.[11] The mid-to-late-nineteenth-century court cases in Ontario and New Jersey under consideration in this chapter reflect a relatively mature stage in the development of lunacy investigation law—one that still drew heavily on its English antecedents, though it had adapted to the context of mainly rural communities largely populated by settlers of European origin.[12]

Lunacy investigation law, whether in the form of testamentary capacity or *non-compos mentis* trials, represented contests over property in which the rational decision-making power of (mainly) men was thrown into question.[13] In these trials, wills and other legal documents reflected the author's authority over how their property was to be distributed amongst family members. On the grounds that a man did not have mental capacity to govern himself at the point of making a certain legal document, his authority was challenged and, in many cases, subordinated. The Ontario testamentary capacity cases questioned and scrutinized the rational decision-making powers of a man's property distribution towards the end of his life, a challenge to masculine identity that struck at the heart of propertied male authority. Similarly, New Jersey's lunacy trials involved men whose mental capacity to govern themselves and their property was challenged at various stages of adulthood. In these cases, if found to be *non-compos mentis*, a guardianship process ensued in which two committees were established—one to take over the management of a man's person and the other to manage his property. In nineteenth-century New Jersey, the process of guardianship was managed through the orphan's court, further signalling the infantilization of male authority. Both legal processes, designed to maintain the integrity of property in the face of irrational behaviour, marked a severe blow to male control and masculine identity, regardless of the court's final decision. In New Jersey and Ontario, mental incapacity cases and masculinity informed one another in colonial settings until well past the mid-nineteenth century.[14]

The intimacy of relationships between property-owning men (as heads of households, as brothers, as sons, etc.) and women (as wives, as sisters, as daughters, etc.) and, more rarely, legal contests over women's property in the face of female mad behaviour, helped to construct and perpetuate a "hegemonic masculinity" of the sort described by Raewyn Connell and others. In a recent overview of this concept, Connell and J.W. Messerschmidt developed a "renovated" analysis that allowed for a broader consideration of the "historical construction and reconstruction of hegemonic masculinities,"[15] and that took into account "the agency of subordinated groups," as well as "the mutual conditioning of gender dynamics and other social dynamics."[16] Drawing on the work of Lynne Segal, Mark C. Carnes, Clyde Griffen, and John Tosh, Robert Rutherdale and Peter Gossage note that "masculinity histories are plural and relational, even as they apply to the masculine power men exert over other men."[17] Put another way, "masculinity carries a heavy ideological freight, and…it makes socially crippling distinctions not only between men and women, but between different categories of men—distinctions which have to be maintained by force, as well as validated through cultural means."[18]

The study of masculinity, intimacy, madness, and the courts in New Jersey and Ontario certainly fits well within this updated conceptualization of hegemonic masculinity. Cases from both New Jersey and Ontario highlight women's subordinate position to men in the structure of property ownership and law, which is a major assumption about masculinity. These civil court cases also highlight the relationships between "different categories of men" in masculinity's formation and preservation. In nineteenth-century *non compos mentis* and testamentary capacity trials, the complex relationships that harbour and shape masculine identity come into view in illuminating ways. The precise contours of masculine identity that lunacy investigation law helped to perpetuate were shaped by the nuances of history, place, and culture.

In the three sections that follow, the details of several court cases that took place between 1837 and 1885 are considered for what they reveal about the intersections of masculinity, intimacy, family, and the courts. The first section explores how certain core male attributes connected to success in nineteenth-century North America were reinforced by lunacy investigation law. The second section assesses the intimate social relationships of the household, how they informed the decision to use the courts to assess mental capacity, and how they affected court proceedings. The third section examines how contests over property and rational thought played out in the male civil court system of juries, judges, and lawyers.

## *Health and Work*

Physical strength and "vigour of body" were central to manliness in the Victorian period. In England, physical strength and virtue were mutually imbricated, with physical qualities such as being "sturdy" and "robust" carrying moral connotations.[19] Strength and virtue enjoyed an even closer association in the popular image of the colonies, the lands of "enhanced masculine vigour"[20] in which men could expect liberation from circumstances threatening to their manliness. In such a context, "to be weak was to be less than a man."[21] In our court cases, there is a clear association between physical health and capacity, though judges displayed a more nuanced understanding of this association than did plaintiffs and their lawyers.[22] The plaintiffs in one Ontario case claimed that the testator "was so weakened by [physical] suffering...that he could not and did not understand any matter of business," including the business of distributing his property.[23] In this example, there is a clear connection between physical disability and business incapacity.

The commercialization of society during the Victorian period saw professions and businesses supplant land ownership as areas of financial success. This change was echoed by a shift from an aristocratic to a bourgeois sense of manliness. John Tosh describes it as a "[t]ransition from masculinity as reputation to masculinity as interiority."[24] An individual man's "self-control, hard work, and independence" were emphasized rather than his aristocratic connections.[25] Victorian culture emphasized supposedly male characteristics such as rationality, constancy, and activeness.[26] According to historian Stephan Collini, "to be known as a man of character was to possess the moral collateral which would reassure potential business associates or employers."[27] Collini argues that men consciously and unconsciously drew upon their gender roles for personal or economic advancement in the nineteenth century.

In the cases studied for this chapter, a challenge to a man's mental capacity was, in effect, a challenge to his sovereignty and the sovereignty of his property. To maintain sovereignty over themselves and their property, men had to maintain a display of rational behaviour and business capacity. Failure to manage property and assets, make sound financial decisions, and run a farm successfully were cited as evidence of incapacity in petitions and judgements alike.[28] In cases with women property owners, business savvy was similarly cited as indicative of capacity.[29] Failed business capacity was so integral to understandings of mental incapacity that every lunacy petition in New Jersey and Ontario stated *pro forma* that the person under suspicion "has been so far deprived of his reason and understanding that he is rendered altogether unfit and unable to govern himself or to manage his affairs."[30] The fact that business capacity was so embedded in the bureaucracy of lunacy trials is indicative of the extent to which business functionality was associated with mental capacity. In the New Jersey case we cited at the outset, when a medical professional witness was asked his opinion about whether his patient was "of sound and disposing mind and memory," he answered as previously noted: "I can't answer that question. I am not sufficiently acquainted with his money matters to answer it."[31] The emphasis on business capacity is unsurprising when we remember the extent to which a man's status was connected with economic function. However, in the era of mental health professionalization, it is striking to see a medical professional abdicating medical expertise.

In the 1845 New Jersey case of Lloyd Vanderveer, Vanderveer's brother petitioned for Vanderveer's property to be removed from his control. According to this brother, Vanderveer "at times refused for several days to take any food: He is also entirely indifferent as to his property—refuses to talk about his property or make any disposal thereof."[32] Vanderveer was institutionalized for a few months, and his affairs were placed in the care of his brother and cousin. After his institutionalization, he lived with various family members, including his mother and this brother, and finally with his own family "consist[ing] of a wife, and two children."[33] Vanderveer's brother saw him daily during that time, and said:

> I consider him now a man of sound mind, a little hypochondriac upon the subject of his bodily health but a very little so. He is altogether capable of transacting business. Of this I have no doubt. His mind is clear and as capable [of doing] business as ever it was. I have conversed with him a good deal on the subject of his affairs and business and have had the best opportunities of forming an opinion with regard to the state of his mind and his capacity for reasoning. I think he might be safely entrusted with the management of his property and the transaction of business. He has been I think, for four or five months entirely capable of transacting business.[34]

Vanderveer's brother was not the only family member monitoring his recovery. According to Vanderveer's father-in-law:

> I was at his house a week from last Monday and conversed with him for some time upon business. Upon both these occasions, he understood himself perfectly well and his mind seemed clear. I consider him as capable of transacting business as he has been for the last five years, or in fact as long as I have known much about him. I think he might be safely entrusted with the management of his affairs and property. He has been living with his family and keeping house since about the first of April.[35]

A number of observations can be drawn from the testimony of Vanderveer's brother and father-in-law. The first is the connection drawn between his attitude towards his body and his capacity. Vanderveer's hypochondria was considered suspect, as it alluded to an unusual relationship with his body. It was not as threatening, however, as his earlier outright rejection of food, which was interpreted as a refusal to safeguard his physical health, and thus considered evidence of incapacity. On the other hand, Vanderveer's return to living with his wife and children indicated a certain measure of restored responsibility.

In this case, the petitions of the brother and father-in-law are striking in their display of masculine control, measure, and strength. Both of these men intervened when their struggling family member lost control, seemingly rescuing him through his confinement and rehabilitating him upon his release. The archival material highlights the contrast between the men in the family who could maintain control and the man who failed to do so. There also seems to be a kind of collective effort to retain family agency through any means necessary, including appealing to the court for the power to manage a brother's affairs while he was confined. In Vanderveer's case, the perspectives preserved in the archives do not betray the opportunism and competition amongst family members that we see in other cases.

In the 1854 New Jersey case of Philip Hutle, a petition was put forward to establish insanity exceeding one year. According to a brother-in-law, Hutle "does not seem to care for anything—[he] is afraid that his mother or sister will poison him and he is believed by all who know him to be insane and that he is constantly growing worse. He owns a house and is worth about $1000 as near as I can judge."[36] This case does not call into question any legal documents created or signed by Philip. Rather, Philip's relatives seem to have petitioned for him to be declared insane as a way of protecting themselves against future financial harm. His indifference was cited as a cause for concern—how could someone who "does not seem to care for anything" be expected to look after the interests of his family? Philip's sister and a different brother-in-law said:

> He is a shoe maker by trade...[and] before said time worked at his trade industriously and was saving and economical of his earnings...but that during the year before last Christmas he was

very irregular in his work and acted very frequently as a person insane: that he seemed to be afraid that his mother or some one in the house would poison his bread and seemed afraid to eat or drink…and since Christmas last he has scarcely worked at all that he lies in Bed a great part or all of the night…that he will not talk and avoids if he can seeing anybody…that he will not take the medicine which the doctor gives him and acts in all respects as if he had lost his mind and become insane.[37]

Again, in the case of Hutle we see concern over his refusal to take medicine, which can be interpreted as an abdication of his physical health. Antisocial behaviour, such as avoiding people, was also treated with suspicion. How could someone recognize and fulfill his manly obligations when he so clearly lacked a manly countenance? How could someone care for his dependents when he displayed an unnatural mistrust of them?

### *Family Relations*

In many cases, being incapable of acting in one's own financial interests was enough to inspire a relative to seek legal means of relief from an inappropriate or unadvised business decision made by a family member. A will's provisions and how it was judged gives us a window into societal expectations of how men related to their nearest and dearest. According to the judge in one case, "strangeness and anomaly in the provisions of a will are not per se grounds upon which the Court refuses to carry them out."[38] By this statement, the judge meant to say that the content of the will in question ought not to sway his assessment of its validity. However, some judges did quite the opposite, frequently referring to the provisions of legal documents in order to justify or void their legitimacy. For example, in the 1875 Ontario case of *Wilson v. Wilson*, the wife of the testator alleged that her husband's sister and lawyer exercised undue influence over the writing of his last will shortly before his death. The will privileged the financial wellbeing of the testator's mother and sister over that of his wife and unborn child. According to the judge, "it would be hard to conceive a more unlikely provision for a father to make advisedly."[39] The judge suggested that the court should invalidate the will because it was unlikely that the testator would knowingly neglect an unborn child. In this statement, the judge inferred that fathers ought to make greater provisions for their kin than for other family members, and held that upholding such an expectation was in the best interest of this father. The father's negligence or lack of awareness discredited his will. Wilson's mental incompetence had rendered him incapable of being a "responsible family man."[40]

Speculation on the rationale of a will's provisions also occurred in the 1866 Ontario case, *Martin v. Martin*.[41] In this case, the testator decided to prioritize providing for his youngest son instead of distributing his property evenly to all of his children. The judge defended the testator's decision. After all, the testator did not have the means to "give farms to all his children."[42] The judge also justified the priority given to the testator's youngest son, pointing out that this was the child "whom he was about to leave without the paternal care which all his other sons had enjoyed up to maturity."[43] This interpretation rings with incredulity: how could the other sons be so ungrateful for the in-kind gifts of their poor, hardworking father?

A closer look at the *Martin v. Martin* case shows an interesting flexibility of the courts in understanding a patriarch's role in the family. Martin's wife and his close friend, Mr. Starr, encouraged the testator to make a will when a mental weakness prevented him from doing so independently. The judge understood the interventions of these intimate relations as a good-willed effort to help him fulfill his familial responsibilities. According to the testimony of Mr. Starr:

> After some part of the will was drawn his wife and son [Warner] came into the room. I think he sent for them. They suggested some things, I believe, but I cannot give any particulars. I stayed outside of the room at this time...He got very weak before the will was finished, and his mind was wandering; I therefore suggested that the finishing of it should be postponed until next morning.[44]

According to his own testimony, the friend operated with a certain discretion: he did not put himself in the room with the family when the will was being made, but he did intervene when it was appropriate and necessary to do so. Mr. Starr's testimony suggests a kind of hierarchy of intimacy, where Martin's wife ought to have more privileged access to her husband than the husband's friend. Ultimately, Martin's sovereignty over his property is seemingly represented in his physical signature on the will. Apparently, Mr. Starr "raised [Martin] up in his bed," whereupon Martin "signed the will with his own hand."[45] In this symbolic moment, the testator's friend went as far as to physically enable the signing of the will, but the testator retained executive control. The court allowing for Mr. Starr's compensation for his friend's physical frailty seems to contrast previously explored examples of the connection between physical capacity and mental capacity; however, the context of this older man's deathbed is quite unlike the middle-aged environs of Vanderveer and Hutle.

Testimony was also given by Reverend Dr. Thornton, who was called upon by Mrs. Martin to act as a lawyer during the making of Martin's will. According to Reverend Dr. Thornton's testimony, sometimes the testator gave instructions for the will "without any suggestion." Other times "Mrs. Martin suggested the subject, and he endeavored to say what he wished done."[46] And, "Sometimes when he had difficulty in explaining himself he would say to Mrs. Martin 'you know.' She would then explain, and he assented."[47] In the judge's opinion, "it was surely natural that his wife, who was with him always during his illness and before, should understand him readily, though Dr. Thornton did not."[48] This deference to the wife's interpretation, both on the part of Reverend Dr. Thornton and the judge, suggests that an intimate relationship could lend a certain expertise to an understanding of another person's business affairs. The judge saw the widow as always acting in the best interests of her husband and rejected the plaintiff's claim that she exercised undue influence on the testator. In the judge's opinion, "she had a wife's faith in his justice and judgment...and made no attempt...to substitute her own wishes for his."[49] Nevertheless, he went on to ponder the futility of trying to regulate the involvement of wives in their husbands' affairs. Quoting a precedent case, he asked, "[w]hat law can decide what is the degree of influence which a wife can exercise over a husband sufficient to invalidate acts done under it?...Hundreds of wills have been made under the influence of wives, apparently unjust, sometimes towards children, sometimes towards relatives, &c."[50] Despite expressing confidence in Martin's widow, this is a cynical take on the role of wives generally.

In general, family members were trusted witnesses as long as judges inferred that they had the best interests of the family in mind. Testimony provided by close family members was given much weight, as we saw in the New Jersey cases of Lloyd Vanderveer and Philip Hutle. In *Ingoldsby v. Ingoldsby*, the judge noted: "It is a circumstance entitled to some weight, that the mother and brother of the testator, the former in constant, and the latter in frequent intercourse with him, and who could have no motive for supporting such a will as he was making, both thought him of sufficient capacity to make a will."[51] Here, the judge put forth two reasons for trusting these witnesses: that they were intimate relations of the testator, and that they did not seem to be acting out of self-interest. The judge was most impressed by the testator's brother, who "gave his evidence intelligently and dispassionately."[52] In the cases of Lloyd Vanderveer and Philip Hutle, an absence of passion was cause for concern. Here, it is the attribute of a reliable witness. Judges often expressed disappointment when family members were not able to give testimony. In *Martin v. Martin*, the judge said that it was "unfortunate" that the testator's widow died before the case went to court, as she "could probably have furnished important information on many parts of the case."[53] In this case, the judge was convinced of her credibility because he saw her as operating in the best interests of her family while her husband was alive.

Two further cases highlight how the courts regulated business decisions which threatened to harm the decision-makers themselves. The 1876 Ontario case *Watson v. Watson* follows a miserly old man who, apparently angry with his son Richard with whom he lived, transferred all of his property to another son, William. Shortly thereafter, frustrated by his new financial dependence on William, the father started a civil action to recuperate the property. The father claimed that at the time of the transfer he was suffering from a fit "of mental depression, during which he was not competent to transact intelligently his business."[54] William, for his part, claimed that his father "was as capable of judgment as at any time during his life," and that thus he should not be granted relief for the consequences of his decision.[55] William's legal counsel said that as William was the only child to take responsibility for the father's care, "it cannot be wondered at that the father desired to benefit [William] in preference to any of the other members of his family."[56] The father's legal counsel responded: "the improvidence of the transaction is alone sufficient to induce the Court to say it shall not be allowed to stand."[57] Ultimately, the judge declared the deed invalid, not "on the ground that the defendant exercised any undue influence" nor because "the plaintiff was incapable of understanding the nature of the act he was doing," but because the consequences of the act were not made clear to him, and his well-being was not secured as he "intended and expected."[58] The judge agreed with the father that he ought not to be held responsible for making sound decisions about his own financial well-being.

A somewhat parallel 1869 Ontario case, *Campbell v. Belfour*, investigates the debt repayments ninety-year-old Bethina Campbell made on behalf of her deceased son. When Campbell came to understand the "disaster" that two of her many repayments represented for her financial situation, she started a court action to recover the money spent.[59] After her death, her heirs continued with the lawsuit. The plaintiffs claimed that the woman was "in such a state of mental incapacity by reason of her age and infirmity, and of grief for the loss of her son, as to be incapable of understanding" the documents she signed, and that the documents ought to be declared invalid.[60] The judge decided that the one or two contracts that Campbell took on that were considered business "disasters" (unfavourable to her financial interests), were not cause enough to think that she was mentally incapable.[61] In the judge's opinion, an expensive gift given to one's child did not require the same "due deliberation, explanation and advice" required by an expensive gift given to someone else.[62] An irresponsible financial exchange may be invalidated if made outside of the family, but within the family it was deemed appropriate. The judge applied his opinion directly to the mother's payment of her son's debts: "If, therefore, I am to treat the note as a gift, it was the gift of a small proportion of her means, by a mother, to pay a creditor of her deceased son."[63] This case echoes the reinforcement of family priorities seen in *Wilson v. Wilson*. Here, legal authorities deemed it just that Campbell compromise her financial situation for a deceased child, while in *Wilson v. Wilson*, a man was criticized by legal authorities for failing to compromise his duty to other beneficiaries for the sake of an unborn child. In *The Purchase of Intimacy,* Viviana Zelizer explores the court's "complex process of matching certain forms of intimacy to particular types of economic transactions," a process that includes "discriminat[ing] sharply between appropriate and inappropriate matchings."[64] This process is in full view here, with the judge deciding that the transaction was valid, largely because of the particular mother-son relationship between the parties involved. Thus, he measured the weight of the intimacy of their relationship against that of the rationality of a business deal. The judge noted that he may have decided differently if Campbell was of a humbler station and education and if her decisions had been more disastrous. In his opinion, the court ought to award more protection to a woman less capable of making a good decision due to a lack of education.[65] The judgment in this case implied that every competent person of basic education was expected to be able to balance financial responsibility with family duty. It seems evident here and in other contexts that to issue a judgment required engagement with complex gendered hierarchies.

## *Intimacy, Court Relations, and Mental Capacity*

As the examples so far have demonstrated, the civil legal system played an important role in arbitrating intimate familial relationships that touched upon mental capacity and manliness in nineteenth-century Ontario and New Jersey. In the court cases under study, we have encountered people who were embedded in intimate contexts of family affairs, including those of a financial nature, that were personal, relational, and private. The appearance of these cases in court is intriguing. Legal documents, such as wills, deeds, and other contracts, are exceptionally formal expressions of relations between people. In studying lunacy investigation cases, we have peered into intimate spaces formalized through both the inking of contracts and the interpretation of those contracts in court. It is important that we not naturalize the archival material we are studying. In bringing family matters like these to court, individuals were requesting that the state arbitrate an intimate dispute. Family members brought each other to court because they desired, or thought that they required, state involvement.

In both Ontario and New Jersey, this intimacy of engagement with the law was, as with other legal investigations, an inevitable aspect of the public nature of legal inquiry through the chancery court. In the case of rural New Jersey, from the early nineteenth century, lunacy trials were often held in the taverns of local innkeepers—the makeshift courts of the day. These trials were publicly attended and, when a jury was included, twelve local property-owning men helped to adjudicate decisions that affected the everyday lives of people in their community. This formed a kind of regulatory legal arena in which the public, the jury and the legal experts all contributed. Ontario shared similar elements with its New Jersey counterpart. In Ontario, the chancery court was established in 1837 with a surprisingly "wide jurisdiction,"[66] which grew more broad still by the middle of the century. Until 1850 its activities were restricted to the town of Toronto but thereafter provision was made for cases to be heard in "such localities as the said Judges may consider necessary and expedient for the purpose of promoting as far as possible the local administration of Justice."[67] In Ontario, some cases were brought to a full trial while others were "decided by arbitrators" followed by "consent judgment from the Court."[68] Nevertheless, in both jurisdictions the authority of the legal process intersected with mental state and masculinity in significant respects.[69]

Although perhaps obvious, the legal authorities involved in the distribution of justice in cases of mental capacity during the period under study were men—from judges, to masters, registrars, lawyers, through to legal clerks.[70] This all-male legal administration certainly affected the response to legal cases, including those relating to mental capacity. The cases under study reveal direct examples of the effects of male authority in the legal process. For example, in the 1876 case of *Watson v. Watson* mentioned earlier in the chapter, after hearing testimony from both parties, Vice Chancellor William Proudfoot called the plaintiff in the case, Mr. Watson, before him to verify what he could not by sifting through the conflicting tangle of legal arguments. Proudfoot interviewed the seventy-five-year-old Watson, determining that "he was so deaf that questions were put to him in writing. He read them readily without spectacles and gave intelligent answers. He did not appear more infirm than persons of his age usually are."[71] Thus, in the opinion of the Vice Chancellor, Watson was old and deaf but suffered no mental incapacity. The problem, he concluded, was that Watson, "had come to live with [the] defendant [Watson's son], and expected to continue there,"[72] and Watson's son did not make the economic arrangement clear enough for his deaf father to understand.

Although Proudfoot claimed that he made his conclusion "from the whole evidence"[73] it is clear that his interview with Watson was the basis for his legal decision. Here, Proudfoot was acting as a kind of surrogate male authority in an attempt to force a family to treat their father in a manner in which he deserved in old age, despite the fact that Watson was clearly a disagreeable man to live with. Although this Vice Chancellor determined that there was no mental incompetence in this case, Proudfoot still stood in to rebalance a problem that he connected to Watson's declining faculties—in this case, his hearing. This aside, in Proudfoot's view Watson's masculinity was still very much intact, as evidenced by his familiarity with "legal phraseology"[74] and his mental intelligence to bargain once his physical impairment was taken into account.

In cases like this, judges and other legal authorities built understandings of mental capacity that were linked to community perceptions but that also reflected a professionally distinct view. As a part of the Chancery Court and the law of equity, male legal experts drew upon case precedent for examples and arguments to help them reason their way through cases they were tasked with resolving. As with other topics in law, over time, the layering of legal precedent through the judgements of male authority resulted in a body of expertise that was drawn upon to resolve cases of mental capacity. In Ontario and New Jersey, the body of legal precedent upon which early and mid-nineteenth century cases were considered was English and it stretched back into the early eighteenth century.

The Ontario case of *Ingoldsby v. Ingoldsby* stands out as a particularly good example of how precedent helped to establish a body of expertise in the courts' legal management of property, men, and masculinity. This was a classic case of a debate over the mental state of someone at the point of making a will. The will was contested by a family member (a son of the defendant) who was concerned that the will was allowing other family members to dispose of property in a way that compromised the plaintiff's interests. Complicating this case was the fact that Ingoldsby senior, who made the will, displayed erratic behaviour as a young man and was considered to be "eccentric" later in life. In his approach to the case, the Chancellor, John Spragge, drew on two English trial precedents that dealt with contested wills in the face of insane behaviour, but then had the following to say: "In giving my views of the case at the close of the argument, I proceeded upon the law as laid down in *Waring v. Waring* (a) and *Smith v. Tebbitt* (b.). I had not seen the latter case of *Banks v. Goofellow* (c.)."[75] Spragge proceeded to quote at great length from the wisdom of English judge Sir Alexander Cockburn and his expostulations on the *Banks v. Goodfellow* case. He concluded that Cockburn's long consideration of the possibility that a man could make a will during a sane period despite at other times being mentally incompetent was now the gold standard upon which similar cases would be judged.

This and other cases highlight the scales of masculine authority that are visible when taking chancery legal process into local and imperial context. The precedent upon which colonial and post-colony Chancery Court authorities drew in contexts like Ontario and New Jersey for their wisdom in cases of mental competence was located in the imperial centre—England—where the traditions of civil law were centuries old. The legal authority of notable men like Cockburn, who was Lord Chief Justice of Queen's bench in England at the time of the 1873 *Ingoldsby v. Ingoldsby* case in Guelph, Ontario, reminded local authorities like Spragge of the pecking order of intelligence on matters of law and mental capacity. Colonial officials might adjust legal wisdom emanating from the centre to suit the peculiarities of each case, but the power of English legal male authority over such decisions was clear enough.[76] In turn, legal authorities in Ontario and New Jersey used their experience and expertise to remind plaintiffs and defendants of their own importance through their judgments which inevitably did not conform to the interests of all participants in the legal process. All of the cases under study here and elsewhere demonstrate this linkage between English and colonial/post-colony legal power in relation to cases of mental capacity.[77]

## *Conclusion*

For historians in the twenty-first century, there are two ways in which lunacy investigation law reveals intimate struggles over masculinity. First, the purpose of the law itself—the removal of control from men over their property—compromised male authority and male identity. Second, the content of the law—the legal process, paperwork, testimony, and in some cases, the public nature of the trial—further emasculated those men who were under legal scrutiny. Moreover, these intimacies of masculinity reflect community, class, and gender dynamics that have been funneled through the state legal apparatus, thus complicating how we may read the legal archive that was produced. Finally, the voices of those men whose masculine credentials were in question were almost never preserved in the archive. Whether the subjects of these trials were still alive (as in the case of New Jersey civil trials in lunacy) or dead (as in the case of Ontario's trials of testamentary capacity), their contributions to the socio-legal construction of masculinity remains largely invisible from the records.

The system of expertise that male legal officials built through precedent in response to mental incapacity was, for the most part, inaccessible to the lay individuals and their families who were subject to the law. Judges wielded extraordinary power in their interpretation of the evidence laid before them relating to mental competence and male behaviour. Moreover, as the foregoing cases demonstrate, these legal decisions betrayed the arbitrary and at times contradictory ways in which masculinity was encoded into the legal process. Trials revealed a range of often competing evidence concerning male behaviour. Yet, despite multiple narratives of masculinity that legal investigations and trials generated, judges were remarkably consistent in their use of the law to reinforce the masculine qualities of rational self-conduct and the responsible management of personal capital.[78]

Characteristics of Victorian masculinity were also reinforced at the crossroads of civil law and community. Local perceptions of manliness and mental capacity informed legal decisions. The very public nature of much of the trial process, and the measures of manliness and mental capacity of witnesses with an intimate knowledge of those men whose mental capacity was being questioned, pulled the legal process inwards towards the everyday masculinities of local cultures. In Ontario and New Jersey, perceptions of manly behaviour in the community often reflected local concerns about physical strength and the capacity for effective hard work. Witnesses' perceptions of what it meant to be a man in mid-to-late nineteenth-century Ontario and New Jersey were ultimately judged by legal authorities who incorporated witness testimony into a body of expertise that stretched across the Anglo-American world. The recasting of local evidence into "legalese" created a professional language that would have been difficult for the average citizen of Ontario and New Jersey to comprehend. Nevertheless, trials of mental capacity reveal histories of intimacy, family, and justice that tied the masculinities of local community to those embedded in the transnational legal process in profound ways.

# PART 4

# *Marriage Regulation*

*Where domestic and sexual intimacies are concerned, regulating marriage has long been one of the primary roles of the state. In recent years, moral and cultural understandings of matrimony have broadened, and the influence of religious rules, rituals, and restrictions has receded in many jurisdictions, especially liberal democracies swept up in the secularization movement of the twentieth and twenty-first centuries. What more important topic could there be than marriage, then, to study from a legal, historical, and transnational perspective? The three contributors to this section do this in compelling ways, situating the institution of marriage squarely at the intersection of the intimate and the global. In the process, they reveal both the power of the state to police the boundaries of legal matrimony and the resolve of certain individuals—and certain couples—who actively challenged those boundaries.*

*The level of immigration to Australia in the nineteenth and early twentieth centuries makes it yet another place, like South Africa (Chapter 4) and Western Canada (Chapter 9), where people from across the globe assembled and formed sexual and domestic partnerships, legally and otherwise. As Mélanie Méthot shows in Chapter 11, the severe criminal sanctions against bigamy reveal the central place of heterosexual marriage in that country's official landscape of morality. The sheer number of bigamy cases (Méthot has found records for over 1,500) reveals something about the risk of marriage breakdown in Australia. But the close analysis of testimony and judgments as well as newspaper accounts for two especially well-documented cases opens a fascinating window onto the intimate worlds of women accused of breaking the rules in such a fundamental way.*

*Like Méthot, Ginger Frost (Chapter 12) and Gail Savage (Chapter 13) make use of legal sources while also drawing from multi-sited archives and non-traditional sources. These two chapters are also united in their focus on the contested identities of European women married to foreign nationals during the global conflicts of the twentieth century. By raising "difficult questions about the relationship between marriage and citizenship status, especially for wives," Savage articulates the central issue that animates and connects these two essays.*[1] *In Chapter 12, Frost examines the experience of British women married to German or Austrian men during the First World War. Although born and raised in the United Kingdom, these women became "enemy aliens" when the war began in 1914. Their husbands were subject to internment or even repatriation, meaning separation, the loss of a breadwinner, confiscation of property, and other legal and material challenges, the traces of which she has located in Home Office records, minutes of the Poor Law guardians, and elsewhere.*

*In Chapter 13, similarly, Savage recounts the particular problems of Soviet women who married foreign nationals during the Second World War. Authorities in Moscow resolved any ambiguity over the citizenship of these women by declining to recognize all such marriages and by refusing them permission to leave the USSR to join their foreign husbands. Individual cases documented in diplomatic archives, especially those of the British Foreign Office, reveal the suffering endured by women and men in these circumstances, but also their creativity and resourcefulness. Through newspaper coverage, some of these stories also entered the realm of public debate, generating strong criticism of the repressive Soviet regime, contributing to Cold-War tensions, and suggesting fascinating links between the intimate lives of these couples and the larger dynamic of contemporary international politics.*

# CHAPTER 11

# Bigamy Prosecutions in Victoria, Australia

## *The Press Coverage and the Case Files*

*Mélanie Méthot*

On a Saturday in April 1884, twenty-two-year-old George Adams married seventeen-year-old Amelia Coulson, the mother of his infant daughter. By 1890, the young couple had added two more children to their family. According to the official records, despite the spouses living in different towns, the Coulson-Adams couple had another three children together between 1893 and 1896.[1] Amelia's bigamy file reveals that under a completely different identity she married police constable Hugh O'Donnell in May 1892. A short month later, the groom informed authorities that his bride had committed bigamy. Local and distant newspapers picked up the story. Genealogists lose her trace until 1895 when the Public Service Board investigated the conduct of a warder named Walter Sydney Green. The Board alleged that Green was living with Amelia who had served a term of imprisonment for bigamy.[2] Two years later, Green came under investigation for the same allegations and once again Amelia's bigamy made it into newspapers.[3] George Adams, Amelia's legal husband, travelled 300 kilometres to Sale to testify against Green.[4]

In 1894 at age seventeen, Lily Strike married Edmund Charles Chalmers, a man a quarter of a century older than her and thrice a widower. Their union lasted barely two years. Civil registry reveals that Lily later married thirty-four-year-old Richard Henry Hammersley without first obtaining a divorce from Chalmers, thus opening her to a charge of bigamy.[5] The couple welcomed a daughter a mere seven months after their marriage.[6] Another daughter soon followed as well as two sons.[7] In

1905, Chalmers successfully filed for divorce and, three weeks after the case was heard, Hammersley denounced Lily's bigamy.[8]

I discovered Amelia Coulson and Lily Strike via the ample press coverage of their respective cases. Victorian courts prosecuted 241 bigamists between 1850 and 1906; nearly three quarters were men.[9] The Australian press mentioned every single case; a few of the bigamists even garnered more than fifty mentions. Amelia's and Lily's stories obviously appealed to a wide readership, since twenty-eight different newspapers reported on the case of Amelia, while Lily's saga appeared in the pages of thirty-one newspapers from a number of cities and small towns across Australia. Focusing on the legal troubles of the two women illuminates family and gender roles in Victoria at the turn of the twentieth century and showcases the two young women's agency.[10]

In this chapter, I analyze the discourses that emerged from both the print media and the legal case files. As Mary Anne Poutanen observes in Chapter 8 of this volume, court documents describe circumstances at specific moments. Although historians note the silences, we can still identify narratives even if (or because of) the courtroom and, as Shelley Gavigan reminds us in Chapter 9, this arena "is seldom fair or neutral terrain."[11] Even official civil documents, such as birth registrations, prove that individuals tried to construct a narrative conforming to social respectability. Husbands had a clear duty to provide for their wives and children, and with this responsibility came a certain authority. Amelia's and Lily's husbands described the independent spirit of their young spouses and their own husbandly attempts to control them. The press hesitated to ascribe guilt to a female bigamist, but when presented with incriminating facts, colonial inhabitants found it harder to sympathize with a mother who displayed a lack of maternal instinct. Comparing the reporting of Lily's divorce to the successive bigamy charge reveals different narratives: while newspapers did not hesitate to paint a negative portrait of the deserting wife in the divorce case, more articles sided with the accused in the bigamy inquiry. Through embellishment, omission, repetition, and other narrative devices, journalists crafted these stories to appeal to popular prejudices and readers' taste for a juicy story. Press reports and court testimony point to the resolve of the young women who abandoned their legal husband and followed their heart. If not necessarily in love with their newer spouse, the two young women nevertheless acted to escape their unhappy marriages.

### *Amelia Coulson: Marriage Expectations, Witness Testimony, and Press Reports*

Only a month after a woman calling herself Amelia Minnie Green married Constable Hugh O'Donnell, the new groom suspected his wife had committed bigamy and he informed the police. At the preliminary hearing, the Reverend Alexander Moore confirmed that he had officiated at Amelia's 1884 marriage and produced a document proving the father of the young bride had given his written consent.[12] In bigamy prosecutions, marriages had to be proven not only with official marriage certificates but often by the testimony of the celebrant and, if possible, of the two witnesses who had signed the registry. Spouses could not testify at trial until the *Crimes Act of 1891* introduced the possibility. The prosecution called on George Adams, Amelia's legitimate husband, to testify. He obliged, travelling with their three young children the sixty-five kilometres separating Geelong from Melbourne.

George's five-page deposition shows he was working as a labourer.[13] He confirmed he had married the defendant at her father's residence. He gave details of their married life, stating they "lived together as man and wife for about 6 years and 3 months." He mentioned the three children "born of the marriage." He acknowledged they "ceased to live together" fifteen months earlier, specifying that Amelia "had left me before and I allowed her back once after she had been away for 3 months." George's deposition exposes his wife's transgressions and highlights his authority as a husband. With all his paternal magnanimity, he "allowed" her back. He added that she again left after five weeks of cohabitation and did not return. He drew attention to the fact that: "The youngest child was 7 months old when she left home." George stressed that Amelia left on her own account, and he once more referred to paternal authority norms, emphasizing that "she left against my wish and she did not return home and I never saw her until last Monday in court." George's testimony suggests that while Amelia displayed her independent spirit by leaving her young family behind, going against normal expectations of motherhood, he, as head of the family unit, never relinquished his patriarchal authority.

George's answers to the cross-examination bring to light Australian society's expectations of marriage or, at the very least, what the defence attorney thought would work in convincing a judge not to indict. Unfortunately, the deposition does not include the questions Amelia's defence attorney asked. Rather, George's statements follow one after the other as if they were recited without interruption. George first referenced his treatment of Amelia: "I did not illtreat my wife as I know of." With a touch of humility, he said: "I was a medium man. I always provided her with sufficient food." The obligation of a husband to provide for his wife seemed to be at the forefront of the attorney's mind, establishing women's economic dependency. The next answer reinforces what others have argued in terms of the medicalization of childbirth. George replied: "I did not think she required a Dr. for any of her three children, she did not ask for one."[14] George acknowledged Amelia's autonomy when he specified "she did not ask for one," implying that if she did, he would have obliged. If George retained the prerogative of final decision-making, the reference to his wife's desires exhibits a degree of input.

Juxtaposing George's statements with the press accounts, one can infer the questions the defence attorney was firing at him. Insinuating that Amelia needed a doctor after the birth of one child, the defence attorney may have then proceeded to needle George: Wasn't she in the hospital after the birth of your last child? To which George replied: "She went to the Geelong hospital being sick with rheumatic fever." The following question could have been: Didn't she return to live with her parents after the birth of the first child? George said: "After the birth of the first child she did not go to her people." Next the defence attorney may have asked something akin to: Isn't it true that her father came to see you and discussed your treatment of her? To which George replied: "Accused's father never complained to me about my conduct to her. Up to the time she first left me, I looked upon my wife as a straightforward honest woman. After she had left me about a fortnight, I met my wife with a man named Green." George's testimony paints himself as a loving husband and emphasizes Amelia's lack of maternal instinct (the youngest child having been only seven months), misplaced agency (she habitually left him against his will), and lack of moral character (she was with another man).

The final part of the cross-examination is the most startling. George admits freely and, it seems, without shame, that he tried to stab his wife and was only unsuccessful because of a technicality. "I never stabbed her," he affirmed, only to admit in the next breath: "I tried to stab her, but I missed her. I tried to stab her with a carving knife after she was caught with Green by her sister near the International Hotel. Green got away over a fence" (painting his rival as a coward) "and I forced the accused into a cab and drove out to her sister's place" (admitting he used force). "Nobody was present when I attempted to stab my wife but she and me. The carving knife went through a locket she was wearing at the time." Nothing came out of his admission in court of assault with a deadly weapon. Perhaps people felt George was justified in his response; after all, his wife had committed adultery. His testimony concludes with George confirming: "I knew about her second marriage when she was arrested." Despite living in different cities, George rapidly found out about his wife's transgressions. Amelia's and George's inner circles visibly intersected. Although he admitted knowing that Amelia had committed bigamy, George did not lodge a complaint.

The deposition of Thomas Brady, George's brother-in-law, gives a better sense of the defence's legal strategy. Amelia's attorney claimed that her first marriage was invalid because, as a minor, Amelia had not received her father's consent. Her counsel argued that Henry Coulson's written consent was a forgery. It was a long shot since the couple had lived in the vicinity of Coulson's house for more than six years and their union had yielded three children. The *Victorian Law Reports* devoted space to the strategy:

> At the trial her counsel proposed to adduce evidence that the consent produced at the time of her first marriage (as required by sec 14 of the *Marriage Act* 1890) was a forgery, and that the prisoner believed at the time that she entered into the second marriage that this forged consent rendered her first marriage invalid, and that she had reasonable ground for thus believing, inasmuch as her husband had told her after the marriage that the marriage was invalid.[15]

Justice Higinbotham refused to admit the evidence on the grounds that, "even if true, it would not exonerate the prisoner."[16] The Chief Justice was decidedly skeptical of Amelia's claim, especially since she lied profusely on her second marriage licence, proving she knew she had something to hide. Amelia could have been desperately hiding from her violent husband; however, neither legal nor press narratives suggests that interpretation.

The brother-in-law testified that the marriage took place at the house of the bride's mother, and also that her father had left the house the preceding Monday. The detail suggests that although marriage played a significant role in bringing respectability to families, the actual celebration did not require the presence of important members of the family, unless the father really did not give his consent. When cross-examined by the prosecution, Brady vouched for George: "Adams was Secretary to the Laborer's Union. He is a very kind man." George's sister testified next, confirming that, as official witness to the ceremony, she signed the registry. She added: "I remember the first child was born."[17] Shorter than George's statement, the two-page testimony of Amelia's second husband also shines a light on some aspects of turn-of-the-twentieth-century marriage in Victoria. Hugh O'Donnell stated first that he had known the accused for about six months. He mentioned the confusion over Amelia's names, declaring she went by the name of Clark but married under Green, both false names. The prosecution called on the two persons who witnessed the union. They affirmed they were present and signed the marriage certificate. It seems they did not know the groom or the bride. In sum, the depositions and exhibits suggest that the defence would have a hard time claiming victimhood for this bigamist who had abandoned her husband and children. The most damning evidence was the second marriage certificate: notwithstanding the numerous lies, it directly linked Green to Amelia. A jury found her guilty and Chief Justice Higinbotham sentenced her to twelve months imprisonment with hard labour.[18] Witnesses painted Amelia as an active agent rather than as a passive victim of a violent husband, albeit an agent who ran into the arms of another man.

The June preliminary hearing depositions outline the contours of the August trial. Bigamy dossiers rarely include trial transcripts. As Fabienne Giuliani's essay (Chapter 15) in this volume also shows, journalists have often functioned as informal court reporters, taking down the testimony verbatim and even noting audience reactions. They mentioned when members of the gallery fainted (generally women), sobbed, or showed some sign of emotion, or when the audience laughed, hissed, or applauded. The press reports thus provide tantalizing details about courtroom activity. Still, one has to decipher facts from impressions. The reporters all heard the same thing or read the same court report but tended to digest the information differently. Journalists catered to their personal bias, or even took artistic license, adding or changing details for dramatic effect. In three instances, newspapers printed "O'Donnell was in a frantic state when he discovered that his wife had a husband living."[19] *The Age* reported the opposite: "He was not much hurt by what had happened. He laid the information because he conceived it to be his duty as constable to do."[20]

While the accuracy of the reporting is open to question, bigamy coverage nonetheless shows that journalists lingered around police stations and court houses, reporting every step of criminal procedures. O'Donnell informed authorities of his wife's bigamy on 11 June 1892. Over the next few days, even before depositions were recorded, newspapers shared details of the case. Eight newspapers related Amelia's bigamy in their 13 June edition, five others covered the story on the fourteenth, while both the *Bendigo Advertiser* and *Argus* published a second account on that day. The story made it into papers published in New South Wales, Western and South Australia. By 21 June, ten more papers had picked up the story. Some newspapers included very little. The *Sydney Daily Telegraph* opted to report (wrongly) that for the marriage performed at St. Francis Church, the accused had not signed the marriage certificate, prompting the defence to ask for a discharge.[21] Other papers devoted more space to the case and as a result some common themes emerge from the coverage.

Most newspapers claimed that the union of Amelia and George produced two children before George testified that they had, in fact, three living children. Few were as judgmental as *The Age*, which printed: "The mother deserted both husband and offspring about two years ago and came to Melbourne." Instead, most included the information matter-of-factly: "The accused was married to George Adams at Geelong in 1884, and there were two children by the marriage."[22] Throughout the different stages of the proceedings, writers referred to Amelia's youth and sometimes to her beauty. Her occupation as a barmaid was no longer featured once the depositions were taken, nor the possible defence of insanity. From the legal file, we know the defence contested the validity of the father's written consent. Journalists, however, focused on the lack of signatures on the marriage certificates.

Contrary to the pre-trial coverage, no themes stand out in the fifteen post-trial accounts. Five newspapers mentioned that Amelia deserted her husband, four talked about the children, and two revisited George's attempted stabbing. Even after the jury found Amelia guilty, the *Ballarat Star* could not bring itself to blame the young female bigamist, concluding its short summary with: "Her defence was that she thought her first marriage was illegal, as it was performed without her father's consent. According to the evidence, her first husband, Adams, had beaten her cruelly, trying to stab her on one occasion with a carving knife."[23] The *Geelong Advertiser*, the local paper from the married couple's official residence, is the only paper alluding to troubles that George may have had with the law. The article provides what seem like verbatim questions and answers:

> Mr. Smith [defence counsel]: Did you get into difficulties with the police?
> Witness: What do you mean[?]
> His Honour: I am glad to say that it is now made the duty of the judge not to permit vexatious questions.
> Witness: I have never been in gaol; if that's what you mean.
> Mr. Smith: Were you absent under compulsion from home in custody of the police?
> His Honour: Don't answer that. I hold it to be a vexatious question.
> Mr. Smith: Did you supply a doctor upon the occasion of the birth of your first child?
> Witness: No[.]
> Mr. Smith: Did you ever supply a nurse?
> Witness: Yes, one of the best nurses in the colony...[24]

Allusions to brushes with the law may have been enough to cast a shadow of doubt on George's good character. The next day, however, the same paper changed its tone, providing a summary highlighting that the two marriages were proven. It explained that the defence's strategy was to argue the first marriage was not valid because it was performed without the consent of the bride's father. By adding the judge's comments, the paper abandoned the previous day's unsympathetic tone toward the legal husband: "The Chief Justice, in passing sentence, said that when the prisoner went through the second marriage, she must have known she had something to conceal or she would not have given a false name." The reporter inserted: "Mrs. Adams appeared a good deal staggered by the sentence, but after a brief struggle she regained the mastery of her features and seemed quite tranquil and composed as she was escorted from the dock."[25] In this last account, Amelia no longer appears as a frail victim, but more as a woman in control.

*The Age* included most of what one reads in the depositions with few mistakes.[26] The court reporter provided features not available in the original deposition regarding the courtship between Hugh and Amelia. One wonders if the details are accurate or simply another journalistic flourish. The reporter wrote: "[O'Donnell] did not see her after that until she telephoned to him to see her at the Tower Hotel and he did so." This detail reinforces the image of an assertive woman who pursued O'Donnell. Also new to the story, O'Donnell testified that he "was married on the Thursday night, and on the Friday morning the accused went away to Warragul."[27] The *Argus* put a different spin on the courtship, stating: "When she was being wooed by O'Donnell," taking away the agency *The Age* gave Amelia. *The Argus* also specified that when she was arrested, Amelia was in warder Green's company, emphasizing her moral failings.[28]

Clearly, newspapers reported information very differently, sometimes wrongly, other times conforming to a bias. The popularity of one "fact" does not make it "truer," but it does indicate where public interest lay. In her role as Mrs. George Adams, Amelia Coulson was a mother of three young children who had failed to meet the expectations of motherhood. She proved she had no maternal instinct by "abandoning her three children, one of whom was only seven months old."[29] For this, perhaps even more than for her adultery, she deserved to serve a sentence of hard labour in prison.

The civil record confirms Amelia knew what she was doing. Although living with Green, she identified George as the father of her three other children.[30] Amelia understood that she was still George's legal wife even if she no longer lived with him. She likely adopted a completely new identity after the Public Board investigated Green's conduct a second time, which would explain why we lose track of her in the records.

### *Lily Strike: Marriage Expectations, Divorce, Bigamy Files, and Press Reports*

First married in 1894 to the widower Edward Charles Chalmers, young Lily Strike Chalmers stayed with her much older husband less than two years. In 1896, she wed Richard Hammersley, with whom she would have five children. It was only when her legitimate husband petitioned for a divorce in 1905 that Richard informed authorities of Lily's offence. If the coverage of Amelia's case started with a portrait of the offender as victim and deteriorated with time, Lily experienced the opposite. Dealing first with the divorce proceedings, the press reported the outlook of a deserted husband seeking to break the legal bonds uniting him to his undisciplined wife. It was only when the bigamy charge materialized that newspapers explored the circumstances of the marriage breakdown and painted Lily in a different light.

The divorce file confirms that Chalmers successfully obtained a divorce from Lily in 1905.[31] The decree was granted on the grounds that Lily had left Chalmers without just cause or excuse. Her husband refers in his affidavit to his own mobility, working first at the hotel in town, then at the City Brewery in Bendigo for about twelve months before he left in March 1896 for Western Australia and finally came back to Victoria in September 1898. He is precise about his movements and even more so when he describes his young wife's actions: "After the said marriage we lived together until Easter 1895 at the said hotel, during that time I several times found her kissing other men and remonstrated with her. She said she would do as she liked." Chalmers paints the image of a not so virtuous woman, but at the same time of a feisty girl who stood up to him despite her very young age (or because of it!). Regardless of his mention of "remonstrances," one does not see him as an authoritarian husband. He then adds:

> On one occasion about Christmas 1894 I went into a room in the hotel and as I came in, I saw a man whom I could not recognize disappear out of another door apparently holding up his trousers with his hands and the said Lily Chalmers was standing up. I then suspected that she had improper relations with such man and I accused her of it—she did not deny my accusation out [and] said she would do what she liked—I still continued to live with her as man and wife as I was very fond of her and thought I might be mistaken until Easter 1895 when she said she did not like me and would not live with me anymore, she went home to her parents.[32]

Chalmers' account is truly fascinating. Attacking his wife's virtue as one was expected to do in divorce proceedings, he simultaneously reveals his own vulnerability ("as I was very fond of her") and lack of authority ("she would do what she liked"). He also points to a great deal of audacity in her replies and actions. The image he paints of himself is not very flattering, which may convince the historian he was truthful in his declarations, yet he did lie in his affidavit about her age, stating she was thirty-three years old, when according to their marriage certificate (for which he provided a copy for the divorce petition) she was barely twenty-nine. The discrepancy obscured the fact that he had married Strike when she was seventeen. His next affidavit affirmation certainly brings his honesty into question whilst simultaneously adding a little drama to his story:

> Afterwards about the middle of the year 1896 upon the solicitations of her family she came to live with me at Bendigo and we lived together as man and wife for about two months—first at the London Hotel and then in High Street, until one night we were staying together in the hotel and we were in the bedroom prior to retiring when she picked up a razor of mine which was in the room and called out loudly that I was going to cut her throat and this brought up a number of people to the room and she refused to stay with me and left—I had not then or at any other time threatened to do her any violence and her action was only done, to the best of my belief, by her to make a disturbance. I did not know where she went to, although I made inquiries to find her whereabouts, until the end of the year 1896 when I heard she was an actress with Frank Clarks Theatrical Company, and I saw and spoke to her in Mitchell street Bendigo and asked her to come back and live with me—and she answered[:] No, I can never live with you anymore, it's no use asking me and as she went away she pulled a locket off my watch chain and put a silk handkerchief into my pocket—I have never seen her since.[33]

At first glance, the husband's story fits with his earlier depictions. Strike displays considerable agency and Chalmers his own vulnerability and lack of authority. Chalmers does not seem concerned with his own appearance as a cuckold or weak husband. But why did he include the story about the razor? Was he afraid that she would mention the incident if she testified or, even more damning, that witnesses to the scene would refer to it? Was Chalmers pre-empting an attack in which he would appear to be the person at fault? If his telling was a true account, it shows how desperately Lily wanted to leave him; and if it was a tactic to control the portrayal of the incident, Lily had grounds to leave him. Other statements do not help his cause. Chalmers points out that Lily returned to her family who took her back even if she had not behaved like a proper wife. He thus acknowledges how Lily's family supported her in her decision to leave him. Chalmers also mentions how he made frequent inquiries to her family "to try and get her address but they have either refused or been unable to give me the same." He states that her sister even told him: "It was no use making inquiries again as Lily would never live with you again." Once more, the statement provides some degree of agency to Lily. Despite all this rejection, it seems Chalmers did not hold a grudge against his young wife as he specifies in his affidavit: "Except as set out in paragraph 6 hereof, I have never suspected or know of any adultery or improper conduct on the respondent's part."[34]

His affidavit paints a man in love with his spirited wife. He waited a long time to divorce because, as he stressed, he did not have the "necessary funds" to institute proceedings. Chalmers' silence on his wife's bigamy, his specifications that the two instances were the only two "misbehaviors," and the constant reference to his desire to make a home with Lily, all suggest a firm commitment to the marriage. Chalmers' marital experiences generally confirm his lifelong devotion to matrimony. At twenty-two, he married sixteen-year-old Margaret Anderson.[35] Margaret died after giving birth to four children.[36] Not yet thirty and the father of young children aged between seven and three, Chalmers was eager to marry again as he needed a wife to take care of his little ones. Not a year passed before he married Margaret's sister, twenty-year-old Mary Anderson.[37] The new Anderson-Chalmers couple had two children (1884, 1886) before Mary died in childbirth. Chalmers did not remain a widower for long and married his third wife in 1893.[38] Unfortunately she died "after a long and painful illness."[39] At forty-two and the father of five children, he embraced matrimony once more and married Lily. Chalmers remained effectively single, but formally married, for a decade before he decided to petition for a divorce. Not long after he was officially free to remarry, he married a woman closer to his age.[40]

The documents included in the bigamy file add yet another layer to Lily Strike's fascinating matrimonial saga.[41] The civil record shows that Richard and Lily stayed together notwithstanding the bigamy accusation.

They went through a formal, legal, and religious marriage ceremony in 1913. The couple even welcomed two more daughters, one in 1908 and another in 1922. Considering the sequence of events, especially the fact that Lily had left her home to work as a barmaid a few months before the bigamy charge, it is possible Richard was trying to force her to return to the matrimonial bed. Lily was arrested at Carisbrook, a town situated about 160 kilometres away from her normal residence. In his deposition Richard specified: "On the 11th September last she left me to take a position as a barmaid."[42]

Unfortunately, as in Amelia's file, the depositions only include the replies from cross-examinations and never the exact questions. To Lily's counsel's interrogation he replied: "We lived together for 8 years. Four children were born of the marriage, she did not tell me after the first child was born that she was married." The civil record indicates that she did use her legal name for the next children instead of Cristal, the name she had given when she married Hammersley. Lily's counsel was trying to demonstrate that Richard had known about his mate's marital status for some time, hence diminishing the possible harm. Richard, however, had to insist that he did not know his wife was the wife of another man since he could be prosecuted for knowingly marrying a person he knew was already married. If Lily was found guilty, a prison sentence would be detrimental to the family stability. Lily, mother of four little ones, comes across as a determined woman who left her home to earn a living, to provide for her children when her husband did not have work.

We rarely hear from the accused themselves in these bigamy files. The statement from the detective who arrested Lily gives a glimpse of her personality. When he told Lily he was preparing the case against her, the detective testified that she replied: "I want to get it through as soon as possible." When the detective confronted her with the first marriage, she acknowledged that she had married Chalmers in 1894 and quickly added, "but I was underage at the time and it was not a lawful marriage and I did not have my father's consent." If indeed true, the statement reinforces her independent nature and her willingness to defy paternal authority. Lily also confirmed her union to Richard: "I was married to Hammersley all right, but I did not think I was legally married the first time." According to her 1894 marriage certificate, her father had given written consent, although we cannot be sure her parents attended the ceremony since her sister and brother served as witnesses and not her parents. Like Chalmers about the age of his wife, Lily had a "faulty" memory. It is possible that she truly believed her marriage to Chalmers was invalid, but she still made two false statements on her 1896 marriage license (her age and her last name). If Lily knew that she needed her father's consent to marry Chalmers, in order to make her union to Richard valid, as a minor, she should have asked for her father's permission. Instead, she lied about her age.

The entire episode indicates her relations with Richard could not have been the best, not only because he was the informant, but also because he did not post her bail. Instead, it was her brother and his wife who helped her. They posted securities of fifty pounds each, while Lily herself was responsible for one hundred pounds, attesting once more that she enjoyed a certain degree of independence. Lily's employment as a barmaid in a remote town conjures the image of a strongminded woman. Judge Hodges must have considered Lily's young age and the fact that her legitimate husband had moved on. Although not part of the dossier, one can imagine Richard told the judge he would take her back. In the end, the Court found her guilty, but by sentencing her to a nominal imprisonment (until the rising of the court), it recognized the harm was minimal.

Like Amelia, Lily's matrimonial saga attracted substantial press coverage. Many Australian dailies and weeklies picked up her story, sometimes adding their own twist, other times relaying the bare minimum. That thirty-one editors decided to print the feature indicates the level of interest in the story. In her monograph *Scandal in the Colonies*, comparative colonial history scholar Kirsten McKenzie explains the role of the Australian press in diffusing scandalous information. She mentions "the routine circulation of metropolitan and colonial newspapers through the entire imperial network and the systematic inclusion by editors of extracts by other publications."[43]

In the reports dealing with Chalmers' petition for divorce, six themes stand out—some Chalmers articulated in his affidavit, but others the reporters formulated themselves. These themes were Lily's bigamous union, her deserting the home, her low morality, kissing other men, Chalmers' matrimonial past (his three previous wives), and his kindness. If the main divorce narrative sympathizes with the husband who did everything to take good care of his wife, one notices a difference in the portrayal of Lily in the bigamy articles. Some reporters chose to paint her in a positive light by identifying her as a victim, while others continued to describe the husband as a poor fellow wronged by his independent wife.

Fifteen newspapers reported on the divorce proceedings. In six succinct paragraphs, *The Age* related important information on the case, such as the occupation and age of the petitioner. The reporter misspelled her name and wrongly stated that she was thirty-two years old, an understandable error since that is what Chalmers had claimed. Someone during the proceedings must have said something about Lily's age, finding the question of youth an important mitigating factor. The writer identified Chalmers' legal team and gave the details about their brief union. In the next paragraph, Lily's "low morality" surfaces as the reporter shared that Chalmers "found his wife kissing other men," but we also learn that, as a good patriarch, Chalmers "remonstrated with her," to no avail since "she said she would do as she liked." In this account, Lily does not conform to the cult of true womanhood, categorically refusing submissiveness. The next line further denotes her crafty temperament: "His wife picked up a razor and called out that he was trying to cut her throat." After mentioning that witnesses arrived after being alarmed by her screams, the reporter simply wrote next: "The respondent refused to stay with him any longer." Despite Lily 's deception and the fact that Chalmers heard she joined "Frank Clark's Variety Company," the benevolent Chalmers still tried to fulfill his husbandly duty "asking her to come back," but again she refused. The reporter did not deviate from the negative portrayal of the young spouse, but he, like Chalmers, also attributed a great deal of agency to her by emphasizing her refusals.

Perhaps afraid his affidavit would not convince the judge his wife lacked moral integrity, Chalmers seems to have claimed during the proceedings that even when they lived together, she "used to take off her rings and pass herself off as a single woman among the young men in the neighborhood,"[44] unless the detail shows artistic license from the writer. According to *The Age*, Chalmers testified that "she told him that she hated him and would not live with him any longer." In the divorce file, there is no mention of "hate." The journalist added that, according to the petitioner, his wife had disappeared and he had only recently discovered her whereabouts. The article concludes by stating Chalmers also just discovered she had committed bigamy. It is possible that it is only when Chalmers petitioned for divorce that Richard found out about his purported wife's past matrimonial story. Lily's own family, however, present at the trial and bailing her out, would have known that the marriage with Richard could not have been legal unless she had been avoiding them during all those years and only reconnected during her ordeal. The patriarchal discourse of the time, although already shaken by the ideas of the New Woman,[45] seeps through as Chalmers repeatedly referenced his responsibility to provide for his family, and according to conventions, Lily's duty to obey her husband. Marriage, in the minds of the legal elite of the time, such as the judge who granted the divorce to Chalmers, served an important function. Hodges contended: "It ought not to be outside the power of Parliament to protect women and the marriage tie and let fellows of this stamp [husbands who abuse their wives] understand they are the worst possible offenders against the community that we have."[46]

Variations in the newspaper accounts suggest that reporters took liberties with the facts. Twelve articles mentioned Lily was the fourth wife of Chalmers, something not indicated in the divorce file, which could entice sympathy either for the young Lily or for the poor fellow who kept losing his wives. Seven accounts did not even mention that she deserted him, and only one paper, *The Bendigo Times*, stated Lily kissed other men.[47] Articles were often matter of fact, yet some included more details, thereby revealing what their authors considered important. In one article, the author seems to highlight the difference in age (fifty-three and thirty-two). The journalist paraphrased the testimony of the petitioner's daughter, who told the court that her father had married four times. Then he quoted the Chief Justice asking: "What became of them" and her reply: "He was very unfortunate through ill-health." The judge also asked if her father had been happily married with all of them, to which she retorted: "Yes; except with the last, through whom the home was broken up." The daughter unequivocally blamed Lily for the dissolution of the union. The reporter contended the judge granted the decree because of the bigamy, but also added Lily and Richard had four children, hence presenting the idea that Lily would not return to Chalmers since she had a family of her own. The article concluded with: "The woman seemed to be one who regarded only her own inclinations and wicked disposition, and not her obligations to society or anybody else."[48] The well-placed "seemed," despite the presence of the other harsh words, opens the possibility that there was more to the testimony than met the eyes. In contrast, the *Bendigo Independent* left little room for interpretation. Elizabeth Chalmers described her father as "soft-hearted" and "very kind" and declared: "I would never have left the home except for Lily. She broke up the family. She would fly into a passion before you could speak to her." Specifying that Justice Madden thought the ordinary evidence of desertion was not very strong in this case, after all Chalmers admitted to moving around a lot in his affidavit, he nevertheless ordered a *decree nisi* remarking that: "She appeared to be one of the class of women who were below all morality and law, defying both in her desire to gratify her sensual and wicked disposition and not her obligations to society or anybody else."[49] The paper accepted Chalmers' version.

If half of the articles on the Chalmers' divorce paint Lily as a deceptive, immoral woman who was entirely to blame for the breakdown of the marriage, some did not condemn the young woman. In fact, keeping their accounts to a minimum, they nearly absolved her. The *Border Watch* printed only: "Edward Chalmers, who obtained a divorce from his wife on Thursday, in the Melbourne Divorce court, on the ground of desertion, had previously buried three wives," raising the possibility that the fourth wife may have deserted him because she was scared for her life.[50]

Three weeks after Chalmers received his divorce, the police arrested Lily on a charge of bigamy. The thirty-one articles dealing with the bigamy accusation present yet another picture of the situation. Eight themes emerge: Lily's young age when she married Chalmers, her pleasing appearance, her fainting in court, her occupation, her status as Chalmers' fourth wife, her bigamous union yielding four children, the circumstances under which the first union dissolved (she left him, they parted, then divorced) and finally, her having left illegitimately or for an engagement. Contrary to the divorce accounts, the nature of most of the bigamy articles tends to make the reader side with the accused. The courts and society often took into consideration mitigating factors such as a woman's need to secure financial support or the importance of legitimizing offspring.[51]

Under the heading "Young Woman Charged with Bigamy," one journalist wrote: "A well-dressed young woman, Lily Strike, was committed for trial at the City Court to-day on a charge of bigamy. During the proceedings, she fell unconscious on the floor of the court, but after a quarter of an hour's absence from the court she recovered."[52] Readers would have sympathized with the good-looking woman who fainted, exposing her "frail" status. Lily differed from Amelia, who had quickly regained her composure. Taking a similar tone, the *Bendigo Independent* printed: "Charges of bigamy against the gentler sex are not common, but there was one at the City court to-day." The journalist also took the time to describe Lily: "A tall woman of respectable appearance." Before the journal mentioned that she fainted when she found out she was committed for trial, it stated that the first husband had already obtained a divorce from the defendant.[53] The tone of some articles takes a no-guilt approach: "Within two years of marriage they parted," the journalists steering clear of Lily's desertion. The formulation suggests the spouses consented to the separation.[54] One is left wondering who was the victim? Since the unlawfully married couple had made a life for themselves and now had four children to look after, should the court punish the offender?

While some reporters clearly sympathized with the bigamist, others kept their tone neutral.[55] When the reporter insisted on the young age of the accused: "Accused was married when only 16 years of age to Charles Chalmers," the adverb "only" inserted before her (incorrect) age served to underscore Lily's innocence. The importance of her youth came up once more as the reporter specified: "She is now only 27 years of age, not 35 years, as reported in yesterday's Star."[56] Youth could be considered a mitigating cause for erring behaviour.

The emphasis on Lily's youth and her pleasing appearance worked to attract support, especially when articles mentioned the fact that she was Chalmers' fourth wife. Only two of the twenty-one articles which mentioned her status as fourth wife did not note her age. The reference to her four children with Richard also played in her favour. She may have left her first husband, but she now seemed committed to fulfill her social role as a wife and a mother.

Lily's occupation as a barmaid appears in twenty-seven articles. Sometimes the information is presented inoffensively, the reporter simply stating how she had gone to Carisbrook "under engagement as a barmaid" although the tone on this particular question varies between articles. *The Argus* incorporated all the other "positive" themes, stating (wrongly): "Last month Chalmers obtained a divorce and about three weeks ago the woman left Hammersley and her children and came to Carisbrook."[57] According to Richard's information and complaint, she had left him three months earlier. If Lily did indeed abandon her husband and children, she was committing a very grave moral offense. A working woman in early twentieth-century Australia would certainly be ostracized for leaving behind her children and husband. More articles, however, simply wrote that she left for work. Neglecting to mention that her husband and children stayed behind, these accounts painted her as a virtuous woman. Historian Catherine Bishop notes that working women in Australia maintained an equally important status within the family because often the husband could not find permanent work.[58] Some reports highlighted Lily's feminine side and frail nature, while others stressed her refusal to conform to gender roles. Four articles simultaneously portrayed her as a victim and a strong, independent woman. For instance: "Accused states that Hammersley did this [issued a warrant] because she did not provide him with money as was her custom."[59] The remark draws sympathy for the young resourceful woman, while the second husband appears as a scoundrel who did not fulfill his husbandly responsibility.

Like the divorce coverage, the treatment of Lily's bigamy is not uniform. Still, the tendency of journalists to include facts about Lily's young age, her pleasing appearance, her status as Chalmers's fourth wife, her four children, her fainting when she heard she would have to stand trial, and her "parting" from Chalmers, all worked together to paint an overall positive portrait of Lily Strike.

## *Conclusion*

The application of bigamy law in Victoria in the late nineteenth and early twentieth centuries proves that the courts viewed husbands as having the sole responsibility to provide for their family and believed that most bigamous women could be excused, as did the Australian press.[60] Amelia Coulson benefitted first from the favourable prejudice towards female bigamists, with newspapers highlighting the possible insanity defence and the ill-treatment she received. As evidence of Amelia deserting her husband and young children surfaced, however, it was harder to excuse her offence. Similarly, the initial coverage of the Chalmers' divorce tended to side with the husband. The reports on the bigamy, however, often painted Lily in a favourable light. To the court and society, Lily's bigamy had not created innocent victims, and therefore she did not deserve to be punished severely. It was better to have a functioning family unit than to punish a bigamous woman. Her punishment is representative of how Victorian courts dealt with women accused of bigamy. Contrary to Lily, Amelia did not deserve absolution. She abandoned a "loving" husband

and her young children to consort with a man of questionable character.[61] Despite her husband's admitted violent outburst, she was at fault. George was able to control his image of a wounded husband throughout the proceedings and again in 1897 when he testified at Green's disciplinary hearing. If Lily successfully disappeared from Chalmers' radar, Amelia was under the constant gaze of George or his entourage.

Scrutinizing different types of sources allows the researcher to add layers to our understanding of marriage and gender roles in Australia. Lily and Amelia exercised considerable agency by leaving behind their legal husbands. Amelia never recovered socially because she had abandoned her children. Lily fared better as she remained true to her vows to Richard and she continued to take care of her children. After Richard's death, Lily waited five years and married a third time. She lived with her last husband until he passed away in 1945. Feisty, independent, and resourceful, Lily nevertheless seems to have felt more at ease married.

## CHAPTER 12

# "Quite English, Except by Marriage"

## *British-Born Wives in Transnational Families in Britain, 1914–1927*[1]

*Ginger Frost*

Throughout the nineteenth century, Britain was the destination for immigrants across Europe, particularly during stressful economic times or political upheavals. As with most economic migrations, the majority of the incomers were single men who settled, got jobs, and married local women. By 1900, for instance, 60,000 Germans lived in Britain, primarily near the docks in South and East London, the majority of whom intended to stay. Some of these men went through the process of naturalization, but many did not bother. Historians have estimated that 5,000 Englishwomen were married to German citizens in 1914; had the First World War not occurred, their stories would have matched those of women married to immigrants throughout the Victorian period. Unfortunately, changes in British law in the late nineteenth century and a devastating global conflict early in the twentieth transformed the lives of these multinational households.[2]

In English common law, nationality came from birth on British soil, either of oneself or one's father (if "legitimate") or mother (if "illegitimate"), or by naturalization. This status was unaffected by marriage for either partner. In 1844, the British reformed the law to grant automatic British nationality to any woman married to a British man, thus making Britain a recipient, but not a donor, of new citizens through marriage. In part to remove this anomaly, Parliament passed another naturalization law in 1870 that de-naturalized British-born women if they married citizens of other states. This brought Britain in line with other European nations, thereby decreasing potential conflicts of law, but imposed a disability for British-born women. At the base of both statutes was the assumption that women were subsumed into their husbands' lives and national loyalties, a problematic idea when the husband was an immigrant who had chosen to remain in the UK permanently.[3]

In the immediate aftermath of the 1870 act, few men and women in multi-national marriages had any concern about issues of citizenship. The coming of the First World War, though, exposed them to popular hostility and governmental control. A British-born woman married to a German, Austrian, or Turkish man was an "enemy alien" along with her husband. She did not automatically regain her nationality if widowed or divorced but had to apply for naturalization. Even worse, rather than decreasing conflicts of law, this policy added them, since the German and Austrian laws of nationality removed citizenship after ten years' absence from the country. As a result, a German-born man who had lived in the UK for a decade was neither British nor German; though his children could claim British citizenship by birth, neither he nor his wife could do so.[4] British-born women married to foreign men were outraged to discover that they were no longer British citizens. As Helen Irving has stated, de-naturalized women felt strong grief when stripped "of their native citizenship" through no fault of their own.[5]

The legal fiction of "coverture" of nationality, which presumed the wife and husband were one in the law, was a major reason for these restrictions, but to this was added a sense of rivalry over British women that persisted into the twentieth century. Many local men (and other women) disapproved of women who married "out." Wendy Webster described the assumption that British women should form relationships only with British men as "sexual patriotism."[6] This assumption that British women marrying "out" was somehow an insult to British men was present at low levels in most periods, but these anti-alien attitudes grew stronger during wars or economic downturns. Women consorting with the enemy during war was deplorable, but sexual relationships were utterly demeaning.[7] In other words, for "sexual patriots," women were at fault for having chosen foreign husbands in the first place. Mild disapproval before the war changed to anger, legal restrictions, and violence after it began. This legal and social background allowed those overseeing the problems of "enemy alien" families to impose hardships on British-born women that would have been unacceptable in times of peace. In other words, the state's interference in the lives of its citizens was particularly harmful when applied to the intimate realm of marriage. Only by studying non-traditional sources, such as poor-law minutes and government documents, can the historian see the full effects of these policies.

## *War and Transnational Marriages*

At the beginning of the First World War, Parliament passed another nationality act, making one concession to women's concerns. If a woman's husband decided to change his nationality through naturalization, she had the right to declare her intention to retain her British nationality if she did so in a "reasonable" amount of time. Otherwise, the law was mostly concerned with ensuring that a British subject in one dominion was a British subject everywhere. Given the years of negotiation to effect this, officials were reluctant to repeal or amend the act to benefit married women, a prioritization that showed the importance of the empire and dominions on domestic politics. After the war, in 1918, the British had to pass an ameliorative law allowing wives of enemy aliens to apply for re-naturalization on favourable terms, cutting the five-year residency requirement for them. This change came from the dire experiences of British-born wives of Germans, Austrians, and Turks during the war.[8]

The British pushed through an act to control the movement of "enemy aliens" in August 1914; at this point, for the first time, wives of such men realized they were no longer British citizens. In the immediate aftermath, the state arrested some aliens, but later released many long-term residents as the emergency faded. After the sinking of the *Lusitania* in May 1915, however, anti-German riots broke out in major cities, and authorities began mass internment and deportations. British-born wives of enemy aliens were not interned with their husbands, but they were deprived of their breadwinners for the duration of the war. The War Office decided to support the families of interned men through grants administered through poor-law boards, locally elected committees that oversaw aid to paupers. The government was emphatic that the money was not poor relief, and the national government reimbursed the unions for everyone they supported. Nevertheless, poor-law guardians treated these women with disdain, combining their class bias with anti-German sentiment.[9]

Since most of the families of "enemy aliens" were poor, the war was one long struggle against destitution. Half of the families affected by internment were in the deprived East End of London; others clustered in the poorest districts of ports like Liverpool.[10] By 1918, Stepney Union, for example, had dozens of families of German nationals receiving aid as well as twelve families of Russian deportees (mostly Jewish refugees who had refused to serve with British forces allied with the tsar). Conflict between the boards and British-born wives of aliens was endemic. Guardians resisted giving aid to healthy and/or "German" women on principle, while the wives disputed both these characterizations. The Stepney Guardians wrote to the Local Government Board (LGB) in March 1915, asking about the eligibility of Elizabeth Bergin for the grant: "This woman is...able-bodied, without children...the Guardians are of opinion that Mrs. Bergin...can obtain work, by asking for it." The LGB replied that, as Bergin's husband was in regular work before internment, she was eligible. The Stepney Guardians again protested that she could "maintain herself by work...Furthermore on the last occasion she appeared before them...she was intoxicated...." The Guardians apparently carried their point, as Bergin was not on the list of wives receiving allowances in September 1915.[11] The LGB asserted that the guardians' expectations were unrealistic: "You will realise that widespread prejudice on the part of employees exists against any employment of relatives of alien enemies...."[12] Yet the Stepney Union insisted that wives of aliens could find work if they wished to do so.

The reasons for this response were related to their view of aid as means-tested. The law supported this, as it often reduced amounts if wives received money from their husbands or kin. Poor-law guardians disliked the idea of the allowances being a "right"; to them, poor-law relief required both destitution and humility.[13] They complained that as soon as the provider was interned, "the wife is informed as a matter of course that an allowance awaits her at the Guardian's office and the wife in every case comes forward to demand it...She is then placed in a better position than the British widow—who is generally required if able-bodied to maintain herself and at least one child."[14] In response, the LGB modified the rules of support in January 1915, allowing the guardians to consider women's ability to earn as a factor.[15] The guardians were quick to take advantage of this flexibility.

Stepney Union, notoriously anti-alien, was not alone in its attitude towards "enemy" wives and children. The list of unions that regarded wives of enemy aliens with hostility during the war was long.[16] Class and nationality biases made the process humiliating for the wives. In May 1918,

Maude Schubert asked the Foreign Office (FO) for help in her dispute with the Edmonton Union, explaining, "One of the Guardians told me I should not have married a German, but having done so my German friends should keep me…I was never so insulted in my life." Schubert's husband intended to bring them to Germany, which explained the hostile reception; a woman willing to move to enemy territory was not someone patriotic Britons should assist.[17] The FO forwarded the letter to the Local Government Board, who sent the complaint to the Guardians of Edmonton for a response. They argued that the Relieving Office saw expensive furniture in Schubert's home and insisted she should sell it before they gave her aid.[18]

Women's reaction to these conflicts revealed the emotional and financial toll of the war. Wives of "enemy aliens" frequently fell into destitution because of war inflation and the loss of their breadwinners. Any antagonistic behaviour by the guardians was likely to get an angry response from women who were embarrassed about having to deal with the poor law. On top of that, many were used to respectful treatment and regarded themselves as patriots. For poor-law guardians, these women's marriages to enemy aliens had removed the protective cloak of middle-class identity, exposing them as possible traitors and spongers from the public purse. One reason for this prejudice may have been that these women had to do manual labour to survive. In 1918, Mrs. Muller lost half of her pay as a charwoman and asked for an increase in her allowance from her union in Sussex, where she was rudely rebuffed. Her complaint showed she was an educated woman, despite her low-status work: "I am more than surprised to know that the Guardians wrote and said I am in a position to find employment and so help to keep myself… As I have two children, ages ranging 5 ½ years and 7 ½, it is difficult to leave them…."[19] Similarly, Mrs. H.L. Schoeneweiss claimed the Alcester Union fought every step of the way against giving her an increase. The guardians "tried to make out that my father employed me, which was very untrue."[20] Despite letters from the LGB, the two unions steadfastly refused to increase the grants.[21]

The situation was so troubled that internees complained to the LGB in October 1918. They noted that "a large number of the Guardians seem unable to understand the position of affairs, having frequently taken up a distinctly hostile attitude towards our wives, and thus the very administration of this grant has become objectionable." The letter pointed out that many British-born wives were in poor health and had small children, so had difficulty finding work, even should an employer overlook their nationality. As a result, they sold off their assets and took low-paid jobs, while, at the same time, watching prices spiral out of control with war inflation. The national government was sympathetic but, having handed over control of the funds to the local unions, it had limited control. One civil servant insisted, in July 1918, "I fail to see why a British-born woman, if she is worth cultivating, should be expected to sell up her home before she can receive assistance—I should have thought the object of the assistance would be to enable her to maintain her home ties...." Poor-law boards refused to see this bigger picture.[22] Such attitudes forced women to choose between their loyalties rather than helping them retain both.

The ripple effect caused by these financial struggles was another grievance, since the wives' families often had to fill the void left by absent breadwinners. In February 1917, Jeanette Hauter wrote to the Home Office (HO) about the sudden cessation of her allowance from the Stepney Union: "I...have been living since with my brother and sister who both have a large family, so that under the present circumstances I am an additional burden...I have been told on several occasions that he (my brother) can not provide for me any longer." The LGB referred the letter to the guardians, the very people who had withdrawn the allowance without explanation.[23] It did the same with Mrs. Silvermann, whose husband was in a Stratford internment camp. Her son was serving in the British forces, and that was the only income she had. She appealed for some allowance, and was referred, as usual, back to the union. The only way to get around this obstruction was to be as public as possible. When the Toxteth (Liverpool) guardians refused help to Mrs. J.M. Bruhn, she contacted the LGB and the local press, making enough of a fuss that the board granted her six shillings a week. Nevertheless, the dissidents on the board tried to overturn that decision at the next meeting; their motion failed by a single vote.[24]

Complicating the struggle to survive were other rules. A British-born woman married to an enemy alien had to register with police weekly, could not go more than five miles away from where she registered without a permit, and was not allowed to travel to restricted districts. This entailed grave hardship for any woman whose natal family lived in one of those areas, as she could not live with kin. Additionally, a woman in receipt of any extra money was required to inform the LGB; if not, she was prosecuted, as Daisy Rosenbaum was in March 1919. The public trustee who ran her husband's company gave the money to her brother-in-law, who had forwarded a loan to her. She stated, "she had no idea that she was not entitled to the money in the same way as a soldier's wife was entitled to a separation allowance." Fortunately, the jury found her not guilty.[25] Women also did not always understand the restrictions on their movements. In October 1914, Dora Gerster was found guilty of going more than five miles away from her home without telling the police and got a month's imprisonment.[26] Eventually, women adapted to the new regime, but their resentment over having to register with police every week did not fade.

The riots over the sinking of the *Lusitania* in May 1915 showed even more viscerally the precarious position of women married to German or Austrian men. The destruction was particularly bad in London and Liverpool but spread to many areas of the country.[27] In Birkenhead, near Liverpool, the wife of an interned Austrian was warned that a mob was coming and so left with as many of her valuables as she could carry. "The crowd," according to the newspaper, "visited the shop and quickly demolished everything they could get their hands on." The same mob subsequently "rendered homeless a woman and her five children whose husband and father, an alien, had been sent from the town...." In the wake of the destruction, most rioters received small fines or were bound over to keep the peace; in contrast, the women and children made homeless went to the workhouse.[28] This violence towards British-born women married to "enemy alien" men was the most serious consequence of the assumption that women were absorbed into their husbands' nationalities. Despite being born in, living in, and, in most cases, having never left Britain, they became targets whenever the war went badly.

## *Living Abroad*

As difficult as the situation was in Britain, both German-born wives of British men and British-born women married to "enemy aliens" also had problems if they lived abroad. German-born wives of British men interned in Germany or British POWs in Germany, like British-born women married to "enemy aliens," were primarily in danger of starvation. The Germans supported German-born wives of interned British men, but the amounts were not generous and had less buying power as the war dragged into its third and fourth years. The Goschen Fund, a charity, was set up to help them, but the grants were inadequate. The Prisoners of War Department argued with the Foreign Office (FO) about this issue in 1917, saying that the British had to top up German support for women married to British subjects there if they did not want a mass migration to Britain: "Talking of falling between two stools…it seemed so heartless to send them away empty handed, as some of them are really starving…."[29] Circumstances could also derail even the small grants offered. If the man was released to a neutral country such as The Netherlands, the grant stopped, though many ex-prisoners could not find employment.[30] The British thus urged women to come to Britain, where they could get allowances, and some women did so.[31] Relief workers in Germany supported the women's claims of poverty; one wrote in June 1917: "I have often been struck…with the pinched appearance of the women, and often of the children also, although it may be accepted that the children only go short in the last resort."[32]

Families separated by war presented another continual dilemma—who should support them? The FO heard an appeal in February 1915 for a Mrs. Vox, a British-born wife of a German husband. In an unusual twist, her husband lived in London with his sister while Mrs. Vox struggled to survive in Berlin. Her husband wrote to the German government for help, saying he had understood the Germans would support her as his wife. At first, they agreed, but then they reversed themselves, probably because his absence for over ten years meant he had lost his German nationality: "she was called to the Embassy in Berlin where they told her again that she was not a German, and [they] could therefore do nothing for her…My poor wife…is not only in bad state of health, but is destitute…" The British urged her to come to Britain, but she had no money for the journey. Eventually, they decided to grant "a suitable amount" to help her survive where she was.[33]

Both British-born wives of enemy aliens and foreign-born wives of Englishmen were especially vulnerable if they lived in central Europe. Some British-born women were on holiday or visiting in-laws when the war began. Others were married to British men working abroad and were trapped on the wrong side of the battle lines. The war was more mobile in the East than on the Western Front, and women caught there could be in danger of battle as well as starvation. In July 1915, when the Austrians invaded Italy, several wives of British POWs interned in Austria lost their support, as the American Consul at Trieste, which distributed the funds, hastily decamped. The British responded that such women should be repatriated to Britain immediately.[34] Austrian territories were a particular problem, as no charity existed there. In 1915, Mrs. Forrester, a British subject by marriage, but an Austrian by birth, appealed for help. She had six children but was left without support when the war began, as her husband John had gone to Russia on business. As the Consul explained, "The British Government will not relieve the foreign-born wives of British subjects, and yet she is regarded by the police authorities as an English woman." The British considered bringing her to the UK, but the transport of seven people—mother and six children—discouraged them. So, the British consul undertook an investigation to find the errant Mr. Forrester, while giving a small grant to his wife. They eventually found the husband working in Odessa and he agreed to a monthly maintenance payment.[35]

Women and families easily fell between the conflicting claims of different governments, unable to assert a right to relief from either. The British took the position that they supported the British-born wives of enemy aliens living in the UK, so the Austrians and Germans should support Austrian- and German-born wives of British men, but some cases remained problematic. Mrs. Flandorfer was British-born but had married an Austrian man. She was living in Karlsbad with her two children in August 1915, while her husband, who had been in Britain when the war broke out, was interned on the Isle of Man. The British pressed the Austrians to support her, but Otto had lived in Britain twenty years and both of his children were British-born. Thus, the Austrians refused this request on the grounds that he had lost his citizenship by living out of the country for two decades. In the meantime, Otto's wife was desperate: "She speaks no German and is unable to get any work since she says everyone says she is English and they will employ no foreigners…" The Austrians argued that, as the children were British, some small amount from Britain was appropriate. The British, for their part, pointed out that they helped Austrian-born women in the same situation, so the Austrians should return the favour. The file ended with no resolution for the Flandorfer family, caught on opposite sides of the front when the war began.[36]

One reason countries struggled with what to do with such women was that these cross-national marriages showed the artificiality of national labels. Transnational partners saw themselves as Europeans, able to feel affection and loyalty to more than one place. Unfortunately, the war forced them into a single category. The Reiser family was an example of a hybrid nationality. German-born Michale Reiser worked as a tailor in Paris with his British-born wife when the war began. Though he was a naturalized citizen, French authorities interned him. Anna, his wife, was the mother of his three sons, two British-born and one born in France. As she was considered "to all extent and purposes British," the French allowed her to remain. But in 1915, she was informed that she was being deported either to Spain or Switzerland. She begged the British consul for help:

> Mrs. Reiser does not wish to go to Spain, having no relations there, and nothing to live on…On the other hand, were she sent to Switzerland, she is afraid that she may be sent to Germany, where she absolutely refuses to go, having no relations…in that country, and, not being able to speak one word of German… As this lady is quite English, except by marriage, and as all her relations are English, I beg, on her behalf, that Your Excellency will use your influence…to allow her to land in England.[37]

Rather than taking in another poor family, the British lobbied the French to allow her to stay where she could earn her living. As she wrote again from Bordeaux in January of 1918, the French apparently agreed.[38]

Deporting a woman who was "quite English, except by marriage" to a country where she knew no one was inherently irrational. Like so many of the women caught in the war, Reiser was neither British nor German nor French, but all three. Indeed, the nationality with the least legality was German, since her husband was a naturalized French citizen, and she was both British-born and French by marriage. For their part, two of the children were born in Britain and one in France. Yet Mrs. Reiser was almost deported to a fourth country, one that had no relation to any of these nationalities but did have the advantage of being neutral. The British (and French) law determined that the British-born children were also "German," basing this on the father's birthplace, not his domicile, naturalization, choice of wife, or workplace. The war forced such families to accept a narrow legal identity, and, ironically, not even the one they preferred. The French state, like the British, assumed that men retained emotional ties to the lands of their births, while ignoring the possibility that the men's wives might also retain emotional ties with theirs.

## *Aftermath*

War classifications were hard to shake even after the guns stopped, since the long peace negotiations left multinational families in limbo. As soon as the armistice came into effect, some British-born wives lobbied to return to the UK. They were unpopular with the defeated populations of Germany and Austria, and they were also unable to survive in the increasingly dire economic situation. Moreover, government funds supporting them disappeared, and British charities also wrapped up their work. The FO was unwilling to readmit German or Austrian subjects until the formal end of the war, which was not until April 1921 for some of the belligerents. Gladys Guttmann, married to a Hungarian, lived through the war in Szenicz with her son Leo. In late November 1918, she asked the British embassy to let her live with her sister, Rebecca O'Dea, in England. O'Dea also wrote to the embassy, saying Gladys was "in great want" in Hungary. Two weeks later, the FO received the request of Emily Umlauft in Vienna to come back to the UK. Though her family had lived in England since 1885, and her two sons were British born, the Foreign Office refused her request as well as that of Guttmann. Nevertheless, Guttmann somehow boarded a transport to Britain, arriving in January 1919, to the irritation of the FO. One must applaud Guttmann's refusal to accept continued expatriation, but she was an exception.[39] Most women married to enemy aliens waited years to return.[40]

Reuniting broken families was a drawn-out process, and the separations took an emotional toll, particularly if the husband had accepted repatriation. According to Panikos Panayi, eighty-four percent of interned enemy aliens were repatriated by October 1919, decimating the German community in England, which dropped from 60,000 in 1914 to 22,254 in 1919. Towards the end of the war, enthusiasm for repatriation waned, due to the problem of British-born wives and children. The British set up a committee to deal with these cases in 1918. The committee considered 4,300 applications and allowed 3,890 to remain, overwhelmingly men who had long resided in the country and who had British families.

Two-thirds of the women allowed to stay were British-born wives of German men. As Panayi put it, this percentage shows "the number of broken families caused by the deportation process."[41]

Repatriation was "voluntary," but most men agreed to leave the camps. Since Germany removed German nationality from any man who had lived out of the state for ten years, repatriated men had to re-apply for German citizenship after they arrived. By and large, during the war, the men went alone, since going abroad to enemy territory was not enticing to British-born wives. Most had never been out of the UK, did not speak German, and faced hostility from in-laws. In addition, the majority had British-born children whom the British government preferred to remain. Thus, the government's policy was never to repatriate a British-born wife against her will, and Germany and Austria followed similar practices.[42] In a war that had horrific casualties, neither side was anxious to deport children. All the same, the economic conditions, low allowances, and riots pushed many women to consider leaving.

The decision to stay or to go depended on class and education. Well-off women likely had travelled to Germany before and could at least speak French. Their husbands were in a better position to keep them, so being reunited with their husbands may have been worth the sacrifice. For poorer women, the key was survival. If they were starving, they had little choice but to follow their breadwinners. Once a woman decided to go, the government insisted that she provide a letter showing she had somewhere to live and adequate support. The government also warned women receiving allowances that they gave up their right to them by leaving the country.[43] Wives of repatriated Germans and Austrians, thus, had to make a difficult choice. If they remained in Britain, they might never see their husbands again, but they did have their natal families and neighbours to support them. If they left for Germany/Austria, they were reunited with their husbands but were strangers in a land hostile to Britain.

Unsurprisingly, many women who followed their husbands to Germany or Austria between 1917 and 1919 returned within a year or two with their children in tow. Conditions in Germany between 1918 and 1923 were disastrous. Government officials admitted as much to each other in 1920 when discussing how much aid to give women who "found circumstances such that they would rather come back" after initially leaving.[44] Mrs. Webber asked for help from the Ministry of Health (MH) in such a situation. She was married to a German man and had eight children when the war began. Her husband was interned and repatriated, and in January 1919, she joined him in Germany. "As her husband found difficulty in maintaining her, she returned to England with her children…She says she is now living with her eight children (another being expected shortly) in one room lent to her in her mother's house…." Webber wanted an allowance like she had during the war, which was not possible. She was also counting on her husband's return as a salesman for a cigarette company, but that could not occur in the immediate future. The civil servant complained, "This is the third case that has come to our notice in which a wife has gone to Germany and after some time returned with her family…in a destitute condition." The MH could do little to help, as the Treasury denied the funding; Britain's own economic woes in the early 1920s did little to encourage generosity. As one official insisted in 1920, "I don't see that the State can reasonably be asked to provide the means of remedying the woman's mistake."[45]

In other words, once a man was repatriated, a lifetime separation was possible, since the process to return was complicated. The government passed another Aliens Restriction Act in 1919 that continued the harsh policies of the war. As David Cesarani put it, "it was a sop to the violent, hysterical and unremitting anti-German feeling that had been fostered during the war…All former enemy aliens could now be deported unless a newly established aliens advisory committee deemed them exempt."[46] The Aliens Committee also considered applications for re-admittance from 1919 to 1931. None were admitted for five years (the statute forbade return for three), so the position of British-born women living without their repatriated husbands was a running problem. Discussions about reducing the expenditure on these families was common, but the only way to do so was to restore the breadwinners, an unpopular choice. Some German men were security risks, while others were rivals for jobs with British dockers, miners, or sailors.[47] After 1920, the Ministry of Labour (ML) had to approve all applicants, and this was no mere formality. As a result, Germans who returned were those who produced jobs for British workers or could live on the earnings of their wives and children.

The 1919 law's effect on transnational families is laid bare in government documents, which show how strictly civil servants and MPs applied its provisions. A typical file from the Foreign Office contains the minutes of the deliberations from 1927, a year with fifty-nine applications.

Each applicant was a deported German/Austrian with a British-born wife and/or children. Twenty-six were accepted, most for limited periods (six months was standard), and under the condition that they not work. Twenty-three were refused, often for the third or fourth time. The others had no recorded decision (seven) or were asked to apply first to the Ministry of Labour (three). In sixteen cases, the British-born wives had decided to accompany their husbands to Germany only to return to Britain in the early 1920s. In three cases, the British-born wife had died, and one had been divorced. Thus, in almost thirty percent of the cases involving current British-born wives, the women were living in Britain while their husbands lived in Germany. When the parents were not apart, they were separated from their children (the latter had either returned without their parents or had not left). The applications ranged from men who had been in Britain for two years to forty-four years before the war. The median was thirteen years, and twenty-one of the applicants (over a third) had lived in Britain at least twenty years before the war began (six were thirty years or more). The committee decisions reflected sympathy with fractured families but only those that met their criteria for return.

The family of John William Peterson was typical. Peterson was born in 1870 and lived in the UK as an adult for so long that he lost his German nationality. He married a British-born woman with whom he had five daughters and two sons. He was interned during the war and repatriated in 1917. When he arrived in Germany, he applied for naturalization, as otherwise he was stateless. His wife and three of his children went with him, but they returned in 1922. Peterson tried several times to rejoin his family but was refused repeatedly. He was, however, allowed to visit his family in August 1926, and was then given an extension for another month on the understanding that he not take employment. At that point, his son made another plea that his father be allowed to remain, saying "the children were prepared to keep him." Five of the children were unmarried and supporting their mother, and the police "formed the opinion that they were respectable and hard-working…" After several refusals, the subcommittee allowed Peterson to rejoin his family permanently in 1927.[48]

Those who were refused permission to return had a variety of problems, especially economic competition. Christopher Rentz, who had a British-born wife and three British-born children, had lived in the UK for twenty-nine years before the war. He repatriated in 1917, and his wife and younger daughter went with him, but Mrs. Rentz brought their daughter back to live with relatives in 1920. Rentz, a chef, was refused when he applied to return in 1919, 1920, 1921, and 1927, always because he would take the job from a British worker.[49] Character issues also scuttled applications. Walter Freier lived in the UK for twenty-five years before the war, but the HO reported that he was "a thoroughly bad lot" and rejected his petition.[50] Emil Jung, a waiter, married a British woman and had a son. He had lived in the UK for twelve years before the war, was interned in 1915, and repatriated in 1919. His wife and child followed him to Germany but came back to Britain in 1924. Jung applied to rejoin his family in 1927, but according to the police, he was pro-German, lazy, drunken, and violent. The decision to refuse him was easy.[51]

Those accepted had passed tests of economic means and character. Ernst Koch, a baker, lived in the UK for six years before he was interned. He had a British-born wife and son who went with him to Germany in January 1919. The wife "returned later leaving the boy behind," but taking with her their daughter who was "presumably born in Germany." In February 1923, he applied to return to the UK to work with his old employer. He was given limited visas throughout 1924. His bakery had done well by 1927 (employing British workers), so the committee allowed him to remain.[52] Other successful applicants had lived in Britain far longer than they had in Germany, and some had sons in the military. Frank May, born in 1853, had a British-born wife and four sons in the British army, two of whom were killed in service. He had lived in Britain for forty-four years before the war but was still interned and repatriated in 1915. His wife did not go to Germany with him and now asked that he be allowed to return. He had two sons and a son-in-law willing to support him. Given the family's sacrifices for Britain during the First World War, May was allowed to return "without any condition."[53] Such stories are eloquent testimonies to the emotional price paid by multi-national families during and after the war. They also, again, emphasize the complex mix of nationalities in certain families.

The end of hostilities could have brought relief, but the Treaty of Versailles caused additional problems. The treaty allowed the victorious powers to confiscate the property of "enemy aliens" to pay German reparations, and this included the property of British-born wives of such men.[54] The British courts even included women who married Germans *after* the armistice, as the case of *Fasbender v. Attorney General* (1921) showed. The plaintiff in the case was a former Mary Dawson, born in Lincoln, who became engaged to Ernest Fasbender, a German national, before the war. As soon as the war was over, she went to Germany and married him, on 3 November 1919. Her property in England was seized by the Public Trustee after the treaty came into effect on 10 January 1920. Fasbender's loyalty to her fiancé was deemed disloyalty to her country, despite the end of hostilities. What made this case even sadder was that the marriage did not last. Mary Fasbender returned to Britain in 1927, having divorced her husband, and petitioned for naturalization.[55]

The problems for women who had their property seized continued for years. In 1927, Muriel Koenig wrote to barrister Chrystal Macmillan about her difficulties. She lived in England with her daughter, but her husband was in Germany: "My husband writes that our being English makes it impossible for us to go to Germany as it would mean disaster to him…[but t]his law makes it most difficult for me to earn a living." Koenig's husband, though, could not support two households, and later pressured her to go to Germany by refusing to send an allowance. She could not rely on her family property, since the British government seized it, "saying it is Germany [sic] money, though it is in fact British money left me by my adopted Mother and Aunt…"[56] No legal remedies existed, and the aggressive actions of the husband did little to heal the growing rift with his wife. In 1928, Helena Normanton, a barrister, estimated that 2,000 cases of distress after the war were related to the loss of property by British women married to enemy aliens.[57]

The divisions shown by these cases sometimes followed pre-existing tensions in the family, but in most cases, the internments and deportations were the main culprits in the disintegration of these marriages. Bitterness grew in some interned men, or the separated wives looked elsewhere for comfort. In one of the FO applications for the return of a repatriated German, that of Georg Neumeier, the wife had twins in 1917 while her husband was interned. Their fate is not recorded, but Mrs. Neumeier followed her husband to Germany in 1919, only to return to Britain soon after. Neumeier was one of those allowed to return to the UK, so perhaps the marriage survived.[58] Other couples were not so fortunate. Charles Krauss was an Austrian who came to England in 1908 and married a British-born woman in 1911. He was interned for most of the war, and his wife stopped visiting or writing him after 1916. In 1919, she wrote him that she was pregnant with her lover's child. Krauss sued for divorce while still interned (in April 1919), and the two were divorced in 1920. This marriage was a casualty of Krauss's long absence from his family, probably one of many.[59] Such stories showed the hollowness of the Home Office's insistence that "the unity of the family" required British women's denationalization. On the contrary, the intervention of the state into the intimate lives of husbands and wives, parents and children, had dire consequences for family unity. Unspoken assumptions about women's loyalty led to harsh penalties for those deemed "unpatriotic."

## *Conclusion*

When the First World War broke out, those married to "enemy aliens" suffered discrimination and poverty, their position heavily influenced by gender. A British man married to a German woman saw little change in his family's treatment, though neighbours might shun his wife if she showed pro-German leanings. But a woman married to an "enemy alien" faced destitution, discrimination, and violence. Women were often surprised to discover that they were no longer British. Their husbands were victimized as well, but, in their cases, they had chosen to move abroad and not to seek naturalization; the initiative remained with them. Women, as Helen Irving has pointed out, were treated the same way as men who joined foreign militaries, as people who had "betrayed" their national allegiance.[60] Class status did not protect women; years of war often reduced middle-class women to poverty. Women discovered that their marriage to a "foreigner" overcame all other factors, including their patriotism, natal kin, or the attitudes of their husbands. Families were often not reunited for a decade after the war, and some never recovered. The First World War was a family tragedy on many levels, and the forced separation of so many multi-national households was another strand of that disaster.

The emotional wounds in these cases resulted from governments' insistence that couples choose between their love of their spouses and their love of their countries. If the marriage was already dead, the British-born woman easily chose her nation (or vice versa); as one woman, estranged from her German husband for twenty years before 1914, insisted, she was "heart and soul an Englishwoman."[61] But for others, the choice was wrenching, a break with one allegiance or another. The fact that more than one loyalty could exist in a person or family at the same time threatened combatant nations and confused and annoyed bureaucrats. Unfortunately, wartime anti-alienism continued well after the signing of the peace treaty, forcing more and more transnational families to break apart or face expatriation.[62] National "coverture" was a legal fiction that was increasingly out of date in the post-war world, but its effects remained strong into the 1940s. The British did not change the law of nationality for married women until 1948, after a second world war again revealed the consequences of reducing married women to adjuncts of their husbands. For too many multinational families, total war, and the governmental intervention that accompanied it, resulted in the severing of intimate ties.

CHAPTER 13

# The "Moscow Widowers"

## *Marriage, Citizenship, and the Soviet Wives of British Subjects in the Aftermath of the Second World War*[1]

*Gail Savage*

The Second World War drove an unprecedented movement of populations. The combination of military deployments to far-flung battle fields, the frantic efforts of refugees to escape persecution or bombing, the internment of foreign nationals, and the incarceration of prisoners of war together produced a mingling of many people who would otherwise never have encountered one another. A surge of marriages across national lines accompanied these population movements, despite the often-determined resistance of authorities. The British war bride represents a popularly remembered face of this phenomenon.[2] The presence of thousands of Canadian troops in the UK from 1939 produced 44,886 marriages between members of Canadian forces and UK women through 1946. In addition, the liberation of the Netherlands by Canadian troops produced an additional 1,886 marriages with Dutch women.[3] American forces did not reach the UK until 1942, but they came in very large numbers, and Anglo-American marriages totaled approximately 40,000 by the end of 1946.[4] Australian women also married Americans in large numbers.[5] And Australian and British men in their turn married foreign women during tours of duty abroad.[6] When armed forces demobilized, servicemen returning to their homes wished to take their wives with them, and the political salience of veterans meant that their wishes were by and large accommodated by authorities, reluctantly or not.

Even the marriages among allies with a shared language raised difficult questions about the relationship between marriage and citizenship status, especially for wives. Such large numbers of newly acquired spouses seeking to leave one country and to enter another challenged the regulation of marriage, citizenship, and immigration in many different jurisdictions. All the Anglophone Allied powers found that they had to make some significant adjustments to the laws governing immigration to accommodate the political pressure exerted by returning veterans.[7] The passage of such legislation during and immediately following the war underscores the contrarian position of the Soviet Union on these matters. Under Soviet law, married women retained their original citizenship, and the Soviet Union, as a matter of general policy, did not permit its citizens to relinquish their citizenship or even to travel abroad without explicit permission. Although Western allies pressured the Soviet government to allow Soviet women who had married foreign men to reunite with their husbands, Soviet authorities resolutely refused to authorize exit visas for many such women. In 1947, the Soviet government went even further by promulgating a revision of Soviet law so that it absolutely forbade any marriage between a Soviet citizen and a foreign national.[8]

This chapter considers the travails generated by marriages between Soviet women and British subjects during the Second World War. Relatively few such marriages took place, but those that did occur caused considerable trouble and, in doing so, left a rich archival record. British Foreign Office files document the posture of officials towards this issue and their efforts on behalf of these couples, while also making it possible to piece together the fates of some of these men and women. These cases show not only the efforts expended by states seeking to exert their power over their citizens but also the creativity of individuals who sought to shape their own lives in the midst of global war. The analysis will focus on those couples who married during the war, considering marriages of Allied prisoners of war to Eastern European women as well as the marriages to Soviet women of servicemen and civilians stationed or located in the Soviet Union. The chapter will then discuss the rationale for the policies adopted by the British on behalf of the Soviet wives of British subjects.

## *War Marriages and Soviet Wives*

As the Soviet armies pushed back German forces in the final days of the Third Reich, they overran prisoner of war (POW) camps in Eastern Europe, especially Poland. Soviet forces, focused on pressing forward with their military campaign, did not pause to provide more than cursory care for these men, often leaving them to fend for themselves as best they could. In addition, the Soviet government refused access to the area by Allied forces to collect the now-freed POWs. The Soviets allowed access only to Odessa, the port on the Black Sea designated as the embarkation point for the repatriation of POWs. Consequently, thousands of POWs made their own way through the chaotic landscape of Eastern Europe to Odessa.[9] And a few of these men turned up accompanied by wives. Soviet authorities refused to allow the embarkation of wives along with their husbands, leaving Allied authorities to deal with the ramifications of reuniting their repatriated men with their wives. Under British law, the wife of a British subject became a British subject herself, so the British, in particular, campaigned for the release of these women, sometimes engaging in lengthy and tedious negotiations to secure their release. In this they were only partially successful and, in some cases, the arguments made by British authorities on behalf of these women were undermined by the behaviour of the parties themselves.

British records docket twenty-four cases involving ex-POWs, although the uncertainties of the time and the place suggest caution in treating this number as a definitive total. Of these twenty-four, the British managed to extricate eight women to join their husbands. Although a relatively small group, the backgrounds of the men suggest the heterogeneous nature of Allied forces under the broad umbrella of British oversight. The preliminary listings of cases of interest included three Australians, two South Africans, and a US citizen serving in the Canadian forces. The purported wives also represented a range of nationalities, including Poles, Silesians, and Austrians, as well as Russians, although Soviet authorities claimed them all as Soviet citizens.[10] The Soviets regarded marriages between Soviet citizens and foreigners with suspicion and were reluctant to grant permission for the women to leave, while the British, who enfolded foreign-born wives into the citizenship status of their British husbands, gave the marriages the benefit of the doubt and sought to keep married couples together. As Ginger Frost found in the context of the First World War (see Chapter 12 in this volume), national identity and interests understood in gendered terms subjected the private lives of these couples to the intrusion of officialdom, often with devastating results for the happiness of the couples involved. Approximately twenty additional marriages took place between British subjects and Soviet women during the war. Most of these were servicemen assigned to duties in the USSR, including six members of the RAF working in the Air Section of the British Military Mission in Moscow. The list also included a few civilians, journalists, and members of embassy staff. Most of these wives were eventually allowed to leave, although usually not until after the end of hostilities, a delay that caused considerable anguish for the couples involved and probably led to the collapse of some of the marriages.

A consideration of the cases in which the British were not able to secure the release of the women on their POW list illuminates the difficulties posed by these cases. Several men repudiated their marriages, some of which may never have taken place. The linked cases of Private Harry Elwell and Rifleman J.A. Maggs illustrate the origins of some of these purported relationships.[11] Elwell and Maggs appear together in an April 1945 memorandum that recapitulates their original story to authorities. They had escaped from Stalag 344 with the assistance of two Russian women. After making their way through the Russian lines, they went to Częstochowa in Poland, where each couple married under the auspices of Soviet military authorities, who then sent them on to Odessa. According to the men, their marriage papers had been lost in a train crash in one version of events, or retained by Soviet authorities in another version. Upon his return to Britain, Maggs visited the Foreign Office to initiate a search for his wife. His sincerity impressed British authorities. When the British Embassy in Moscow wrote the Foreign Office in November 1945, T. Sharman told them that he had authorized a certificate that Mrs. Maggs would be issued a British visa, even though the Maggs' marriage had not yet been proven. He observed: "It seems obvious from Rifleman Maggs' anxious enquiries that he held the form of marriage concluded by him and his wife in Poland to be a valid one." And Sharman also asked for authorization to issue a certificate to Mrs. Elwell, which led British authorities to contact Elwell to obtain his wife's home address.[12]

The story of these two couples then took a decided turn when Elwell denied that any such marriage had taken place. In a lengthy letter, he explained the circumstances that had led to this misunderstanding. Elwell had been a prisoner of war since Dunkirk and had spent most of his time in Upper Silesia. After war broke out between Germany and the Soviet Union, Russian women were brought to the camp as slave labour, and Elwell made the acquaintance of Irene Kisenko in September 1944. At the approach of the Russian army, the Germans intended to move the prisoners westward, but Elwell, Maggs, and two women, Irene Povlovna Kisenko and Maria Andrukhova, determined to escape together and make their way eastwards to the Russian lines, which they succeeded in doing in January 1945. Because Soviet authorities were holding single women for military duty, Elwell passed off Irene as his wife, but he insisted that he had never actually married her, and he furthermore insisted that the story that Maggs had told them was untrue in respect of the marriage. Although grateful for Irene's assistance in their mutual escape, Elwell wished to establish his status as a single man.[13] A Foreign Office official in London noted: "Mr. Elwell may happily call himself a single man. This letter amply confirms Mr. Napier's suspicions that Mr. Sharman in Moscow is making too liberal a use of the term married wife, and that Russian obstructionism is justified."[14] Later Maggs too repudiated his marriage, writing early in 1946 that he did not want any further inquiries to be made: "…as this was no marriage, I only try to do my best for her… In fact, I have hopes of getting married this year over here now…and I am sorry if I have caused you so much trouble regarding this case." The Moscow Embassy then wrote Maria Andrukhova (Mrs. Maggs) to withdraw her application for a passport, thus ending the matter.[15]

The tangled story of Maggs and Elwell had caused trouble for British officials in London and Moscow, but at least the truth of the purported marriages had emerged before these cases had been pressed too strenuously to Soviet authorities. More embarrassing was the case of Private H.P. Seaborne, a South African serving in the British forces who became a prisoner of war in Poland. There he met Halina Lipiaewa while both were working at a paper factory. Halina and another young woman helped some of the men escape by cutting a wire fence, provided that the POWs took the women with them.[16] They travelled together to Odessa as a married couple. There, Soviet authorities refused to let her embark and sent her back to her home village. The British made arrangements with the South African government to send Mrs. Seaborne by air to Cairo and arranged with the Americans for sea transport from Cairo to South Africa. Then they traced her to her home village. In September 1945, Mrs. Seaborne's name was included on a list of eight wives given permission to leave, and she was put on her way to her husband's hometown of Port Elizabeth, South Africa. This narrative seemed to be unfolding towards a happy ending until South African authorities alerted the Dominions Office that Private Seaborne married someone else just before her arrival. They requested that the British Embassy in Moscow look into the validity of the earlier marriage.[17]

The British embassy in Moscow responded to this development with some consternation. The Embassy warned the Foreign Office: "if facts are as stated, I feel we must take the bull by the horns, explain very soon to the Soviet Government, and if she wishes, offer to repatriate her to her home in Ukraine."[18] Officials in Moscow realized that the record of the Seaborne marriage had never been scrutinized and told the Foreign Office that "It is necessary to clear up this case satisfactorily or it may have a disastrous effect on the other Soviet wives of British subjects."[19] Accordingly, the Foreign Office instructed the embassy in Warsaw to investigate. Officials in Poland reported back that they could not find any record of the marriage. They talked to a Roman Catholic priest who remembered a British soldier and a Ukrainian woman, but the priest had refused to enact any marriage. From the British point of view, this was the worst possible outcome, as the so-called wife and British subject was not a wife at all, and therefore not a British subject. This sequence of events would be regarded with suspicion by the Soviets, who already suspected that these claimed marriages were no more than a ruse to facilitate the otherwise unauthorized exit of Soviet citizens. However, in South Africa Seaborne and his "wife" both found happy endings, just not together. Seaborne's South African marriage was valid. South African authorities agreed that Halina Lipaewa could stay in South Africa. They later reported that "Mrs. Seaborne," termed the "blond ballerina" in the British press,[20] was under contract to work in South African theatres. She was happy to stay in South Africa; South Africa was happy to let her stay. And she was already making plans to bring her mother to join her. The Foreign Office breathed a collective sigh of relief and hoped that the case could be regarded as closed.[21]

However, the Seaborne case did come back to haunt Foreign Office efforts on behalf of the wives of other British subjects, just as officials feared. Soviet officials deployed the example of Seaborne in their opposition to permitting the wife of Brigadier Gordon Redvers Way to leave the Soviet Union. Way had married Ketevna Nedareishvili in September 1942 at Tiflis (now Tbilisi), where he was involved in talks with his Soviet counterparts on shared intelligence issues. There he met Ketevna, a ballerina and telegraphist specialist, and married her, but after returning to his duties he never saw his wife again. His case became the longest running unresolved case. Way's rank and position gave him an advantage in advocating for himself, and he dedicated himself to effecting a reunion with his wife with considerable energy and ingenuity over several years. He frequently visited and wrote to Foreign Office officials. He similarly pressed War Office officials. His advocacy contributed to raising the question of British subjects married to Soviet women at the very highest of levels. Mrs. Churchill went to Moscow in the spring of 1945 with this issue on her list. After Clement Attlee's electoral victory in July, as Prime Minister he raised the question with Stalin at Potsdam on 1 August. Way became increasingly unhappy as the Soviets released other wives but remained adamant about refusing either to allow him to visit his wife in Tiflis or to allow her to exit. When the Foreign Office again raised his case in 1946, Deputy Foreign Minister Andrey Vyshinsky said that he could not offer hope in the matter, expressing the worry that Mrs. Way would be "jilted" as Mrs. Seaborne had been.[22]

The details of other cases point to the chaos in Europe at the close of the war, as some of the purported wives of POWs seemed to simply disappear. This proved to be a disastrous outcome for Private J. Cummins. Cummins recapitulated the story of his marriage to Irmgard Gunter, "…a Polish girl I married after escaping from a prison camp in Poland with her help and her Folks at home." He explained: "…she is the only person I have got in the world my parents I never seen & I have been brought up in a Catholic convent in Eire and there I was Born."[23] Like the other wives who managed to reach Odessa, Mrs. Cummins had not been permitted to embark with her husband. But she had reportedly evaded Soviet authorities and managed to get aboard the SS *Staffordshire* the night before its departure for the UK. Soon after his repatriation to England, Cummins asked the British Prisoners of War Relatives Association for help finding his wife. They wrote to the War Office, which in turn pressed the Foreign Office to take some action. Lt. Col. Hammer underlined the urgency of the case: "Cummins who is a simple uneducated man, is acutely distressed, as his wife is his only relative."[24] Cummins himself wrote several letters during the autumn of 1945, pleading for help finding his wife, "…the only person I have belong to me that I can call my own…."[25] Foreign Office officials traced her to a reception camp in Italy, but early in September authorities there reported to the War Office that she had left the camp voluntarily and had formed a relationship with a soldier stationed locally. Authorities in Naples described

Mrs. Cummins' marriage certificate as of "dubious origin," and they did not plan further action.[26] It is not clear whether this information was passed along to Cummins at that time, and he continued to be bereft at his wife's disappearance. In letter after letter, he pressed officials to greater efforts to find her. Cummins last heard from his wife on 6 August 1945, and although he had not seen his home for four years he was "waiting for my wife to come to me to go home."[27] Tiring of waiting, Cummins wanted to go look for her, saying: "…what have I got after my… serving abroad nothing the one I had is gone and not her fault or mine so I will follow her…."[28] He then went to a local police station to talk to a detective about tracing his wife, but he could not tell them anything about his wife's whereabouts, concluding: "I think it is a shame leaving my wife in Naples begging her to keep herself alive and I do not no [sic] if she is dead or alive."[29] Continuing investigation did not find any sign of Mrs. Cummins.[30]

Although Cummins did not give up on his lost wife, others found that the passage of time weakened once strong connections. Driver F.R. German of the Royal Army Service Corps claimed to have married in Archangel in western Russia on 10 January 1942.[31] His purported wife denied the marriage, and the marriage was not registered so officials doubted its validity.[32] But German insisted on the marriage's validity, and he wrote to Winston Churchill requesting his help in getting his wife out of the Soviet Union, citing the role of the 1940 Republican presidential candidate Wendell Willkie in extricating the Soviet wife of an American soldier.[33] German had no documents to prove his marriage, but he adamantly denied allegations by British intelligence that his wife had led him on in staging a pretended ceremony. He stressed the suffering of his wife and child in Archangel and pleaded that they be brought to England.[34] The status of the marriage continued to be under question during 1944. The War Office kept the Foreign Office apprised of the precarious situation of Miss Trifanova/Mrs. German. The Foreign Office thought the lack of registration invalidated the marriage, but the War Office relayed the couple's insistence that they regarded themselves as married.[35] While the matter continued under discussion, the British Embassy and authorities in Archangel made arrangements to provide food to German's so-called wife and their child, as they were already doing for other women in similar situations.[36]

Sometime in late 1945 or early 1946, German fell out of touch with Trifanova, who then made inquiries about him, leading Archangel once again to get in touch with the Foreign Office about the case. The Foreign Office, reluctant to get involved, decided to ascertain German's feelings about renewing attempts to bring his "wife" to England.[37] This elicited a long, anguished letter from German, in which he explained his change of heart. Shocked at hearing about his "wife" after a long interlude of silence, German protested that he had done all he could to bring her and his child to England and spent all he had to keep them. Constant worry had led to his collapse. He explained: "I had considered things hopeless and so since then my life as [sic] changed so much that it would be impossible for me to marry her if she came here and although I am being torn apart at this moment there really isn't anything I can do about it for I am in love with someone else and to her I owe so much for during my illness it was only her that kept me going…." He closed his letter "with an ache in my heart for as I sit here it seems that someone as [sic] just returned from the dead and actually is not real. Please do your best for me Sir if you have to give her my reason and let her down as lightly as possible for in her mind she is probably thinking that I am dead and it would be better if she believed that." A Foreign Office official's note on the letter read: "This will not help the case of the Soviet wives either."[38] The Moscow Embassy duly notified Miss Trifanova of German's decision.[39]

Sometimes the marital relationship did not survive the reunion. Flight Sergeant Thomas Percival Clarke of the Royal Air Force was among the most persistent of the husbands. He was attached to the RAF Air Mission in Moscow, where he met and married Natalia Vasilievna on 17 January 1943. Clarke wrote many letters to the Foreign Office to advocate for his wife's release.[40] Clarke's mother and father lobbied Winston Churchill on his behalf, and his mother wrote the king.[41] Clarke also lobbied several MPs, including Brendan Bracken and Louis Tolley, especially after his wife's name did not appear on the earliest list of wives permitted to leave, although she ultimately did receive permission to join him in 1945. Clarke's expressed devotion to and activism on behalf of his wife impressed Foreign Office officials, but Moscow Embassy officials worried about the sincerity of Mrs. Clarke's attachment to her husband. Sharman described her as "an attractive looking girl with expensive tastes… living with a senior member of an Allied Embassy and…a regular guest at diplomatic parties." Perhaps she would become unsatisfied with her RAF Sergeant once reunited with him.[42] London colleagues rebuked this gossip and the bias it suggested, but it turned out to be prescient.[43] Once reunited after several years of separation, their relationship broke down almost at once, and the wife returned to the Soviet Union with the Dynamo Football club, which was then in England on a good will tour.[44] This created an opportunity for anti-British propaganda. The 1943 marriage between Zinaida Mikhaislovna Scholohova and Sergeant Kenneth Garrison Liddell, also of the RAF, suffered a similar fate. Mrs. Liddell separated from her husband soon after their 1945 reunion. She too became a subject of Soviet concern, but at first she was not similarly eager to leave London, where she was making a good income.[45] But in the end she also returned to the Soviet Union.

A few civilian names appeared on the list, including three journalists and a clerk at the British Embassy. One prominent case among these couples consumed considerable consular work. Ronald Matthews (1903–1967), correspondent for the *Daily Herald,* was one of several journalists covering the Soviet Union who married Russian women.[46] Matthews met his wife, Tanya Svetlova (1913–1999) when she became his secretary during his assignment to Moscow.[47] Western journalists depended upon Russian language assistants to carry out their work in the Soviet Union during the war, and Matthews was no exception. After divorcing her first husband, Tanya Svetlova married Matthews on 31 October 1942 and filed the forms and papers to request her release from Soviet citizenship on 10 November 1942. Although Ivan Maisky, Soviet ambassador to the UK until 1943, had assured Matthews that the process would not take long, the Soviet bureaucracy made no response for months. Growing impatient and dissatisfied with the efforts of the British embassy in Moscow to help him, in June 1943 Matthews wrote to his MP, A.P. Herbert, to urge him to raise a question in Parliament to draw attention to his case. By the end of the year, a Moscow Embassy official described Matthews as "reduced to a highly nervous condition" by the delay. Having lost hope in the procedure to obtain a release from Soviet citizenship, Matthews petitioned Minister of Foreign Affairs Vyacheslav Molotov for permission for his wife to leave the country on her Soviet passport in order to travel to England to provide support to Matthews' bereaved mother. To the apparent surprise of everyone, this expedient worked, and Ronald and Tanya Matthews successfully departed from the Soviet Union in early

February 1944, despite a last-minute attempt by officials at the airport to separate the couple and retain Tanya and the Matthews' infant son in the Soviet Union.[48] Tanya Matthews then settled with her son in Cairo while Matthews went on to cover the Normandy invasion and the campaigns in Europe during the summer of 1944.

Although Tanya Matthews was safely out of the Soviet Union, the Matthews' difficulties with state authorities continued. It soon became clear that Tanya Matthews would neither leave Cairo to travel onward to the UK nor return to the Soviet Union, as had been implied by the award of an exit visa. Her very public avowal of her plans troubled both the British embassy in Cairo and Foreign Office officials. The Foreign Office, in particular, worried that the apparent violation of the terms of the agreement to allow her departure might compromise their ongoing efforts to win the release of other Soviet wives of British subjects. Lord Kinnear, UK ambassador to Egypt, asked the Foreign Office to put pressure on Matthews to get his wife to leave Cairo.[49] This proved difficult, as Ronald and Tanya Matthews were no more amenable to British authority than they had been to Soviet authority. The Foreign Office's letter to Matthews, urging him to bring his wife to the UK took some time to reach him, as he was moving quickly from place to place while covering the Normandy campaign and then suffered serious injuries in an accident. His reply, when Matthews finally composed it, indignantly rejected the position of the Foreign Office. In Matthews' view, the Foreign Office had bungled the early attempts to extricate his wife from the Soviet Union, there had never been any undertaking for Tanya Matthews to return to the Soviet Union, and if there had been the Soviet Union itself, by the behaviour towards the Matthews family upon their departure, would have negated any such agreement. In addition, he noted, it was unsafe for his wife to go to England at that time, and she would remain in Cairo.[50] Despite this response, which officials might well have regarded as churlish and unappreciative of their efforts on his behalf, officials continued to work in support of Tanya Matthews' petition for release from Soviet citizenship.[51]

Not all couples suffered unhappy endings. Only eight of the POW couples were reunited, but most of the couples who married in the Soviet Union during the war were ultimately allowed to leave in the second half of 1945 or early 1946. As detailed above, the wife of Brigadier Way and the wife of Driver German were two notable exceptions. In addition, two wives arrived in Britain but elected to return to the Soviet Union, Mrs. Clarke and Mrs. Liddell. In contrast, the case of Corporal Joseph Francis York, also of the RAF, suggests that some of these relationships proved resilient despite long separations and difficult challenges. This case also suggests the extent of the effort expended on these cases by officials. York married Lucille Williamovna Rautiainen née Toivonen on 4 May 1942. Lucille had been born an American citizen in Michigan, but her family had brought her to the USSR as a young girl, and she had surrendered her American passport and become a Soviet citizen in April 1937. Her case became one of special interest for British Ambassador Sir Archibald Clark Kerr[52] because she suffered from diabetes, and York and Clark Kerr wanted her in Moscow so she could be provided with proper medical care. Soviet authorities denied this request, but Lucille came to Moscow anyway, and Clark Kerr had to intervene with Andrey Vyshinsky, who served as Deputy Foreign Minister under Molotov, to keep her there.[53] With Vyshinsky, Clark Kerr adopted a knowing, patriarchal tone, readily conceding that "it is difficult to condone this unhappy woman's return to Moscow without a pass and that, in so doing she has been guilty of an act of folly, (not, I may say, uncommon in women), which exposes her to the rigours of the law." Clark Kerr begged that an exception be made for her, despite her "stupidity," noting her improved health since she had been able to have proper treatment and how much he would appreciate such "an act of compassion."[54] Whether or not this flattery proved decisive for Vyshinsky, Mrs. York remained in Moscow, working at the Military Mission.

Meanwhile, in England, York continued to lobby on behalf of his wife as years passed. In 1945, he turned to his MP R.L. Paget, who wrote to Foreign Secretary Ernest Bevin about the case. Mrs. York finally received permission to join her husband, who wrote a letter of gratitude to the Foreign Office, thanking officials for their "untiring efforts and sympathetic help."[55] Lucille York was not the only American among the Moscow wives. RAF Sergeant Edgar Frederick Parr married Stella Dolgum on 24 October 1942. Stella had been born in New York City, but had surrendered her American passport to become a Soviet citizen in 1941. Parr, like York, actively lobbied on behalf of his wife, despite his posting in Ceylon (now Sri Lanka), writing to Winston Churchill as well as Foreign Office officials. Mrs. Parr, like Mrs. York, was finally allowed to leave the USSR. Mrs. Parr was one of the three wives who received permission to leave the Soviet Union in January 1946.[56] This was the last round of permissions authorized by the Soviets, although the British kept up the pressure to gain further releases.

## *Love and Marriage and Foreign Policy*

In April 1948, Sir Maurice Peterson,[57] who had taken over as British Ambassador to the Soviet Union from Clark Kerr in 1946, had a meeting with Vyshinsky that focused entirely on the issue of the Soviet-born wives of British subjects. Peterson tried once again to persuade Vyshinsky of the importance of the matter. He also asked Vyshinsky to explain the Soviet point of view, as he claimed that he had trouble understanding it. Vyshinsky did not believe this rhetorical claim, saying: "Soviet attitude towards the Soviet wives had been explained many times and was based on Soviet law. He did not think there could be any real misunderstanding." Vyshinsky reiterated this view later in the meeting, saying: "…that he was convinced I realized how the matter really stood and that it was unnecessary to go over it again and again."[58]

By 1948, Vyshinsky might have been forgiven for this sentiment, as the British had indeed brought up this issue over and over again. Since 1943, many high-level contacts between British and Soviet officials had discussed the position of Soviet women married to British subjects. In June 1943, Ambassador Clark Kerr reported making several personal appeals to Molotov on behalf of these couples, at that time eight in number. Also in June, Sir Alexander Cadogan spoke to Ivan Maisky, Soviet ambassador to the UK, about the issue, and Clark Kerr followed up with Maisky in August. Towards the end of the year, around the time of the Teheran Conference, Foreign Secretary Eden sent a personal message to Molotov from Cairo, asking him to use his influence to obtain exit visas for these women, the number of which had grown to twelve. This initiative at least elicited a reply, and Molotov responded that consideration of such cases by the Praesidium of the Supreme Soviet, the body that had jurisdiction over such matters, had practically ceased because of wartime conditions. British officials concluded that not much could be accomplished until the end of the war. Tellingly, Molotov expressed his surprise that such "a minor question" would attract Eden's personal attention.[59]

As soon as practicable, the British returned to the matter, driven in part by public opinion. During her spring 1945 tour of the Soviet Union, Mrs. Churchill sought to bring the issue to the attention of Mrs. Molotov.[60] In May 1945, chargé d'affaires Frank Roberts raised the issue with Vyshinsky. Roberts reminded Vyshinsky that, as the war had ended, the time had come to deal with these cases. He suggested that releasing these wives would allay the personal hardships suffered by the couples and contribute to good will between the UK and the Soviet Union.[61] Clark Kerr had further conversations with Molotov in June 1945, and, in July, requested that the Dean of Canterbury bring Stalin's attention to the subject. Clark Kerr's account of this conversation suggested that Stalin might take some action.[62] These discussions paved the way for a private discussion between Clement Attlee and Stalin at Potsdam in August 1945, which seemingly proved decisive in the release of some of the wives in the autumn and winter of 1945.[63]

The tedium of this listing, which is not exhaustive, demonstrates that the British brought up the matter again and again, much to the exasperation of the Soviets. The disagreement between the UK and the USSR had several different components. First, the two nations had opposing views about the nature of nationality. In its simplest terms, the British recognized dual nationality and the Soviets did not. In the 1948 meeting described by Peterson, Vyshinsky explained that, given the British view of dual nationality: "If the wives went to the United Kingdom they could be claimed as British subjects. His point seemed clearly to be that it was against Soviet law to allow the wives to go to a country in which such a contention could be sustained."[64] This clash places the possession of women at the centre of establishing national identity. The harsh treatment of British women who had married foreigners identified as enemies after the outbreak of the First World War described by Ginger Frost contrasts with the insistence of British authorities that the foreign wives of British subjects were also British, a position that Soviet authorities could not accept. The relationship between gender and citizenship provides the through line linking these different situations. The question of the citizenship status of the Eastern European women who married British ex-POWs also provided another platform for a struggle over the expanded claims of Soviet citizenship over territories in Eastern Europe. The British and the Americans resisted these claims and moved to protect these women from Soviet authorities, in so far as that was possible. They agreed that Soviet interrogators should not have access to women claiming to be wives of Allied servicemen until those claims had been investigated. British officials firmly rejected the Soviet claim that the term "Soviet" could be applied to Poles from east of the Curzon line, a view shared by the Americans.[65]

In addition, political pressures animated both governments. In a memorandum describing a conversation between Vyshinsky and Maxwell Hamilton, chargé d'affaires of the United States, Vyshinsky put the Soviet position on denying exit visas to Soviet women married to foreigners in historical context. Hostile émigré populations had sustained anti-revolutionary movements after the French Revolution and the Russian Revolution, and consequently the Soviet government sought to avoid sustaining such groups. In addition, the Soviet government insisted on closely examining each case on its alleged merits to make sure that the women involved did not use marriage as a cover for avoiding their responsibilities as citizens.[66] The British, in contrast, had to deal with public opinion. The aggrieved husbands and members of their families wrote to their local Members of Parliament. They wrote to the prime minister, to the foreign secretary, and to the king. MPs regularly presented Parliamentary Questions that compelled officials to prepare formal responses. The emotional appeal of families, ex-POWs, and returning servicemen on behalf of wives left behind, meant the government could not ignore the issue. In addition, officials tended to agree that the separation of husbands and wives represented a genuine grievance with which they sympathized. In 1943, the Foreign Office instructed the Moscow Embassy to pursue the issue because "on grounds of humanity, we think it important that everything possible should be done to prevent the separation of these wives from their husbands." Officials also wished to avoid seeing the matter raised in public, as "The subject is naturally one on which personal feelings are inclined to run high...."[67] Two years later, in 1945, an embassy official dealing with a particularly difficult case involving the wife of a POW incarcerated by Soviet forces used the same kind of language in discussing "the unhappy case" that involved him "in a long struggle against the usual inertia and inhumanity."[68] In addition, the husbands often expressed a sense of rejection by an erstwhile ally. T.P. Clarke, who campaigned so diligently on behalf of his wife only to be rejected by her in the end, expressed this sentiment in a letter to Louis Tolley, MP, complaining that the Soviets "...appear to have quickly forgotten service rendered in connection with the Arctic convoys."[69]

In the months immediately following the end of the war, Foreign Office officials enjoyed some modest successes in extricating some of the wives from the Soviet Union, but many Soviet wives continued to languish. And new marriages continued to take place. At the same time the Soviet position hardened. No additional wives obtained exit visas after February 1946. In 1947, the Soviet Union underlined its intransigence on this issue by passing a law that forbade the marriage of Soviet citizens with foreigners. This step led to a storm of international criticism and a confrontation at the United Nations. The marriage prohibition brought the Soviet Union in conflict with the Universal Declaration of Human Rights. In addition, citizens of other countries had encountered the Soviet refusal to release Soviet women who had married foreign men. The son of the Chilean ambassador to the USSR was not permitted to take his wife with him, when his father came to the end of his term and the family returned to Chile. The Chileans later led the challenge to the USSR that came before the UN.[70] The issue was taken up again in the conference on the international position of married women, and in 1954, after the death of Stalin, the USSR repealed this legislation, although Soviet women who married foreigners continued to occupy a very precarious position and few were allowed to leave.

During wartime, especially war on a global scale, government authorities typically subordinated the intimate, private lives of individuals to wartime public policy enacted to keep friends and enemies apart. Political and military leaders might wish to set aside the intimate lives of ordinary people, but the questions of power and authority raised by those wishing to carry on their lives have left traces in the archives. These fragmentary narratives, however incomplete, remind us that although state power—even authoritarian state power—can and often does limit the choices exercised by individuals, they nevertheless can exhibit a scope for creative resistance. As these personal stories suggest, such individuals sometimes carved out a space for themselves despite the best efforts of government officials to thwart them. And in turn, the emotions generated by these episodes can seep into the realm of high politics, in this case, by contributing to the breakdown of the alliance between the British and the Soviets that ushered in the Cold War.[71]

# PART 5

# *Everyday Violence*

*Our final section consists of three chapters united in their focus on domestic, sexual, and intimate-partner violence. In studies located on three different continents, these contributors in turn discuss the troubling circumstances in which Canadian women were accused of infanticide, the growing opprobrium around abusive fathers in nineteenth-century France, and the state's responses to violence against women in late twentieth-century Guatemala. Where, we might ask, does each of these case studies fall along what Jane Nicholas calls "a continuum of daily violence against women and children" understood as more or less ordinary in these patriarchal societies but which, from the perspective of victims and survivors, constituted nothing less than "a state of terror"?*[1]

*Nicholas sets the stage in Chapter 14 with her study of a century's worth of criminal case files for women accused of infanticide in Ontario. She makes a fascinating argument about how the everyday violence experienced by girls and women ("a particular conception of white legitimate suffering bodies") informed the compassion and judicial clemency typically displayed in these cases, even for women disadvantaged by class, race, and ethnicity. This essay offers a deep reading of the troubling story of Annie Robinson, who was convicted of infanticide and sentenced to be hanged in November, 1909. It also draws our attention to the power of emotions in legal proceedings, revealing how "embodied performances of correct emotions" by women accused of infanticide were critical to their prospects for judicial mercy.*[2]

*Violence inflicted on the bodies of girls and women—this time, more explicitly, sexual violence—is the focus of Chapter 15, by Fabienne Giuliani. The context is nineteenth-century France and the emphasis is not so much on individual cases as on the social, cultural, and political construction of a new public menace. Giuliani's central character is* *the working-class father as sexual predator and child abuser—*le père infâme*—as revealed in social inquiries, court records, and especially as the century progressed, in sensational newspaper accounts. The resonance with the Nicholas chapter could not be stronger; indeed, it would be difficult to imagine a more "despicable" pattern of paternal abuse than the one revealed in the Robinson case. And by engaging with the growing literature on fatherhood, including failed fatherhood, as the expression of historically specific understandings of masculinity, Giuliani offers an interesting bridge to a number of other essays in this collection, especially those by Garneau (Chapter 5) and Chilton and Moran (Chapter 10).*

*With Emilee Lord and John Wertheimer's Chapter 16, on violence against women and domestic abuse in Guatemala at the turn of the twenty-first century, finally, we find a challenge to the prevailing scholarship on these issues. Most studies of sexual and domestic violence in Guatemala have suggested that authorities in that country have tended to turn a blind eye to the issue because of "a corrosive blend of corruption and machismo."*[3] *Using a creative methodology to assemble a small archive of public-opinion interviews, Lord and Wertheimer argue that public awareness around these forms of everyday violence has in fact grown since the 1980s. And while the problem certainly persists, Guatemala's legislative and judicial efforts to combat violence against women have been more effective than most scholars will allow.*

## CHAPTER 14

# Suffering for Compassion

## *Everyday Violence and Infanticide in Ontario, 1820–1920s*

*Jane Nicholas*

"The tradition of the oppressed teaches us that the 'state of emergency' in which we live is not the exception but the rule."[1]

Annie Robinson was scheduled to be executed on 24 November 1909.[2] She had been sentenced two months earlier for killing two infants, born about one week apart in March 1908 to two of her unmarried daughters, Jessie and Ellen. The father of both infants was Robinson's husband, James, the girls' father. When Annie testified to killing one of the infants, she wept stating, "I was just in such a state of sorrow for the child on the bed—for Jessie. And the shame—of it being her child, and her own father, which just driv [sic] me that I didn't realize—what I was doing at the time."[3] Annie's expression of the suffering of her children and herself is documented throughout the lengthy court transcripts. The girls lived in a state of fear in the small rural and remote village of Hugel in northern Ontario. They had been sexually abused since they were small children, and Ellen had, in fact, given birth to a child by her father in 1906, and was pregnant again at the time of the trial. She was seventeen years old. The abuse was horrifyingly persistent and a part of the girls' everyday life. In his charge to the jury, Justice Magee acknowledged the "long suffering" and "ill-treatment" of Annie, Jessie, and Ellen, but dismissed its significance, telling the jury the only issue to consider was Annie's actions.[4]

Annie Robinson's capital case file, read alongside criminal assize and coroners' files on infanticide in Ontario between 1820 and the 1920s, provides a mediated glimpse of how everyday violence toward girls and women manifested in infanticide.[5] If legislation required investigations to determine culpability in infant deaths, the exercise of the law reveals a near willful desire to find white women not guilty, making Annie's death sentence rare and unusual.[6] Building from cultural anthropologists' and historians' investigations of everyday violence and suffering, this chapter assesses how levels of violence were adjudicated through the suffering body, wherein compassion was exercised toward women perpetrators of infanticide, who were deemed to be morally legitimate victims of excess violence.[7] Work by historian Constance Backhouse has proven that desperate women found compassionate courts in nineteenth-century Canadian infanticide cases.[8] That white women who violently shunned motherhood generally found mercy remains perplexing in a culture wherein white women's highest calling was motherhood within legal marriage. Yet, as cultural anthropologist Miriam Ticktin argues, compassion is a response to an "embodied performance" that makes an actor "recognizable" as a "morally legitimate suffering body."[9] Through the collective suffering, courts often found certain white women deserving of compassion; they had suffered enough and suffered publicly.

Tracing the overwhelming continuities in the adjudication of infanticide investigations in late nineteenth- and early twentieth-century Ontario reveals the durability of a particular conception of white legitimate suffering bodies. This conception revolves around the axis of female sexual respectability, nobility, and a public articulation of appropriate emotions in the face of everyday violence. Focusing on the suffering body in infanticide investigations reveals how family violence created a near-constant state of exception in which colonial and Canadian women lived; a state of exception perhaps best articulated by anthropologist Michael Taussig's phrase "terror as usual," with its nod to the habituation of violence. To Taussig, the state of terror is only revealed accidentally through an especially ugly or poignant example that flares brightly and quickly burns out.[10] Annie Robinson's case burned as a contained, ignominious example revealing the typicality of the state of exception and what might be described as everyday terror. Focusing in particular on the homicide trials of Annie Robinson in September of 1909, I argue this curious pattern played out as a result of the informal recognition of the terror as usual in girls' and women's lives as part of the measuring of moral legitimacy through the body—and significantly, the white body.[11] As long as certain women could establish that they were morally legitimate suffering bodies and that the pattern of violence was not triggered by them, the law recuperated them by lessening penalties and punishments; but not without first measuring their respectability and conduct through their pain and suffering. In the face of family violence, white women like Annie Robinson embodied a fine balance of duty, obligation, suffering, and appropriate shame. Infanticide was then an extension of the realm of everyday family violence within this state of emergency.

## *Reading the Robinson Case File*

For historians, court records are stimulating and challenging in part because of the requirement to give voice to suffering.[12] Historical case files are both abundant and sparse. Thousands of files have been preserved (with files improving as the state apparatus developed in Upper Canada, Canada West, and Ontario), but many are incomplete and, of the ones that are comprehensive, many contain only portions of dialogue transcribed by clerks. This follows an established, well-noted pattern of deficits of "the case file": its fragmentary nature, its authorship by people in positions of power, its way of capturing inauthentic "voice" or occluding it entirely, and its general distortions by the very nature of its production for the purposes of state bureaucracies or institutions.[13] Against these issues, historians have argued for its methodological value in regard to the agency of vulnerable populations.[14] The Robinson case file suffers some of the well-documented issues historians have noted of this type of evidence. It is partial, with frustrating silences and gaps, and was produced for the purposes of recording the means to justice as opposed to what actually happened. As Shelley Gavigan notes in Chapter 9, court records of speech compelled in various judicial offices and locations leading to "scrutiny and judgment, then and now" hardly exist on "fair or neutral terrain."[15] Yet, the Robinson file remains the only documentation of the case and the lives of its participants, save some surprisingly sparse newspaper reporting.

While the limits of the case file make it difficult to access the thoughts and experiences of Annie, Jessie, or Ellen, their case is valuable in its stark revelation of the moral judication of suffering. Ethical considerations remain. Following Backhouse's work, I have used the real names here, given the time that has lapsed.[16] The Robinson trial has already received some limited attention in the historiography.[17] In her study of child sexual abuse in Victorian England, Louise A. Jackson writes, "We have a duty to our subjects to 'use them as a source' in a responsible way, to render their accounts with subtlety, to acknowledge the interconnectedness of body, pain, experience, voice."[18] I have followed Jackson in attempting an analysis that speaks to issues of violence, the body, and justice. Focusing on the body and emotions refines our understanding of the Robinson case and the perplexing acceptance of infanticide.[19]

## *Family Violence, Infanticide, and Cultural Violence in Ontario*

Family violence was ordinary in nineteenth- and early twentieth-century Ontario. Various acts of violence were socially acceptable and permitted by law, including corporal punishments of children, servants, and wives.[20] Asymmetrical power relations formally and informally structured households and legal authority to discipline family members fell to male heads of household, who could exert control physically, economically, financially, and emotionally.[21] Both men and women perpetrated violence, and issues of gender, class, race, and age formed a complicated matrix of who could reasonably execute violence on other household members in the name of discipline. Physical discipline was often regarded as necessary to correct behaviour and to punish infractions, although common law provisions provided some protection against "excessive cruelty." Defining and proving excess, if one survived it, remained complicated. Nineteenth- and twentieth-century courts became spaces where women sought protection and legal remedy to violence and denial of support.[22] Nonetheless, domestic violence against women, children, and servants was recurring, and women also committed violence against children and other women.[23] While under hegemonic white, Anglo-Protestant domestic ideology women were expected to be earthly angels, yet they lived in a society that enshrined violence in law and socially accepted it, making them—sometimes at once—both victim and perpetrator.

Infanticide took on new import alongside "the discovery of child mortality" in the nineteenth century.[24] Three interrelated factors seem to have been at play. First, infant death needed to be parsed from adult death and removed from the realm of nature in order for it to be identified as a social, if not a political problem.[25] The increased use of vital statistics created a sense of the scale of infant mortality and helped to recognize infant deaths as premature; that is, taken from the realm of nature, where such deaths were expected, and situated within culture with its expectation of sustained biological life.[26] If infant death had been reshaped from something natural and mundane to stand as "the most sensitive index…of social and sanitary progress," the infant figured as issue, but only unevenly as individual.[27] By 1909, first-wave feminists and reformers were attending to child and maternal health but with blinkered (and sometimes eugenical) perspectives that excluded many children. The disabled, the "illegitimate," and other "lesser-bred" children were not publicly mourned as lost future citizens; they were economic and physical threats to the well-being of the nation and the family and sometimes dismissed as better off dead.[28] While the status of some infants rose then, and their deaths were seen as unnatural losses, infanticide slithered along.

Second, the rising status of physicians as the professional interpreters of the body meant that they could reputedly isolate and name a cause of death. Significantly, they could also at least wager whether or not a child had been born alive, was stillborn, died in the process of being born, or was not viable, although decisive conclusions remained elusive.[29] Coroners' files reveal the very real struggle to prove an infant had lived prior to its death. Indeed, the very questions of the beginning and end of life were provisional, making it difficult to conclude two important though basic facts: the infant had lived, and the death was unnatural.[30]

Third, the development of the state—a rapid development in colonial Canada in the nineteenth century—created an apparatus of registrations, official paperwork, and offices imbued with power over the administration of life, the official naming of death, and the meting out of punishment. The coroners' office, for example, went from local authority to mediate gossip and allay fears to quasi-grand jury "providing rapid responses to high-stakes cases of suspicious and violent death."[31] As a result of these three factors, in a relatively short sixty or so years, cause of death in coroners' files for unidentified infants went from "a visitation from God" in the 1840s to highly technical and specific declarations.[32] By 1896, for example, one Toronto physician's post-mortem of a newly born male child included details of length and weight, as well as an individual analysis of the major internal and external organs. He reported that the child was "well nourished" and "born at full term." He concluded that the "child was born alive"; "could not have lived long—probably less than two hours"; was "not very long dead when found"; and that there could have been "no physician in attendance."[33] Such specific declarations were not always the case and post-mortems were not always conducted. By 1902, finding infant bodies, especially in larger counties like York, was greeted with a near bureaucratic sigh of habituation.

Many victims of infanticide who appear in legal records were "illegitimate."[34] Infanticide registered as a woman's issue hinging on respectability, victimization, and birth control, the latter of which was legally and morally proscribed.[35] Indeed, the striking thing about the criminal and coroner files—and the strange exception of the Robinson case—is that so few of the cases address how women got pregnant, leaving the stark impression of the biological impossibility that they did so themselves. The relations of the sexes, however, were such that women's bodies were sites of profound discipline and that purity, chastity, and morality were deemed to be their greatest gifts and the easiest to spoil. Cases of seduction and rape in the period reveal the commonness of the experience and the impossible bind women faced of having their own reputations adjudicated as part of the alleged course of justice.[36] Without legal access to birth control, both women's pursuit of pleasure and their victimization left them vulnerable. An infant for an unmarried woman was a remarkable danger to her emotional and economic well-being. Formalized Christian marriage legitimated not only the children who came afterward but also the woman. Under colonial and Canadian law, children belonged to their fathers, except when they were illegitimate, and then they were their mother's alone. While not all single mothers became social outcasts, single motherhood could be a disaster for women, who were dismissed from respectable work and subsequently lost their place in society, or became outcasts living on the social, moral, and economic margins of society.[37] Women's respectability was often calculated in toto by way of sexuality.

Most of the women and girls investigated for infanticide were unmarried and described as youthful, although records of actual age are spotty at best. Some lived with their family of origin who, in turn, assisted with varying degrees of awareness with the delivery and disposal of the body. The Robinson family fits this general pattern, although with the acknowledged violence of incest. The female culture of birthing and dying in many of these cases of infant death was difficult for the law to pierce. When family members assisted women in concealing a birth and death of a child, it was typically mothers and sisters, who seemed to do so shrouded by silence.

A few examples highlight these points. In 1858, Catherine Graham gave birth silently and alone in a household that included her mother, father, and a sister, Matilda. While both sisters claimed that Matilda had no knowledge of the birth, Catherine reported that Matilda brought her the scissors she used to cut the umbilical cord. For almost eighteen hours, Catherine kept the baby in bed with her before leaving the child by a fence post in the middle of the night. Although her mother witnessed the discharge of the placenta, Catherine recalled: "when it fell my mother picked it up and put in in the pot—she did not say anything."[38]

Both married and unmarried sisters aided. In 1861, when Eleanor Strachan was on trial for infanticide, her married sister Eliza Winks admitted to taking the infant's body in a carpetbag and disposing of it in the St. Lawrence River.[39] More than fifty years later, in 1917, unmarried sisters Alice and Annie Douglas were tried for the murder of Annie's newborn. Annie admitted to giving the infant turpentine, which Alice reportedly brought to her. Both Annie and her sister were found not guilty; at the time Annie was twenty-one and Alice seventeen.[40]

Similarly, Gladys and Doris Neabel were sisters living together in the same household when they hastened the death of Gladys' infant in 1923.[41] Gladys was found guilty of concealment in the death of her child and Doris pled guilty to the unlawful disposition of a dead body. They were both unmarried. Gladys was eighteen years old and Doris was fourteen. The indictment outlined how Doris took the infant and left it "under a stump in an open field" in order to conceal the fact that Gladys had given birth. In response to the guilty verdict and plea, the community protested. Two hundred and seventy-four rate payers signed a petition to request leniency. It described the girls as: "two young daughters of Daniel Neabel" and as "young girls of tender years of respectable parents" and further described the family as "well respected by everyone who know them."[42] As in many other case files from coroner or criminal proceedings, no one asked how Gladys got pregnant. Silence could recuperate familial respectability.

Over the course of almost a century, infanticide remained a crime reacted to with leniency, even with the rising need to protect infants from "premature" death. When Annie Robinson was sentenced to death, the court's seeming lack of compassion sparked outcry. Church authorities, women's groups like the Women's Christian Temperance Union and suffrage associations, as well as ordinary citizens wrote letters, signed petitions, and supported motions to request both clemency and subsequently the early release of Annie Robinson from prison.[43] There was no doubt that Annie contributed to the infants' deaths. Like many other girls and women, she admitted to it. Contrary to the spoken words of Justice Magee, however, her actions were only a small part of the adjudication of justice. What is unique to the lengthy Robinson case file is the subtle piercing of the silence on terror, suffering, and violence.

### *The Case of Annie Robinson*

James Robinson and Annie Mathieson were likely married some time in 1888 when Annie was about twenty-four years old and James about twenty-six. One year later, Annie gave birth to her first child. By 1905, she had given birth to ten living children and most of her marriage had been spent either pregnant or recovering from pregnancy and childbirth. It was, by Annie's testimony, around this time that James had taken to drink—a not insignificant fact given the temperance movement at the time.[44] In 1906, Annie's second daughter, Ellen, gave birth to her first child by her father, who was absorbed into the family.[45] By the fall of 1909, Jessie and Ellen had collectively given birth to five children, although both were still in their teen years.[46] Nevertheless, Robinson seems to have been a well-connected and respected man, who largely kept his family isolated on the bush farm and away from the community. The children attended school in winter, but otherwise rarely left the farm beyond weekly church attendance.[47]

By the summer of 1909, the appearance of respectable and hardworking bush farmers had given way to local gossip and authorities investigated. "Generally disbelieved" gossip about James slowly formed into concern about his unmarried, pregnant daughters who were never seen with an infant. A local Methodist minister made a complaint to J.J. Kelso of the Children's Aid Society in early August. Local authorities decided not to wait.[48] In an ill-conceived attempt to clear his reputation, James Robinson invited the local men to see the farm. On the morning of 9 August 1909, Ernest Albert Wright, a local merchant tailor and magistrate, and Dr. John Albert Dixon, the local doctor and coroner, attended to the farm. Until that point, Wright testified that James Robinson had been seen as a man of good standing in the community, who was "an honest and virtuous man" and one with a reputation that would take more than rumor, scandal or "a woman's talk" to besmirch.[49] As he testified, infant bodies did it.

By the time Wright and Dixon arrived at the farm, James had fled. Annie immediately broke down and took them to a gravesite near the barn where three bodies were discovered. When the men returned much later that night with police constable John Bole and a liveryman named Samuel Wilson, Annie broke down further, losing consciousness and crying and choking. She was violently "assisted" by way of "20, 30, or 40" closed-fisted punches to the back by one of the men, who had brought her outside.[50] Over the course of the night she told details of the case and was removed from the farm in the morning, after the men had breakfast, a meal likely made by Annie and/or her daughters.

The confession was as strange as the entire investigation. Questions emerged about the sobriety of the investigators. Annie's brother Peter Mathieson described his one criticism of the investigation and legal proceedings as arising "from the more or less drunken condition of those who went to my sister's home and placed her under arrest."[51] Indeed, the word "investigation" might imply a more formal, thoughtful pattern of fact-finding when the testimony revealed chaos. At trial, few of the men could accurately recount the events or their order, lending credibility to the stories they had been drinking. There was a serious question of whether Annie's confession was admissible. It was unclear what capacity the men were acting in: curious neighbour or legal authority. More than once Annie was described by the men investigating as being "in terror" during the night. The confession was also incorrectly dated as being given on 9 August, although it was given, recorded, and signed on the tenth. It was also unclear when Annie was arrested.

The physical evidence was also questionable. The three bodies removed from the single gravesite near the barn were almost indistinguishable from one another and no one could say which body was which or even in what order they had come out of the ground. Further, there were three infant bodies but only two were subject to the two separate murder cases against Annie; and only one was the subject of a coroner's inquest. The doctor and coroner testified that he could not identify which was Ellen's child or which was Jessie's. The matter seemed to be a small one as it raised little attention in the course of the trials. In spite of the problems with the confession and the physical evidence, however, Annie's confession stood. The problems of memory, physical evidence, and the means of confession were set aside for the men. The discrepancy in crediting men's word and women's word in the trial is striking.

Annie Robinson testified to killing the infants and, despite a substantial effort of her defence counsel to have her confession disallowed, she was convicted in two separate trials of homicide and sentenced to death as required by the Criminal Code. The case against Annie Robinson hinged upon the level and type of violence she faced as well as the girls' role in their own victimization. The adjudication of justice became a measurement of the morally legitimate suffering body against largely unarticulated standards of everyday violence.

## *The Trials of Annie Robinson*

During both trials Jessie and Ellen testified for the Crown. Each faced a long examination on abuse. As Backhouse argues, while most women and girls suffered in private, "one of the greatest mythologies embedded in law" was that women made accusations of sexual assault frivolously.[52] Girls, like Jessie and Ellen, would be vigorously questioned, with their own actions coming under scrutiny. Such was the uneven balance in gendered respectability: girls' and women's was almost constantly under question, even when clearly victims, while men, like James Robinson, maintained theirs in the wake of gossip until bodies were brought up from the ground. This contributed to the durable myth of girl/woman as temptress that shaded rape and incest trials, sparking claims that victims entrapped, lured, or otherwise provoked assaults.[53] Jessie's and Ellen's testimony in this homicide case, then, paralleled sexual assault cases of the period, with their behaviour and their observations of their mother's emotions and deportment under scrutiny in spite of the fact that they were victim witnesses. It was precisely the continuation from incest to infanticide that rendered their own bodily suffering—and the question of its legitimacy—so significant.

Both the Crown and the defence went to great lengths to attempt to measure the level and types of violence, most especially physical violence. The girls reported that their father threatened them with violence and poisoning, that he had kicked and beaten them, and that he threatened to shoot one of the girls if she left the farm. Threats, however, did not necessarily register as legitimate suffering, and the persistent question remained whether or not they had suffered physically and excessively.

Annie, Jessie, and Ellen each recounted violence in the home, but nothing especially heinous given the accepted levels of everyday violence. Importantly, all faced significant questions regarding their own role in the abuse, but the questioning was longer and more invasive for the girls. Jessie and Ellen were asked repeated questions about whether or not and when they had disclosed the abuse to Annie. Jessie's cross-examination by the defence is indicative:

> Question: Now why didn't you tell your mother sooner?
> Answer: I was afraid of father.
> Question: Why were you afraid of your father?
> Answer: He threatened to beat me.
> Question: If you told?
> Answer: Yes sir.
> Question: And you were living in the same house with him and your mother?
> Answer: Yes sir.
> Question: And this was going on?
> Answer: Yes.
> Question: Did your father ever beat you?
> Answer: No, he never beat me.
> Question: Well then if he never beat you—
> Answer: Not for that.
> Question: If he never beat you why did you submit to him, why did you give way to him if he never beat you?
> Answer: I was afraid.[54]

The wording of the questions was clearly confusing as Jessie answered a specific question about being beaten for disclosing the abuse that turned into a statement of not being beaten at all. Her short answer "Not for that" was disregarded. At other points, in both trials, the word terror is used to describe the feelings of Annie, Jessie, and Ellen. Terror was, however, contested by the Crown Attorney who repeatedly asked about the infliction of physical beatings.

Later, after the trials, Sudbury Crown Attorney J.H. Clary provided further facts, likely that emerged from James Robinson's trial, to Minister of Justice A.B. Aylesworth and asserted that "terror dominated" in the home.[55] In spite of this, and although the girls reported that the sexual abuse started at around the age of five in Ellen's case and eight or nine in Jessie's, suspicion remained that they had somehow been accomplices in their own victimization for having allowed it to continue. Jessie's testimony is again indicative of the assessment of her role in her own victimization:

> Q: From what you saw of your own home, who would be master of the household, who controlled the household, your father or your mother?
> A: Father.
> Q: Now I suppose your father would have something to do with you at various places, inside the house and out?
> A: Yes, sir.
> Q: In the fields?
> A: All over.
> Q: If he would call you would you go?
> A: No, not until he would get cross with me.
> Q: And when he would get cross?
> A: I would go.
> Q: What would you do?
> A: I would have to go.
> Q: And that was the state of affairs in your home?
> A: Yes sir.

In spite of her clear attempt to refuse her father, Jessie was seen as complicit. As feminist social historians assert, victims of domestic abuse, sexual assault, and incest faced a host of hurdles to being believed. One of these related to the age of the victim, who after sixteen was greeted with increased doubt.[56] Indeed, by the time they were old enough to come forward and speak about the abuse, girls were less likely to be believed or were seen to be complicit. To his credit, Annie's defence attorney tried to ensure that their father's terrifying control was included in the trial even if it did not always appear as undue physical abuse in every instant.[57]

Both girls were testifying under difficult physical conditions. Jessie had given birth about seven weeks earlier to a child who died, and Ellen was heavily pregnant, and would give birth within weeks of the trial.[58] With their own morality in question, doubt crept into the legitimacy of their suffering. Even people sympathetic to Annie questioned her daughters' actions. Letters, petitions, and newspaper editorials often portrayed Annie as an innocent victim, who desperately tried to save her family from shame and disrepute. The bluntest effort to save Annie and criticize her daughters was the resolution passed by the International Order of The King's Daughters and Sons (Province of Ontario) that declared their support for "the unfortunate woman, Mrs. Robinson, who in her mother love tried to hide the guilt of her infamous husband and irresponsible daughters."[59] Many statements simply bypassed her daughters altogether.

Annie was bound by terror, sadness, and shame. When examined during the trial, Annie Robinson reported that even after she knew her husband was raping her daughters, she could not speak of it; not to her mother, not to her mother-in-law, not to anyone. When asked about this oppressive silence she replied, "I was borne down with sorrow and shame."[60] Jessie testified that, when her mother found out about the incest, her mother was "heart-broken." Ellen testified to the following:

> Q: Did you ever catch your mother when she would be crying alone? Did you ever see your mother when she would be crying quietly to herself?
> A: No. She nearly always cried when she started to talk to us.
> Q: Were there plenty of tears in that home?
> A: Yes.

Annie's reputation as a well-raised, religious, and virtuous woman broken down by years of abuse and terror was carefully established at trial. The defence in the first trial rested on Annie's testimony that began with her respectable upbringing in a kind, church-going, "middling poor" farm family. Questions regarding marriage were carefully laid out to reveal that Annie had been a dutiful wife in all regards: raising James's children, working in the fields, and never refusing her husband's sexual advances, although he was difficult to satisfy.[61] With the birth of Ellen's first baby, Annie knew of her abuse and yet could not leave. With ten children, Annie faced the gut-wrenching choice of leaving some or all of the children behind or sending them off without her. She tried the latter with Jessie, but James found her and brought her back to the farm.[62]

Further emotional internal conflict is revealed in the treatment of at least one of the infants. Immediately after Jessie's baby was born, Annie washed, dressed and fed him; actions not atypical in other cases.[63] As she did this, Jessie cried on the bed. Annie recalled: "She was crying - - - crying and lamenting, and said 'Oh, if I had not made do this this would not have happened,' and lamenting over this two or three times, or maybe more, and she said, 'Oh mother, if this could only be kept hid.'"[64] Annie put the child under the mattress and clothing where it suffocated. Not long after she went to rescue the child. He was dead.

After the trial, the Crown Attorney for Sudbury wrote the Minister of Justice with more details. At least one of the younger sisters was also being abused by James Robinson and at his later trial he was found guilty of rape of the youngest daughter and incest against Ellen and Jessie. His pattern of abuse included his selection of one of the girls in the only and shared bedroom, whom he would abuse while the others were present.[65] Although physical violence was carefully measured at the trial, this missed the emotional pain and embodied terror of witnessing and weaponized it as complicity.

In concluding his charge to the jury at the first homicide trial, Magee called Annie's behaviour into question for apparently allowing the abuse to occur and cautioned against over-sympathizing with her situation. He stated:

> Something many be said that it was weakness of character, if we so call it, that that was the real reason that allowed this wickedness to go on in her family for the gratification of her husband, but for the ruin of her own children, the fruit of her own body. There is sympathy of course for these children, but can one sympathise very much with a woman who allowed this to go on, and allowed her affection for a man who must have lost her respect, if it was affection for him, allowed her to let her own children be ruined by him during all these years. We must not lose our common sense in our sympathy. At the same time one is quite ready to acknowledge that this woman had many a trial and no doubt many and many a night of sorrow as she thought over this. She apparently was not to blame, so far as we know, for any of these acts of her husband, but we cannot admit that she was not to blame for allowing her children to be so treated and so brought up by the man who should have been their pattern in virtue and right conduct.[66]

Embodied emotions of shame, terror, and sorrow mattered very much, but the appeal to "common sense" attempted to dislocate the acts of homicide from the acts of abuse and the "stickiness" of the emotions associated with them.[67] In spite of Magee's attempt to parse character, emotions, and action, the three were formed in tandem, forging the morally suffering legitimate body at the heart of the case. Judgment of Annie Robinson was inseparable from the measurement of the embodied and emoted everyday violence and the state in which she and her daughters lived.

The jury disagreed with Magee. At the end of this first trial, the jury returned a verdict of not guilty "on the ground that she was not responsible for her action at the time the deed was committed."[68] The jury seemed to have seen Annie as a broken woman, defeated by her circumstances. The judge was testy in his response and returned the jury to deliberate on strict orders to reconsider the spoken evidence, within the strict letter of the law especially regarding insanity. The jury struggled with the charge. While they deliberated, James A. Mulligan and Magee had a terse exchange wherein Mulligan asked for the case to be reserved on the grounds that Annie had been deprived of a trial by jury. After nearly four hours of deliberation, and one further attempt to find her not guilty, the jury returned with a guilty verdict but with a recommendation for mercy. Justice Magee announced the mandatory death penalty and Annie Robinson's life expectancy was suddenly reduced to two months. She broke down in sobs, bent over and huddled in the corner of the dock. *The Globe* reported: "There is no doubt that every effort will be made to have the sentence commuted. Feeling here is very strong for her."[69] Another trial for the second infant began the next day and ended with the same result.

Local and national communities pled for mercy. As with other trials of women convicted of murder, some quarters of Canadian society struggled with the very idea of executing women.[70] Perhaps it was the commonness of infanticide combined with the seemingly harsh punishment in capital cases that made death so unpalatable. Perhaps, as a white woman whose respectability had been shattered through (at least to some) no fault of her own, death seemed too high a price to pay. Perhaps it was the respectability of Annie's brothers—one a Presbyterian minister and one a bachelor farmer—who stepped in to care for the children and promised to take in Annie as well; who also tracked down and apprehended a fleeing James Robinson, ensuring a trial that revealed more extensive details of his abuse of his wife and daughters as well as his own alleged role in encouraging Annie to commit infanticide.[71] Perhaps it was some of the hundreds of petitioners and letter writers, including a conflicted but still supportive Helen MacMurchy—a well-known physician and public health reformer—who pled for mercy. Unlike others who were firm in their support of Annie, MacMurchy wrote with mixed feelings but ultimately asserted her support "because the circumstances of this case are so abhorrent and beyond all description vile and dreadful that one would gladly forget them all. But the fact that they are so awful constitutes the poor woman's strongest plea. Certainly, the other criminal should be dealt with before his wife suffers the penalty of the law, and I am not sure that she should so suffer."[72] To writers like MacMurchy, Annie Robinson figured as an exception—a woman whose circumstances were deemed to be horrific and rare. At the very end of it all, Annie spent less than two years in prison for the murder of two of her grandchildren. A national community and the Cabinet spared her life because of the appalling and extraordinary circumstances for her actions. It is true that Annie and her daughters experienced horrible violence that offended moral sensibilities of the time. The crux of the problem, however, was that Annie, Ellen, and Jessie's circumstances reflected ordinary, everyday violence that was far too common in early twentieth-century Ontario.[73]

## *Suffering and Redemptive Acts of Compassion*

Then and now it would be easy to dismiss the Robinson case as aberrant and cast James as a despicable monster: a quintessential "*père infâme*" in Fabienne Giuliani's terms.[74] Abjection and disavowal create false distance, however understandable the rejection may be for the attempt to maintain the fiction of a civilized society. More accurately, the Robinson case stands as an exemplar. Within the wider context of family violence, we can trace at least some infanticide cases along a continuum of daily violence against women and children that constituted a state of terror. For Annie, Ellen, and Jessie, the deaths of two infants were bound with their own experiences of violence, terror, and abuse, and inseparable from them. Read alongside other cases, we can see the influence of the lack of birth control, the exaltation of purity, and the punishment of "illegitimacy." The Robinson case, while dramatic, indicates a wider pattern that many more infants' deaths followed: seduction, rape or incest, murder, disposal of the body, and later discovery of it. Recourse to justice could be gained through embodied performances of correct emotions to reveal moral legitimacy in what amounted to a performance of the normality of terror. All of this reveals the fine gradations of "life" in nineteenth- and early twentieth-century Canada, and how violence and emotions contributed to those gradations. Publicly airing the suffering of girls and women for their alleged shame provoked redemptive acts of compassion, but in the end, bartering pain for compassion was a poor substitute for the formal legal recognition of life with dignity for girls and women.

## CHAPTER 15

# Despicable Fathers

## *Constructing the Image of France's Poor and Incestuous* Pères Infâmes, *1804–1889*[1]

*Fabienne Giuliani*

On 15 November 1885, one of the inside pages of *Le Petit Parisien* reported on "the arrest of a wretched man, accused of having had relations with his daughter and having forced her into prostitution. This odious character, whose life has been but a long series of disgraceful acts, is named François Sardaigne. He…describes himself as a tailor; in reality, he has always lived off his daughter and his wife."[2] This brief story provides a snapshot of how incest was imagined in late nineteenth-century France: a crime committed by poor, alcoholic, and lazy fathers against their daughters. This understanding of incest as a crime of poverty, geographically concentrated in northern and eastern France, remains embedded in the collective imagination more than a century later.[3]

And yet, incest is not a primarily working-class or socially determined phenomenon.[4] Nor was this any less true at the turn of the nineteenth century, when incest had recently been decriminalized following the adoption of France's first Penal Code in 1791. Having previously been defined as sexual relations between biological relatives or between individuals with a spiritual or familial bond, the crime of incest was associated with the arbitrary administration of justice under the ancien régime and was left off the list of criminal offences drawn up by members of the Constituent Assembly. Indeed, it had formerly applied to both members of an incestuous couple, a couple that might consist of two consenting adults or an adult violently forcing a young girl into sexual relations. This broad definition of incest disappeared during the French

Revolution. Instead, the concept of rape, which had already existed in criminal law under the ancien régime, was used to prosecute men who vaginally penetrated girls. In other words, after 1791, incest—insofar as it involved a violent sexual act committed by a male relative against a young girl—came to be treated as rape. Although not forgotten, the other form of incest—involving consensual sexual activity between adults—was no longer criminalized. This chapter does not address this second notion of incest that existed at the turn of the nineteenth century. Rather, it focuses on one form of incestuous violence, namely sexual activity forced on a child by a parent who, by virtue of the latter's age or role within the family unit, had authority over the victim.

Other forms of incestuous violence, which are not discussed below, include those committed against children by brothers, uncles, or grandfathers—and, in rarer cases, by women or children against other family members. My goal is therefore not to undertake an anthropological study of incest in the nineteenth century. Rather, I focus on the type of assault most frequently cited in reports of incestuous violence, namely attacks by fathers against their children, regardless of the latter's gender. Furthermore, this dominant form of incestuous violence is also the one that first attracted the attention of social science researchers in the late 1970s. In keeping with the feminist struggles of the period, the earliest such works published in the United States analyze the father-daughter relationship through the lens of male domination. In a 1977 article, Judith Herman and Lisa Hirschman argued "that the greater the degree of male supremacy in any culture, the greater the likelihood of father-daughter incest."[5] Linda Gordon drew similar conclusions in her groundbreaking effort to historicize incest, using the records of child welfare agencies in Boston. As with Herman and Hirschman's work, Gordon's analysis focuses on the father-daughter relationship and ultimately argues that the study of such violence "requires a feminist perspective, that is, one that takes into account the whole system of gender relations in our society."[6] In the 1990s, the emerging concept of gender made it possible to further develop this feminist reading of incestuous violence. Take, for example, Anne-Marie Sohn's 1989 profile of incestuous fathers in France[7] and Marie-Aimée Cliche's analysis of incestuous violence in Quebec society during the nineteenth and twentieth centuries. The latter scholar concludes that her work "tends to validate the feminist interpretation of incest as an extreme manifestation of the patriarchal system."[8]

Indeed, the feminist conception of gender as an integral component of "a broader network of linkages encompassing sex, age, sexuality, hierarchies, roles, etc."[9] is key to approaching and understanding incestuous acts, since the latter occur within a context of male domination and patriarchal power. Nevertheless, incestuous violence can remain difficult to analyze. For instance, in addition to hierarchies and domination, family life is also shaped by affection and bonds that the notion of gender can only partially explain. As Judith Butler notes, "It is not simply that sexuality is unilaterally imposed by the adult...but that the child's love, a love that is necessary for its existence, is exploited and a passionate attachment abused."[10] For this reason, both a familial and a gendered lens must be applied in order to interpret the full diversity of variables at play when studying incestuous violence from an intersectional perspective. For if incest constitutes gender violence, it also constitutes generational violence committed by parents against their children or by older family members against younger ones—situations where the existing role of protector or educator can make it easier to impose adult sexuality using threats, violence, or blackmail. Finally, incest also constitutes a form of emotional violence that occurs within the private sphere: a context hidden from public view where family members express and experience emotions among themselves. A sacred space, the home serves as the primary location where the secret of incest is cultivated and perpetuated through coercion. The three forms of oppression most closely associated with cases of incestuous violence are therefore gender (male) dominance, emotional dominance, and generational dominance.

This chapter focuses on the figure of the father, that is to say on society's conception of those men who took on responsibilities associated with fatherhood—including both biological fathers and surrogates, such as stepfathers. With the adoption of the Civil Code of 1804, such father figures were placed at the pinnacle of French society. The family, the central institution of nineteenth-century French society, changed considerably over the decades with the introduction of new practices such as cohabitation and birth control. Coupled with growing industrialization, these new modes of family life proved worrisome to the country's elites, giving rise to many anxious discourses on the living conditions of working-class and poor families. Concerns about fathers featured prominently among these anxieties. Passed less than a century after paternal power was so clearly enshrined in the Civil Code, an 1889 French law provided for the possibility of stripping fathers of their authority when they neglected their responsibilities. However, this intrusion of the state into the private sphere was not intended to target all men or all households. All of which raises the question of how certain fathers, who had been so mighty in the eyes of the law at the turn of the nineteenth century, came to be seen as monsters, wretches, and vile figures whom the state had to keep in check in order to protect against the threat of incest.

Fatherhood, after all, is also a social construction. That is why John Tosh encourages historians "to turn from masculinity as a set of cultural attributes to consider masculinity as a social status, demonstrated in specific social contexts."[11] Since the 1990s, American and Canadian historians have been especially careful to recognize how "fatherhood is, indeed, a social construction…and it is a construction that changes over time in response to economic, political, cultural, and social change."[12] Far from being monolithic, fatherhood therefore encompasses multiple "faces" (*visages*), to adopt the term coined by John Demos in the 1980s and used more recently by Peter Gossage. As a result, when reconstructing the concept, historians must consider a "range of roles, expectations, and responsibilities that can vary over time, as well as across social and geographic space."[13] Ultimately, nineteenth-century French discourses coalesced to construct a new understanding of incest and paternity, an understanding that by the 1880s had come to associate these two concepts with the private lives of the poor. And to some extent, the figure of the wretched father helped to reinvent the taboo surrounding incest in French society.

In the pages that follow, I seek to historicize the emergence in France of this new social construction of incest based on the figure of the poverty-stricken father. More specifically, I analyze how medical, political, and legal discourses produced between 1804 and 1889 came to be reflected in concrete measures. All of these texts, I should add, were produced by male members of France's social and intellectual elite: men who, because of their position, had significant influence in society. Their writings can therefore provide valuable insights into both elite representations of an era and the means by which those views were disseminated within the population. No such analysis, however, is without bias. For a historian, it remains difficult to concretely measure the diffusion and the impact of these ideas among the French population and especially within the peasant and working-class majority, members of which rarely produced written discourse. In this sense, the press, whose circulation increased dramatically during the nineteenth century, is a precious source embodying a relay between elite discourses and the general population. With all of this in mind, this chapter draws extensively on judicial records, in the form of Assize Court case files, as well as a significant collection of newspaper articles in order to demonstrate, in a nuanced way, the wider impact of elite discourses around family, fatherhood, poverty, and sexual violence.

In the end, this multifaceted approach makes it possible to identify three main periods in the emergence of the figure of the wretched, incestuous father. First, between 1804 and 1832, fathers were cast as the guardians of the family home and placed at the pinnacle of society. Between 1832 and 1875, elite discourses expressed a great deal of concern regarding the behaviour of poor working-class fathers. Finally, between 1875 and 1889, the image of the vile, incestuous father mired in poverty came to be embraced by public opinion. Amplified by the press, this new understanding of incest and poverty led to the adoption of protective laws.

## *Defenders of the Home (1804–1832)*

In the early nineteenth century, as the First French Empire was taking shape, a common elite opinion held that the French Revolution had upset the natural order of the family, leaving France on the brink of moral collapse. Based on their reforms to marriage and family law, revolutionary leaders were accused of "calling on the population to abandon all sense of modesty and to embrace a distasteful promiscuity," thereby bringing about "the loss of respect for morals and the destruction of all paternal and familial bonds among men."[14]

Re-establishing paternal authority was therefore seen as a necessary step toward restoring order in French society. Jean-Étienne-Marie Portalis, known as the father of the Civil Code, argued that paternal authority represented "a kind of public office to which it is important, especially in free states, to give some scope. Yes, there is a need to make fathers into veritable magistrates."[15] In this way, the family was perceived as a microcosm. It was the very foundation of French society, insofar as it produced children who, in turn, would become adults capable of contributing to the nation's development. However, the family was not seen as an egalitarian institution. Rather, it "needs to be governed. The husband, the father has always been considered the head of household. Marital authority, paternal authority: these are republican institutions."[16] In 1804, these ideas came to be enshrined in Book I, Title IX of the Civil Code, under the heading *De la puissance paternelle* (Of Paternal Authority). In particular, Article 373 specified that, within a family, such authority rested with the father alone for the duration of the marriage.[17] The turn of the nineteenth century therefore witnessed the legal recognition of almost wholly unfettered paternal authority. For instance, a father could be convicted of assault and battery on his child and still retain full parental authority.

Linda Gordon and Paul O'Keefe argue that legislating male dominance in this way serves to promote incestuous violence: "The pattern that we found most consistently associated with incest was extreme male domination of the family."[18] By granting fathers such power, French authorities were essentially helping to conceal cases of incest by preventing the state from intervening in the private sphere. Such a degree of paternal authority was also recognized in other North Atlantic countries. For instance, Ulf Drugge notes how, in contemporary Sweden, "the master's possibility to exercise power within his household and uphold discipline was regulated by law. Thus, punishment of family members was allowed, at least to a certain extent, and was meant to be exerted exclusively by the master."[19] However, this idea of unilateral male power sanctioned by legal norms needs to be nuanced, since competing paternal identities also emerged during the same period. In fact, recent historiography points to a construction of fatherhood that stood in direct opposition to that of the tyrannical father. In his work on Quebec, Peter Gossage contrasts the idea of fathers being invested with great authority by culture and the Civil Code to an emerging model of fatherhood based on an ability to provide for the family (*le père pourvoyeur*).[20] Likewise, Margaret Marsh discusses the birth of a male domestic identity in the United States during the second half of the nineteenth century,[21] and John Tosh associates the arrival of this "modern" model of fatherhood in England with "the requirements of an entrepreneurial, urbanizing society."[22]

Meanwhile, in France, the desire to restore paternal authority as the foundation of society clashed with a new expectation, rooted in the Enlightenment and the Penal Code of 1791, that crimes causing bodily injury would be punished—especially when the victims were children.

This utilitarian approach to law was reflected in the Penal Code of 1810, which definitively redefined sexual violence exclusively in terms of rape (as had been done more tentatively in the Penal Code of 1791). To begin with, Article 331 of the new Penal Code introduced the category of *attentat à la pudeur* (indecent assault), which served to criminalize sexual violence other than that involving the penetration of a girl by an adult man. Furthermore, Article 333 recognized abuse of authority as an aggravating factor in such crimes, stipulating that persons convicted of assaulting someone under their authority would be sentenced to perpetual hard labour.[23] Legislators also established an age threshold (Article 332), treating crimes committed against individuals under the age of fifteen more seriously. This reflected a trend observed over the course of the French Revolution and throughout the nineteenth century whereby age emerged as a distinct category of governance.[24]

By treating sexual crimes committed by individuals in a position of authority more seriously, the new Penal Code focused attention on incestuous fathers. Such men began to appear before by the Assize Court established in 1808 to hear the most serious cases, and their public trials culminated with a judgment handed down by an all-male jury. But starting in 1810, trials for incestuous violence were conducted behind closed doors, in accordance with the constitutional provision requiring judicial proceedings to be held in secret when they posed a threat to public order and morals. This secrecy had an impact on public perceptions of incest, since it meant that transcripts of trial proceedings did not appear in the new publications dedicated to covering legal affairs. The need to protect society from scandal meant that no details were published on the crimes of these fathers, despite the provisions for public court proceedings included in the Penal Code. Such cases were therefore rarely mentioned in factums and the popular press prior to 1832. Only those fathers whose crimes were especially heinous and wide-ranging sometimes appeared in such publications. Examples include Claude Jouffrot, an incestuous father who had children with his daughter and forced her to poison her mother in 1830. From its opening lines, the account inspired a sense of outrage by underscoring the extreme nature of Jouffrot's crimes: "Since the courts began taking such care to punish the worst offenders, never have proceedings been conducted with such solemnity. Even the judges shook with horror, and the public was frightened by the appearance of a man of that age, whose hair was beginning to turn white."[25]

In any case, judicial proceedings were generally not initiated until after a scandal broke and the surrounding community expressed its disapproval. For instance, in 1813, the mayor of Les Essarts, a commune in the Seine-et-Oise department, wrote to the court regarding a scandal that was enveloping his community: "The people are saying that on the 26th of last month in the afternoon, a certain Charles Colas, a labourer from Mauregard…sought to have his way with his unfortunate child to satisfy not his passion but his rage by trying to violate her."[26] That same year, with regard to a different case, the public prosecutor of Versailles reported on "rumblings…that Chevalier, married for eleven years and father to six living children, had for several years been engaged in incestuous relations with his eldest daughter, then aged 7 or 8, and had allegedly sought to rape her. Chevalier's conduct having become the subject of chatter within the commune, the deputy who learned of these rumours had Chevalier's wife and daughter appear before him."[27] Although these proceedings were initiated after the scandal broke and heard behind closed doors, they still troubled certain contemporary observers who saw them as drawing attention to bad behaviour and contributing to social decline. For example, in 1820, Chrestien de Poly, vice-president of the Court of the Seine, expressed his unease with the very existence of such trials that, although conducted in secret, nevertheless showcased incestuous violence: "It seems as if everyone is working to make it more visible, more notorious, more contagious."[28]

In fact, some fathers were able to leverage both their legal status and the fear of scandal when faced with going before the courts. For instance, Louis Tassu, a notary accused of raping his daughter and committing infanticide, wrote to the Minister of Justice asking that the proceedings against him be dropped. Tassu's correspondence emphasizes the various public offices he had held, in order to make the accusations brought against him by his daughter seem impossible and unthinkable. He was a good father, a good public official. He described himself as "a forty-four-year-old upstanding citizen and the tender and kind father of six children…having exercised the important duties of a notary in Meaux with honour and integrity for nearly fifteen years, and called during this time to serve as a substitute judge…exercising his public duties with zeal and devotion to both his sovereigns and his fellow citizens for a period of four years."[29] This appropriation by fathers of the discourses surrounding fatherhood supports Linda Gordon's contention that, "the incest itself…

is also evidence for the existence of an extremely male-dominant family power structure,"[30] in which fathers are perfectly aware of the role assigned to them by society.

Between 1804 and 1832, as paternal authority was being reaffirmed, the fact that these powerful and exemplary fathers were beginning to appear before the courts, accused of committing acts of violence against their children, created a tension within French society that would prove difficult to resolve.

## *Dangerous Fathers (1832–1875)*

Following the adoption of the new Penal Code, the Assize Court heard larger numbers of cases involving incestuous violence. Official crime statistics, which began to be kept in 1826, confirmed the fears of French authorities by showing a measurable increase in the prevalence of rape, a crime previously associated with the "world of villages and hamlets, those locations left behind by progress."[31] In response, the Penal Code was amended in 1832 to better address the threat of sexual violence. The corresponding crimes were divided into three categories. Article 331 covered indecent assault against a child under the age of eleven. Article 332 covered indecent assault with violence as well as rape, both of which were aggravated if committed on a child under the age of fifteen. (At the time, rape was defined in such a way that it could only be committed against a girl or a woman; the notion of indecent assault with violence therefore served to criminalize sexual violence committed anally). Finally, Article 333 was reworked to clearly address crimes committed by those individuals who, in French society, held authority over children. It now specified that parents who assaulted their own children faced a defined period of hard labour, in the case of those crimes defined in Article 331, or perpetual hard labour, in the case of those crimes defined in Article 332.[32] In this way—and without actually using the word "incest"—the 1832 amendments established rape and indecent assault with violence committed by a parent as the most serious of sexual offences.

This marked an important turning point, since the state had come to acknowledge, by way of criminal law, that fathers could abuse their authority and commit sexual violence against their own children. But whereas the legislation left open the possibility that any father could henceforth be subject to prosecution, the publication of several studies served to produce a much narrower view of who might commit such crimes. As France became increasingly industrialized during the first half of the nineteenth century, the re-establishment of the Académie des Sciences Morales et Politiques in 1832 gave rise to extensive research on the social conditions of workers. The authors of these studies, often medical doctors who were partial to hygiene theory, observed the lifestyles of working-class families in emerging industrial centres, mainly located in northern and eastern France. Their reports provided lengthy descriptions of housing and expressed concerns over the lack of privacy endured by family members. For instance, this is how Louis-René Villermé's very lengthy 1840 study summed up the situation on Rue des Étaques in Lille:

> I would prefer to add nothing more to this hideous portrait that immediately reveals the profound misery of the poor inhabitants; but I must mention that many of the beds I just described were shared by individuals of both sexes and of very different ages, most of them shirtless and repulsively dirty. Fathers, mothers, the elderly, children, adults are all squeezed together, all piled on top of one another. I will say no more and leave it to the reader to complete the picture. But I warn him that if he intends to hold steadfast in the truth, his imagination must not shrink from any of the disgusting mysteries that occur within these impure layers, amid darkness and drunkenness.[33]

This idea that workers' private lives posed a danger could also be found in the work of Adolphe Blanqui, who declared "that their unsanitary housing conditions are the source of all the miseries, all the vices, all the calamities of their social state…With very few exceptions, one can establish the moral standing of a family of workers simply by inspecting the rooms they inhabit."[34]

Around 1850, indictments drawn up by prosecutors against incestuous fathers also began to make a connection between the moral state of the working class and the possibility of incest. One such document stated that, "Jean Cadio is a brutal drunkard and immoral to the point of lacking even a trace of fatherly feelings."[35] Another described "Devien, a wheelwright from Vernon," who "is habitually drunk. His bad behaviour, laziness, and violence toward his wife have earned him the worst of reputations in the town where he lives."[36] In this way, the vocabulary used by magistrates around 1850 resembled that used by social researchers around 1840. The introduction of a new legal process—the home visit—also reflected the level of familiarity of those working in the justice system with expert studies published just a few years earlier. Indeed, around 1850, magistrates began probing the living conditions of families as part of their efforts to prove incest. In this way, the intimate spaces of the poor, where entire families shared a single bedroom, became both a cause and evidence of incest in the eyes of the law. In 1847, the home of a man named Quentin, accused of raping his daughter, was inspected by the magistrate in charge of the investigation:

> The interior of the dwelling, with its untiled and otherwise uncovered floor, contains but the following pieces of furniture: a wooden chest, two chairs, a doorless two-compartment wardrobe or sideboard with no shelves in the upper compartment, a feather bed for sleeping, a bolster, two pillows, a set of sheets and a woollen blanket, all placed on boards separated from the ground by two lengths of wood twenty centimetres thick.[37]

A man name Placet, accused in 1858 of raping his daughter, lived in similar conditions:

> The dwelling of the accused and his daughter is set apart from any other dwelling…It is surrounded by ruins, old buildings and various hovels, within a vaulted cellar…This vault contains no furniture, and along the two walls opposite the door, is a space filled with straw and surrounded by large stones, without sheets or blankets, or any other form of bedding: the accused tells us that the space on the left is his bed and the space on the right is his daughter's.[38]

Beginning in 1856, concerns about incest, first expressed by social researchers and later taken up by legal professionals in the context of their investigations, were fed by debates between proponents of the theory of consanguinity (the *anticonsanguinistes*) and those of the theory of degeneracy (the *consanguinistes*). In an address to the Académie Impériale de Médecine on 29 April 1856, Dr. Prosper Menière introduced France to the medical theory of consanguinity, that is to say the idea that children born to biologically related parents are at greater risk of defects and diseases. Menière was concerned about the acceptance of consanguineous marriage in France, "because it can be easily demonstrated that this is the main cause of racial decay."[39] According to this theory, which gave rise to the anti-consanguinity movement in France, incest was dangerous and harmful regardless of the social context in which it occurred. But the following year, Benedict-Augustin Morel published an alternate theory—that of degeneracy—according to which "practicing dangerous or unhealthy occupations and living in overpopulated or unhealthy conditions subjects the body to new causes of decay and consequently degeneration."[40] Based on this theory, Morel embraced the ideas put forward a few years earlier regarding working-class housing: it was not inbreeding that caused defects but rather an individual's living environment. In France, most medical doctors came to share this view, whereas the theory of consanguinity largely fell out of favour as the century drew to a close. Protecting against degeneracy therefore meant ensuring a healthy home and living environment. Around 1860, the idea that the state should be able to intrude into the private lives of working-class (and therefore poor) families became widespread among the elites. For example, Paul Bernard, a former magistrate, called for a firmer approach:

> I wish to clearly state that because I have too often, in the course of my duties, witnessed incest in the family home, I must firmly argue for overlooking legal scruples. Over the last three decades, the habit of cohabitation has become increasingly common in manufacturing centres, to a frightening extent, and the indifference of men and women to any and all family ties has led them to unashamedly enter into the most odious and criminal liaisons.[41]

Bernard's impatience with the justice system reflects the fact that it remained reluctant to investigate suspected cases of incestuous violence, even as support for child protection measures increased. In 1860, for instance, several residents of one Marseille neighbourhood wrote directly to the public prosecutor, accusing a man named Davin of raping his daughter. For his part, the local police commissioner, who had been refusing to open an inquiry, explained that "things seemed so serious that I did not think I should investigate any further…so as not to have the facts of the case come to light."[42] The fact that Davin, who worked as a merchant, enjoyed a good social standing, and was well integrated into the community only inspired further reticence. Marie-Aimée Cliche notes a similar reluctance to open investigations in Quebec, "especially when the accuser had a bad reputation and the accused was held in public esteem."[43]

Although there was growing recognition of paternal incest by the 1860s, both public anger and legal proceedings focused on just one category of fathers, leaving other manifestations of the crime unexamined. And as Rachel Devlin notes, "what needs to be better understood is… the ways in which acknowledged acts of incest have been important in establishing and maintaining patriarchy as well."[44] The way that incestuous violence was being discussed and portrayed in France, namely through a social and medical lens, therefore served to justify the intrusion of the state into the private lives of poor working families, since "by making the absolute crime of incest the point of origin of every little abnormality, one strengthened the urgency of external intervention, of a kind of mediating element of analysis, control, and correction."[45]

## *Despicable Fathers (1875–1889)*

This interference by the state in the intimate lives of the poor came about during the final quarter of the nineteenth century. Previously, the social construction of incest based on the figure of the poor father had remained an elite phenomenon. But after 1875, it became a widespread feature of public opinion. The spread of this new way of seeing incest coincided with the dawn of the age of mass culture, which implies the arrival of an entirely new cultural regime whose social and political influence reached virtually all segments of society.[46] In this context, news coverage was able to reach new audiences thanks to higher literacy levels and the growth of a low-cost, high-circulation popular press. The latter began covering sexual violence in the 1880s, although such reports "tended to become more exhaustive over time, alongside the growing use of euphemistic language."[47] Inconspicuous but nevertheless present, these news items shared a consistent form and narrative: the texts were short—around two or three paragraphs—and consistently referred to sexual relations involving a father and a daughter. Using familiar rhetorical devices, they refrained from describing the criminal act itself and avoided using the word "incest," preferring roundabout and morally charged expressions like “shameful conduct” and “abominable crime.” As for the father, he was portrayed as wretched, disgraceful, and idle. On 10 September 1884, the inner pages of *Le Petit Journal* included one such account of incestuous violence. Under the headline “A Monster,” it briefly explained how “the police in Andruick (Pas-de-Calais) have just put an end to a horrible scandal. They captured a wretched man who had been abusing his daughter since she was thirteen years old, making her a mother on two occasions.”[48]

On 14 November 1885, the *Gazette des Tribunaux* presented another case in very similar terms: “Sometimes, the disgraceful father allowed himself to be moved by his child’s tears, but then he forced her to perform obscene acts and Fanny, overcome by fear, dared not complain. The silence emboldened the wretched man: one day, he raped his daughter, and threatened to kill her if she told anyone.”[49] At times, these stories served to implicitly construct a generalized portrait of the fathers involved. Presented as idle drunkards, they would have naturally been associated with the world of poverty. In some cases, the text explicitly referred to the father’s social condition. For instance, on 29 December 1887, *Le Petit Parisien* reported that, “The public prosecutor’s office in Le Havre is currently busy with a shameful case of incest that was uncovered in recent days. For the past seven years, a shepherd from Angerville, a widower with four children, has been abusing one of his daughters, who has already had two children in that time. This wretched father, upon seeing his daughter fall pregnant for a third time, wanted to force her to find work.”[50] These press reports consistently associated the fathers involved with poverty, whether through references to their occupations or their morals. The consistent use of the adjective “wretched” (*misérable*) is also significant. It drew a connection between a father’s social circumstances and the disgraceful acts he committed. It encouraged readers to despise these worthless men and turn away from them. In this way, incest came to be understood as an exceptional crime rooted in masculine poverty, one that society should avoid dwelling on so as to prevent it from spreading.

This new vision of incest was even reflected in the growing number of reports made to legal authorities, reports that tended to adopt the same language as stories published in the press. In 1892, the public prosecutor of Meaux received an anonymous letter informing him that, “Shameful things are happening in Beaubry near Prévillers. I refer to a father who abuses his child of 10 or 12 years of age; the mother told me about it in the presence of a witness. I do not want to give my name having waited for her to report this monster as she told me she would…I urge you to address this urgently; the child talks of taking her own life."[51] Heightened public awareness of incest therefore reflected a vision that had originated with the elites, showing how "political devices circulated through society gradually, rather than all at once."[52] Similar processes were underway in England during the same period. For example, Kim Stevenson describes how, across the Channel, "the revelation of incestuous relationships amongst the urban poor by the Victorian social explorers, child crusaders and moral campaigners including Mearns, Shaftesbury and Booth did much to educate the public and bring incest 'into the light of day.'"[53]

This process, which brought together various discourses surrounding incest, was further bolstered toward the end of the century by the emerging field of criminology. In this context, Alexandre Lacassagne—a physician and criminologist from Lyon who was considered an expert on incest—produced a synthesis of the medical debates described above and called for state intervention in the private lives of workers and the poor. According to Lacassagne, "it is not consanguinity that is either healthy or unhealthy, but rather the environment in which it occurs. Consanguinity in a proper social environment is not the same as consanguinity in an unwholesome social environment."[54] He went on: "When such unions happen to produce cripples, aside from the fact that the latter become burdens on society, one sees the authors of such marriages demanding asylums for the insane, institutions for the deaf and dumb, hospitals of all kinds—in a word, establishments where they hide their cripples: they rid themselves of their degenerate progeny, but at the expense of the community."[55] In providing this new perspective on the theories of consanguinity and degeneracy, Lacassagne was perfectly aligned with the social defence movement that spread through France around the turn of the twentieth century. The view was that French society had to guard against incest because the latter represented a threat to its future.

On 24 July 1889, these anxieties surrounding parenthood among the poor culminated in the passage of legislation providing for the automatic loss of parental authority in cases where parents raped their children. The new law also established the principle of pre-emptive forfeiture for parents "who, due to their habitual drunkenness, notorious and disgraceful behaviour, or abuse, jeopardize the health, safety or morality of their children."[56] This provision was clearly aimed at socially disadvantaged parents: those whose living conditions did not allow them to conceal their violence, alcoholism, neglect, and promiscuity; those who scandalized and endangered society. The growing sense of insecurity that marked the end of the century was what justified these preventive and protective measures. Beggars, thieves, and repeat offenders may have been the most despised figures in French society at the time, but behind them lurked the figure of the wretched, incestuous father, relegated to the shadows because of the special danger he posed, and from whom society felt the need to protect itself. After all, "faced with a potential risk or danger, not only could preventive action based on a legitimizing scientific discourse be taken, but it would be better accepted and deemed more acceptable than a repressive response."[57]

## *Conclusion*

At the dawn of the twentieth century, French society followed the lead of its elites by adopting a new understanding of incestuous violence. Perceived in the late eighteenth century as a crime committed by a couple engaging in sexual activity that went against the natural or religious order, incest came to be seen as a monstrous crime committed by destitute men against their daughters. Completed around 1880, this shift in perspective had occurred over the course of a century marked by complex but convergent elite discourses that consistently associated the crime of incest with poor, working-class fathers. The complexity of these discourses lay in the fact that, although the Civil Code had established paternal authority as a central pillar of French society, amendments to the Penal Code helped bring to light cases where fathers wielded this power in a disgraceful manner.[58] Meanwhile, the convergence of discourses reflected the growing alignment between political and legal opinion with regard to the socially determined nature of incestuous violence. The studies conducted by experts around 1840, the spread of Morel's theories after 1857, and the everyday work of magistrates after 1860 all contributed to the masculine social construction of incestuous violence adopted by public opinion after 1880. Incest came to be understood as a crime committed by a wretched father in the privacy of his home, whereby he failed to live up to the role conferred on him by the Civil

Code of 1804—and public opinion held that French society needed to be protected against such men.

But it is important not to allow this narrow understanding to distract from the fact that it also "indicates a far more complex patriarchal system of oppression."[59] Indeed, "men's institutional positioning through the division of labour in employment, in the family, and as citizens, is key to understanding their place in power relations and why they are both oppressors and oppressed."[60] The nineteenth-century elite that publicly debated the problem of incest in France was entirely male. Men were the ones who adopted legislation and presided over the courts. They were the experts, the doctors, the jurors, and the researchers. But male power is variable: "It contains contradictions and forms of heterogeneity, and the perpetuation of a patriarchal social order comes at the cost of constant adjustments."[61] By making poor fathers the sole focus of the discourse on incestuous violence, members of France's male elite not only distanced themselves from the incestuous "other" but also introduced a series of assumptions that served to protect other members of the family and of society. Hinging on ideas about social status, gender, and the family, these assumptions rendered unthinkable the idea that various social groups and family members were even capable of incest: fathers who were not poor or working-class; mothers and other women; as well as brothers and sisters, uncles and aunts, grandfathers and grandmothers. Such a situation most certainly brings to mind the warning issued in 1977 by Judith Herman and Lisa Hirschman: "Because the taboo is created and enforced by men, we argue that it may also be more easily and frequently violated by men."[62]

The question of the taboo surrounding incest appears even more relevant in light of how incestuous violence once again disappeared from public discourse around 1890, in stark contrast to the growing interest in the topic during the previous decades.[63] Amid much more circumspect coverage of incest in the press, the end of the nineteenth century also saw the emergence of medical categories that made it even easier for incestuous fathers of all kinds to deny their crimes: the figure of the lying child and that of the hysterical woman. These categories provided evidence for new medical theories arguing that mothers were prone to manipulating their children in order to falsely accuse their husbands before the courts. And such ideas persisted well into the first half of the twentieth century.

As a result, when Violette Nozière was charged with the murder of her working-class father in 1933, her descriptions of the incestuous violence she had suffered at his hands won her little public support. Instead, she was widely portrayed as a bad daughter.[64] The system had therefore come to protect all men, whereas "social, symbolic or even legal attacks on such authority required…significant effort."[65] It is therefore not surprising that, amid the feminist struggles of the 1970s and the publication of the first accounts by French incest victims in 1986,[66] the figure of the poor incestuous father once again came to feature prominently in the country's collective imagination, and once again served to protect other perpetrators of incestuous violence.

CHAPTER 16

# Violence against Women, the Law, and Public Opinion in Guatemala

*Emilee Lord and John Wertheimer*

At Christmas time, 2018, in Quetzaltenango, Guatemala's second-largest city, a man sat on a park bench near a massive, twinkling tree, watching children throw little firecrackers and shrill with delight as they popped. Perhaps in the spirit of the season, he agreed to participate in a public opinion survey. The questions concerned Guatemala's high-profile 2008 "Law Against Femicide and Other Forms of Violence Against Women." Upon hearing the topic, he tossed off a firecracker of his own: "I used to beat women." But, he insisted, no more. "It makes me sad to see women treated that way."[1] Mr. Park Bench's professed change of heart echoed the responses of many other survey participants.

Scholars tell different stories. They tend to portray Guatemala's legal campaign against gendered violence as a total dud. In works with titles such as "Crimes without Punishment," scholars argue that, thanks to Guatemala's corrosive blend of corruption and machismo, the nation's efforts to combat gendered violence have "not reduced levels of violence against women."[2] Some even contend that gender-violence legislation, far from weakening Guatemala's "culture of violence…at its patriarchal core," has actually served to "uphold" that culture.[3] The scholarly "general consensus" is unmistakable: "[I]mpunity for these crimes continues unabated."[4] There is an "epidemic of impunity."[5] Abusive Guatemalan men enjoy "total impunity."[6] In sum, scholars conclude, "[j]ustice has taken a sabbatical in Guatemala."[7]

We believe that these scholars overstate the futility of Guatemala's legal efforts against gendered violence. Our dissenting argument reflects our distinctive research approach. The sociologists, political scientists, and legal scholars who write about this topic typically zoom in on the most recent phase—the most active phase—of the story. When they do stretch their chronologies backward, they focus not on the legal system's response to gendered violence in previous eras, but rather on tragic episodes in Guatemalan history generally—the Spanish Conquest, the US-backed military coup of 1954, the bloody civil war of 1960 to 1996. Scholars invoke such episodes in an effort to explain how, in Guatemala, "gender-based violence became normalized."[8] By contrast, our archives-based examination of Guatemala's legal treatment of violence against women stretches back to the mid-twentieth century, decades before the nation paid concerted attention to the problem. Framed in this broader way, Guatemala's recent legal record appears more substantial than it does when considered in chronological isolation.

We also introduce public-opinion research to the mix of investigative methods. Scholars typically approach Guatemala's recent efforts to combat gendered violence through some combination of government statistics, which inevitably show high and rising caseloads;[9] anecdotes from the press and elsewhere, which often are horrific and sometimes are sensational;[10] and the testimonies of human rights workers, non-governmental organizations, and others whose advocacy interests incline them toward distressing narratives.[11] Our public-opinion-based research corroborates some prevailing assumptions, but also suggests that existing studies have underestimated the effectiveness of the Guatemalan legal system's recent efforts to combat gendered violence.[12] Guatemalan women's rights reformers have worked hard. Although huge challenges remain, the knowledge that past reforms have made at least some headway should inspire continued struggle.

## *Gendered Violence and the Law in Guatemala: Historical Background*

Guatemala's robust recent efforts to combat gendered violence contrast starkly with its previous indifference. Prior to 1964, formidable cultural and institutional barriers shielded domestic abuse from public scrutiny. Intrafamilial violence in Guatemala may have been as widespread then as it would later become, but few people noticed. The prevailing domestic ideal was the patriarchal family, in which men commanded, women obeyed, and the state maintained a respectful distance.[13] Domestic abuse was widely tolerated. The doors behind which it occurred remained closed.

Many Guatemalans, including many women, thought of wife-beating as something akin to child-spanking: a family matter not subject to legal oversight. Several factors combined to discourage victimized women from seeking legal recourse. Many feared additional physical punishment.[14] Those who depended economically on abusive male breadwinners hesitated to blow the whistle, fearing economic consequences. A generalized culture of acceptance inclined many victims to stoicism. One Guatemalan woman recalled her sister telling her, "You chose your husband. Now you must deal with the consequences."[15]

Guatemala's legal institutions reflected these underlying cultural assumptions. Although general-application criminal laws (akin to "assault and battery") technically applied, their enforcement required victims or witnesses to press charges. This rarely happened, especially when altercations occurred in domestic spaces, as was typical. Aside from these general-application criminal laws, domestic violence was largely unregulated. No laws or courts targeted it. No judges, prosecutors, or police units were specially charged or trained to deal with it. No nongovernmental organizations offered support. Domestic violence remained shrouded, a problem that had no name.

The few "assault-and-battery"-type cases that were filed, often by protective fathers against abusive sons-in-law, were not taken very seriously. Abusive men often casually admitted guilt, as criminal penalties were light and a record of spousal abuse brought no shame to the abuser. Indeed, wife-beating appears to have been consistent with the day's code of masculinity. One mid-century husband was so drunk at the time of his wife's beating that he remembered nothing. Upon learning that his wife had been battered, however, he readily claimed responsibility, figuring that, because he was the husband, the battering must rightly have been done by him.[16]

This situation altered somewhat with the passage of Guatemala's Family Court Act of 1964. The goal of this statute was to combat family disintegration, which reformers blamed for poverty, juvenile delinquency, and other ills. The Act created new tribunals with "exclusive jurisdiction over all matters relating to the family."[17] Significantly, the long list of family-related issues over which the new courts had jurisdiction—divorce, annulment, child custody, child support, and so forth—did not include intrafamilial violence.[18] Domestic abuse was not yet a salient legal issue, even among family-law reformers. Nevertheless, by urging aggrieved family members to seek judicial intervention of any sort, the law empowered the government to breach patriarchal walls as never before.

Both men and women took advantage of the new law, but they did so in different ways. Men generally sought to use the new family courts to reinforce fraying relationships, thereby buttressing their control over women. Women, by contrast, generally used family-court litigation to achieve independence after conjugal relationships had fractured. Above all, women used family courts to help them secure child support.

Evidence of domestic violence abounds in family-court cases from these early years, but most of it is indirect. Women mentioned the physical abuse that they suffered not to press criminal charges against perpetrators, but rather to bolster their claims to other things. For example, an abused wife named Juana supplemented her family-court divorce petition with a physician's note testifying to the injuries that she had suffered at the hands of her husband.[19] Many other women mentioned intimate-partner abuse in the context of child-support cases. In September of 1965, María Sacalxot testified that, "[o]n the fourteenth of this month…I was subject to mistreatment at the hands of my husband, especially physical blows." She escaped and found refuge elsewhere for the night. When she returned home the next day, her husband received her with another beating and kicked her out of the house. Concluding that no peaceful accord with her husband was possible, Maria moved in with her adoptive mother. She hoped that the family court would make this new arrangement workable by ordering her husband to pay child support.[20]

Again and again, in cases such as Juana's and Maria's, family court judges heard evidence of gendered violence but did nothing to punish it criminally. That was by design. The Family Court Act of 1964 conceptualized the family as a crime-free zone. Although the new courts enjoyed authority over "all issues relating to the family,"[21] they were civil courts only. The idea that something could be both family-related and criminal confounded the statute's scheme. Indeed, family court judges were encouraged to keep families together whenever possible, even if it meant urging battered women to reunite with their abusers.

Nevertheless, family courts initiated several trends in the direction of legal action against domestic violence. They encouraged women to litigate. From the start, women dominated the family court docket. Year after year, women initiated over eighty percent of family court cases. In theory, at least, women did not need to be rich in order to file suit, since Article 15 of the Family Court Act provided legal aid to poor women.[22] The act breached the domestic sphere as never before. It enabled women to pursue deadbeat dads for child support, which made it easier for them to escape abusive homes and still feed their children. Family courts also frequently granted restraining orders and police protection to battered women. Although domestic violence, as a criminal matter, remained formally beyond their reach, the new tribunals nonetheless produced a modest decrease in patriarchal power and corresponding increases in state power and women's power.

In 1996, Guatemala took a bigger step toward confronting domestic abuse when it adopted a "Law to Prevent, Sanction, and Eradicate Intrafamilial Violence."[23] This law's passage resulted from international as well as domestic factors. International organizations, including the United Nations, made women's rights and gendered violence major points of emphasis during these years.[24] Treaty obligations mattered, too. "Because Guatemala has subscribed to" various "international juridical instruments," the national legislature explained when passing a law designed to protect women, "we must emit adequate national legislation."[25]

Guatemala's fledgling women's movement pushed hard for the 1996 law. During the previous decade, the movement had strengthened substantially and had broadened its focus beyond formal legal equality to such "private" issues as gender roles and intimate-partner violence.[26] In this same year, 1996, Guatemala's thirty-six-year civil war, which took an estimated 200,000 lives, ended with the signing of peace accords.[27] The peace process—with its anti-violence emphasis, its support for human rights, its robust attention to women's issues, and its accompanying spirit of endless possibility—blew wind into the sails of anti-domestic-violence initiatives.[28]

Like the previous Family Court Act, the Intrafamilial Violence Law of 1996 was technically gender neutral. Both men and women could be victims—or perpetrators.[29] And the new law, like the old one, offered civil remedies only. It added no new crimes. Its provisions were protective, not punitive. They included restraining orders, court-ordered removals of aggressors from family homes, provisional suspension of aggressors' child custody, decommissioning of arms, and mandatory anti-violence therapy for aggressors.[30] These measures were to apply independently of any criminal processes that might simultaneously arise under other laws.[31]

Guatemalan family members, especially women, immediately found the 1996 intrafamilial violence law useful. In 1999, 1,300 intrafamilial violence cases were filed nationally, mostly by comparatively well-to-do women in the Guatemala City area. By 2008, case volume had exploded to 24,000, and had spread across the nation and its social classes. By then, an average of sixty-five intrafamilial violence cases were filed, somewhere in Guatemala, every day. Although the per capita rate of such cases remained substantially higher in the United States than in Guatemala,[32] the Guatemalan numbers were rising quickly, bringing the problem out of the shadows and helping the Central American nation qualify for the *Toronto Star*'s "Ten Worst Countries for Women" list in 2008.[33] In a similar spirit, scholars pointed to the explosion of abuse cases and concluded that the law was not working.[34] In a way, however, the burgeoning caseload suggested that it was working.

In 2008, Guatemala adopted an even stronger measure against gendered violence: the "Law against Femicide and Other Forms of Violence against Women." Unlike previous reforms, this new statute was criminal, not civil. And unlike predecessors, it was a gender-specific measure. Only women could be victims; only men could be perpetrators.[35] It created several new crimes, the most severe of which was "femicide"—the killing of a woman "within the framework of unequal power relations between men and women."[36] The 2008 law also criminalized many "other forms of violence against women," including physical, sexual, psychological, and economic violence. Punishments were serious: from twenty-five to fifty years, non-commutable, for femicide; and from five to twelve years, commutable, for the other crimes.[37]

The Femicide Law also created new institutions, many of which would wind up being staffed by women. Specialized "Femicide" Courts, both trial-level and appellate, soon appeared in areas populous enough to justify them. The law also called for the creation of dedicated prosecutors' offices specializing in violence-against-women cases; publicly funded consciousness-raising campaigns; *pro bono* legal counsel for poor victims; special victims' units in police stations that specialized in gendered-violence cases; and comprehensive support systems for female victims, complete with childcare and psychological counseling.[38]

Although the 2008 Femicide Law did not end gendered violence in Guatemala, it was not a dead letter. Women quickly found the law useful and invoked it frequently. During the law's first six years, as institution-building and consciousness-raising occurred nationwide, annual case volume increased each year, from about 12,000 in 2008 to around 50,000 in 2013.[39] Thereafter, about 50,000 violence-against-women cases were filed annually. This figure represented about fifteen percent of all criminal cases filed in the country.[40] Admittedly, many gendered-violence cases petered out before reaching trial. But the same thing happened in all criminal cases. Our analysis of all criminal cases filed in the department of Totonicapán in 2010 and 2011 revealed that violence-against-women cases were actually slightly more likely than other sorts of cases to advance to trial.[41]

Other scholars point to the high volume of violence-against-women cases and conclude that there is "No Justice for Guatemalan Women."[42] We agree that much work remains. The high case volume indeed demonstrates the continued pervasiveness of violence against women. But the robust litigation record also indicates that women are no longer willing to suffer abuse in silence. Only about 0.5 percent of the cases arising under the 2008 femicide law involve actual killings. The other 99.5 percent involve other forms of violence against women: physical, sexual, psychological, and economic. In order for these other forms of violence to generate prosecutions, victims must be willing to press charges.[43] The increasing case volume indicates women's increased willingness to denounce mistreatment.

## *Public Opinion of the Femicide Law*

One way to measure a criminal statute's impact is to consider the cases that arise under it. Another is to consider the cases that do not arise, owing to the statute's success in discouraging the criminalized behaviour. This second phenomenon is important, but difficult to measure. One way to explore it is to ask regular citizens how aware they are of the law and how effective they think the law has been at changing people's habits. In December of 2018, seeking to conduct this sort of research, Emilee Lord, a student at Davidson College in the United States, traveled to Guatemala to talk to the sorts of regular people who sit on park benches. She did most of her interviewing in the city of Quetzaltenango (population around 180,000 at the time), though she also did a bit of comparative work in Guatemala City (population around one million), and the mountainous village of Cantel (population around 36,000). She asked open-ended questions about violence against women and the 2008 femicide law. Participation was optional and confidential. Emilee generally chose to interview people who were sitting alone, or in small groups, often waiting for others. The mix of interview subjects was as unscientifically random as one might expect, given the methodology. Surprisingly, all forty-five people whom Emilee approached—twenty-five men and twenty women—agreed to participate. Emilee's unthreatening foreignness may have put people at ease. The topic's broad resonance helped, too. Everyone had heard of the law, and everyone had stories to tell about it. Many participants launched into lengthy tales involving relatives, acquaintances, or themselves.

The questions were open-ended, such as: "What impact do you think the 2008 'Law against femicide and other forms of violence against women' has had?" "To what extent are the police a resource for women under this law?" "How has the situation of women changed in your lifetime?" We sorted respondents into three categories: those who believed that Guatemala's laws against gendered violence consistently worked, those who believed that they sometimes worked, and those who believed that they did not work. We then used common-sense quantification[44] to determine if respondents' opinions correlated in any meaningful way with their sex, age, education level, or ethnicity. Just as importantly, we listened carefully to their stories.

Before discussing the results of our study, we should acknowledge its limitations. Constraints of time and money limited the number of survey participants. More interviews, conducted in more parts of the country, with a more diverse range of interviewers and interviewees, would have been preferable. Emilee's identity as a young, white, female foreigner may have affected people's responses. The interviews' locations may have skewed the sorts of people interviewed. A more varied team of questioners and a truly randomized sampling of survey subjects could correct for this bias.

What we have constructed is less an airtight statistical study than a capacious historical archive, a snapshot of opinions in one corner of the country at one moment in time. While our findings may not be *statistically* significant, they nonetheless seem *historically* significant, as all people's lived experiences inherently are. We have assembled a modest collection of revealing conversations—conversations that, whatever their quantitative limitations, arguably illuminate the inner lives of Guatemalan women as few numerical measures could. In what follows, we try to make sense of what we found. We urge other scholars to conduct similar studies, reinforcing or challenging our conclusions, as the case may be.

### GENDER

Men were significantly more likely than women to believe that the femicide law was working well. Over half of the men whom we interviewed—fifty-five percent—expressed a high degree of confidence in the law's effectiveness. "Women are well protected" by the law, said one male respondent.[45] Another added that Guatemalan legal authorities "take instances of domestic abuse more seriously these days. They take notice and they apply the law."[46] The law works "quite well," said a third.[47]

Female respondents were substantially more skeptical. Just fifteen percent of them believed that the law worked consistently. The rest split about evenly between those who thought that the law sometimes worked and those who thought it did not work. Women's views also tended to be more nuanced and less categorical than men's views. Male optimists were prone to unconditional statements, such as, "The law works." By contrast, female optimists, who were scarcer than their male counterparts, were also quicker to acknowledge that the law had shortcomings as well as strengths. Female pessimists, meanwhile, typically acknowledged that the law had some virtues, though they believed that implementation flaws—too many exceptions for the wealthy, too little support for Indigenous women—were serious. One forty-two-year-old entrepreneur from Guatemala City captured this nuance. She noted approvingly that the femicide law gave women rights and "is very well known by women." "The problem is," she observed, that even though women "have the rights," many hesitate to invoke them, because they "do not feel a sense of self-worth," due to the "machismo that has existed in Guatemala for years."[48]

### AGE

Generational differences also mattered. Guatemala is the youngest country in Latin America.[49] Almost half of the population is under nineteen years of age.[50] Our average respondent, by contrast, was about forty years old. Our collection of interviews skewed so old because we followed Institutional Review Board guidelines, which required our respondents to be at least eighteen years old. The urban setting may also have contributed to our age imbalance, since city residents, who tend to have better health care and higher living standards than their rural counterparts, may also enjoy longer lifespans.[51] For analytical purposes, we divided our pool into "older" and "younger" categories by sorting the people whom we interviewed by age and drawing a line through the middle of the list, which happened to be about forty years of age.

Among male respondents, youth correlated with the belief that the law was effective. This was true among both supporters and opponents of the law, who disagreed on the law's desirability but agreed that it was effective. This may reflect the generational profile of abusers. Men in their twenties are the most likely cohort to be accused of violating the 2008 law, followed by men in their thirties, forties, and so on, down the testosterone curve.[52] It seems probable, therefore, that younger male respondents were more likely than their elders to have experienced the law's restrictions personally.

Some testimonials suggest that gender norms may be evolving among younger Guatemalan men. One young man, a barista, told of witnessing a husband beating his wife on the street one day. Rather than accepting this as normal behaviour and looking away, as earlier eyewitnesses might have done, the barista summoned the police. A patrolman arrived, pinned the husband against a wall, and prepared to make an arrest. Just then, the barista was surprised to see the wife intervene. "This is not your problem," she said. "Everything is fine here." The barista concluded that the nation's legal structures were adequate, but that the broader culture provided a weak foundation upon which to build.[53] Other young men, however, believe that the law is too effective. These young men represent an emerging backlash against gender-specific reform. A twenty-two-year-old waiter complained that the law's penalties were too harsh and that it unfairly applied only when victims were female, providing no help to men abused by women.[54] This young man also was convinced that the law's criminal penalties were draconian.

Older men were more skeptical of the 2008 law's effectiveness. These men were less likely than their juniors to have had personal run-ins with the law. Their deeper historical memories may also have inclined them to doubt the possibility of rapid change. "In recent years, and we are talking about the last five years," one highly educated older respondent acknowledged, the nation's institutions "have started to help women a little more than before—but the process is a little slow."[55] Women's advances take so long, he said, because, regardless of what the law books say, men learn gender roles at home, as children. On the surface, the new law might appear to be blossoming promisingly, but "You have to see the roots of the tree, not only its flowers."[56] Other older men agreed that the law's effectiveness was limited—by scarce national resources, by a culture of *machismo*, and by the difficulty of effecting broad social change overnight. These challenges were especially acute in rural areas, these older men thought.[57]

Age correlated much less strongly with women's views than with men's. Among female respondents, the strongest generational correlation was between youth and pessimism: the exact opposite of the male result. Female optimists—those who believed that the law consistently worked—distributed fairly evenly across the age range. Female moderates—those who believed that the law sometimes worked—also divided fairly evenly between young and old. But female pessimists skewed young. The likely explanation is the mirror image of the male story discussed above. The youngest women in our study were the most likely to have experienced recent physical abuse.[58] Young women—for our purposes, those under forty—were thus more likely than older women to have personally experienced the law's failure to prevent abuse, or to have peers who had personally experienced this failure. They also might be the most likely to have been exposed to feminist theories, and therefore the least accepting of intimate-partner abuse, be it emotional, verbal, or physical. This group understands the massive cultural challenge lurking below the legal challenge. One twenty-four-year-old Indigenous woman, a mother of four, considered the law to be an overall failure, but blamed its lack of effect on "men's stubborn heads," not the law itself.

Views regarding gendered violence, however, are not generationally static. They cross-pollinate within families. One sixty-eight-year-old grandmother explained that her husband, a typical *machista*, had originally been abusive to her, in part because he knew that she was economically dependent and therefore would not leave him. When her daughter was young, this woman advised her to get a good education and achieve economic independence before marrying, so that she would never be beholden to any man. The daughter succeeded, and her success inspired this woman, by then in her forties, to "find the spark." She returned to school, got a degree, and secured a job as a schoolteacher. Her husband's emotional abuse continued, but her new financial independence gave her the strength to pack her bags and leave him. He "cried and cried—in the typical way," she said. Ultimately, she agreed to return if he met her demands: that he accompany her to church weekly, that he let her manage her own money, and that he never raise his voice to her again. The man agreed, though his yelling never really stopped. Two decades later, on the park bench, reflecting on this story, this woman proudly reported that she sees the same spark in her granddaughter, who, when observing her grandfather's ill temper, intervenes, saying, "Why are you yelling at grandmother this way? Please stop."[59]

This grandmother readily acknowledged, however, that violence against women remains a serious problem in Guatemala. She accounted for some women's continued acceptance of it by invoking a fast-food analogy. "It's like *Pollo Campero*," she said, referencing a popular Guatemalan equivalent to Kentucky Fried Chicken. Many Guatemalan women suffer abuse their entire lives because "they do not know anything else but the grease in the air. They don't know the grease stinks because they have never known anything else. The blemishes on their skin—and all the problems greasy food causes—obesity—all of it—they don't know that there are other options. That there is a better life. It's the same with marital abuse." This grandmother's family story shows that change is possible. Her fast-food analogy suggests that more change is needed.

## EDUCATIONAL LEVELS

We divided respondents into three educational groupings: high (any university training), intermediate (secondary school or a licensing program), and low (from just a few years of primary school through some high school or vocational training).[60] In the aggregate, our interviewees turned out to be far more highly educated than the national average, perhaps because we interviewed mostly in cities, where education levels tend to be high. About forty percent of our respondents ranked at the "high" level, far above the national average of about ten percent. Additional interviews in rural communities, where education levels are lower, and where nearly half of Guatemalans live, would be necessary to balance the pool.[61]

Respondents with the least education tended to believe that Guatemala's laws against gendered violence are effective. Sixty percent of this group thought that the law consistently worked. These respondents were also the least likely to equivocate. Only ten percent fell into the intermediate "sometimes" category, in part because low-education interviewees typically provided clipped answers. Though some threw in personal stories, most replied tersely and categorically.

Compared with low-education respondents, intermediate-education respondents were more voluble and seemed more comfortable speaking with foreigners. Their opinions regarding the law's effectiveness divided evenly. About twenty percent of the intermediate group reported that the law consistently works, sixty percent reported that it sometimes works, and twenty percent reported that it does not work.

High-education respondents said the most and had the lowest opinion of the law's effectiveness. A plurality (forty-four percent) of high-education respondents believed that the law does not work. The rest divided evenly between "consistently works" and "sometimes works." Multiple high-education respondents invoked Guatemalan history. For example, an elderly, PhD-bearing sociologist, who spoke for over an hour, embedded personal stories within critical theoretical frames. He saw the widespread mistreatment of Guatemalan women as a legacy of the machismo-inflected, pro-capitalist government established by a US-backed military coup in 1954.[62] Violence against Guatemalan women was rampant, he reasoned, "because justice is null in a country as corrupt as this." He cited high poverty rates and low education levels, especially in rural areas, as factors that exacerbate the mistreatment of women, especially Indigenous women.

Although our collection of interviews is relatively small, it does suggest an intriguing pattern. Formal educational levels in Guatemala appear to be inversely proportional to belief in the femicide law's effectiveness. If that finding is accurate, the over-representation of highly educated Guatemalans in our study may have caused us to under-estimate the public's sense of the law's effectiveness.

It is worth pointing out that a respondent's belief in the law's effectiveness does not necessarily indicate his or her support for the law. Some interviewees, especially female interviewees, who said that the law does not work were disillusioned supporters. Some other respondents, especially male respondents, on the other hand, reported that the law consistently worked but were dissatisfied with the results, which they considered to be too severe and unfair to men.

### ETHNICITY AND URBAN/RURAL DIFFERENCES

We invited interviewees to self-report their ethnicities. Most did. Two of every three self-identified as "Ladino," which, in Guatemalan parlance, means a mix of Indigenous and Spanish heritage.[63] Just over a quarter self-reported as Indigenous.[64] This constitutes a slight over-representation of Ladinos—a likely result of our city-based interviews, since Indigenous Guatemalans tend to be underrepresented in cities.[65]

Most Ladinos found the 2008 law against femicide and other forms of violence against women to be at least somewhat effective. Just eight out of twenty-nine Ladinos (twenty-eight percent) said that the law did not work.[66] Indigenous respondents were more skeptical. Almost half—nine out of twenty—thought that the law did not work. This skepticism likely reflects Guatemala's long-standing, systemic neglect of Indigenous rights and interests, as well as the tendency of the nation's Indigenous people to live in rural areas, beyond the easy reach of legal institutions.[67] Much work remains to be done to spread legal protections to Indigenous communities. Despite the general pessimism of Indigenous respondents, however, it is worth noting that a majority of them still thought that the law worked either sometimes or consistently. And some Indigenous respondents thought that the situation was improving. One said that awareness of the 2008 law had increased in her community within the past six months, thanks to the introduction of Indigenous-language women's rights workshops.[68] These multi-language workshops had helped her and other women to learn about the legal resources available to them. This woman's testimony suggests the possibility that the 2008 law may grow increasingly effective in rural and Indigenous communities, as information and institutions spread from urban centers, and as women increasingly regard the law as a functioning protector.

## *Conclusion*

In 2017, the United Nations examined the effectiveness of anti-gendered-violence efforts in Latin America and the Caribbean.[69] Guatemala scored near the top in terms of legislation passed and national plans adopted.[70] It also scored well when it came to establishing institutions and procedures to implement these measures.[71] The UN report gave special recognition to Guatemala and one other nation for the "promising" steps that they had recently taken "in relation to the theme of punishment of violence against women and/or gender."[72] Guatemala was commended for five things in particular: creating "specialized units…in the justice sector" to handle such cases, "working to increase awareness of violence against women," providing free and "culturally relevant" legal assistance, seeing cases through to completion, and offering "trained and sensitized personnel" capable of providing services in Indigenous languages as well as Spanish.[73]

The UN report's positive view contrasts dramatically with the bleak portrait painted by most scholars. Our research suggests a middle view. About one-third of our survey subjects agreed with scholars that Guatemala's anti-gendered-violence effort had failed. Two-thirds of respondents, however, agreed with the UN that the law worked either sometimes or consistently. Needless to say, there is a difference between respondents' perceptions of Guatemalan reality and that reality itself. But the difference between the nuanced perceptions of our interview subjects and the wholly negative perceptions of scholars is notable. In this case, popular perceptions may well be more accurate.

Mistreatment of women and the sexism underlying it remain problems in Guatemala, as elsewhere. But it seems inaccurate to dismiss the 2008 femicide law and the legal system's other efforts to combat gendered violence as utter failures. Many men fear the law's consequences and have changed their behaviour. Many women believe that the law offers them protection. About 50,000 Guatemalan women invoke the law annually. They would not do so if the law were as ineffective as most scholars say. Although the interview archive that we assembled is far from definitive, it suggests that the substantial energy that Guatemala has devoted to this problem has indeed made a difference. Guatemalan efforts to improve women's lives through legal reform may have not been wholly successful, but neither have they been total failures.

# NOTES

## INTRODUCTION

1 CBC Digital Archives, "There's no place for the state in the bedrooms of the nation," https://www.cbc.ca/player/play/1260871747995, accessed 6 October 2022. See also Angus McLaren and Arlene Tigar McLaren, *The Bedroom and the State: The Changing Practices and Politics of Contraception and Abortion in Canada, 1880–1997*, 2nd ed. (Toronto: Oxford University Press Canada, 1997).

2 "Family life is sometimes presumed to be a realm so private and intimate as to be beyond the law's power," writes American legal scholar Jill Elaine Hasday. "But in fact, one of the law's most important and far-reaching roles is to govern family life and family members." Jill Elaine Hasday, *Family Law Reimagined* (Cambridge, MA: Harvard University Press, 2014), 1. This is a vast literature, but see also John Eekelaar, *Family Law and Personal Life* (Oxford: Oxford University Press, 2007); Stephen Cretney, *Family Law in the Twentieth Century: A History* (Oxford: Oxford University Press, 2005); Maaike Voorhoeve, ed., *Family Law in Islam: Divorce, Marriage and Women in the Muslim World* (London: I.B. Tauris & Co. Ltd., 2012); Kenneth M. Cuno and Manisha Desai, *Family, Gender, and Law in a Globalizing Middle East and South Asia* (Syracuse: Syracuse University Press, 2009).

3 For a recent reappraisal of Trudeau's omnibus legislation as it applied to the criminality (or otherwise) of same-sex intimacies, see Tom Hooper, "Queering '69: The Recriminalization of Homosexuality in Canada," *Canadian Historical Review* 100, no. 2 (May 2019): 257–73.

4 Gail Savage, "The 'Moscow Widowers': Marriage, Citizenship, and the Soviet Wives of British Subjects in the Aftermath of the Second World War," see below, Chapter 13.

5 Mélanie Méthot, "Bigamy Prosecutions in Victoria, Australia: The Press Coverage and the Case File," see below, Chapter 11.

6 The present volume, in fact, offers a surprisingly rare opportunity to compare research findings across subfields, which historians have traditionally defined by geography, time period, and subject matter. We will refer at greater length below to the vast and deeply textured literature in this field, but our point for the moment is simpler: that most of this work has tended to reflect and

reinforce the narrower spatial, temporal, and jurisdictional boundaries that characterize both history and legal studies as fields of scholarly research.

7 Peter Gossage, *Families in Transition: Industry and Population in Nineteenth-Century Saint-Hyacinthe* (Montreal and Kingston: McGill-Queen's University Press, 1999); Peter Gossage, "On Dads and Damages: Looking for the 'Priceless Child' and the 'Manly Modern' in Quebec's Civil Courts, 1921–1960," *Histoire sociale/Social History* 49, no. 100 (November 2016): 603–23; Peter Gossage and Robert Rutherdale, eds., *Making Men, Making History: Canadian Masculinities across Time and Place* (Vancouver: UBC Press, 2018); Lisa Moore, "Civic Identities in Conflict: Montreal's Anglophone and Francophone Private School Girls," in *Making the Best of It: Women and Girls of Canada and Newfoundland during the Second World War*, eds. Sarah Glassford and Amy J. Shaw (Vancouver: UBC Press, 2020) 89–108; Lisa Moore, "'The said accused is adjudged a juvenile delinquent': Girls and Young Women before the *Cour de bien-être social* of Montreal, 1950–1977" (PhD diss., Concordia University, in progress); and Peter Gossage and Lisa Moore, "Marriage, Property, and the Law in a Square-Mile Family: The Case of Annie Stevenson Anderson v. David Morrice, 1884–85," in *Montreal's Square Mile: The Making and Transformation of a Colonial Metropole*, ed. Dimitry Anastakis, Elizabeth Kirkland, and Donald Nerbas (Toronto: University of Toronto Press, 2024) 147–74.

8 Adele Perry, *On the Edge of Empire: Gender, Race and the Making of British Columbia, 1849–1871* (Toronto: University of Toronto Press, 2001); Sarah Carter, *The Importance of Being Monogamous: Marriage and Nation Building in Canada to 1915* (Edmonton: University of Alberta Press, 2008); Carolyn Strange and Tina Loo, *Making Good: Law and Moral Regulation in Canada, 1867–1939* (Toronto: University of Toronto Press, 1997). Some of the international scholarship in this area is discussed below, but see in particular Jisoo M. Kim, *The Emotions of Justice: Gender, Status, and Legal Performance in Choson Korea* (Seattle: University of Washington Press, 2015) and Alecia Simmonds, "Intimate Jurisdictions: Reflections upon the Relationship between Sentiment, Law and Empire," in *Transnationalism, Nationalism and Australian History*, ed. Anna Clark, Anne Rees, and Alecia Simmonds (Singapore: Palgrave Macmillan, 2017).

9 *Family and Justice in the Archives: Histories of Intimacy in Transnational Perspective—Famille et justice dans les archives: Perspectives transnationales sur les histoires de l'intimité*, Concordia University, Montreal, Quebec, Canada, 5–7 May 2019, co-chairs Peter Gossage and Eric H. Reiter, https://familyandjustice.cieq.ca/, accessed 6 October 2022.

10 Several contributors, moreover, employ an explicitly transnational lens in their essays to observe the ways in which domestic intimacies played out in legal proceedings. James Moran and Emma Chilton (Chapter 10), for instance, investigate the commonalities between understandings of masculinity and legal capacity in nineteenth-century Canada and the United States, which grew out of a shared inheritance of English lunacy investigation law. In their essays,

moreover, Riyad Koya, Lorena Rizzo, Ginger Frost, and Gail Savage (Chapters 3, 4, 12, and 13 respectively) explore how transnational mobility and marriage were regulated by legal proscriptions related to racial and national identities.

11 We thank French historian Anne-Emanuelle Demartini for this elegant turn of phrase. Demartini, "Récits d'inceste dans les archives judiciaires de l'affaire Violette Nozière (1933–1934)," paper presented at the 2019 symposium *Family and Justice in the Archives: Histories of Intimacy in Transnational Perspective* (see details in endnote 9, above).

12 Robert Darnton, *The Great Cat Massacre and Other Episodes in French Cultural History* (New York: Basic Books, 1984); Natalie Zemon Davis, *Fiction in the Archives: Pardon Tales and Their Tellers in Sixteenth-Century France* (Stanford: Stanford University Press, 1987); Arlette Farge, *La vie fragile: Violence, pouvoirs et solidarités à Paris au XVIIIe siècle* (Paris: Hachette, 1986).

13 Michael Grossberg, *Governing the Hearth: Law and the Family in Nineteenth-Century America* (Chapel Hill: University of North Carolina Press, 1985); Constance Backhouse, *Petticoats and Prejudice: Women and Law in Nineteenth-Century Canada* (Toronto: Osgoode Society and Women's Press, 1991).

14 Arlette Farge, *Le goût de l'archive* (Paris: Seuil, 1989); Carolyn Steedman, *Dust* (Manchester: Manchester University Press, 2001); Ann Laura Stoler, *Along the Archival Grain: Epistemic Anxieties and Colonial Common Sense* (Princeton: Princeton University Press, 2009).

15 Patricia Seed, *To Love, Honor, and Obey in Colonial Mexico: Conflicts Over Marriage Choice, 1574–1821* (Stanford: Stanford University Press, 1988); Shannon McSheffrey, *Marriage, Sex, and Civic Culture in Late Medieval London* (Philadelphia: University of Pennsylvania Press, 2006).

16 Joan Sangster, *Regulating Girls and Women: Sexuality, Family, and the Law in Ontario, 1920–1960* (Oxford: Oxford University Press, 2001); Mary Anne Poutanen, *Beyond Brutal Passions: Prostitution in Early Nineteenth-Century Montreal* (Montreal and Kingston: McGill-Queen's University Press, 2015); Nora Jaffary, *Reproduction and Its Discontents in Mexico: Childbirth and Contraception in Mexico, 1750–1905* (Chapel Hill: University of North Carolina Press, 2016).

17 Thierry Nootens, *Fous, prodigues et ivrognes: Familles et déviance à Montréal au XIXème siècle* (Montreal and Kingston: McGill-Queen's University Press, 2007).

18 On inheritance, see Bettina Bradbury, *Caroline's Dilemma: A Colonial Inheritance Saga* (Kensington, Australia: NewSouth Publishing, 2019); and Peter Gossage, "Tangled Webs: Remarriage and Family Conflict in 19th-Century Quebec," in *Family Matters: Papers in Post-Confederation Canadian Family History*, ed. Edgar-André Montigny and Lori Chambers (Toronto: Canadian Scholars Press, 1998), 355–76; Matthew Gerber, *Bastards: Politics, Family, and Law in Early Modern France* (New York: Oxford University Press, 2012); Rachel G. Fuchs, *Contested Paternity: Constructing Families in Modern France* (Baltimore: Johns Hopkins University Press, 2008). On the guardianship of children, see Gossage, "On Dads and Damages"; Sylvie Perrier, *Des*

*enfances protégées: La tutelle des mineurs en France, 17e–18e siècles* (Saint-Denis: Presses Universitaires de Vincennes, 1998); and Viviana A. Zelizer, *The Purchase of Intimacy* (Princeton: Princeton University Press, 2005). On spousal conflicts and family allowances, see Margo De Koster, *Chers enfants: Les allocations familiales en Belgique, 1921–1945* (Tielt: Lannoo, 2001); and Thierry Nootens, *Genre, patrimoine et droit civil: Les femmes mariées de la bourgeoisie québécoise en procès, 1900–1930* (Montreal and Kingston: McGill-Queen's University Press, 2018). On the family as economic unit, see Julie Hardwick, *Family Business: Litigation and the Political Economies of Daily Life in Seventeenth-Century France* (Oxford: Oxford University Press, 2009); and Susan M. Socolow, *The Merchants of Buenos Aires, 1778–1810: Family and Commerce* (Cambridge: Cambridge University Press, 2009).

19 Christopher Lasch articulated this view in the title of his influential 1977 book: Christopher Lasch, *Haven in a Heartless World: The Family Besieged* (New York: Basic Books, 1977).

20 Constance Backhouse, *Carnal Crimes: Sexual Assault in Canada, 1900–1975* (Toronto: Irwin Law for Osgoode Society for Canadian Legal History, 2008).

21 Marie-Aimée Cliche, *Maltraiter ou punir: La violence envers les enfants dans les familles québécoises, 1850–1969* (Montréal: Boréal, 2007); Cliche, *Fous, ivres ou méchants? Les parents meurtriers au Québec, 1775–1965* (Montreeal: Boréal, 2011); Anne-Emanuelle Demartini, *Violette Nozière, la fleur du mal: Une histoire des années trente* (Ceyzérieu: Champ Vallon, 2017); Fabienne Giuliani, *Les liaisons impossibles: Histoire de l'inceste dans la France du XIXème siècle* (Paris: Publications de la Sorbonne, 2014); Elaine Farrell, *"A Most Diabolical Deed": Infanticide and Irish Society, 1850–1900* (Manchester: Manchester University Press, 2013); Cliona Rattigan, *"What else could I do?" Single Mothers and Infanticide, 1900–1950* (Dublin: Irish Academic Press, 2012).

22 Roderick Phillips, *Putting Asunder: A History of Divorce in Western Society* (Cambridge, UK: Cambridge University Press, 1988); James G. Snell, *In the Shadow of the Law: Divorce in Canada, 1900–1939* (Toronto: University of Toronto Press, 1991); see also Norma Basch, *Framing American Divorce: From the Revolutionary Generation to the Victorians* (Berkeley: University of California Press, 1999). There is a rich literature, moreover, examining marital breakdown through civil suits for separation of bed and board (*séparation de corps et de biens*) in the Quebec context. See Marie-Aimée Cliche, "Les séparations de corps dans le district judiciaire de Montréal de 1900 à 1930," *Revue canadienne droit et société* 12, no. 1 (1977): 71–100; Cliche, "Les procès en séparation de corps dans la région de Montréal, 1795–1879," *Revue d'histoire de l'Amérique française* 49, no. 1 (Summer 1995): 3–33; Sylvie Savoie, "Les couples séparés: Les demandes de séparation aux 17e et 18e siècles," in *Les marginaux, les exclus et l'autre au Canada aux 17e et 18e siècles*, ed. André Lachance (Saint-Laurent, QC: Fides, 1996), 245–82; Savoie, "Women's Marital Difficulties: Requests of Separation in New France," *The History of the Family* 3, no. 4 (1998): 473–85; Catherine Gélinas, "La violence conjugale

dans le district judiciaire de St-François entre 1866 et 1893 d'après les procès en séparation de corps" (master's thesis, History, Université de Sherbrooke, 2000).

23 Sangster, *Regulating Girls and Women*; Tamara Myers, *Caught: Montreal's Modern Girls and the Law, 1869–1945* (Toronto: University of Toronto Press, 2006); Joëlle Droux, *Enfances en difficulté: De l'enfance abandonnée à l'assistance éducative (1892–2012)* (Geneva: FOJ/SRO Kundig, 2012); David Niget, *La naissance du tribunal pour enfants: Une comparaison France-Québec (1912–1945)* (Rennes, Presses de l'Université de Rennes, 2009); Véronique Blanchard and David Niget, *Mauvaises filles, incorrigibles et rebelles* (Paris: Textuel, 2016); Jean Trépanier and Xavier Rousseaux, *Youth and Justice in Western States, 1815–1950: From Punishment to Welfare* (Cham: Palgrave Macmillan, 2018); Elizabeth Clapp, *Mothers of All Children: Women Reformers and the Rise of Juvenile Courts in Progressive Era America* (University Park: Pennsylvania State University Press, 1998); David S. Tanenhaus, *Juvenile Justice in the Making* (New York: Oxford University Press, 2004).

24 Laura Hanft Korobkin, *Criminal Conversations: Sentimentality and Nineteenth-Century Legal Stories of Adultery* (New York: Columbia University Press, 1998); William M. Reddy, *The Invisible Code: Honor and Sentiment in Postrevolutionary France* (Berkeley: University of California Press, 1997); Eric Reiter, *Wounded Feelings: Litigating Emotions in Quebec, 1870–1950* (Toronto: University of Toronto Press for Osgoode Society for Canadian Legal History, 2019); Julie-Marie Strange, *Death, Grief and Poverty in Britain, 1870–1914* (Cambridge: Cambridge University Press, 2005). See also Mary Louise Kete, *Sentimental Collaborations: Mourning and Middle-Class Identity in Nineteenth-Century America* (Durham, NC: Duke University Press, 2000).

25 Kathryn A. Sloan, *Runaway Daughters: Seduction, Elopement, and Honor in Nineteenth-Century Mexico* (Albuquerque: University of New Mexico Press, 2008); Eric Reiter, "From Shaved Horses to Aggressive Churchwardens: Social and Legal Aspects of Moral Injury in Lower Canada," in *Essays in the History of Canadian Law XI: Quebec and the Canadas*, ed. G. Blaine Baker and Donald Fyson (Toronto: University of Toronto Press for the Osgoode Society for Canadian Legal History, 2013), 460–502. See also Alexandra Shepard, *Accounting for Oneself: Worth, Status and the Social Order in Early Modern England* (Oxford: Oxford University Press, 2015).

26 Jane E. Mangan, *Transatlantic Obligations: Creating the Bonds of Family in Conquest-Era Peru and Spain* (New York: Oxford University Press, 2015); Jessica M. Marglin, *Across Legal Lines: Jews and Muslims in Modern Morocco* (New Haven: Yale University Press, 2016). For a gendered discussion of family identity, see also Gossage and Rutherdale, *Making Men, Making History*.

27 There is quite a different "public/private" dichotomy in legal studies, however, which we embrace somewhat more readily, if not unreservedly, and to which we will return below.

28 Lauren Berlant, "Intimacy: A Special Issue," *Critical Inquiry* 24, no. 2 (1998): 283.

29 The idea of "intimate publics" is also incorporated by Suzanne Lenon into her recent work on race and inheritance, including "the inheritance of intimacies," in Western Canada. Suzanne Lenon, "Inheritance's Intimacies and Social Change," *Canadian Review of Sociology* 54, no. 3 (2017): 366–68, citation at p. 367. Wiegman used the expression as the title for a 2002 article but did not develop its conceptual possibilities to any extent. See Robyn Wiegman, "Intimate Publics: Race, Property, and Personhood," *American Literature* 74, no. 4 (December 2002): 859–85. For a primer on Berlant's framing of this idea, see Lauren Berlant and Jay Prosser, "Life Writing and Intimate Publics: A Conversation with Lauren Berlant," *Biography* 34, no. 1 (Winter 2011): 180–87.

30 Zelizer, *The Purchase of Intimacy*; Zelizer, "Do Markets Poison Intimacy?," *Contexts* 5, no. 2 (2006): 33–38.

31 Zelizer, "Do Markets Poison Intimacy?," 34.

32 Michelle A. McKinley, "Illicit Intimacies: Virtuous Concubinage in Colonial Lima," *Journal of Family History* 39, no. 3 (2014): 205. McKinley's 2016 monograph about enslaved persons in Peru focuses on their use of the Spanish colonial court system to seek "fractional freedoms" for themselves and, just as often (especially in cases involving women), for their sons and daughters. Her subtitle for that book suggests its focus on individual agency and on the legal dimensions of family, kinship, and domesticity for these enslaved people, for whom no legally sanctioned or morally idealized "private sphere" can be thought to have existed. Michelle A. McKinley, *Fractional Freedoms: Slavery, Intimacy, and Legal Mobilization in Colonial Lima, 1600–1700* (Cambridge, UK: Cambridge University Press, 2016).

33 Ann Laura Stoler, "Tense and Tender Ties: The Politics of Comparison in North American History and (Post) Colonial Studies," *Journal of American History* 88, no. 3 (December 2001): 829.

34 Stoler, *Carnal Knowledge and Imperial Power: Race and the Intimate in Colonial Rule* (Berkeley: University of California Press, 2010), 9.

35 This is an area in which Canadian feminist scholars have made major contributions. See for example Jennifer S.H. Brown, *Strangers in Blood: Fur Trade Company Families in Indian Country* (Vancouver: University of British Columbia Press, 1980); Sylvia Van Kirk, *'Many Tender Ties': Women in Fur-Trade Society in Western Canada, 1670–1870* (Winnipeg: Watson & Dwyer, 1980); Perry, *On the Edge of Empire*; Robin Brownlie and Valerie J. Korinek, eds., *Finding a Way to the Heart: Feminist Writings on Aboriginal and Women's History in Canada* (Winnipeg: University of Manitoba Press, 2012).

36 See the contributions by Fabienne Giuliani (Chapter 15), Shelley Gavigan (Chapter 9), and Mélanie Méthot (Chapter 11) in this volume.

37 See the essays below by Isabelle Bouchard (Chapter 1) and Chandra Murdoch (Chapter 2) on inheritance, by Jean-Philippe Garneau (Chapter 5) on guardianship, and by Juandrea Bates (Chapter 6) on adolescents seeking autonomy.

38 Reiter, *Wounded Feelings*. See also Alecia Simmonds, "Introduction: Affective Encounters in the Archives," *Law&history: Journal of the Australian and New Zealand Law and History Society* 6, no. 2 (November 2019): 1–8; Alecia

Simmonds and Eric H. Reiter, "The Legal History of Emotions," in *The Routledge History of Emotion in the Modern World*, eds. Katie Barclay and Peter Stearns (London: Routledge, 2023), 423–39.

39 The meaning we attach to the "justice" in our title is captured by the third paragraph of the *OED*'s definition: "The administration of law; due legal process; judicial proceedings." *Oxford English Dictionary* (online), s.v. "justice," paragraph I.3.a, consulted 6 October 2022. Readers looking for essays on the broader idea of justice as it has emerged and evolved in Western and other intellectual traditions already have plenty of material on which to draw. The political philosopher David Johnston, for instance, has published a brief history of Western ideas on justice, beginning with Plato and finishing with twenty-first-century ideas of social justice and global justice. While Johnston is dismissive of what he calls "strictly legal justice," he nonetheless describes it as "the obvious form in which people usually encounter something resembling justice in the everyday world." David Johnston, *A Brief History of Justice* (Chichester, UK and Malden, MA: Wiley-Blackwell, 2011), 4.

40 Douglas Hay, "Crime and Justice in Eighteenth- and Nineteenth-Century England," *Crime and Justice* 2 (1980): 45–84.

41 Donald Fyson, *Magistrates, Police, and People: Everyday Criminal Justice in Quebec and Lower Canada, 1764–1837* (Toronto: University of Toronto Press for the Osgoode Society for Canadian Legal History, 2007), 5.

42 For important contributions to the literature on social, legal, and moral regulation, see Jean-Marie Fecteau, *The Pauper's Freedom: Crime and Poverty in Nineteenth-Century Quebec*, trans. Peter Feldstein (Montreal and Kingston: McGill-Queen's University Press, 2017), especially chapter 1, "The Concept of Regulation," 9–36; and Robert Menzies and Dorothy E. Chunn, eds., *Regulating Lives: Historical Essays on the State, Society, the Individual, and the Law* (Vancouver: UBC Press, 2002).

43 Eric Reiter, personal communication, 4 April 2021.

44 Hay, "Crime and Justice in Eighteenth- and Nineteenth-Century England," 47.

45 "In short, at the highest levels of abstraction, public law is the law that pertains to government—for example, constitutional separation of powers or administrative procedure; or to the vertical relation between the government and individuals to the extent that government imposes an obligation owed to it on individuals—for example, criminal law; or directly confers a right or entitlement on the latter … or guarantees such individual right or entitlement…." Michel Rosenfeld, "Rethinking the Boundaries between Public Law and Private Law for the Twenty-First Century: An Introduction," *International Journal of Constitutional Law* 11, no. 1 (2013): 125.

46 Such topics and approaches are well represented in the present volume; see, among others, Chapter 8 (on prostitution); Chapter 11 (on bigamy); Chapter 14 (on infanticide); and Chapter 15 (on incest).

47 For an important and illustrative Canadian example, see Karen Dubinsky and Franca Iacovetta, "Murder, Womanly Virtue, and Motherhood: The Case

of Angelina Napolitano, 1911–1922," *Canadian Historical Review* 72, no. 4 (1991): 505–31. See also Riyad Koya's discussion of femicide amongst Indian indentured labourers in Mauritius, Chapter 3 in this volume.

48 See, for example, in the Canadian context Perry, *On the Edge of Empire* and especially Carter, *The Importance of Being Monogamous*.

49 Lorena Rizzo, "The Materiality and Visuality of Intimacy in a South African Colonial Archive," Chapter 4 in this volume. Riyad Koya takes a similar approach in his study of Indian indentured labourers in nearby Mauritius, characterizing them as "strangers before the law"; see below, Chapter 3.

50 "Private law," according to legal scholar Michel Rosenfeld, "traditionally encompasses the common law of contract, torts, and property that regulates relations among individuals." Rosenfeld, "Rethinking the Boundaries between Public Law and Private Law," 125.

51 Grossberg, *Governing the Hearth*, ix.

52 This approach is well represented in the studies cited above. For a handful of close-to-home examples, see Reiter, *Wounded Feelings*; Nootens, *Genre, patrimoine et droit civil*; Bradbury, *Caroline's Dilemma*; and Gossage, "On Dads and Damages."

53 The critics include Michel Rosenfeld, who describes the distinction as "unwieldy," especially in the twenty-first century context of globalization and privatization. He also quotes fellow legal scholar Paul Verkuil, who has compared the public/private dichotomy in law to "a dysfunctional spouse" in that it "has been around forever, but it continues to fail as an organizing principle." Rosenfeld, "Rethinking the Boundaries between Public Law and Private Law," 125.

54 Supreme Court of Canada, Foley v. Marcoux, [1957] S.C.R. 650, 1 October 1957; cited in Gossage, "On Dads and Damages," 619–20. One of Shelley Gavigan's great insights, moreover, is the extent to which "improper intimacies" can be discovered in the records left behind by criminal trials that brought the state's power to bear on theft, extortion, mischief, or perjury: offences against public order that don't necessarily "shout" (as she puts it) gender or family relations (see below, Chapter 9).

55 Jean-Philippe Garneau, "Administering Minor Children's Inheritance: Domestic Authority and Masculinities in Lower Canada, 1825–1835," Chapter 5 in this volume, 105.

56 Savage, "The 'Moscow Widowers,'" 258.

57 Simmonds, "Introduction: Affective Encounters in the Archives," 1–2.

58 Jacques Derrida, *Archive Fever: A Freudian Impression*, trans. Eric Prenowitz (Chicago: University of Chicago Press, 1996); Steedman, *Dust*; Stoler, *Along the Archival Grain*. For Athanasiou, the archive refers to "a historically and politically qualified constellation of the spectral remains—including cultural imaginaries, written and unwritten artefacts, epistemic genres and structures, technologies of monumentality, everyday snippets, discursive formations and affective states [...rather than] a mere repository of historical data." And furthermore, "the archive actively regulates the possibility of memory-work within prevailing matrices of power and knowledge." Athena Athanasiou, "Gendered Intimacies of the Nationalist Archive," in *Agonistic Mourning:*

*Political Dissidence and the Women in Black*, ed. Athena Athanasiou (Edinburgh: Edinburgh University Press, 2017), 93–94.

59 Lorena Rizzo, "The Materiality and Visuality of Intimacy in a South African Colonial Archive," Chapter 4 in this volume, 100; emphasis added.

60 Shelley A.M. Gavigan, "Improper Intimacies, Impossible Promises, and the Prerogatives of Patriarchy: Family and Justice in Nineteenth-Century Criminal Courts in Canada's North-West Territories," Chapter 9 in this volume, 186.

61 See, among many other studies, Louise Dechêne, *Habitants et marchands de Montréal au XVIIe siècle* (Paris: Éditions Plon, 1974); Gérard Bouchard, *Quelques arpents d'Amérique: Population, économie, famille au Saguenay, 1838–1971* (Montreal: Boréal, 1996); Benoît Grenier, *Seigneurs campagnards de la Nouvelle-France: Présence seigneuriale et sociabilité rurale dans la vallée du Saint-Laurent à l'époque préindustrielle* (Rennes: Presses de l'Université de Rennes, 2007); Bradbury, *Wife to Widow*; Robert Sweeny, *Why Did We Choose to Industrialize? Montreal, 1819–1849* (Montreal and Kingston: McGill-Queen's University Press, 2015); Nootens, *Genre, patrimoine et droit civil.*

62 Steedman, *Dust*, 46.

63 Quoted in Riyad Sadiq Koya, "Strangers before the Law: The Intimate Lives of Indian Indentured Labourers in Colonial Mauritius," Chapter 3 in this volume, 77.

64 Steedman, *Dust*, 47. Mélanie Méthot makes a similar point very clearly in her discussion of the witness testimony provided in Australian bigamy trials. See Méthot, "Bigamy Prosecutions in Victoria, Australia: The Press Coverage and the Case Files," Chapter 11 in this volume.

65 Gavigan, "Improper Intimacies," 186.

66 Louise A. Jackson, *Child Sexual Abuse in Victorian England* (New York and London: Routledge, 2013), 12.

67 We are most familiar with the Canadian contributions to this area of research, which include Gary Kinsman and Patrizia Gentile, *The Canadian War on Queers: National Security as Sexual Regulation* (Vancouver: UBC Press, 2010); Lyle Dick, "The 1942 Same-Sex Trials in Edmonton: On the State's Repression of Sexual Minorities, Archives, and Human Rights in Canada," *Archivaria* 68 (January): 183–217; Lyle Dick, "The Queer Frontier: Male Same-Sex Experience in Western Canada's Settlement Era," *Journal of Canadian Studies* 48, no. 1 (Winter 2014): 15–52; Dominic Dagenais, *Grossières indécences: Pratiques et identités homosexuelles à Montréal, 1880–1929* (Montreal and Kingston: McGill-Queen's University Press, 2020).

68 The historical literature on aging and the elderly is significant and growing. Some exemplary (again, Canadian) contributions are Bradbury, *Wife to Widow*; Megan Jean Davies, *Into the House of Old: A History of Residential Care in British Columbia* (Montreal and Kingston: McGill-Queen's University Press, 2003); Aline Charles, *Quand devient-on vieille? Femmes, âge et travail au Québec, 1940–1980* (Québec: Les Presses de l'Université Laval, 2007); James Struthers, "Framing Aging Through the State: Canada's Two Senate Committees on Aging, 1963–1966 and 2006–2009," *Canadian Review of Social Policy* nos. 68–69 (2012–2013): 1–9.

## PART ONE

1 For an important exploration of "contact zones" in the context of Canadian settler-colonialism, see Katie Pickles and Myra Rutherdale, eds., *Contact Zones: Aboriginal and Settler Women in Canada's Colonial Past* (Vancouver: UBC Press, 2005).

2 Lorena Rizzo, "The Materiality and Visuality of Intimacy in a South African Colonial Archive," Chapter 4 in this volume, 85.

## CHAPTER 1

1 This chapter was translated from the original French by Steven Watt. The author would like to thank the Université du Québec à Trois-Rivières (UQTR), which provided funding for the initial stages of this research project through the Fonds institutionnel de recherche (FIR), as well as the Fonds de recherche du Québec, Société et culture (FRQSC), which awarded her a *Research Support for New Academics* grant. Thanks as well to Dannick Rivest, Alexandre Marchand, and Audrey Tremblay for collecting and transcribing the sources on which this study is based.

2 These lands are in the northern part of the ancestral territory of the Abenaki. Spanning territories that now comprise Canada and the United States, the Ndakina extends, from north to south, the New England coastline to the St. Lawrence River and, from east to west, the Chaudière River to the Richelieu River and Lake Champlain. Geneviève Treyvaud and Michel Plourde, *Les Abénakis d'Odanak, un voyage archéologique* (Odanak, QC: Musée des Abénakis, 2017), 30.

3 Sylvie Dépatie, "La seigneurie de l'île-Jésus au XVIIIe siècle," in *Contributions à l'étude du régime seigneurial canadien*, ed. Sylvie Dépatie, Mario Lalancette, and Christian Dessureault (LaSalle: Hurtubise HMH, 1987), 57.

4 The chiefs were the ones to appoint these legal representatives and define their powers. Such appointments were formalized before a notary. Procuration from the Abenaki to Augustin Gill, 28 October 1811, doc. 1280, S31, CN401, Bibliothèque et Archives nationales du Québec, Trois-Rivières (BAnQ-TR); Revocation of procuration from Simon Obomsawin et al. to Augustin Gill, 23 October 1829, doc. 1122, S74, CN603, Bibliothèque et Archives nationales du Québec, Vieux-Montréal (BAnQ-VM); Revocation of procuration from Simon Obomsawin et al. to Augustin Gill, 2 November 1829, doc. 1126, S74, CN603, BAnQ-VM; Procuration from the Indians of the village of St. François to Louis Gill, 9 July 1832, doc. 6158, S78, CN603, BAnQ-VM; Resignation of Louis Gill, 10 February 1855, doc. 2549, S14, CN603, BAnQ-VM.

5 On the adoption of captives by the Abenaki of Odanak following raids carried out in New England, see Evan Haefeli and Kevin Sweeney, *Captors and Captives: The 1704 French and Indian Raid on Deerfield* (Amherst: University of Massachusetts Press, 2004); Jean Barman, *Abenaki Daring: The Life and Writings of Noel Annance, 1792–1869* (Montreal: McGill-Queen's University Press, 2016): 19–38. On the link between war and adoption into Indigenous communities, see Brett Rushforth, *Bonds of Alliance: Indigenous and Atlantic*

*Slaveries in New France* (Chapel Hill: University of North Carolina Press, 2012): 15–71.

6 Stéphanie Béreau, "Joseph-Louis Gill 'Magouaouidombaouit,'" in *Vivre la conquête*, ed. Gaston Deschênes and Denis Vaugeois (Quebec City: Septentrion, 2013), 2:100–112.

7 Burial of Augustin Gill, 4 June 1851, reel 4123, ZA314, BAnQ-TR.

8 Brian Gettler, "En espèce ou en nature? Les présents, l'imprévoyance et l'évolution idéologique de la politique indienne pendant la première moitié du XIXe siècle," *Revue d'histoire de l'Amérique française* 65, no. 4 (2012): 414.

9 On the importance of kinship for access to community resources, see Heidi Bohaker, "'Nindoodemag': The Significance of Algonquian Kinship Networks in the Eastern Great Lakes Region, 1600–1701," *The William and Mary Quarterly*, 63, no. 1 (January 2006): 23–52.

10 John C. Weaver, *The Great Land Rush and the Making of the Modern World, 1650–1900*, (Montreal: McGill-Queen's University Press, 2003); Allan Greer, *Property and Dispossession: Natives, Empires and Land in Early Modern North America* (Cambridge: Cambridge University Press, 2018).

11 Karine Gentelet, Jeremy Webber, and Pierre Noreau, "Le droit foncier en regard des réalités autochtones," *Recherches amérindiennes au Québec* 46, nos. 2–3 (2016): 78. On Indigenous legal traditions in Canada, see John Borrows, *Canada's Indigenous Constitution* (Toronto: University of Toronto Press, 2010).

12 See, for instance, Rolande Bonnain, Gérard Bouchard, and Joseph Goy, eds., *Transmettre, hériter, succéder: La reproduction familiale en milieu rural, France-Québec, XVIIIe–XIXe siècles* (Paris: École des hautes études en sciences sociales; Lyon: Presses universitaires de Lyon, 1992); Gérard Bouchard, *Quelques arpents d'Amérique: Population, économie, famille au Saguenay, 1838–1871* (Montreal: Boréal, 1996); Sylvie Dépatie, "La transmission du patrimoine au Canada (XVIIe–XVIIIe siècle): Qui sont les défavorisés?," *Revue d'histoire de l'Amérique française* 54, no. 4 (Spring 2001): 558–570; Allan Greer, *Peasant, Lord, and Merchant: Rural Society in Three Quebec Parishes, 1740–1840* (Toronto: University of Toronto Press, 1985).

13 Isabelle Bouchard, "L'organisation des terres autochtones de la vallée du Saint-Laurent sous le Régime britannique," *Journal of the Canadian Historical Association*, New Series 27, no. 1 (2016): 31–59. On changes to land tenure during the nineteenth century, see Susan M. Hill, *The Clay We Are Made Of: Haudenosaunee Land Tenure on the Grand River* (Winnipeg: University of Manitoba Press, 2017); Daniel Rück, *The Laws and the Land: The Settler Colonial Invasion of Kahnawà:ke in Nineteenth-Century Canada* (Vancouver: UBC Press, 2021).

14 Christian Dessureault, Thomas Wien, and Gérard Bouchard, "À propos de *Quelques arpents d'Amérique* de Gérard Bouchard," *Revue d'histoire de l'Amérique française* 50, no. 3 (Winter 1997): 407.

15 On the use of the family reconstitution model for studying Indigenous families and their relationships to the land, see Brenda Macdougall, *One of the Family:*

*Metis Culture in Nineteenth-Century Northwestern Saskatchewan* (Vancouver: UBC Press, 2010).

16 Louis Lavallée, "La vie et la pratique d'un notaire rural sous le régime français: Le cas de Guillaume Barette, notaire à La Prairie entre 1709–1744," *Revue d'histoire de l'Amérique française* 47, no. 4 (1984): 499–519; 516; Jean-Philippe Garneau, "Droit et 'affaires de famille' sur la Côte-de-Beaupré: Histoire d'une rencontre en amont et en aval de la Conquête britannique," *Revue juridique Thémis* 34 (2000): 515–61; Donald Fyson, "Judicial Auxiliaries Across Legal Regimes: From New France to Lower Canada," in *Entre justice et justiciables: Les aux auxiliaires de la justice du Moyen-Âge au XXe siècle*, ed. Claire Dolan (Quebec City: Presses de l'Université Laval, 2005), 389–91; David Gilles, "Le notariat canadien face à la Conquête anglaise: L'exemple des Panet," in *Les praticiens du droit du Moyen Âge à l'époque contemporaine*, ed. Vincent Bernaudeau et al. (Rennes: Presses Universitaires de Rennes, 2008), 189–207. On other colonial contexts where French civil law was applied after British conquest, see Riyad Sadiq Koya's contribution to this collection (Chapter 3).

17 Procuration from the Abenaki to Joseph Gamelin, 17 January 1800, unnumbered doc., S88, CN603, BAnQ-VM. On the concept of "dish" or "common pot," see Victor P. Lytwyn, "A Dish with One Spoon: The Shared Hunting Grounds Agreement in the Great Lakes and St. Lawrence Valley Region," in *Papers of the Twenty-Eighth Algonquian Conference (*Winnipeg: University of Manitoba, 1997), 210–27; Lisa Brooks, *The Common Pot: The Recovery of Native Space in the Northeast* (Minneapolis: University of Minnesota Press, 2008), 3–8.

18 I consulted the records of twenty-three notaries who worked in the region. Augustin Gill is named in a total of 182 notarial deeds. In addition to the fifty-eight deeds where he is described as acting in a personal capacity (as a party), he appears in others as the legal representative responsible for managing the "seigneurial" lands of the Abenaki of Odanak (fifty-eight) or Wôlinak (four); as the representative of a third party (tutor, curator, executor or legal representative) (thirty-five); in his capacity as a chief (eighteen); or as an interpreter (five) or witness (four).

19 Until 1848, even though the Abenaki mission had a separate church, its baptisms, marriages, and burials were recorded in the parish register of Saint-François-du-Lac. Catholic Civil Register, Saint-François-du-Lac, 1687–1899, Superior Court Fonds, Judicial District of Richelieu, ZA314, BAnQ-TR. My research also involved accessing the *Infrastructure intégrée des microdonnées historiques de la population du Québec* (IMPQ).

20 Procuration from the Abenaki Indians to Joseph Gamelin, 17 January 1800, unnumbered doc., S88, CN603, BAnQ-VM; Procuration from the Abenaki Indians to Henry Rousseau, 3 February 1810, doc. 1097, S31, CN401, BAnQ-TR.

21 For example, Grant from Joseph Gamelin to André Liorgeau, 15 January 1802, unnumbered doc., S88, CN603, BAnQ-VM.

22 Marriage of Augustin Gill and Marie Plamondon, 1 May 1797, reel 4120, ZA314, BAnQ-TR.

23 Obligation from Raphaël Bourque to Augustin Gill, 3 February 1810, unnumbered doc., S35, CN401, BAnQ-TR; Free gift from Augustin Gill (and his wife) to Louis Cartier *dit* Lafrance, 8 June 1814, doc. 1195, S25, CN603, BAnQ-VM.

24 For example, Conveyance from François Lemaître Duhaime to Augustin Gill, 2 November 1810, doc. 1173, S31, CN401, BAnQ-TR; Sale of pastureland from Augustin Gill to Louis Allard, 4 March 1820, doc. 3182, S78, CN603, BAnQ-VM.

25 Transfer and conveyance of pastureland from Augustin Gill and Louis Cartier *dit* Lafrance for the benefit of Louis Cartier, his son, 4 March 1820, doc. 2791, S25, CN603, BAnQ-VM; Statement by Augustin Gill, 11 July 1829, doc. 2969, S31, CN401, BAnQ-TR.

26 Married on 3 February 1777, Félicité Girard died on 2 December 1781 in Ancienne-Lorette. IMPQ, civil register couple #9937104.

27 Survey report to the seigneur of Saint-François, 11 July 1783; Survey report to Joseph Gill, 12 August 1783, unnumbered doc., S20, CA401.

28 Marriage between Jean Plamondon and Catherine Gill, 17 November 1783, reel 4119, ZA314, BAnQ-TR. That same day, Plamondon surveyed an island for his father-in-law and two members of the Gamelin family. Survey report to Joseph Gill, Pierre Gamelin, and Joseph Gamelin, 17 November 1783, unnumbered doc., S20, CA401.

29 In April 1782, Jean Plamondon, the surviving spouse, was appointed tutor and Étienne Auclair, a maternal uncle, was appointed subrogate tutor. Since the latter had both children in his care, he was appointed ad hoc tutor three years later. Tutorship of the minor children of Jean Plamondon and the late Marie-Félicité Girard, 15 and 19 April 1782, D5743, S1, CC301, Bibliothèque et Archives nationales du Québec, Quebec City (BAnQ-QC); Assembly of friends for the tutorship of the minor children of Jean Plamondon and the late Marie-Félicité Girard, 11 May 1784, D6080, S1, CC301, BAnQ-QC; Petition and assembly of relatives and friends for the minor children of Jean Plamondon and the late Marie-Félicité Girard *dit* Breton, 25 April 1785, D6235, S1, CC301, BAnQ-QC.

30 Assembly of relatives and friends for Jean and Marie, minor children of Jean Plamondon and the late Marie-Félicité Girard *dit* Breton, 4–10 January 1791, D7034, S1, CC301, BAnQ-QC. On the role played by assemblies of relatives and friends in the appointment of tutors to minor children, see Jean-Philippe Garneau's contribution to this collection (Chapter 5).

31 Marriage contract, 27 April 1797, unnumbered doc., S88, CN603, BAnQ-VM.

32 Joseph-Anselme Maurault, *Histoire des Abénakis, depuis 1605 jusqu'à nos jours* (Sorel, QC: Atelier typographique de la Gazette de Sorel, 1866), 353; Inventory of property for the estate of the late Jean Plamondon and Catherine Gill, 10 March 1810, doc. 1107, S31, CN401, BAnQ-TR; IMPQ, civil register couple #9715867.

33 Marie Plamondon's brother's son (Jean) married one of Augustin's nieces (Monique), and one of Augustin and Marie's sons (David) married a granddaughter of Jean Plamondon and Catherine Gill. Marriage of Jean Plamondon

and Monique Gill, 25 June 1832, reel 4121, ZA314, BAnQ-TR; Marriage of David Gill and Caroline Plamondon, 24 November 1845, reel 4122, ZA314, BAnQ-TR.

34 Benoît Grenier, *Seigneurs campagnards de la Nouvelle France: Présence seigneuriale et sociabilité rurale dans la vallée du Saint-Laurent à l'époque préindustrielle* (Rennes: Presses universitaires de Rennes, 2007), 222.

35 Grant from Marguerite Hertel to the Abenaki and Sokokis Indians, 23 August 1700, unnumbered doc., S2, CN601, BAnQ-VM. This location is confirmed by Gédéon de Catalogne's 1709 map of the region (D197, SS2, S4, P600, BAnQ-QC).

36 Suzanne was the daughter of Antoine Gamelin (the militia captain) and Angélique Hertel. She married Joseph-Louis in Baie-du-Febvre on 2 November 1763. The groom had previously been married to an Abenaki woman named Marie Jeanne. Reel 4125, Saint-Antoine-de-la-Baie-du-Febvre, 1686–1773, ZA314, BAnQ-TR. Strangely, the marriage contract was signed after the ceremony, rendering it invalid under French civil law. Marriage contract, 30 November 1763, unnumbered doc., S80, CN401, BAnQ-TR; Claude-Joseph De Ferrière, *La science parfaite des notaires* (Paris: Chez Veuve Savoye, 1771), 1:252.

37 Marriage between Joseph Gamelin, and Catherine Annance, February 1768, reel 4119, ZA314, BAnQ-TR.

38 Catherine Annance (died in 1801) was the daughter of Gabriel Annance and Marie Appoline Gill, the latter being the sister of Joseph Louis. Maurault, *Histoire des Abénakis,* 348; Barman, *Abenaki Daring*, XXVI, 26–27.

39 Marriage of François-Louis Gill and Suzanne Gamelin *dit* Chateauvieux, 3 May 1802; Marriage of Antoine Gill and Isabelle Gamelin, 21 February 1803, reel 4120, ZA 314, BAnQ-TR.

40 Sale from Louis Cartier to Augustin Gill, 19 April 1797, unnumbered doc., S88, CN603, BAnQ-VM. Note that French units of currency, especially the *livre de vingt sols*, were still widely used in the (British) colony of Lower Canada at this time.

41 Obligation from Augustin Gill to Joseph Gamelin, 9 March 1798; Quittance from Louis Cartier and his wife to Augustin Gill, 19 April 1798, unnumbered doc., S88, CN603, BAnQ-VM.

42 Quittance from Augustin Gill and Marie Plamondon to Jean Plamondon, 17 February 1800, unnumbered doc., S88, CN603, BAnQ-VM; Obligation from Jean Plamondon to Joseph Gamelin, 2 April 1804, unnumbered doc., S88, CN603, BAnQ-VM; Offer of specifications from Augustin Gill and Marie Plamondon to Jean Plamondon, 3 April 1804, unnumbered doc., S88, CN603, BAnQ-VM; Quittance from Augustin Gill and his wife to Jean Plamondon, 7 May 1804, unnumbered doc., S88, CN603, BAnQ-VM.

43 Marriage contract, 27 April 1797, unnumbered doc., S88, CN603, BAnQ-VM.

44 Augustin Gill also acquired some pastureland in the fief of Saint-François. However, this land was sold or transferred before the household began to implement its inheritance strategies.

45 Grant from Henry Rousseau to Augustin and Thomas Gill, 21 May 1810, doc. 1132, S31, CN401, BAnQ-TR; Conveyance from François Lemaître to Augustin Gill, 2 November 1810, doc. 1173, S31, CN401, BAnQ-TR.

46 Grant from Joseph Gamelin to Thomas and Louis Gill, 19 February 1803, doc. 1389, S27, CN603, BAnQ-VM.

47 Sale with right of redemption ("*droit de réméré*") clause from César Annance to Augustin Gill, 23 January 1829, doc. 2920, S31, CN401, BAnQ-TR.

48 Filing by Augustin Gill of various deeds of sale, 16 November 1824, unnumbered document, S6, CN401, BAnQ-TR.

49 Baptism of Marie Félicité Gill, 7 August 1799; Burial of Félicité Gill, 17 August 1801; Baptism of Augustin Gill Jr., 8 December 1802; Baptism of Louis Gill, 21 April 1805; Baptism of Félicité Gill, 21 July 1807; Baptism of Élie Gill, 27 September 1809; Baptism of David Gill, 11 November 1811; Baptism of Félix Gill, 2 May 1814, reel 4120, ZA314, BAnQ-TR.

50 Augustin Jr. married Angèle Caya in Baie-du-Febvre on 16 April 1825. IMPQ, civil register individual #13331871.

51 Augustin Jr. was provided with an additional property located in the seigneurie of Pierreville. Conveyance and release from Augustin Gill and his wife to Augustin and Louis Gill, 1 April 1825, doc. 4707, S78, CN603, BAnQ-VM.

52 Greer, *Peasant, Lord, and Merchant*, 77.

53 Sale of a piece of land from Hugh Heney and others to Augustin Gill, 4 March 1825, doc. 4658, S78, CN603, BAnQ-VM; Sale from Jean-Baptiste Cartier and Jean Lemire to Augustin Gill, 9 March 1825, doc. 4667, S78, CN603, BAnQ-VM.

54 This requirement appears to have been met, as the section of land ceded to Louis contained several buildings by the time of his marriage. Marriage contract between Louis Gill and Adèle Manseau, 23 November 1832, doc. 6216, S78, CN603, BAnQ-VM.

55 It is unclear how Augustin Gill Sr. acquired this land.

56 Gift from Augustin Gill and Marie Plamondon to their minor children Élie, David, and Félix Gill, 13 May 1829, doc. 2950, S31, CN401, BAnQ-TR.

57 Gift from Joseph Gamelin to Augustin Gill, 29 September 1824, unnumbered doc., S6, CN401, BAnQ-TR; Will of Joseph Gamelin, 29 September 1824, unnumbered document, S6, CN401, BAnQ-TR; Quittance and release from François Plamondon, David and Félix Gill, heirs of the late Joseph Gamelin, to Stephen Bernard, 9 June 1835, doc. 8003, S25, CN603, BAnQ-VM.

58 Renewal deed ("*Titre nouvelle*") from Élie Gill to François Legendre, 8 March 1841, doc. 2692, S74, CN603, BAnQ-VM; Renewal deed ("*Titre nouvelle*") from Félix Gill to François Legendre, 26 March 1841, doc. 2708, S74, CN603, BAnQ-VM.

59 On the use of the deed of gift for ensuring the material security of ageing parents, see Greer, *Peasant, Lord, and Merchant*, 76–81.

60 Inter-vivos gift from Augustin Gill and Marie Plamondon to their minor children Élie, David, and Félix Gill, 13 May 1829, doc. 2950, S31, CN401, BAnQ-TR.

61 Ibid.

62 For example, see Dépatie, "La transmission du patrimoine dans les terroirs en expansion: Un exemple canadien au XVIIIe siècle," *Revue d'histoire de l'Amérique française* 44, no. 2 (Fall 1990): 187–89, 197; Bouchard, *Quelques arpents d'Amérique*, 212.

63 Conveyance and release from Augustin Gill and his wife to Augustin and Louis Gill, 1 April 1825, doc. 4707, S78, CN603, BAnQ-VM. The transferred land represented the share (*la légitime*) that she could "expect to inherit from the Estate of the aforementioned father and mother," that is to say "half of what the heirs would have received if the assets had been divided equally." Dépatie, "La transmission du patrimoine dans les terroirs en expansion," 172.

64 Félicité was the only one of Augustin Gill's children considered to be an "Indian." Pierre-Paul Osunkhirhine to William McCulloch, 26 July 1833, pp. 34408–34409, reel C-11466, vol. 87, RG10, LAC.

65 Marriage between Stanislas Vassal and Félicité Gill, 13 August 1822, reel 4120, ZA314, BAnQ-TR.

66 While serving as a lieutenant and interpreter at Saint-François (Odanak), Vassal fought in the War of 1812 alongside the Abenaki. Department staff list for 1814, 2 November 1813, pp. 182948–182950, reel C-13396, vol. 627, RG10, LAC; Petition from Stanislas Vassal to George Dalhousie, 11 July 1822, pp. 93901–93902, reel C-2567, vol. 199, RG1 L3L, LAC.

67 Prior to his marriage, he wintered for three years along the Columbia River as a clerk and hunter. Employment contract between Stanislas Vassal and Thomas Thain, 16 April 1818, S29, CN601, BAnQ-VM. This information was found in the *Voyageurs Contracts Database*, which is managed by Nicole St-Onge and Robert Englebert, and hosted by the Société historique de Saint-Boniface https://archivesshsb.mb.ca/en. After marrying Félicité Gill, Vassal worked in Haute-Mauricie region for the Hudson's Bay Company and the King's Posts Company. François Antaya, "Chasser en échange d'un salaire: Les engagés amérindiens dans la traite des fourrures du Saint-Maurice, 1798–1831," *Revue d'histoire de l'Amérique française* 63, no. 1 (Summer 2009): 18.

68 Claude Gélinas, "La Mauricie des Abénaquis au XIXe siècle," *Recherches amérindiennes au Québec* 33, no. 2 (2003): 54.

69 Pierre-Paul Osunkhirhine to William McCulloch, 26 July 1833, pp. 34408–34409, reel C-11466, vol. 87, RG10, LAC. Stanislas Vassal died on 13 January 1854, at the age of seventy-two. He was buried in the mission cemetery. Burial of Stanislas Vassal, 14 January 1854, reel 4142, ZA314, BAnQ-TR.

70 Antaya, "La traite des fourrures dans le bassin du Saint-Maurice: Les conditions de travail des engagés au début du XIXe siècle (1798–1831)" (master's thesis, Université du Québec à Trois-Rivières, 2007), 155.

71 Obligation from Stanislas Vassal to Augustin Gill, 11 July 1829, doc. 2968, S31, CN401, BAnQ-TR.

72 Statement by Augustin Gill, 11 July 1829, doc. 2969, S31, CN401, BAnQ-TR. His business activities do not appear to have been successful, since his widow renounced the community of property, deeming it "more of a burden than a benefit." Renunciation by Félicité Gill of the community of property between herself and her late husband, Henry Vassal, 10 April 1854, doc. 2330, S14, CN603, BAnQ-VM.

73 Augustin Gill appears to have married an Abenaki woman in 1790, with whom he apparently had a daughter named Suzanne (1791–1864). His marriage contract with Marie Plamondon does not provide the given name of his first wife. Maurault, *Histoire des Abénakis,* 353.

74 Gift from Augustin Gill and Marie Plamondon to their minor children Élie, David, and Félix Gill, 13 May 1829, doc. 2950, S31, CN401, BAnQ-TR.

75 On the relation between marital status and inheritance practices up to the end of the nineteenth century, see Diane Gervais, "Succession et cycle familial dans le comté de Verchères, 1870–1950," *Revue d'histoire de l'Amérique française* 50, no. 1 (Summer 1996): 88–89.

76 Gift from Augustin Gill and his wife to Jacques Joseph Gill, 15 July 1811, doc. 1261, S31, CN401, BAnQ-TR.

77 Marie was the daughter of Michel Gill, son of François Gill *dit* Langoumois, and Marie-Anne Lemaître *dit* Lottinville. Marriage contract between Jacques Joseph Gill and Marie Gill, 17 July 1811, doc. 1262, S31, CN401, BAnQ-TR; Marriage between Marie Gill and Jacques Joseph, 29 July 1811, reel 4120, ZA314, BAnQ-TR.

78 Baptism of an unnamed child, 21 July 1812, reel 4120, ZA314, BAnQ-TR.

79 In his marriage contract, Jacques Joseph is described as the natural son of François Joseph Gill and Agnès. However, neither parent is identified in his marriage record. Apart from his marriage to Marie Gill, he has no clear connection to the Gill family tree. This deed of gift could be seen as a willingness to consider the "alternative family structures and relations of care outside of the immediate family," as Chandra Murdoch puts it in her contribution to this collection (Chapter 2, 53).

80 The couple would eventually build a home on the property and establish a farm that featured multiple buildings (milkhouse, barn, cowshed, and stable). Inventory of Jacques Joseph Gill, 1 June 1830, doc. 1203, S74, CN603, BAnQ-VM.

81 Grant from Joseph Gamelin to Thomas and Louis Gill, 19 February 1803, doc. 1389, S27, CN603, BAnQ-VM.

82 Gift from Augustin Gill and his wife to Jacques Joseph Gill, 15 July 1811, doc. 1261, S31, CN401, BAnQ-TR; Notice of Protest from Jacques Joseph Gill, husband of the late Marie Gill, against Augustin Gill, 16 July 1830, doc. 1226, S74, CN603.

83 He was likely taught to read and write by Jesuit missionaries. Béreau, "Joseph-Louis Gill," 102–106. On the unique culture of schooling that developed within the Indigenous communities of the St. Lawrence Valley, see Thomas Peace, "Borderlands, Primary Sources, and the Longue Durée: Contextualizing Colonial Schooling at Odanak, Lorette and Kahnawake, 1600–1850," *Historical Studies in Education* 29, no. 1 (Spring 2017): 8–31.

84 However, Augustin was not among them. Mathieu Chaurette, "Les premières écoles autochtones au Québec: Progression, opposition et luttes de pouvoir, 1792–1853" (master's thesis, Université du Québec à Montréal, 2011), 65–66.

85 Benjamin Sulte, *Histoire de Saint-François-du-Lac* (Montréal: L'Étendard, 1886), 109. Augustin Gill served as an interpreter in the preparation of many notarial deeds, because he "understood the Abenaki language very well." Will of Ursule Gill, 20 June 1835, doc. 1794, S74, CM603, BAnQ-VM.

86 Félicité is the only one of the couple's children who did not have a marriage contract. However, she signed her name to several other notarial deeds. Marriage contract between Augustin Gill Jr. and Angèle Caya, 23 April 1825, doc. 4721, S78, CN603, BAnQ-VM; Marriage contract between L. Gill and A. Manseau, 23 November 1832; Marriage contract between Élie Gill and Adélaïde Crevier Descheneaux, 23 July 1836, doc. 6814, S78, CN603, BAnQ-VM; Marriage contract between David Gill and Caroline Plamondon, 20 November 1845, doc. 3160, S74, CN603, BAnQ-VM; Marriage contract between Félix Gill and Marie Théodosie Rousse *dit* Comptois, 25 February 1848, doc. 906, S14, CN603, BAnQ-VM.

87 This schoolteacher had attended Dartmouth College in New Hampshire. On his school in Odanak, see Chaurette, "Les premières écoles autochtones," 27–31, 45–46. Born between 1802 and 1814, the couple's children were unlikely to have attended the school established at Saint-François-du-Lac between 1803 and 1809. Claude Bellavance, Yvan Rousseau and Jean Roy, eds., *Histoire du Centre-du-Québec* (Quebec City: Presses de l'Université Laval, 2013), 370.

88 Since 1819, treasurers appointed by the chiefs had been responsible for holding the seigneurial dues collected by their legal representative. Quittance from the Abenaki to Augustin Gill, 2 December 1824, doc. 229, S74, CN603, BAnQ-VM.

89 For example, Quittance from Ignace Portneuf et al. to Louis Gill, 20 January 1837, doc. 1997, S74, CN603, BAnQ-VM; Account of Louis Gill for the Seigneurie of Saint-François, 16 October 1843, pp. 46025–46038, reel C-13379, vol. 597, RG 10, LAC.

90 Conveyance and release from Augustin Gill and his wife to Augustin and Louis Gill, 1 April 1825, doc. 4707, S78, CN603, BAnQ-VM.

91 Voyageur Contract between Louis Gill and Stanislas Vassal, 25 January 1828, doc. 825, S74, CN603, BAnQ-VM.

92 With respect to the transfer of know-how, the couple's other sons were by no means left to their own devices. David and Félix collaborated on carpentry projects, including work done on the mission presbytery in 1845. For example, see Specifications for work to be completed by David and Félix Gill for Simon Obomsawin et al., 11 December 1844, doc. 3060, S74, CN603, BAnQ-VM.

93 As prescribed in the deed of gift, this exchange was approved by their father a few days later (20 December). Exchange between Louis Gill and Augustin Gill Jr., 11 November 1841, doc. 2790, S74, CN603, BAnQ-VM.

94 Procuration from the Indians of the Village of Saint-François to Louis Gill, 9 July 1832, doc. 6158, S78, CN603, BAnQ-VM.

95 In notarial deeds, individual members of the Odanak community would identify themselves as an "Abenaki Indian" (*sauvage abénakis*) where notaries normally recorded a man's profession. Some also declared an occupation, normally that of hunter. Other documents also note the position a person held within the community, such as chief.

96 On the relationship between race and property, see Cheryl I. Harris, "Whiteness as Property," *Harvard Law Review* 106, no. 8 (1993): 1709–1791; Brenna

Bhandar, *Colonial Lives of Property: Law, Land, and Racial Regimes of Ownership* (Durham, NC: Duke University Press, 2018).

97 Louis Gill served as a school trustee, a justice of the peace and a summary court commissioner. Sale from Maxime Grondin to the Corporation d'éducation de St. François, 26 June 1847, doc. 756, S14, CN603, BAnQ-VM; Lease for a pew in the church of Saint-François-du-Lac from Pierre Gauthier to Louis Gill, 16 September 1849, doc. 1292, S14, CN603, BAnQ-VM; Will of Louis Gill, 9 July 1858, doc. 3263, S14, CN603, BAnQ-VM

98 Charles Gill, *Notes historiques sur l'origine de la famille Gill de Saint-François du Lac et Saint-Thomas de Pierreville et histoire de ma propre famille* (Montreal: E. Senécal, 1887), 53.

99 This gift was made before she married Charles Barbeau in Saint-Thomas-de-Pierreville on 17 July 1859. Her eldest son (William) left the province in the 1840s. Act of notoriety regarding the absence of William Vassal, 3 April 1854, doc. 2324, S14, CN603, BAnQ-VM; Gift from Félicité Gill, widow of Stanislas Vassal, to Henry Vassal, 14 July 1859, doc. 3505, S14, CN603, BAnQ-VM; IMPQ, civil register couple #9301588.

100 Marie-Line Audet, "Protéger, transformer: L''agent des sauvages' et la réserve des Abénaquis de la rivière Saint-François (Québec), 1873–1889" (master's thesis, Université du Québec à Trois-Rivières, 2011), 19–21.

101 Petition from the Gill family to Matthew W. Aylmer, 16 March 1833, pp. 34110–34112, reel C-11031, vol. 86, RG10, LAC.

102 On the legal definition of Indian status from 1850, see for example, Ted Binnema, "Protecting Indian Lands by Defining *Indian*: 1850–76," *Journal of Canadian Studies* 48, no. 2 (2014): 5–39.

103 The intergenerational transfer of individual land allotments of the Abenaki families was affected by the colonial system of inheritance laws. For more on its implementation through the Indian Act, see Chandra Murdoch's contribution to this collection (Chapter 2).

## CHAPTER TWO

1 I would like to thank the Osgoode Society for Canadian Legal History for supporting this research through the R. Roy McMurtry Fellowship in Legal History, as well as the editors, Dr. Heidi Bohaker, Dr. Brian Gettler, Dr. Daniel Newman, and the members of the Humanities Dissertation Writing Group for their helpful comments on earlier drafts of this work. Due to the number of communities involved in this research, and restrictions on time due to the ongoing COVID crisis, I have not consulted with the communities involved and take full responsibility for any errors in interpretation this might entail. This is not the standard practice, nor acceptable to many, in the field of Indigenous history or Indigenous studies. Thus, I see this work not as an end point in a research study, but as the very beginning of an effort to understand these issues and I welcome comment and critique. Because communities and families were not consulted, I have removed names from my descriptions of the cases in my text. I understand that this is an imperfect solution, in that it renders invisible

the people involved. However, I strongly felt that this outweighed any potential harm of using names without consultation or permission, despite these being a part of the public record through Library and Archives Canada.

2 Today reserves make up just 0.2 percent of the land mass claimed by Canada. Arthur Manuel and Grand Chief Ronald Derrickson, *The Reconciliation Manifesto: Recovering the Land, Rebuilding the Economy* (Toronto: James Lorimer and Company Ltd., 2017).

3 An Act to amend and consolidate the laws respecting Indians (The Indian Act), S.C. 1876, c. 18 (39 Vict.).

4 See Isabelle Bouchard, "Land Ownership and Inheritance among the Abenaki of Odanak: The Process of Family Reproduction in the Gill Household," Chapter 1 in this volume.

5 I use "Indian Agent" as the Indian Act does to denote commissioners, superintendents, and agents of other offices acting under the instructions of the Superintendent General. The Indian Act, S.C. 1876, c. 18, s. 11 (39 Vict.).

6 An Act respecting Indians (The Indian Act), R.S.C. 1985, c. 1-5, s. 42-50.1.

7 The Council went by various names over the years, although with much political continuity. To simplify, I use "The Grand General Indian Council of Ontario" or "The Grand General Council" in this chapter. Indigenous communities from Quebec also participated in early meetings. The Ontario communities that participated in the councils I examine are Aamjiwnaang First Nation (formerly Chippewas of Sarnia), Akwesasne (formerly St. Regis), Alderville First Nation (formerly Alnwick), Beausoleil First Nation (formerly Christian Island), Bkejwanong (formerly Walpole Island), Chippewas of Georgina Island (formerly Snake Island), Chippewas of Kettle and Stoney Point, Chippewas of Nawash Unceded First Nation (formerly Cape Croker), Chippewas of Rama First Nation, Chippewas of the Thames (formerly Caradoc), Delaware Nation at Moraviantown (formerly Moravians of the Thames), Garden River First Nation, Hiawatha First Nation (formerly Rice Lake), Unspecified Manitoulin Island, Lake Superior, and Lake Huron First Nations, Mississaugas of the New Credit (formerly New Credit), Mississaugas of Scugog Island First Nation, Mohawks of the Bay of Quinte, Munsee-Delaware First Nation (formerly Muncey of the Thames), Oneida Nation of the Thames, Saugeen First Nation, Shawanaga First Nation, Six Nations of the Grand River, Wasauksing First Nation (formerly Parry Island), Wiikwemkoong First Nation (formerly Wikwemikong). In my text I have used the names of reserves from the nineteenth century as they appear in the records.

8 See for instance Lynn Gehl, "The Queen and I: Discrimination Against Women in the 'Indian Act' Continues," *Canadian Woman Studies* 20, no. 2 (Summer 2000): 64–69; Kathleen Jamieson, *Indian Women and the Law in Canada: Citizens Minus* (Ottawa: Advisory Council on the Status of Women, 1978); Bonita Lawrence, "Gender, Race, and the Regulation of Native Identity in Canada and the United States: An Overview," *Hypatia* 18, no. 2 (2003): 3–31, and *"Real" Indians and Others: Mixed-Blood Native Peoples and Indigenous Nationhood* (Vancouver: UBC Press, 2004); and Genevieve Painter,

"Partial Histories: Constituting a Conflict between Women's Equality Rights and Indigenous Sovereignty in Canada" (PhD diss., University of California Berkeley, 2015), https://escholarship.org/uc/item/59c8k7c0. On the effects of the imposition of monogamous marriage see Sarah Carter, *The Importance of Being Monogamous: Marriage and Nation Building in Western Canada to 1915* (Edmonton: University of Alberta Press, 2008). For residential school history see *Canada's Residential Schools, The History, Part 1: Origins to 1939, The Final Report of the Truth and Reconciliation Commission of Canada, Volume 1* (Montreal and Kingston: McGill-Queen's University Press, 2015).

9 *Reclaiming Power and Place: The Final Report of the National Inquiry into Missing and Murdered Indigenous Women and Girls, vol. 1a* (National Inquiry into Missing and Murdered Indigenous Women and Girls, 2019), 251.

10 On inheritance, see Mary-Ellen Kelm and Keith D. Smith, *Talking Back to the Indian Act: Critical Readings in Settler Colonial Histories* (Toronto: University of Toronto Press, 2018), 5; John Leslie and Ron Maguire, *The Historical Development of the Indian Act* (Ottawa: Indian and Northern Affairs, 1978), 62 and 82; and Susan M. Hill, *The Clay We Are Made Of: Haudenosaunee Land Tenure on the Grand River* (Winnipeg: University of Manitoba Press, 2017), 193–97. On the DIA and surveillance see Jarvis Brownlie, "Intimate Surveillance: Indian Affairs, Colonization, and the Regulation of Aboriginal Women's Sexuality," in *Contact Zones: Aboriginal and Settler Women in Canada's Colonial Past*, ed. Katie Pickles and Myra Rutherdale (Vancouver: UBC Press, 2005), 160–78; and Keith D. Smith, *Liberalism, Surveillance, and Resistance: Indigenous Communities in Western Canada, 1877–1927* (Edmonton: Athabasca University Press, 2009).

11 An Act to encourage the gradual Civilization of the Indian Tribes in this Province, and to amend the Laws respecting Indians (The Gradual Civilization Act), S.C. 1857, c. 26, s. 10. Changes to this law are outlined below.

12 Dower provisions stipulated that widows would receive a life interest in one third of the property. See Philip Girard, Jim Phillips, and R. Blake Brown, *A History of Law in Canada, Volume 1: Beginnings to 1866* (Toronto: Osgoode Society for Canadian Legal History and University of Toronto Press, 2018), 355 and 357. Married women were excluded from owning property until 1884. See Lori Chambers, *Married Women and Property Law in Victorian Ontario* (Toronto: Osgoode Society for Canadian Legal History and University of Toronto Press, 1997); and Constance Backhouse "Married Women's Property Law in Nineteenth-Century Canada," *Law and History Review* 6, no. 2 (Fall 1988): 211–57.

13 Canadian provinces share a unified system of criminal law, first codified in 1892. Private law in most provinces, including Ontario, follows the British common-law tradition; the exception is Quebec (formerly Lower Canada), where a legal order based on French civil law prevails. See the contributions to the volume by Isabelle Bouchard (Chapter 1) and Jean-Philippe Garneau (Chapter 5). See also Girard et al., *A History of Law in Canada*, chapters 2 and 3, 42–80.

14 For an overview of the work of the Grand General Council, see Norman D. Shields, "Anishinaabek Political Alliance in the Post-Confederation Period: The Grand General Indian Council of Ontario, 1870–1936" (master's thesis, Queen's University, 2001); and "The Grand General Indian Council of Ontario and Status Legislation," in *Lines Drawn Upon the Water: First Nations and the Great Lakes Borders and Borderlands*, ed. Karl S. Hele (Waterloo: Wilfred Laurier University Press, 2008): 205–18.

15 Shields traces their political organizing to 1936. Shields, "Anishinaabek Political Alliance."

16 For an overview of Six Nations political history see Hill, *The Clay We Are Made Of.*

17 The most northern delegates were from the North Shore of Lake Huron and Manitoulin Island.

18 The Munsee-Delaware First Nation and the Delaware Nation at Moraviantown communities were also represented. Anishinaabeg is the plural form of Anishinaabe, the Ojibwe spelling for the name of the people who include Ojibwe, as well as "Chippewa, Odawa, Potawatomi, Algonquin, Saultaux, Nipissing and Mississauga First Nations, as well as some Oji-Cree and Métis." Karl Hele, "Anishinaabe," in *The Canadian Encyclopedia*, Historica Canada, article published 16 July 2020; last edited 16 July 2020, https://www.thecanadianencyclopedia.ca/en/article/anishinaabe.

19 The Gradual Civilization Act, S.C. 1857, c. 26, s. 10.

20 An Act for the gradual enfranchisement of the Indians, the better management of Indian Affairs, and to extend the provisions of the Act 31st Vict., Chapter 42 (The Gradual Enfranchisement Act), S.C. 1869, c. 6 (32–33 Vict.).

21 Ibid., s. 13.

22 Ibid., s. 13–14.

23 Ibid., s. 9.

24 *The General Council of the Six Nations and Delegates from different Bands in Western and Eastern Canada, June 10, 1870* (Hamilton: The Spectator Office, 1870), 25.

25 Subject to approval of council and the Superintendent General. The Indian Act, S.C. 1876, c. 18, s. 8 (39 Vict.).

26 Ibid., s. 9.

27 Ibid.

28 *Minutes of the 7th Grand General Indian Council held upon the New Credit Indian Reserve, Near Hagersville Ontario, from September 13th to September 18th, 1882* (Hagersville: Hagersville Book and Job Room, 1883), 15–16.

29 Ibid., 16

30 Ibid.

31 Ibid., 17.

32 An Act to further amend "The Indian Act, 1880," S.C. 1884, c. 27, s. 5 (47 Vict.).

33 *Minutes of the Eighth Grand General Indian Council held upon the Cape Crocker Indian Reserve, County of Bruce, From September 10th to Sept 15th, 1884* (Hagersville: The Indian Publishing Company, 1884), 16.

34 Lawrence Vankoughnet to Robert Sedgewick, 11 February 1892, 764-1, vol. 3947, file 123, Record Group 10 (RG10), Library and Archives Canada (LAC), Ottawa.
35 Ibid.
36 Ibid.
37 An Act to further amend the Indian Act, S.C. 1894, c. 32, s. 1 (57–58 Vict.).
38 An Act to further amend "The Indian Act, 1880," S.C. 1884, c. 27, s. 5 (47 Vict.).
39 Ibid. This was similar to the Gradual Civilization and Gradual Enfranchisement Acts where it was stipulated that she "live respectfully" in order to reside on her husband's property until her children reached majority.
40 An Act to further amend the Indian Act, S.C. 1894, c. 32, s. 1 (57–58 Vict.).
41 Ibid.
42 *Minutes of the Thirteenth Grand General Indian Council of Ontario and Quebec, held upon the Moraviantown Indian Reserve from 16th to 20th of October, 1894* (Wiarton: The Wiarton Canadian Office, 1894), 17.
43 Ibid.
44 Ibid.
45 Ibid.
46 See the following examples from RG 10, LAC: C-9666, vol. 2989, file 215,320; C-9665, vol. 2974, file 209,900; C-9663, vol. 2946, file 199,050; and C-9662, vol. 2896, file 182,145.
47 Hill, *The Clay We Are Made Of*, 196. Most of the cases I found where bands dealt with inheritance after 1894 were from Six Nations (ten out of fifteen). Other cases were from Tyendinaga, C-9661, vol. 2839, file 172,121, RG10, LAC; Moravians of the Thames, C-9662, vol. 2896, file 182,145, RG10, LAC; and Sarnia, C-9666, vol. 2989, file 215,320, RG10, LAC, and C-9665, vol. 2974, file 209,900, RG10, LAC.
48 This too was subject to approval but generally accepted by the Department, as far as I can tell from the records.
49 C-12780, vol. 2221, file 43,288, RG10, LAC.
50 Ibid. The Department refused approval on the grounds that other young men on the reserve needed the property.
51 C-12783, vol. 2419, file 86,444, RG10, LAC.
52 J.T. Gilkison to Superintendent General of Indian Affairs, 23 September 1884, C-12781, vol. 2273, file 54,672, RG10, LAC.
53 Ibid.
54 Ibid.
55 J.T. Gilkison to Superintendent General of Indian Affairs, 8 December 1884. C-12781, vol. 2273, file 54,672, RG10, LAC.
56 J.T. Gilkison to Superintendent General of Indian Affairs, 15 December 1884. C-12781, vol. 2273, file 54,672, RG10, LAC.
57 J.T. Gilkison to Superintendent General of Indian Affairs, 31 December 1884. C-12781, vol. 2273, file 54,672, RG10, LAC.
58 George Burbridge to Lawrence Vankoughnet, 11 October 1885, C-12781, vol. 2273, file 54,672, RG10, LAC. The second husband in his claim demonstrated concern for the sons and a willingness that their interests be accounted for.

59 The Chiefs in Council, Oneida, 28 March 1882, C-12770, vol. 2184, file 37,004, RG10, LAC.

60 George Burbridge to Superintendent General of Indian Affairs, 13 December 1882, C-12770, vol. 2184, file 37,004, RG10, LAC. The legal loophole was closed in 1894 to cover widowers. An Act to further amend the Indian Act, S.C. 1894, c. 32, s. 20.5 (57–58 Vict.).

61 C-9665, vol. 2987, file 214,399, RG10, LAC.

62 Ibid.

63 William McFarlane to Superintendent General of Indian Affairs, 1 May 1900, C-9665, vol. 2987, file 214,399, RG10, LAC.

64 Memorandum to the Deputy Minister, 3 October 1894, C-12791, vol. 2742, file 146,087, RG10, LAC.

65 Hayter Reed to E.D. Cameron, 5 February 1894, C-12791, vol. 2742, file 146,087, RG10, LAC.

66 See, for example, C-12784, vol. 2517, file 106,465, RG10, LAC.

67 D.J. McPhee to Superintendent General of Indian Affairs, 13 January 1897, C-9662, vol. 2896, file 182,029, RG10, LAC.

68 Hayter Reed to D.J. McPhee, 21 January 1897, C-9662, vol. 2896, file 182,029, RG10, LAC.

69 C-9664, vol. 2959, file 205,222, RG10, LAC.

70 E.D. Cameron to Secretary of Indian Affairs, 29 December 1898, C-9664, vol. 2959, file 205,222, RG10, LAC.

71 See all of the following documents in C-9664, vol. 2959, file 205,222, RG10, LAC: E.D. Cameron to Secretary of Indian Affairs, 29 December 1898; E.D. Cameron to Secretary of Indian Affairs, 12 January 1899; E.D. Cameron to J.D. McLean, 19 April 1898; E.D. Cameron to Secretary of Indian Affairs, 25 April 1899; E.D. Cameron to Secretary of Indian Affairs, 14 July 1906.

72 Frank Pedley to [Gordon?] J. Smith, Indian Superintendent, 6 June 1908, C-9664, vol. 2959, file 205,222, RG10, LAC.

73 C-9663, vol. 2939, file 196,761, RG10, LAC.

74 J.D. McClean to E.D. Cameron, 4 April 1898, C-9663, vol. 2939, file 196,761, RG10, LAC.

75 On tensions and overlap between Haudenosaunee and Indian Act principles of family law see Hill, *The Clay We Are Made Of*, 194–95.

76 H.C. to Deputy Superintendent General, 11 May 1895, C-12792, vol. 2759, file 150,470, RG10, LAC.

77 See Kim Anderson, *Life Stages and Native Women: Memory, Teachings, and Story Medicine* (Winnipeg: University of Manitoba Press, 2011); Brenda Child, *Holding Our World Together: Ojibwe Women and the Survival of Community* (New York: The Penguin Group, 2012); and Hill, *The Clay We Are Made Of*, 53–76.

78 Hill, *The Clay We Are Made Of*, 53–76; Madeleine Whetung, "(En)gendering Shoreline Law: Nishnaabeg Relational Politics Along the Trent Severn Waterway," *Global Environmental Politics* 19, no. 3 (August 2019): 16–32; Deborah McGregor, "Indigenous Women, Water Justice and Zaagidowin (Love)," *Canadian Woman Studies* 30, issue 2/3 (2013): 71–78.

79 Ebenezer Watson to Superintendent General of Indian Affairs, 21 February 1883, C-12780, vol. 2206, file 41, 622, RG10, LAC. Another example from 1883 can be found in C-12780, vol. 2206, file 41,622, RG10, LAC.

80 Telegram to J.D. McLean from L.N., 30 September 1898, C-9662, vol. 2918, file 186,900, RG10, LAC; M.F. to Clifford Sifton, no date, received by Department 27 April 1897, C-9661, vol. 2882, file 179,779, RG10, LAC; A.S. McDougall to Deputy Superintendent General of Indian Affairs, 7 April 1897, C-9661, vol. 2882, file 179,779, RG10, LAC. For examples contesting band decisions, see Mrs. A.R. and Mrs. E.J. to Deputy Superintendent of Indian Affairs, 17 May 1899, C-9665, vol. 2974, file 209,900, RG10, LAC; and H.C. to Deputy Superintendent General, 11 May 1895, C-12792, vol. 2759, file 150,470, RG10, LAC.

81 Thomas Gordon to Superintendent General of Indian Affairs, 7 September 1882, C-12779, vol. 2194, file 38,957, RG10, LAC.

82 M.J.T. to the council of the Muncey Reserve, 30 November 1895, C-12793, vol. 2796, file 158,512, RG10, LAC.

83 Ibid.

84 M.T. to W.F. Romm, M.P., 29 December 1895, C-12793, vol. 2796, file 158,512, RG10, LAC.

85 M.L. to Lawrence Vankoughnet, 11 May 1888, C-12782, vol. 2401, file 83,326, RG10, LAC.

86 Frank Pedley to Inspector of Indian Agencies, 4 July 1903, C-9666, vol. 2989, file 215,320, RG10, LAC.

87 John Cameron, Barrister, Notary Public and Commissioner to Thomas Gordon, 15 August 1894, C-12793, vol. 2765, file 152,688, RG10, LAC; Report by E.D. Cameron on his investigation, 14 March 1895, C-9659, vol. 2798, file 159,852, RG10, LAC; G.E. Deroch to George Anderson, 21 January 1899, C-12793, vol. 2779, file 156,252, RG10, LAC; George L. Taylor, Barrister, Notary Public to Superintendent General of Indian Affairs, 18 February 1897, C-9662, vol. 2896, file 182,145, RG10, LAC; Leitch and Pringle to Deputy Superintendent General, 12 December 1896, C-9663, vol. 2935, file 195,838, RG10, LAC; Pardee and Shaughnessy Solicitors for the Bank of Montreal and the Huron and Lambton Loan and Savings Company to Superintendent General of Indian Affairs, 7 September 1899, C-9665, vol. 2986, file 213,666, RG10, LAC; E.D. Cameron to Secretary of Department of Indian Affairs, 29 December 1898, C-9664, vol. 2959, file 205,222, RG10, LAC. In the matter of the claim to the S.E. lot of the S ½ of lot 26 con. 1 Tuscarora, J.W. Bowley for claimant Frederick John Hill, C.G. claiming for him, C-9662, vol. 2918, file 186,830, RG10, LAC. Notaries were also hired at times for wills to be written, these are not counted here.

88 I found at least fifteen files containing these more extensive investigations. For examples, see Report by E.D. Cameron on his investigation, 14 March 1895, C-9659, vol. 2798, file 159,852, RG10, LAC; E.D. Cameron to Secretary of Department of India Affairs, 29 December 1898, C-9664, vol. 2959, file 205,222, RG10, LAC; and E.D. Cameron to Secretary, 31 January 1899, C-9664, vol. 2962, file 206,213, RG10, LAC.

89 For an overview of the legal profession during this time period see Christopher Moore, *The Law Society of Upper Canada and Ontario Lawyers, 1797–1997* (Toronto: University of Toronto Press, 1997), 135–85.

90 Hayter Reed to John Scoffield, 13 March 1897, C-9662, vol. 2899, file 184,147, RG10, LAC.

91 See, for example, Lawrence Vankoughnet to Matthew Hill, 10 February 1888, C-12782, vol. 2401, file 83,326, RG10, LAC; Hayter Reed to John Beattie, 19 January 1897, vol. 2895, file 182,145, RG10, LAC; and C-9661, vol. 2881, file 179,003, RG10, LAC.

92 See, for example, C-9665, vol. 2986, file 213,666, RG10, LAC.

93 C-12780, vol. 2238, file 45,797, RG10, LAC. In this case it should be noted that the transmission of property was initially brought to the Indian Agent at the request of the family through the Chief.

94 A. Power to Deputy Superintendent General of Indian Affairs, 28 September 1883, C-12780, vol. 2238, file 45,797, RG10, LAC.

95 E. Newcombe to Deputy Superintendent General of Indian Affairs, C-9659, vol. 2803, file 161,186, RG10, LAC.

96 Michelle McKinley's use of the term "architecture of paternalism" was instructive to my thinking throughout this essay. Michelle McKinley, *Fractional Freedoms: Slavery, Intimacy, and Legal Mobilization in Colonial Lima, 1600–1700* (New York: Cambridge University Press, 2016), 5.

97 Manuel and Derrickson, *The Reconciliation Manifesto*, 185.

## CHAPTER THREE

1 My thanks to Peter Gossage and Eric Reiter for inviting me to the Family and Justice in the Archives Symposium, and to Rachel Berger for recommending my invitation. Three anonymous reviewers have offered generous comments that have assisted me in revising this chapter. Peter Gossage and Lisa Moore have been delightful to work with as editors for this volume. I dedicate this chapter to David Lieberman, from whom I learned so much about legal history.

2 The cases I discuss in this chapter are drawn from Colonial Office (CO) records of the British government held at The National Archives (TNA) at Kew. These records are held in bound volumes, CO 167/283 and 167/304. For Virapatrim's case, see CO 167/283, file no. 2400. The trial transcript is identified as the Trial of Any [sic] Apin, alias Virapatrim, an Indian Labourer, for the murder of an Indian woman named Thelamey [?], held before the Court of Assize at Port Louis, Mauritius, Port Louis, dated 8 April 1847 (hereafter, Trial of Andy Apin). The transcript is enclosed in Despatch no. 129 Judicial, dated 1 June 1847, from William Gomm to Secretary of State.

3 I.M. Cumpston, *Indians Overseas in British Territories, 1834–1854* (London: Dawsons of Pall Mall, 1969), 178; Prahbu P. Mohapatra, "Longing and Belonging: The Dilemma of Return among Indian Immigrants in the West Indies 1850–1950" (New Delhi: Center for Contemporary Studies, Nehru Memorial Museum and Library, Research-in-Progress Papers, "History and Society," Third Series, Number XXX, 1998), 32.

4 Georg Simmel, "The Stranger," in *On Individuality and Social Forms: Selected Writings*, ed. Donald N. Levine (Chicago and London: University of Chicago Press, 1971), 144.

5 Marina Carter and Khal Torabully, *Coolitude: An Anthology of the Indian Labour Diaspora* (London: Anthem Press, 2002), 161.

6 Clare Anderson, *Convicts in the Indian Ocean: Transportation from South Asia to Mauritius, 1815–53* (New York: St. Martin's Press, Inc., 2000), 6.

7 Ibid., 8.

8 Richard B. Allen, *Slaves, Freedmen, and Indentured Laborers in Colonial Mauritius* (Cambridge: Cambridge University Press, 1999), 12.

9 Satyendra Peerthum's research has uncovered 110 individual labour contracts engaged between 1826 and 1834, prior to the abolition of slavery. Satyendra Peerthum, "'A Cheap Reservoir of Mankind for Labour': The Genesis of the Indentured Labour System in Mauritius, 1826–1843," in *Angajé: The Early Years: Explorations into the History, Society and Culture of Indentured Immigrants and Their Descendants in Mauritius*, Volume 1, ed. Vijayalakshmi Teelock et al. (Port Louis, Mauritius: Aapravasi Ghat Trust Fund, 2012), 160.

10 *British Parliamentary Papers* (hereinafter "*BPP*"), 1875, C. 1115, Report of the Royal Commissioners Appointed to Enquire into the Treatment of Immigrants in Mauritius, 27. Cited by Anderson, *Convicts*, 7.

11 Monique Dinan, *Mauritius in the Making Across the Censuses 1846–2000* (Port Louis, Mauritius: Nelson Mandela Centre for African Culture, 2002), 6.

12 Carter and Torabully, *Coolitude*, 53.

13 Ibid., 54.

14 Allen, *Slaves, Freedman, and Indentured Laborers*, 58–59.

15 See Despatch from Governor Sir William Nicolay to Lord Glenelg, dated 23 January 1836, in *BPP*, 1837–38, nos. 180, 232, "Orders in Council for the Better Regulation and Enforcement of the Relative Duties of Masters and Employers, and Articled Servants, Tradesmen, and Labourers in the Colonies of British Guiana and Mauritius," 47. This episode is discussed by Radhika Mongia in *Indian Migration and Empire: A Colonial Genealogy of the Modern State* (Durham and London: Duke University Press, 2018), 26–32.

16 Hollier Griffiths to G.F. Dick, Colonial Secretary, dated 20 November 1835, in *BPP*, nos. 180, 232, 49.

17 See Riyad Sadiq Koya, "Slavery, Abolitionism, Indentured Labour: The Problem of Exit and the Border Between Land and Sea in Colonial India," in *South Asian Migrations in Global History: Labour, Law, and Wayward Lives*, ed. Neilesh Bose (London and New York: Bloomsbury Academic, 2021), 118; Mongia, *Indian Migration and Empire*, 29–30.

18 Memorandum by P. D'Epinay, dated 5 January 1836, in *BPP*, 1837–38, nos. 180, 232, 59.

19 Dinan, *Mauritius in the Making*, 6–7.

20 Despatch no. 151 from W.M. Gomm to Secretary Gladstone, dated 17 August 1846, in *BPP*, 1847, no. 325, "Immigration of Labourers into the West India Colonies and the Mauritius," 204.

21 Marina Carter, *Servants, Sirdars and Settlers* (Oxford, UK: Oxford University Press, 1995), 23.

22 Ibid., 194.

23 This moment of extended surveillance in post-abolition Mauritius might be compared to the project of surveillance, classification, and identification embarked upon by the South African state after 1910, as discussed by Lorena Rizzo in Chapter 4 of this volume.

24 Allen, *Slaves, Freedman, and Indentured Laborers*, 65.

25 The Chamber of Agriculture of Mauritius suggested in 1872 that the return passage was necessary at the earlier stages of indenture in that the Indian labourer was a "stranger" to the population of Mauritius "… in the midst of which he necessarily found himself as it were exiled." "Report of the President of the Chamber of Agriculture as Chairman of the Committee Appointed on the Occasion of the Royal Commission of Enquiry, in *BPP* 1875, C. 1115, Report of the Royal Commissioner, Appendix D at 254.

26 On the role of labour intermediaries connecting workers to labour markets, see Tirkanthar Roy, "Sardars, Jobbers, Kanganies: The Labour Contractor and Indian Economic History," *Modern Asian Studies* 42, no. 5 (2008): 971–98; Crispin Bates and Marina Carter, "Sirdars as Intermediaries in Nineteenth-Century Indian Ocean Indentured Labour Migration," *Modern Asian Studies* 51, no. 2 (2017): 462–84.

27 Arjan de Haan argues that the preservation of rural ties "unsettled" migrant workers. De Haan, "Unsettled Settlers: Migrant Workers and Industrial Capitalism in Calcutta," *Modern Asian Studies* 31, no. 4 (1997): 919.

28 My thanks to Peter Gossage for suggesting an important comparison to the work of Adele Perry. See Perry, *On the Edge of Empire: Gender, Race, and the Making of British Columbia, 1849–1871* (Toronto, Buffalo, and London: University of Toronto Press, 2001). See also Ann Laura Stoler, *Capitalism and Confrontation in Sumatra's Plantation Belt, 1870–1979*, Second Edition (Ann Arbor: University of Michigan Press, 1995) and *Carnal Knowledge and Imperial Power: Race and the Intimate in Colonial Rule* (Berkeley, Los Angeles, and London: University of California Press, 2010).

29 Nayan Shah, *Stranger Intimacy: Contesting Race, Sexuality, and the Law in the North American West* (Berkeley, Los Angeles, and London: University of California Press, 2011).

30 J.P. Woodcock, "Paper laid before the Right Honorable the Governor General of India in Council by Mr. J.P. Woodcock of the Bengal Civil Service," in *BPP*, 1837–38, nos. 180, 232, 121.

31 Report of T. Hugon upon Subject of Indian Emigration to Mauritius, in *BPP*, 1840, no. 331, Copies of Correspondence addressed to the Secretary of State in the Colonial Department relative to the Introduction of Indian Labourers into the Mauritius, 191. Hugon's remarks foreshadowed extensive debates on the kidnapping of women that would plague the indentured labour system. For an example, see Koya, "Slavery, Abolitionism," 113–14; Samita Sen, "'Without His Consent?': Marriage and Women's Migration in Colonial India," *International Labor and Working-Class History* no. 65 (2004): 77–104.

32 Report of T. Hugon upon Subject of Indian Emigration to Mauritius, in *BPP*, 1840, no. 331, 191.

33 Carter, *Servants, Sirdars and Settlers*, 91.
34 Despatch from J.M. Higginson to H. Labouchere, dated 22 April 1856, Text of Ordinance enclosed in file no. 6536, no. 79 Legislative, CO 167/375, TNA.
35 Governor Nicolay adopted this position at an early stage. Letter from Colonial Secretary G.F. Dick to Mauritius Committee, dated 3 January 1840, in *BPP*, 1840, no. 331, 7. See also Charles Anderson, *Outlines of a Plan Submitted to Her Majesty's Government for the Purpose of Establishing an Authorized Committee to Regulate and Carry on the Introduction of Indian Laborers at Mauritius* (London: Nichols, Printer, 1840), 2.
36 Carter, *Lakshmi's Legacy*, 47–50.
37 Carter, *Servants, Sirdars and Settlers*, 88.
38 Carter, *Lakshmi's Legacy*, 32.
39 Ibid., 33; see also Hugh Tinker, *A New System of Slavery: The Export of Indian Labour Overseas 1830–1920*, Second Edition (London: Hansib Publishing Limited, 1993), 203.
40 Carter, *Servants, Sirdars and Settlers*, 242.
41 Ibid., 243.
42 Crispin Bates and Marina Carter, "Tribal Migration," in *Dalit Movements and the Meanings of Labour in India*, ed. Peter Robb (Delhi: Oxford University Press, 1993), 176.
43 Carter, *Servants, Sirdars and Settlers*, 239.
44 Ashrufa Faruqee, "Conceiving the Coolie Woman: Indentured Labour, Indian Women and Colonial Discourse," *South Asia Research* 16, no. 1 (1996): 62.
45 On the role of the Protector in the allocation of women, see Carter, *Servants, Sirdars and Settlers*, 241.
46 Ibid., 246.
47 John Scoble, *Hill Coolies: A Brief Exposure of the Deplorable Condition of the Hill Coolies in British Guiana and Mauritius, and of the Nefarious Means by which they were Induced to Resort to these Colonies* (London: Harvey and Darton, 1840), 27.
48 Ibid., 30.
49 Carter, *Servants, Sirdars and Settlers*, 91.
50 Letter from John Scoble to Baron Stanley, Secretary of State for the Colonies, received 11 November 1845, enclosure 2 in Despatch from Secretary Gladstone to Governor W.M. Gomm, dated 24 February 1846, in *BPP*, 1847, no. 325, "Immigration of Labourers," 163; Anil Persaud, "The Civility of Things: 'Unnatural Practices' and the Making of Value(s) in the British Sugar Colonies," *Wadabagei* 10, no. 3 (2007): 32.
51 Letter from John Scoble to William Ewart Gladstone, Secretary of State for the Colonies, dated 12 January 1846, enclosure 4 in Despatch from Secretary Gladstone to Governor W.M. Gomm, dated 24 February 1846, in *BPP*, 1847, no. 325, "Immigration of Labourers," 164.
52 Circular from G.F. Dick, Colonial Secretary, to Stipendiary Magistrates, enclosure 1 in Despatch no. 121 from Governor W.M. Gomm to Secretary Gladstone, dated 30 June 1846, in ibid.

53 The Colonial Regulations, according to Henry Jenkyns, consisted of circulars issued by the Secretary of State of the Colonies to colonial governors. The regulations were intended, he notes, for "the information and guidance of governors." From at least 1862, the Colonial Regulations were published as a discrete section of The Colonial Office List. Chapter XV, section 1 pertains to criminal trials. The pertinent regulation reads: "Whenever a capital sentence shall have been executed a report of it must be transmitted to the Secretary of State." Arguably, this report served to bind the subject to the sovereign, the capital sentence being a matter of the Crown's justice. Henry Jenkyns, *British Rule and Jurisdiction Beyond the Seas* (Oxford: at the Clarendon Press, 1902), 100.

54 For Mauritius, the correspondence is preserved within the series "CO 167," containing "original correspondence relating to Mauritius" from 1778 to 1951." Description taken from the website of the National Archives at Kew, https://discovery.nationalarchives.gov.uk/details/r/C4358, accessed 23 February 2021.

55 Carolyn Steedman, *Dust: The Archive and Cultural History* (New Brunswick, NJ: Rutgers University Press, 2000).

56 Farge evokes the historian's process of culling, copying, and now digitizing documents from a longer series, by which a new "series" is created. "This series," she continues, "becomes the object of research." Having assembled a new series of documents, the texts are to be "scrutinized," to "discover discrepancies, perhaps even the unique." Arlette Farge, *The Allure of the Archives* (New Haven and London: Yale University Press, 2013), 63–65.

57 On the significance of these wider narratives, see also Carter and Torabully, *Coolitude*, 51 and 100; Gaiutra Bahadur also notes the frequency of the sexual violence against women "throughout the sugar colonies." Gaiutra Bahadur, *Coolie Woman: The Odyssey of Indenture* (Chicago and London: University of Chicago Press, 2014), 108–10. See also Basdeo Mangru, "The Problem of Indian Wife Murders," in *The Elusive El Dorado: Essays on the Indian Experience in Guyana* (Lanham, MD: University Press of America, 2005), 33–50; Prabhu P. Mohapatra, "'Restoring the Family': Wife Murders and the Making of a Sexual Contract for Indian Immigrant Labour in the British Caribbean Colonies, 1860–1920," *Studies in History* 11, no. 2 (1995): 227–60; Arunima Datta, *Fleeting Agencies: A Social History of Indian Coolie Women in British Malaya* (Cambridge: Cambridge University Press, 2021). On the trope of "sexual jealousy," the classic essay is by Brij V. Lal, "Veil of Dishonour: Sexual Jealousy and Suicide on Fiji Plantations," *Journal of Pacific History* 20, no. 4 (1985): 135–53.

58 William Gomm to Secretary of State, dated 11 June 1847, file no. 2405 Mauritius, Despatch no. 129 Judicial, CO 167/283, TNA.

59 James Wilson to Governor, dated 11 April 1847, in Ibid.

60 William Gomm to Secretary of State, dated 30 December 1848, file no. 3195 Mauritius, Despatch no. 317 Judicial, CO 167/304, TNA.

61 Recalling Robert Cover, who insisted that "Legal interpretation takes place in a field of pain and death." Cover, "Violence and the Word," in *Narrative, Violence, and the Law: The Essays of Robert Cover*, Paperback Edition, ed.

Martha Minor, Michael Ryan, and Austin Sarat (Ann Arbor: University of Michigan Press, 1995), 203.

62 See Alexander Wood Renton and George Grenville Phillmore, eds., *Burge's Commentaries on Colonial and Foreign Laws Generally and in their Conflict with each other and with the Law of England*, Volume 1, New Edition (London: Sweet & Maxwell, 1905), 201–02.

63 Ibid., 203.

64 The 1838 ordinance was not confirmed by the Crown; Ordinance 24 of 1845 confirmed and maintained the Penal Code, finally received Crown approval. Ibid., 202.

65 See Frederic William Maitland, "The Early History of Malice Aforethought," in *The Collected Papers of Frederick William Maitland*, Volume I, ed. H.A.L. Fisher (Cambridge: at the University Press, 1911), 304–28.

66 Renton and Phillmore, *Burge's Commentaries*, 200. For further discussion of the Mauritian legal system under slavery and indenture, see Nandini S. Boodia-Canoo, *Slavery, Indenture and the Law: Assembling a Nation in Colonial Mauritius* (London and New York: Routledge, 2023).

67 Hannah Weiss Miller, *Subjects and Sovereigns: Bonds of Belonging in the Eighteenth-Century British Empire* (New York: Oxford University Press, 2017), 163.

68 Cited in Julia Stephens, *Governing Islam: Law, Empire, and Secularism in South Asia* (Cambridge: Cambridge University Press, 2018), 25.

69 J. Duncan M. Derrett, "The British as Patrons of the Śāstra," in *Religion, Law and the State in India* (London: Faber and Faber, 1968), 234–35.

70 See, for example, Scott Alan Kugle's discussion of the codification of Sharīʿa in "Framed, Blamed, and Renamed: The Recasting of Islamic Jurisprudence in Colonial South Asia," *Modern Asian Studies* 35, no. 2 (2001): 257–313.

71 On the *Juge d'Instruction*, see Morris Ploscowe, "Development of Inquisitorial and Accusatorial Elements in French Procedure," *Journal of Criminal Law and Criminology* 23, no. 3 (1932): 373–75.

72 Carter and Torabully write, "The clerks and other officials who recorded the names of migrating Indians were frequently of a different ethnic background and invested them with their own curious spellings. The resulting distortions have produced a set of unique names which are common to diaspora Indians descended from the nineteenth-century indentured labourers whether they are Indo-Trinidadian, Indo-Mauritian or Indo-Guyanese. They are part of a continuing 'coolie' heritage." Carter and Torabully, *Coolitude*, 136.

73 This case is also discussed by Marina Carter in *Servants, Sirdars and Settlers*, 243.

74 Quotes in this section are taken from the "Trial of Andy Apin," cited above. The transcripts are unpaginated. Where possible, I locate quotes within the transcript.

75 Ibid., testimony of Andy Apin.

76 Ibid., testimony of Gustave Giquel.

77 Ibid., testimony of Carpaye.

78 Ibid., testimony of Gustave Giquel.

79 Ibid., testimony of Frederick Gustave Gimel.

80 Translated, "I have killed my wife." Ibid., testimony of Frederick Gustave Gimel.

81 Ibid., testimony of Gustave Giquel.

82 Ibid., argument for Prisoner by Celicourt Anselme.

83 Ibid., note by James Wilson, Chief Judge, Court of Assize.

84 For a further description of this case, see Carter, *Servants, Sirdars and Settlers*, 241.

85 The notes of the presiding judge and other documents are enclosed within William Gomm to Secretary of State, dated 18 December, 1848, file no. 2621 Mauritius, Despatch no. 310, CO 167/304, TNA. The "notes" are presented as a narrative of the trial and are not clearly demarcated with respect to individual testimony.

86 Notes of the Presiding Judge on the trial *Reg. v. Beecon*, 12 December 1848, identification of the Prisoner.

87 Ibid., testimony of Gones Gontaye.

88 Ibid., testimony of Joseph Marie Cordonau.

89 Ibid., testimony of Cordonau.

90 Extract from the Minutes of the Registry of the Court of Appeal, Mauritius, file no. 2621 Mauritius, CO 167/304, TNA.

91 Ibid.

92 Ibid.

93 Memorial of Clement Ulcoq to William Maynard Gomm, dated 13 December 1848, Port Louis, file no. 2621, CO 167/304, TNA. On malice aforethought, see Maitland, "The Early History."

94 S.B. Mookerji notes that Hindus were known as "Malabars" and Muslims as "Lascars" in eighteenth-century Mauritius. Mookerji, *The Indenture System in Mauritius* (Calcutta: K.L. Mukhopadhyay, 1962), 12.

95 Brief mention is made of this case by Carter, *Servants, Sirdars and Settlers*, 243.

96 All materials pertaining to Valoo's trial are enclosed with Gomm to Secretary of State, dated 30 December 1848, file no. 3195, Despatch no. 317 Judicial, CO 167/304, TNA. The trial transcript within the file is identified as Mauritius December Assizes, contd., Monday, 18 December 1848.

97 Ibid., testimony of Aristide Aubin.

98 Brumeau's statement is located in Extract from the Minutes of the Registry of the Court of Appeal Mauritius, file no. 3195, CO 167/304, TNA. All quotes in this paragraph are from this unpaginated Extract.

99 Ibid.

100 Ibid., Extract from Ordinance no. 6 of 1838, being the Penal Code of Mauritius.

101 Ibid., The Humble Petition of Gojunday Valoo.

102 Ibid., Judges Chambers, Court House, letter dated 20 December 1848, from S. Villiers Surtees to William Gomm.

103 Kymlicka argues that liberals offer a distinction between voluntary and non-voluntary immigration to argue that voluntary immigrants have an obligation

to integrate with the host society. See Will Kymlicka, *Multicultural Citizenship* (Oxford: Clarendon Press, 1995): 61–62.

104 W.M. Gomm to Reverend Bishop Collier, dated 28 December 1848, file no. 3195 Mauritius, CO 167/304, TNA.

105 Jacques Derrida, *Before the Law: The Complete Text of* Préjugés (Minneapolis and London: University of Minnesota Press, 2018), 30.

106 Ibid., 53.

107 On Hugon's appointment, see Carter, *Servants, Sirdars and Settlers*, 155. The Protector of Immigrants played a significant role in surveilling the family under indenture, only partially gestured to in this chapter. The Protector might be contrasted to the role of the Indian Agent in Canada, as discussed in Chandra Murdoch's contribution to this volume (Chapter 2).

108 Carter writes of the "seclusion of women from the state" in *Lakshmi's Legacy*, 137–42.

109 Gesturing here to Jacques Derrida, *Of Hospitality: Anne Dufourmantelle Invites Jacques Derrida to Respond*, trans. Rachel Bowlby (Stanford, CA: Stanford University Press, 2000).

## CHAPTER FOUR

1 The classification of individuals based on racial origin and gender is also examined in detail by Riyad Koya (Chapter 3 in this volume) within the context of colonial Mauritius. On the disenfranchisement of subjects based on marriage and nationality, see the contributions of Ginger Frost (Chapter 12) and Gail Savage (Chapter 13) in this volume.

2 Lorena Rizzo, "Gender and Visuality: Identification Photographs, Respectability and Personhood in Colonial Southern Africa in the 1920s and 1930s," *Gender & History* 26, no. 3 (2014): 688–708; Lorena Rizzo, *Photography & History in Colonial Southern Africa: Shades of Empire* (London: Routledge, 2020).

3 Lisa Lowe, "The Intimacies of Four Continents," in *Haunted by Empire: Geographies of Intimacy in North American History*, ed. Ann Laura Stoler (Durham, NC: Duke University Press, 2006), 204.

4 Western Cape Archives and Record Service (KAB), PIO 1 – 147 E, file on Marie Schiffer Lafite. Note E in the archival reference relates to the filing order and the category of European.

5 KAB IRC 1/2/4 73 C, Eva & Lai Wing. The C identifies the family as Chinese.

6 Lauren Berlant, "Intimacy: A Special Issue," *Critical Inquiry*, 24, no. 2 (1998): 281–88.

7 Melanie Micir, "Abandoned Lives: Impossible Projects and Archival Remains," in *The Passion Projects* (Princeton: Princeton University Press, 2019), 51.

8 Athena Athanasiou, "Gendered Intimacies of the Nationalist Archive," in *Agonistic Mourning: Political Dissidence and the Women in Black* (Edinburgh: Edinburgh University Press, 2017), 111; Allen Feldman, "Memory Theatres, Virtual Witnessing, and the Trauma-Aesthetic," *Biography* 21, no. 1 (2004): 163–202.

9 Jacques Derrida, "Archive Fever in South Africa," in *Refiguring the Archive*, ed. Carolyn Hamilton, Verne Harris, Michèle Pickover, Graeme Reid, Razia Saleh and Jane Taylor (Dordrecht, Boston, and London: Kluwer Academic Publishers, 2002), 38–82.

10 Athanasiou, "Gendered Intimacies," 89.

11 Nadine Attewell, "Looking in Stereo: School Photography, Interracial Intimacy, and the Pulse of the Archive," *Asian Diasporic Visual Cultures and the Americas* 4 (2018): 19–44; Æsa Sigurjónsdóttir, "Dissecting Patriarchy in the Intimacy of the Archive Through the Work of Ramesh Daha, Tatiana Lecomte, and Miranda Pennell," *Eikon* 100 (2017): 57.

12 Sean Field, *Oral History, Community, and Displacement: Imagining Memories in Post-Apartheid South Africa* (New York: Palgrave Macmillan, 2012), 160. For a critical discussion of empathy and historical method, see Austin Harrington, "Dilthey, Empathy, and Verstehen: A Contemporary Reappraisal," *European Journal of Social Theory* 4, no. 3 (2001): 311–29.

13 Meltem Ahiska, "Occidentalism and Registers of Truth: The Politics of Archives in Turkey," *New Perspectives on Turkey* 34 (2006): 9–29.

14 Bernard Magubane, *The Making of a Racist State: British Imperialism and the Union of South Africa, 1875–1910* (Trenton, Asmara: Africa World Press, 1996).

15 Saul Dubow, "South Africa and South Africans: Nationality, Belonging, Citizenship," in *The Cambridge History of South Africa*, ed. Robert Ross, Anne Kelk Mager, and Bill Nasson (Cambridge: Cambridge University Press, 2011), 17–65.

16 John Lambert, "South African British? Or Dominion South Africans? The Evolution of an Identity in the 1910s and 1920s," *South African Historical Journal* 43, no. 1 (2000): 197–222. The parallels with Canada's Indian Act, which in 1876 had significantly restricted the property rights of Indigenous people in another recently established British Dominion, will be hard to miss for readers of Chandra Murdoch's contribution to this volume (Chapter 2).

17 Radhika Viyas Mongia, "Race, Nationality, Mobility: A History of the Passport," *Public Culture* 11 (1999): 527–56.

18 Martin Chanock, *The Making of South African Legal Culture 1902–1936: Fear, Favour, and Prejudice* (Cambridge: Cambridge University Press, 2001).

19 Martin Chanock, "Writing South African Legal History: A Prospectus," *Journal of African History* 30 (1989): 278.

20 Audie Klotz, *Migration and National Identity in South Africa, 1860–2010* (Cambridge: Cambridge University Press, 2013); Jonathan E. Klaaren, "Migrating to Citizenship: Mobility, Law, and Nationality in South Africa, 1897–1937" (PhD diss., Yale University, 2004). The PhD was published as Jonathan E. Klaaren, *From Prohibited Immigrants to Citizens: The Origins of Citizenship and Nationality in South Africa* (Cape Town: University of Cape Town Press, 2017). I am using the unpublished dissertation here.

21 Nancy Rose Hunt, "The Affective, the Intellectual, and Gender History," *Journal of African History* 55 (2014): 331–45.

22 Athanasiou, "Gendered Intimacies," 114.

23 Ken Plummer, "The Square of Intimate Citizenship: Some Preliminary Proposals," *Citizenship Studies* 5, no. 3 (2001): 237–53.

24 Athanasiou, "Gendered Intimacies," 104.

25 The main racial divide in the nineteenth century Cape was "white/European" and "other than white/European." For a more detailed discussion of the use of racial categories and ethnonyms, especially the specifications of "coloured" see Vivian Bickford-Smith, *Ethnic Pride and Racial Prejudice in Victorian Cape Town: Group Identity and Social Practice, 1875–1902* (Cambridge: Cambridge University Press, 1995), 23, 30.

26 Bickford-Smith, *Ethnic Pride*, 10–17.

27 Bickford-Smith, *Ethnic Pride*, 20.

28 Martin Legassick, "The State, Racism, and the Rise of Capitalism in the 19th Century Cape," *South African Historical Journal* 28, no. 1 (1993): 329–68; Nigel Worden, "Diverging Histories: Slavery and its Aftermath in the Cape Colony and Mauritius," *South African Historical Journal* 27, no. 1 (1992): 3–25.

29 Bickford-Smith, *Ethnic Pride*, 28–30.

30 Shula Marks, "Class, Culture, and Consciousness in South Africa, 1880–1899," in *The Cambridge History of South Africa*, ed. Robert Ross, Anne Kelk Mager, Bill Nasson (Cambridge: Cambridge University Press, 2011), 102–56.

31 Bickford-Smith, *Ethnic Pride*, 92–96.

32 Hermann Giliomee, "The Non-racial Franchise and Afrikaner and Coloured Identities, 1910–1994," *African Affairs* 94, no. 375 (April 1995): 199–225.

33 Saul Dubow, *Racial Segregation and the Origins of Apartheid in South Africa, 1919–1936* (New York: Palgrave Macmillan, 1989), 20–23.

34 Milton Shain, "Diamonds, Pogroms and Undesirables—Anti-alienism and Legislation in the Cape Colony, 1890–1906," *South African Historical Journal* 12, no. 1 (1980): 13–28.

35 Maynard W. Swanson, "The Sanitation Syndrome: Bubonic Plague and Native Policy in the Cape Colony, 1900-1909," *Journal of African History* 18, no. 3 (1977): 387–410.

36 Bickford-Smith, *Ethnic Pride*, 212.

37 Vivian Bickford-Smith, Elizabeth van Heyningen, Nigel Worden, eds., *Cape Town in the 20th Century: An Illustrated Social History* (Cape Town: David Philip Publishers, 1999), 71.

38 Shula Marks and Stanley Trapido, "The Politics of Class, Race and Nationalism," in *The Politics of Class, Race and Nationalism in Twentieth Century South Africa*, ed. Shula Marks and Stanley Trapido (London, New York: Routledge, 1987), 1–70.

39 Sally Peberdy, *Selecting Immigrants: National Identity and South Africa's Immigration Policies 1910–2008* (Johannesburg: WITS University Press, 2009), 34.

40 Ann Laura Stoler, "Colonial Archives and the Arts of Governance," *Archival Science* 2 (2002): 87–109.

41 Bickford-Smith, *Ethnic Pride*, 23–25. European and white had been synonyms throughout the nineteenth century in the Cape. The terms often obscured

rather than specified differences of ancestry and geographical origin, and people of mixed descent sometimes managed to be accepted as white/European, at times thanks to marriage and familial association.

42 Viyas Mongia, "Race, Nationality, Mobility," 132.

43 Peberdy, *Selecting Immigrants*, 32. Peberdy focuses on Indian immigration, which was how the South African government coined the issue. However, immigrants from Mauritius, St. Helena, and Madeira were likewise affected by the restrictive legal regimes.

44 Uma Dhupelia-Mesthrie, "The Passenger Indian as Worker: Indian Immigrants in Cape Town in the Early Twentieth Century," *African Studies* 68, no. 1 (2009): 111–34; Andrew Macdonald, "The Identity Thieves of the Indian Ocean: Forgery, Fraud and the Origins of South African Immigration Control, 1890s–1920," *Proceedings of the British Academy* 179 (2012): 253–76; Uma Dhupelia-Mesthrie, "Split-Households: Indian Wives, Cape Town Husbands and Immigration Laws, 1900s to 1940s," *South African Historical Journal* 44, no. 4 (2014): 635–55.

45 David Lincoln, "Mauritian Settlers in South Africa: Ethnicity and the Experience of 'Creole' Émigrés, ca. 1875–1920," *Immigrants and Minorities* 13, no. 1 (1994): 1–11.

46 Patrick Eisenlohr, "Creole Publics: Language, Cultural Citizenship, and the Spread of the Nation in Mauritius," *Comparative Studies in Society and History* 49, no. 4 (2007): 968–96. From the archival file, the specificities of Marie Schiffer Lafite's self-identification within the registers of early twentieth century Mauritian social formation remain unclear. Like "coloured," "creole" would predominantly refer to people of mixed African-Euro background, but still included more complex identities that complicated the binary of Black and white, especially in contexts of former slave-societies and long histories of South Asian immigration.

47 Peberdy, *Selecting Immigrants*, 38.

48 Lincoln, "Mauritian Settlers," 7.

49 Karen Harris, "Paper Trail: Chasing the Chinese in the Cape (1904–1913)," *Kronos* 40 (November 2014): 136.

50 Peter Richardson, "The Recruitment of Chinese Indentured Labour for the South African Gold Mines, 1903–1908," *Journal of African History* 18, no. 1 (1977): 85–108.

51 Thembisa Waetjen, "Drug Dealing Doctors and Unstable Subjects: Opium, Medicine and Authority in the Cape Colony, 1907–1910," *South African Historical Journal* 68, no. 3 (2016): 342–65.

52 Harris, "Paper Trail," 134.

53 Uma Dhupelia-Mesthrie, "The Form, the Permit and the Photograph: An Archive of Mobility between South Africa and India," *Journal of Asian and African Studies* 46 (2011): 650–62; Yoon Jung Park, "Sojourners to Settlers: Early Constructions of Chinese Identity in South Africa," *African Studies* 65 (2006): 201–23.

54 I would argue here that "white respectability" was lodged precisely in the entitlement to attest to "Black respectability." See also Ann Laura Stoler,

"Making Empire Respectable: The Politics of Race and Sexual Morality in 20th-Century Colonial Cultures," in *Dangerous Liaisons: Gender, Nation and Postcolonial Perspectives*, ed. Ann McClinton, Amir Mufti, and Ella Shohat (Minneapolis: University of Minnesota Press, 1997), 334–73.

55 Park, "Sojourners to Settlers."

56 Harris, "Paper Trail," 144, 152. According to figures provided by Harris, less than ten percent of Chinese men married non-Chinese women.

57 A.J. Christopher, "To Define the Indefinable: Population Classification and the Census in South Africa," *Area* 34 (2002): 401–08.

58 Giliomee, "The Non-Racial Franchise." There was no sense of inner-Chinese ethnic and racial differentiation. See Harris, "Paper Trail," 150.

59 Pierre L. van den Berghe, "Miscegenation in South Africa," *Cahiers d'Etudes Africaines* 1 (1960): 68–84; Jeremy Martens, "Citizenship, 'Civilisation' and the Creation of South Africa's Immorality Act, 1927," *South African Historical Journal* 59, no. 1 (2007): 223–41.

60 Pei-Chia Lan, "Migrant Women's Bodies as Boundary Markers: Reproductive Crisis and Sexual Control in the Ethnic Frontiers of Taiwan," *Signs Journal of Women in Culture and Society* 33, no. 4 (2008): 833–61.

61 Harris, "Paper Trail," 134, 147.

62 Dhupelia-Mesthrie, "The Form, the Permit," 657.

63 Elizabeth Edwards, "Introduction: Observations from the Coal-Face," in *Raw Histories: Photography, Anthropology and Museums*, ed. Elizabeth Edwards (Oxford and New York: Berg, 2001), 1–21.

64 John Tagg, "A Means of Surveillance: The Photograph as Evidence in Law," in *The Burden of Representation* (Minneapolis: University of Minnesota Press, 1993), 66–102. For the well-established critique of Tagg's argument see, for example, Jens Jäger, "Photography: A Means of Surveillance? Judicial Photography 1850–1900," *Crime, History & Societies* 5, no. 1 (2001): 27–51.

65 See for example Paul Landau, "Empires of the Visual: Photography and Colonial Administration in Africa," in *Images and Empires: Visuality in Colonial and Postcolonial Africa*, ed. Paul Landau and Deborah Kaspin (Berkeley, Los Angeles, and London: University of California Press, 2002), 141–71.

66 Lorena Rizzo, "Policing the Image: the Breakwater Prison Albums, Cape Town, in the Late Nineteenth and Early Twentieth Centuries," *Social History* 41, no. 3 (2016): 285–303.

67 See Harris, "Paper Trails," 138, for the photographic registration of Chinese, and Dhupelia-Mesthrie, "The Form, the Permit" for Indian immigrants and indentured labourers.

68 Rizzo, "Visual Aperture: Bureaucratic Systems of Identification, Photography and Personhood in Colonial Southern Africa," *History of Photography* 37 (2013): 263–82.

69 John Peffer and Elizabeth L. Cameron, eds., *Portraiture and Photography in Africa* (Bloomington and Indianapolis: Indiana University Press, 2013).

70 Erin Haney, "Portraits in the World," in *Photography and Africa* (London: Reaktion Books, 2010), 57–89.

71 I use affective here not as something that is separate from politics but pertains to it and denotes the conflicting realms of affect, meaning, and being in the domain of the nation's archive. See Athanasiou, "Gendered Intimacies," 98.

72 Athanasiou, "Gendered Intimacies," 106.

73 Keith Breckenridge, *Biometric State: The Global Politics of Identification and Surveillance in South Africa, 1850 to the Present* (Cambridge: Cambridge University Press, 2014).

74 Zeynep Gürsel, "Portraits of Unbelonging: Photography, the Ottoman State and the Making of Armenian Emigrants," eikones NOMIS Public Lecture, University of Basel, 22 February 2019; Homi Bhabha, *The Location of Culture* (London, New York: Routledge, 2004), 90. Athanasiou refers to Bhabha's argument as well, without however elaborating on the analogy between the racialized nation and historical narration. Athanasiou, "Gendered Intimacies," 89.

75 John Comaroff, "Reflections on the Colonial State, in South Africa and Elsewhere: Factions, Fragments, Facts and Fictions," *Social Identities: Journal for the Study of Race, Nation and Culture* 44, no. 3 (1998): 321–61.

76 Athanasiou, "Gendered Intimacies," 98.

## PART TWO

1 Masculinity and fatherhood are themes to which we will return elsewhere in this volume, notably in Chapter 10, by Emma Chilton and James Moran, and Chapter 15, by Fabienne Giuliani.

2 For broad, transnational perspectives on juvenile justice and on the system of specialized tribunals that emerged around the turn of the twentieth century, see Jean Trépanier and Xavier Rousseaux, eds., *Youth and Justice in Western States, 1815–1950: From Punishment to Welfare* (Cham: Palgrave MacMillan, 2017); and William S. Bush and David S. Tanenhaus, eds., *Ages of Anxiety: Historical and Transnational Perspectives on Juvenile Justice* (New York: New York University Press, 2018).

## CHAPTER FIVE

1 This chapter was translated from the original French by Steven Watt. A somewhat modified French-language version was published recently as Jean-Philippe Garneau, "La tutelle des enfants mineurs au Bas-Canada: Autorité domestique, traditions juridiques et masculinités," *Revue d'histoire de l'Amérique française* 74, no. 4 (2021): 11–35.

2 On the important connection between institutions and masculinities, see Raewyn Connell, "A Thousand Miles from Kind: Men, Masculinities and Modern Institutions," *Journal of Men's Studies* 16, no. 3 (2009): 237–52. More generally, see also Peter Gossage and Robert Allen Rutherdale, eds., *Making Men, Making History: Canadian Masculinities across Time and Place* (Vancouver: UBC Press, 2018); Matthew McCormack, *The Independent Man: Citizenship and Gender Politics in Georgian England* (Manchester: Manchester University Press, 2005); John Tosh, *Manliness and Masculinities in Nineteenth-Century*

*Britain: Essays on Gender, Family and Empire* (Harlow: Pearson Longman, 2005); Alain Corbin, Jean-Jacques Courtine, and Georges Vigarello, *Histoire de la virilité. Tome 2: Le triomphe de la virilité: Le XIXe siècle* (Paris: Seuil, 2011); E. Anthony Rotundo, *American Manhood: Transformations in Masculinity from the Revolution to the Modern Era* (New York: Basic Books, 1993).

3 For a recent study linking the transatlantic world and masculinities, see Elizabeth Mancke and Colin Grittner, "From Communal to Independent Manhood in Liverpool, Nova Scotia, ca. 1760–1820," *Histoire sociale/Social History* 52, no. 106 (2019): 257–80.

4 See, for instance, the interesting case of legal and ethnic pluralism in nineteenth-century Mauritius discussed by Riyad Koya in Chapter 3 of this collection.

5 I use this term broadly to describe individuals who were themselves born in the British Isles (including Ireland) or whose parents were born there.

6 The 1825 census shows that the Irish community already accounted for more than 4,000 of Montreal's roughly 22,500 urban residents. Altogether, people with origins in the United Kingdom (thirteen percent of whom reported being born in the colony) accounted for approximately forty-two percent of the city's population. They lived alongside smaller minorities of German, Italian, Jewish, and African descent, as well as Indigenous peoples. "Dénombrement du Comté de Montréal fait en 1825 par MM. Louis Guy et Jacques Viger…," Private Fonds P694, Bibliothèque et Archives nationales du Québec, Vieux Montréal (hereafter BAnQ-VM). And although it was overwhelmingly French Canadian, the countryside was nevertheless home to significant Anglo-Celtic enclaves, such as those in the seigneuries of Beauharnois and Argenteuil, as well as in villages like William Henry (Sorel) and Terrebonne.

7 Gillian I. Leitch, "The Importance of Being English? Identity and Social Organisation in British Montreal, 1800–1850" (PhD diss., Université de Montréal, 2007).

8 The historical literature on the family in Lower Canada is rather sparse. It tends to either focus on a single cultural group or to study the elites with little regard for cultural factors. That being said, a certain number of studies do address cultural distinctions with regard to behaviour and family strategies. Significant examples include Sherry Olson and Patricia A. Thornton, *Peopling the North American City: Montreal 1840–1900* (Montreal and Kingston: McGill-Queen's University Press, 2011); Nancy Christie, "'He is the Master of His House': Families and Political Authority in Counterrevolutionary Montreal," *William and Mary Quarterly* 70, no. 4 (2013): 341–70.

9 Granted, in the Province of New York, the legal practices and customs of the already established Dutch settlers persisted long after the conquest. However, Anglicization gained ground after 1720, with the general application of the victor's brand of positive law—English common Law. David E. Narrett, *Inheritance and Family Life in Colonial New York City* (Ithaca, NY: Cornell University Press, 1992).

10 A portion of the private law currently in force in Quebec can still be traced back to France, despite the significant hybridization that occurred with codification

in 1866–1867 (just prior to Canadian Confederation). In particular, see Evelyn Kolish, *Nationalismes et conflits de droits: Le débat du droit privé au Québec (1760–1840)* (LaSalle, QC: Éditions Hurtubise HMH, 1994); Brian Young, *The Politics of Codification: The Lower Canadian Civil Code of 1866* (Montreal and Kingston: McGill-Queen's University Press, 1994).

11 Under the British regime, the age of majority fell from twenty-five to twenty-one. Hilda Neatby, *The Administration of Justice under the Quebec Act* (Minneapolis: University of Minnesota Press, 1937), 329. Certain ordinances passed under the French regime clarified the situation in certain specific cases. *Édits, ordonnances royaux, déclarations et arrêts du Conseil d'État du Roi, concernant le Canada* (Quebec City, P.E. Desbarats, 1803), vol. 1, 438–41, 557–59, 563–67.

12 These authors provide much more useful information than the Custom of Paris itself, which merely glosses over provisions governing the tutorship of minors, such as those in articles 240 and 241 (pertaining to community of property). In particular, see Jean Meslé, *Traité des minorités, tutelles et curatelles…* (Paris: Mouchet, 1735).

13 Numerous studies have explored this question. For preindustrial Quebec, they include Christian Dessureault, *Le monde rural québécois aux XVIIIe et XIXe siècles: Cultures, hiérarchies, pouvoirs* (Montreal: Fides, 2018); Gilles Paquet and Jean-Pierre Wallot, *Un Québec moderne 1760–1840: Essai d'histoire économique et sociale* (Montreal: Éditions Hurtubise HMH, 2007).

14 Tutorship was also present in regions that did not abide by the community of property regime or equality of inheritance. See among others: Guy Brunet, "Le juge et l'orphelin: Des assemblées de parents aux conseils de famille, XVIIIe–XIXe siècles," *Annales de démographie historique* 1 (2012): 225–47. On guardianship, see William Blackstone, *Commentaries on the Laws of England* (Oxford: Clarendon Press, 1765), vol. 1, chap. 17.

15 Kolish, *Nationalismes et conflits de droit.*

16 Like the Defender of the Minor in Buenos Aires at the end of the nineteenth century, discussed in Chapter 6 by Juandrea Bates, the *procureur du roi* did not intervene on his own authority in family disputes. In fact, most tutorship proceedings were non-confrontational in Lower Canada.

17 Kolish, *Nationalismes et conflits de droit*; Jean-Pierre Wallot, "Plaintes contre l'administration de la justice (1807)," *Revue d'histoire de l'Amérique française* 19, no. 4 (1966): 551–60; 20, no. 1 (1966): 28–43; 20, no. 2 (1966): 281–90; 20, no. 3 (1966): 366–79.

18 In particular, see Nancy Christie and Michael Gauvreau, "Marital Conflict, Ethnicity, and Legal Hybridity in Postconquest Quebec," *Journal of Family History* 41, no. 4 (2016): 430–50; Jean-Philippe Garneau, "Poursuivre son mari en justice: Femmes mariées et coutume de Paris devant la cour du Banc du roi de Montréal (1795–1830)," in *Canada's Legal Past: Looking Forward, Looking Back*, ed. Lyndsay Campbell, Ted McCoy, and Mélanie Méthot (Calgary: University of Calgary Press, 2020), 149–77; Marie-Aimée Cliche, "Les procès en séparation de corps dans la région de Montréal 1795–1879," *Revue d'histoire de l'Amérique française* 49, no. 1 (1995): 3–33; Evelyn Kolish, "Some Aspects

of Civil Litigation in Lower Canada, 1785–1825: Towards the Use of Court Records for Canadian Social History," *Canadian Historical Review* 70, no. 3 (1989): 337–65.

19 Bettina Bradbury, *Wife to Widow: Lives, Laws, and Politics in Nineteenth-Century Montreal* (Vancouver: UBC Press, 2011).

20 However, see Claude Champagne, "La pratique testamentaire à Montréal (1777–1825)," *Cahiers de Thémis* 1 (1972): 1–98; Thierry Nootens, *Genre, patrimoine et droit civil: Les femmes mariées de la bourgeoisie québécoise en procès, 1900–1930* (Montreal and Kingston: McGill-Queen's University Press, 2018).

21 Tutorships and Curatorships Fonds, Superior Court and former jurisdictions, 1795–1975, CC601, S1, BAnQ-VM.

22 The court's jurisdiction covered all or part of the following areas: Lanaudière and the Laurentians on the North Shore, Vaudreuil-Dorion and the islands surrounding Montreal, the entire Montérégie region, and a slice of the Eastern Townships.

23 These data are based on the index to the tutorship and curatorship case files. I would like to thank the Centre d'histoire des régulations sociales at UQÀM for giving me access to the FileMaker database created using this index.

24 In particular, I consulted the parish registers available on the website of Généalogie Québec (https://www.genealogiequebec.com). Unfortunately, whereas Catholic church records are fairly complete, those of Protestant churches have far more gaps. Furthermore, it is much harder to determine lines of descent using Protestant church records, especially in the case of women, since the names of the spouses' parents are rarely provided, widows often used the name of their deceased husband and, in the case of baptismal records, the mother's surname is rarely given.

25 With regard to lawyers who addressed the court in English and French—and often both—see Jean-Philippe Garneau, "The Lawyers, the Courtroom and the Public Sphere: Defending the French Law Tradition in British Quebec at the Turn of the Nineteenth Century," *Quaderni storici* 47, no. 3 (2012): 797–824.

26 "Tutelle des mineurs de A. McDonald," 2 August 1825, CC601, S1, BAnQ-VM.

27 For example, see "Tutelle des mineurs de Nicholas Redhead," 5 October 1832, CC601, S1, BAnQ-VM.

28 Other cases involved a range of circumstances such as absence, insanity, and unclaimed inheritances.

29 According to the 1831 census, the population of the district of Montreal was just under eighty percent French Canadian. However, French Canadians made up only about half of the urban population. See Appendix O.o. in the *Appendix to the XLIst Volume of the Journals of the House of Assembly of Lower-Canada* (Quebec City: Nelson and Cowan, [1832]).

30 Nearly eighty-five percent of appointments involved a rural family, whereas the 1831 census shows that the countryside accounted for about ninety percent of the district's population (*Appendix to Journals of the House of Assembly of Lower-Canada*, Appendix O.o.).

31 Jean-Philippe Garneau, "Le rituel de l'élection de tutelle et la représentation du pouvoir colonial dans la société canadienne du XVIIIe siècle," *Bulletin d'histoire politique* 14, no. 1 (Fall 2005): 45–56.

32 In addition to the 127 Montreal-based cases from 1825 and 1835 where a tutor was appointed, I identified another 184 such cases in 1831 and 1832. In the latter year, Montreal experienced a cholera epidemic. In compiling this expanded sample, I relied on the research conducted by Alexandre Michaud-Guindon for his master's thesis, titled "Familles montréalaises et élection de tutelle au temps du choléra: Genre, appartenance ethnique et pratique judiciaire" (Université du Québec à Montréal, 2019).

33 The socio-professional categories used in this table are rather broad and imprecise. The one titled "Public Figures and Other Elites" is based on a range of often vague designations (e.g., "gentleman" and "bourgeois") or titles that do not reflect a socio-professional activity (e.g., "seigneur"). It encompasses military officers, members of the clergy, and senior civil servants. The "Tradesmen and Service Providers" category covers various sectors of activity. In addition to actual tradesmen (engaged in manufacturing, construction, food production, etc.), it encompasses individuals working in hospitality, food services, education, and transportation (with the exception of carters, who fall under "Workers and Day Labourers"). Not surprisingly, the sample does not include any domestic servants (who made up about one-fifth of the urban population according to the 1825 census). Jean-Paul Bernard, Paul-André Linteau, and Jean-Claude Robert, "La structure professionnelle de Montréal en 1825," *Revue d'histoire de l'Amérique française* 30, no. 3 (1976): 383–415.

34 Derived from the French "*les classes populaires*," the term "popular classes" is widely used by Quebec historians to denote labourers, small farmers, and others who shared a broadly plebeian experience, especially during the early nineteenth century. Mary Anne Poutanen (Chapter 8) uses the same term to describe people of modest means who navigated the criminal justice system in early nineteenth-century Montreal.

35 In particular, see "Tutorship of Thomas Wiley et al.," 18 November 1835, CC601, S1, BAnQ-VM. Janice Harvey, "Agency and Power in Child Charity: A Study of Two Montreal Child Charities, 1822–1900," in *Agency and Institutions in Social Regulation: Towards an Historical Understanding of their Interaction*, ed. J.-M. Fecteau and J. Harvey (Montreal: Presses de l'Université du Québec, 2005), 328–42.

36 Nicolas-Benjamin Doucet, *Fundamental Principles of the Laws of Canada*, 2 vols. (Montreal: John Lovell, 1842).

37 Regarding this infamous election, see James Jackson, *The Riot That Never Was: The Military Shooting of Three Montrealers in 1832 and the Official Cover-up* (Montreal: Baraka Books, 2010).

38 See the biography of the couples' son: Pierre B. Landry, "Bagg, Stanley Clark," in *Dictionary of Canadian Biography*, vol. 10 (Toronto/Quebec City: University of Toronto/Université Laval, 1972), last modified 2018, http://biographi.ca/en/bio/bagg_stanley_clark_10E.html.

39 Claude Champagne reports that only twelve wills of English-speaking women were submitted for validation before the Prerogative Court of Montreal between 1777 and 1825. See Table 4 in *La pratique testamentaire*. However, some English-speaking women had their wills drawn up by a notary. See Bradbury, *Wife to Widow*, 151–69.

40 Bradbury, *Wife to Widow*, 63–68.

41 "Tutelle des enfants mineurs de Nathaniel Smith," 28 June 1825, CC601, S1, BAnQ-VM. In the same fonds, see also "Tutelle des enfants mineurs de Hix Salls," 9 April 1835.

42 Nicolas-Benjamin Doucet was careful to remind his English-speaking readers of this fact. See *Fundamental Principles*, vol. 2, 41.

43 R.J. Morris, *Men, Women and Property in England, 1780–1870: A Social and Economic History of Family Strategies amongst the Leeds Middle Class* (Cambridge: Cambridge University Press, 2005).

44 I found about twenty such cases, including seven from 1835, which suggests that they did not become less common over time.

45 Curatorship dated 25 July 1825 and authorization 29 July 1825, S1, CC601, BAnQ-VM.

46 In subsequent proceedings, a sister of the minor children participated in the assembly of relatives and friends. "Autorisation d'Antoine Deniger," 28 October 1825, S1, CC601, BAnQ-VM.

47 "Procuration de Pélagie Larochelle (tutrix) à Andrew Porteous," 1 August 1825, S187, CN601, BAnQ-VM.

48 Sylvie Perrier, *Des enfances protégées: La tutelle des mineurs en France (XVII^e–XVIII^e siècles): Enquête à Paris et à Châlons-sur-Marne* (Paris: Presses universitaires de Vincennes, 1998).

49 "Tutelle des mineurs Bessette," 13 March 1835; "Tutelle des mineurs Morrier," 30 June 1835, S1, CC601, BAnQ-VM. In cases where fathers happened to arrange for a relative to be appointed tutor, the intention was often to buy out the minor children's maternal inheritance rights.

50 "Tutelle des mineurs Martel," 2 September 1823; new tutorship, 23 April 1825; authorization, 29 April 1825, S1, CC601, BAnQ-VM.

51 "Tutelle des mineurs Stirrat," 7 October 1825, S1, CC601, BAnQ-VM.

52 "Tutelle *ad hoc* de F. Deniger," 20 December 1825, S1, CC601, BAnQ-VM. Regarding John Trim, see Frank Mackey, *Black Then: Blacks and Montreal, 1780s–1880s* (Montreal and Kingston: McGill-Queen's University Press, 2004), 65-75.

53 In my extensive but by no means exhaustive use of parish registers, I found no cases where a tutor provides such consent for the minor child of a widow.

54 Mackey, *Black Then*, 249.

55 The following are just a few of the many studies to have highlighted connections between gender and either nation or empire: Jeffery Vacante, *National Manhood and the Creation of Modern Quebec* (Vancouver: UBC Press, 2017); Sarah Carter, *The Importance of Being Monogamous: Marriage and Nation Building in Western Canada to 1915* (Edmonton: University of Alberta Press,

2008); Adele Perry, *On the Edge of Empire: Gender, Race, and the Making of British Columbia, 1849–1871* (Toronto: University of Toronto Press, 2001); Mary Beth Norton, *Founding Mothers and Fathers: Gendered Power and the Forming of American Society* (New York: Alfred A. Knopf, 1996).

56 Mothers who were appointed either as a sole tutor or jointly with a new husband account for more than half of the 303 tutorships authorized in the district of Montreal in 1825 and 1835. The remaining proceedings exclusively involved French-speaking fathers, with one possible exception (a widower whose late wife was French Canadian but whose own ethnocultural background is unclear).

57 Jan Noel, "A Man of Letters and Gender Troubles of 1837," *Canadian Historical Review* 98, no. 3 (2017): 505–53.

58 Raewyn Connell, "A Thousand Miles from Kind."

59 Tosh, *Manliness and Masculinities*, 66–68.

60 M.B. Norton, *Founding Mothers*.

61 Mancke and Grittner, "From Communal to Independent Manhood."

62 In Lower Canada, the political disputes of the 1830s had escalated by 1837 into armed rebellion against British imperial rule, led by the aforementioned Louis-Joseph Papineau. There is a considerable literature on this topic, but see especially Allan Greer, *The Patriots and the People: The Rebellion of 1837 in Rural Lower Canada* (Toronto and Buffalo: University of Toronto Press, 1993).

## CHAPTER SIX

1 [Maria Elena and Ana Maria] Galuzzi, "De la patria potesdad," G 1917-1918, no. 178, Division Poder Judicial (DPJ), Archivo General de la Nación (AGN).

2 Galluzzi, "De la patria potestad," AGN.

3 Donna J. Guy, *Sex and Danger in Buenos Aires: Prostitution, Family, and Nation in Argentina* (Lincoln: University of Nebraska Press, 1991); Karen Mead, "Gendering the Obstacles to Progress in Positivist Argentina, 1880–1920," *The Hispanic American Historical Review* 77, no. 4 (1997): 645–75; The Argentine Republic, *Código civil de la República Argentina* (Buenos Aires: Pablo Coni, 1874).

4 Galluzzi, "De la patria potestad," AGN.

5 Ibid.

6 Ibid.

7 My study is based on a sample composed of 300 cases that were tried in Buenos Aires Civil Courts between 1870 and 1930. These records are now housed in the Archivo General de la Nación (AGN) and the Archivo General de las Tribunales (AGT), both in Buenos Aires, Argentina. This sample includes cases involving *entrega*, physical custody, *nombremiento de tutor*, a request to name a tutor, *patria potestad,* requests by parents to assert parental authority, or requests by others to strip parents of authority over their children. This sample includes ninety-two cases lodged by minors against a parent or guardian. Eighty-one of those ninety-two were lodged after 1890. The total

number of cases filed during this time remains unknown. Civil court records now housed in the AGN have been indexed. However, these only represent a small percentage of cases. The vast majority remain in the basement of the AGT where the records of tens of thousands of civil court proceedings from this period remain unindexed, filed by last name without regard to chronology or case type, making them extremely difficult for historians to use. I discovered, however, that the papers of the Defender of the Minor, housed in the AGN, included thousands of references to cases in which a minor appeared as the subject of court proceedings—though these institutional records often provided little more than the minor's name and a one-sentence summary of the case. I cross-checked the names in the Defender of the Minor records with those in the Civil Archive and located 1,705 previously unused cases dating from 1870 to 1930. I then pooled these with the cases indexed in the AGN and selected fifty cases from each decade at random for my sample.

8 Fernando Rocchi, *Chimneys in the Desert: Industrialization in Argentina During the Export Boom Years* (Stanford: Stanford University Press, 2006), 155.

9 For a general history of this period, see Ezequiel Gallo, "Society and Politics," in *Argentina Since Independence*, ed. Leslie Bethell (Cambridge: Cambridge University Press, 1993), 76–112; Rock, *Argentina*, 170–76.

10 For the growth of Buenos Aires, James Scobie, *Buenos Aires: Plaza to Suburb, 1870–1910* (New York: Oxford University Press, 1974), Chapter 3. For workers' movements, see Ronaldo Munck, "Cycles of Class Struggle and the Making of the Working Class in Argentina, 1890–1920," *Journal of Latin American Studies* 19, no. 1 (1987): 19–39. For the January 1919 Tragic Week see David Rock and Mario dos Santos, "Lucha civil en la Argentina-la semana trágica de enero de 1919," *Desarrollo económico* (1971): 165–215.

11 Julia Rodriguez, *Civilizing Argentina: Science, Medicine, and the Modern State* (Chapel Hill: University of North Carolina Press, 2006).

12 Diego de la Fuente, dir., *Segundo censo de la República Argentina: Mayo 10 de 1895* (Taller Tipográfico de la Penitenciaría Nacional, 1898), Tomo II, "Población."

13 María Carolina Zapiola, "'¿ Es realmente una colonia?¿ Es una escuela?¿ Qué es?' Debates parlamentarios sobre la creación de instituciones para menores en la Argentina, 1875–1890," in *Las políticas sociales en perspectiva histórica: Argentina, 1870–1952*, ed. Daniel Lvovich and Juan Suriano (Buenos Aires, Argentina: Prometeo UNGS, 2006).

14 Scobie, *Buenos Aires*, 11–13.

15 Ibid., 24–28.

16 Ibid., 200–203.

17 Donna J. Guy, "Women, Peonage, and Industrialization: Argentina, 1810–1914," *Latin American Research Review* 16, no. 3 (1981): 65–89.

18 Ricardo Cicerchia, "Minors, Gender, and Family: The Discourses in the Court System of Traditional Buenos Aires," *The History of the Family* 2, no. 3 (1997): 331–46.

19 Maximiliano Ricardo Fiquepron, "Los vecinos de Buenos Aires ante las epidemias de cólera y fiebre amarilla (1856–1886)," *Quinto sol* 21, no. 3 (2017): 2.

20 Scobie, *Buenos Aires*, 112–17.
21 Rock, *Argentina*, 165. Urban crowding is described in Scobie, *Buenos Aires*, 150–54.
22 Walter, *Politics and Urban Growth in the City*, 18.
23 Ibid., 19; Scobie, *Buenos Aires*, 168.
24 Walter, *Politics and Urban Growth in the City*, 23.
25 Donna J. Guy, "CLAH Lecture: Harrods Buenos Aires. The Case of the Unwanted Dresses, 1912–1940," *The Americas* 77, no. 3 (2020): 351–60.
26 Scobie, *Buenos Aires*, 117–20.
27 Carlos Faustimo, "Entrega de un hijo," F 1904, no. 178, DPJ, AGT.
28 Hector Mendez, "Entrega," M 1910, DPJ, AGN.
29 Constancia Satari "Solicitando entrega de una menor," C 1904, DPJ, AGT.
30 Rock, *Argentina*, 331.
31 Jose Moya, *Cousins and Strangers: Spanish Immigrants in Buenos Aires, 1850–1930* (Berkeley: University of California Press, 1998), 373–75; Ruggiero, *Modernity in the Flesh*, 93–94.
32 Luz de Carmen Novo, "De entrega," N 1904, 1908, DPJ, AGT.
33 L. Martel, "Reclusion de un hijo," M 1899, no. 189, DPJ, AGT.
34 Celica Guarneri, "Reclusion De Un Hijo," 1914, G 1914, no. 144, DPJ, AGN.
35 Dr. Rosario Guevara De Castro, "Solicita La Reclusion De Su Hija La Menor Margarita Castro," G 1912, no. 106, DPJ, AGT.
36 Moya, *Cousins and Strangers*, 56.
37 Scobie, *Buenos Aires*, 137, 140–42.
38 The civil code required that minors get parental approval to wed. Orphaned or abandoned youths could petition courts to gain judicial approval for their nuptials when parents were not available. These cases, like family disputes, are lodged in Buenos Aires' Archivo General de la Nación as well as the city's Archivo General de los Tribunales.
39 Cicerchia, "Minors, Gender, and Family."
40 Matteo Rossi, "Entrega de una hija," 1914, R 143, DPJ, AGT.
41 Doña Luisa Garré, "Solicitando, La Entrega De Una Menor," 1914, L 17.2785, DPJ, AGT.
42 Pablo José Rosa, "De patria potestad," 1899, R 1682, DPJ, AGT.
43 Rosa, "De patria potestad," AGT.
44 Hector Fernandez, "De Entrega," 1908, G 1899, no. 1329, DPJ, AGT.
45 Martin Vega de Costa, "Solicitando Se Le Nombre Tutor," 1907, V 1907, no. 73, DPJ, AGN.
46 Cicerchia, "Minors, Gender, and Family," 334.
47 Garré, "Solicitando, La Entrega De Una Menor," AGT.
48 Feijoo, "Las trabajadoras porteñas a comienzos del siglo"; Rocchi, *Chimneys in the Desert*.
49 Galluzzi, "De la patria potestad," AGN.
50 Moreno Flora, "De patria potestad," M 1901, no. 1639, DPJ, AGT.
51 Galluzzi, "De la patria potestad," AGN.
52 Guzman Reales, "Entrega," M 1907, no. 762, DPJ, AGT.
53 Reales, "Entrega," AGT.

54 Kathy Peiss, *Cheap Amusements: Working Women and Leisure in New York City, 1880 to 1920* (Philadelphia: Temple University Press, 1986); Mary E. Odem, *Delinquent Daughters: Protecting and Policing Adolescent Female Sexuality in the United States, 1885–1920* (Chapel Hill: University of North Carolina Press, 2000).

55 Juan Pablo Solis, "De la patria potestad," 1915, S 1915, no. 3284, DPJ, AGT.

56 Maria Blanca, "Solicitando Tutor," 1914, B 1913, no. 02637, DPJ, AGN; Juan Mendez, "Cerrar patria potestad," 1917, M 1914, no. 7432, DPJ, AGT.

57 Article 393 specifically prohibited siblings from exercising *patria potestad.* Articles 292 and 367 established considerable barriers against allowing siblings to act as legal guardians in any capacity.

58 Manuel Guiloff, "Solicitando La Entrega De Sus Hijos," 1918, G 178, AGN.

59 Teresa Sol Paulina, "De Tutor," 1912, P 1912, no. 0273, DPJ, AGT.

60 Santiago Patricio, "Entrega De Menor," 1916, P 1916, no. 44318, DPJ, AGT.

61 Solis, "De la patria potestad," AGT.

62 Donna J. Guy, "Parents Before the Tribunals," in *Latin America*, ed. Elizabeth Dore and Maxine Molyneux (Durham, NC: Duke University Press, 2000), 172–93.

63 Solis, "De la patria potestad," AGT.

64 Galluzi, "De la patria potestad," AGN.

65 Rock, *Argentina,* 158–63.

66 Mead, 26.

67 Blanca, "Solicitando Tutor."

68 Ibid.

69 Francisco Guzmaras, "Solicitando Tutor De Un Menor," 1915, G 144, 1914-1915, DPJ, AGN.

70 Bianca Premo, *Children of the Father King: Youth Authority and Legal Minority in Colonial Lima* (Chapel Hill: University of North Carolina Press, 2005), 3.

## CHAPTER 7

1 Ben B. Lindsey, "The Parenthood of the State" (paper presented at the Fifty-Ninth Annual Meeting of the National Education Association, Des Moines, Iowa, 1921), 42–43.

2 Ibid., 52–53.

3 Over the years, scholars have examined the multidirectional influences of reformers, state officials, and voluntary associations who initiated and implemented these reforms. Central to tracing movements of ideas, knowledge, and expertise on social policy across Western countries are: Daniel T. Rodgers, *Atlantic Crossings: Social Politics in a Progressive Age* (Cambridge: Harvard University Press, 1998); Seth Koven and Sonya Michel, eds., *Mothers of a New World: Maternalist Politics and the Origins of Welfare States* (New York: Routledge, 2013).

4 Over the past two decades, several anthologies examined similarities and differences between attitudes towards delinquent children and youth in North

America and Europe, with most recent accounts also exploring juvenile justice under colonial administrations. See: Heather Shore and Pamela Cox, eds., *Becoming Delinquent: British and European Youth, 1650–1950* (Aldershot: Ashgate Dartmouth, 2002); Jean Trépanier and Xavier Rousseaux, eds., *Youth and Justice in Western States, 1815–1950: From Punishment to Welfare* (Cham: Palgrave MacMillan, 2017); William S. Bush and David S. Tanenhaus, eds., *Ages of Anxiety: Historical and Transnational Perspectives on Juvenile Justice* (New York: New York University Press, 2018).

5 Parents figure more prominently in historical studies that examine the policing of girls' and young women's sexuality. Scholars who explore the construction of female delinquency emphasize the utility that parents found in the juvenile court and its ancillary institutions as they struggled to control their daughters. Such studies include: Mary E. Odem, *Delinquent Daughters: Protecting and Policing Adolescent Female Sexuality in the United States, 1885–1920* (Chapel Hill: University of North Carolina Press, 1995); Joan Sangster, *Girl Trouble: Female Delinquency in English Canada* (Toronto: Between the Lines, 2002); Pamela Cox, *Gender, Justice, and Welfare: Bad Girls in Britain, 1900–1950* (New York: Palgrave Macmillan, 2003); Tamara Myers, *Caught: Montreal's Modern Girls and the Law, 1869–1945* (Toronto: University of Toronto Press, 2006). For additional studies that evaluate the agentive power of parents, see: David Niget, "The Price of Virtue: Socio-Judicial Regulation of Juvenile Sexuality in France During the First Half of the Twentieth Century," in *Youth and Justice in Western States, 1815–1950*, 333–64, and Trépanier, "Children and Their Families in the Montreal Juvenile Delinquents Court, 1912–1950: Actors or Spectators of Their Own Fate?," in *Youth and Justice in Western States*, 365–88.

6 On the creation of Chicago's juvenile court, see: Anthony M. Platt, *The Child Savers: The Invention of Delinquency* (Chicago: University of Chicago Press, 1969); David S. Tanenhaus, *Juvenile Justice in the Making* (New York: Oxford University Press, 2004). For a gendered analysis of the contributions of Chicago's and Denver's courts to the development of this legal system, see: Elizabeth Clapp, *Mothers of All Children: Women Reformers and the Rise of Juvenile Courts in Progressive Era America* (University Park: Pennsylvania State University Press, 1998). Juvenile courts in the segregated South remain relatively understudied. Two central texts that trace the history of the juvenile justice systems of Memphis, Tennessee, and Texas respectively are: Jennifer Trost, *Gateway to Justice: The Juvenile Court and Progressive Child Welfare in a Southern City* (Athens: University of Georgia Press, 2005); William S. Bush, *Who Gets a Childhood? Race and Juvenile Justice in Twentieth-Century Texas* (Athens: University of Georgia Press, 2010).

7 Julian W. Mack, "The Juvenile Court," *Harvard Law Review* 23, no. 2 (1909): 104.

8 Richard S. Tuthill, "History of the Children's Court in Chicago," in *Children's Courts in the United States: Their Origin, Development, and Results*, ed. Samuel J. Barrows (Washington: Government Publishing Office, 1904), 3.

9 Julian W. Mack, "Welcoming Address: The Day of the Child," in *The Child in the City: A Series of Papers Presented at the Conferences Held During the Chicago Child Welfare Exhibit*, ed. Sophonisba P. Breckinridge (Chicago: Hollister Press, 1912), 6.

10 Emma O. Lundberg and Katharine F. Lenroot, *Juvenile Courts at Work: A Study of the Organization and Methods of Ten Courts* (US Government Printing Office, 1925), 1.

11 For a sample of contemporary publications on the city and its effects on children, see: Jane Addams, *The Spirit of Youth and the City Streets* (New York: Macmillan Company, 1909); Ben B. Lindsey and Harvey J. O'Higgins, *The Beast* (New York: Doubleday, Page & Company, 1910); Breckinridge, *The Child in the City*.

12 David J. Rothman, *Conscience and Convenience: The Asylum and Its Alternatives in Progressive America* (Boston: Little, Brown, 1980); Victoria Getis, *The Juvenile Court and the Progressives*; Michael Willrich, *City of Courts: Socializing Justice in Progressive Era Chicago* (Cambridge: Cambridge University Press, 2003).

13 James D. Schmidt, *Industrial Violence and the Legal Origins of Child Labor* (New York: Cambridge University Press, 2010); Tracy L. Steffes, *School, Society, and State: A New Education to Govern Modern America, 1890–1940* (Chicago: University of Chicago Press, 2012); Kriste Lindenmeyer, *A Right to Childhood: The U.S. Children's Bureau and Child Welfare, 1912–46* (Urbana: University of Illinois Press, 1997).

14 On the "best interest of the child" doctrine, see: Susan Tiffin, *In Whose Best Interest?: Child Welfare Reform in the Progressive Era* (Westport: Greenwood Press, 1982).

15 A main argument against the power this new system possessed was that it trampled children's constitutional rights. On the US Supreme Court case that enshrined children's entitlement to the same procedural safeguards as adults, see: David S. Tanenhaus, *The Constitutional Rights of Children: In Re Gault and Juvenile Justice* (Lawrence: University Press of Kansas, 2011).

16 Influential works that engage with the theory and history of social control and disciplinary power through the study of regulation of family and private life include Jacques Donzelot, *The Policing of Families* (New York: Random House, 1979) and Christopher Lasch, *Haven in a Heartless World: The Family Besieged* (New York: Basic Books, 1977).

17 On women's involvement in the creation and operation of the nation's new juvenile courts, see: Clapp, *Mothers of All Children*. On the role women played in the development of child-centred government policies and the rise of the welfare state primarily in North America and Europe, see: Koven and Michel, eds., *Mothers of a New World*.

18 Michael Grossberg, "Changing Conceptions of Child Welfare in the United States, 1820–1935," in *A Century of Juvenile Justice*, ed. Margaret K. Rosenheim, et al. (Chicago: University of Chicago Press, 2002), 22–3.

19 Scholars who engage with these questions include: Platt, *The Child Savers*; Rothman, *Conscience and Convenience: The Asylum and Its Alternatives in Progressive America*; Eric Schneider, *In the Web of Class: Delinquents and Reformers in Boston, 1810s–1930s* (New York: New York University Press, 1993). More recently, studies have focused on how intersecting notions of gender and race shaped the experiences of juvenile court subjects and the level of access children had to an idealized vision of juvenile justice. Odem, *Delinquent Daughters*; Miroslava Chávez-García, *States of Delinquency: Race and Science in the Making of California's Juvenile Justice System* (Berkeley: University of California Press, 2012); Tera Eva Agyepong, *The Criminalization of Black Children: Race, Gender, and Delinquency in Chicago's Juvenile Justice System, 1899–1945* (Chapel Hill: University of North Carolina Press, 2018).

20 Platt, *The Child Savers*, xvii–xix.

21 Notwithstanding the move towards an emphasis on environmental factors, one of the changes brought about by this scientific turn was also the adoption of eugenicist beliefs to inform the course of treatment of populations that were deemed beyond reform. On the simultaneous development of the modern system of "urban courts" and the rise of discourses that linked criminality and hereditary traits, see: Khalil Gibran Muhammad, *The Condemnation of Blackness: Race, Crime, and the Making of Modern Urban America* (Cambridge, MA: Harvard University Press, 2011); Michael Willrich, "The Two Percent Solution: Eugenic Jurisprudence and the Socialization of American Law, 1900–1930," *Law and History Review* 16, no. 1 (1998).

22 Julia Lathrop, "Introduction," in *The Delinquent Child and the Home: A Study of the Delinquent Wards of the Juvenile Court of Chicago*, ed. Sophonisba P. Breckinridge and Edith Abbott (Russell Sage Foundation, 1912), 5.

23 Ibid.

24 An example of the first Chicago "History of the Case" form can be found in: Timothy David Hurley, *The Juvenile Court Record* 3, no. 1 (January 1902): 6–7.

25 Different versions of probation officer schedules used in home inspections can be found in: Appendix VI, Breckenridge and Abbott, *The Delinquent Child and the Home*, 333–43.

26 Ibid.

27 Ibid., 268.

28 Ibid., 269.

29 J.J. McManaman, "The Juvenile Court," *The Juvenile Court Record* 5, no. 11 (December 1904): 6.

30 Breckenridge and Abbott, *The Delinquent Child and the Home*, 269.

31 Ibid., 274.

32 Quoted in: David J. Rothman, "The Progressive Legacy: Development of American Attitudes toward Juvenile Delinquency," in *Juvenile Justice: The Progressive Legacy and Current Reforms*, ed. LaMar Taylor Empey (Charlottesville: University Press of Virginia, 1979), 51.

33 T.D. Hurley, *Origins of the Illinois Juvenile Court: Juvenile Courts and What They Have Accomplished* (Chicago: Visitation and Aid Society, 1907), 56.

34 "Instructions of Judge Curtis D. Wilbur to the Probation Officers, April 7, 1909," in *Report and Manual for Probation Officers of the Superior Court Acting as Juvenile Court*, ed. Board of Supervisors Los Angeles County (Los Angeles: Commercial Printing House, 1912), 58.

35 Hurley, *Origins of the Illinois Juvenile Court*, 57.

36 Breckinridge and Abbott, *The Delinquent Child and the Home*.

37 Victoria Getis refers to Breckenridge, Abbott, and their colleagues at the Chicago School of Civics and Philanthropy as leaders in the movement from functionary social work to policy social work, bringing scientific methods to the study of social problems. Victoria Getis, *The Juvenile Court and the Progressives* (Urbana: University of Illinois Press, 2000), 133–38.

38 Breckenridge and Abbott, *The Delinquent Child and the Home*, 170–73.

39 Ibid, 19.

40 Anna Schultz to Judge Ben Lindsey, undated; R.C. Hukill to Judge Ben Lindsey, 20 June 1916; Statement of Probation Officer, 21 June 1916, Colorado State Archives (CSA), Denver, CO, Denver Juvenile Court Records (DJCR), Box 24867, Case no. 8735. Names of children and parents who appear in the sealed juvenile court case files were changed.

41 CSA, DJCR, Box 24864, Case no. 8234.

42 Similarly, see Chapter 6 of this volume for Juandrea Bates' discussion of the potential that legal petitions hold to reveal minors' work experiences, social networks, and generational conflict.

43 Shelby County Archives (SCA), Memphis and Shelby County Juvenile Court Records, Social Files (MSCJCR-SF), Box 7, Case no. 260.

44 SCA, MSCJCR-SF, Box 15, Case no. 580.

45 CSA, DJCR, Box 24867, Case no. 8705

46 CSA, DJCR, Box 24861, Case no. 7640

47 CSA, DJCR, Box 24867, Case no. 8735.

48 SCA, MSCJCR, Legal Files (MSCJCR-LF), Box 12, Case no. 3457.

49 Eva Price to Eddie Dunbar, 29 September 1913, CSA, DJCR, Box 24935, Case no. 1626.

50 CSA, DJCR, Box 24868, Case no. 8922.

51 Historical and contemporary debates over parental liability laws examine both tort and criminal cases as different avenues through which parents could be held responsible for their children's actions to both deter and punish caretakers for failing to control their dependents. See: Linda A. Chapin, "Out of Control: The Uses and Abuses of Parental Liability Laws to Control Juvenile Delinquency in the United States," *Santa Clara Legal Review* 37 (1996): 621; Peter Gossage, "On Dads and Damages: Looking for the 'Priceless Child' and the 'Manly Modern' in Quebec's Civil Courts, 1921–1960," *Histoire sociale/Social History* 49, no. 100 (2016): 603–23. Contributory laws were also used to police adults who were not the children's parents, many of whom were brought before the court for sexual offenses.

52 Ben B. Lindsey, "The Juvenile Laws of Colorado," *The Green Bag* 18 (1906): 126.

53 What the designation "any other person" meant—whether it referred only to a person acting as the child's caretaker or not—quickly became a contentious question. The Colorado Supreme Court provided a narrow definition of this designation in *Gibson v. People*, 44 Colo. 600 (1908).

54 CGA, S.L. 1903, Ch. 85, pp. 178–86.

55 As Michael Willrich shows, desertion and failure to support one's family were criminalized in every state of the union by 1915. In some states it was a misdemeanor while in others a felony. Michael Willrich, "Home Slackers: Men, the State, and Welfare in Modern America," *The Journal of American History* 87, no. 2 (2000): 460, 472.

56 CGA, S.L. 1905, Ch. 81, pp. 163–165; CGA, S.L. 1911, Ch. 179, pp. 527–32.

57 Lindsey, "The Juvenile Laws of Colorado," 129.

58 CSA, DJCR, Box 24932, Case nos. 1006, 1042, 1065, 1155; Box 24935, Case no. 1635; Box 24936, Case nos. 1747, 1785; Box 24937, Case no. 1945.

59 CSA, DJCR, Box 24944, Case no. 3078; Box 24943, Case no. 3031.

60 CSA, Colorado State Supreme Court Case File, Box 39146, Case no. 5905. Supplemental Abstract of Record and Brief of Defendant in Error, 23–24.

61 Sanford Bates, "Possibilities and Methods of Increasing Parental Responsibility for Juvenile Delinquents," *Journal of the American Institute of Criminal Law and Criminology* 12 (1921).

62 Lindsey, "The Parenthood of the State," 52.

63 Fabienne Giuliani's analysis in Chapter 15 of this volume provides a valuable reminder of the class-based assumption prevalent in the construction of parental delinquency, creating identification between poverty and deviancy while allowing others to distance themselves from the latter classification.

64 This finding echoes Jean-Philippe Garneau's and Juandrea Bates' conclusions in Chapters 5 and 6, respectively, which show how families' engagement with the legal regimes that regulated their lives helped shaped not only their own experiences but the institutions they encountered.

## PART THREE

1 Mary Anne Poutanen, *Beyond Brutal Passions: Prostitution in Early Nineteenth-Century Montreal* (Montreal and Kingston: McGill-Queen's University Press, 2015).

2 Mary Anne Poutanen, "Intimacies in the Neighbourhood: Revisiting Sex Commerce, Families, and Criminal Court Records in Early Nineteenth-Century Montreal," Chapter 8 in this volume, 163.

3 Shelley A.M. Gavigan, *Hunger, Horses and Government Men: Criminal Law on the Aboriginal Plains* (Vancouver and Toronto: UBC Press for the Osgoode Society for Canadian Legal History, 2012).

4 Emma Chilton and James Moran, "Civil Law, Mental Capacity, and Masculinity in Transnational Context," Chapter 10 in this volume, 199.

CHAPTER 8

1 Bibliothèque et Archives nationales du Québec, Vieux-Montréal (BAnQ-VM), TL32 S1 SS1, Deposition of Adélaide Cinqmars, 12 February 1841.

2 Bettina Bradbury, *Wife to Widow: Lives, Laws, and Politics in Nineteenth-Century Montreal* (Vancouver: UBC Press, 2011), 99.

3 BAnQ-VM, Lovell's Directory, 1842.

4 Library and Archives Canada (LAC), Record Group (RG) 31, Census Returns, Montreal, City of Montreal, 1842.

5 BAnQ-VM, Lovell's Directory, 1843, 1844, 1845; BAnQ-VM, CN601, Greffes de notaire J.D. Vallée, Bail, 23 February 1844.

6 BAnQ-VM, CN601, Greffes de notaire J.D. Vallée, Testament, 6 February 1846.

7 Bradbury, *Wife to Widow*, 374.

8 BAnQ-VM, CN601, Greffes de notaire Charles Desève, Obligation, 16 December 1834.

9 Lorena Rizzo, "The Materiality and Visuality of Intimacy in a South African Colonial Archive," Chapter 4 in the present volume.

10 For age of marriage in Lower Canada, see Peter Gossage, "Family Formation and Age at Marriage in Saint-Hyacinthe Quebec, 1854–1891," *Histoire sociale/Social History* 24, no. 47 (1991): 69. For more on the relationship between marriage age and sexual maturity, consider Leah Leneman and Rosalind Mitchison, *Sin in the City: Sexuality and Social Control in Urban Scotland 1660–1780* (Edinburgh: Scottish Cultural Press, 1998), 5.

11 Timothy J. Gilfoyle, *City of Eros: New York City, Prostitution, and the Commercialization of Sex, 1790–1920* (New York: Norton, 1992), 99.

12 BAnQ-VM, TL32 S1 SS11, Indictment, 16 July 1822, 18 July 1822; Sentence, 19 July 1822.

13 LAC, Census of 1825, Lower Canada.

14 *La Minerve*, 30 November 1829.

15 BAnQ-VM, TL32 S1 SS1, Deposition of Robert Wood and William Wilson, 17 February 1837.

16 LAC, RG4 B 14, Police Registers, vol. 38, 15 February 1837.

17 BAnQ-VM, CN 601, Greffes de notaire Peter Lukin, 15 December 1829.

18 BAnQ-VM, TL32 S1 SS11, Indictment, 12 January 1832.

19 BAnQ-VM, TL32 S1 SS1, Deposition of Robert Wood, 17 February 1837.

20 BAnQ-VM, CN 601, Greffes de notaire Henry Griffin, 23 September 1830. Portneuf is located on the north shore of the St. Lawrence River, about 200 kilometres downstream from Montreal.

21 BAnQ-VM, TL32 S1 SS1, Deposition of Etienne Benêche *dit* Lavictoire, 7 May 1831.

22 I use the term "popular class" to describe a diverse plebeian reality in early nineteenth-century Montreal. It is derived from the French *"les classes populaires"* and widely employed by Quebec historians.

23 Donald Fyson, *Magistrates, Police, and People: Everyday Criminal Justice in Quebec and Lower Canada, 1764–1837* (Toronto: University of Toronto Press, 2006).

24 *Montreal Herald*, 9 October 1821.

25 BAnQ-VM, TL32 S1 SS1, Deposition of Thomas Adams, 8 November 1840.

26 Marilynn Wood Hill, *Their Sisters' Keepers: Prostitution in New York City, 1830–1870* (London: University of California Press, 1993), 292.

27 BAnQ-VM, TL32 S1 SS1, Deposition of Joseph Auger, 8 May 1833; Deposition of Adelphe Delisle, 21 July 1824.

28 BAnQ-VM, TL32 S1 SS1, Deposition of William Lemon, Henri Latreille, and Marie-Anne Labonne, 24 April 1815.

29 BAnQ-VM, TL32 S1 SS1, Deposition of Charles Leclerc, 26 July 1825.

30 Judith Walkowitz, *Prostitution and Victorian Society: Women, Class, and the State* (New York: Cambridge University Press, 1980), 25–26.

31 Luddy, "An Outcast Community."

32 Wood Hill, *Their Sisters' Keepers*, 296–97.

33 Judith Fingard, *The Dark Side of Life in Victorian Halifax* (Porter's Lake, NS: Pottersfield Press, 1989). The relationship between sex workers and soldiers has been explored in a number of key studies. See, for example, Katherine Crooks, "'Profits, Savings, Health, Peace, Order': Prostitution, Urban Planning and Imperial Identity in Halifax, Nova Scotia, 1898–1912," *The Journal of Imperial and Commonwealth History*, 46, no. 3 (2018): 446–72; Philippa Levine, "Sexuality, Gender, and Empire," in *Gender and Empire*, ed. Philippa Levine (Oxford: Oxford University Press, 2004), 133–37; Philippa Levine, *Prostitution, Race and Politics: Policing Venereal Disease in the British Empire* (New York: Routledge, 2003); Maria Luddy, "An Outcast Community: The 'Wrens' of the Curragh," *Women's History Review* 1, no. 3 (1992): 341–55; Walkowitz, *Prostitution and Victorian Society*; and Frances Finnegan, *Poverty and Prostitution: A Study of Victorian Prostitutes in York* (New York: Cambridge University Press, 1979).

34 Fingard, *The Dark Side of Life*, 98.

35 BAnQ-VM, TL32 S1 SS1, Deposition of James King, 2 July 1824.

36 BAnQ-VM, TL32 S1 SS1, Deposition of Thomas Rousby, 20 November 1823.

37 BAnQ-VM, TL32 S1 SS1, Deposition of Jean Dérouin, 26 October 1831.

38 BAnQ-VM, TL32 S1 SS1, Depositions of Thomas Critchley and Adam Elder, 19 April 1842.

39 BAnQ-VM, TL32 S1 SS1, Deposition of Mary Ann Turner, 12 March 1841.

40 Cited in Ian C. Pilarczyk, "'Justice in the Premises': Family Violence and the Law in Montreal, 1825–1850" (PhD diss., McGill University, 2003), 234, n607.

41 BAnQ-VM, TL32 S1 SS1, Deposition of Louise Corbeille, 31 October 1836.

42 Gregory Thomas Smith, "The State and the Culture of Violence in London, 1760–1840" (PhD diss., University of Toronto, 1999): 163.

43 Bradbury, *Working Families*, 178–80.

44 Harvey, "To Love, Honour and Obey," 129.

45 Stephen Robertson, "What's Law Got to Do with It? Legal Records and Sexual Histories," *Journal of the History of Sexuality* 14, no. 2 (January/April 2005): 163.

46 A Jackeen is a derogatory name given to a Dubliner. The *Oxford English Dictionary* defines it as: "A contemptuous designation for a self-assertive

worthless fellow." *The Compact Edition of the Oxford English Dictionary* (Oxford: Oxford University Press, 1971). I wish to thank colleague and Irish scholar D'Arcy Ryan and Dubliner Kevin Whelan for their assistance.

47 BAnQ-VM, TL32 S1 SS1, Depositions of George Mackin and Hypolite Simon, 4 August 1837.

48 Joel Best, *Controlling Vice: Regulating Brothel Prostitution in St. Paul, 1865–1883* (Columbus: Ohio State University Press, 1998), 70.

49 Clare A. Lyons, *Sex among the Rabble: An Intimate History of Gender and Power in the Age of Revolution, Philadelphia, 1730–1830* (Chapel Hill: University of North Carolina Press, 2006), 340.

50 Sherry Olson, "Feathering Her Nest in Nineteenth-Century Montreal," *Social History/Histoire sociale* 33, no. 65 (May 2000): 1–35.

51 Best, *Controlling Vice*, 59.

52 BAnQ-VM, TL32 S1 SS11, Presentment of the Grand Jury, 18 January 1840.

53 BAnQ-VM, TL32 S1 SS1, Depositions of William Hall and Adelphe Delisle, 7 June 1824.

54 LAC, MG24 B 173, James Reid Papers, vol. 3, 19 February 1819.

55 Frank Mackey, *Done with Slavery: The Black Fact in Montreal* (Montreal and Kingston: McGill-Queen's University Press, 2010), 243.

56 BAnQ-VM, TL32 S1 SS1, Depositions of John George Dagen, Christopher Byrne, and Benjamin Wicklin, 14 April 1825.

57 Mackey, *Done with Slavery*, 243.

58 BAnQ-VM, TL32 S1 SS1, Deposition of Patrick Graham, 8 May 1820.

## CHAPTER 9

1 I appreciated the opportunity to have participated in the Family and Justice in the Archives Symposium. I am honoured by the invitation to contribute to this collection and deeply appreciative of the vision, commitment, and encouragement (and hard work) of Peter Gossage and Lisa Moore. Sincere thanks to Nisaa Khan for her excellent research assistance, to Law Librarian Daniel Perlin and linguist-cum-archivist Zachary O'Hagan for their assistance, to Karen Andrews for wise counsel, and to my best reader, Amy Deverell, who made time for this when she had none. I am particularly grateful to Bruce Farrer, of the Qu'Appelle Historical Society and Secretary, Qu'Appelle Masonic Lodge no. 6 AF & AM, for generously sharing his knowledge of Qu'Appelle's history and photographs from the Qu'Appelle Lodge's collection. The financial support from Osgoode Hall Law School's Research Program for Senior Scholars is gratefully acknowledged. The research presented in this chapter is both an excerpt of the longer paper prepared for the Family and Justice in the Archives symposium and part of an ongoing larger project on law and justice in the nineteenth-century lower courts in what is now the Province of Saskatchewan.

2 The 1884–1885 Census of the three Provisional Districts of the NWT (Assiniboia, Alberta, and Saskatchewan) revealed that Saskatchewan, the largest, was the least populated district: the total population was 10,746, of whom

5,373 resided in the sub-district of Prince Albert. *Census of the Three Provisional Districts of the North-West Territories 1884–85* (Ottawa: Maclean, Roger & Co, 1886), Table 1, 2–3.

3 See *Census of Canada, 1880–81* (Ottawa: Maclean, Roger & Co, 1882), Volume I, Table III, 300–301, where 1,075 Indians are reported living in the sub-district of Prince Albert but no reference to Métis numbers.

4 This included 1,745 Indian and 2,156 Métis [French, English, "Scotch," and Irish]. See *1884–5 Census of the NWT*, Table 3, 10–11.

5 See for example, Alan B. Anderson, *Settling Saskatchewan* (Regina: University of Regina Press, 2013), 243–44; Paget James Code, "Les Autres Métis: The English Métis of the Prince Albert Settlement 1823–1886" (master's thesis, University of Saskatchewan, 2008).

6 Code, "Les Autres Métis," 45–46. See also "Town of Prince Albert," in *McPhillips Alphabetical & Business Directory of the Saskatchewan District, together with Brief Historical Sketches …* (Qu'Appelle, NWT: The "Progress" Book & Job Office, 1888), 31–46F. The Métis may have been the first settlers of the district, but the prominent settlers profiled in the Directory appeared to have been white male "immigrants" from Eastern Canada.

7 His name does not appear in the 1881 Census of Canada as a resident of the North-West Territories.

8 For instance, in the winter of 1882, nine Edmonton men had been charged with "malicious injury to property" for the destruction of J.M. Bannerman's house; all nine were acquitted in June by Magistrate Richardson when the Prosecutor failed to appear: Canada Sessional Papers, 1883, vol. 10, no. 23, Annual NWMP Case Returns for 1882, Appendix D, 42. This case has been studied by Bruce Ziff and Sean Ward, "Squatters' Rights and the Origin of the Edmonton Settlement," in *Essays in the History of Canadian Law: A Tribute to Peter N. Olive*, ed. Jim Phillips, R. Roy McMurtry, and John T. Saywell (Toronto: University of Toronto Press for the Osgoode Society for Canadian Legal History, 2008), 452–53.

9 George Finlay, et al. (1882), file 156, First Series, 1876-1886, Court Records (CR), Regional Justice Centre, Department of the Attorney General (AG), Provincial Archives of Saskatchewan (PAS), Regina. In the 1881 Census of Canada, North West Territories, District of Saskatchewan, Sub-District Prince Albert, item number 112184, 44, https://central.bac-lac.gc.ca/.item/?app =Census1881&op=pdf&id=e008212243, his name is spelled "Findlay"; he is listed as having been born in Scotland, aged thirty-two, whose occupation is listed as farmer. His wife, Charlotte Findlay, item number 112185, is listed as being twenty-six and having been born in Manitoba. No record of Charlotte Findlay can be found in the 1891 Census. Her brother John J. Pocha named one of his daughters Charlott, possibly in her memory. 1901 Census of Canada, The Territories, District of Saskatchewan, Sub-District of Kirkpatrick, Item Number 1018638, 1, https://central.bac-lac.gc.ca/.item/?app=Census1901&op =&img&id=z000182632.

10 Deposition of John M. Cameron in George Finlay (1882). The formal Information is not found in the court record but J.P. Campbell's notes of the

depositions and cross-examination of Cameron and his four witnesses at the hearing can be found, as well as George Finlay's Recognizance authorizing his release pending trial later that fall.

11 Ibid.

12 In the court record, the handwritten spelling of their surname appears as "Pothieu." Their signatures are on the document, only an "X" in place of a signature. However, a third deponent, Charles "Pothieu" signed his name, "Charles Pocha." The 1881 Census of Canada for the Saskatchewan District of the North-West Territories contains no one named "Pothieu." However, there are several entries in both the 1881 and 1891 Censuses for Pocha family members, including Joseph and Mathilda Pocha and their children. The Pocha family was said to be a prominent Métis family in the Prince Albert area. See Code, "Les Autres Métis," 29. I have elected to use Code's spelling as it appears to be their correct family name rather than the family name transcribed in J.P. Campbell's handwritten notes.

13 Deposition of John M. Cameron, in George Finlay (1882).

14 Ibid. It is not clear from the transcript just when Cameron's apology was signed.

15 Ibid.

16 Deposition of Joseph Pocha, in George Finlay (1882).

17 W.C. McKay, "Early History Noble Redmen," *Prince Albert Daily Herald*, 15 December 1923, quoted by Code, "Les Autres Métis," 43. Code includes the Pochas as members of the English Métis of the Prince Albert settlement, although the Census records list them as of French origin.

18 Deposition of Mathilda Pocha, in George Finlay (1882).

19 Ibid.

20 The 1882 North-West Mounted Police (NWMP) Case Returns indicate that the case was committed for trial, but that Cameron's prosecution failed. Canada, Sessional Papers of the Dominion of Canada (CSP), 1883, vol 10, no. 23, Annual NWMP Case Returns for 1882, Appendix D, 41. Thomas Righton is named as "J. Righter" and William Craigie appears as "Craggie."

21 *The Prince Albert Times and Saskatchewan Review*, 1 November 1882, 5, col. 1.

22 Census of Canada, 1891, North-West Territories, District of Saskatchewan, sub-District Prince Albert, Item number 4774328, 30, https://central.bac-lac.gc.ca/.item/?app=Census1891&op=pdf&id=30953_148228-00573.

23 Felice Batlan, "Engendering Legal History," *Law & Social Inquiry* 30 (2005): 823, at 837.

24 George Finlay (1882).

25 James G. Chalmers (1898), file 166, IR 19, R1286, Supreme Court of the North-West Territories (Criminal) Records (SCNWT), PAS.

26 John McLeod (1889), file 8, SCNWT (Criminal), IR 19, R1286, PAS.

27 Richard Crispen (1898), file 191, SCNWT (Criminal), IR 19, R1286, PAS.

28 Fanny Haman (1897), file 162, SCNWT (Criminal), IR 19, R1286, PAS. Shame and stigma associated with pregnancy and illegitimacy that may follow "improper intimacies" are implicated not only in this perjury case, but also in the

prosecution of Baptiste Robillard for perjury, having denied under oath that he had had sexual connection with a young woman but having previously signed an acknowledgement of paternity of her child. See Shelley A.M. Gavigan, *Hunger, Horses, and Government Men: Criminal Law on the Aboriginal Plains* (Vancouver: UBC Press and The Osgoode Society for Canadian Legal History, 2012), 106–109.

29 A precursor to the Royal Canadian Mounted Police (RCMP), the North-West Mounted Police (NWMP) was a paramilitary police force established in 1873 to enforce the law and administer justice in the Northwest Territories.

30 For a fuller account of the administration of justice in the NWT in this period, see Gavigan, *Hunger, Horses, and Government Men*, 33–49.

31 Provincial Archives of Saskatchewan (PAS): Department of the Attorney-General, Reginal Judicial Centre, Court Records First Series, 1876–1886, Files 1-282 [A-G (GR11-1) CR-Regina, 1st Series, 1876–1886; Supreme Court of the North-West Territories (Criminal) Records, IR 19, R1286; Department of Attorney General, Supreme Court of the North-West Territories, Court Records (Justices of the Peace), CR-JP 1897–1904.

32 Including the issue of naming or anonymizing the men, women, and children involved as Informants, Accused, Complainant, Victim, Witness—to which no single approach has been taken. See, for example, Dorothy E. Chunn, "Secrets and Lies: The Criminalization of Incest and the (Re)Formation of the 'Private' in British Columbia," in *Regulating Lives: Historical Essays on the State, Society, The Individual, and The Law*, ed. John McLaren, Robert Menzies, and Dorothy E. Chunn (Vancouver: UBC Press, 2002), 120–44, 141, fn 1; Constance Backhouse, *Carnal Crimes: Sexual Assault Law in Canada, 1900–1975* (Toronto: Irwin Law and The Osgoode Society for Canadian Legal History, 2008), 4–5; Jacqueline Briggs, "Exemplary Punishment: TRL MacInnes, the Department of Indian Affairs, and Indigenous Executions, 1936–52," *Canadian Historical Review* 100, no. 3 (September 2019): 398, 401; Geoffrey Reaume, *Remembrance of Patients Past: Life at the Toronto Hospital for the Insane, 1870–1940* (Toronto: University of Toronto Press, 2009). Reaume used pseudonyms for the patients whose files he read and stories he told.

33 *Qu'Appelle Progress*, 28 June 1894, p. 1, col. 2 (online).

34 The *Criminal Code*'s marginal note for the section described the offence as "unlawfully defiling women" and, for the most part, created offences directed at those who procured or drew women into prostitution. *Criminal Code 1892*, S.C. 1892, c. 29, s. 185 (55-56 Vict.). In its record of the Shaw prosecution, the NWMP used this short name for the offence. See *The Annual Report of the Commissioner of the NWMP for 1897*, CSP 1898, no. 15, "Annual Return of Criminal Cases tried in the North-West Territories from December 1st, 1896 – November 30th, 1897," Appendix KK at 244, which recorded that Wilson charged George Shaw with the offence of "defiling a woman" and that the charge was dismissed by H. Gisborne J.P. on 11 January 1897 at Qu'Appelle. The court documents give the date as 9 January 1897.

35 Deposition of Cst. M.J. Della Torre, in George Shaw (1897), Court Records, Justices of the Peace (CR-JP) 1897-1904, SCNWT, Department of Attorney General, PAS [No file number].

36 Bruce Farrer, Qu'Appelle Local History Society, telephone conversation with author, 28 January 2021.
37 George Shaw (1897).
38 John McLaren, "Recalculating the Wages of Sin: The Social and Legal Construction of Prostitution, 1850–1920," *Manitoba Law Journal* 23 (1995): 524–55.
39 Adultery could be a ground for divorce; alienation of affection was a tort.
40 Deposition of William Wilson, in George Shaw (1897).
41 Deposition of Mrs. W. Wilson, in George Shaw (1897).
42 Ibid.
43 *Qu'Appelle Progress,* 14 January 1897, p. 4, col. 3.
44 Census of Canada, 1901, NWT, Assiniboia East District, Sub-District Winlaw, Item no. 1034778, 3, https://central.bac-lac.gc.ca/.item/?app=Census1901&op=pdf&id=z000181697.
45 Census of Canada, 1901, NWT, District of Eastern Assiniboia, Sub-District Qu'Appelle, Item no. 981052, 9, https://central.bac-lac.gc.ca/.item/?app=Census1901&op=pdf&id=z000181216.
46 Census of the North West Provinces, 1906, Province of Saskatchewan, Assiniboia East District, Qu'Appelle Sub-District, 17, https://central.bac-lac.gc.ca/.item/?app=Census1906&op=pdf&id=e001210238
47 *Qu'Appelle Footprints*, at 366, 374, 380. Wilson was awarded contracts to build local schools and churches, including the Grassmere School in 1906 ($775.00), at 366; Vernon School in 1903 ($1,500.00), 374; St Thomas Anglican Church addition in 1903 ($550.00), 380.
48 Bruce Farrer, Secretary, Qu'Appelle Lodge no. 6 AF & AM, e-mail correspondence to author, 22 January 2021.
49 Ibid., and telephone conversation with author, 11 January 2021.
50 Farrer, e-mail correspondence to author, 2 February 2021.
51 An Act to amend and consolidate the laws respecting Indians (The Indian Act), S.C. 1876, c. 18, s. 3 (39 Vict.): "The term "Indian" means First. Any male person of Indian blood reputed to belong to a particular band; Secondly. Any child of such person; Thirdly. Any woman who is or was lawfully married to such person.
52 Chandra Murdoch, "Inheritance and the Indian Act: Political Action and Women's Property on Southern Ontario Indian Reserves, 1857–1900," Chapter 2 in this volume, quotation at p. 57.
53 Sarah Carter, *Imperial Plots: Women, Land, and the Spadework of British Colonialism on the Canadian Prairies* (Winnipeg: University of Manitoba Press, 2016), 4. See also Carter, *The Importance of Being Monogamous: Marriage and Nation Building in Western Canada to 1915* (Edmonton and Athabasca: University of Alberta Press and AU Press, 2008), 22–27.
54 *Rathwell v Rathwell* [1974] SJ No 2 at para 21 (Sask QB), per Disbery, J. Disbery's judgment was overturned but a clearer expression of patriarchal hubris by a prairie judge is hard to imagine.
55 See for example, Joy Parr, *Labouring Children: British Immigrant Apprentices to Canada, 1869–1924* (Toronto: University of Toronto Press, 1994), xvi (citing Phyllis Harrison's work).

56 Their family name is also spelled "Crispin" in the 1901 Census of Canada. If "Crispin" was the correct spelling of Richard's name, it is possible he is the same R. Crispin who had been tried in Regina for perjury on 13 March 1897 by Justice of the Peace William Trant; the charge was dismissed. See *Annual Report of the Commissioner of the North-West Mounted Police 1897*, Appendix KK, Return of Criminal and other Cases tried in the North-West Territories from 1 December 1896 to 30 November 1897, 243 at 246 (CSP 1898, vol. 12, no. 15).

57 See the entry for Joseph Glenn and his family in the 1901 Census of Canada, The Territories, District of Assiniboia East, Sub-District Indian Head, Item Number 933492, 12, https://central.bac-lac.gc.ca/.item/?app=Census1901&op=pdf&id=z000180850.

58 Letter from Mrs. Annie Crispen to her husband, 17 March 1898, in Joseph Glenn (1898), file 187, SCNWT (Criminal), IR 19, R1286, PAS.

59 Ibid.

60 Letter from Richard Crispen to his wife, 27 March 1898, in Joseph Glenn (1898).

61 Entry in Annie Crispen's notebook, 17 April 1898, in Joseph Glenn (1898).

62 Ibid.

63 Deposition of Richard Crispen in Joseph Glenn (1898).

64 Ibid.

65 Richard Crispen (1898), file 191 SCNWT (Criminal), Coll R1286, PAS.

66 Letter from R. Crispen to J. Glenn, dated "Aug," Exhibit (A), in Joseph Glenn (1898).

67 Deposition of Joseph Glenn in Richard Crispen (1898).

68 Ibid.

69 Ibid.

70 Ibid.

71 *The Regina Leader*, 15 December 1898, 10, col 5.

72 "Richard Crispin; Blackmailer Perjurer and General Bad Lot, Sentenced to Twelve Years," *The Regina Leader*, 4 October 1911, 3, cols 1–3. The newspaper also incorrectly stated that Crispin was sentenced to serve twelve years when in fact he had been sentenced for two offences to seven years and five years to be served concurrently, not consecutively.

## CHAPTER 10

1 Cross-examination of Dr. James Kennedy, New Jersey State Archives (NJSA), Chancery Court (CC), Lunacy Case Files (LCF), case of Philip Lerch 1835–1839.

2 Cross-examination of Dr. James Kennedy, NJSA, CC, LCF, case of Philip Lerch 1835–1839.

3 John Tosh, *Manliness and Masculinities in Nineteenth-Century Britain: Essays on Gender, Family and Empire* (Harlow: Pearson Longman, 2005), 67; 66–68.

4 Tosh, *Manliness and Masculinities*, 68.

5 Although defined in relation to the peculiarities of time and place, rational behaviour in relation to self-conduct and capital management was nevertheless consistently tied to the economic interests of male authority.

6 New Jersey became an English colony in 1664 and one of the first American States after the American Revolutionary period. Ontario's nineteenth-century history was more complex, starting as the British colony of Upper Canada (1791–1841), then Canada West (1841–1867), and subsequently the Canadian province of Ontario.

7 Civil trials in lunacy of the sort found in the New Jersey State Archives were also held in nineteenth-century Ontario. However, thus far these legal documents have not been found in significant numbers or collected archivally. Cases of testamentary capacity such as those found in Ontario in Chancery Reports were dealt with in New Jersey as civil trials in lunacy.

8 James Moran, *Madness on Trial: A Transatlantic History of English Civil Law and Lunacy* (Manchester: Manchester University Press, 2019), 31–48.

9 Moran, *Madness on Trial*, 117–39.

10 The phrase is borrowed from Christopher Tomlins, "Law's Empire: Chartering English Colonies on the American Mainland in the Seventeenth Century," in *Law, History, Colonialism: The Reach of Empire*, ed. Diane Kirkby and Catharine Coleborne (Manchester: Manchester University Press, 2001), 26–45.

11 The literature on law's empire is vast. See for example, Kirkby and Coleborne, *Law, History, Colonialism*; John Carrier Weaver, *The Great Land Rush and the Making of the Modern World: 1650–1900* (Montreal and Kingston: McGill-Queen's University Press, 2003); and Mindie Lazarus-Black and Susan Hirsh, eds., *Contested States: Law, Hegemony and Resistance* (New York: Routledge University Press, 1994).

12 Some Ontario judges made a great effort to separate a person's sanity from his capacity to write legal documents. However, despite their protestations, the trials over which they presided still contain telltale attributes of lunacy investigation. For example, *Chancery Reports* (CR), *Upper Canada* (UC), Case of Ingoldsby v. Ingoldsby, 1873.

13 Some trials and court procedures involved struggles around women's property. In New Jersey, for example, of the 1,800 lunacy trials examined in other research, approximately eight percent focused on women's property. See Moran, *Madness on Trial*, 140–66.

14 From mid-century forward with the arrival and development of lunatic asylums, these institutional options for the mad, along with their developing psychiatric professional expertise, began to serve as a parallel arbiter of irrational behaviour (male and female), mixing in complex ways with lunacy investigation law. James Moran explains how this process unfolded in New Jersey in *Madness on Trial*, 206–31. In Upper Canada (Ontario) some preliminary research suggests an equally interesting process; see G. Landry, "Commissions of Lunacy in Upper Canada, 1860–1910," (Honours thesis, University of Prince Edward Island, 2016). Volker Hess traces an equally complex but remarkably similar coming together of civil law and asylum committal in nineteenth-century Germany. See Volker Hess, "Bookkeeping Madness: Archives and Filing Between

Court and Ward," in *Knowledge Making: Historians, Archives and Bureaucracy*, ed. Barbara Brookes and James Dunk (New York: Routledge, 2020), 22–45. Thierry Nootens does the same for Quebec, in his analysis of the law of civil interdictions in Quebec. Thierry Nootens, *Fous, prodigues et ivrognes: Familles et déviance à Montréal au XIX siècle* (Montreal and Kingston: McGill-Queen's University Press, 2007).

15 R.W. Connell and James W. Messerschmidt, "Hegemonic Masculinity: Rethinking the Concept," *Gender and Society* 19, no. 6 (December 2005): 846.

16 Connell and Messerschmidt, "Hegemonic Masculinity," 848.

17 Peter Gossage and Robert Rutherdale, "Introduction," in *Making Men: Making History: Canadian Masculinities Across Time and Place*, ed. Peter Gossage and Robert Rutherdale (Vancouver: UBC Press, 2018), 3.

18 Tosh, *Manliness and Masculinities*, 44.

19 Tosh, *Manliness and Masculinities*, 73.

20 Tosh, *Manliness and Masculinities*, 186.

21 Tosh, *Manliness and Masculinities*, 185. See also J.A. Mangan and James Walvin, eds., *Manliness and Morality: Middle-Class Masculinity in Britain and America, 1800–1940* (Manchester: Manchester University Press, 1987); Andrew Holman, *A Sense of their Duty: Middle Class Formation in Victorian Ontario Towns* (Montreal and Kingston: McGill-Queen's University Press, 2000), 153.

22 See CR, UC, Case of Emes v. Emes, 1865; and CR, UC, Martin v. Martin, 1866.

23 CR, UC, Case of Emes v. Emes, 1865, 327.

24 Tosh, *Manliness and Masculinities*, 72.

25 Tosh, *Manliness and Masculinities*, 32. Variances in codes of manliness are attributed in part to religion and occupation.

26 Tosh, *Manliness and Masculinities*, 69.

27 Stefan Collini, *Public Moralists: Political Thought and Intellectual Life in Britain, 1850–1930* (Oxford: Oxford Universty Press, 1993), 106; quoted in Tosh, *Manliness and Masculinities*, 76.

28 Examples of cases in which inability to work was considered a sign of incapacity include, NJSA, CC, LCF, Case of Isaac Bogert, 1850; NJSA, CC, LCF, Case of Isaac Morris, 1844; NJSA, CC, LCF, Case of Benjamin v. Mulford, 1865; CR, UC, Martin v. Martin, 1866; NJSA, CC, LCF, Case of Philip Lerch, 1835–1839; NJSA, CC, LCF, Case of Lloyd Vanderveer, 1845; and NJSA, CC, LCF, Case of Philip Hutle, 1954.

29 CR, UC, case of Rachel Bailey, 1856. Another woman's business savvy is celebrated in CR, UC, case Campbell v. Belfour 1869.

30 NJSA, CC, LCF, Case of Benjamin Mulford, 1865.

31 Cross-examination of Dr. James Kennedy, NJSA, CC, LCF, case of Philip Lerch, 1835–1839.

32 NJSA, CC, LCF, Case of Lloyd Vanderveer, 1845.

33 NJSA, CC, LCF, Case of Lloyd Vanderveer, 1845.

34 NJSA, CC, LCF, Case of Lloyd Vanderveer, 1845.

35 NJSA, CC, LCF, Case of Lloyd Vanderveer, 1845.

36 NJSA, CC, LCF, Case of Philip Hutle, 1854.
37 NJSA, CC, LCF, Case of Philip Hutle, 1854.
38 CR, UC, Miller v. Miller, 1877, 231.
39 CR, UC, Wilson v. Wilson, 1875, 57.
40 For a full discussion of what Robert Rutherdale and Peter Gossage describe as "responsible family manhood," albeit for a later period, see Robert Rutherdale, "Three Faces of Fatherhood as a Masculine Category: Tyrants, Teachers, and Workaholics as 'Responsible Family Men' During Canada's Baby Boom," in *What is Masculinity? Historical Dynamics from Antiquity to the Contemporary World*, ed. John H. Arnold and Sean Brady (Basingstoke: Palgrave Macmillan, 2011), 323–48; Peter Gossage, "Visages de la paternité au Québec, 1900–1960," *Revue d'histoire de l'Amérique française* 70, nos. 1–2 (Spring/Fall 2016): 53–82.
41 Interestingly, the judgement of Martin v. Martin echoes the sentiment that the provisions of a will should not weigh heavily in an investigation of its validity. CR, UC, Martin v. Martin, 1866, 517.
42 CR, UC, Martin v. Martin, 1866, 516.
43 CR, UC, Martin v. Martin, 1866, 516.
44 CR, UC, Martin v. Martin, 1866, 509.
45 CR, UC, Martin v. Martin, 1866, 506.
46 CR, UC, Martin v. Martin, 1866, 509.
47 CR, UC, Martin v. Martin, 1866, 509.
48 CR, UC, Martin v. Martin, 1866, 509.
49 CR, UC, Martin v. Martin, 1866, 513.
50 CR, UC, Martin v. Martin, 1866, 514. Quoted case: Stulz v. Schoeffle, 16 Jur. 909.
51 CR, UC, Ingoldsby v. Ingoldsby, 1873, 141–42.
52 CR, UC, Ingoldsby v. Ingoldsby, 1873, 141–42.
53 CR, UC, Martin v. Martin, 1866, 506.
54 CR, UC, Watson v. Watson, 1876, 70. Note that someone claiming that they themselves were incapable to transact business was less common in civil law, where generally people want to be seen as having full control of their faculties and thus full control of their property. Claiming your own incapacity is more common in the criminal legal tradition; so much so that insanity pleas have become a trope.
55 CR, UC, Watson v. Watson, 71.
56 CR, UC, Watson v. Watson, 75.
57 CR, UC, Watson v. Watson, 76.
58 CR, UC, Watson v. Watson, 79.
59 CR, UC, Campbell v. Belfour, 1869, 113.
60 CR, UC, Campbell v. Belfour, 1869, 110.
61 CR, UC, Campbell v. Belfour, 1869, 113.
62 CR, UC, Campbell v. Belfour, 1869, 112.
63 CR, UC, Campbell v. Belfour, 1869, 113.
64 Viviana Zelizer, *The Purchase of Intimacy* (Princeton: Princeton University Press, 2005), 52.

65 CR, UC, Campbell v. Belfour, 1869, 114.

66 For an analysis of the creation of the Court of Chancery in broad historical context in the colony, see Elizabeth Brown, "Equitable Jurisdiction and the Courts of Chancery in Upper Canada," *Osgoode Hall Law Journal* 21, no. 2 (September 1983): 275–314.

67 See Robert Cooper, *The Rules and Practice of the Court of Chancery of Upper Canada: Comprising the Orders of 1850 and 1851, with Eplanatory* [sic] *Notes Referring to the English Orders and Decisions* (Toronto: A.H. Armour and Co., 1851), 12.

68 Brown, "Equitable Jurisdiction," 291.

69 As Brown notes, "in 1853, equitable jurisdiction was granted to the County Courts for the first time." See, Brown, "Equitable Jurisdiction," 302. This and other mid-century reforms established more parity between Ontario and New Jersey in how the chancery court was used.

70 See Constance Backhouse, "Lawyering: Clara Brett Martin, Canada's First Woman Lawyer," in *Petticoats and Prejudice: Women and Law in Nineteenth-Century Canada* (Toronto: Osgoode Society and Women's Press, 1991), 293–326. For a comparative study including Canada and the United States, see M.J. Mossman, *The First Women Lawyers: A Comparative Study of Gender, Law and the Legal Professions* (Oxford: Hart Publishing, 2006).

71 CR, UC, Watson v. Watson, 78.

72 CR, UC, Watson v. Watson, 78.

73 CR, UC, Watson v. Watson, 78.

74 CR, UC, Watson v. Watson, 78.

75 CR, UC, Case of Ingoldsby v. Ingoldsby, 1873, 132.

76 This might sound like an absurdity in the case of New Jersey, which since 1776 had formed part of the United States of America in defiance of English rule. Nevertheless, as an independent state in the US, New Jersey adopted almost all of the common law and statute law of England well into the nineteenth century. See Moran, *Madness on Trial*, 129–30.

77 These intersections of law, community, and masculinity are highlighted in longer trials of lunacy in New Jersey in which the defendant, having been found *non compos mentis* for a period of time was later able to successfully reverse this decision through an appeal or *traverse* of the earlier trial. See, for example, the case of Philip Lerch, 1835–1839.

78 The essays in this book authored by Mélanie Méthot (Chapter 11), Fabienne Giuliani (Chapter 15), and Shelley Gavigan (Chapter 9) offer nuanced interpretations of how courts and other institutions have reckoned with gendered acts and articulations of family responsibility and duty.

## PART FOUR

1 Gail Savage, "The 'Moscow Widowers': Marriage, Citizenship, and the Soviet Wives of British Subjects in the Aftermath of the Second World War," Chapter 13 in this volume, 257.

CHAPTER 11

1 Victoria Records of Birth, Death and Marriage (VRBDM) 1893-5606, 1894-31622, and 1896-13511.

2 "Items of news," *Mount Alexander Mail*, 30 September 1893, 3.

3 *Bairnsdale Advertiser and Tambo and Omeo Chronicle*, 13 May 1897, 2. "Charges against a Gaol Warder," *The Age*, 12 May 1897, 6. "Alleged Misconduct of a Warder," *Argus*, 12 May 1897, 6. *Mount Alexander Mail*, 15 May 1897, 2.

4 "Alleged Misconduct of a Warder," *The Argus*, 12 May 1897, 6.

5 Public Record Office Victoria (PROV), 30-P0-1410.

6 VRBDM 1897-8923.

7 VRBDM 1899-7654, 1901-9174, 1904-15229.

8 VRBDM 1908-9234, 1913-7523.

9 Data collected in Trove and from the Prosecution Project. The Trove database is a collaboration between the National Library of Australia and hundreds of partner organizations in that country; https://trove.nla.gov.au/. Based at Griffith University in Queensland, the Prosecution Project is working to digitize the archival records of criminal trials in all regions of Australia. See M. Finnane, A. Kaladelfos, A. Piper, Y. Smaal, R. Blewer, L. Durnian, et al., *The Prosecution Project Database*, https://app.prosecutionproject.griffith.edu.au/web/. Be it in the United Kingdom, Australia, New Zealand, or Canada, more men were prosecuted for bigamy; and judges tended to impose lighter sentences on bigamous women. Rebecca Probert, *Divorced, Bigamist, Bereaved?* (Kenilworth, UK: Takeaway (Publishing), 2015), 143; David Cox, "'Trying to Get a Good One' Bigamy Offences in England and Wales, 1850–1950," *Plymouth Law and Criminal Justice Review* 4 (2012): 1–32; Maria Luddy, "Marriage, Sexuality and the Law in Ireland," in *Cambridge Social History of Modern Ireland*, ed. E.F. Biagini and M.E. Daly (Cambridge: Cambridge University Press, 2017), 348; Timothy J. Gilfoyle, "The Hearts of Nineteenth-Century Men: Bigamy and Working-Class Marriage in New York City, 1800–1890," *Prospects* 19 (1994): 141; Raewyn Dalziel, "The Privileged Crime: Policing and Prosecuting Bigamy in Nineteenth-Century New Zealand," *New Zealand Journal of History* 51, no. 2 (2017): 6; Mélanie Méthot, "Bigamy in the Northern Alberta Judicial District, 1886–1969: A Socially Constructed Crime that Failed to Impose Gender Barriers," *Journal of Family History* 31, no. 3 (2006): 260; L.M. Friedman, "Crimes of Mobility," *Stanford Law Review* 43, no. 3 (1991): 637–58; Ginger Frost, "Bigamy and Cohabitation in Victorian England," *Journal of Family History* 22, no. 3 (1997): 287; D.M. Turner, "Popular Marriage and the Law: Tales of Bigamy in Eighteenth-Century Old Bailey," *London Journal* 30, no. 1 (2005): 17; Bernard Capp, "Bigamous Marriage in Early Modern England," *The Historical Journal* 52, no. 3 (2009): 547; Peter Gilmore, "'Said to Have Left His Wife in Ireland': Adultery, Bigamy and Desertion in Ulster Presbyterian Migration to Pennsylvania, 1780–1815," *Journal of Backcountry Studies* 6, no. 1 (2011): 2; Annalee Lepp, "Dis/membering the Family: Marital Breakdown, Domestic Conflict, and Family Violence in Ontario 1830–1920" (PhD diss., Queen's University, 2001), 221.

10 I employ the term "agency" in this chapter as it has been defined by historians like Lynn M. Thomas, encompassing not only meaningful action but "the motivations that undergird, motivations that exceed rational calculation and articulated intention to include collective fantasies, psychical desires and struggles just to get by." Lynn M. Thomas, "Historicising Agency," *Gender and History* 28, no. 2 (2016): 335.

11 Shelley A.M. Gavigan, "Improper Intimacies, Impossible Promises, and the Prerogatives of Patriarchy: Family and Justice in Nineteenth-Century Criminal Courts in Canada's North-West Territories," Chapter 9 in this volume, 186.

12 PROV 30-P0-895, "Deposition of Minister Alexander Moore," 20 June 1892.

13 The following four paragraphs are based on information drawn from the husband's deposition; see PROV 30-PO-895, "Deposition of George Adams," 20 June 1892.

14 Lisa Featherstone, "The Value of an Infant: The Rise of Paediatrics in Australia, 1880–1910," *Health and History* 10, no. 1 (2008): 110–33; Lynette Finch, "Caring for Colonial Infants: Parenting on the Frontiers," *Australian Historical Studies* 29, no. 110 (1998): 112.

15 Reg. v. Adams, *Victoria Law Reports* 18 (1892): 566–68, https://www.austlii.edu.au/cgi-bin/viewdoc/au/cases/vic/VicLawRp/1892/104.html, accessed 13 November 2023.

16 Ibid.

17 Her daughter having been born before marriage may explain why Amelia may have returned to her paternal home after the birth rather than to George. Frank Bongiorno explains how rates of premarital pregnancy rose at the end of the nineteenth century, prompting guardians of public virtue to comment negatively on girls ready to surrender their virginity and men willing to "debauch" a woman before marriage. Bongiorno, *The Sex Lives of Australians* (Collingwood: Black, Inc., 2015), 155–56.

18 PROV 516-P0002, vol. 11, no. 6117, 197.

19 "A Woman Arrested for Bigamy," *Geelong Advertiser*, 13 June 1892, 3; "Charge of Bigamy," *Argus*, 13 June 1892, 6. *Mount Alexander Mail*, 15 June 1892, 2.

20 "Peculiar Bigamy Case," *Age*, 21 June 1892, 6.

21 "Peculiar Case of Bigamy," *Sydney Daily Telegraph*, 21 June 1892, 5. The same text appeared in three Adelaide newspapers: *Advertiser*, the *Express and Telegraph*, and *South Australian Chronicle*, 21 June 1892, 5 and 3; and 25 June 1892, 2.

22 "A Case of Bigamy," *Age*, 13 June 1892, 2; "A Charge of Bigamy," *Express and Telegraph*, 14 June 1892, 3.

23 *Ballarat Star*, 2 August 1892, 3.

24 "A Woman Tried for Bigamy," *Geelong Advertiser*, 1 August 1892, 4.

25 *Geelong Advertiser*, 2 August 1892, 3.

26 By 1890 the *Age* was selling 100,000 copies a day, making it one of the world's most successful newspapers.

27 "Peculiar Bigamy Case," *Age*, 21 June 1892, 6.

28 "Alleged Bigamy," *Argus*, 21 June 1892, 3.

29 Ibid.

30 VRBDM 1893-5606, 1894-31622, and 1896-13511.

31 PROV, VPRS 283-P0-154, "Charles Chalmer's affidavit," 9 August 1905.

32 Ibid.

33 Ibid.

34 Ibid.

35 VRBDM 1875-2113.

36 "Family Notices," *The Ballarat Star*, 4 February 1882, 2.

37 VRBDM 1883-6445.

38 VRBDM 1893-2148.

39 "Family Notices," *Bendigo Advertiser*, 24 September 1894, 2.

40 "Family Notice," *The Australasian*, 5 May 1906, 60. VRBDM, 1906-4459.

41 PROV 30-PO-1410.

42 PROV 30-PO-1410, "Deposition of Richard Henry Hammersley," 15 February 1906. The information in the following three paragraphs is also drawn from this deposition.

43 Kirsten McKenzie, *Scandal in the Colonies: Sydney and Capetown 1820–1850* (Melbourne: Melbourne University Press, 2004), 7.

44 "Divorce Court," *The Age*, 9 November 1905, 6.

45 Sharon Crozier-De Roza, "Identifying with the Frontier: Federation New Woman, Nation and Empire," in *Changing the Victorian Subject*, ed. Maggie Tonkin, Mandy Treagus, Madeleine Seys, and Sharon Crozier-De Rosa (Adelaide: University of Adelaide Press, 2014), 45.

46 "Erring Spouses," *Observer*, 18 November 1905, 48.

47 "Intercolonial News," *Barrier Miner*, 10 November 1905; "Chalmers v. Chalmers," *Bendigo Independent*, 10 November 1905, 3; "Divorce Court," *Argus*, 10 November 1905, 8; "Erring Spouses," *Observer*, 18 November 1905, 48; "Erring Spouses," *Evening Journal*, 10 November 1905, 2; "Erring Spouses," *Register*, 10 November 1905, 5; "Victoria," *Newcastle Morning Herald and Miners' Advocate*, 10 November 1905, 5; *Maitland Daily Mercury*, 10 November 1905, 2; "A Much Married Man," *Singleton Argus*, 11 November 1905, 5; *Clarence and Richmond Examiner*, 18 November 1905, 2; "Victoria," *Maitland Weekly Mercury*, 18 November 1905, 10.

48 "Erring Spouses," *Register*, 10 November 1905; and *Observer*, 18 November 1905. There is a very similar account in "Divorce Court," *Argus*, 10 November 1905.

49 "Chalmers vs Chalmers," *Bendigo Independent*, 10 November 1905, 3.

50 *Border Watch*, 15 November 1905, 3.

51 Mélanie Méthot, "Female Bigamists: Their Particular Position in the Canadian Courts and Media," *Women's History* 28, no. 4 (2019): 532–51.

52 "Young Woman Charged with Bigamy," *Express and Telegraph*; and "Alleged Bigamy," *Zeehan and Dundas Herald*, 14 December 1905, 3. Sellwood (2016) discusses the phenomenon, as does Victoria Bates for the Victorian era. See Victoria Bates, "Under Cross-Examination She Fainted: Sexual Crime and Swooning in the Victorian Courtroom," *Journal of Victorian Culture* 21, no. 4 (2016): 456–70.

53 "Melbourne," *Bendigo Independent*, 14 December 1905, 4. In "Alleged Bigamy," the *Ballarat Star* included nearly the exact same information, omitting only the fainting part, 14 December, 1905, 4. In "Police Court Episode," the *Australian Star* only mentions her youth and that she "fell unconscious to the floor" and "remained unconscious for half an hour," 14 December 1905, 7.

54 "Bigamist Charged. A Remarkable Case," *Mount Alexander Mail Star*, 6 December 1905, 2; *Maryborough Chronicle Wide Bay and Burnett Advertiser*, 12 December 12 1905; "Barmaid Bigamist," *Morning Post*, 12 January 1906, 4; "Young Woman Charged with Bigamy. Becomes a Barmaid," *Express and Telegraph*, 6 December 1905, 4; "A Much-Married Woman," *Kalgoorlie Miner*, 7 December 1905, 2; "Bigamy Charged. Young Woman Remanded," *Geelong Advertiser*, 6 December 1905, 4; "A Remarkable Bigamy Case," *Daily Telegraph*, 6 December 1905, 5.

55 "Alleged Bigamy," *Ballarat Star*, 7 December 1905, 6.

56 "A Charge of Bigamy," *Ballarat Star*, 6 December 1905, 6.

57 "Alleged Bigamy," *Argus*, 5 December 1905, 6; "Charge of Bigamy: A Woman Arrested," *Bendigo Advertiser*, 5 December 1905, 3. (The journalist reported she was 35 years old.)

58 Catherine Bishop, "Women on the Move: Gender, Money-Making, and Mobility in Mid-Nineteenth-Century Australasia," *History Australia* 11, no. 2 (2014): 48.

59 "Victoria," *Barrier Miner*, 6 December 1905, 1.

60 As I have shown elsewhere, the Canadian courts and press had the same attitude towards women who committed bigamy. See Méthot, "Bigamy in the Northern Alberta Judicial District."

61 Newspapers reported in October and November 1894 about Green's possible involvement with a jail scandal. "Alleged Conspiracy," *Gippsland Times*, 25 October 1894, 3; *Gippsland Farmers' Journal*, 26 October 1894, 2; *Advocate*, 27 October 1894, 7; "A Gaol Scandal," *Herald*, 1 and 2 November 1894, 4 and 5. Green was apparently dismissed. *Gippsland Farmers' Journal*, 6 November 1894, 2.

## CHAPTER 12

1 The author expresses her thanks to Liverpool University Press, which has granted permission to reprint material from *Mixed Marriage: Class, Religion, Race, and Nation in England, 1837–1939* (2024).

2 J.C. Bird, *Control of Enemy Alien Civilians in Great Britain, 1914–1918* (New York: Garland, 1986), 174; Panikos Panayi, *The Enemy in Our Midst: Germans in Britain During the First World War* (Oxford: Berg, 1991), 10–13, 80; Laura Tabili, *Global Migrants, Local Culture: Natives and Newcomers in Provincial England, 1840–1939* (Basingstoke: Palgrave Macmillan, 2011), 52–53.

3 Helen Irving, *Citizenship, Alienage, and the Modern Constitutional State: A Gendered History* (Cambridge: Cambridge University Press, 2016), 41–47, 82–84.

4 M. Page Baldwin, "Subject to Empire: Married Women and the British Nationality and Status of Aliens Act," *Journal of British Studies* 40, no. 4 (October 2001): 522–66; Irving, *Citizenship,* 109; 125–30.

5 Irving, *Citizenship*, 256–57.

6 Wendy Webster, *Mixing It: Diversity in World War II Britain* (Oxford: Oxford University Press, 2018), 197–222.

7 Brian K. Feltman, "'We Don't Want Any German Off-Spring After These Prisoners Left Here': German Military Prisoners and British Women in the First World War," *Gender & History* 30, no. 1 (January 2018): 110–30.

8 Baldwin, "Subject to Empire," 522–56; Irving, *Citizenship*, 109; 125–30.

9 Panayi, *Enemy in Our Midst*, 80; David Cesarani, "An Alien Concept? The Continuity of Anti-Alienism in British Society before 1940," *Immigrants and Minorities* 11, no. 3 (November 1992): 34–37.

10 Irving, *Citizenship*, 137–38; Laura Tabili, "Outsiders in the Land of their Birth: Exogamy, Citizenship, and Identity in War and Peace," *Journal of British Studies* 44, no. 4 (October 2005): 796–815.

11 London Metropolitan Archives (LMA), Stepney Board of Guardians (hereafter STBG), STBG/L/98/26, Letterbook, 1915, 31 March 1915, 4; STBG/L/81/2, Minute Book, 1914–15, 15 April 1915, 701; STBG/L/98/26, Letterbook, 1915, 5 June 1915, 280; STBG/L/100/9, Correspondence with Local Government Board, 1915–17, 30 September 1915. Anti-alienism in Stepney predated the war; see *Times*, 12 January 1911, 8.

12 STBG/L/100/9, Correspondence with the LGB, 1915–17, 1 March 1916.

13 STBG/L/98/26, Letterbook, Stepney Union, 1915, f. 661, 7 August 1915, Stepney Union to LGB.

14 STBG/L/98/26, Letterbook, Stepney Union, 1915, f. 813, 14 September 1915, Stepney Union to LGB.

15 The National Archives (TNA), Foreign Office Records (FO) 383/462, Circular from the LGB, 9 December 1915.

16 Liverpool Public Library, West Derby Union Records, 353 WES/1/48, 191-17, Roll 726, f. 445, 4 July 1917.

17 TNA, FO 383/310, 1917–18, 24 May 1918, Maude Schubert to Swiss Legation.

18 TNA, FO 383/310, 1917–18, 21 June 1918, Local Government Board to Prisoners of War Department.

19 TNA, FO 383/310, 1917–18, 6 June 1918, M. Muller to Swiss Legation; see also 23 July 1918, Relieving Officer report. His reason for recommending against the increase was "there is plenty of work of various kinds to be had."

20 TNA, FO 383/310, 1917–18, 24 June 1918, Mrs. H.L. Schoeneweiss to Swiss Legation.

21 TNA, FO 383/310, 1917–18, 22 August 1918, LGB to FO.

22 TNA, FO 383/310, 1917–18, 3 July 1918, Prisoners of War Department to Home Office.

23 STBG/L/100/9, LGB Correspondence, 1916–17, 3 February 1917, Mrs. Jeanette Hauter to HO, forwarded to Stepney Union, 19 February 1917.

24 Liverpool Public Library, Toxteth Union Records, 353 TOX/1/10 Minute Books, Toxteth Union, 1915–17, 6 January 1916, f. 206.

25 *Times*, 5 March 1919, 5; 3 April 1919, 9.

26 *Times*, 24 October 1914, 3.

27 Tabili, "Outsiders," 796–815; Nicoletta Gullace, "Friends, Aliens and Enemies: Fictive Communities and the Lusitania Riots of 1915," *Journal of Social History* 39, no. 2 (Winter 2005): 345–67.

28 *Liverpool Daily Post*, 12 May 1915, 5; see also 10 May 1915, 7; 1 May 1915, 3; 13 May 1915, 3, 5; 14 May 1915, 10; 15 May 1915, 8.

29 TNA, FO 383/317, 4 September 1917, L. van Rappard to Mr. Aveling.

30 TNA, FO 383/317, 3 October 1917, Foreign Office to Local Government Board.

31 TNA, FO 383/317, 12 January 1917.

32 TNA, FO 383/317, Memorandum, 29 June 1917.

33 TNA, FO 383/37, 1915–17, 2 February 1915, Edward Lowry to Mr. Acland; 10 February 1915, Foreign Office to Lowry; 13 May 1915, Alworth Vox to Foreign Office; 21 May 1915, Foreign Office to Vox.

34 TNA, FO 383/3, 2 July 1915, Vice-Consul, Vienna, to Consul, Milan; 15 July 1915, FO to Consul.

35 TNA, FO 383/3, 22 June 1915, Alfred Halstead, Consul General to U.S. Ambassador; 13 July 1915, FO to U.S. Embassy; 27 October 1915, Report on John Forrester; 5 November 1915, FO to U.S. Ambassador; 11 November 1915, British Consul, Odessa, to FO.

36 TNA, FO 383/3, 30 August 1915, Vienna Consul to U.S. Ambassador, including copy of a letter from Austria, dated 26 August 1915; 28 September 1915, FO to American Embassy.

37 TNA, FO 383/17, 9 February 1915, British Consul, Bordeaux to Paris Consul.

38 TNA, FO 383/17; 13 February 1915, HO to Brighton Police; 5 April 1915, French reply; 7 April 1915, HO to Bordeaux Consul; FO 383/143, 18 January 1918, Reiser to Francis Bertie, FO.

39 TNA, FO 383/477, November 1918–March 1919, 27 November 1918, Spanish Embassy to FO; 3 January 1919, Rebecca O'Dea to Prisoners of War Department; 30 January 1919, Rebecca O'Dea to PWD; 2 December 1918, Spanish Embassy to FO; 8 February 1919, Home Office to Spanish Embassy; 27 January 1919, Thomas Andrews to FO; 10 March 1919, FO to Spanish Embassy.

40 *Times*, 12 November 1921, 4.

41 Panikos Panayi, *Prisoners of Britain: German Civilian and Combatant Internees During the First World War* (Manchester: Manchester University Press, 2012), 278–79. See also Panayi, "An Intolerant Act by an Intolerant Society: The Internment of Germans in Britain During the First World War," in *The Internment of Aliens in Twentieth Century Britain*, ed. David Cesarani and Tony Kushner (London: Frank Cass, 1993), 53–75.

42 Bird, *Control of Enemy Aliens*, 169–99; *Times*, 14 September 1918, 3.

43 TNA, Treasury Office Records, T1/12567/21247 British-Born Wives of Germans, 1919–20; Home Office to Treasury, 24 January 1920; TNA, FO 383/411, Repatriation of German Wives and Families, 1918, 11 October 1918, War Office to Dr. Markel, London.

44 TNA, Home Office Records (HO), T1/12567/21247, 27 January 1920, A.D. Lowry to Millar.

45 TNA, Ministry of Health Papers, MH 57/203, 28 November 1919; HO, T1/12567/21247, 27 January 1920, Lowry to Millar.

46 Cesarani, "An Alien Concept," 38–39.

47 TNA, HO 45/19966, Aliens Interdepartmental Committee Minutes, 1919, vol. 1; quote from Memo #25, presented at 29 March 1919 meeting; for a typical discussion of the Russian families, see 28 November 1919 Minutes.

48 TNA, FO 372/367, Subcommittee Meeting of the Home Office, 14 January 1927, f. 5.

49 TNA, FO 372/367, Home Office Subcommittee Meeting Minutes, 18 February 1927, f. 27.

50 TNA, FO 372/367, Home Office Subcommittee Meeting, 14 January 1927, f. 16.

51 TNA, FO 372/367, Home Office Subcommittee Meeting Minutes, 13 May 1927, f. 56.

52 TNA, FO 372/367, Subcommittee Meeting of the Home Office, 14 January 1927, f. 13.

53 TNA, FO 372/367, Subcommittee Meeting of the Home Office, 7 July 1927, f. 74.

54 TNA, HO 45/9282/1749E, Naturalization Act, 1870–72; Irving, *Citizenship*, 78–79.

55 *Times*, 10 November 1921, 4; 25 November 1921, 4; 27 July 1922, 5; *Solicitors' Journal and Weekly Reporter* 66 (12 August 1922): 704–05; "The Operation of the Treaty Charge," *Solicitors' Journal and Weekly Reporter* (20 January 1923): 243–44; for her naturalization, see HO 334/106/15483.

56 London School of Economics (LSE), Chrystal Macmillan Papers, 5NMW/B/01, Box 1, Correspondence, 1921–33, 15 March 1923, M. Koenig to C. MacMillan; 10 October 1923, M. Koenig to C. MacMillan.

57 LSE, Helena Normanton Papers, 7HLN/C/03, "The Birthright of Nationality," *Good Housekeeping* (July 1928), cutting, 143.

58 TNA, FO 372/367, Home Office Subcommittee Meeting Minutes, 7 July 1927, f. 79. No divorce under this name occurred between 1919 and 1940.

59 TNA, Divorce Petitions, J77/1444/4485, 1919–20; *Times*, 1 July 1919, 4; 8 July 1919, 4.

60 Irving, *Citizenship, Alienage, and the Modern Constitutional State*.

61 *Solicitors' Journal and Reporter* 732 (1917).

62 *Justice of the Peace*, 95 (1931), 266.

## CHAPTER 13

1 I would like to acknowledge the Faculty Development Fund of St. Mary's College of Maryland for their support of this project. Also, thanks to my colleague Jeff Eden who provided valuable advice and assistance in the preparation of this essay. The phrase "Moscow Widowers" is borrowed from The National Archives (TNA), Foreign Office (FO) 369/3299, "Repatriation to the United

Kingdom of Mrs. Lucille York," Joseph York to R.L. Paget, MP, 5 August 1945. York so described the group of men waiting to be reunited with their Soviet-born wives.

2 Elfrieda Berthiaume Shukert and Barbara Smith Scibetta, *War Brides of World War II* (Novato, CA: Presidio Press, 1988); Jenel Virden, *Good-bye, Piccadilly: British War Brides in America* (Urbana and Chicago: University of Illinois Press, 1996).

3 C.P. Stacey and Barbara M. Wilson, *The Half-Million: The Canadians in Britain, 1939–1946* (Toronto: University of Toronto Press, 1987), 138–40.

4 David Reynolds, *Rich Relations: The American Occupation of Britain 1942–1945* (London: Phoenix Press, 1996), 421–22.

5 Marilyn Lake, "The Desire for a Yank: Sexual Relations between Australian Women and American Servicemen during World War II," *Journal of the History of Sexuality* 2, no. 4 (April 1992): 624–25.

6 For instance, see an account of British servicemen in Austria marrying Austrian women: Lukas Schretter, "Making Friends, Making Families: Post-World War II Marriages between Austrian Women and British Soldiers, 1945–1955," *Geneaology* 6 (2022): 74.

7 For the American case, see Philip E. Wolgin and Irene Bloemraad, "'Our Gratitude to Our Soldiers': Military Spouses, Family Re-Unification, and Postwar Immigration Reform," *Journal of Interdisciplinary History* 41, no. 1 (Summer 2010): 27–60.

8 George Ginsburg, *The Citizenship Law of the USSR* (The Hague, Boston, and Lancaster: Martinus Nijhoff Publishers, 1983), 52–60.

9 For a detailed account of the diplomatic issues at stake concerning Allied POWs under Soviet control, see Arieh J. Kochavi, *Confronting Captivity: Britain and the United States and their POWs in Nazi Germany* (Chapel Hill: University of North Carolina Press, 2005), 225–79. Frank Costigliola estimates that 7,000 British and American POWs came under Soviet control at the end of the war, "'Like Animals or Worse': Narratives of Culture and Emotion by U.S. and British POWs and Airmen behind Soviet Lines, 1944–1945," *Diplomatic History* 28, no. 5 (November 2004): 750. For a detailed near-contemporary description of the situation from an American point of view, see John R. Deane, *The Strange Alliance: The Story of Our Efforts at Wartime Co-operation with Russia* (New York: Viking Press, 1947), 182–201.

10 TNA, FO 369/3297. See the list of cases and explanation provided by T. Sharman of the Moscow Embassy to the Foreign Office, 5 June 1945.

11 TNA, FO 369/3702, "Case of Mr. Elwell," communication from Moscow to FO, 26 January 1946.

12 TNA, FO 369/3296; FO 369/3301, T. Sharman to Foreign Office, 22 November 1945.

13 TNA, FO 369/3301, Elwell to Foreign Office, 31 December 1945.

14 TNA, FO 369/3301, "Case of Mr. H. Elwell," note on cover, illegible initials, 4 January 1946.

15 TNA, FO 369/3702, "Soviet Wives: Maria Andrukhova (Mrs. Maggs)," Maggs to FO, n.d.; Embassy to Andrukhova, 20 February 1946.

16 TNA, Dominions Office (DO) 35/1160, "Soviet born wives of British and Commonwealth POWs," clipping, *Daily Mail*, 25 February 1946; "Girl from Russia Doesn't Know She is Unwanted: Ex-P.O.W. Denies Marriage," *The Courier and Advertiser*, 23 February 1946, 3.

17 TNA, FO 369/3703 South Africa House to Dominions Office, 6 April 1946.

18 TNA, DO 35/1160, "Soviet born wives of British and Commonwealth POWs," Telegram Moscow to Foreign Office.

19 TNA, FO 369/3703, Moscow to Foreign Office, 23 April 1946.

20 "The Blond Ballerina Arrives," *Dundee Courier*, 25 February 1946, 3.

21 TNA, FO 369/3704, Warsaw to Foreign Office, 28 May 1946; Foreign Office to Dominions Office, 13 August 1946.

22 TNA, FO 369/3703, "Mrs. Way (and other Soviet wives of British subjects)," draft memorandum, 23 April 1946.

23 TNA, FO 369/3301, "Repatriation of Private Cummins's wife," letter from Cummins, 26 November 1945.

24 TNA, FO 369/3299, Lt. Col. V.M. Hammer to G.C. Allchin, 9 May 1945.

25 TNA, FO 369/3299, Cummins, 26 September 1945.

26 TNA, FO 369/3299, Cipher telegram to War Office, 5 September 1945.

27 TNA, FO 369/3299, Cummins, 6 October 1945.

28 TNA, FO 369/3299, Cummins, 17 October 1945.

29 TNA, FO 369/3300, Cummins, 24 October 1945.

30 TNA, FO 369/3301, Communication from Consulate General Naples, 8 November 1945; FO 369/3299, Telegram, 12 November 1945.

31 For an analysis of the Soviet attitude towards such marriages, see Liudmila Novikova, "Criminalized Liaisons: Soviet Women and Allied Sailors in Wartime Arkhangel'sk," *Journal of Contemporary History* 55, no. 4 (2020): 745–63.

32 TNA, FO 369/2903, 1 October 1943; 8 October 1943, 27 November 1943.

33 TNA, FO 369/2903, German to Winston Churchill, 18 August 1943. German did not remember the anecdote about Willkie accurately. In 1942, at the request of President Roosevelt, Wendell Willkie embarked on a world tour of allies that included the Soviet Union; see Samuel Zipp, *The Idealist: Wendell Willkie's Wartime Quest to Build One World* (Cambridge, MA: Belknap Press, 2020). Later in 1943, American journalist Eddy Gilmore, who was in love with a Russian woman, asked Willkie to intervene when Soviet authorities ordered her out of Moscow. Willkie's direct appeal to Stalin led to the couple being permitted to reunite and marry in Moscow, but the woman was not allowed to leave the Soviet Union until much later. Eddy Gilmore, *Me and My Russian Wife* (London: W. Foulsham & Co. LTD., 1954), 112–13. For contemporary coverage of this episode see: "Love Conquers," *New York Times*, 15 July 1943, 20.

34 TNA, FO 369/2903, German to Foreign Office, 13 October 1943.

35 TNA, FO 369/3025, "Description of living conditions in Russia of wife of a British soldier," 1 June 1944; Foreign Office to Moscow, 16 June 1944.

36 TNA, FO 369/3025, "Release from Soviet citizenship," Moscow Embassy to Foreign Office, 30 July 1944.

37 TNA, FO 369/3702, "Case of alleged marriage between Driver German and Miss L. Trifanova," 12 March 1946.

38 TNA, FO 369/3704, "Driver German and Miss Trifanova," German to Foreign Office, 18 June 1946; note by Graham, 24 June 1946.

39 TNA, FO 369/3705, "Driver German and Miss Tiranova."

40 TNA, FO 369/3025, T.P. Clarke to Sir Alexander Cadogan, 3 February 1944 and 16 August 1944; FO 369/3296, T.P. Clark to Sir Alexander Cadogan, 13 May 1945.

41 TNA, FO 369/3296, Mrs. Clark to Winston Churchill, 13 March 1945; FO 369/3297, T.G.M. Clarke (father) to Winston Churchill, 30 May 1945; FO 369/3298, Mrs. Clark (mother) to King George, 13 June 1945.

42 TNA, FO 369/3300, "Proposed repatriation of Mrs. Clarke," Sharman to Allchin, 18 September 1945.

43 TNA, FO 369/3300, "Proposed repatriation of Mrs. Clarke," note on cover, 28 September 1945.

44 Ronald Kowalski and Dilwyn Porter, "Political Football: Moscow Dynamo in Britain, 1945," *International Journal of the History of Sport* 14, no. 2 (August 1997): 100–21. See also Peter Beck, "Britain and the Cold War's 'Cultural Olympics': Responding to the Political Drive of Soviet Sport," *Contemporary British History* 19, no. 2 (2005): 169–85, which places the Dynamo tour in the context of the developing cold war.

45 TNA, FO 369/3703, "Soviet Wives," sub file "Case of Mrs. Liddell," copy of letter Mr. F.K. Roberts, Moscow Embassy, to M. Vyshinsky, 7 March 1946.

46 As we have seen above, American journalist Eddy Gilmore also married a Russian woman after the intervention of Wendell Willkie, although it took years for American authorities to get permission for the couple to leave the Soviet Union. See Gilmore, *Me and My Russian Wife*. British journalist Paul Winterton, who also worked in Moscow during the war, later wrote a novel based on the Gilmore romance under the name of Peter Bax. *Came the Dawn* (1949), also published under the title *Two If By Sea*, was the basis for the 1953 film "Never Let Me Go," starring Clark Gable and Gene Tierney. The heroine of both the novel and the film was portrayed as a ballerina.

47 See Tanya Matthews, *Journey between Freedoms* (Philadelphia: Westminster Press, 1951), 270–78, for her version of these events.

48 TNA, FO 369/3025, Moscow to Foreign Office, 29 January 1944.

49 TNA, FO 369/3025, Cairo to Foreign Office, 5 July 1944; Foreign Office to Ronald Matthews, 20 July 1944.

50 TNA, FO 369/3025, Matthews to Under Secretary of State Foreign Office, 5 October 1944.

51 TNA DO 35/1160, Moscow to Foreign Office, 21 August 1945; Paris to Foreign Office, 27 August 1945.

52 Donald Gillies, *Radical Diplomat: The Life of Archibald Clark Kerr, Lord Inverchapel, 1882–1951* (London: I.B. Tauris, 1999).

53 TNA, FO 369/3025, Archibald Clark Kerr to Vyshinsky, 23 April 1944, 11 May 1944; Vyshinsky to Clark Kerr, 18 May 1944; Clark Kerr to Vyshinsky, 23 May 1944; Vyshinsky to Clark Kerr, 31 May 1944; Clark Kerr to Vyshinsky,

3 June 1944. Arkady Vaksberg, *Stalin's Prosecutor: The Life of Andrei Vyshinsky* (New York: Grove Weidenfeld, 1990).

54 TNA, FO 369/3025 Archibald Clark Kerr to Vyshinsky, 3 June 1944.

55 TNA, FO 369/3300, "Repatriation of Mrs. York," York, 9 October 1945.

56 TNA, FO 369/3702, Dekanozov to Clark Kerr, 23 January 1946. Passports were approved for Mrs. Inkpin, Mrs. Parr, and Mrs. Holland. Vyshinsky approved passports for Mrs. Brand, Mrs. Bunn, Mrs. Clarke, and Mrs. Edwardes in October 1945. FO 369/3301, "Grant of Soviet foreign passports." The first round of releases was during September 1945, when passports were approved for Mrs. Elvin, Mrs. Johnson, Mrs. Lamb, Mrs. Liddell, Mrs. Smith, Mrs. York, Mrs. Okulaitch (Canadian), and Mrs. Seaborne. FO 369/3300, Clark Kerr to Foreign Office, 1 September 1945.

57 Maurice Peterson, *Both Sides of the Curtain: An Autobiography* (London: Constable, 1950).

58 TNA, FO 447/72. "General Discussion of Soviet wives," Peterson memorandum of meeting with Vyshinsky, 20 April 1948.

59 TNA, FO 369/3296, "Russian Wives in the U.S.S.R. of British subjects," historical memorandum, 24 January 1945.

60 TNA, FO 369/3296, Telegram Moscow to Foreign Office, 24 May 1945.

61 TNA, FO 369/3298, "Soviet Wives of British subjects," letter Roberts to Vyshinsky, 25 May 1945; FO 181/1082, Roberts telegram Moscow to FO, 13 June 1945.

62 TNA, FO 369/3298, "Soviet wives of British subjects," Clark Kerr cyphers to FO, 13 June 1945 and 9 July 1945.

63 TNA, FO 369/3701, "Soviet Wives of BSS," Thomas Brimelow memorandum, 11 November 1945.

64 TNA, FO 447/72, Peterson memorandum, 20 April 1948.

65 TNA, FO 369/3297, "Release of Soviet wives of British subjects from Soviet Citizenship," Clark Kerr telegram, 8 June 1945; FO 369/3298, "Soviet wives of British Subjects," Halifax note to US State Department, 4 July 1945.

66 TNA, FO 369/3025 "Memorandum of conversation on May 25th, 1944." A copy of this memorandum is also printed in *Foreign Relations of the United States* [FRUS]: Diplomatic Papers, 1944, Europe, Volume IV, Document 802. The issue of marriages between American citizens and Soviet citizens continued to aggravate American-Soviet relations throughout the Cold War. See Rósa Magnúsdóttir, "Divided Spouses: Soviet-American Intermarriage and Human Rights Activism during the Cold War," in *Intermarriage from Central Europe to Central Asia: Mixed Families in the Age of Extremes*, ed. Adrienne Edgar and Benjamin Frommer (Lincoln: University of Nebraska Press, 2020), 309–32. Soviet ambivalence and hostility towards mixed marriages was not limited to those involving men of Western nations; it also extended to marriages between Russians and citizens of other Communist countries. See Benjamin Tromly, "Brother or Other? East European Students in Soviet Higher Education Establishments, 1948–1956," *European History Quarterly* vol. 44, no. 1 (2014): 80–102, for marriages between Eastern Europeans and Russians; and Elizabeth McGuire, *Red at Heart: How Chinese Communists Fell in Love with*

*the Russian Revolution* (Oxford: Oxford University Press, 2018) for marriages between Chinese and Russians.

67 TNA, FO 369/2903, Cipher FO to Moscow, 4 August 1943.

68 TNA, FO 369/3299, Sharman to Allchin, 25 August 1945.

69 TNA, FO 369/3299, Clarke to Alderman Louis Tolley, MP, 9 August 1945.

70 George Barrett, "Assembly to sift Soviet Wives' Case: Refusal to let them leave Russia with Alien Husbands up in U. N. Tomorrow," *New York Times*, 24 April 1949, 25.

71 Recently, diplomatic history has expanded its reach to include the emotional life. See Frank Costigliola, *Roosevelt's Lost Alliances: How Personal Politics Helped Start the Cold War* (Princeton: Princeton University Press, 2012).

## PART FIVE

1 Jane Nicholas, "Suffering for Compassion: Everyday Violence and Infanticide in Ontario, 1820–1920s," Chapter 14 in this volume, 290.

2 Ibid., quotations at pp. 276 and 291.

3 Emilee Lord and John Wertheimer, "Violence against Women, the Law, and Public Opinion in Guatemala," Chapter 16 in this volume, 311.

## CHAPTER 14

1 Walter Benjamin, "Theses on the Philosophy of History," in *Illuminations: Essays and Reflections*, ed. Hannah Arendt (New York: Harcourt Brace Jovanovich Inc., 1968), 257.

2 *King v. Annie Robinson*, Criminal Assizes, Sudbury, Ontario, Fall 1909, Library and Archives Canada (LAC), Record Group (RG) 13, vol. 1484 (1, 2, 3), file 417A/CC49; 1909–11 (case of Annie Robinson). Hereafter cited as Robinson capital case file.

3 Robinson capital case file.

4 Robinson capital case file.

5 On infanticide in Canadian history, see W. Peter Ward, "Unwed Motherhood in Nineteenth-Century English Canada," *Historical Papers* 161 (1981): 34–56; Constance Backhouse, "Desperate Women and Compassionate Courts: Infanticide in Nineteenth-Century Canada," *The University of Toronto Law Journal* 34, no. 4 (Autumn 1984): 447–78; Marie-Aimée Cliche, "L'infanticide dans la région de Québec, 1660–1969," *Revue d'histoire de l'Amérique française* 44, no. 1 (Summer 1990): 31–59; Constance Backhouse, *Petticoats and Prejudice: Women and Law in Nineteenth-Century Canada* (Toronto: The Women's Press, 1991), chapter 4; Andrée Levesque, "Mères célibataires et infanticides à Montréal, 1914–1930," in *Femmes et justice pénale, XIX$^{e}$–XX$^{e}$ siècle*, ed. Christine Bard, Frédéric Chauvaud, Michelle Perrot, and Jacques-Guy Petit (Rennes: Presses universitaires de Rennes, 2002); and Ian C. Pilarczyk, "'So Foul A Deed': Infanticide in Montreal, 1825–1850," *Law and History Review* 30, no. 2 (May 2012): 575–634.

6 The overwhelming majority of cases I have collected (over 300) do not explicitly mention race with the exception of a small handful of coroners' files that note race when it was a woman of colour. The invisibility of whiteness, despite its lack of biological or stable social foundation, is characteristic of Canadian history wherein whiteness is largely presumed and often left uninterrogated. In a small number of coroners' inquest files that address race, the women had fled justice. Women of colour would likely face a far less generous moral calculus in measuring their suffering. For an analysis involving an early criminal case of an Anishnaabe woman accused of infanticide from Upper Canada see Backhouse, *Petticoats and Prejudice*, 112–24.

7 My thinking has been influenced by work in anthropology on everyday violence and child death. See Nancy Scheper-Hughes, *Death Without Weeping: The Violence of Everyday Life in Brazil* (Berkeley: University of California Press, 1992), especially chapters 7 and 8; and Philippe Bourgois, "Families and Children in Pain in the U.S. Inner City," in *Small Wars: The Cultural Politics of Childhood*, ed. Nancy Scheper-Hughes and Carolyn Sargent (Berkeley: University of California Press, 1999), 331–51. The term "everyday violence" appears as the title in chapter 2 of Marie-Aimée Cliche's *Abuse or Punishment? Violence Toward Children in Quebec Families, 1850–1969*, trans. W. Donald Wilson (Waterloo, ON: Wilfrid Laurier University Press, 2014).

8 Backhouse, "Desperate Women and Compassionate Courts," and Backhouse, *Petticoats and Prejudice*, chapter 4.

9 Miriam Ticktin, *Casualties of Care: Immigration and the Politics of Humanitarianism in France* (Berkeley: University of California Press, 2011), 3–4, 12–13. In regard to the nascent field of the history of emotions, Ticktin's concept most closely aligns with Monique Scheer's practice theory, which understands emotions to be embodied and reflective of historically specific emotional regimes (along with attendant gestures) that provoke affective responses. See Scheer, "Are Emotions a Kind of Practice (and Is That What Makes Them Have a History)? A Bourdieuian Approach to Understanding Emotions," *History and Theory* 51, no. 2 (2012): 193–220.

10 Mick Taussig, "Terror As Usual: Walter Benjamin's Theory of History as a State of Siege," *Social Text* 23 (Autumn/Winter 1989): 3–20.

11 On the significance of anti-black racism in domestic violence trials, see Barrington Walker, "Killing the Black Female Body: Black Womanhood, Black Patriarchy, and Spousal Murder in Two Ontario Criminal Trials, 1892–1894," in *Sisters or Strangers? Immigrant, Ethnic, and Racialized Women in Canadian History*, ed. Marlene Epp and Franca Iacovetta (Toronto: University of Toronto Press, 2004), 89–107. For a telling story of racial injustice in a different and later case see Constance Backhouse, *Carnal Crimes: Sexual Assault Law in Canada* (Toronto: The Osgoode Society, 2008), chapter 8.

12 Elaine Scarry, *The Body in Pain: The Making and Unmaking of the World* (New York: Oxford University Press, 1985), 3–10. For recent work on Scarry, see Lina Minou and Tomas Macsotay, "Introduction," *Cultural History* 8, no. 1 (2019): 1–6. Scarry's reflection on the law was in regard to civil litigation, which often seeks to measure "pain and suffering" in search of financial remedy.

13 These issues are well-addressed in Franca Iacovetta and Wendy Mitchinson, *On the Case: Explorations in Social History* (Toronto: University of Toronto Press, 1998). For a related close reading of a capital case file involving child death see Peter Gossage, "*La marâtre*: Marie-Anne Houde and the Myth of the Wicked Stepmother in Quebec," *Canadian Historical Review* 76, no. 4 (December 1995): 563–97.

14 Backhouse, *Petticoats and Prejudice*; Backhouse, *Carnal Crimes*; Constance Backhouse, *Colour-Coded: A Legal History of Racism in Canada, 1900–1950* (Toronto: University of Toronto Press, 1999); and James Walker, *Race, Rights, and the Supreme Court of Canada* (Waterloo: Wilfrid Laurier Press, 1997).

15 Shelley A.M. Gavigan, "Improper Intimacies, Impossible Promises, and the Prerogatives of Patriarchy: Family and Justice in Nineteenth-Century Criminal Courts in Canada's North-West Territories," Chapter 9 in this volume, 186.

16 Backhouse, *Carnal Crimes*, 4. Gavigan discusses this issue as well and provides references to work taking other approaches to naming. See Gavigan, Chapter 9 in this volume, 186 and 384, n30.

17 Karen Dubinsky, *Improper Advances: Rape and Heterosexual Conflict in Ontario, 1880–1929* (Chicago: University of Chicago Press, 1993), 60–63.

18 Louise A. Jackson, *Child Sexual Abuse in Victorian England* (New York and London: Routledge, 2013), 12.

19 Backhouse and Mitchinson note the discrepancy between abortion and infanticide by highlighting the harshness with which abortion was treated in the same period. Backhouse asserts it was the implication of professional doctors as well as the tendency to presume that it was middle-class women, purportedly the mothers of the nation, who sought abortions. Mitchinson notes that infants were not especially significant beings. See Backhouse, "Involuntary Motherhood," 98–99, 109; and Wendy Mitchinson, *The Nature of Their Bodies: Women and Their Doctors in Victorian Canada* (Toronto: University of Toronto Press, 1991), 143–44. Abortion could be done privately, while infanticide required a full pregnancy and delivery. Nineteenth-century legislation made concealment of a pregnancy and not seeking medical attention crimes, further criminalizing keeping pregnancy a secret.

20 While laws prohibited rape and incest, scholars have convincingly demonstrated the high bar of proof and the pattern of disbelief of victims that hindered reporting and prosecution. For historical work in Canada on domestic violence against women and children and the difficulty in securing justice see, for example, Backhouse, *Petticoats and Prejudice*; Lori Chambers, *Married Women and Property Law in Victorian Ontario* (Toronto: University of Toronto Press, 1997); Karen Dubinsky and Franca Iacovetta, "Murder, Womanly Virtue, and Motherhood: The Case of Angelina Napolitano, 1911–1922," *Canadian Historical Review* 72, no. 4 (1991): 505–31; Dubinsky, *Improper Advances*; Annalee Lepp, "Dis/membering the Family: Marital Breakdown and Family Violence in Ontario, 1830–1920" (PhD diss., Queen's University, 1996); Neil Sutherland, *Children in English-Canadian Society: Framing the Twentieth-Century Consensus* (Waterloo, ON: Wilfrid Laurier University

Press, 2000), chapter 1; and Charlotte Neff, "Government Approaches to Child Neglect and Mistreatment in Nineteenth-Century Ontario," *Histoire sociale/Social History* 41, no. 81 (May 2008): 165–214.

21 Backhouse, *Petticoats and Prejudice*; Elizabeth Jane Errington, *Wives and Mothers, School Mistresses and Scullery Maids: Working Women in Upper Canada, 1790–1840* (Montreal and Kingston: McGill-Queen's University Press, 1995); and Chambers, *Married Women and Property Law*.

22 Lepp, "Dis/membering the Family."

23 Lorna R. McLean and Marilyn Barber, "In Search of Comfort and Independence: Irish Immigrant Domestic Servants Encounter the Courts, Jails, and Asylums in Nineteenth-Century Ontario," in Epp and Iacovetta, *Sisters or Strangers?*, 139. The capacity to discipline servants is mentioned in Errington, *Wives and Mothers, School Mistresses and Scullery Maids*, 120; and, on violence toward children, see Cliche, *Punishment or Abuse*.

24 On the "discovery" in global context see, Scheper-Hughes, *Death without Weeping*, 273–76.

25 George Emery, *Facts of Life: The Social Construction of Vital Statistics, Ontario 1869–1952* (Montreal and Kingston: McGill-Queen's University Press, 1993), chapter 2.

26 I use the term biological life following Agamben, Ticktin, and others who distinguish between the simple biological fact of life and life lived with access to the polis, rights, and dignity. Agamben argues that "homo sacer" can be subjected to violence and death with impunity. Giorgio Agamben, *Homo Sacer: Sovereign Power and Bare Life* (Stanford: Stanford University Press, 1998). See also Lucia Mantilla Gutierrez, "The Biopolitical Construction of Infancy and Adulthood: The Child as Paradigm and Utopia," *Global Studies of Childhood* 6, no. 2 (2016): 211–21.

27 Quoted in Cynthia Comacchio, *Nations Are Built of Babies: Saving Ontario's Mothers and Children, 1900–1940* (Montreal and Kingston: McGill-Queen's University Press, 1993), 16.

28 On eugenics, see Angus McLaren, *Our Own Master Race: Eugenics in Canada, 1885–1945* (Toronto: McClelland and Stewart, 1990). On threats to nation and family see, Jane Nicholas, *Canadian Carnival Freaks and the Extraordinary Body* (Toronto: University of Toronto Press, 2018). On the strain—emotional and economic—placed on families, see Veronica Strong-Boag, *Fostering Nation: Canada Confronts Its History of Childhood Disadvantage* (Waterloo, ON: Wilfrid Laurier University Press, 2011).

29 Mitchinson, *The Nature of Their Bodies*, especially chapters 1, 6, and 7. For a specific example regarding parsing of cause of death, see Archives of Ontario (AO), MS 7566, RG 22-5895, Unknown (female child-Catherine Dark), York, 1894.

30 This is evident in many of the case files where doctors cannot definitely prove the child lived or that it died an unnatural death. It is also evident in an interesting pattern that emerges from case files from York country in the 1890s. Increasingly, physicians seem wary of signing death certificates without a coroners' inquest, even in cases of sickness and disease, causing an uptick in inquests.

31 Myles Leslie, "Reforming the Coroner: Death Investigation Manuals in Ontario, 1863–1894," *Ontario History* 100, no. 2 (Autumn 2008): 237.

32 AO, RG 22-3888 Container B270622 file 1841, inquest into the death of the body of a female child, Newcastle, 1841.

33 AO, MS 7606, RG 22-5895, Unknown (Male Infant), York, 1896.

34 Backhouse, *Petticoats and Prejudice*, 113.

35 Mitchinson, *The Nature of Their Bodies*.

36 Backhouse, *Carnal Crimes*.

37 For mistresses' perspectives which reveal the problem, see Errington, *Wives and Mothers, School Mistresses and Scullery Maids*, 56. An example from the coroners' files is AO, RG 22-2995, Leeds and Grenville, CP/CA Inquests 1890–93, Box 6 Barcode B232447 File Unknown Infant (Female), 1890.

38 AO, MS 8477, RG 22-392-0-3617, Criminal Assize Clerk, Criminal Indictment Files, Middlesex County, 1858 Graham, Catherine, Killing Illegitimate Child.

39 AO RG 22-392-0-3195, Criminal Assize Clerk Criminal Indictment Files, Leeds & Grenville County, Strachan, Eleanor Infanticide, 1861.

40 AO, MS 8502, RG 22-392-0-5209, Criminal Assize Clerk Criminal Indictment Files, Peterborough, 1917.

41 AO, MS 8462, RG 22-392-0-2602, Criminal Assize Clerk Criminal Indictment Files, Huron, Neabel, Doris, 1923; AO, MS 8462 RG 22-392-0-2603, Criminal Assize Clerk Criminal Indictment Files, Huron, Neabel, Gladys, 1923.

42 Ibid.

43 Robinson capital case file.

44 Robinson capital case file. On temperance and social purity, see Mariana Valverde, *The Age of Light, Soap, and Water: Moral Reform in English Canada, 1885–1925* (Toronto: University of Toronto Press, 2008), 58–61. It was likely important that James was seen as a drinker in the petitions for clemency and release for Annie. Drunkenness was associated with abusive behaviour and first-wave maternal feminists saw the issue as central to securing women's public and private roles and security in Canadian society. Gail Cuthbert Brandt et al., *Canadian Women: A History*, 3rd edition (Toronto: Nelson, 2011), 122. The association of incest, abuse, poverty, and drunkenness is one of long standing; see Chapter 15 in this volume, where Fabienne Giuliani tracks its development in France over the course of the nineteenth century.

45 The child was a girl and never named in the case file. Her birth seems not to have been officially registered, unlike all of the other Robinson children.

46 Ellen's first child was born in 1906, lived, and became part of the household. Jessie and Ellen each gave birth in March 1908, and Ellen was pregnant again at the time of Annie's trial in 1909. Jessie testified that she had two children, although only one is accounted for in the trial. A third infant corpse was discovered and exhumed with the two that were the subject of Annie's charges but was barely discussed in the case file.

47 Robinson capital case file.

48 "Two Infants Murdered," *The Globe*, 11 August 1909, 5.

49 Robinson capital case file.

50 Robinson capital case file.

51 Robinson capital case file, letter from Peter Mathieson to A.B. Aylesworth, 24 November 1909.

52 Backhouse, *Carnal Crimes*, 15, 171; and Joan Sangster, *Regulating Girls and Women: Sexuality, Family, and the Law in Ontario, 1920–1960* (Don Mills, ON: Oxford University Press Canada, 2001), 28–29.

53 Backhouse, *Carnal Crimes*, 172.

54 Robinson capital case file.

55 Robinson capital case file, J.H. Clary letter to A.B. Aylesworth, 11 October 1909. James Robinson's criminal case file has eluded me so far, but newspapers reported on it. The trial was held in Sudbury in October 1909. *The Globe*, for example, reported that Robinson was charged with murder, rape, and incest, in addition to other charges. Annie was called to testify against him. While the jury deliberated, Robinson entered guilty pleas on the rape and incest charges in exchange for other charges (minus the murder charge) being withdrawn by the Crown. The jury found him not guilty of murder. Justice Magee sentenced him to twenty-eight years in jail for rape and incest. James Robinson died in the Kingston Penitentiary in 1925. See "Acquitted of Murder Change," *The Globe*, 30 October 1909; and Cameron Willis, Report on James Robinson from the Penitentiary Museum research service, prepared on 20 December 2019.

56 Sangster, *Regulating Girls and Women*, chapter 2; and Backhouse, *Carnal Crimes*.

57 Robinson capital case file.

58 On Jessie's earlier delivery, see Robinson capital case file, J.H. Clary letter to A.B. Aylesworth, 11 October 1909. By the time of her father's trial on 28 October 1909, Ellen had recently given birth. She testified from her hospital bed. This was her third child, and the only one born to either her or her sister that received professional medical attention. On Ellen's, see "James Robinson Stands his Trial," *The Globe*, 29 October 1909.

59 Robinson capital case file, letter from Mrs M.S. Savage to A.B. Aylesworth, 5 October 1909.

60 Robinson capital case file.

61 Robinson capital case file.

62 Robinson capital case file.

63 A significant number of infant bodies were found wrapped in some sort of cloth or paper, and typically for the former, a woman's apron. The aprons could be used to track down the women and represented a significant risk of discovery if the body was found and reported to authorities.

64 Robinson capital case file.

65 Robinson capital case file.

66 Robinson capital case file. Blaming mothers for not guarding daughters, or for not intervening, cast men's abuse as mothers' failure. See Sacco, *Unspeakable: Father-Daughter Incest in American History* (Baltimore: Johns Hopkins University Press, 2009), chapter 4.

67 On emotions as sticky, see Sara Ahmed, *The Cultural Politics of Emotion*, second edition (New York: Routledge, 2015), 14.

68 Robinson capital case file.

69 "Mrs. Robinson Sentenced—To be hanged for the murder of two grandchildren," *The Globe*, 25 September 1909.

70 Iacovetta and Dubinsky, "Murder, Womanly Virtue, and Motherhood"; Gossage, "*La marâtre*."

71 "The Capture of Jas. Robinson," *Ottawa Citizen*, 16 September 1909.

72 Robinson capital case file, letter from Helen MacMurchy to A.B. Aylesworth, 26 October 1909. Helen MacMurchy was a Canadian physician, public health reformer, and the first Chief of the Child Welfare Division of the federal Department of Health during the 1920s. She was also a prominent eugenicist who helped to establish the Canadian National Committee on Mental Hygiene, an organization that advocated for the sterilization of "feedble-minded" individuals.

73 Accurate statistics are nearly impossible to gather because of the prohibitions on disclosure and the lack of accurate recording and archiving. Legal cases from Ontario in regard to domestic abuse, incest, rape, and sexual assault provide a window on the commonness of such violence. See Lepp, "Dis/membering the Family"; and Sangster, *Regulating Girls and Women*. For a comparable study in the US which reveals the prevalence of father-daughter incest during the nineteenth century, see Sacco, *Unspeakable*, chapter 1. As other chapters in this volume reveal, violence was not limited to or unique to Ontario or this particular period. See especially the contributions to this volume by Mary Anne Poutanen (Chapter 8), Fabienne Guiliani (Chapter 15), and Emilee Lord and John Wertheimer (Chapter 16).

74 See below, Chapter 15.

CHAPTER 15

1 This chapter was translated from the original French by Steven Watt.

2 "[L]'arrestation d'un misérable, accusé d'avoir eu des rapports avec sa fille et de l'avoir livrée à la prostitution. Ce personnage odieux, dont la vie n'est qu'une longue suite d'ignominies s'appelle François Sardaigne. Il…se dit ouvrier tailleur: En réalité il a toujours vécu aux dépens de sa fille et de sa femme." *Le Petit Parisien*, 15 November 1885.

3 In 2008, during a professional soccer match between Paris Saint-Germain and RC Lens, Parisian fans taunted their Northern opponents with a banner that read, "Pédophiles, chômeurs, consanguins: Bienvenue chez les Ch'tis" (Pedophilia, Unemployment, and Inbreeding: Welcome to the Sticks).

4 Véronique Le Goaziou, "Les viols en justice: Une (in)justice de classe?," *Nouvelles questions féministes* 32, no. 1 (2013): 16–28.

5 Judith Herman and Lisa Hirschman, "Father-Daughter Incest," *Signs: Women in Culture and Society* 4, no. 3 (Summer 1977): 741.

6 Linda Gordon, "Incest and Resistance: Patterns of Father-Daughter Incest, 1880–1930," *Social Problems* 33, no. 4 (Spring 1986): 254.

7 Anne-Marie Sohn, "Les attentats à la pudeur sur les fillettes en France (1870–1939) et la sexualité quotidienne," in *Violences sexuelles*, ed. Alain Corbin (Paris: Imago, 1989), 71–111.

8 "[T]end à confirmer la problématique féministe qui considère l'inceste comme une manifestation extrême du système patriarcal." Marie-Aimée Cliche, "Survivre à l'inceste dans les maisons du Bon-Pasteur de Québec, 1930–1973," *Nouvelles pratiques sociales* 14, no. 2 (Winter 2001): 129.

9 "[I]ndissociable du genre, maillage plus large qui noue ensemble sexe, âge, sexualité, hiérarchies, rôles, etc." Agnès Fine, Christiane Klapisch-Zuber, and Didier Lett, "Liens et affects familiaux," *Clio: Femmes, Genre, Histoire* 34 (2011): 7.

10 Judith Butler, *The Psychic Life of Power: Theories in Subjection* (Stanford: Stanford University Press, 1997), 7–8.

11 John Tosh, "What Should Historians do with Masculinity? Reflections on Nineteenth-Century Britain," *History Workshop* 38 (1994): 184.

12 Robert L. Griswold, "Introduction to the Special Issue on Fatherhood," *Journal of Family History* 24, no. 3 (Summer 1999): 252.

13 "[G]amme de rôles, d'attentes et de responsabilités dynamique dans le temps, variable dans l'espace social ou géographique." Peter Gossage, "Visages de la paternité au Québec, 1900–1960," *Revue d'histoire de l'Amérique française* 70, nos. 1–2 (Summer/Fall 2016): 57. See also John Demos, "The Changing Faces of Fatherhood," in *Past, Present and Personal: The Family and the Life Course in American History* (New York: Oxford University Press, 1986), 41–67.

14 "[A]ppelant ainsi les populations à l'oubli de toute pudeur et à une rebutante promiscuité…éteindre à la fois le respect des mœurs et anéantir parmi les hommes tous les rapports de paternité et de filiation." Frédéric Portalis, introduction to *Discours, rapports et travaux inédits sur le Code civil* by Jean-Étienne-Marie Portalis (Paris: Joubert, 1844), xxv.

15 "[U]ne sorte de magistrature, à laquelle il importe, surtout dans les états libres, de donner une certaine étendue. Oui, on a besoin que les pères soient de vrais magistrats." J.-É.-M. Portalis, "Discours préliminaire sur le projet de Code civil, 1er pluviôse an IX," in *Discours sur le Code civil*, 24.

16 "[D]oit avoir son gouvernement. Le mari, le père en a toujours été réputé le chef. La puissance maritale, la puissance paternelle sont des institutions républicaines." J.-É.-M. Portalis, "Discours de présentation du Code civil prononcé le 3 frimaire an X," in *Discours sur le Code civil*, 105.

17 "[L]e père seul exerce cette autorité durant le mariage," *Code civil* (Paris: De l'imprimerie de la République, 1804), 92.

18 Linda Gordon and Paul O'Keefe, "Incest as a Form of Family Violence: Evidence from Historical Records," *Journal of Marriage and Family* 46, no. 1 (February 1984): 32.

19 Ulf Drugge, "Family Trauma Through Generations: Incest and Domestic Violence in Rural Sweden in the Nineteenth Century," *Journal of Family History* 33, no. 4 (Fall 2008): 412.

20 Gossage, "Visages de la paternité," 58.

21 Margaret Marsh, "Men and Masculine Domesticity, 1870–1915," *American Quarterly* 40, no. 2 (June 1988): 165–88.

22 John Tosh, "Masculinities in an Industrializing Society: Britain, 1800–1914," *Journal of British Studies* 44, no. 2 (April 2005): 342. Tosh is prominent among

the historians who have shown that the attributes of paternity are plural and constantly evolving over time, a theme which is taken up by several other contributors to this volume. In Chapter 5, for instance, Jean-Philippe Garneau analyzes the different ways of legalizing father's guardianship according to the social class and ethnicity of those involved. And in Chapter 10, Emma Chilton and James Moran study the nuances of male attributes in the context of civil cases treating their mental capacity.

23 "[L]a peine sera celle des travaux forcés à perpétuité, si les coupables sont de la classe de ceux qui ont autorité sur la personne envers laquelle ils ont commis l'attentat," *Code pénal* (Paris: P. Didot l'Aîné et F. Didot, 1810), 81.

24 Michel Bozon and Juliette Rennes, "Histoire des normes sexuelles: L'emprise de l'âge et du genre," *Clio: Femmes, Genre, Histoire* 42 (2015): 9.

25 "[D]epuis que les tribunaux s'occupent soigneusement à punir les grands coupables, jamais procédure n'avait eu plus de solennité, les juges même frémissaient d'horreur, et le peuple était effrayé à l'aspect d'un homme de cet âge, dont les cheveux commençaient à blanchir." Jugement de la Cour d'assises du département de la Meurthe séant à Nancy, qui condamne à la peine de mort, Claude JOUFFROT, âgé de 62 ans, et sa fille, MARGUERITE, âgée de 17 ans, pour crime de parricide, 1830, Factum fonds (8-FM-1532), Bibliothèque Nationale de France (BNF).

26 "[L]a voix publique m'informe que le 26 du mois dernier après midi le nommé Charles Colas journalier à Mauregard…a voulu se servir de sa malheureuse enfant pour satisfaire non pas à sa passion mais à sa rage en voulant l'habiter." Letter from the mayor of Les Essarts with information for the Court, 10 June 1813, Colas case, records of Assize Court proceedings (2U114), Archives départementales des Yvelines (ADY).

27 "[U]n bruit sourd…que Chevalier, marié depuis 11 ans et père de 6 enfants vivant, avait depuis plusieurs années un commerce incestueux avec sa fille aînée alors âgée de 7 à 8 ans et aurait cherché à la violer. La conduite de Chevalier étant devenu le sujet de la conversation de la commune, l'adjoint instruit par ces bruits fit comparaître devant lui la femme et la fille Chevalier." Indictment, 24 August 1813, Chevalier case, records of Assize Court proceedings (2U115), ADY.

28 "[I]l semble que toute le monde se donne la main comme de concert, pour la rendre plus grande, plus notoire et plus contagieuse." Jean-Prosper Chrestien de Poly, *Essai sur la puissance paternelle* (Paris: Adrien Egron, 1820), 1: 93.

29 "[U]n citoyen recommandable âgé de 44 ans et père tendre et bon de six enfants…ayant exercé avec honneur et probité des fonctions importantes de notaire à Meaux pendant près de 15 années, appelé pendant cet intervalle à une magistrature de juge suppléant…magistrature qu'il remplit avec zèle et dévouement tant à ses souverains qu'à ses concitoyens pendant 4 ans." Letter from Tassu to the King and the Minister of Justice, 7 July 1832, Tassu case, records of Assize Court proceedings (2U237), ADY.

30 Gordon, "Incest and Resistance," 258.

31 "[M]onde des villages et des hameaux, ces lieux oubliés du progrès." Georges Vigarello, *Histoire du viol: XVI*[e]*-XX*[e] *siècles* (Paris: Seuil, 1998), 131.

32 Jean-Baptiste Duvergier, *Code pénal annoté, édition de 1832* (Paris: A. Guyot et Scribe, 1833), 51.

33 "[J]e voudrais ne rien ajouter à ce détail des choses hideuses qui révèlent, au premier coup d'œil, la profonde misère des malheureux habitans ; mais je dois dire que, dans plusieurs des lits dont je viens de parler, j'ai vu reposer ensemble des individus des deux sexes et d'âges très différens, la plupart sans chemise et d'une saleté repoussante. Père, mère, vieillards, enfans, adultes, s'y pressent, s'y entassent. Je m'arrête…le lecteur achèvera le tableau, mais je le préviens que s'il tient à l'avoir fidèle, son imagination ne doit reculer devant aucun des mystères dégoûtans qui s'accomplissent sur ces couches impures, au sein de l'obscurité et de l'ivresse." Louis-René Villermé, *Tableau de l'état physique et moral des ouvriers employés dans les manufactures de coton, de laine et de soie* (Paris: Jules Renouard et Cie, 1840), 1: 83.

34 "[O]se affirmer que l'insalubrité de leurs habitations est le point de départ de toutes les misères, de tous les vices, de toutes les calamités de leur état social…. A peu d'exception près, on pourrait juger de la valeur morale d'une famille d'ouvriers par la seule inspection du local qu'elle habite." Adolphe Blanqui, *Des classes ouvrières en France pendant l'année 1848* (Paris: Firmin Didot frères, 1849), 74–75.

35 "Jean Cadio est brutal ivrogne et immoral au point de n'avoir pas conservé les moindres sentiments d'un père." Indictment, 14 January 1848, Cadio case, records of Assize Court proceedings (5U150), Archives départementales de Loire-Atlantique (ADLA).

36 "Devien, charron à Vernon…se livre habituellement à l'ivrognerie. Son inconduite sa paresse et les violences auxquels il se porte envers sa femme lui ont fait acquérir la plus triste réputation dans la commune qu'il habite." Indictment, 15 April 1868, Devien case, records of Assize Court proceedings (UP51644), Archives départementales de Seine-et-Marne (ADSM).

37 "[L]'intérieur du logement non carrelé, ni crêpe, ni plateforme n'est garni que des meubles ci après : un coffre en bois, deux chaises, une armoire ou buffet à deux compartiments dépourvus de ses volets et des tablettes du compartiment supérieur, un lit composé d'un lit de plumes, un traversin, deux oreillers, une paire de draps et une couverture en laine, le tout placé sur des planches séparées du sol par deux morceaux de bois de deux décimètre d'épaisseur." Information gathered by the justice of the peace for the canton of Marines, November 1847, Quentin case, records of Assize Court proceedings (2U369), ADY.

38 "[L]'habitation de l'inculpé et de sa fille est isolé de toute autre habitation…. Elle consiste, au milieu de ruines, de vieux bâtiments de toute espèce de masures d'un caveau voûté…. Aucun meuble n'existe dans ce caveau, dans chacun des deux angles opposés au côté dans lequel existe la porte d'entrée nous trouvons un certain espace rempli de paille et entouré de grosses pierres sans draps ni couvertures ou autre effet de literie : l'inculpé nous désigne l'espace à gauche comme étant son lit et l'espace à droite comme étant celui de sa fille." Minutes of the visit to the home of the accused by the judge and the public prosecutor, 11 May 1858, Placet case, records of Assize Court proceedings (2U460), ADY.

39 "[C]ar il est facile de démontrer que là se trouve la principale cause de la détérioration des races." Prosper Menière, *Du mariage entre parents considérés comme cause de la surdi-mutité congénitale, lu à l'académie de médecine séance du 29 avril 1856* (Paris: Desprez, 1856), 5–6.

40 "[L]'exercice de professions dangereuses ou insalubres, l'habitation dans des centres trop populeux ou malsains, soumettent l'organisme à de nouvelles causes de dépérissement et conséquemment de dégénérescence." Benedict-Augustin Morel, *Traité des dégénérescences physiques, intellectuelles et morales de l'espèce humaine* (Paris: Baillières, 1857), 50.

41 "Je déclare hautement que j'ai vu trop fréquemment l'inceste assis au foyer domestique, pendant que j'exerçais mes fonctions, pour ne pas réclamer avec fermeté contre les scrupules de la loi. L'habitude de vivre en concubinage s'est propagée depuis trente ans au milieu des centres manufacturiers, dans des proportions effrayantes, et l'indifférence des hommes et des femmes pour tous les liens de la famille les a amenés à contracter sans honte des liaisons plus odieuses et plus criminelles." Paul Bernard, *Histoire de l'autorité paternelle en France* (Montdidier: Imprimerie administrative Radenez, 1863), 468.

42 "[L]es choses me paraissaient tellement graves que je n'ai pas crû devoir pousser plus loin mes investigations...pour ne pas donner l'éveil des recherches exercées dans cette affaire." Police commissioner of Marseille's fifth arrondissement to the public prosecutor, 19 November 1860, Davin case, records of Assize Court proceedings (208U4/68), Archives départementales des Bouches-du-Rhône (ADBR).

43 "[S]urtout quand le dénonciateur est affligé d'une mauvaise réputation tandis que la personne accusée jouit de l'estime générale." Marie-Aimée Cliche, "Un secret bien gardé: l'inceste dans la société traditionnelle québecoise, 1858–1938," *Revue d'histoire de l'Amérique française* 50, no. 2 (Fall 1996): 207.

44 Rachel Devlin, "'Acting out the Œdipal Wish': Father-Daughter Incest and the Sexuality of Adolescent Girls in the United States, 1941–1965," *Journal of Social History* 38, no. 3 (Spring 2005): 612. In Chapter 14 of this volume, Jane Nicholas demonstrates how infanticide investigations in Ontario were perceived through the suffering body of the women involved. In France, incest cases were more often adjudicated through the social and living status of the fathers.

45 Michel Foucault, "12 March 1975," in *Abnormal: Lectures at the Collège de France, 1974–1975*, trans. Graham Burchell (London: Verso, 2003), 267–68. Originally published as *Les anormaux: Cours au Collège de France: 1974–1975* (Paris: Gallimard/Le Seuil, 1999).

46 Dominique Kalifa, *La culture de masse en France: Tome 1: 1860–1930* (Paris: La Découverte, 2001), 1.

47 "[O]nt tendance à s'appesantir avec le temps, parallèlement à la domination croissante de l'euphémisme." Anne-Claude Ambroise-Rendu, "Les récits d'abus sexuels sur enfants depuis le 19e siècle jusqu'à aujourd'hui: Du fait divers au problème de société," *Les Cahiers du journalisme* 17 (Summer 2007): 243.

48 "[L]a gendarmerie d'Andruick (Pas-de-Calais) vient de mettre fin à un horrible scandale. Elle s'est emparée d'un misérable qui abusait de sa fille depuis que

celle-ci avait l'âge de treize ans et qui l'a rendue deux fois mères." *Le Petit Journal,* 10 September 1884.

49 "[Q]uelquefois le père infâme se laissait toucher par les larmes de son enfant, mais alors il se livrait sur elle à des obscénités, et Fanny, sous l'empire de la crainte, n'osait se plaindre. Ce silence enhardit le misérable : un jour, il viola sa fille, et menaça de la tuer si elle parlait." *La Gazette des Tribunaux,* 14 November 1885.

50 "[L]e parquet du Havre est saisi en ce moment d'une honteuse affaire d'inceste découverte ces jours-ci. Depuis sept ans, un berger d'Angerville, resté veuf avec quatre enfants, abusait d'une de ses filles, laquelle, depuis cette époque, a eu déjà deux enfants. Ce misérable père, la voyant enceinte pour la troisième fois, voulut la forcer à se placer." *Le Petit Parisien*, 29 November 1887.

51 "Il se passe des choses honteuses à Beaubry près de Prévillers je parle d'un père qui abuse de son enfant âgée de 10 à 12 ans sa mère m'en a parlé devant témoin je ne veux pas me nommer ayant attendu qu'elle dénonce ce monstre comme elle me l'avait dit…je vous prie de vous occuper au plus vite l'enfant parle de se détruire." Anonymous report to the Public Prosecutor of Meaux, 1892, Rozé case, records of Assize Court proceedings (UP51816), ADSM. Punctuation added for clarity.

52 "[Q]ue les mécanismes politiques n'ont pas été diffusés d'un seul coup dans les relations sociales, mais lentement." Jean-Clément Martin, "Violences sexuelles, étude des archives, pratique de l'histoire," *Annales: Histoire, Sciences Sociales* 51, no. 3 (1996): 656.

53 Kim Stevenson, "'These are cases which it is inadvisable to drag into the light of day': Disinterring the Crime of Incest in Early Twentieth-Century England," *Crime, History and Societies/Crime, Histoire et Sociétés* 20, no. 2 (2016): 3.

54 "[C]e n'est pas la consanguinité qui est saine ou morbide, c'est le terrain sur lequel elle se produit. Il y a une consanguinité de milieu social sain et une consanguinité dans un milieu social pathologique." Alexandre Lacassagne, "Consanguinité," in *Dictionnaire encyclopédique des sciences médicales*, ed. Amédée Dechambre (Paris: Masson, 1877), 695.

55 "[S]i de ces unions naissent des infirmes quelconques, outre que ce sont des non-valeurs pour la société, on voit les auteurs de pareils mariage réclamer en même temps des asiles d'aliénés, des institutions de sourds-muets, des hôpitaux de toutes sortes, en un mot des établissements où ils cachent leurs infirmes: Ils se débarrassent de leurs produits dégénérés, mais au frais de la collectivité." Lacassagne, "Consanguinité," 712.

56 "[Q]ui, par leur ivrognerie habituelle, leur inconduite notoire et scandaleuse ou par des mauvais traitements, compromettent soit la santé, soit la sécurité, soit la moralité de leurs enfants." *Loi sur la protection des enfants maltraités ou moralement abandonnés,* 24 July 1889, Article 2.

57 "[A]u nom d'un possible risque ou danger, l'action préventive, fondée sur un discours scientifique légitimant, va pouvoir s'exercer, mieux acceptée, plus acceptable qu'une intervention répressive." Martine Kaluszynski, "Le retour de l'homme dangereux," *Penal Field/Champ pénal* 5 (2008), https://doi.org/10.4000/champpenal.6183.

58 See also Chapter 16 in this volume, in which Emilee Lord and John Wertheimer present a similar analysis of the 2008 "Law Against Femicide and Other Forms of Violence Against Women" in Guatemala.

59 Drugge, "Family Trauma," 427.

60 Caroline New, "Oppressed and Oppressors? The Systematic Mistreatment of Men," *Sociology* 35, no. 3 (2001): 741.

61 "[I]l comporte des contradictions et des formes d'hétérogénéité, et la pérennité d'une organisation patriarcale de la société n'est possible qu'aux prix d'adaptations incessantes." Christine Guionnet, "Analyser la domination masculine, ses ambivalences et ses coûts: Intérêt et enjeu d'une étude en terrain sensible," *Savoir/Agir* 26, no. 4 (2013): 48.

62 Herman and Hirschman, "Father-Daughter Incest," 740.

63 Odile Roynette, "La construction du masculin: De la fin du 19e siècle aux années 1930," *Vingtième siècle: Revue d'histoire* 75, no. 3 (2002): 89.

64 Anne-Emmanuelle Demartini, "L'affaire Nozière: La parole sur l'inceste et sa réception sociale dans la France des années 1930," *Revue d'histoire moderne et contemporaine* 56, no. 4 (2009): 190–214.

65 "[S]'attaquer socialement, symboliquement, voire judiciairement à une telle autorité exige...un effort important." Dorothée Dussy and Léonore Le Caisne, "Des maux pour le taire: De l'impensé de l'inceste à sa révélation," *Terrain* 48 (February 2007): 14.

66 Eva Thomas, *Le viol du silence* (Paris: Aubier, 1986).

## CHAPTER 16

1 Emilee Lord conducted person-on-the-street interviews in Quetzaltenango, Cantel, and Guatemala City, Guatemala, in December of 2018. The interview described here took place in the *parque central* (central park) of Quetzaltenango, on 23 December 2018. Due to privacy considerations and Institutional Review Board (IRB) restrictions, we withhold the names of her interview subjects. Interview notes are in Emilee's possession. Note that for this project, we scrupulously followed Davidson College's IRB protocol, which entailed an application to and approval from a campus review board, a training course that both of us took, restrictions on the interview pool (no subjects under eighteen years of age), agreement to change the names of all interviewees (which we have done), and signed permission forms from all interviewees (those forms remain on file and are available upon request). For more on Davidson College's IRB process, see: https://www.davidson.edu/offices-and-services/human-subjects-irb/hsirb-application.

2 Karen Musalo and Blaine Bookey, "Crimes without Punishment: An Update on Violence against Women and Impunity in Guatemala," *Hastings Race and Poverty Law Journal* 10 (2013): 279.

3 Susan A. Berger, *Guatemaltecas: The Women's Movement, 1986–2003* (Austin: University of Texas Press, 2006), 47, referring to Guatemala's 1996 law against intrafamilial violence. See also Mazariegos Matías, "La discriminación contra la mujer, fuente real del decreto número 22-2008 del Congreso de la República

de Guatemala, ley contra el femicidio y otras formas de violencia contra la mujer," *Universidad de San Carolos de Guatemala*, Facultad de Ciencias Jurídicas y Sociales (2009): 70.

4 "The International Violence against Women Act: Could IVAWA Save Guatemala from Femicide?," Council on Hemispheric Affairs, 5 August 2010, https://www.coha.org/the-international-violence-against-women-act-could-ivawa-save-guatemala-from-femicide/. This depressing conventional wisdom reflects a broader and equally depressing proposition: that in places such as Guatemala, reform measures, however well-intended, are doomed to irrelevance, because those societies have no regard for the rule of law. In Guatemala in particular, this broader argument goes, "almost absolute impunity" for lawbreakers prevails generally. It should come as no surprise that violence against women has continued unabated, these scholars argue, for Guatemalan violators act "without repercussion." David Carey Jr. and M. Gabriela Torres, "Precursors to Femicide: Guatemalan Women in a Vortex of Violence," *Latin American Research Review* 45, no. 3 (2010): 145.

5 Natalie Jo Velasco, "The Guatemalan Femicide: An Epidemic of Impunity," *Law and Business Review of the Americas*, 14, no. 2 (2008): 397–424.

6 Hilda Morales Trujillo, "Femicide and Sexual Violence in Guatemala," in *Terrorizing Women: Feminicide in the Américas*, ed. Rosa-Linda Fregoso and Cynthia Bejarano (Durham: Duke University Press, 2010), 127.

7 Valerie M. Hudson and Patricia Leidl, "Guatemala: A Case Study," in *The Hillary Doctrine: Sex and American Foreign Policy* (New York: Columbia University Press, 2015), 143. Hector Ruiz is somewhat more optimistic. In his article, "No Justice for Guatemalan Women: An Update 20 Years After Guatemala's First Violence Against Women Law," he expresses some hope for the future: "Guatemala is poised to be a pioneering leader in the fight against the rampant levels of violence against women in the Northern Triangle region." Unlike the future, however, the present, in Ruiz's estimation, is dire: "A culture of violence and impunity pervades all of Guatemalan society today, harboring an environment in which patriarchal repression is the norm." Héctor Ruiz, "No Justice for Guatemalan Women: An Update 20 Years After Guatemala's First Violence Against Women Law," *Hastings Women's Law Review* 101, no. 29 (2018): 122–23.

8 Carey and Torres, "Precursors to Femicide," 143. See also Velasco, "The Guatemalan Femicide," 400–02; and Hudson and Leidl, "Guatemala: A Case Study," 114–25.

9 See Hudson and Liedl, "Guatemala: A Case Study," 111, 142; Velasco, "The Guatemalan Femicide," 399; "Guatemala Femicide Law: Progress Against Impunity?," The Guatemala Human Rights Commission/USA (2009), 2, http://www.ghrc-usa.org/Publications/Femicide_Law_ProgressAgainstImpunity.pdf. See also Guillermo Díaz Castellanos, "Violencia contra la mujer in Guatemala," *Sociedad y Discurso* 23 (2013): 56, lamenting the low percentage of cases in which perpetrators of violence against women are punished; Ruiz, "No Justice for Guatemalan Women," 122–23; Morales Trujillo,

"Femicide and Sexual Violence in Guatemala," 127; and Musalo and Bookey, "Crimes Without Punishment," 270–79.

10 See, for example, Gabriela Torres, "Bloody Deeds/Hechos sangrientos: Reading Guatemala's Record of Political Violence in Cadaver Reports," in *When States Kill: Terror in the U.S.-Latin American Interstate Regime*, ed. Cecilia Menjívar and Néstor Rodríguez (Austin: University of Texas Press, 2005), 143–69; Velasco, "The Guatemalan Femicide," 397; Hudson and Leidl, "Guatemala: A Case Study," 138; and Mazariegos Matías, "La discriminación contra la mujer," 48.

11 For analysis of the grassroots movements, human rights workers, and NGOs, and public officials whose actions in Guatemala and elsewhere helped produce anti-domestic-violence laws, see Berger, *Guatemaltecas*; and Fregoso and Bejarano, eds., *Terrorizing Women*.

12 For very different sorts of interviews than ours, see Cecilia Menjívar, "Violence and Women's Lives in Eastern Guatemala: A Conceptual Framework," *Latin American Research Review* 43, no. 3 (2008): 109–36.

13 Luisa del Carmen Chinchilla Escobar, "Violencia Intrafamiliar, Aplicación legal en el Juzgado de Primera Instancia de Familia del Municipio de Quetzaltenango" (Quetzaltenango, Guatemala, Mayo de 2001, Facultades de Quetzaltenango, Universidad Rafael Landívar, Facultad de Ciencias Jurídicas y Sociales), 16.

14 John Wertheimer, interview with Maria Virgilia Elizondo Montoya, Quetzaltenango, Guatemala, 25 July 2012. Notes in author's possession.

15 John Wertheimer's interview with Juanita Yax, 25 July 2012, Quetzaltenango, Guatemala. Notes in author's possession.

16 Totonicapán, Juzgado de Paz (1961), no legajo or case number, falta contra las personas case filed by María Calixta Pacheco against Mateo Domingo Tax, author's notebook 2012-01, 24.

17 Family Court Act of 1964 ("Ley de Tribunales de Familia," Decreto Ley no. 206, Guatemala, 1964), arts. 1–2.

18 Ibid.

19 Quetzaltenango, Juzgado de Familia (1965), case #47, research notebook 2011-01, 64–66.

20 Quetzaltenango, Juzgado de Familia (1965), case #443, legajo #3, research notebook 2011-01, 84.

21 "Ley de Tribunales de Familia," Decreto Ley no. 206, art. 1 (Guatemala, 1964).

22 "Ley de Tribunales de Familia," Decreto Ley no. 206, art. 15 (Guatemala, 1964).

23 Decreto no. 97-1996, El Congreso de la República de Guatemala, 28 November 1996, in Coordinadora Nacional para la Prevención de la Violencia Intrafamiliar y contra las Mujeres (CONAPREVI), *Compendio de instrumentos internacionales y nacionales sobre discriminación y violencia contra las mujeres*, 3rd ed. (Guatemala: CONAPREVI, December 2009), 103–10.

24 See United Nations General Assembly Resolution 48/104, "Declaration on the Elimination of Violence Against Women" (1993), http://www.un-documents

.net/a48r104.htm; and The United Nations, Fourth World Conference on Women, "Platform for Action," "Violence against Women," D-1, "Actions to be Taken by Governments" (1995), https://www.un.org/womenwatch/daw/beijing/platform/violence.htm.

25 This wording comes from a different law, but the same impetus applied to the 1996 Intrafamilial statute discussed above. Decreto no. 7-99, 9 March 1999, reprinted in Comisión Presidencial de Derechos Humanos (COPREDEH), *Instrumentos de derechos humanos de protección a la mujer…* (Cosponsored by Cooperación Comunidad Europea) (Guatemala: FONAPAZ, 2003), 158.

26 In 1993, for example, Guatemalan women's leaders persuaded the government to create a commission dedicated to ensuring that the textbooks used in Guatemalan school represented "equal functions for men and women." Acuerdo gubernativo no. 711-93, *Diario de Centro América* 247, no. 86 (16 December 1993): 2417; "Base Legal" (Ofinina Nacional de la Mujer, Miisterio de trabajo y Previsión Social, 2015), 17. "Sex discrimination is learned in the *machista* home," a Guatemalan women's-rights activist wrote in a 1991 editorial. "La mujer exige su lugar en la sociedad," *Telegráfico*, 25 November 1991, reprinted in Oficina Nacional de la Mujer, *Memoria de Labores, 1990–1991* (Guatemala, December 1991): 40.

27 Michael Clodfelter, *Warfare and Armed Conflicts: A Statistical Encyclopedia of Casualty and other Figures, 1492–2015* (Jefferson, NC: McFarland & Co., 2017), 625.

28 Nava San Miguel Abad, interviewed by John Wertheimer, Madrid, Spain, 7 June 2016.

29 Note, however, that the 1996 measure listed women—along with children, the aged, and people with disabilities—among the groups targeted for "special protection." Decreto no. 97-1996, art. 2, el Congreso de la República de Guatemala, 28 November 1996.

30 Ibid., art. 7.

31 Ibid., art. 2.

32 Matthew R. Durose, et al., "Family Violence Statistics, Including Statistics on Strangers and Acquaintances," report prepared for the US Department of Justice, Office of Justice Programs, Bureau of Justice Statistics (June 2005), 1, http://bjs.ojp.usdoj.gov/content/pub/pdf/fvs02.pdf.

33 Olivia Ward, "Ten Worst Countries for Women," *Toronto Star*, 8 March 2008. Guatemala came in at number five.

34 Berger, *Guatemaltecas*; Velasco, "The Guatemalan Femicide."

35 The law defines "femicide" as follows: "The crime of femicide is committed when someone, within the framework of unequal power relations between men and women, kills a woman." By this definition, the perpetrator must logically be a man. "Comete el delito de femicidio quien, en el marco de las relaciones desiguales de poder entre hombres y mujeres, diere muerte a una mujer." *Ley contra el Femicidio y otras Formas de Violencia Contra la Mujer*, Decreto no. 22, 2 May 2008, ch. 4, art. 6.

36 Ibid.

37 Ibid., ch. 4, arts. 6–8.

38 Ibid., ch. 7. For photographs of cartoon characters on the walls of special domestic violence units in police stations and cribs and toys in courthouse offices dedicated to processing the Femicide Law, contact the authors.

39 Ruiz, "No Justice for Guatemalan Women," 107.

40 Instituto Nacional de Estadística de Guatemala, *Estadísticas de Violencia en contra de la Mujer, 2017* (Guatemala, 2018), 4.

41 John Wertheimer, research notebook 2012-02, 84–111, in author's possession and available upon request.

42 Ruiz, "*No Justice for Guatemalan Women*," 122–23.

43 "Cuadros 1.4, Denuncias por los delitos contemplados en la ley contra el femicidio y otras formas de violence en contra de la mujer, por año de registro según tipo de delito. Período 2014–2017," Instituto Nacional de Estadística de Guatemala, *Estadísticas de Violencia en contra de la Mujer, 2017* (Guatemala: 2018), Anexo A.

44 For more on "common-sense quantification" and its application to legal-historical scholarship, see John Wertheimer, "Counting as a Tool of Legal History," in *Making Legal History: Essays in Honor of William E. Nelson*, ed. Daniel Hulsebosch and R.B. Bernstein (New York: New York University Press, 2013), 162–78.

45 Emilee Lord, interview in Quetzaltenango, Guatemala, 11 December 2018.

46 Emilee Lord, interview in Quetzaltenango, Guatemala, 11 December 2018.

47 Emilee Lord, interview in Quetzaltenango, Guatemala, 11 December 2018.

48 Emilee Lord, interview in Quetzaltenango, Guatemala, 21 December 2018.

49 "The World Factbook: Guatemala," *Central Intelligence Agency*, accessed 1 February 2021, https://www.cia.gov/the-world-factbook/countries/guatemala/#people-and-society.

50 Ibid.

51 Ibid.; Pan American Health Organization, "Country Report: Guatemala," *Health in the Americas*, https://www.paho.org/salud-en-las-americas-2017/?page_id=127; Ellen Van de Poel, Owen O'Donnell, and Eddy Van Doorslaer, "What Explains the Rural-Urban Gap in Infant Mortality: Household or Community Characteristics?," *Demography* 46, no. 4 (November 2009): 827–50.

52 Note that teenaged abusers outnumber men in their fifties or sixties, though not men in their twenties, thirties, or forties. Instituto Nacional de Estadística Guatemala, *Estadísticas de Violencia en contra de la Mujer, 2017* (Guatemala, November 2018), 20, https://www.ine.gob.gt/sistema/uploads/2018/11/30/20181130081722emO14nj4jr5XWfNPqRNeFnEgRtxtdjJf.pdf

53 Emilee Lord, interview in Quetzaltenango, Guatemala, 27 December 2018.

54 Emilee Lord, interview in Quetzaltenango, Guatemala, 23 December 2018.

55 Emilee Lord, interview in Quetzaltenango, Guatemala, 12 December 2018.

56 Emilee Lord, interview in Quetzaltenango, Guatemala, 18 December 2018.

57 Emilee Lord, interview in Quetzaltenango, Guatemala, 18 December 2018.

58 Women in their twenties are the most likely decade cohort to suffer abuse, followed by women in their thirties. Instituto Nacional de Estadística Guatemala, *Estadísticas de Violencia en contra de la Mujer, 2017* (Guatemala, November 2018), 11, tables 2.5 and 2.6, https://www.ine.gob.gt/sistema/uploads/2018/11/

30/20181130817220emO14nj4jr5XWfNPqRNeFnEgRtxtdjJf.pdf. Note that female teens are more likely to suffer gendered violence than women in their fifties. Other than that, the numbers decline steadily from the twenties forward.

59 Emilee Lord, interview in Quetzaltenango, Guatemala, 14 December 2018.

60 Men and women are proportionally represented in all three categories. This marks an advance for women. Years ago, women's educational opportunities in Guatemala were disproportionally constrained. That is no longer so. Overall education levels in Guatemala remain low by regional standards but have increased in recent decades. Since 1998, the nation's illiteracy rate has shrunk from thirty percent to thirteen percent, producing a generational divide in education levels. Younger generations tend to have more years of schooling. In 1986, only forty-eight percent of the Guatemalan population was literate. Illiteracy numbers have now decreased to just ten percent in Indigenous male populations, twenty percent in Indigenous female populations, and between five and seven percent for both male and female non-Indigenous populations. See Manuel Orzaco and Marcela Valdivia, "Educational Challenges in Guatemala and Consequences for Human Capital and Development," *The Dialogue*, 2 February 2017, https://www.thedialogue.org/analysis/educational-challenges-in-guatemala-and-consequences-for-human-capital-and-development/.

61 "Guatemala—Rural Population," accessed 31 July 2020, https://tradingeconomics.com/guatemala/rural-population-percent-of-total-population-wb-data.html. Note that thirty-five percent of our respondents ranked at the "intermediate" education level, and twenty-five percent occupied the "low-education" category.

62 Emilee Lord, interview in Quetzaltenango, Guatemala, 23 December 2018.

63 Many people who identify as Ladino have significant quantities of Indigenous DNA. Jens Sochteg, et al., "Genomic Insights on the Ethno-history of the Maya and the 'Ladinos' from Guatemala," *BMC Geometrics*, BioMed Central, 2015, https://doi.org/10.1186/s12864-015-1339-1.

64 The Maya ethnic category subdivides into several distinct Indigenous groups, such as Quiche.

65 According to the CIA's statistics, Ladinos account for 60.1 percent of the total population, followed closely by Indigenous groups with 39.3 percent. "The World Factbook: Guatemala," *Central Intelligence Agency*, 2019. Our slightly lower measure of Indigenous groups may result from our city-based methodology.

66 Note that Ladino men were comparatively likely to believe that the law consistently worked; Ladino women were more likely to report that it worked only sometimes. But neither sex thought the law a total failure. The percentage of Ladino men and women, respectively, characterizing the law to be a total failure was comparably modest—only about twenty-eight percent in both cases.

67 One of the more prevalent ideas expressed by urban respondents was that rural areas, where Indigenous communities tend to be, are disproportionately affected by domestic violence. One-third (fifteen of forty-five) of urban respondents independently identified Indigenous and rural groups as having a

higher risk of violence against women. "Indigenous people are very ignorant of their rights," a typical comment alleged. The police cannot respond swiftly enough to problems in outlying areas, multiple respondents said.

68 Emilee Lord, interview in Quetzaltenango, Guatemala, 27 December 2018.

69 "From Commitment to Action: Policies to End Violence Against Women in Latin America and the Caribbean," *United Nations Development Project and United Nations Women* (Panama, 2017).

70 Of the thirty-three nations included in the study, Guatemala was one of the top five in terms of legislative thoroughness as well as "legislative consistency" in this subject area. Table 12: "Legislative Consistency between domestic violence, intrafamilial violence and violence against women existing in 2016 and policies and/or national plans on domestic violence, intrafamilial violence, gender based violence and violence against women existing in 2016, by country," in United Nations Development Project and United Nations Women, *From Commitment to Action: Policies to End Violence Against Women in Latin America and the Caribbean* (Panama, 2017): 44.

71 United Nations Development Project and United Nations Women, *From Commitment to Action: Policies to End Violence Against Women in Latin America and the Caribbean* (Panama, 2017): 68.

72 Ibid.

73 Ibid., 68–69.

# INDEX